India: Human Development Report

India: Human Development Report

A Profile of Indian States in the 1990s

Abusaleh Shariff

NATIONAL COUNCIL OF
APPLIED ECONOMIC
RESEARCH

(United Nations)

OXFORD
UNIVERSITY PRESS

OXFORD
UNIVERSITY PRESS

YMCA Library Building, Jai Singh Road, New Delhi 110001

Oxford University Press is a department of the University of Oxford.
It furthers the University's objective of excellence in research,
scholarship, and education by publishing worldwide in

Oxford New York
Athens Auckland Bangkok Bogota Buenos Aires Calcutta
Cape Town Chennai Dar es Salaam Delhi Florence Hong Kong
Istanbul Karachi Kuala Lumpur Madrid Melbourne Mexico City
Mumbai Nairobi Paris Sao Paolo Singapore Taipei Tokyo Toronto
Warsaw

with associated companies in

Berlin Ibadan

ISBN 0 19 564762 9

Edited by Usha Tankha
Design: Itu Chaudhuri Design
Printed in India by Omni Advertising and Marketing
and published by Manzar Khan, Oxford University Press,
YMCA Library Building, Jai Singh Road, New Delhi 110 001

Foreword

The goal of all development effort is to raise the level of well-being of all the citizens of a country. Traditionally, per capita income was regarded as the key summary indicator of economic welfare. This has been increasingly questioned in recent years. The United Nations Development Programme (UNDP) for the past ten years has been computing and publishing the Human Development Index (HDI) which is designed to provide a more balanced indicator of human welfare in order to supplement the traditional per capita GNP figures for different countries. However, even the average HDI figure masks much of the variation across different regions and groups of people, specially in large countries such as India. It is thus important to obtain a picture of the levels of living of the disadvantaged regions or groups of people in a country in order to evaluate the success of national development programmes in improving the life of the less well off.

Although India has a more developed statistical system than most of the developing world, it is difficult to obtain an integrated picture of the various dimensions relating to human development. Different sources of data such as the National Population Census, the Sample Registration System, the National Sample Surveys, National Family Health Surveys, and the like, provide different facets of information that are not related to one another. For example, whereas the Population Census provides detailed information on demographic characteristics, it has no information on income, asset ownership, consumption patterns, and other variables. It was thus felt that a multipurpose unified survey covering different facets of human development: levels of living, employment and wages, literacy and education, morbidity, disability, and nutrition, effectiveness of public services such as the public distribution system, education and health care, and demographic characteristics would be useful. Such a unified survey would enable researchers to draw interrelationships between these different variables and thereby better understand the determinants of human development and would ultimately lead to better policy design.

This report is the culmination of four years of intensive work at the National Council of Applied Economic Research. The NCAER conducted this multipurpose survey of 33,000 households in rural India between January and May 1994. The study was commissioned by the Planning Commission, Government of India, and funded and supported by a consortium of United Nations and bilateral agencies: the United Nations Development Programme (UNDP), the United Nations Children's Fund (UNICEF), the United Nations Fund for Population Activities (UNFPA), and the International Development Research Centre (IDRC), Canada/the Canadian International Development Agency (CIDA). The project was actively supported and guided by the Planning Commission. The NCAER is grateful to all these agencies for having reposed sufficient confidence in the organization to undertake this project.

Data are analyzed in this report at the all-India level, by state and population group. The report covers only the rural sector in view of the predominance of the rural population in a country like India. At the outset, a word of caution might not be out of place. A sample of 33,000 households is relatively small for a country as large as India to accurately represent the many different parameters identified both for population groups and states. An attempt has been made to validate the results of this survey by comparing them with other available data. Attention is drawn wherever significant deviations occur. The real value of the findings is to draw attention to specific issues in order to generate debate and encourage further research. This rich mine of data is expected to foster a continued stream of research endeavour through more focused and disaggregated analyses at the micro level. The NCAER intends to support such further research effort.

The report is the joint effort of a host of individuals belonging to NCAER and elsewhere. The full list of those who worked on the project follows. I would particularly like to thank those without whose able leadership and support this project could not have been completed. First, I would like to record my gratitude to my predecessor, Dr S.L. Rao, who had the vision and courage to undertake this large endeavour and to provide encouragement and support to the research team. I would like to thank Dr S.P. Pal who directed this study from the outset until the data collection and compilation stage. Mr I. Natarajan and his team were instrumental in drawing the sample frame for this study. Data analysis and computer support were provided by Dr G.R. Bhowmik and Mr Surajit Baruah. Ms Usha Tankha undertook the editorial responsibility and Mr Itu Chaudhari did the designing work, both bringing their professional skills to shaping this report.

I would also like to record my deep appreciation of the consistent support and help of Mr R. Sudarshan of the UNDP throughout the conduct of this study.

Finally, and most notably I would like to thank Dr Abusaleh Shariff who has so ably directed the study since August 1995. He has had the unenviable task of systematizing this large data set, cleaning it, and analysing it over a period of about 12 months. He has done this with great care and patience.

Rakesh Mohan
Director General, NCAER

India is a country of diversities in the social and economic spheres. Although there are wide variations in rural and urban areas, within rural areas as well, notable differentials exist in the levels of living as measured by indicators of human development such as literacy and schooling, health and longevity, employment and wage security and access to public programmes.

The National Council of Applied Economic Research (NCAER) conducted a survey of 33,000 rural households during 1994 to create a Human Development Profile of India. This report is based on the findings of the multi-purpose survey spread over 1,765 villages and 195 districts in 16 states in India. Multi-stage stratified sampling techniques were used to draw a representative sample. About 90 indicators of human development that reflect various dimensions of levels of living—income and assets, employment and wages, consumption expenditures, literacy, morbidity, undernutrition, demographic rates and health care utilization—are discussed and compared to highlight disparities between the selected states and between the eight selected population groups. The states are grouped in such a way as to represent different regions in the country, including the Northern, Upper Central, Lower Central, Eastern, Western, and Southern regions. The population groups that have been categorized on the basis of household income, poverty line criteria, land ownership, occupation, caste, and religion, household size, adult literacy, and village development, create a comprehensive environment for meaningful interpretation of data.

The report is divided into ten chapters followed by an exhaustive statistical appendix. An introduction in Chapter 1 is followed by a description of the methodology on which the report is based (Chapter 2). Chapters 3 to 5 highlight various aspects of material well-being such as relative income and poverty, assets and distribution of income measured through work participation and wages of different sections of the population, household expenditure and food security. Chapter 6 focuses on aspects of literacy and education transition in India with special emphasis on gender disparity, cost of elementary schooling, and entry of private elementary level schools. Chapter 7 presents parameters relating to health, morbidity, and disability. Chapter 8 deals with demographic parameters and utilization of services, while Chapter 9 discusses the impact of village infrastructure on human development indicators.

A series of 28 village studies (two each in 14 selected states) were also undertaken to understand the qualitative dimension of human development. These will be published separately in four volumes. A synthesis of the village studies, however is included in this report (Chapter 10). The principal purpose of this synthesis is to introduce and validate the data collected in the NCAER/HDI Survey, 1994.

The report reveals some astounding data. Although relative differentials exist, absolute deprivation is high in most parts of rural India. For example, about half the population of rural India is illiterate and suffers from 'capability poverty'; about 40 per cent have extremely low incomes. About 8 per cent of household income is spent on health and primary education alone. A meagre 43 per cent households have domestic lighting, 25 per cent have access to tap water, and only 33 per cent utilize the public distribution system. Bihar, Uttar Pradesh, Madhya Pradesh, Orissa, Rajasthan and West Bengal are the most backward states. The states of Kerala, Tamil Nadu, Karnataka, Andhra Pradesh, Maharashtra, Gujarat, Punjab and Haryana are relatively better off with Kerala ranking first in respect of most human development indicators.

Land is the dominant source of income and economic security; yet it does not substantially improve the HD parameters such as capability, poverty and literacy. Among social groups, Scheduled Castes (SCs) and the Scheduled Tribes (STs) have the lowest levels of income and human development in rural India. The poor spend disproportionately large amounts on health and education. For example, those who are in the lower segment below the poverty line (16 per cent of all households) spend as much as 19 per cent of their annual income on health care alone and another 7 per cent on primary education. The next category of the poor (18 per cent of all households) spend 12 and 4.4 per cent respectively. As a proportion of income the relatively better off spend less on these items. National policies and programmes during the last half a century have not helped the SCs and the STs to emerge from the perennial poverty trap. Level of village development has a clear influence on income and human development.

A determined, concerted and sustained effort to eliminate poverty and social disability is necessary in India. Besides targeted investments in social services, there is a need to enable and empower the poor and the vulnerable to participate meaningfully in the social and economic spheres of India society. Macroeconomic restructuring is an important and essential step towards economic transformation. The belief that a relatively efficient role can be played by the private sector and also that cost recovery is needed to sustain many social service investments is a reality. However, over 50 per cent of India's population is still vulnerable and cannot afford the cost of education and health care. Public action, therefore, is needed to restructure and eliminate the current anomalies in the dispensation of social services so as to target them to the most needy and at the same time recover costs from the better-off by allowing the private sector to cater to the needs of the latter. Synergistic efforts should be made to invest in the rural and agricultural sectors so as to enhance rural incomes and also generate broad based employment opportunities along with guaranteed real wages.

The survey has shown that while absolute deprivation still persists in

India, relative deprivations are narrowing down, albeit slowly. The challenge for India in the next century is to improve the levels of living and concurrently reduce relative deprivation within a limited time-frame.

NCAER is now in the process of implementing a programme of studies in human development using advanced research methods and models to unravel the intricacies of the social and economic inequalities in India. A second survey is envisaged in the year 1999–2000 to enable us to understand changes in the parameters and also create a benchmark at the turn of the century.

Abusaleh Shariff
Principal Economist and Head
Human Development Programme, NCAER

Research Team

Directors

S. P. Pal
(1992–5)

Abusaleh Shariff
(1995–9)

D. V. Rukmini
Senior Statistician
(1992–5)

T. K. Sundari
Senior Economist
(1993)

G. Chakrabarty
Statistician
(1992–6)

Sanjay Kumar
Economist
(1992–5)

Dhirendar Kumar
Economist
(1994–5)

Shanta Venkatraman
Economist
(1992–4)

S. B. Kshatriya
Consultant
(1996)

K. K. Tripathy
Consultant
(1996)

M. K. Arora
Junior Economist
(1992–6)

Tarujyoti Buragohain
Economist
(1995–9)

Rajeshwari
Junior Economist
(1996)

Survey Design

I. Natarajan
Chief Economist

R. K. Shukla
Statistician

Computer Support

G. R. Bhowmik
Systems Analyst

Surajit Baruah
Systems Analyst

Thanks are due to Veena Kulkarni, Chhabi Sinha, A. Jayakumar, P. K. Ghosh and A. C. Mallick for research assistance and to Jaya Kumari, Shanta, and V. K. Kaushik for secretarial support.

Field Work Team

Name	Designation
Ramamani Sunder	Economist
B.L. Joshi	Jr. Economist
A. Razzack	Consultant
N.G. Jagdish	Jr. Economist
Jagdish Sinha	— do —
Veena Kulkarni	Research Assistant
Rajesh Jaiswal	— do —
J.P. Singh	Economist
T.K. Krishnan	— do —
D. Routray	— do —
Y.K. Tanwar	Jr. Economist
H.R. Ameta	— do —
C.R. Roy	— do —
R. Madhavachary	— do —
Bastoo Ram	— do —
Nihal Singh	— do —
V. K. Sharma	— do —
Madhumita Lodh	Consultant
P.K. Ghosh	— do —
R. Raman	— do —
O.P. Sharma	Research Assistant
D.K. Roychoudhury	— do —
A.K. Jain	— do —
S.K. Mondal	— do —
T.Satyanarayana	— do —
B.S. Ch. Prusti	— do —
C. Murthy	— do —
S.K. Bathla	— do —
M.L. Solanki	— do —
G. K. Sinha	— do —
R.S. Landge	Investigator
K.S. Urs	— do —
Inderjeet Singh	— do —
V.B. Saxena	— do —
P.N. Magon	— do —
A. Bindu	Field Supervisor
M.L. Sharma	— do —

Contents

List of Tables

India: Human
Development
Report

1

Introduction

Human development is a process of enlarging people's choices. The most critical of these wide-ranging choices are to live a long and healthy life, to be educated, and to have access to resources needed for a decent standard of living. Additional choices include political freedom, guaranteed human rights, and personal self-respect. Development enables people to have these choices… Human development thus concerns more than the formation of human capabilities such as improved health or knowledge. It also concerns the use of these capabilities.

"The approach to human development encompasses jnana, karma *and* bhakti.*"*

—Amartya Sen

'Human development is the end—economic growth a means. So, the purpose of growth should be to enrich people's lives.'

The quotation highlights some of the thoughts enshrined in the *Human Development Report* that is published annually by the United Nations Development Programme. The report has defined development as a process of increasing people's choices. According to the report the most critical choices that people should have, include a long and healthy life, access to knowledge and income, assets and employment for a decent standard of living. It presents many different types of national level human development parameters of which the Human Development Index (HDI) is noteworthy. This is a composite index encompassing selected information on literacy and education, expectation of life at birth and measures of material well-being. A recent improvement has been to separately compute a 'gender adjusted index'. Such indices are not normally computed at state levels. One sure method of understanding various aspects of human development or quality of life is to know the relative levels of the various components of human development. For example, the various components of 'knowledge' are levels of literacy, school enrolment, causes for non-enrolment and dropping out of school, duration of schooling, costs of schooling and accessibility to schools. Similarly, 'longevity' can be well understood on the basis of information on prevalence of morbidity and mortality, disability, under-nutrition, health care utilization, cost of seeking health care, and the efficacy of public health programmes. The 'material well-being' component can be further disaggregated to encompass various aspects such as level and source of household income, land and asset ownership, work opportunities, employment and wage stability, money and real wages and so on. The quality of life in developing countries is also linked with institutions and public programmes meant to provide for the basic needs of the poor and vulnerable sections of society.

The Indian Economic Scenario

A brief look at the Indian economic scenario provides a backdrop to this survey report. Since Independence, India has made significant progress in several areas of economic and human development, and the economy has diversified substantially. Food production has grown to provide adequate levels of food security; infrastructure development has proceeded apace; a vast pool of trained human resources have been developed; domestic savings and capital formation have increased substantially; a vast network of development institutions has been nurtured; and a high level of technological development has taken place.

However, implementation of the Five Year Plan programmes, particularly in terms of delivery in the social sectors, has been inadequate. Many public programmes are either not implemented or if implemented are not sustainable for want of funds and personnel, and an efficient bureaucratic machinery in the country.

The population of India was about 935 m in 1996.[1] Despite its vast land area, the density of population is very high. India is one of the poorest countries in the world where one-third of the population, that is, about 300 m people, live below the poverty line. There is evidence of substantial income disparities among states, between rural and urban areas, and among various population groups.

After about 40 years of planned development based on the dominance of government and public sector institutions and import substitution strategies, in 1991 India launched a number of structural adjustment programmes intended to improve economic performance through a greater use of market-based incentives and competition. The programme sought to withdraw the state from many areas of activity where the private sector could operate better. The funds thus earned could increasingly be used for social expenditures. To what extent this strategy has actually benefited the vast majority of people and led to greater equity and social justice remains to be seen.

A litmus test to ascertain the health of an economy is to find out how deeply the macroeconomic gains percolate to the masses. The distribution of national income to the people takes place through a number of structural, institutional, policy, and distributional mechanisms. However, the parameters used to assess the impact of macroeconomic gains to individuals need to be clearly established. Human development and better standards of living are not only ends in themselves but essential inputs for promoting economic growth and development. They are the dominant routes for inter-generational transfers that ensure the future growth of a country. While in India there has been a net increase in national wealth both in absolute and per capita terms, it is nonetheless necessary to investigate whether this type of economic prosperity has contributed to human development and the welfare of the masses.

The fast pace of economic growth of the East Asian economies such as South Korea, Taiwan, and Malaysia during the 1980s and 1990s indicated that the two most essential parameters facilitating growth have been high

"One of the primary reasons why economic growth has not had an impact on the lives of ordinary people is the current state of India's backwardness in human development."
—Mahbub ul Haq

Even after 40 years of planned development, more than one-third of India's people are classified as poor.

Human development is an essential input for promoting economic growth and development. It is a dominant route for inter-generational resource transfers.

1 *Report of the Technical Group on Population Projections.* GOI, New Delhi, Sept. 1996.

3

levels of literacy and better health of citizens. Although relatively better access to technology, a high savings rate, and foreign capital inflows contributed to the high growth of these countries, the sustainability of their economic growth has been attributed to higher levels of human development. Enhancement of human capabilities is an essential step forward in ensuring sustained economic and human development of a nation according to the *Human Development Report.* The relative rates of return to primary education, especially among women (even in India) are significant. The returns are manifest not only through an increase in productivity of labour, but also through improvements in technical (direct or market returns) and allocative (indirect or non-market returns) efficiencies in the utilization of scarce resources such as nutrition and health care.

Public policy concerns for human development are always constrained by lack of adequate resources. Besides establishing institutions and building infrastructure, the provision of basic needs requires huge investments as well as high quality administrative and managerial skills. Since practically all human development investments are made by the state governments in India, substantial inter-state variations in this may be expected. In populous and growing economies, keeping pace with the ever increasing demands on facilities is a difficult task. Nonetheless, policy should aim to create structures that ensure that basic human needs are met and also that alternatives and choices are available. Community participation of the diverse population groups in the country is absolutely essential to ensure sustenance of human development in India. Sustained growth will ensue only when the limited resources available for human development are targeted to benefit the most needy, and reach clearly identified areas and population groups. The findings of this research report are intended to help achieve this objective of national and state governance.

Objectives of the Report

This report takes stock of the major indicators of 'human development' in India. While indices such as the Human Development Index (HDI) and Gender Development Index (GDI) incorporate the essence of quality of life principally to order data and make international comparisons, like many others, they often conceal more than what they actually reveal. Such considerations formed the basis for undertaking this multifaceted empirical study to estimate and assess human development indicators for India as a whole, and for the individual states. Thus far, many economic comparisons have been made, largely between geographic areas, basically ignoring the identities of the people concerned. This study is different insofar as it goes a step ahead and bridges this gap by linking data with people belonging to different population groups.

Estimates at the level of state within a large country such as India only highlight the relative overall differentials that are already well known. State level HDIs and GDIs are not very useful for specific policy formulations and programme implementation. Thus, there was a felt need to generate a

Creating structures and institutions which ensure that basic human needs are met and that alternatives and choices are available should be the priority.

Many economic comparisons have largely been made between geographic areas, often ignoring the identities of the people concerned. This report intends to bridge that gap.

number of indicators for certain dimensions of human development so that each one of them could provide a complete set of information useful for targeting and programme implementation.

The human development profile discussed in this report is based on data collected from a rural sample of 33,230 households drawn from 16 states,[2] in a survey conducted between January and May 1994 by the National Council of Applied Economic Research. This survey (henceforth referred to as NCAER/HDI Survey,1994) was commissioned by the Planning Commission and financed by a consortium of international organizations such as the United Nations Development Programme (UNDP), United Nations Children's Fund (UNICEF), United Nations Fund for Population

Irrationally held truths may be more harmful than reasoned errors.

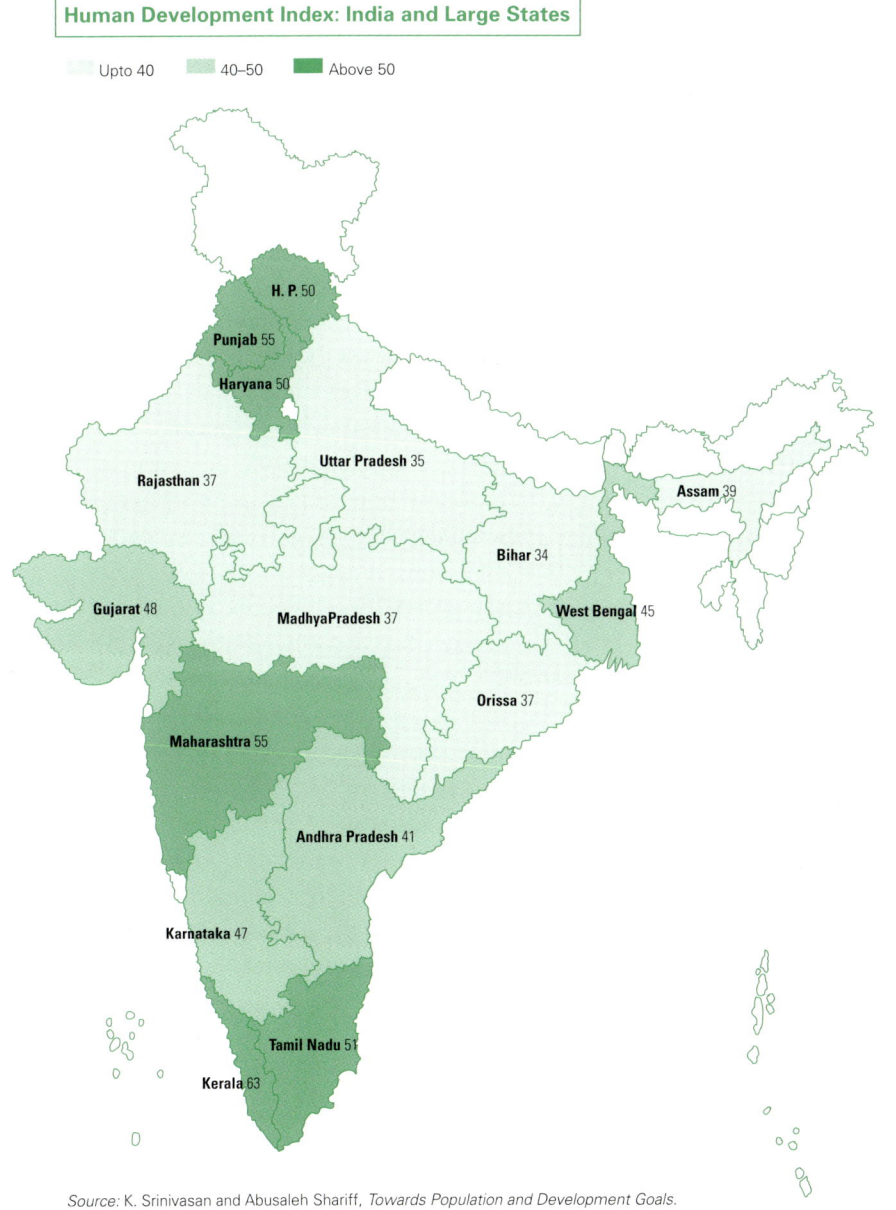

Human Development Index: India and Large States

Upto 40   40–50   Above 50

H. P. 50
Punjab 55
Haryana 50
Uttar Pradesh 35
Rajasthan 37
Assam 39
Bihar 34
Gujarat 48
MadhyaPradesh 37
West Bengal 45
Orissa 37
Maharashtra 55
Andhra Pradesh 41
Karnataka 47
Tamil Nadu 51
Kerala 63

Source: K. Srinivasan and Abusaleh Shariff, *Towards Population and Development Goals.* Oxford University Press, Delhi, 1997.

2 The urban component of this study, a survey of about 2,500 households selected from 16 urban centres, is currently under preparation. The sample of households from all the North-eastern states are presented together.

Activities (UNFPA), and the Canadian International Development Agency (CIDA)/International Development Research Centre (IDRC), primarily to estimate indicators relating to education, health and material well-being at state level for different social groups. Such disaggregation is necessary to reflect the heterogeneous nature of the Indian population and the diversity of experience. Data generated from this survey could provide baseline estimates in future assessments of the impact of structural adjustment and economic reform.

This is therefore a multipurpose survey. A comprehensive survey instrument was canvassed to one or more adult household members by a team comprising one trained female and one male investigator. A comprehensive village schedule was also made to elicit community level variables. In every state, local institutions were entrusted with the task of collecting data. Those involved in this survey from the local institutions as well as the investigators were trained at the level of the state. The survey instrument was translated into the respective state languages. The estimated rates and ratios presented in this report are representative of both the level of the state and all India.

NCAER also undertook 28 village studies (two each in 14 selected states) as a sequel to the above-mentioned survey with the aim of understanding the ground level realities and providing validity to the survey research findings. The staff of NCAER were especially trained to undertake these qualitative studies and were required to stay within the village for extended periods of time. The survey draws upon these village studies to put the estimates and ratios computed from the data in the right perspective. A synthesis of these village studies is presented in Chapter 10.

This NCAER/HDI Survey, 1994 provides an opportunity to undertake comparisons within the country and highlight disparities both between states and different types of population groups. It appears that while inter-state disparities persist, inter-population group disparities appear to be narrowing in the case of certain parameters, but certainly not in levels of income (Tables 1.1 and 1.2). The data reveal considerable disparities both in output and input parameters among the major states; and the levels of income, literacy and village development show considerable differentials in most of the parameters presented in this report.

The principal purpose of this report is to introduce and validate the data collected from the survey. The data are expected to generate investigative and analytical studies both by NCAER and other interested organizations in India and abroad. Box 1.1 presents a summary of the various components of the human development indicator survey and forms of research output.

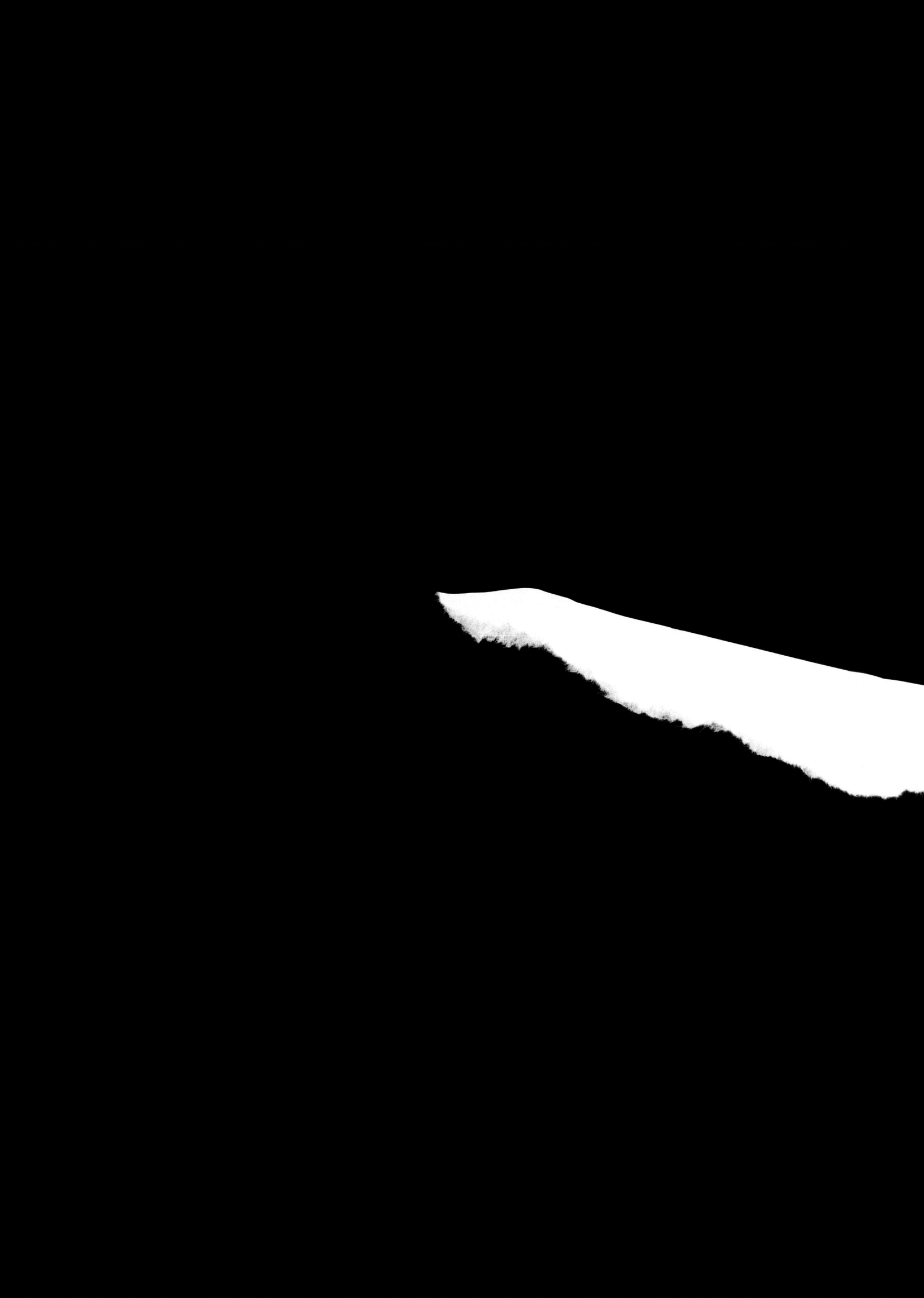

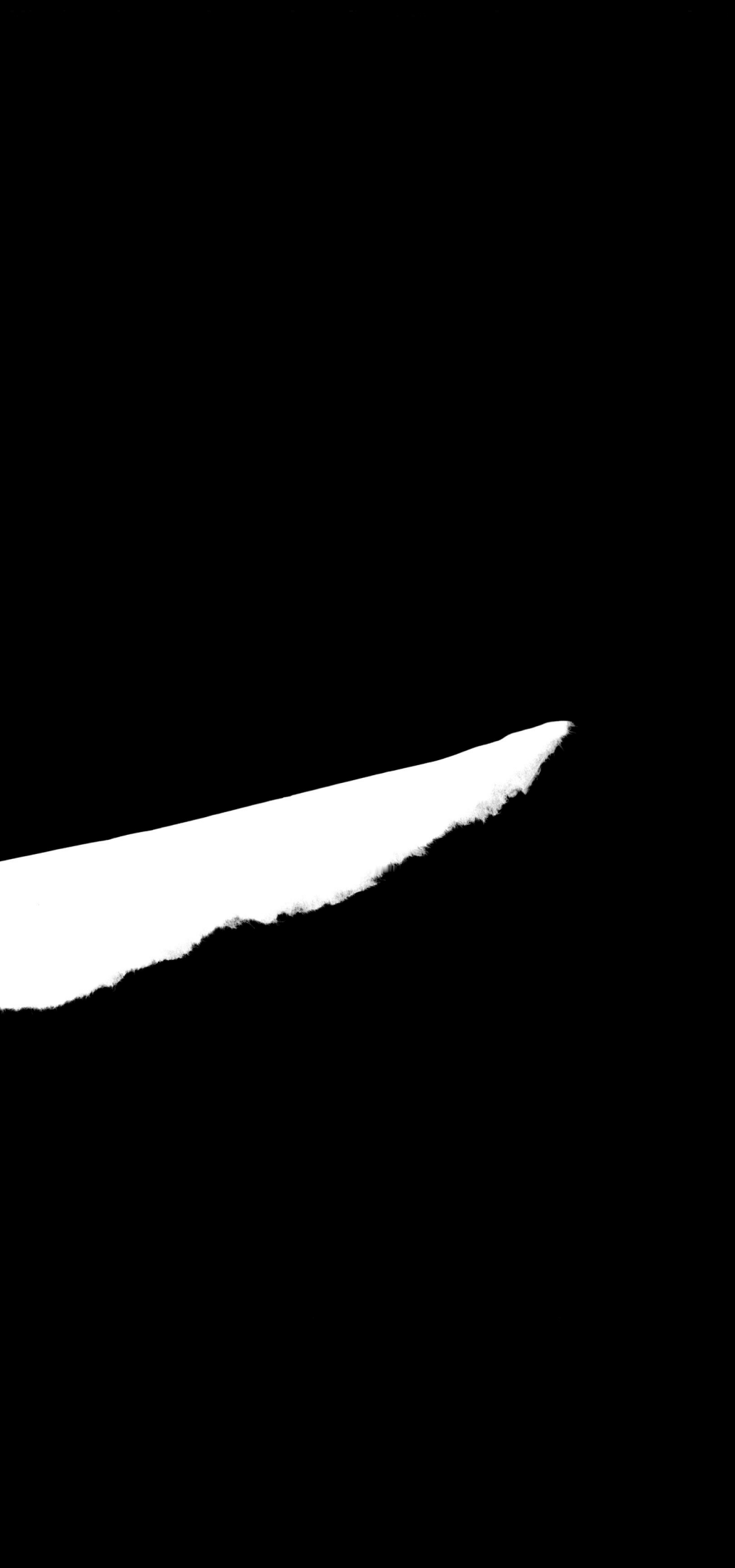

TABLE 1.1

Human Development Profile of Rural India, 1994: Selected Indicators for States

States/Regions	Per Capita Income (Rs per year)	Wage Earning House-holds*	Adult Wage Earners as a Per Cent of Total Adult Earners	Average Wage Per Day (Rs.)		Population Below Poverty Line (per cent)	Capability Poverty Measure (CPM)** (per cent)	Literacy Rate (7+ years)	Ever Enrolment Rate (6–14 years)	Proportion of Total Household Income Spent on		Households using Facilities (per cent)		
				Agri-cultural	Non-Agri-cultural					Education	Health	Electricity	Piped Water	Public Distri-bution System
North														
Haryana	6,368	21	25	42	46	27	47	55	78	3.4	3.5	82	44	9
Himachal Pradesh	4,168	18	16	28	31	45	48	68	93	7.0	-	88	71	76
Punjab	6,380	22	20	35	41	32	36	60	87	3.6	5.8	84	21	6
Upper Central														
Bihar	3,691	26	33	23	26	42	66	44	59	3.0	7.5	10	4	5
Uttar Pradesh	4,185	18	22	20	31	40	61	47	64	2.6	5.9	20	15	5
Lower Central														
Madhya Pradesh	4,166	24	52	17	22	40	56	44	63	1.9	5.4	51	11	34
Orissa	3,028	24	40	18	21	55	55	55	71	2.5	4.2	19	24	5
Rajasthan	4,229	19	27	23	31	40	66	41	61	3.0	6.5	49	28	24
East														
North-Eastern Rg.	5,070	13	19	25	32	33	40	70	81	2.6	3.8	44	9	22
West Bengal	3,157	25	30	23	21	51	53	59	66	3.0	7.0	16	9	11
West														
Gujarat	5,288	30	45	16	29	39	45	59	80	1.9	3.8	72	60	48
Maharashtra	5,525	27	51	15	21	34	46	58	85	2.0	3.4	60	43	51
South														
Andhra Pradesh	5,046	38	54	23	25	21	42	50	80	2.0	6.9	63	31	66
Karnataka	4,769	29	43	17	23	33	48	55	78	2.6	-	63	47	70
Kerala	5,778	37	41	41	40	30	12	90	99	5.7	6.8	61	17	78
Tamil Nadu	5,122	45	52	23	31	34	30	64	88	2.5	6.7	63	50	82
All India	**4,485**	**27**	**38**	**21**	**28**	**39**	**52**	**54**	**71**	**2.7**	**5.3**	**43**	**25**	**33**

* Refers to households which have reported more than 50 per cent of their total income as wages.
** CPM is a simple average of percentage of births unattended by trained health personnel, percentage of stunted children and female illiteracy rate.

TABLE 1.2
Human Development Profile of Rural India, 1994: Selected Indicators for Population Groups

Population Groups	Per Capita Income (Rs per year)	Wage Earning Households*	Adult Wage Earners as a Per Cent of Total Adult Earners	Population Below Poverty Line (per cent)	Capability Poverty Measure (CPM)** (per cent)	Literacy Rate (7+ years)	Ever Enrolment Rate (6–14 years)	Proportion of Total Household Income Spent on Education	Health	Households using Facilities (per cent) Electricity	Piped Water	Public Distribution System
Poverty Line Groups												
Lower Segment Below	1,095	49	53	100	58	44	61	7.3	19.1	28	23	30
Upper Segment Below	2,026	40	49	100	56	46	64	4.4	12.3	31	22	30
Lower Segment Above	3,931	23	38	–	51	54	76	3.0	6.0	45	25	37
Upper Segment Above	11,396	–	16	–	42	67	84	1.7	2.2	61	28	30
Landholding Groups												
Landless Wage Earners	2,308	100	92	68	56	37	60	3.8	10.0	30	29	44
Marginal	3,502	21	37	45	54	53	71	3.3	6.7	36	20	31
Small	4,803	4	22	27	52	55	74	2.3	4.7	45	21	27
Medium	6,516	–	15	16	52	58	76	1.7	3.5	57	25	26
Large	10,930	–	7	11	48	61	78	1.2	2.1	69	32	30
Other Landless	4,111	–	17	37	48	62	76	3.5	8.0	53	31	35
Social Groups												
Caste												
SCs	3,505	31	55	51	60	39	60	2.6	4.9	30	17	38
STs	3,237	47	58	50	68	42	63	2.9	7.0	31	23	32
Religion												
Hindus	4,514	27	38	39	48	53	72	2.6	5.1	43	25	34
Muslims	3,678	24	31	43	56	49	62	2.7	6.6	30	19	22
Christians	5,920	32	43	27	26	81	91	3.1	5.7	60	28	66
Other Minorities	5,427	25	33	34	47	54	79	3.5	5.3	61	21	16
Village Development Groups												
Low	4,045	28	36	43	61	42	60	2.5	5.9	27	14	18
Medium	4,369	27	38	38	53	54	74	2.7	5.4	42	22	33
High	5,079	29	39	33	42	64	81	2.7	4.8	59	38	47
All India	**4,485**	**27**	**38**	**39**	**52**	**54**	**71**	**2.7**	**5.3**	**43**	**25**	**33**

*   Refers to households which have reported more than 50 per cent of their total income as wages.
** CPM is a simple average of percentage of births unattended by trained health personnel, percentage of stunted children and female illiteracy rate.

BOX 1.1

Components of the NCAER/HDI Survey, 1994 and Research Outputs

1. *Sample Survey:* 33,230 rural households
2. *Research Outputs Based on Primary Data :*

   ### Over 100 HDI Estimates for
   a   Rural India as a whole
   b   16 Selected States
   c   8 Population Groups (Rural India)
   d   3 Selected Population Groups for 16 Selected States

   ### Human Development Profile of Key Indicators for
   a   16 Selected States
   b   8 Population Groups (Rural India)
   c   Quick reference summary sheets enlisting key human development
        parameters for Rural India and according to levels of poverty

   ### State Profiles
   A data base for each of the 16 selected states according to 8 population groups

3. **State Profiles based on Secondary Data**
    16 State Reports (available at NCAER.)

4. **Qualitative Data Based on Village Studies**
    28 Village Studies (2 each in 14 selected states) and an all India summary

2

Methodology

Survey research techniques may be as old as the statistical theory of probability. In recent years, however, the need for accurate data both from regular censuses and surveys cannot be overemphasized, not only for economic planning and forecasting, but also for a meaningful audit and review of the national achievements of growth, development, and equity.

This multipurpose survey was intended to collect broad-based data and estimate statistics with a fair degree of reliability.

Since censuses are often only head counts, and at best can collect only limited data on social and economic characteristics, and that too normally at intervals of ten years, surveys are inevitable. By definition, surveys are conducted on a sample basis—generally a representative sample with a fair degree of standard error usually less than 10 per cent. Surveys are useful in providing a database for the estimation of rates, ratios, and proportions of parameters needed for national and regional planning. Often surveys are eye-openers as they delve deeper than a census in providing the much-needed insights to enable us to understand social and economic processes.

Human development by definition is a wide concept encompassing literacy and knowledge, health and longevity, material well-being and levels of disposable incomes. Given these broad parameters, this survey essentially sets out to collect vital data to compute literacy, and enrolment rates, morbidity rates, levels of household and per capita income, movable and immovable asset ownership, wage employment and wage rates, and household expenditures on schooling and health care. This multipurpose survey was not intended to estimate limited statistics with a high degree of accuracy; rather its aim was to collect broadbased data with a fair degree of reliability.

Examples of other multipurpose surveys include the World Bank sponsored Living Standards Measurement Study (LSMS) beginning 1978, the World Fertility Survey (WFS), and subsequently the Demographic and Health Surveys (DHS). The latter are among the largest surveys, primarily to assess demographic and a few socio-economic characteristics of a large number of both developed and developing countries. The celebrated Indianapolis survey undertaken in the 1930s may be regarded as the precursor to most others, and was conducted to assess the state of households in post-Depression USA. A parallel effort, albeit on a much smaller scale, was sponsored by the United Nations in 1952 in India, namely, the Mysore Population Study.

Disadvantages of a Census

One way of knowing the values of parameters such as literacy, child mortality, prevalence of diseases, and poverty is to take a census of the entire population. The information collected from the entire population would enable us to 'calculate' the values of these parameters. The observed values thus calculated would deviate from the actual values only through errors, such as those in measurement and observation and mistakes in recording. All such errors together constitute what is known as the non-sampling error. If considerations of cost are ignored, a census would appear to be the best way of knowing the values of the parameters. Apart from the huge cost incurred in conducting a census, there are however, other difficulties in following this procedure.

If the universe (of which a census is to be taken) is large, and the information to be collected is diverse, as in the present case, it will take a long time to complete the exercise, as also to process and analyse the huge quantity of data collected in the census. Total time taken to collect, process, and analyse the data will often be so long that the estimates will be outdated by the time the findings are available for use. Sometimes quite a number of the population parameters, including its size, may change over the duration of the census.

A large number of persons need to be appointed and trained for collection of data in a census. This increases the possibility of error, and thus increases 'non-sampling errors'. The non-sampling errors may be large enough to make the calculated values of the parameters deviate substantially from their actual values, negating the purpose of conducting the census which entails a huge cost. A sample survey on the other hand, is confined to a scientifically selected section of the universe, takes much less time and employs fewer persons for collection, processing, and analysis of data. It therefore entails less cost. A few trained or experienced persons can be engaged for the purpose. A sample survey has a lower non-sampling error that can be further lowered if the survey is carefully planned and executed.

The 'estimates' of the parameters derived from survey data will no doubt be at variance with the actual value due to 'sampling errors'. This is due to the fact that only a part of the universe has been observed to arrive at these estimates. The sample can be scientifically selected to minimize sampling errors, given the budget in terms of money and time. When the sample is so selected, such errors can be estimated from the data collected in the survey, and we are then aware of the confidence level of these estimates. These considerations suggest that a sample survey conducted under intensive supervision can provide estimates with adequate levels of precision. Moreover, these estimates become available in a shorter time and can be used for formulating timely policies and for other purposes.

Mode of the Survey

Only when a survey project is approved and financial sanctions have been granted, can work on a survey get off the ground and move into full swing.

The most important activity subsequent to the sanction of the project is preparation of the survey instruments.

However, prior to this important step, a good deal of preliminary research and preparatory planning is essential. For instance, in the case of this household survey NCAER had already prepared a project proposal in May 1992 including issues such as the project justification, budget estimates, time schedule for the study, prior obligations and prerequisites and the format of the expected outputs.

The most important activity subsequent to the sanction of the project is preparation of the survey instruments. In this case, since the survey had to be conducted all over the country, the survey instruments were first prepared in English. These instruments were discussed and debated upon in advisory group meetings and two large workshops. The English version of the survey instruments were then translated into nine different languages to be used in different states. The English version was used in Kerala, Orissa, and the North-eastern states. Questionnaires translated into Hindi were used in Uttar Pradesh, Bihar, Haryana, Punjab, Himachal Pradesh, Rajasthan, Madhya Pradesh, and Delhi. For Karnataka, Andhra Pradesh, Tamil Nadu, Maharashtra, Gujarat and West Bengal the survey instruments were translated into the respective state languages, namely Kannada, Telugu, Tamil, Marathi, Gujarati, and Bengali. In many states, local and state level institutions were involved in organizing and collecting the data.

Given the multifaceted nature of the survey instruments, coding and transference of data was undertaken for the final product of income estimates rather than for all the details, which would have increased the size of data manifold.

A number of parameters were pre-coded and also pre-classified. However, pre-coding and pre-classification have advantages and disadvantages. Often both need to be based on prior information or expectations, and one may end up creating unsuitable categories; often some important variables may become less dependable and an analysis would have to rely on data that is available. In this survey, as it turned out, certain important data were not collected in the desirable format. For example, to collect information on income from agriculture, details on landownership by type of ownership, cultivation cycle, pattern of irrigation, crop variety, output per hectare, and prices were collected; these bits of data were used to compute household income which ultimately was noted down on the survey instruments and then transferred into the electronic data directories. Similarly, the education levels of people were collected with the following intervals: illiterate, below primary, middle, secondary and so on. This categorization did not prove very useful because it prevented computation of the mean years of schooling—a very important estimate to undertake meaningful comparisons between states and population groups. Besides, since literacy cut-offs were uniform for the whole of India, it did not enable documentation of state level variations in definitions of levels of literacy.

As far as possible, the definitions of the parameters frequently and commonly referred to were made to match the prevailing standard definitions; this was not however always possible for various technical as well as academic reasons. For example, literacy is defined in the same way as the census defines it, so that the estimates computed by this survey would be comparable; but the same was not possible in the case of enrolment of children at various levels. The survey estimated the net enrolment rates based on actual reporting by household members on the enrolment status of children, rather than the gross enrolment rates given by public statistics based on school level reporting which often is close to or sometimes over 100 per cent. Care was however taken to follow the standard definitions as far as possible when defining household income, per capita income, work participation rates, birth and death rates, morbidity prevalence rates, and the like.

Since this is a multipurpose survey, data were collected using varied reference periods based on some conventional rules. For example, to estimate household income in rural agricultural households, it was considered appropriate to relate cultivation and output information to that of the previous agricultural year. Similarly, to estimate short duration morbidity, occurrence of sickness during the previous 30 days was recorded, but for major morbidity the reference period was the previous one year. Similarly, births and deaths were recorded for the previous one year's reference period, whereas immunization rates were computed using the reporting of immunizations received according to the age of the child. The work participation rates were computed taking the usual annual status into consideration. The actual survey was spread over six months from January to June 1994, and thus most of the data pertains to one year prior to the date of the survey, i.e. 1993–4.

Surveys of this nature and magnitude have to be carefully launched. One of the quality controls in the very early stages is the pre-test of the survey instruments. Since the ultimate quality of data is determined by the relative occurrence of the sampling and non-sampling errors, it is necessary to reduce these errors. Pre-testing is an effort to assess not only the completeness and accuracy of data collection, and to test the suitability of the questions, but also to assess both the investigator and respondent fatigue. In this survey the survey instruments were in two parts. Part One was entitled Socio-economic and Educational Profile of Household and Part Two entitled Health Profile of the Household. The intention was that Part One would be canvassed by a male investigator to an adult male respondent and Part Two would be canvassed by a female investigator to an adult female respondent. In many states, especially in the northern parts of India, adequate numbers of female investigators were difficult to find and it was not always possible to ensure the matching sex combination of investigator and respondent.

Pre-testing was done only in the state of Uttar Pradesh using survey instruments only in English. Since pre-testing was done by experienced staff from NCAER, there is no reason to suspect the formatting, placement, and structure of questions and proformas used in data collection. But in other states the survey instruments were translated into the languages of the

Since this is a multipurpose survey, varied reference periods were used to collect accurate data. By and large the estimates relate to the financial year 1993–4.

respective states and no pre-testing was undertaken at the state level. As a consequence problems arose during the translation which could have been rectified if state level pre-tests of the translated survey instruments had been done. The state level pre-test must be the rule rather than the exception, especially when large-scale national surveys are involved.

It was the primary responsibility of the NCAER core team to ensure training of supervisors belonging both to NCAER and the networking institutions. A detailed training and scheduling plan was prepared for this purpose. In all, about 150 supervisors and about 600 investigators were trained for the purpose of collecting and compiling the data using the survey instruments all over India. The same team of investigators was used to do the house-listing of about 2,00,000 households, of which just over 33,000 households were selected for data collection. The local teams were given overall charge of charting out the field-work plan and the time scheduling of data collection. The state and national level monitoring teams were however in overall charge of ensuring the timely completion of the field operations.

The success of collection, compilation, and interpretation of the data may largely be attributed to the experience of NCAER staff in data processing and coordination of data collection throughout the states. Data coding, especially when the survey instruments did not contain self-coding designs, needed massive data transfer and coding exercises. This was achieved at the regional level. Often excessive centralization or decentralization can cause various practical problems. The regionalization of coding, data entry and consistency checks helped to maintain control over the quality of data as well as to meet time schedules without substantially increasing the cost of operations.

The unit of observation and analysis of this study is the household. Many of the attributes of interest in this study pertain to individuals in households, such as currently pregnant women and children aged 5–12 years. However, preparation of a sampling frame of individuals was considered to be extremely costly both in terms of time and money. As a compromise, households were selected as the final stage of sampling. Even the sampling frame, in the form of a list of all households, is neither available nor easily prepared. A multi-stage sampling design had therefore to be adopted. Multi-stage designs are generally less efficient from the viewpoint of sampling variability than sampling of individual units directly in a uni-stage sample. This loss was more than compensated by utilizing some auxiliary information for stratification and varying the probabilities of selection of sampling units at various stages.

The multi-stage sample design adopted was chosen on considerations of cost, both in terms of money and time, operational feasibility, and the precision of the estimates to be derived for selected population groups.

Sampling error of the estimates derived from survey data depends on the design adopted and the sample size. It also depends on the variability present in the universe from which the sample is drawn. The greater the variability in the universe the less precise will be the estimates derived from a sample. The stratification technique serves to divide the universe into several strata with lower variability within each stratum and consequently greater variability between strata. Since variability within strata is reduced, the relevant parameter within a stratum can be estimated with greater precision. The estimates pertaining to each stratum can then be suitably aggregated to arrive at the estimate pertaining to the universe. The ideal criterion for stratification is the same variable for which an estimate is sought. This is, however, difficult to follow in practice. The second best way is to stratify the universe according to some other variable(s) highly correlated to the variable of interest. The choice of stratification variables depend on the availability of data, and at times such data are collected before selection of the sample.

In a certain situation a stratum itself may be of special interest, for which separate estimates may be needed. A stratified sample readily provides such estimates. The technique of stratification has been used here at the stage of selecting sample districts and sample households from selected villages.

Selection of Sample

It is often advantageous to select sampling units with unequal probabilities instead of drawing a simple random sample. Simple averages as estimates tend to be biased in such cases. However, the bias can be estimated and adjusted to get an unbiased estimate of the parameter. Such unbiased estimates often have lower sampling errors in comparison to the corresponding simple random sample. The technique has been used for selection of districts only by making the probability of selection proportional to the size of the rural population obtained from the 1991 census.

For any scientifically selected sample, sampling errors of the estimates will decrease as the sample size increases. This will be zero for the largest sample size, as in the case of a census. Non-sampling error generally increases with the sample size for reasons discussed above. Total errors in the estimates derived will be the sum of sampling and non-sampling errors. If the sample size is increased, the sampling error decreases while the non-sampling error increases. Sampling error also depends on the actual value of the parameter being estimated. If the actual value is small, as in the case of child mortality, we shall need a larger sample size to estimate the parameter with tolerable precision. However, in this study the absolute magnitude of such estimates is not so important, the real objective being to rank various population groups according to the estimated parameters. In this too there is cause for concern only where the differences are large. A moderately large sample may be adequate for such purposes while a large sample will tend to increase non-sampling error. Further, in a multipurpose survey like this one, different parameters dictate different sample size. The sample size has to be chosen taking account of these variations so as to minimize the total error in the estimate.

Most of the parameters to be estimated out of the data collected through this survey are known to be correlated with income and female literacy. Data on female literacy are available in census publications. Detailed data on

Although the unit of observation and data collection of this survey is the household, information has been collected at individual and village level as well.

A stratified, multistage sampling procedure was adopted to identify the index household.

income are not easily available. However, in rural areas crop cultivation accounts for a major part of the income of a majority of the households. Income from agriculture thus becomes a good proxy for total income. Data on income from agriculture are available in publications of the Centre for Monitoring the Indian Economy. Keeping these and data availability in view, rural female literacy and income from agriculture were chosen as stratification variables for the districts. In each state, districts were cross-classified by income from agriculture and rural female literacy rate to form homogeneous strata in terms of these two variables. The number of such strata in a state was determined on considerations of the range of the stratification variables and the resulting frequency in each stratum. From

Selected Districts for the Survey

Selected Districts

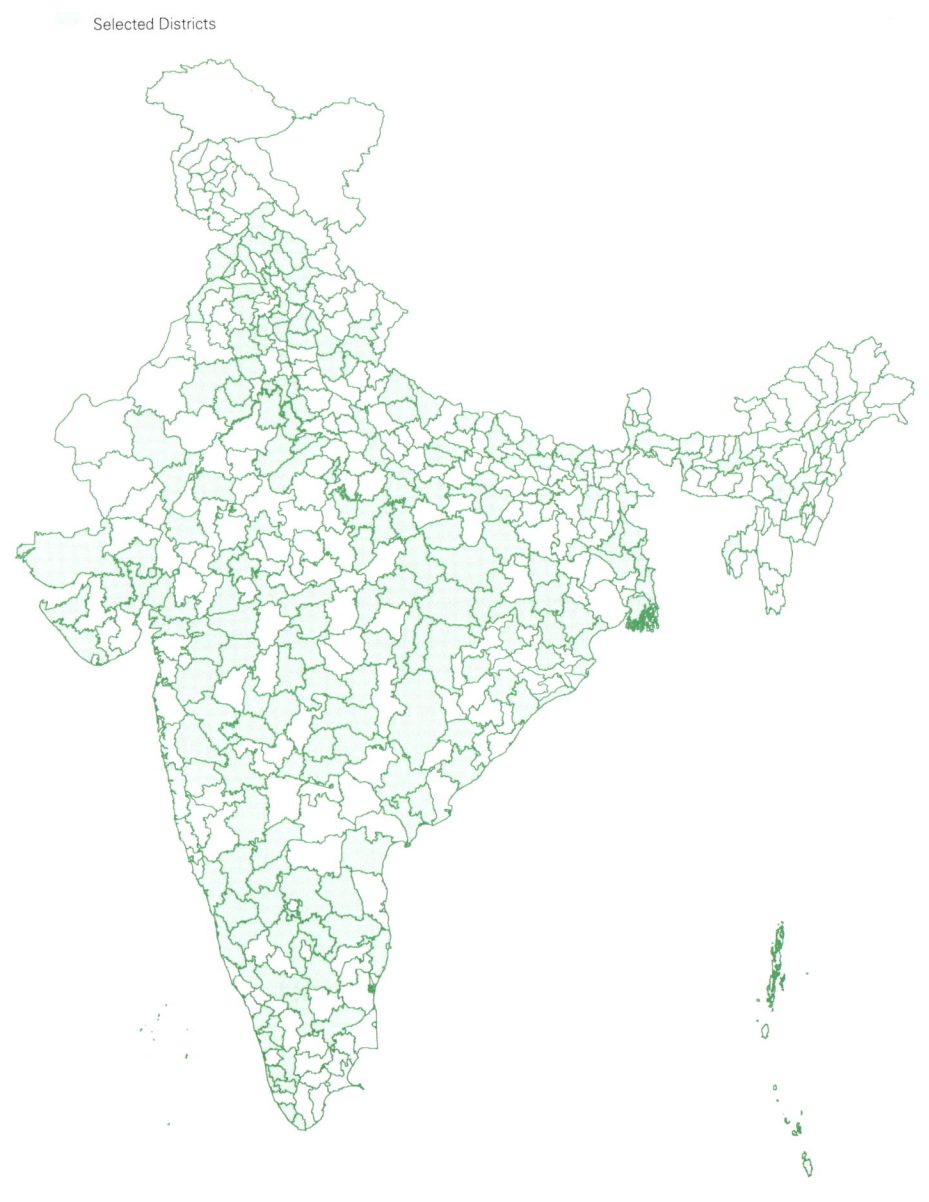

each of these strata a pre-assigned number of districts, depending on the size of the stratum, were selected with probability proportional to the rural population in the district.

A list of all the villages in the selected districts was obtained from census records. A pre-assigned number of sample villages were then selected linear systematically after arranging the villages in a *tehsil* (an administrative block, the level of a district) alternately in ascending and descending order of rural female literacy. The sampling interval in each district was suitably chosen to make the design partially self-weighting.

The households in the sample villages were listed along with some auxiliary information such as religion, caste, major source of income, cultivable land operated where major source of income was cultivation, and other social and demographic attributes of the households. For large villages only a part of the village, selected at random, was listed and sample households selected from these. These attributes of the listed households were used for stratification of the listed households.

The composition of the population in terms of attributes like religion, caste, occupation are different in different states. Also, population groups of interest to this survey are different in different states. The nature and number of strata of households formed in the states were therefore different. Two groups of listed households were separated as Stratum 1 and Stratum 2 in each of the states. These were:

Stratum 1   Households with at least one pregnant woman.
Stratum 2   Households with at least one child aged less than 12 months but no pregnant women.

The remaining households were stratified according to religion, ethnic group, and the occupation of the head of the household. The strata thus formed in various states along with allocation of sample households are shown in Annex I. Sample households from each of the non-empty strata so formed have been selected linear systematically. Sampling intervals were suitably chosen to make the design partially self-weighting. The total number of rural households selected in the sample was 35,130 spread over 1,765 villages and 195 districts in 16 states (see Table 2.1).

The precision of the estimates derived from the sample observations depends upon the sample size and the sample design adopted. Standard deviation of the sampling distribution (the so-called standard error) of these estimates can often be estimated without bias from the sample observations. Estimated standard errors of a few of the estimates pertaining to the states are presented in Annex II. Using the Central Limit theorem and the law of large numbers one can assert with 95 per cent confidence that the corresponding population parameter will lie in the interval $\Omega \pm 2\sigma$, where Ω is the estimate and σ is the standard error derived from the sample observations.

Besides estimating household-level human development parameters, data can be used to analyse intra-household dynamics as well as community factors on the standard and quality of life.

TABLE 2.1
Rural Sample by States

Regions/States	Total Number of Districts	Number of Sample			Households Surveyed
		Districts	Villages	Households	
North					
Haryana	16	11	90	1,808	1,722
Himachal Pradesh	12	8	65	1,260	1,225
Punjab	12	8	70	1,373	1,303
Upper Central					
Bihar	42	12	116	2,338	2,155
Uttar Pradesh	63	23	217	4,251	4,036
Lower Central					
Madhya Pradesh	45	25	217	4,320	4,162
Orissa	13	11	102	2,040	1,971
Rajasthan	27	12	106	2,102	1,984
West					
Gujarat	19	10	88	1,768	1,606
Maharashtra	30	16	151	2,998	2,765
East					
West Bengal	17	8	78	1,560	1,515
North-eastern Region	60	8	66	1,276	1,233
South					
Andhra Pradesh	22	12	113	2,244	2,100
Karnataka	20	15	135	2,747	2,523
Kerala	14	8	75	1,500	1,474
Tamil Nadu	20	8	76	1,545	1,456
All India	**433**	**195**	**1,765**	**35,130**	**33,230**

States and Population Groups

The sampling in each state was done independently so that estimates were obtained in a straightforward manner. Estimates pertaining to other population groups were obtained using the technique of post stratification. Unbiased estimates for various parameters were derived as the weighted sum of individual sample observations, the weights being the inverse of the probability of selection of the unit in the sample. The various population groups for which estimates were made are described below.

Categorization and grouping of populations into various categories is an extremely useful exercise. In this research there is an eightfold categorization of population groups. Each of these categories leads to a better understanding of Indian society. Population groups can be broadly categorized into two types although they are not presented in that order. They are: (a) those that highlight ordering based on economic and asset criteria, such as the household income group, poverty line group category, and landholding size category. In practice these are individual attributes and their identification for either policy purposes or for targeting often becomes very difficult; (b) the other criterion is to identify population groups on the basis of certain community characteristics that broadly reflect relative deprivation between population groups. For example, social groups categorizations based on religion and caste of individuals, occupation groups, literacy, village development index, and state identification conform to this type of categorization. The alternative approach adopted in this research is intended to improve the implementation of policy prescriptions and help direct budget allocations to clearly identifiable population groups and regions rather than individuals, which is less efficient, time consuming, and expensive.

Categorization According to States

All relevant indicators and consequent analysis are presented in three dimensions: (a) according to 16 major states; (b) according to eight different types of population groups; and (c) according to household income decile groups. Fifteen major states and the North-eastern region together comprise the 16 state category. The states are grouped in the following combinations— Northern Region: Haryana, Himachal Pradesh and Punjab; Upper Central Region: Bihar and Uttar Pradesh; Lower Central Region: Madhya Pradesh, Orissa and Rajasthan; Eastern Region: West Bengal and the North-eastern states; Western Region: Gujarat and Maharashtra; and Southern Region: Andhra Pradesh, Karnataka, Kerala, and Tamil Nadu. In this report, however, estimates at the level of these regions are not presented to avoid diversion into state comparisons.

Population Group Classification

Eight types of population groups have been created so as to create a comprehensive environment for meaningful interpretation of data. They are: (i) household income groups, (ii) poverty line groups, (iii) landholding groups, (iv) occupation groups, (v) social groups, (vi) household size groups, (vii) adult literacy groups, and (viii) Village Development Index groups.

For the household income groups, household incomes were computed by adding all monetary receipts and imputed money incomes earned by all members of the households participating in various types of occupations and enterprises. The returns from farming and wage labour activities, income from trade, professions, regular jobs, and rents and remittances were collected directly. The net agricultural income was computed by estimating the gross cultivated area under various crops and by applying village level norms of output and input per hectare and the respective prevailing harvest prices at the level of the village. Although the per capita incomes have been calculated, it was decided to use household incomes to create the income classification. Five household income categories were created using the cut offs created by the standard income surveys of the NCAER. The class intervals of annual household income are: (a) up to Rs 20,000; (b) Rs 20,001 to Rs 40,000; (c) Rs 40,001 to 62,000; (d) Rs 62,001 to 86,000; and (e) above Rs 86,000. The distribution suggests that 58 per cent of all households fall in the less than Rs 20,000 category followed by 27 per cent in the Rs 20,001 to 40,000 category.

To estimate the poverty line it is common practice to estimate the

Besides presenting estimates at state level, estimates are also available for eight carefully defined population groups.

percentage of poor based on a 'head count' using standard definitions. This method entails estimation of the poverty line expressed in terms of the amount of money required to purchase minimum nutrition and a few minimal requirements. After estimating a poverty line, the population below the line is further divided by using the mean income of this group. A similar division of those who are above the poverty line was made. This exercise created four groups identified as: (a) lower segment below the poverty line, (b) upper segment below the poverty line, (c) lower segment above the poverty line, and (d) upper segment above the poverty line. The respective percentage distribution of households adds up to 99.5 < 100.0 respectively.

India being a rural and agriculture-based economy in which the large majority are dependent on land as the principal source of income, a landholding classification is appropriate. All the sample households were therefore grouped as: (a) landless wage earner, (b) landless other occupation, (c) marginal farmer, (d) small farmer, (e) medium farmer, and (f) large farmer. Conventional land size categorizations were used to designate labels such as marginal, small, and the like. In this classification, the landless wage earners were those who owned no land at all but worked at least partly as agricultural wage labourers. A dichotomous category was also created, namely all landowners and all the landless.

Occupation groups are normally created using the reported occupation of the head of the household. This approach does not however capture the essence of recent changes occurring in the realm of transitions in occupation. For example, there have been substantial occupational shifts, diversification of occupations and multiple occupations among all the adult members of a household in the recent past. Therefore, in this study, the occupation groups have been created on the basis of major source of income criteria. The major source of income is that from which the total income of the household is the largest. There may, thus, be a traditional cultivator family, but if its principal source of income is from wage labour it is classified as a wage labour household. In this classification the wage earners may have other sources of income or even may have land but have been reported to be receiving the largest share of household income from wage labour. Although the landless constitute 37 per cent of the population, the landless wage earners are just about 20 per cent.

Two types of social groups were created: one based on reporting according to caste among the Hindus—they are the Scheduled Tribes (STs) and the Scheduled Castes (SCs). The other categorization was based exclusively on religious affiliation. The categories are Hindus, Muslims, Christians, and Other Minorities. All the above categories are based on the reported caste and religion of the head of the household. The presumption is that the remaining members of the household are followers of the religion and caste to which the household head belongs. During the state level discussion Sikhs were found among the Other Minorities category in Punjab.

Household size is a useful parameter and shows considerable variation between states and among the population groups. Three household size categories were created, namely up to 4, 5–7, and 8 and more members and the respective percentages are 33.5, 48.2, and 18.3 respectively.

Adult literacy is a crucial input in human development. There is a substantial variation in literacy between males and females in India. It is expected that different combinations of male and female education may yield different results in human development and welfare. Bearing this in mind, four adult literacy groups were created, namely (a) no literate adult male and no literate adult female, (b) only adult female is literate, (c) only adult male is literate, and (d) both male and female are literate.

A detailed village questionnaire was canvassed across all the 1,765 sample villages. The questionnaire covered economic, social, infrastructural (with emphasis on health, education-related facilities) aspects of the village. The information collected has been used to construct the development index at the village level. The index can be taken as one of the indicators of the level of human development in the rural regions of India.

A detailed village questionnaire was canvassed across the 1,765 sample villages.

Four types of indices were developed for each sample village. These are as follows:

a. Infrastructure and Amenities Index comprising variables such as accessibility of the village, means of media and communication available, presence of basic needs like safe drinking water, electricity.
b. Education Related Index comprising variables such as accessibility of educational institutions, female–male student ratio in primary schools, presence of special schemes like mid-day meals, scholarships.
c. Health Related Index comprising variables such as accessibility to health facilities.
d Other Development Indicators Related Index comprising variables such as proportion of irrigated area to cropped area, number of government/NGO schemes functioning in the village.

An overall composite index as an unweighted average of the above listed sectoral indices was computed. The maximum score assigned to each of the individual indices reflects the focus and the priority of the project. The scores are as given below:

Index type (a)	score 88
Index type (b)	score 87
Index type (c)	score 68
Index type (d)	score 20
Total maximum score	263

Given the maximum score possible, the index of each village was arrived at in the following way:

$$\frac{\text{Score obtained by the village}}{\text{Maximum score}} \times 100$$

Based on the value of the composite index the villages were categorized as follows:

Less developed villages	index value 0–30
Moderately developed villages	index value 31–45
Developed villages	index value 46–100

Finally, the threefold classification of the villages was incorporated as a control variable in the tables describing the characteristics of the sample households.

The profile of indicators, parameters and measures are presented in a particular order to ensure easy flow of discussion. The principal aim of this study is to introduce data, identify and define parameters, highlight their quality, and generate interest among academics and policy-makers. First, all issues are discussed at the level of India and 16 major states followed by a discussion highlighting differentials according to eight population groups. State level estimates for three population groups, namely household income, social group, and village development, index are discussed separately. A detailed state-wise presentation of indicators according to eight population groups can be found in 16 separate volumes by state (forthcoming).

BOX 2.1

The Sample Tree

● **15 States and North-eastern Region**

- Stratified by rural female literacy, income from agriculture
- Probability proportional to rural population

● **Districts 195**

- Linear systematic selection method

● **Villages 1,765**

- Stratified by various economic and demographic attributes
- Linear systematic selection method

● **Households 35,130**

3

Poverty and Relative Income

Material well-being has traditionally been judged in terms of the command people have over income and assets. The literature on this subject abounds in controversies over methodology of data collection and empirical estimation procedures. This report presents indicators that highlight both direct income and assets, and various indirect dimensions of prosperity, such as employment and wage stability, dependency ratio, and consumption expenditures.

His cottage may be frail—its roof may shake—the wind may blow through it—the storm may enter—but an alien idea cannot enter—change agents dare not cross the threshold of the ruined tenant!

Levels of Household Income

This section presents data on the inter-state and inter-group variations in annual total and per capita household income (*see* Table 3.1). The rural per capita Net State Domestic Product (NSDP), indirectly estimated by using CSO data for the year 1993–4, are compared with the survey data and discussed. The Gini ratio based on the distribution of total household income is also estimated.

The NSDP normally contains many types of income that do not accrue at the level of the household. For example, profits both from public and private sector undertakings do not entirely get distributed to households; rather they are directly accounted for to compute domestic product. Similarly, the value added due to mining activities, forest based products, and other natural resources are directly accounted for in the National Accounts while only a nominal proportion may get transferred to the households through wage payment and activities relating to their processing, storage, and transport. Besides, it is also true that direct incomes are normally under-reported due to various practical considerations. For example, the rich wish to understate income to avoid paying large sums of Income Tax. On the other hand, the relatively poor wish to understate household incomes in the hope of becoming eligible for innumerable kinds of direct and indirect subsidies announced by the government under poverty alleviation and other welfare programmes. The perks and subsidies offered to regular salaried employees and returns from investments in banks and securities are less likely to be netted in the household surveys.

For all these reasons, it is expected that directly observed levels of household per capita income would be lower than those implied by the NSDP estimates. Nonetheless, it is useful to validate the observed household income data from the HDI survey with available NSDP estimates. This can be done only at the all India level for reasons that will be explained later.

TABLE 3.1

Levels of Income and Poverty Line by States

Regions/States	Sample Size	Estimated % of Households	Income (Rs per year)		Proportion of Mean PCI	Gini Ratio PCI	Poverty Line (Rs/year)***
			Per Household	Per Capita			
North							
Haryana	1,722	1.9	39,956	6,368 (2)	1.42	0.37	2,818
Himachal Pradesh	1,225	0.8	23,973	4,168 (12)	0.93	0.39	2,818
Punjab	1,303	2.2	37,418	6,380 (1)	1.42	0.39	2,818
Upper Central							
Bihar	2,155	11.5	22,459	3,691 (14)	0.82	0.39	2,535
Uttar Pradesh	4,036	16.1	26,733	4,185 (11)	0.93	0.42	2,557
Lower Central							
Madhya Pradesh	4,162	7.7	25,319	4,166 (13)	0.93	0.41	2,324
Orissa	1,971	4.4	17,208	3,028 (16)	0.68	0.42	2,330
Rajasthan	1,984	5.1	27,184	4,229 (10)	0.94	0.41	2,623
East							
North-eastern Region**	1,233	4.3	28,160	5,070 (7)	1.13	0.34	2,775
West Bengal	1,515	7.9	18,113	3,157 (15)	0.70	0.35	2,642
West							
Gujarat	1,606	4.5	29,356	5,288 (5)	1.18	0.49	2,418
Maharashtra	2,765	8.2	29,929	5,525 (4)	1.23	0.45	2,338
South							
Andhra Pradesh	2,100	9.1	24,776	5,046 (8)	1.13	0.42	1,954
Karnataka	2,523	5.0	27,372	4,769 (9)	1.06	0.49	2,241
Kerala	1,474	3.9	29,101	5,778 (3)	1.29	0.40	2,922
Tamil Nadu	1,456	7.4	23,271	5,122 (6)	1.14	0.43	2,370
All India	**33,230**	**100.0**	**25,653**	**4,485***	**1**	**0.43**	**2,444**

* The all India Rural NSDP estimated indirectly based on CSO figures is Rs 5,036.
** The PCI estimate for Assam represents the North-eastern Region. The correlation coefficient between estimates of per capita income by NCAER and CSO estimates is 0.79. The corresponding rank correlation is 0.80.
*** Poverty lines for 1973–74 estimated by the Planning Commission have been updated using state-specific CPIAL as deflators.

Figures in parentheses are ranks.

One opinion is that consumer expenditure is a better indicator of well-being since consumption is believed to be influenced by past saving as well as prospects of future income. From this point of view the use of consumption data is considered to be more appropriate. However, the object of studying inequality in income or level of living in a poor country is to lay bare the disparities in the opportunities available to different sections of the population to earn a livelihood. Realized consumption often includes public expenditure on services such as health, education, and nutrition, and thus reflects a higher level of well-being than income alone would indicate. Besides, at least in the short-term it is possible that the current consumption has been maintained through liquidation of both movable and immovable assets. In such a case the data on direct income would appear more appropriate for analytical purposes.

The household income estimated from the survey reflects the actual short-term worth of households and their capacity to mobilize funds for immediate expenditure. A comparison of total or per capita household income across states is attempted below. Regional differences in the prices of essential commodities are ignored. The following discussion should be viewed in this perspective.

An average rural household in the country earns Rs 25,653 per year which corresponds to Rs 4,485 per capita. Haryana and Punjab are among the states that recorded high levels of household income at Rs 39,956 and Rs 37,418, respectively, which corresponds to a per capita income of Rs 6,368 and Rs 6,380, respectively. It is also expected that the under-reporting of income is much higher in Punjab and Haryana. Other states whose total as well as per capita household incomes are above the all India average are Maharashtra (Rs 29,299 total household and Rs 5,525 per capita), Gujarat (Rs 29,356 total household and Rs 5,288 per capita), and Karnataka (Rs 27,372 total household and Rs 4,769 per capita). Many states such as Orissa, West Bengal, Bihar, Madhya Pradesh and Himachal Pradesh have low household as well as per capita incomes. Orissa has the least total household income (Rs 17,208) as well as per capita income (Rs 3,028). It is likely, however, that this survey has underestimated the rural income in West Bengal which is less than even the state of Bihar.

Total household income in Kerala has been estimated at Rs 29,101, and the per capita income is considerably higher than the all India average of Rs 5,778 because of small average household size. Other states that have lower total household but higher per capita incomes than the national average are Tamil Nadu and Andhra Pradesh. On the other hand, Rajasthan and Uttar Pradesh which have relatively higher household incomes but lower per capita incomes than the national average suggest large household size. Apart from West Bengal, all low-income states fall in the central region of the country, covering over 50 per cent of India's population.

It is inappropriate to compare the per capita income survey estimates with those provided by the official per capita income estimates given by the Central Statistical Organization. In the first place the NSDP figures are a state level cumulation of the indirect estimates of the value added for a number of sub-sectors across the whole economy which is then divided by the mid-year population. Secondly, the survey estimates are only for rural areas and therefore unsuitable for comparison with per capita NSDP. The routinely published NSDP estimates for all India and states do not give the rural–urban break-up. It is possible, however, to estimate the all India rural NSDP indirectly using the proportion of all India rural and urban shares in NSDP provided by the CSO for the year 1980–1. The rural–urban share of income is rarely published by the CSO, and only at the all India level. Since the share of urban will be substantially different in different states depending upon the rate of urbanization, the ideal solution would be to compute the rural incomes for each state separately. Such estimates are however difficult to undertake without state level break-ups. However, all India average rural per capita NSDP for the year 1994 worked out to be Rs 5,036. This is only about 11 per cent higher than the survey estimate of

Practically all low-income states fall in the central region of the country, covering over 50 per cent of India's population.

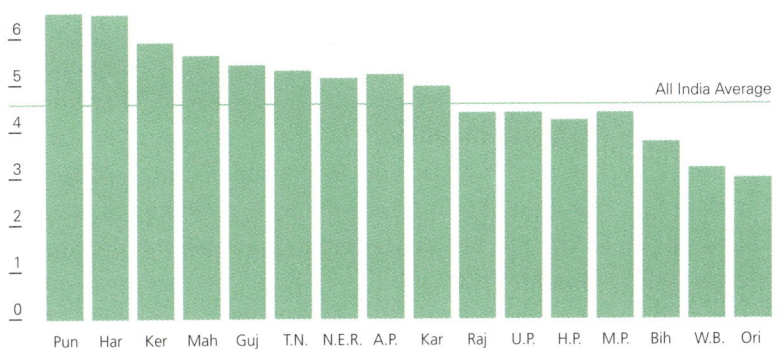

Average Per Capita Income

Among States
Rs '000

Among Poverty Groups
Rs '000

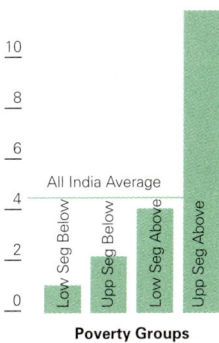

Rs 4,485. The survey has therefore been relatively successful in capturing household incomes.

The reasons for the relatively higher incomes that figure in the CSO estimates have been discussed above. However, the relevant factor accounting for this difference may be the income generated by some sectors of the economy whose value added does not percolate to households due to the indivisibility problem discussed earlier. Besides, it appears that most of the state income in the so-called backward states accrues as a result of primary, domestic, and household activities as opposed to industrial and largely market-based activities in the relatively prosperous states.

While total household and per capita incomes present absolute averages at the level of the state, they do not highlight income inequality within the state. The Gini ratio is a popular index of income inequality within population groups. It ranges between 0 and 1, and the higher value signifies relatively larger income inequality. The Gini ratio for rural India, based on distribution of household according to per capita income, is 0.43, and the ratio ranges between 0.49 in Karnataka and Gujarat to 0.34 in the north-east and 0.35 in West Bengal. It is lower than the national average in Himachal Pradesh, Haryana, Bihar, Orissa, Kerala, Madhya Pradesh, and Rajasthan whereas it is high in Gujarat, Karnataka, and Maharashtra. Generally speaking, the disparity appears low among states with lower per capita income and high among states with relatively higher per capita income with the exception of Haryana and Kerala which present an encouraging picture of higher per capita income with low disparity.

Table 3.2 presents the household and per capita incomes of eight types of population groups (*see* chapter 2 for a detailed categorization of population groups). Obviously, both total household and per capita income increase with the size class of income and poverty categorization. The respective average total household income for the five income classes are Rs 11,027; Rs 28,141, Rs 49,072, Rs 72,178, and Rs 1,47,855, and the respective per capita incomes are Rs 2,192, Rs 4,506, Rs 7,132, Rs 9,309, and Rs 17,865. The household income is about 12.4 times higher for the size class of above

Among Social Groups
Rs '000

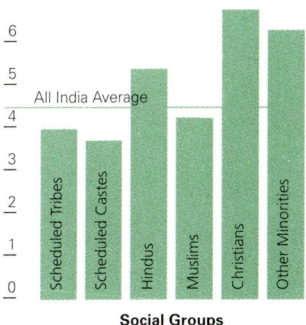

Among Village Development and Household Size Groups
Rs '000

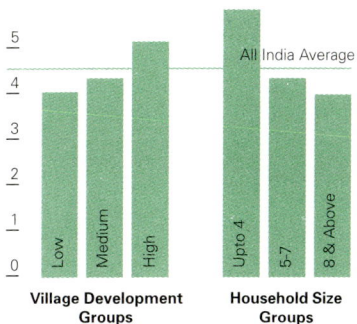

3 The ratio has been estimated using the Trapezoidal rule:

$$G = \sum_{i=1}^{n-1} P_i Q_{i+1} - \sum_{i=1}^{n-1} Q_i P_{i+1}$$

where P_i is the proportion of persons with income Y_i or less and Q_i is their share in income.

Rs 86,000 in comparison with the lowest group; and in the case of per capita income it is seven times larger. The Gini ratio, which presents relative dispersion within the group, is really low only in the highest income category.

The mean levels of household incomes for the four poverty group classifications are Rs 6,950, Rs 12,379, Rs 22,138, Rs 58,100 respectively. Households grouped under the lowest segment below the poverty line (about 16 per cent of the households) have an average per capita income of only Rs 1,095 followed by Rs 2,026 for those in the upper segment below the poverty line (18.5 per cent of all households) which is 24 per cent and 45 per cent of the mean income. Per capita per day availability of income during 1994 worked out to be as low as Rs 3 and Rs 5.5 respectively, which is too low even to replenish the basic caloric requirements for survival. The Gini ratios are extremely low for all the four poverty-based categories, showing a high degree of homogeneity in levels of income within these groups. It may be useful to select these households for a separate analysis.

Income disparity is low among states with low per capita income and high among states with high per capita income. It is greater among the lower income categories.

TABLE 3.2
Levels of Income and Inequality by Population Groups

Population Groups	No. of Sample Households	Income (Rs per year)		Gini Ratio
		Per Household	Per Capita	
Household Income Groups				
Upto 20,000	18,582	11,027	2,192	0.23
20,000–40,000	8,925	28,141	4,506	0.25
40,000–62,000	3,175	49,072	7,132	0.20
62,000–86,000	1,224	72,178	9,309	0.21
Above 86,000	1,324	1,47,855	17,865	0.07
Poverty Line Groups				
Lower segment below	5,256	6,950	1,095	0.16
Upper segment below	6,144	12,379	2,026	0.07
Lower segment above	14,698	22,138	3,931	0.12
Upper segment above	7,132	58,100	11,396	0.17
Landholding Groups				
Landless wage earner	5,834	11,313	2,308	0.30
Marginal	10,521	19,586	3,502	0.39
Small	6,212	29,377	4,803	0.36
Medium	3,282	44,695	6,516	0.37
Large	1,989	85,969	10,930	0.27
Landless others	5,392	21,574	4,111	0.36
Land owners	22,004	31,154	5,108	0.41
Landless	11,226	16,141	3,187	0.34
Occupational Groups				
Cultivators	15,347	32,374	5,408	0.47
Salaried+Prof.+S.Empl.	4,224	35,760	5,857	0.34
Wage earners	8,596	12,580	2,450	0.27
All others	5,063	21,010	3,709	0.36

Contd.

Social Groups				
Caste				
STs	3,770	19,556	3,504	0.42
SCs	7,238	17,465	3,237	0.32
Religion				
Hindus	27,767	25,713	4,514	0.43
Muslims	3,239	22,807	3,678	0.40
Christians	900	28,860	5,920	0.39
Other Minorities	1,324	30,330	5,427	0.48
Household Size Groups				
Up to 4	10,679	18,399	5,687	0.42
5-7	15,846	25,060	4,326	0.41
8 and above	6,705	40,449	4,019	0.43
Adult Literacy Groups				
None literate	9,674	15,271	3,138	0.28
Female literate	1,045	19,060	3,987	0.42
Male literate	10,779	24,367	4,137	0.41
Both literate	11,732	36,187	5,683	0.42
Village Development Groups				
Low	9,724	24,149	4,045	0.42
Medium	13,060	25,173	4,369	0.41
High	10,446	27,628	5,079	0.45
All India	**33,230**	**25,653**	**4,485**	**0.43**

* Estimate not available.

Among Poverty Groups
Rs '000

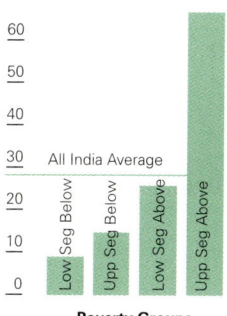

Poverty Groups

It is noteworthy, however, that about 22 per cent of households that fall in the upper segment above the poverty line have a per capita income of Rs 11,396, which is 2.5 times higher than the national average and 10.4 times higher than the per capita income of those in the lower segment below the poverty line.

As expected, per capita household income increases considerably with

Among Social Groups
Rs '000

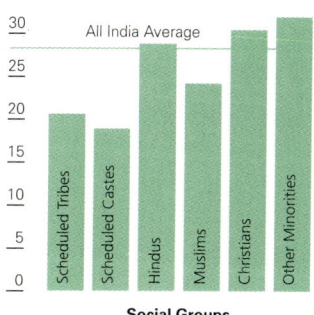

Social Groups

Average Household Income

Among States
Rs '000

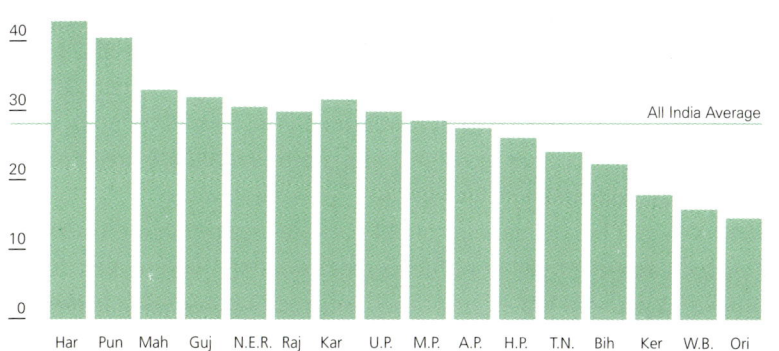

Among Village Development and Household Size Groups
Rs '000

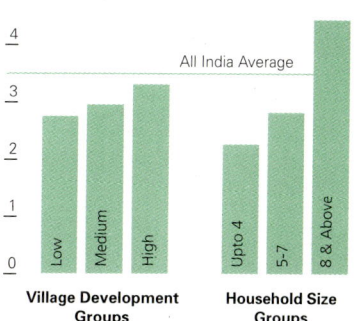

the size of landholding. For example, the landless wage earners have an average total income of Rs 11,313, and a per capita income of Rs 2,308 per annum which is 48 per cent lower than the all India average of Rs 4,485. This difference is only 22 per cent lower for marginal farmers and 7 per cent higher for small farmers, 45 per cent higher for medium farmers, and 144 per cent higher for large farmers. Thus, rural incomes are clearly a function of the size of landownership in India. The Gini ratios among all these categories are moderate.

The levels of income are high for the salaried, professional, and trading classes who constitute about 13 per cent of all rural households. Their per capita income is 31 per cent higher than the national average and 2.4 times higher in relation to wage earners. Wage earners recorded 45 per cent lower per capita income than the all India average. The income of wage earners is only Rs 2,450 per capita per year (Rs 6.70 per day per person) which is about 58 per cent lower than that for the salaried, professionals, and traders, and 55 per cent less than that of farmers. Wage earners are a relatively homogeneous group in terms of levels of income, as is reflected by the Gini ratios.

While household income increases considerably with size of household, the per capita income in fact falls. This phenomenon is because of the differentials in composition in terms of age and sex, as well as number of earning members per household. It is therefore desirable to undertake age-standardized estimates to substantiate most of the above comparisons. However, household size is closely associated with the life cycle issues that enable changes both in the size and composition of households, and in turn affect levels of income. Per capita income is about 30 per cent lower for large households (8 or more members) than for households with 4 or less members.

The levels of income by social groups suggest that both total household and per capita incomes are the least among SCs followed by STs in comparison with the national average. SCs have a total household income of Rs 17,465 and per capita income of Rs 3,237, which is only about 68 per cent of the all India mean household income and 72 per cent of the all India mean per capita income. Similarly, STs have a total household income of Rs 19,556 and a per capita income of Rs 3,504 which are 76 and 78 per cent respectively, of the national average. Although variation is large, the SCs display relatively more homogeneous patterns in levels of income as reflected by the Gini ratio.

Among the religious categories, Christians recorded the highest levels of income, of Rs 28,860 per annum, followed by the Hindus with Rs 25,713, and Muslims with Rs 22,807. The per capita income differentials between religious groups are all the more significant due to the vast differentials in family size. The respective per capita incomes are Rs 5,920 for Christians, Rs 4,514 for Hindus, and Rs 3,678 for Muslims.

The level of adult literacy in a household has a close correlation with the level of income. For example, households that have both literate men and women have 81 per cent higher incomes compared to households in which all adult members are illiterate.

TABLE 3.3

Percentage Distribution of Households by Income Groups

(Survey conducted by NCAER in recent years - All India)

Income Groups	Market Information Survey of Households					Human Development Indicator Survey 1994
	1986	1988	1990	1993	1994	
1	2	3	4	5	6	7
Rural						
Low	73.6	68.8	67.3	65.5	65.4	57.6
Lower Middle	21.4	25.8	23.9	22.6	23.2	26.8
Middle	4.0	4.3	7.1	8.2	7.5	8.9
Upper Middle	0.7	0.7	1.2	2.3	2.5	3.3
High	0.3	0.4	0.5	1.4	1.4	3.4
Total	100.0	100.0	100.0	100.0	100.0	100.0
Urban						
Low	42.1	42.3	37.1	38.4	36.7	NA
Lower Middle	35.8	35.5	34.8	33.0	33.1	NA
Middle	15.2	16.2	17.9	16.1	17.1	NA
Upper Middle	3.8	5.0	6.4	7.6	7.8	NA
High	2.1	3.0	3.8	4.9	5.3	NA
Total	100.0	100.0	100.0	100.0	100.0	NA

Source: Cols. 2 to 6: NCAER, Market Information Surveys of Households. Col. 7: NCAER/HDI Survey, 1994.

Cut-off Levels of Household Income for Various Years

Rs, current prices

Year	Low	Lower Middle	Middle	Upper Middle	High
1986	up to 9,000	9,001–18,000	18,001–30,000	30,001–42,000	Above 42,000
1988	up to 11,000	11,001–22,000	22,001–36,000	36,001–50,000	Above 50,000
1990	up to 12,500	12,501–25,000	25,001–40,000	40,001–56,000	Above 56,000
1993	up to 18,000	18,001–36,000	36,001–56,000	56,001–78,000	Above 78,000
1994	up to 20,000	20,001–40,000	40,001–62,000	62,001–86,000	Above 86,000

Percentage Distribution of Households by States

Income Group: Above Rs 86,000

Per cent

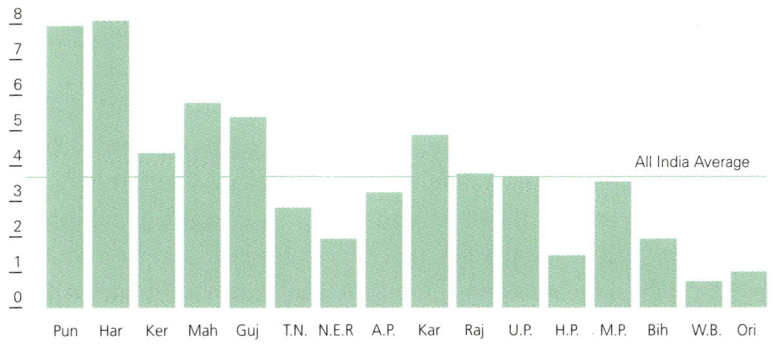

As expected, both the levels of household and per capita income increase with the level of village development. For example, developed villages have 25 per cent higher per capita income than the less developed one. As will be discussed subsequently, the share of income in the developed villages from non-agricultural sources is higher.

The distribution of households by income classes is presented in App. Table A.3.1. For rural India, 58 per cent of households fall below the Rs 20,000 income category, followed by 27, 9, 3.3, and 3.4 per cent in subsequent income categories. It is further apparent that the proportion of households in the 'up to Rs 20,000' category is only 34 per cent in Haryana and 42 per cent in Punjab, whereas it is as high as 74 per cent in Orissa and 71 per cent in West Bengal. The relative proportion of rich households is also high in Haryana, Punjab, and Maharashtra (17.5, 15, and 10 per cent respectively).

Table 3.3 presents the percentage distribution of households by income groups from other surveys conducted by NCAER during 1986–94. The estimates presented in columns 2 to 6 are taken from the series of surveys called the Market Information Survey of Households, and estimates in column 7 are from the present survey. One can see a clear decline in the proportion of low income category households although the transition to the higher income categories has been modest both in terms of percentages and absolute numbers. The income cut-off for successive years have been adjusted taking the rate of inflation into consideration.

While the distribution of household income according to land size categories confirms a direct positive correlation, occupation groups further affirm the relative advantage of the salaried, professional, and business class households. The proportion of ST and SC households in the lowest income category is over 70 per cent in comparison with only 50 per cent of all Hindu households. The share of Hindus in the higher income slabs is substantially higher than that of the STs and SCs discussed above (App. Table A.3.2).

Share and Structure of Household Income

Some interesting observations emerge from the study of the share of household income from various sources for states (Table 3.4). On the whole, agriculture and allied activities contribute to 55 per cent of the total household income in rural India. This is followed by income from salaries and professional services (16.5 per cent), agricultural wages (7.9 per cent), non-agricultural wages (6.3 per cent), petty trade (5 per cent), and other self-employment and artisanship (4.5 per cent).

Karnataka, Madhya Pradesh, Maharashtra and Gujarat show relatively high levels of income from agriculture and allied sources. States in which the share of agriculture is low are: Tamil Nadu, West Bengal, and the North-eastern region. The contribution of both agricultural and non-agricultural wages is relatively high in Tamil Nadu, that of petty business and agricultural wages in West Bengal, salaries and non-agricultural wages in Himachal Pradesh, and salaries and petty business in the North-eastern region.

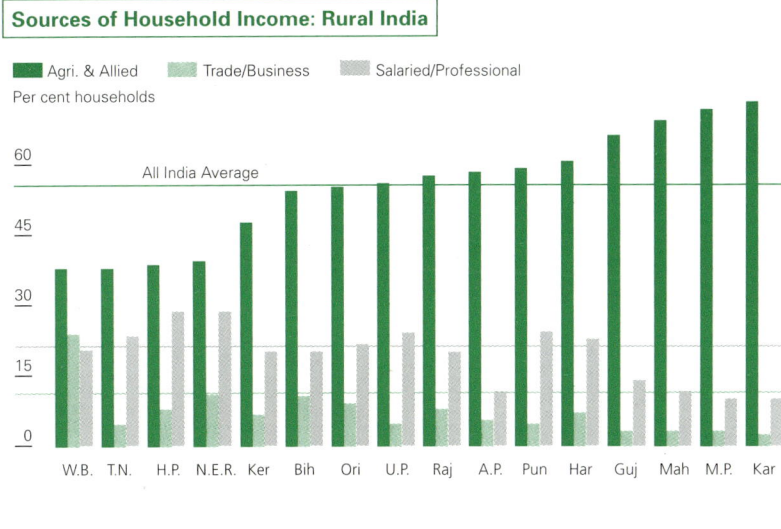

Sources of Household Income: Rural India

■ Agri. & Allied ■ Trade/Business ■ Salaried/Professional

Per cent households

All India Average

W.B. T.N. H.P. N.E.R. Ker Bih Ori U.P. Raj A.P. Pun Har Guj Mah M.P. Kar

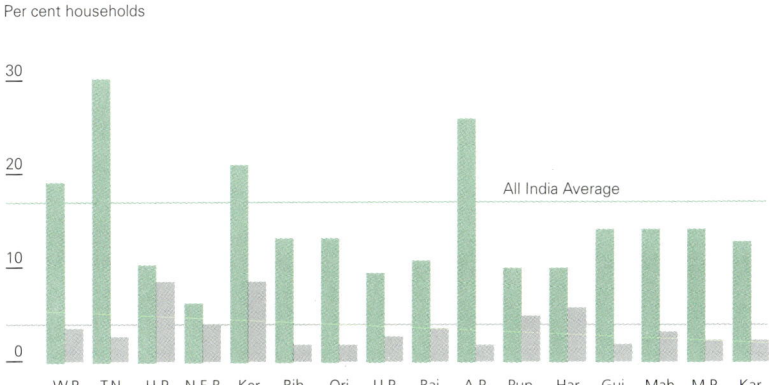

■ Wage (Agri.+Non-agri.) ■ Other Sources

Per cent households

All India Average

W.B. T.N. H.P. N.E.R. Ker Bih Ori U.P. Raj A.P. Pun Har Guj Mah M.P. Kar

TABLE 3.4

Percentage Distribution of Household Income by States

Regions/States	Percentage Distribution w.r.t. Total Household Income										All Sources
	Agr.+Alld. Activities	Artisan/ Ind.Work	Petty Trd. Small Bus.	Orgnd Trd. Business	Salaried Employmt.	Qualified Professn.	Rent/Int. Dividend	Agrl. Wage	Non-agrl. Wage	Other Sources	
North											
Haryana	58.5	2.6	4.1	0.6	20.0	0.5	1.6	3.0	5.5	3.6	100.0
Himachal Pradesh	37.5	5.7	3.1	1.3	29.0	0.5	1.3	0.4	12.1	9.1	100.0
Punjab	56.3	3.8	4.5	0.3	21.6	0.5	2.1	3.2	5.5	2.2	100.0
Upper Central											
Bihar	52.8	5.8	8.7	2.1	15.2	0.8	0.5	6.7	6.4	1.0	100.0
Uttar Pradesh	54.6	7.0	3.1	2.5	21.6	0.5	0.4	2.9	5.7	1.6	100.0
Lower Central											
Madhya Pradesh	69.6	3.5	3.0	0.4	8.7	0.3	0.5	7.3	5.7	1.0	100.0
Orissa	53.5	4.8	6.8	3.5	16.4	0.2	0.8	5.9	7.3	0.8	100.0
Rajasthan	56.0	5.1	3.9	2.2	18.1	0.1	1.4	0.9	9.9	2.5	100.0

Contd.

East										
North-eastern Rg.	37.7	3.8	10.9	6.0	29.2	2.1	1.0	3.3	4.6	1.5	100.0
West Bengal	36.7	4.0	18.7	3.3	18.6	0.8	0.2	12.2	4.4	1.2	100.0
West										
Gujarat	64.8	2.7	2.6	1.5	13.6	0.3	0.6	9.4	3.6	0.7	100.0
Maharashtra	67.2	1.2	3.1	1.0	10.9	0.4	1.2	10.0	3.0	1.9	100.0
South										
Andhra Pradesh	56.0	4.9	2.7	1.0	9.5	0.6	0.3	19.7	4.7	0.5	100.0
Karnataka	69.8	3.9	2.8	0.9	8.9	0.2	0.3	8.9	3.5	0.9	100.0
Kerala	46.5	3.3	3.5	1.8	15.1	0.6	0.7	10.0	10.5	8.1	100.0
Tamil Nadu	36.8	6.3	2.2	1.6	23.0	0.5	0.3	13.0	15.4	0.8	100.0
All India	**55.0**	**4.5**	**5.0**	**1.9**	**16.5**	**0.5**	**0.7**	**7.9**	**6.3**	**1.7**	**100.0**
C.V.	21.0	34.3	80.1	74.6	35.9	81.2	65.2	68.1	49.9	106.8	–

TABLE 3.5

Percentage Distribution of Household Income by Source across Population Groups

Population Groups	Percentage Distribution of Total Household Income										All Sources
	Agr+Alld. Activity	Artisan/ Ind.Work	Petty Trd. Small Bus.	Orgnd Trd. Business	Salaried Employmt.	Qualified Professn.	Rent/Int. Dividend	Agrl. Wage	Non-agrl. Wage	Other Sources	
Household Income Groups											
Up to 20,000	39.1	7.5	7.2	0.7	6.8	0.4	0.7	21.6	14.1	1.9	100.0
20,001–40,000	50.4	5.1	6.5	2.0	19.1	0.6	0.7	6.9	6.6	2.0	100.0
40,001–62,000	56.5	3.6	4.2	2.7	23.9	0.7	0.8	2.3	3.2	2.1	100.0
62,001–86,000	63.6	2.7	3.1	2.9	21.8	0.7	0.7	1.1	1.8	1.6	100.0
Above 86,000	76.6	1.7	1.5	2.1	15.7	0.3	0.5	0.3	0.5	0.7	100.0
Poverty Line Groups											
Lower segment below	38.8	6.2	4.9	0.4	4.4	0.2	0.4	26.6	16.9	1.2	100.0
Upper segment below	38.5	7.4	8.6	1.3	6.5	0.5	0.5	20.1	15.3	1.4	100.0
Lower segment above	48.3	6.1	6.6	1.6	15.1	0.5	0.7	10.6	8.3	2.2	100.0
Upper segment above	64.6	2.6	3.1	2.4	20.4	0.7	0.7	2.0	2.1	1.4	100.0
Landholding Groups											
Landless wage earners	2.8	2.0	0.9	0.1	1.2	0.2	0.2	51.8	40.0	0.8	100.0
Marginal	48.0	5.1	5.5	1.7	18.6	0.6	0.7	9.2	7.4	3.1	100.0
Small	71.9	2.1	2.6	1.8	13.9	0.4	0.4	3.3	2.3	1.2	100.0
Medium	82.2	1.2	1.9	1.4	9.2	0.3	0.4	1.4	1.3	0.7	100.0
Large	90.2	0.8	1.2	0.8	5.2	0.2	0.4	0.3	0.4	0.5	100.0
Landless others	3.2	16.4	17.7	5.3	46.3	1.5	2.0	2.3	2.1	3.2	100.0
Landowners	70.5	2.6	3.1	1.5	12.5	0.4	0.5	4.1	3.3	1.5	100.0
Landless	3.0	11.1	11.5	3.3	29.6	1.0	1.3	20.7	16.2	2.3	100.0
Occupational Groups											
Cultivators	88.1	1.2	1.5	0.5	3.5	0.2	0.3	2.6	1.5	0.7	100.0
Salaried+Prof.+S.Empl.	14.7	1.0	1.2	0.2	77.9	2.3	0.4	0.7	0.8	0.6	100.0
Wage earners	12.0	1.7	0.8	0.1	1.1	0.1	0.1	45.9	37.4	0.7	100.0
All others	13.4	26.4	29.6	12.1	1.9	0.1	3.2	2.2	2.4	8.7	100.0

Contd.

Social Groups											
Caste											
STs	55.6	2.7	3.2	1.5	14.8	0.8	0.5	11.7	8.0	1.0	100.0
SCs	37.7	5.7	5.1	1.0	15.2	0.5	0.5	19.7	13.1	1.5	100.0
Religion											
Hindus	56.1	4.3	4.6	1.8	16.4	0.5	0.6	8.0	6.2	1.5	100.0
Muslims	44.1	8.3	9.9	2.9	14.7	0.8	0.5	7.7	7.4	3.8	100.0
Christians	46.3	2.9	4.1	1.9	23.5	0.4	0.5	9.4	7.8	3.1	100.0
Other Minorities	60.3	3.1	3.7	0.6	17.6	0.8	1.9	5.2	5.0	1.7	100.0
Household Size Groups											
Up to 4	50.9	4.5	4.5	1.3	15.4	0.7	1.1	11.8	7.4	2.4	100.0
5–7	54.9	4.7	5.1	1.9	16.3	0.6	0.6	8.2	6.4	1.4	100.0
8 and above	58.5	4.4	5.3	2.4	17.5	0.4	0.6	4.2	5.1	1.6	100.0
Adult Literacy Groups											
None literate	52.5	5.8	3.4	0.4	3.3	0.2	0.6	19.5	12.3	1.9	100.0
Female literate	51.5	3.8	3.4	1.8	7.5	0.4	0.9	14.3	8.8	7.4	100.0
Male literate	56.9	5.5	4.8	1.3	14.2	0.5	0.5	8.0	7.1	1.3	100.0
Both literate	54.8	3.5	5.8	2.8	23.0	0.7	0.8	3.5	3.5	1.6	100.0
Village Development Groups											
Low	61.2	4.8	3.3	1.3	14.3	0.4	0.5	6.1	6.6	1.4	100.0
Medium	56.0	4.2	5.3	1.7	15.7	0.5	0.7	8.7	5.5	1.7	100.0
High	48.8	4.7	6.1	2.6	19.0	0.7	0.9	8.5	6.8	1.9	100.0
All India	**55.0**	**4.5**	**5.0**	**1.9**	**16.5**	**0.5**	**0.7**	**7.9**	**6.3**	**1.7**	**100.0**

The origin of income and its share in total household income according to population group presents some very instructive insights (Table 3.5). It is clear that prosperity in rural India is closely linked with the size of landownership and exploitation of land. While those in the lowest income category derive only 39 per cent of their income from agriculture, they get 22 and 14 per cent respectively, from agricultural and non-agricultural wages. The share of agricultural income increases from 39 to 50, 57, 64, and 77 per cent in the successive household income categories. The middle income groups receive up to one quarter of their income from salaries and professional services. Similarly, landless wage earners receive 52 and 40 per cent, respectively (92 per cent in all), of income from agricultural and non-agricultural wage employment alone while large landowners derive 90 per cent of their income from cultivation alone. As is to be expected, those in the lower segment below the poverty line receive 44 per cent from wage employment and another 39 per cent from cultivation.

The share of income from agriculture is relatively high among STs in comparison with SCs. The share of income from wage labour (both agricultural and non-agricultural) is highest among SCs at about 33 per cent followed by about 20 per cent among STs.

Among religious groups, the share of income from agriculture for Hindus is high at 56 per cent with salaried and professional activities accounting for about 17 per cent of their income. Christians and Other Minorities also derive a relatively high share of income from salaries and professional employment. Muslims show the lowest share of income from agriculture; their sources of income are however more diversified than other religious groups. Besides having a 44 per cent share from agriculture, Muslims have about double the average share from artisanship and independent work (about 10 per cent), and about double the average share from petty and organized trade. The share of income from salaried and professional services among Muslims is the lowest when compared with any other religious category.

The other interesting feature is that the share of income from agriculture falls with the level of village development. The paradox appears to lie in the fact that while the highest rural incomes in India are indeed drawn from agriculture, agricultural income is least associated with village development. Developed villages receive a higher than average share of income from petty and organized trade, salary and professional services, and both agricultural and non-agricultural labour.

Average Income by Source

The average income per reporting household by source is presented in App. Table A.3.3. The household income from agriculture is highest in Punjab and Haryana with Rs 42,639 and Rs 34,046, respectively followed by Rs 28,160 in Gujarat and Rs 28,390 in Maharashtra. Income from agriculture is meagre in Himachal Pradesh and generally low in West Bengal, Orissa, and Kerala.

Average income level is highest from organized trade followed by salaried and professional services, both averaging close to Rs 26,000 per annum. Income from organized trade is high in Rajasthan, Orissa, Uttar Pradesh, and Gujarat but low in Kerala and West Bengal. A high level of income receipts from salaried employment were reported in Rajasthan, Punjab, Haryana, and Tamil Nadu but these are low in West Bengal.

Average agricultural and non-agricultural wage receipts per reporting household for rural India work out to Rs 6,341 and Rs 7,844 respectively. The highest agricultural wages are to be found in Andhra Pradesh followed by Kerala with Rs 9,900 and Rs 9,461 respectively. The agricultural wage receipt is very low in Rajasthan and Orissa with only Rs 2,279 and Rs 2,956, respectively. The wages from non-agricultural work are highest in Tamil Nadu at about Rs 15,000 followed by Kerala, Haryana, and Punjab. Non-agricultural wage receipts are very low in Orissa and West Bengal. These estimates according to population groups are presented in App. Table A.3.4.

Table 3.6 presents average annual wage income per household, average annual wage income per adult wage earner, average number of person days of work, and average wage per day. It is clear that the average levels of household income, both from agricultural and non-agricultural income are relatively higher in the south Indian states and the states of Haryana and Punjab. Although the daily wage rate in agriculture is relatively high in Punjab and Haryana, the number of days of employment is relatively low. On the other hand, while the daily wage rate is relatively low in the states

Hindus draw a higher proportion of income from agriculture, and salaried and professional activities account for 17 per cent of their income. The share of income from salaried and professional activities is the lowest for Muslims.

Those in the lowest income category derive only 39 per cent of income from agriculture, and 22 and 14 per cent income from agricultural and non-agricultural activities respectively.

of Andhra Pradesh, Karnataka, Tamil Nadu, Maharashtra, and Gujarat, these states offer a larger number of days of employment, thus offering better wage stability for the wage labour households.

On the whole, the role of non-agricultural income even in rural areas is becoming significant. For example, for rural India as a whole, the annual total wage income per household is Rs 7,844 from non-agricultural sources compared with Rs 6,341 from agricultural wage employment. The respective per capita incomes are Rs 4,313 and Rs 2,848. This relatively higher share of income from non-agricultural wages is due both to the relatively higher average wage and relatively larger number of workdays in non-agricultural wage work. The wage rate per day for non-agricultural work is Rs 28 as opposed to Rs 21 for agricultural wage work. The number of work days is also higher (152 days per year) as compared to 137 days of agricultural wage work per annum. Although there is a certain degree of parity in agricultural and non-agricultural wages in Kerala and Andhra Pradesh, non-agricultural wages are higher than the agricultural wages in all other states. Duration of wage employment is considerably higher in

TABLE 3.6

Agricultural and Non-Agricultural Wage Income Across States

Regions/ States	Avg. Annual Wage Income per Household (Rs)		Avg. Annual Wage Income per Earner (Rs)			Average Person Days Worked			Average Wage per Day (Rs)		
	Agriculture	Non-agrl.	Agriculture	Non-agrl.	All	Agriculture	Non-agrl.	All	Agriculture	Non-agrl.	All
North											
Haryana	7,012	11,614	3,152	7,295	5,824	75	157	130	42	46	45
Himachal Pradesh	2,828	8,468	2,147	6,210	5,962	77	199	192	28	31	31
Punjab	6,000	10,246	3,068	6,572	6,087	88	162	159	35	41	38
Upper Central											
Bihar	5,949	6,792	2,771	4,109	3,915	123	161	163	23	26	24
Uttar Pradesh	4,071	8,189	2,189	5,528	4,137	108	179	157	20	31	26
Lower Central											
Madhya Pradesh	4,168	5,159	1,577	2,403	2,312	95	108	124	17	22	19
Orissa	2,956	4,038	1,490	2,434	2,298	85	114	118	18	21	20
Rajasthan	2,279	7,278	1,241	4,546	4,074	53	146	135	23	31	30
East											
North-eastern Rg.	6,731	9,617	4,764	6,625	6,580	190	206	229	25	32	29
West Bengal	6,278	4,354	4,071	2,900	4,479	178	136	199	23	21	22
West											
Gujarat	7,545	72,95	2,348	3,633	3,292	151	126	158	16	29	21
Maharashtra	5,833	57,73	2,495	3,172	2,892	161	148	175	15	21	17
South											
Andhra Pradesh	9,900	92,87	4,208	4,221	4,405	183	169	188	23	25	23
Karnataka	5,892	84,89	2,530	4,049	2,923	146	174	156	17	23	19
Kerala	9,461	11,335	5,295	5,828	6,397	130	146	149	41	40	43
Tamil Nadu	7,745	14,796	2,725	5,898	4,059	119	188	151	23	31	27
All India	**6,341**	**7,844**	**2,848**	**4,313**	**3,768**	**137**	**152**	**160**	**21**	**28**	**24**

Daily Wages from Agriculture and Non-agriculture: All India

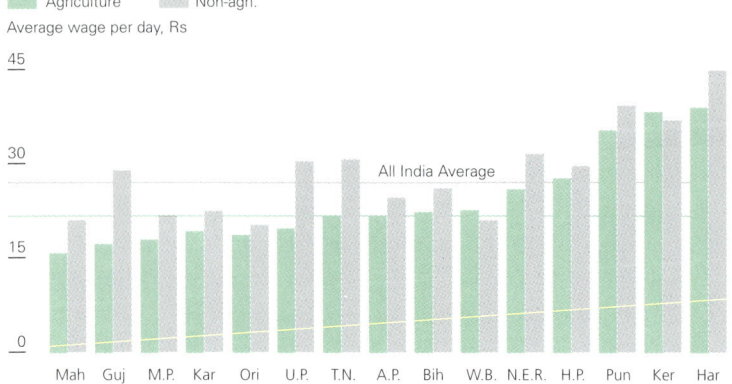

Agriculture ▓ Non-agri.

Average wage per day, Rs

Person Days of Wage Employment: All India

Agriculture ▓ Non-agri.

Average person days worked

States in southern India offer better wage stability by providing a larger number of days of employment than Punjab and Haryana, where wage rate is relatively high but days of employment are low.

non-agricultural work in the states of Haryana, Himachal Pradesh, Punjab, Madhya Pradesh, Orissa and Rajasthan.

Levels and Intensity of Poverty

The simplest measure of poverty is the 'head count ratio' (HCR) which represents the percentage of the population that earns/spends below a certain level of income (expenditure). This level is identified as the poverty line. HCR is estimated on the basis of household expenditures collected by the NSSO through nationally representative sample surveys. Direct income has rarely been used to compute HCR primarily because of the dearth of data on a regular basis. NCAER has for the first time in India collected direct income data from nationally representative sample surveys. In the recent past NCAER has collected direct income data through the Rural Economic Demographic Survey of 1980–1, Market Information Survey of Households beginning 1985–6 on an annual basis, and now through its first Human Development Indicator Survey,1994.

The percentage of population below the specified poverty line is a measure of the *incidence* of poverty, that is, how many are poor. Sen's

Wage Income and Wage Earners

Distribution of Annual Wage Income: Rural India

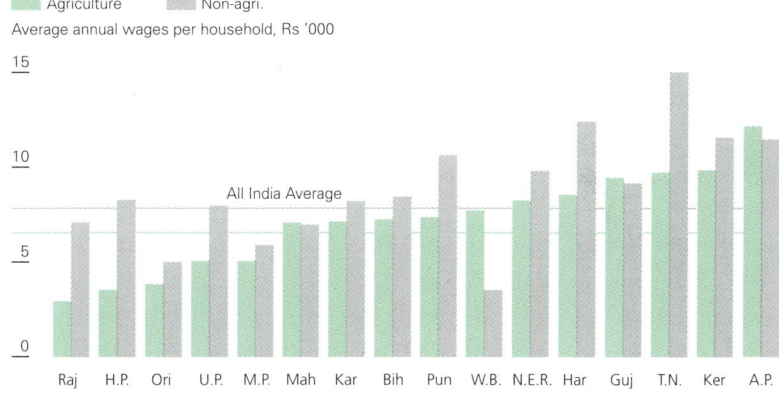

■ Agriculture   ■ Non-agri.

Average annual wages per household, Rs '000

Distribution of Wage Earners: Rural India

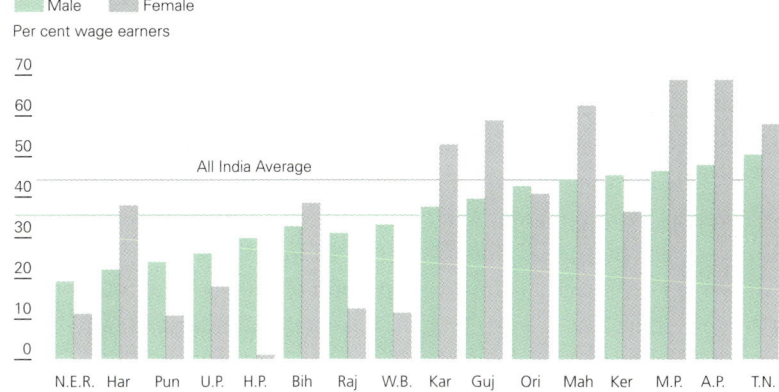

■ Male   ■ Female

Per cent wage earners

poverty measure on the other hand presents the intensity of poverty which is derived as follows:

Let $(y_1, y_2, y_3, \ldots \ldots y_n)$ be the vector of incomes,
z is the poverty line,
n is the total number of persons of which q are poor,
$q/n = H$ is the Head Count Ratio,
G_p is the Gini Coefficient of distribution of income among the poor,

The poverty gap I is defined as

$$I = \sum_{i=1}^{q} (z - yi)/qz$$

Sen's poverty measure is then given by

$$P_s = H[I + (1 - I)G_p]$$

The measure P_s has a number of desirable properties. However, being a function of the Gini coefficient among the poor, this and other similar

Among Village Development Groups

Per cent poor

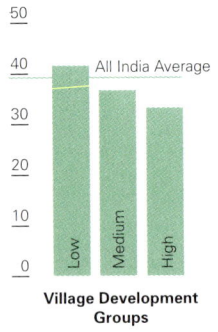

Village Development Groups

Among Household Size

Per cent poor

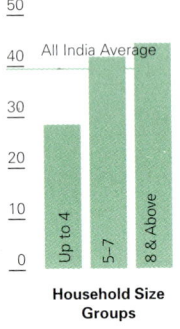

Household Size Groups

Among Social Groups

Per cent poor

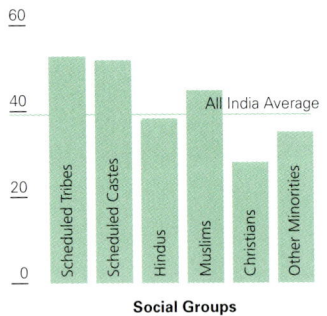

Social Groups

measures are not additively decomposable over population subgroups. A measure advanced by Foster, Greer, and Thorbecke in 1984 is *additively* decomposable apart from satisfying the desirable properties suggested by Sen. The measure is popularly known as the FGT index and is given by

$$FGT = H [I^2 + (1 - I)^2 C_p^2],$$

where C_p^2 is the squared coefficient of variation of distribution of income among the poor.

In the following section poverty estimates are made using the HDI survey data of 1994 and generally following the methodology suggested by the Expert Committee on Poverty Estimates, 1989. The poverty lines presented in Table 3.7 have been computed by updating the state level poverty lines given by the Expert Committee using the 'Consumer Price Index for Agricultural Labour' (CPIAL) as an inflator for the respective states.

In rural India the poverty line is estimated to be Rs 2,444 per year. This level is high in states such as Kerala, Punjab, Haryana, Himachal Pradesh, and the North-eastern states, which suggests higher levels of prevailing prices in those states. Andhra Pradesh, Karnataka, Maharashtra, Madhya Pradesh, and Orissa recorded lower levels of poverty. On the basis of the poverty line measure, the HCR for rural India was estimated to be 39 per cent in 1994. The highest percentage of poor are found in Orissa (55 per cent), followed by West Bengal (51 per cent), Himachal Pradesh (45 per cent), Bihar (42 per cent), and Uttar Pradesh, Madhya Pradesh, and Rajasthan (40 per cent each). A lower proportion of the poor are found in Andhra Pradesh, Haryana, Kerala, Punjab, Karnataka, Tamil Nadu, and Maharashtra.

The levels of HCR from the NCAER 1994 survey were compared with the HCR computed by the Expert Group for 1993–94. Keeping in view the fact that these estimates are derived from survey data and therefore are subject to sampling and other errors the divergence between the two sets of estimates is not wide. However, NCAER estimates an HCR of 32 per cent for

Incidence of Poverty: Head Count Ratio

Among States

Per cent poor

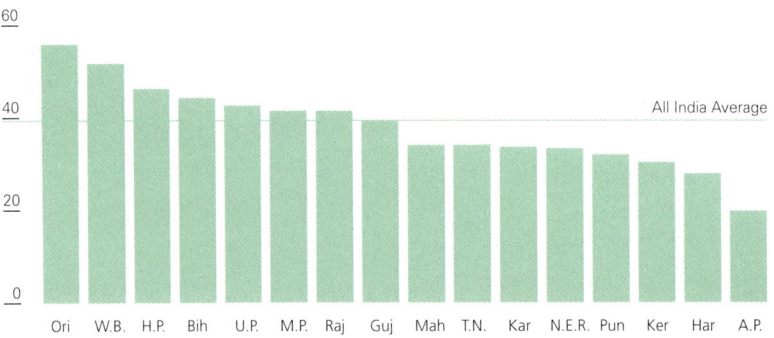

TABLE 3.7

Estimated Poverty Parameters for States

Regions/ States	Poverty Line (Rs per year)**	Head Count Ratio (%)		Mean Income of the Poor (Rs per year)	Gini Among the Poor	Poverty Indices	
		NCAER 1994	Expert Group*** (Rural)1993–4			Sen	FGT
North							
Haryana	2,818	27	28	1,922	0.17	0.11	0.03
Himachal Pradesh	2,818	45	30	1,713	0.22	0.23	0.09
Punjab	2,818	32	12	1,771	0.19	0.15	0.05
Upper Central							
Bihar	2,535	42	58	1,587	0.19	0.21	0.08
Uttar Pradesh	2,557	40	42	1,535	0.22	0.22	0.09
Lower Central							
Madhya Pradesh	2,324	40	41	1,605	0.16	0.15	0.05
Orissa	2,330	55	50	1,319	0.23	0.30	0.12
Rajasthan	2,623	40	27	1,672	0.18	0.20	0.08
East							
North-eastern Rg.*	2,775	33	45	1,976	0.13	0.12	0.03
West Bengal	2,642	51	41	1,745	0.17	0.24	0.09
West							
Gujarat	2,418	39	22	1,495	0.20	0.19	0.07
Maharashtra	2,338	34	38	1,595	0.16	0.13	0.04
South							
Andhra Pradesh	1,954	21	16	1,396	0.14	0.08	0.02
Karnataka	2,241	33	29	1,357	0.19	0.18	0.08
Kerala	2,922	30	26	1,999	0.18	0.13	0.04
Tamil Nadu	2,370	34	33	1,470	0.20	0.16	0.06
All India	2,444	39	37	1,591	0.19	0.18	0.07

Notes :   * Represents Assam.
          ** Poverty lines for 1973–74 estimated by the Planning Commission have been updated using state specific CPIAL as deflators.
          *** Planning Commission, *Report of the Expert Group on Estimation of Proportion and Number of Poor*, Perspective Planning Division, New Delhi, 1993.

Percentage Distribution of Households by States

Poverty Groups

Lower Segment Below Poverty Line   Upper Segment Above Poverty Line

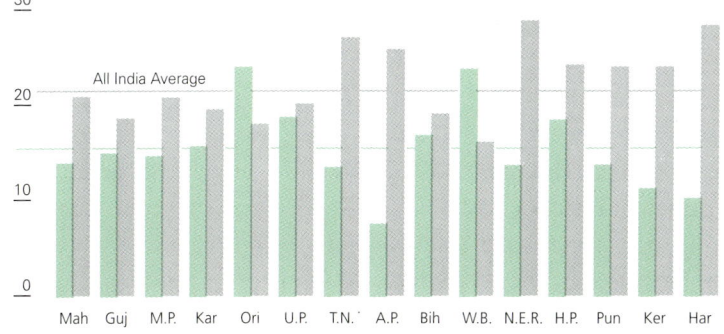

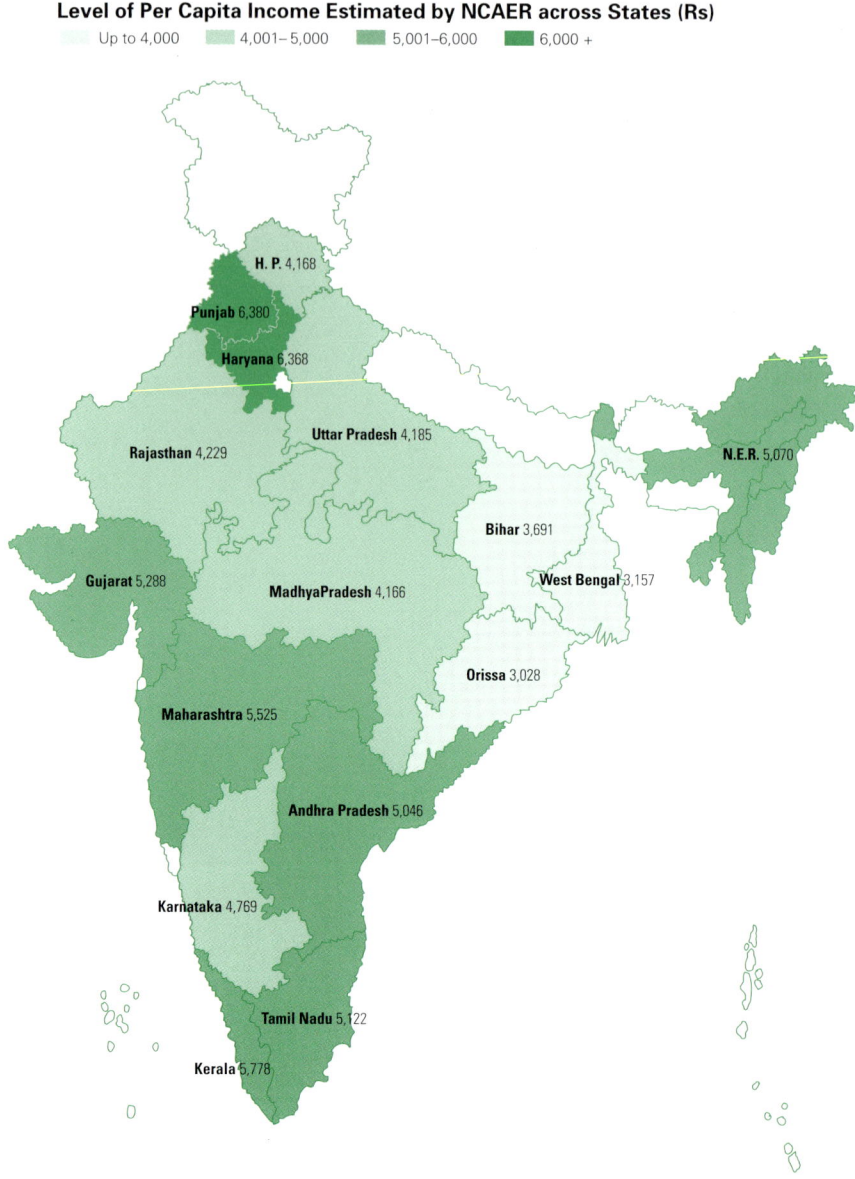

Level of Per Capita Income Estimated by NCAER across States (Rs)

Up to 4,000   4,001– 5,000   5,001–6,000   6,000 +

H. P. 4,168

Punjab 6,380

Haryana 6,368

Uttar Pradesh 4,185

Rajasthan 4,229

N.E.R. 5,070

Bihar 3,691

West Bengal 3,157

Gujarat 5,288

MadhyaPradesh 4,166

Orissa 3,028

Maharashtra 5,525

Andhra Pradesh 5,046

Karnataka 4,769

Tamil Nadu 5,122

Kerala 5,778

Punjab compared with only 12 per cent estimated by the Expert Group. This may partly be due to higher under-reporting of household income in Punjab. The NCAER computations also seem to have underestimated HCRs for the state of Bihar.

The mean household income of those below the poverty line is Rs 1,591 per annum which is only 33 per cent of the overall per capita income of Rs 4,485 for rural India. This income is around one quarter of the per capita incomes of Punjab, Karnataka, Maharashtra, and Gujarat, and over 40 per cent of that of Orissa, Kerala, and Madhya Pradesh. The depth or intensity of poverty, as measured by the Sen Index, was found to be alarmingly high in the states that registered higher incidence of HCR and Gini. The states of

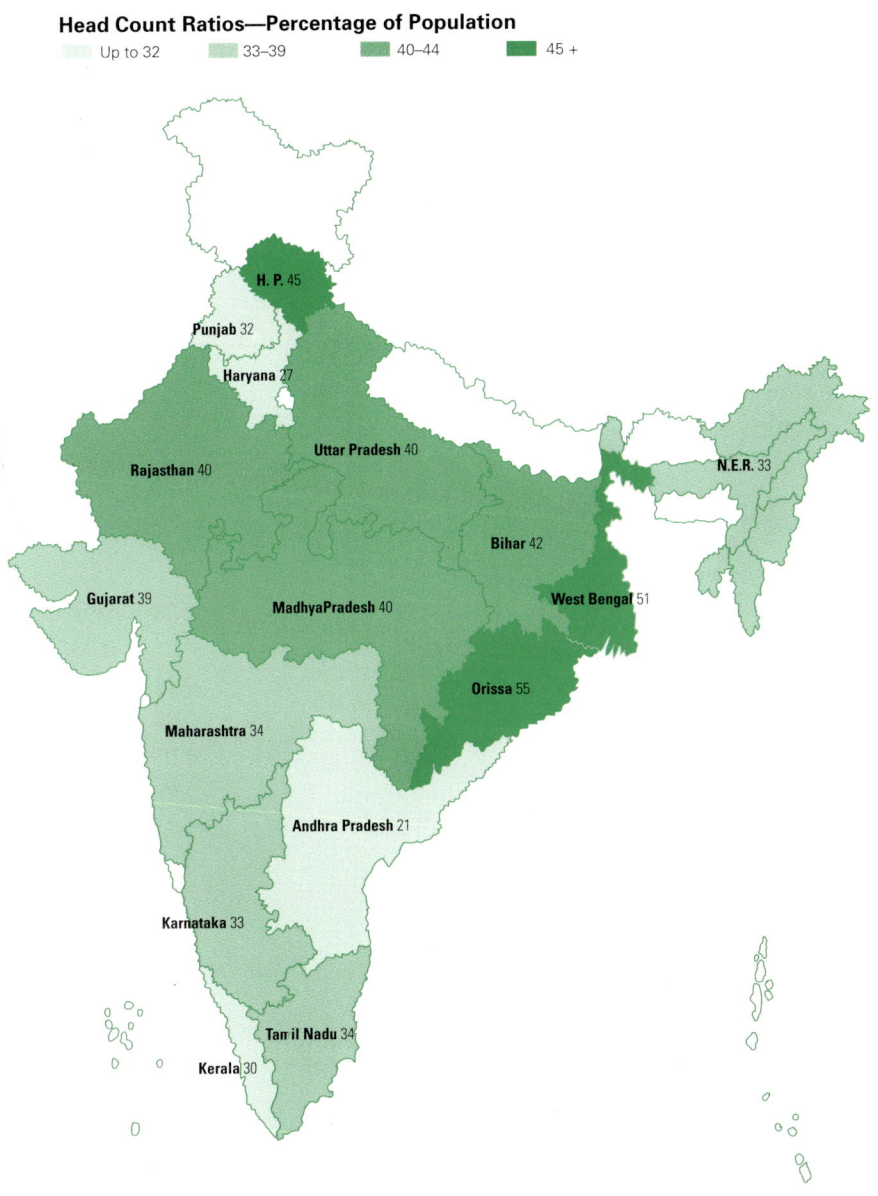

Head Count Ratios—Percentage of Population

Up to 32   33–39   40–44   45 +

H. P. 45
Punjab 32
Haryana 27
Rajasthan 40
Uttar Pradesh 40
N.E.R. 33
Bihar 42
Gujarat 39
MadhyaPradesh 40
West Bengal 51
Orissa 55
Maharashtra 34
Andhra Pradesh 21
Karnataka 33
Tamil Nadu 34
Kerala 30

Haryana, Maharashtra, Andhra Pradesh, and Punjab registered a lower Sen Index than the national average. Similarly, Orissa, Uttar Pradesh, Kerala, and Rajasthan have a higher Sen Index largely due to the wider disparity of income among the poor which is a matter of concern.

A simple distribution of households according to poverty groups is presented in App. Table A.3.1. As a clear extension of a discussion on distribution of household income, Orissa and West Bengal have almost one quarter of their rural households in the lower segment below the poverty line. Andhra Pradesh has the least number of households in this category. This is a manifestation of lower levels of consumer price index reported from Andhra Pradesh. However, from this data it is apparent that even in

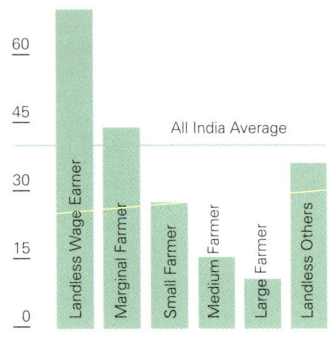
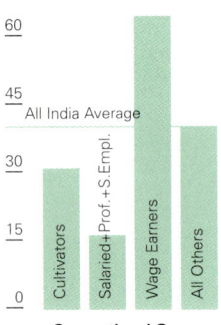
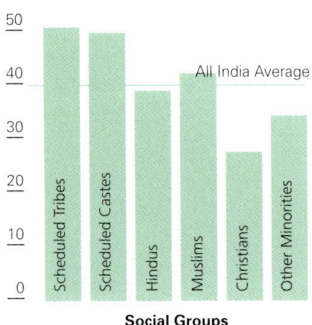
TABLE 3.8

Estimated Poverty Parameters by Population Groups

Population Groups	Head Count Ratio	Mean Income of the Poor	Gini Among Poor (Rs per year)	Poverty Indices Sen	FGT
Household Income Groups					
Up to 20,000	69	1,553	0.19	0.34	0.13
20,001–40,000	13	2,011	0.08	0.03	0.01
40,001–62,000	2	2,226	-	-	-
62,001–86,000	-	-	-	-	-
Above 86,000	-	-	-	-	-
Poverty Line Groups					
Lower segment below	100	1,092	0.16	0.63	0.33
Upper segment below	100	1,980	0.06	0.22	0.04
Lower segment above	-	-	-	-	-
Upper segment above	-	-	-	-	-
Landholding Groups					
Landless wage earner	68	1,493	0.20	0.35	0.14
Marginal	45	1,581	0.19	0.21	0.08
Small	27	1,714	0.16	0.11	0.04
Medium	16	1,657	0.17	0.07	0.02
Large	11	1,641	0.19	0.05	0.02
Landless others	37	1,685	0.17	0.16	0.05
Landowners	31	1,619	0.18	0.14	0.05
Landless	52	1,559	0.20	0.25	0.09
Occupational Groups					
Cultivators	31	1,578	0.20	0.15	0.06
Salaried+Prof.+S.Empl.	16	1,817	0.14	0.06	0.02
Wage earners	65	1,525	0.20	0.32	0.12
All others	38	1,714	0.15	0.15	0.05
Social Groups					
Caste					
STs	51	1,609	0.18	0.24	0.08
SCs	50	1,561	0.19	0.24	0.09
Religion					
Hindus	39	1,587	0.43	0.19	0.05
Muslims	43	1,650	0.17	0.19	0.06
Christians	27	1,664	0.18	0.12	0.04
Other Minorities	34	1,503	0.19	0.17	0.07
Household Size Groups					
Up to 4	26	1,679	0.18	0.11	0.04
5–7	41	1,589	0.19	0.19	0.07
8 and above	43	1,552	0.20	0.21	0.08

Contd.

Adult Literacy Groups					
None literate	45	1,743	0.13	0.17	0.05
Female literate	43	1,552	0.18	0.21	0.08
Male literate	39	1,590	0.19	0.19	0.07
Both literate	27	1,659	0.18	0.12	0.04
Village Development Groups					
Low	43	1,552	0.20	0.21	0.08
Medium	38	1,603	0.18	0.18	0.06
High	33	1,662	0.18	0.15	0.05
All India	**39**	**1,591**	**0.19**	**0.18**	**0.07**

Haryana and Punjab over 10 per cent and 14 per cent of households, respectively, live in abject poverty. Earlier it was stated that the average household wage income (both agricultural and non-agricultural) in Haryana and Punjab is not the highest among the states mostly because of the fewer number of person days of work at least in the case of agriculture. Thus we may assume that the landless wage earners in Haryana and Punjab are as poor as their counterparts in other states.

Table 3.8 presents poverty estimates according to population groups. HCR among the less than Rs 20,000 category is 69, and in the Rs 20,001–40,000 category it is 13 per cent. HCR declines substantially as landholding size increases. HCR, which is 68 per cent for the landless, decreases to 45 for the marginal, 27 for the small, 16 for the medium, and to only 11 among the large farmers. HCR is low (16 per cent) among the salaried and professional class. The intensity of poverty is high among the relatively poor and landless although the disparity within groups is low.

Both incidence and intensity of poverty are higher among STs and SCs in comparison with the national average. HCR is about 50 among STs and SCs in comparison with only 39 for rural India. The Sen Index is as high as 0.24 among STs and SCs in comparison with only 0.18 among the rural population as a whole. HCR is 43 per cent among the Muslims in comparison with only 27 among the Christians and 39 among the Hindus. The Sen Index was found to be low only among the Christians.

However, the intensity of poverty is highest among the households classified as belonging to the lower segment below the poverty line with a Sen Index of 0.63 and FGT of 0.33, the highest for any category of population group. These indices are 0.22 and 0.04 in the upper segment below the poverty line category. Levels of village development are related with poverty. Less developed villages have higher HCR and also a higher Sen Index.

Less developed villages have both higher incidence and intensity of poverty.

"Nearly one-third of the total number of absolute poor in the world live in India. What is more distressing is that while 46 per cent of India's people survive in absolute poverty… about two-thirds are 'capability poor', i.e. they do not receive the minimum level of education and health care necessary for functioning human capabilities."
–Mahbub ul Haq

Principal Findings

I Level of Income

1 The mean household income for rural India as a whole is Rs 25,653 per year which corresponds to a per capita income of Rs 4,485. All the low income states fall in the Central region of the country which covers about 50 per cent of the country's population. Punjab, Haryana, and Kerala exhibit relatively higher levels of income but also high income disparities.

2 Over 58 per cent of all rural households fall into the less than Rs 20,000 per annum income category with Rs 6 per day to meet their minimum requirements; those with an income above Rs 86,000 per annum constitute only 4 per cent of the population. Their household income is 13 times higher than that of the poorest class.

3 Levels of income are closely related to ownership of land. The income of wage labourers is 58 per cent lower than that of salaried persons and professionals, and 77 per cent lower than that of large farmers.

4 Literacy and level of village development have a bearing on household income. The income of households where both adult males and females are literate is 58 per cent higher than that of households with illiterate adults. Households in developed villages also generally have a higher level of income.

5 Both total household and per capita income are low for the SCs and STs, 68 per cent and 76 per cent that of the all India average respectively. Muslims as a religious category have low levels of income, especially when measured in per capita terms.

II Level of Poverty

6 The poverty line for rural India as a whole is Rs 2,444 per capita per year. The percentage of the population below the poverty line is estimated to be 39 (in 1994). Poverty is highest in Orissa (55 per cent), West Bengal (51 per cent), and Himachal Pradesh (45 per cent). The incidence of poverty is low in Andhra Pradesh, Haryana, Punjab, and Kerala.

7 The mean household income of the poor has worked out to be Rs 1,591 per annum. The HCR among the less than Rs 20,000 category is 69, and in the Rs 20,001–40,000 category is 13 per cent. The HCR declines substantially as landholding size increases. The HCR is only 16 per cent among the salaried and professional class. The highest HCR is about 51 per cent among STs and the lowest is 27 per cent among Christians and both literate groups. The incidence of poverty is highest among both the lower and upper segment below poverty line groups.

III Source of Income

8 The major share of income (55 per cent) in rural India comes from agriculture and allied activities followed by income from salaries and professions (16.5 per cent). The share of income from agriculture is highest in states like Karnataka, Maharashtra, and Gujarat and lowest in Tamil Nadu, West Bengal, and the North-eastern region.

9   Only 39 per cent of income in poor households comes from agriculture while in the higher income groups over 77 per cent of income is derived from agriculture. Over 90 per cent of the income of landless labourers comes from wage employment. SCs have a large share of their income coming from wage labour; Muslims earn their income from artisanship, independent work, petty and organized trade.

10 The average household incomes for the four poverty groups considered are Rs 6,950, Rs 12,379, Rs 22,138, and Rs 58,100 respectively. Of households belonging to the upper segment above the poverty line, about 22 per cent have a per capita income of Rs 11,396 which is 2.5 times the national average and 10.4 times the income of the lower segment below the poverty line.

4

Assets and Distribution of Income

While the money income earned during a reference period is identified as current income, ownership of moveable and fixed assets is identified as permanent income. Permanent income may be considered to reflect the economic worth of households and is also an index of economic security.

Ownership of Assets and Amenities

Size of Landholding and Livestock

India continues to be an agricultural society and land, draught and milch animals are the household assets that determine the level of living of the majority of rural population. Table 4.1 presents data on land and livestock according to major states. On the whole, 63 per cent of rural households reported ownership of land. This proportion is as high as 91 per cent in Himachal Pradesh, 84 per cent in Rajasthan, 79 per cent in Kerala, and 76 per cent in Madhya Pradesh and Uttar Pradesh. The lowest percentage that reported ownership of land was 34 per cent in Tamil Nadu; surprisingly it was only 44 per cent in Punjab followed by 53 per cent in West Bengal.

The average size of landholding for India as a whole is only 4.5 acres per reporting household. The landholding size is significantly higher in Punjab (7.5 acres), Rajasthan and Gujarat (7 acres each), Madhya Pradesh (6.5 acres), and Maharashtra (6.3 acres), whereas it is the lowest in Kerala (only

Size of Land Holding

Among States: All India

Reporting Hh.　Total Hh.

Land per household (acres)

Among Village Development and Household Size Groups

Land per household (acres)

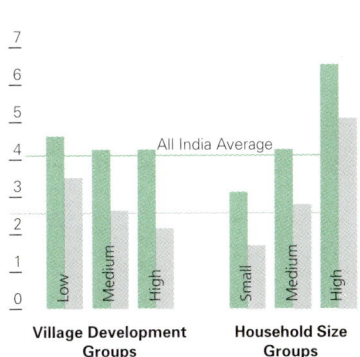

Village Development Groups | Household Size Groups

Among Social Groups

Land per household (acres)

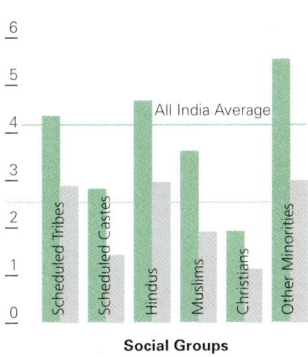

Social Groups

Among Poverty Groups

Land per household (acres)

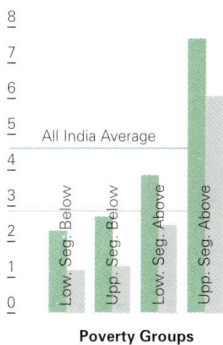

Poverty Groups

0.9 acres), Himachal Pradesh (1.7 acres), Tamil Nadu and West Bengal (2.8 acres each). The average size of landholding for all rural households is 2.8 acres; it is highest in Rajasthan (6 acres) followed by Madhya Pradesh (4.9 acres). The level and pattern of ownership conform to estimates presented by the Agriculture Census.

Ownership of draught animals was reported by 33 per cent of all rural households. A higher proportion of households own draught animals in Madhya Pradesh, Himachal Pradesh, Orissa, and the North-eastern region. The proportion of households reporting ownership of draught animals was lowest in Kerala (only 2.6 per cent), Tamil Nadu (10.4 per cent), and Haryana (19 per cent).

The average number of draught animals owned per reporting household is only 2.8 for rural India; the number is very high in the North-eastern region whereas it is around 2.5 in most of the states. While the ownership of draught animals may be seen to reflect the level of agricultural backwardness, ownership of milch animals reflects rural entrepreneurship and also the level of supply of milk-based nutrients. Overall, 48 per cent of rural households reported owning milch animals. This ownership was very high in Himachal Pradesh (86 per cent), Haryana (78 per cent), Punjab (75 per cent), Uttar Pradesh (65 per cent), and Rajasthan (71 per cent). Ownership of both draught and milch animals is generally low in the southern states except Karnataka. The average ownership is 2.3 cattle heads; it is generally higher in the northern states, the North-eastern region, and Orissa. However, in Gujarat—where 'Operation Flood' evolved and paved the way for self-sufficiency in milk production in India and also for enhancing the export of milk-based products — the ownership of milch cattle does not show any unique characteristics. The success of Operation Flood may be said to be largely attributed to the quality of milch cattle owned and the cooperative marketing structure of milk and milk products (Table 4.1).

The proportion of households owning land is strongly associated with household income. Both the proportion of reporting households and the average size of landholding increase considerably as household income increases (App. Table A.4.1). The proportion of households owning land

Land and Livestock Ownership

By Poverty Line Groups

Per cent

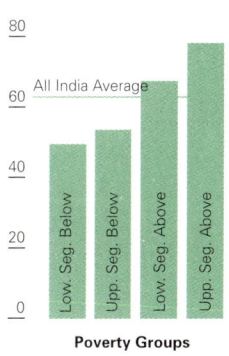

Poverty Groups

By Social Groups

Per cent

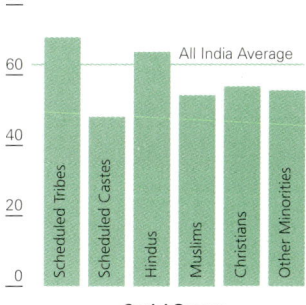

Social Groups

TABLE 4.1

Land and Livestock Owned by Households across States

Regions/States	Land Holdings			Draught Animals			Milch Animals		
	% Rep Households	Average per Reporting Household (acres)	Average per Household (acres)	% Rep Households	Average per Reporting Household (number)	Average per Household (number)	% Rep Households	Average per Reporting Household (number)	Average per Household (number)
North									
Haryana	57.6	5.8	3.4	18.8	2.4	0.5	77.6	2.3	1.8
Himachal Pradesh	91.1	1.7	1.5	55.6	2.3	1.3	85.7	2.5	2.2
Punjab	44.3	7.5	3.3	26.0	1.8	0.5	74.8	2.6	2.0
Upper Central									
Bihar	59.8	3.7	2.2	37.5	2.7	1.0	42.0	2.4	1.0
Uttar Pradesh	75.6	3.4	2.5	31.0	2.0	0.6	64.9	1.9	1.2
Lower Central									
Madhya Pradesh	76.1	6.5	4.9	57.1	2.5	1.4	62.2	2.5	1.6
Orissa	71.7	3.5	2.5	52.6	2.8	1.5	38.3	3.0	1.2
Rajasthan	84.3	7.1	6.0	22.9	1.9	0.4	71.2	1.9	1.4
East									
North-eastern Rg.	63.1	3.9	2.5	52.5	7.2	3.8	57.5	5.2	3.0
West Bengal	53.0	2.8	1.5	35.3	3.3	1.2	33.8	2.4	0.8
West									
Gujarat	55.3	7.0	3.9	27.3	1.9	0.5	50.8	1.9	1.0
Maharashtra	65.4	6.3	4.1	36.0	2.4	0.9	43.8	2.1	0.9
South									
Andhra Pradesh	51.3	4.4	2.3	27.4	2.4	0.6	36.4	2.2	0.8
Karnataka	64.1	5.9	3.8	39.2	2.3	0.9	45.0	2.1	1.0
Kerala	78.7	0.9	0.7	2.6	2.9	0.1	24.1	1.5	0.4
Tamil Nadu	34.4	2.8	1.0	10.4	2.0	0.2	21.5	1.8	0.4
All India	**63.4**	**4.5**	**2.8**	**33.1**	**2.8**	**0.9**	**48.3**	**2.3**	**1.1**
C.V.	22.7	43.3	48.3	46.2	46.5	87.3	36.3	33.5	51.9

increases from about 52 per cent in the lowest income category to about 94 per cent in the highest income group. The holding size also increases from 2.5 to 4.2, 6.2, 9.2, and 16.6 acres respectively for the five successive income groups. The average holding size for marginal, small, medium, and large farmers is 1.3, 3.8, 7.5 and 21.8 acres respectively. For all cultivators the average is 5.6 acres. The other occupation groups that own land in India are the salaried, the professionals, and traders. The proportion of households owning land as well as size of holding have a strong association with poverty groups. Similarly, household size and landownership are positively related. The relatively less developed villages have more households reporting landownership and also relatively larger size of holdings. Thus there seems to be a negative relationship between higher dependence on agriculture alone for income and level of village

Ownership of Land and Income from Agriculture

Among States

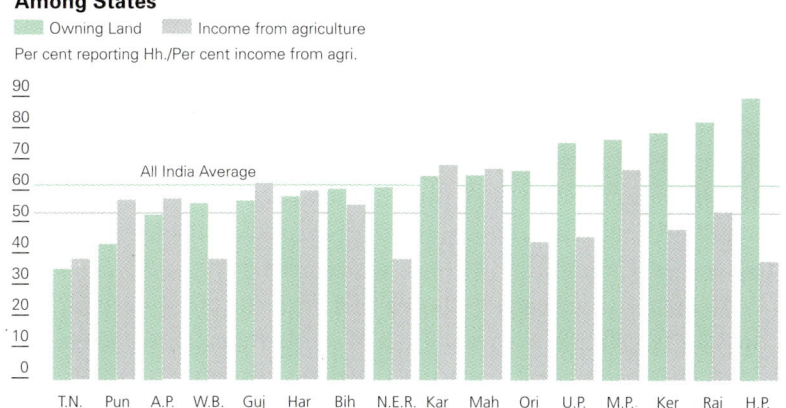

Owning Land ▢ Income from agriculture ▢
Per cent reporting Hh./Per cent income from agri.

Among Poverty Groups

Per cent reporting Hh./Per cent income from agri.

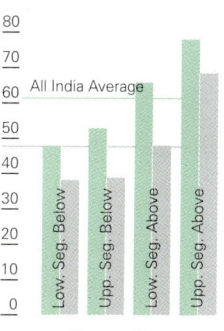

Poverty Groups

development. This aspect needs further investigation using the NCAER/HDI 1994 data set.

STs reported higher ownership of land (69 per cent) with an average size of holding of 4.3 acres compared with SCs who owned the least land (only 47 per cent) reporting an average size of only 2.8 acres The landownership pattern seems to conform to the historical and domiciliary or residential patterns that affect specific caste groups in India. Predictably, STs who normally live in remote, hilly, and forest areas by and large report a higher proportion of ownership but the land size is relatively small.

A comparison of religious groups suggests that Hindus are the most landed with about 65 per cent reporting ownership of land followed by Christians and Muslims. About 57 per cent Muslims are landed. Other minorities, mainly Sikhs in Punjab, own the largest size of land with 5.5 acres followed by Hindus with 4.6 acres. Christians have the smallest size of holding with 2.0 acres and they largely live in the state of Kerala.

It is clear that a relatively smaller proportion of SC and Muslim households own land, and the average size of landholding is also smaller. Since land continues to be the basis of economic prosperity in rural areas and is a fixed asset, it is important that the landless and small landholders are targeted under various non-agricultural income-generating activities. As with the case of land, livestock ownership is also positively related to income and poverty group categories, and inversely related to the level of development of the village.

Among Village Development and Household Size Groups

Per cent reporting Hh./Per cent income from agri.

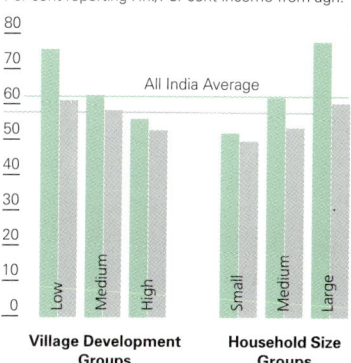

Village Development Groups   **Household Size Groups**

Among Social Groups

Per cent reporting hh./Per cent income from agri.

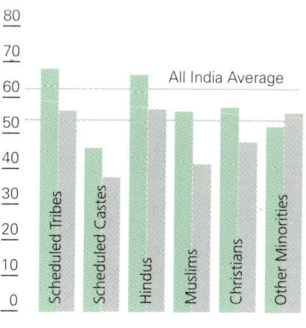

Social Groups

Ownership of House and Consumer Durables

Table 4.2 shows the percentage of rural households that own a house, a bicycle, a television set, a radio/transistor radio, an electric fan, and a motorcycle/scooter.

House Ownership: Ownership of a house or a dwelling structure is very high in India. A dwelling unit can be one of many types such as a *pucca* (brick and mortar) house, a thatched structure or a hutment. With regard to quality of housing, it can be seen from App. Table A.4.2 that about 53 per cent of all dwellings identified were *kutcha* (thatched) houses which excludes the semi-*pucca* houses. Orissa, Bihar, Madhya Pradesh, and Karnataka reported a very high proportion of *kutcha* houses, whereas Punjab, Tamil Nadu, Kerala, and Gujarat reported lower proportions of those. The incidence of house ownership is high in rural India also because of lack of lease and rental markets as well as due to cultural factors such as low physical mobility among the population.

Bicycle: Fifty-four per cent of all rural households own bicycles. This compares well with the data from another survey, the MISH survey, conducted by the NCAER during 1993–4, which estimated that 50 per cent of rural households owned bicycles during that year.[1] Bicycle ownership is high in the states of Punjab, Haryana, Uttar Pradesh, Bihar, and Madhya Pradesh,[2] and low in Himachal Pradesh and Kerala. Bicycle ownership appears to be influenced by the levels of disposable income as well as utility of the asset. Generally speaking, bicycle ownership is low in the western and southern states, the so-called relatively developed states, and higher in the less developed central states. This seems to reflect the levels of development and accessibility to other modes of transport such as the roads and railways, and the cost and affordability of such a mode of transport. The

Land continues to be the basis of economic prosperity in rural areas and since land is fixed and finite, it is important that the landless and small landholders are targeted for non-agricultural income-generating activities.

Households in Punjab and Haryana have reported very high levels of both productive and utility moveable assets.

1 The Market Information Surveys of Households (MISH) are regularly conducted by NCAER to estimate the market demographics of goods in India. Data presented here pertains to the MISH survey of 1993–4.
2 Data not presented.

Ownership of Selected Consumer Durables

Distribution among States

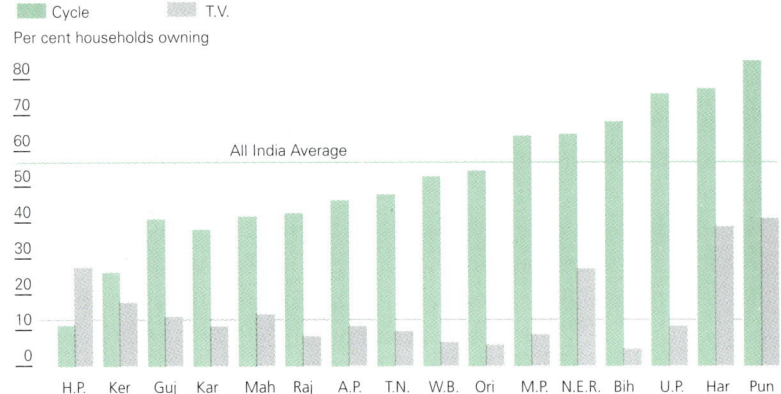

Distribution among States

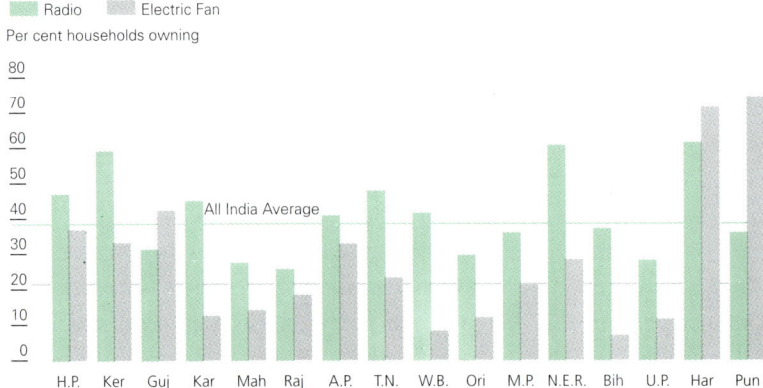

exceptions to this generalization are Himachal Pradesh and Kerala where bicycle ownership is low largely because both states have a higher proportion of hilly terrain where cycling is difficult. In the states of Punjab and Haryana the high levels of bicycle ownership are largely due to the high income and flat terrain which make it possible to own and operate bicycles with ease.

TABLE 4.2
Ownership of House and Selected Consumer Durables by States

| Regions/States | Percentages of Households Owning | | | | | | |
	House	Bicycle	Tele-vision	Radio/ Transistor	Electric Fan	Motorcycle/ Scooter	Sewing Machine
North							
Haryana	99.3	75.0	40.3	59.7	73.1	6.1	53.0
Himachal Pradesh	97.2	11.8	27.9	47.2	37.1	3.3	61.7
Punjab	97.5	80.0	38.6	37.3	75.4	13.4	63.7
Upper Central							
Bihar	98.6	63.1	5.6	36.9	4.4	2.8	7.2
Uttar Pradesh	97.8	72.9	8.2	27.3	10.0	2.6	15.4
Lower Central							
Madhya Pradesh	97.8	62.3	9.8	36.5	20.5	4.0	7.8
Orissa	96.4	55.8	6.4	29.8	13.4	2.0	2.0
Rajasthan	98.4	41.5	8.1	23.1	19.4	2.8	13.1
East							
North-eastern Rg.	98.1	62.5	24.4	59.7	25.7	12.0	4.7
West Bengal	91.4	53.1	7.7	41.4	7.9	0.6	0.2
West							
Gujarat	93.9	37.7	14.1	31.7	43.2	5.6	2.1
Maharashtra	92.9	40.9	14.1	28.1	17.5	4.6	7.3
South							
Andhra Pradesh	94.4	44.3	12.1	41.8	32.1	3.6	4.6
Karnataka	93.7	38.4	9.9	44.4	14.3	3.3	7.4
Kerala	93.6	26.9	18.5	60.0	32.8	3.9	9.2
Tamil Nadu	89.1	48.1	10.5	48.0	22.2	4.2	1.8
All India	**95.5**	**54.1**	**11.8**	**37.7**	**20.3**	**3.9**	**9.7**
C.V.	3.0	34.8	67.0	28.0	72.4	70.2	129.8

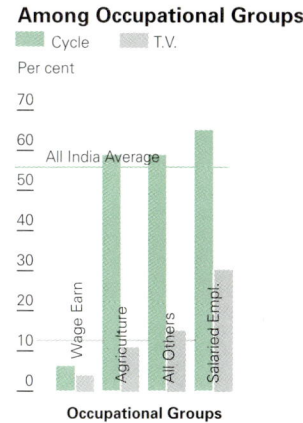

Among Occupational Groups
Cycle   T.V.
Per cent

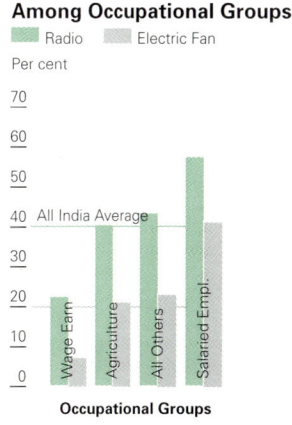

Among Occupational Groups
Radio   Electric Fan
Per cent

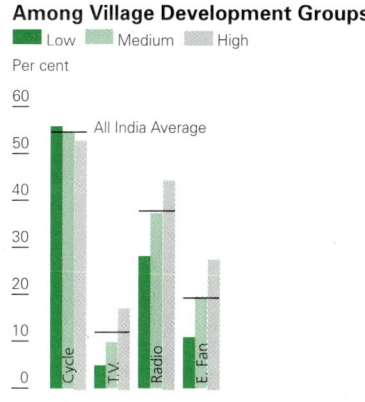

Among Village Development Groups
Low   Medium   High
Per cent

Radio and Television Set: The second most frequently owned asset is a radio/transistor radio. About 38 per cent of rural households own these. The MISH survey also estimated the same percentage for 1993–4. This ownership is high in the southern states, the North-east, Himachal Pradesh, and Haryana. Indeed, Kerala has the highest level of ownership which points to a relationship between literacy level and exposure to the media.

About 12 per cent of Indian households own television sets in rural India. The MISH survey also estimated the same percentage for 1993–4. Ownership of television sets was found to be higher in Haryana, Punjab, the

North-east, and Kerala. The proportion owning colour television sets is high in Haryana and Punjab while that owning black and white television sets is high in Kerala and the North-east. Ownership of television sets is as low as 5.6, 6.4 and 7.7 per cent respectively in Bihar, Orissa, and West Bengal. Ownership of fans is also highest in Punjab and Haryana, and lowest in Bihar, West Bengal, and Uttar Pradesh. The ownership and use of television sets and fans is dependent on the availability of electricity for domestic use. West Bengal is one of the states that has a low proportion of rural households that have electric connections.

Scooter and Motorcycle: About 4 per cent of Indian households own two-wheeled power driven machines. The MISH survey estimates this to be 3.3 per cent. Scooter or motorcycle ownership is high in Punjab (13 per cent of the households) and the North-eastern states (12 per cent). The other state where the ownership is high is Haryana. Motor cycle ownership is lowest in West Bengal (only 0.6 per cent of households).

As was the case for states, the variation between population groups in regard to ownership of houses is low. However, as expected, the percentage of houses that are *kutcha* declines consistently and sharply from a high of 66 per cent to only 20 per cent according to household income categories. Similar trends are noticeable in the poverty line categorization. The village development index is also associated with the percentage of *kutcha* houses which declines from 67 per cent to 46 per cent. Over 70 per cent of landless labourers live in *kutcha* houses, so also STs and SCs (74 and 67 per cent respectively). While only 34 per cent of Christians and 55 per cent of Hindus reported living in *kutcha* houses, 66 per cent of Muslims reported doing so (Table 4.6).

As expected, ownership of assets such as bicycle, radio/transistor radio, electric fan, television set, and scooter were all positively related to household income, poverty line and occupation. For example, households with an annual income of less than Rs 20,000, landless wage earners, those in the lower segment below the poverty line, and STs have low levels of ownership of assets while the comparably better off groups have very high levels of ownership. Television set, fan, and scooter ownership increases substantially with the level of development of the village.

Sewing Machine: About 10 per cent of all rural households own a sewing machine, which is considered to be a productive asset used to generate income. There are substantial inter-state variations in its ownership; for example, the ownership is very high in the northern states of Punjab, Haryana, and Himachal Pradesh ranging between 53 to 64 per cent of households. It appears that in these states a sewing machine is not entirely used as a productive asset; rather, high ownership reflects higher purchasing capacity associated with the practice of gifting this asset during marriages. Sewing machine ownership is almost negligible in West Bengal, Tamil Nadu, Orissa, and Gujarat.

Inter-group analysis (App. Table A.4.8) reveals that the ownership of this asset is related to household income. However, it is interesting to note that about 15 per cent of landless households who do not undertake wage-earning activities do own this asset in anticipation of pursuing a career as professional tailors. The ownership of a sewing machine is relatively high among Muslim households in comparison with their Hindu counterparts. Similarly, its ownership is high among large households and developed villages.

Ownership of Productive Assets

Information on ownership of productive assets, especially in rural areas, provides clues to growth patterns in agriculture and the use of technology. Information in this survey was collected with regard to the ownership of agricultural implements such as irrigation tube-well, thresher, winnower, bullock cart, electric generator, and tractors. Information on ownership of a biogas plant was also collected. It may be noted that the proportions computed relate to all households, but if they were computed, for example, only as a proportion of the landed, then the estimates would be considerably higher.

TABLE 4.3
Distribution of Households Owning Productive Assets by States

Regions/States	Percentages of Households Owning						
	Tube-well	Gene-rator	Thre-sher	Winn-ower	Bullock-cart	Tractor	Biogas Plant
North							
Haryana	20.3	1.9	7.1	5.6	14.0	8.6	0.5
Himachal Pradesh	8.1	1.2	2.9	5.1	0.1	2.4	2.5
Punjab	64.6	1.8	8.9	1.8	19.3	13.5	0.6
Upper Central							
Bihar	9.5	1.5	6.4	1.0	2.9	1.7	0.2
Uttar Pradesh	12.8	0.8	5.4	1.8	7.5	4.2	0.7
Lower Central							
Madhya Pradesh	7.9	0.5	3.3	1.1	29.4	2.5	0.6
Orissa	1.3	0.1	0.2	1.0	12.1	1.5	0.7
Rajasthan	13.2	0.6	1.3	0.3	8.7	3.2	0.2
East							
North-eastern Rg.	13.7	0.4	0.7	0.3	1.2	1.3	0.3
West Bengal	12.5	1.5	2.6	0.3	10.9	1.2	0.7
West							
Gujarat	3.6	0.1	0.2	0.8	11.2	2.1	2.6
Maharashtra	1.6	0.1	1.2	0.6	21.0	1.7	4.4
South							
Andhra Pradesh	3.2	0.5	0.3	0.3	16.9	2.7	1.3
Karnataka	7.0	0.4	1.0	1.4	14.9	2.6	1.5
Kerala	0.3	0.1	0.6	0.3	0.3	1.3	0.9
Tamil Nadu	3.3	0.4	0.0	0.0	3.0	0.6	0.5
All India	**9.1**	**0.7**	**2.7**	**1.0**	**11.1**	**2.6**	**1.1**
C.V.	129.1	82.6	104.8	118.4	74.5	100.1	96.7

TABLE 4.4

Distribution of Households Owning Productive Assets by Population Groups

Population Groups	Percentages of Households Owning						
	Tube-well	Gene-rator	Thre-sher	Winn-ower	Bullock-cart	Tractor	Biogas Plant
Household Income Groups							
Up to 20,000	4.1	0.0	0.7	0.4	5.9	0.0	0.4
20,001–40,000	11.8	0.8	3.6	0.9	14.1	2.4	1.0
40,001–62,000	19.1	1.7	5.3	2.4	21.0	5.3	2.7
62,001–86,000	24.0	2.3	8.9	3.2	26.7	7.7	3.0
Above 86,000	33.4	3.1	18.2	6.1	34.6	21.7	6.5
Poverty Line Groups							
Lower segment below	4.4	0.0	1.0	0.5	5.6	0.0	0.6
Upper segment below	5.4	0.3	0.8	0.4	6.4	1.0	0.3
Lower segment above	8.3	0.7	2.5	0.8	11.4	2.1	0.9
Upper segment above	17.5	1.4	6.0	2.2	18.9	6.1	2.5
Landholding Groups							
Landless wage earner	2.0	0.0	0.0	0.0	1.3	0.0	0.3
Marginal	6.6	0.3	1.2	0.5	7.0	1.4	0.7
Small	12.0	1.1	5.2	1.4	18.4	2.9	1.6
Medium	21.0	2.2	7.6	2.3	33.8	6.7	2.3
Large	24.9	2.8	13.9	5.9	43.4	16.0	4.8
Landless others	8.2	0.3	0.3	0.1	1.1	1.2	0.4
Landowners	11.6	1.0	4.2	1.5	16.9	3.7	1.5
Landless	4.9	0.2	0.1	0.1	1.2	0.7	0.3
Occupational Groups							
Cultivators	13.0	1.2	5.1	1.7	21.4	4.4	1.8
Salaried.+Prof.+S.Empl.	12.4	0.9	2.3	0.7	3.9	2.5	1.1
Wage earners	2.2	0.0	0.0	0.0	2.8	0.0	0.3
All others	7.6	0.3	0.9	0.5	2.8	1.6	0.4
Social Groups							
Caste							
STs	2.8	0.2	0.6	0.4	10.7	1.3	1.0
SCs	5.4	0.3	0.8	0.4	5.9	1.0	0.6
Religion							
Hindus	8.3	0.6	2.6	1.0	11.6	2.6	1.2
Muslims	8.5	1.2	2.6	0.9	8.2	1.8	0.4
Christians	3.3	0.1	0.8	0.7	1.3	0.6	0.5
Other Minorities	40.5	1.4	7.2	1.4	15.7	8.6	0.4
Household Size Groups							
Up to 4	5.1	0.4	1.0	0.4	6.8	1.4	0.7
5–7	9.3	0.6	2.4	0.9	10.9	2.2	1.0
8 and above	16.2	1.6	6.8	2.0	19.7	6.0	1.9
Adult Literacy Groups							
None literate	3.8	0.2	0.9	0.3	7.6	0.8	0.3

Contd.

Female literate	5.8	0.4	1.2	0.9	8.4	2.0	1.0
Male literate	8.7	0.6	2.4	0.9	11.7	2.5	0.6
Both literate	14.3	1.2	4.8	1.6	13.8	4.4	2.1
Village Development Groups							
Low	8.9	0.7	3.4	1.1	11.6	2.5	0.5
Middle	9.6	0.8	3.0	1.1	11.4	2.7	1.1
High	8.9	0.6	1.7	0.7	10.4	2.6	1.6
All India	**9.1**	**0.7**	**2.7**	**1.0**	**11.1**	**2.6**	**1.1**

Bullock-carts continue to be used as a mode of transport in rural India. However, in 1994 only about 11 per cent of all rural households owned a bullock-cart in comparison with about 2.6 per cent of the households who owned a tractor (Table 4.3). About 9 per cent of all households owned tube-wells which is an indicator of assured supply of water for cultivation. Only a small proportion of households owned generators, winnowers and threshers. As expected, one finds considerable inter-state variation in the ownership of these productive assets. The states that had experienced the Green Revolution or those that had accepted HYV technology had a higher proportion of households owning these items. Tractor ownership is the highest in Punjab (13.5 per cent) followed by Haryana (8.6 per cent). The only two other states owning more tractors than the national average are Uttar Pradesh and Rajasthan. Similarly, power generator sets are extensively used in Punjab (65 per cent) followed by Haryana (20 per cent), while the national average is only about 9 per cent of households.

The ownership of a bullock-cart is as high as 30 per cent in Madhya Pradesh, followed by around 20 per cent each in Maharashtra and Punjab. Bullock-carts are also fairly common in Haryana, Andhra Pradesh, and Karnataka.

Just above one per cent of all rural households own a biogas plant. However, biogas plants are most numerous in Maharashtra (about 5 per cent) followed by Gujarat and Himachal Pradesh (about 2.5 per cent of households).

Ownership of productive assets according to the socio-economic characteristics of households is presented in Table 4.4. Asset ownership has a strong positive association with economic status. Similarly, household size also shows a positive and significant association with ownership of productive assets which is because large families are more likely to own cultivable land. Asset ownership is much higher among other minorities, mostly Sikhs. The level of village development does not show any clear association with asset ownership.

Ownership of bicycle rises with income. Ownership of other assets like television set, radio, motorcycle/scooter rises with income as well as the level of development of the village. Across states, variations in ownership of bicycles are much narrower than that of other assets. That is to be expected as the bicycle is considered a necessity in rural areas that lack other transport facilities. A large proportion of households owns radios across states. This is one of the cheapest source of entertainment in rural areas.

Punjab, Haryana, and UP have recorded high ownership of assets such as tractors, tube-wells and generators. Sixty-five per cent of households in Punjab use power generators compared to about 9 per cent for the whole of India.

Television sets and motorcycles/scooters are owned by the richer sections of the population, because only they can afford these assets. Consequently, the proportion owning these assets varies widely across states depending on their general prosperity.

Domestic Amenities

Kitchen: Recent research that focuses on gender, female status, and autonomy of the household, explores the concept of control and use of physical space. Having a separate kitchen symbolizes autonomy for female members within the Indian sociocultural context. This study therefore examines the distribution of 'separate kitchen' (App. Table A.4.3) along with ownership and quality of domestic amenities such as electricity, water, and toilets (Table 4.5). As mentioned earlier, large proportions of houses in states located in central parts of India namely, Orissa, Bihar, Uttar Pradesh, Madhya Pradesh, West Bengal Karnataka are *kutcha*. Only about 43 per cent of houses have a separate kitchen in rural India. States with a high proportion of such houses are Kerala, Himachal Pradesh, the North-east, Karnataka, and West Bengal. The central states of Uttar Pradesh, Bihar, Madhya Pradesh have low proportions of houses with a separate kitchen.

Households having a separate kitchen may be important both from the health and hygiene point of view and also from a gender perspective. A multivariate analysis of anthropometric data has shown that households having a separate kitchen exhibit considerable positive gains in regard to combating under-nutrition both among boys and girls.[3] Having a separate kitchen in the home enables women to enjoy privacy and control over space which is so necessary in child and personal care activities, such as breastfeeding, and more autonomous control over food preparation and distribution. Mother's education on the other hand has been seen to only influence boys' education and not their health.

Electricity: Domestic use of electricity is a good indicator of development. On the whole only 43 per cent of rural households were

Existence of a separate kitchen in a household symbolizes autonomy for female members through the control and use of physical space.

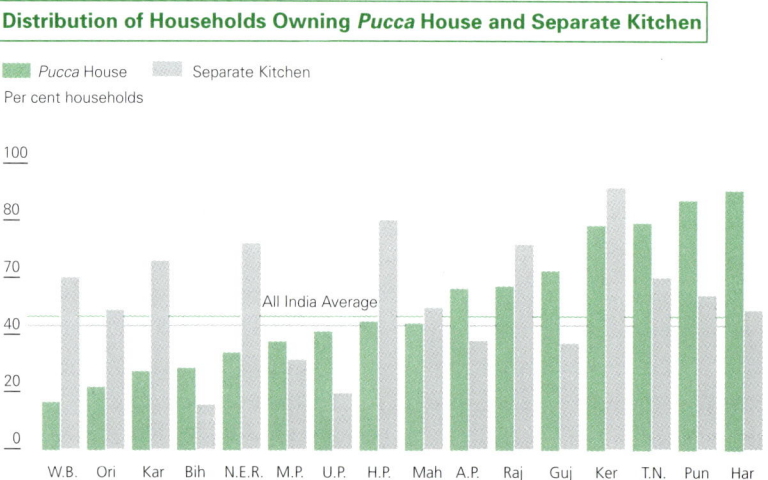

Distribution of Households Owning *Pucca* House and Separate Kitchen

■ *Pucca* House ■ Separate Kitchen

Per cent households

3 Abusaleh Shariff, 'Women and Child Health', in M. Krishnaraj, R. Sudarshan and A. Shariff (eds) *Gender, Population and Development.* Oxford University Press, Delhi, 1998.

Households Having Access to Protected Water and Piped Water

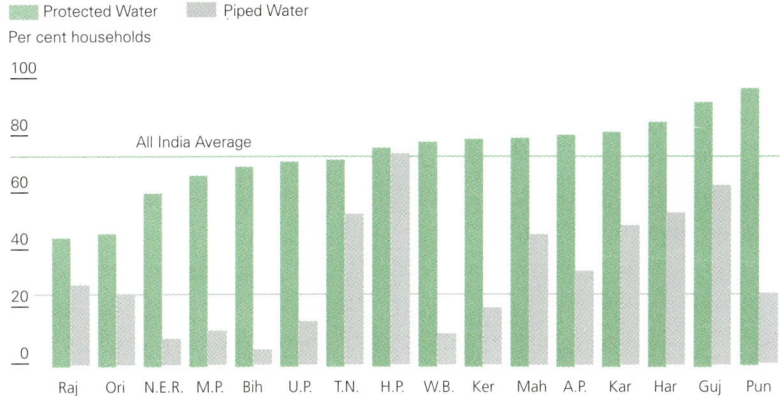

TABLE 4.5

Amenities Available in Households by States

Regions/States	Percentages of Households Owning					
	Kutcha House	Separate Kitchen	Electric Connection	Protected Water	Piped Water	Toilet
North						
Haryana	13.8	45.3	81.9	84.0	44.3	8.0
Himachal Pradesh	57.5	80.9	88.0	73.9	70.6	16.2
Punjab	18.1	48.8	83.5	96.1	21.0	19.8
Upper Central						
Bihar	71.7	15.9	9.8	68.8	3.6	7.3
Uttar Pradesh	58.1	18.1	20.1	70.0	14.7	10.7
Lower Central						
Madhya Pradesh	60.7	32.3	50.4	65.9	11.0	5.5
Orissa	80.0	45.3	18.8	48.6	24.4	3.8
Rajasthan	44.4	38.8	49.1	46.8	28.4	4.0
East						
North-eastern Rg.	66.5	74.0	44.1	61.9	8.7	68.0
West Bengal	82.8	61.1	15.6	77.5	9.1	22.2
West						
Gujarat	37.4	48.5	71.9	87.8	59.7	21.9
Maharashtra	55.7	51.7	59.7	79.3	43.3	5.4
South						
Andhra Pradesh	44.7	40.3	63.1	79.6	31.2	15.2
Karnataka	74.1	66.5	63.0	80.2	46.5	10.6
Kerala	25.2	89.1	61.1	79.2	16.7	63.1
Tamil Nadu	22.4	55.7	63.0	71.6	49.9	11.1
All India	**55.4**	**42.4**	**42.9**	**72.0**	**24.8**	**15.3**
C.V.	42.6	38.9	45.9	17.3	64.4	102.8

found to have electric connections. The proportion of houses connected with electricity was very low in Bihar (9.8 per cent) followed by West Bengal (15.6 per cent), Orissa, and Uttar Pradesh. Domestic use of electricity is as high as

88 per cent in Himachal Pradesh, 83 per cent in Punjab, and 81 per cent in Haryana. The southern and western states have a moderate range of 60 to 70 per cent (*see* also App. Table A.4.4).

Protected and Piped Water: The proportion of households having access to protected water for the best part of the year was 72 per cent. The sources include piped water, tube-wells, protected wells and regular supply from tanker trucks. The proportion of households having a regular supply of piped water was 25 per cent for rural India. The incidence of piped water supply was high in Himachal Pradesh (71 per cent) followed by 60 per cent

The SCs and STs are a considerably disadvantaged group in comparison with all others in terms of ownership and accessibility to amenities such as electricity, piped water, and toilets.

Amenities Available in Households

Percentage of Households having Electric Connection

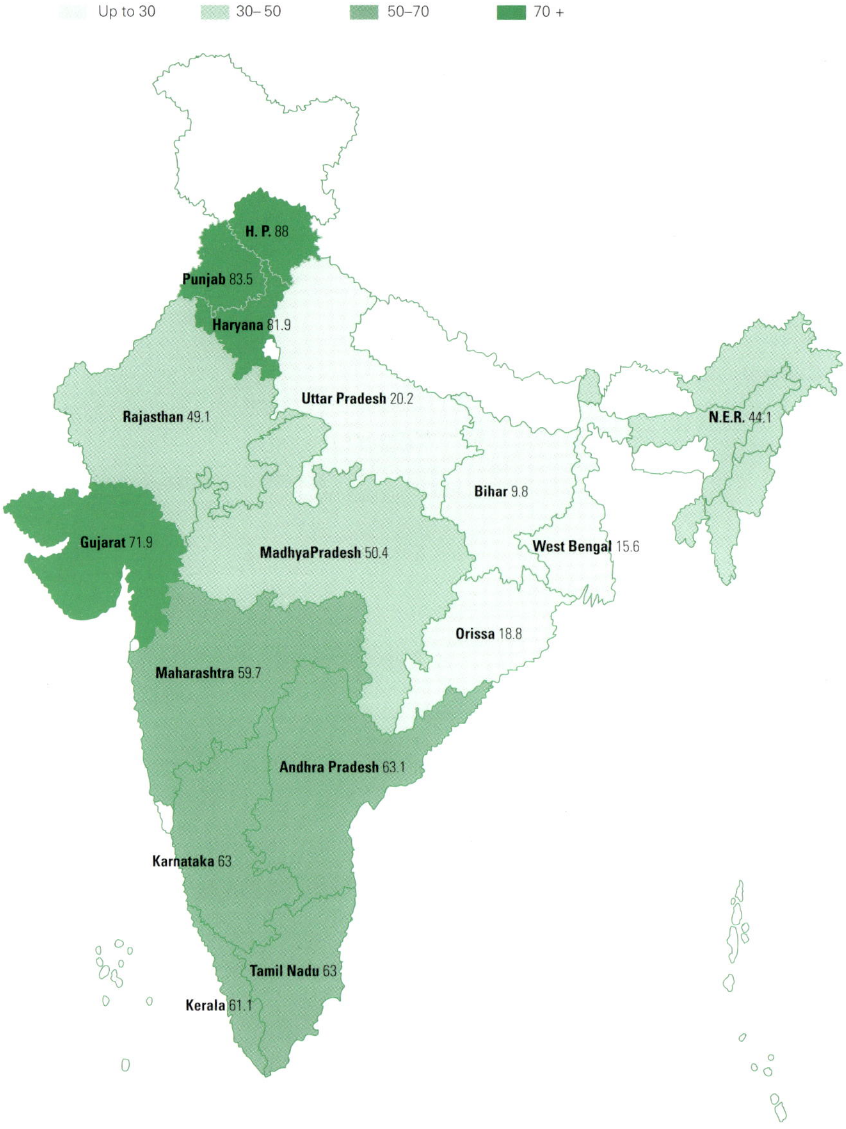

| Up to 30 | 30–50 | 50–70 | 70 + |

H. P. 88
Punjab 83.5
Haryana 81.9
Rajasthan 49.1
Uttar Pradesh 20.2
N.E.R. 44.1
Bihar 9.8
Gujarat 71.9
MadhyaPradesh 50.4
West Bengal 15.6
Orissa 18.8
Maharashtra 59.7
Andhra Pradesh 63.1
Karnataka 63
Tamil Nadu 63
Kerala 61.1

in Gujarat, 50 per cent in Tamil Nadu, 47 per cent in Karnataka, and 44 per cent in Haryana. Piped water supply was lowest in Bihar (only 3.6 per cent), the North-east (8.7 per cent), West Bengal (9.1 per cent), and Kerala (17 per cent). Kerala is a special case where potable water is available from natural lakes and springs which reduces the dependence on piped water supply (App. Table A.4.5 and A.4.6).

Toilets: Overall only 15 per cent of rural households in India have access to private toilets. The proportion is higher in the North-east and Kerala (68 and 63 per cent respectively), whereas in all other states it is about 10 to 15 per cent. In Punjab and Gujarat the percentage is about 20 per cent. Both income and cultural factors determine the presence of a toilet in or near a residential quarter in India (App. Table A. 4.7).

As expected, all household amenities and access to electricity and water increase as levels of income increase. This is true of the poverty line categories too. While the presence of a kitchen, electricity, and toilets

Percentage of Households having Piped Water

Up to 10   10–25   25–45   45 +

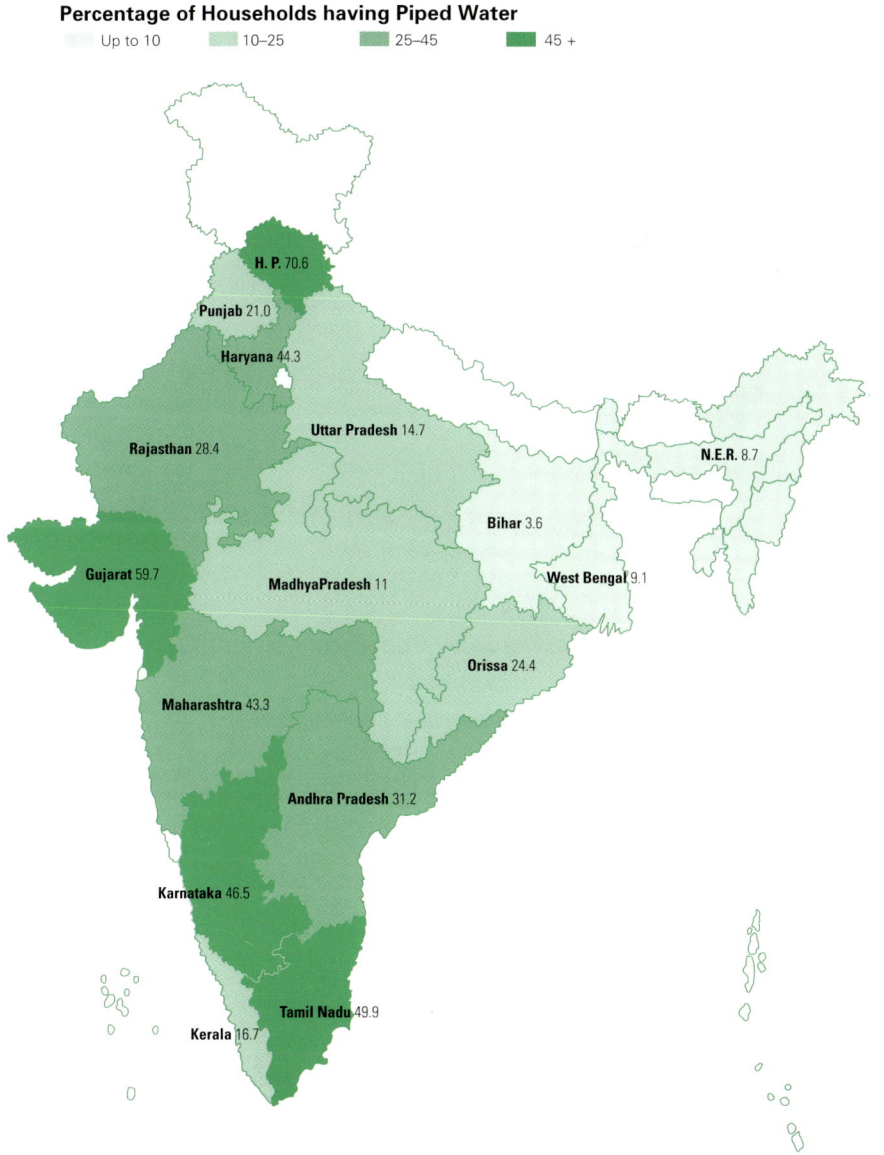

H. P. 70.6

Punjab 21.0

Haryana 44.3

Rajasthan 28.4

Uttar Pradesh 14.7

N.E.R. 8.7

Bihar 3.6

Gujarat 59.7

MadhyaPradesh 11

West Bengal 9.1

Orissa 24.4

Maharashtra 43.3

Andhra Pradesh 31.2

Karnataka 46.5

Tamil Nadu 49.9

Kerala 16.7

Percentage of Households having Separate Kitchen

Up to 35   35–55   55–80   80 +

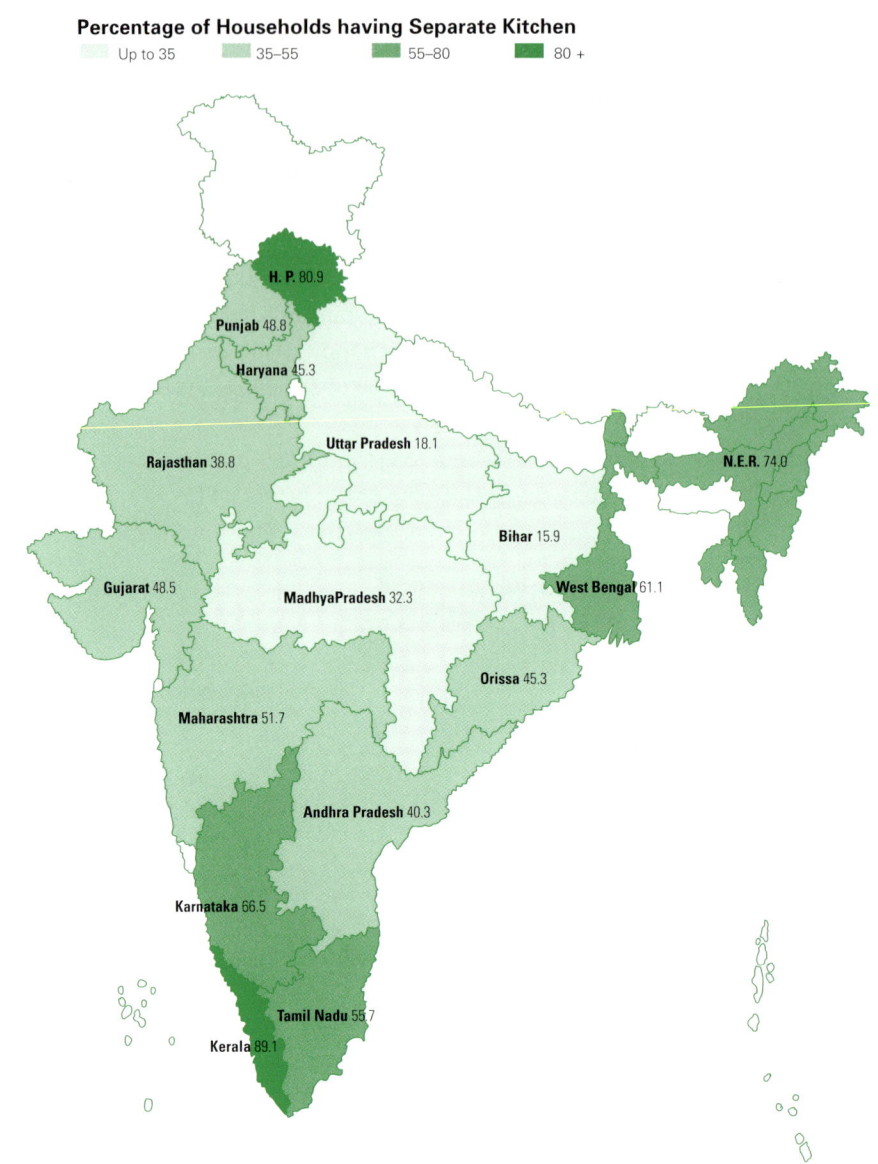

H. P. 80.9
Punjab 48.8
Haryana 45.3
Rajasthan 38.8
Uttar Pradesh 18.1
N.E.R. 74.0
Bihar 15.9
Gujarat 48.5
MadhyaPradesh 32.3
West Bengal 61.1
Orissa 45.3
Maharashtra 51.7
Andhra Pradesh 40.3
Karnataka 66.5
Tamil Nadu 55.7
Kerala 89.1

TABLE 4.6

Amenities Available in Households by Population Groups

Population Groups	Percentages of Households Owning					
	Kutcha House	Separate Kitchen	Electric Connection	Protected Water	Piped Water	Toilet
Household Income Groups						
Up to 20,000	66.4	33.5	32.6	69.6	23.4	10.0
20,001–40,000	47.0	47.8	49.8	74.8	25.5	19.1
40,001–62,000	34.4	61.9	63.4	74.9	27.2	26.8
62,001–86,000	28.1	68.1	71.8	76.5	28.4	29.4
Above 86,000	19.5	72.1	79.6	78.8	33.5	32.3
Poverty Line Groups						
Lower segment below	70.8	31.3	27.7	67.0	22.7	9.6
Upper segment below	68.8	33.7	30.6	69.9	21.6	9.9

Contd.

Lower segment above	53.0	42.2	44.8	72.9	25.4	14.4
Upper segment above	37.3	58.5	60.7	75.6	28.1	26.2
Landholding Groups						
Landless wage earner	70.7	28.4	29.7	74.5	28.5	6.5
Marginal	57.4	39.9	36.2	69.5	20.2	15.6
Small	52.8	44.6	44.5	69.1	21.3	14.1
Medium	46.2	55.1	56.5	70.6	24.9	17.0
Large	31.2	67.5	69.4	75.3	31.6	18.7
Landless others	49.1	46.3	53.5	76.5	30.9	24.4
Landowners	52.4	45.5	44.0	70.0	22.1	15.6
Landless	60.8	36.6	40.9	75.4	29.6	14.9
Occupational Groups						
Cultivators	53.4	44.6	44.2	69.6	22.7	14.0
Salaried+Prof.+S.Empl.	35.4	55.3	62.0	73.7	30.2	29.9
Wage earners	69.3	30.9	29.8	73.2	25.8	7.2
All others	52.6	45.8	45.6	75.2	24.8	20.9
Social Groups						
Caste						
STs	74.0	34.4	29.7	61.6	17.2	12.2
SCs	66.6	30.1	30.7	72.8	22.6	8.3
Religion						
Hindus	55.2	41.5	43.2	71.1	25.3	13.2
Muslims	65.9	44.7	30.0	78.1	19.4	26.7
Christians	34.2	68.8	59.9	64.7	27.8	50.3
Other Minorities	43.0	42.7	60.5	83.2	20.6	14.1
Household Size Groups						
Up to 4	58.1	37.9	41.1	72.1	28.0	14.5
5–7	55.7	43.5	42.8	71.6	23.3	16.1
8 and above	49.7	47.4	46.3	72.7	23.2	15.0
Adult Literacy Groups						
None literate	73.8	23.3	22.6	68.2	19.0	5.2
Female literate	51.9	49.8	50.9	75.3	29.4	16.9
Male literate	56.3	36.3	39.7	69.7	23.5	8.4
Both literate	39.1	63.7	62.2	76.9	30.6	30.2
Village Development Groups						
Low	66.5	28.2	26.6	64.4	13.7	8.2
Medium	54.4	42.7	42.2	71.3	22.2	14.9
High	45.9	55.7	58.6	79.7	38.3	22.4
All India	**55.4**	**42.4**	**42.9**	**72.0**	**24.8**	**15.3**

increases steeply, access to protected water is relatively equitable across population groups.

STs and SCs are a considerably disadvantaged group in comparison with all other social groups as regards ownership of and accessibility to amenities such as an electricity connection, piped water, and toilets. The proportion of households living in *kutcha* houses is considerably higher among SCs, followed by STs.

About 70 per cent of Christians reported having separate kitchens in their houses and also seemed to have a higher proportion of toilets in their homes. The survey revealed that most of the Christians belonged to Kerala, the North-east, and Tamil Nadu. While the percentage of Muslims having a separate kitchen was marginally lower, the electric connections were substantially lower; only 30 per cent in comparison with 43 per cent for Hindus. Muslims have a relatively higher proportion of toilets and access to protected water; however, next only to the Christians. Accessibility to piped water, on the other hand, is better among the Christians and Hindus with 28 and 26 per cent respectively among the reporting households in comparison with only 19 per cent among Muslims.

The proportion of households with access to amenities also increases with the level of village development. Even equitable distribution of protected and piped water supply may be said to be strongly associated with the level of village development. Indeed, the data on village level amenities were graded to compute the village development index. Data on the village development index computed using village level information and household level reporting about amenities were cross-classified. It is interesting to note that the availability of potable water and piped water differ considerably in accordance with the village development index. These estimates are presented in Table 4.6.

App. Tables A.4.2 to A.4.7 present the cross-tabulations of home ownership, percentage of *kutcha* homes, percentage of houses with separate kitchen, households having electric connections, access to protected and piped water and toilet ownership according to states. The patterns within states are more or less similar to that in rural India as a whole.

Economic Asset Index

A composite asset index has been constructed using a range of productive and utility assets commonly owned by rural households in India. Productive assets include agricultural implements, bullock-cart, irrigation pump-set, tractor as against the utility assets that are commonly used household assets such as radio, fan, television, and the like. The individual assets were first given differentiated weights, and these weights were subsequently adjusted so that the cumulative asset index value ranged between 0 and 100. Thus, if a household owned all the assets included in the computation of this index it would take a value of 100. The average productive, utility, and total asset index are 4.9, 5.9, and 5.4 respectively.

The highest index values both for productive and utility assets were found for the states of Punjab and Haryana. While the southern states have above average utility assets, the productive asset index is below the national average. Since most of the productive assets are agricultural implements and gadgets, the relatively high productive asset index of Punjab and Haryana may be attributed to higher ownership of power tractors in these states. Tractors take the maximum value in the list of ownership of productive assets used in this analysis. The ownership of productive assets is also related both to cultivation practices and intensity of cultivation which vary

Adult WPR in States

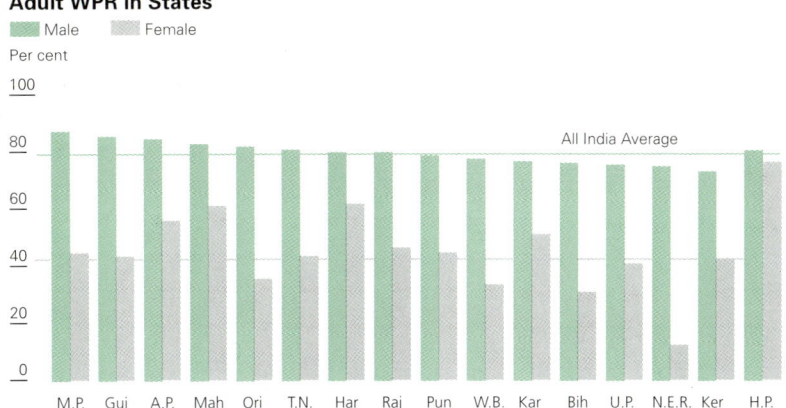

By Poverty Groups

Per cent

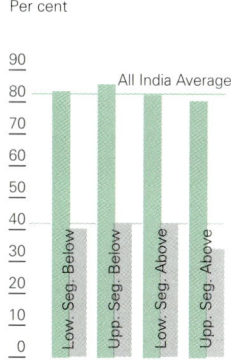

Poverty Groups

widely between groups. The utility assets may indeed reflect the relative positions in levels of prosperity of households in the respective states.

The asset index is strongly related to levels of household income and also with the poverty line categories. Landless wage earners have only 0.9 as an index of productive assets whereas it is as high as 3.3, 6.7, 12.1, and 17.4 respectively for the four landed categories. The utility index also increases according to landholding but not as steeply as it does for productive assets. Productive asset value is only 2.4 and 2.7 respectively for STs and SCs. While Christians have low productive assets they have a substantially higher ownership index of utility assets. Other minorities, comprising largely Sikhs, Jains, and Buddhists have very high levels of productive assets. This is largely because of the large number of Sikhs from Punjab in the Other minorities category. The trend is similar for utility asset ownership. Productive asset ownership is high among the agriculturists followed by the salaried, professional, and trade categories whereas the utility asset ownership is higher in the latter category. On the whole, the level of village development does not influence the level of productive assets but it does affect utility assets. The pattern within states is similar to that in rural India as a whole. Both the indices rise with prosperity in terms of income as well as the level of development of the villages. Marginal variation across social groups is perhaps a reflection of the relative levels of prosperity of these groups.

By Level of Village Development and Household Size Groups

Per cent

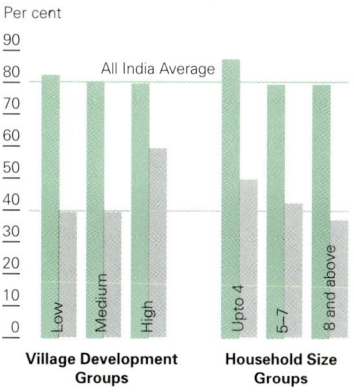

Village Development Groups   Household Size Groups

Distribution of Income

Workforce Participation Rate (WPR)

One mechanism through which the fruits of macroeconomic growth get distributed to people and affect their quality of life is employment that leads to consequent gains in income. Therefore, the capacity of the economy to generate additional employment and sustain money wage returns requires careful consideration. Below, estimated Work Participation Rates (WPRs) from this survey are discussed.

Table 4.7 presents WPRs by sex in states. App. Table A.4.10 and A.4.11

Adult WPR by Social Groups

Per cent

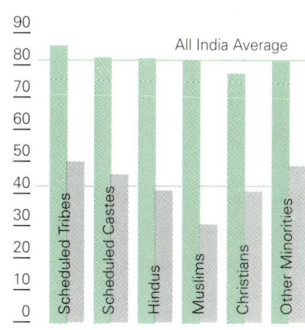

Social Groups

TABLE 4.7

Work Participation Rate (Percentage) by Sex Across States

Regions/ States	Usual Status					Usual and Subsidiary Status				
	Male	Male 1991 Census	Female	Female 1991 Census	F/M Col 3/ Col 1	Male	Male 1991 Census	Female	Female 1991 Census	F/M Col 8/ Col 6
	1	2	3	4	5	6	7	8	9	10
North										
Haryana	50.6	47.9	13.2	11.3	0.26	50.9	48.5	14.9	12.6	0.29
Himachal Pradesh	51.9	49.7	37.7	34.8	0.73	52.3	50.5	48.9	36.6	0.93
Punjab	52.9	53.4	9.3	6.8	0.18	53.2	55.0	28.8	4.4	0.54
Upper Central										
Bihar	48.4	48.0	9.1	15.7	0.19	49.1	48.9	19.0	16.3	0.39
Uttar Pradesh	48.5	49.4	7.4	12.9	0.15	48.8	50.5	20.6	14.2	0.42
Lower Central										
Madhya Pradesh	53.8	52.2	28.0	32.5	0.52	54.0	54.0	28.3	39.3	0.52
Orissa	55.3	53.7	15.9	20.8	0.29	56.0	54.7	24.8	22.6	0.44
Rajasthan	47.6	49.1	10.6	27.0	0.22	48.0	50.1	25.8	33.3	0.54
East										
North-eastern Rg.	45.1	48.6	4.6	39.3	0.10	46.8	-	8.9	-	0.19
West Bengal	51.8	51.4	7.4	11.7	0.14	53.4	52.1	20.4	13.1	0.38
West										
Gujarat	56.3	54.4	21.6	27.1	0.38	56.4	54.9	29.5	35.6	0.52
Maharashtra	53.7	52.0	33.7	33.0	0.63	53.9	53.2	38.3	46.1	0.71
South										
Andhra Pradesh	58.2	55.4	36.8	34.8	0.63	58.3	57.9	37.8	42.5	0.65
Karnataka	54.5	53.9	31.2	29.3	0.57	54.9	56.0	32.5	36.6	0.59
Kerala	53.6	47.8	28.5	16.9	0.53	53.7	47.9	29.1	16.9	0.54
Tamil Nadu	57.6	57.0	27.1	30.9	0.47	58.2	58.3	29.1	38.5	0.50
All India	**51.9**	**51.6**	**18.4**	**22.7**	**0.35**	**52.4**	**52.6**	**26.0**	**26.8**	**0.50**
C.V.	6.8	5.5	56.1	41.3	53.5	6.4	-	34.3	-	32.6

present WPRs and adult WPRs for major states. Two types of WPRs are estimated, one based on usual status[3] and the other reporting work participation, if any, for those whose usual status is domestic chores, students, and non-workers which can be termed `subsidiary status work participation'.

For the country as a whole the usual status male and female WPRs are 51.9 and 18.4 per cent respectively. A noteworthy aspect is that the coefficient of variation for male WPR is only 6.8 while for the female WPR it is 56 per cent, suggesting a wider variation in usual status employment of women across states. Female WPRs range from a low of 4.6 followed by 9.1 and 9.3 per cent in the North-eastern states, Bihar, and Punjab to a high of 38, 37 and 31 per cent respectively in Himachal Pradesh, Andhra Pradesh, and Karnataka. The male WPR is high in Andhra Pradesh, Tamil Nadu, and Gujarat and low in the North-east, Rajasthan, Uttar Pradesh, and Bihar (Table 4.7).

3 Usual Status Work Participation Rate is estimated by recording what normally individuals do for a living for at least half the year. When the reported activity is 'household duties' or 'student' for example, a further probe is conducted to find out if they have undertaken productive work at all even when the normal activity is considered unproductive. Such an activity is considered to be a subsidiary activity.

All the usual status male WPRs closely match the rates for all the states available from the Census of 1991. The usual status female WPRs are, however, relatively lower when compared with similarly defined rates from the 1991 Census. While the survey appears to have underestimated the usual status female WPRs in the North-eastern states, the Census underestimates female WPRs in the case of Kerala.

A question posed to individuals who had reported 'domestic chore', 'student' or 'unemployed' was whether they had participated in any activity that might be described as 'unpaid family work' but which would have contributed to the ultimate income of the household. While only about 0.5 per cent of men reported positively, in the case of women the additional 8 per cent answered affirmatively at the all India level. Thus the usual and subsidiary status female WPR worked out to be 26 per cent for India as a whole with a considerably low coefficient of variation of 34.3 per cent. This percentage matches well with 26.8 per cent estimated by the 1991 Census. While this rate increases only marginally in the case of the four southern states, the increase is substantial in West Bengal, Rajasthan, Uttar Pradesh, Punjab, Bihar, and Orissa. This discrepancy appears to be largely due to cultural factors regulating female work that needs further investigation. Overall, the female–male sex ratio for usual status WPR which was only 0.35 improved to 0.50 when subsidiary work was included (Table 4.7).

While overall participation rate is affected by the extent of participation of children in the labour force, the adult WPRs for persons aged 15–59 present a relatively more stable estimate. The usual status adult WPRs worked out to be 82.7 and 29.5 per cent respectively for males and females with a very low coefficient of variation for males and a high coefficient of variation for females. WPRs for males and females according to the extended definition are 83 and 41 per cent respectively. There was about 12 per cent increase in the WPRs among females, due to inclusion of subsidiary status (App. Table A.4.9).

The usual status adult male WPR decreases marginally while female participation rate decreases considerably as household income increases.

While there are large variations in female work participation between states, male participation rates are fairly uniform.

Landless wage earning households and marginal farmers report high Work Participation Rate.

Female Work Participation Rate among States

Usual Status   Usual & Subsidiary
Per cent workers (15–59 years)

Work Participation Rate (%) Among Females Both in Usual and Subsidiary Status

Up to 20   20–30   30 +

H. P. 48.9

Punjab 28.8

Haryana 14.9

Rajasthan 25.8

Uttar Pradesh 20.6

N.E.R. 8.9

Bihar 19.0

Gujarat 29.5

MadhyaPradesh 28.3

West Bengal 20.4

Orissa 24.8

Maharashtra 38.3

Andhra Pradesh 37.8

Karnataka 32.5

Tamil Nadu 29.1

Kerala 29.1

Female WPR decreases as the landholding size increases.

Variation in female WPR by social groups is phenomenal.

While the male WPR decreases from about 85 to 79 per cent, the female WPR falls from a high of about 36 to 19 per cent for the lowest and highest household income categories respectively.

A similar decline although not as steep can also be found in the case of poverty line group classification among both the usual status and usual and subsidiary status adult female WPRs. The adult male participation rates on the other hand are relatively more stable across poverty line classifications. Although this gives credence to the argument that the truly poor households cannot afford to remain unemployed, it should be recognized that further investigation and extended analysis of this data is desirable to address the issue of poverty, work and earnings.

The male WPR varies according to land size, being highest for landless wage earners, 89 per cent, and lowest for the large landholder, 76 per cent. The male WPR only marginally falls according to different landed categories, such as the marginal, small, medium, and large farmers. Adult female WPRs show considerable variation for the land size categories. Females in landless wage earning households have a fairly high WPR of 52 per cent followed by the marginal farmers, 31 per cent, small farmers, 24 per cent, medium farmers, 22 per cent, and large farmers, 21 per cent. It is clear that female work participation decreases as landholding size increases, presumably because hired labour substitutes female members of the household. The notable fact in all this is the very high participation of females belonging to wage earning households in the workforce, which is evident both in the landless wage earner and wage earner categories presented in App. Table A.4.9.

Another observed trend is that adult male WPR falls according to household size from above 87 per cent to 81 per cent. But adult female WPR falls substantially from 40 per cent to only 21 per cent in the small and the large household size category. A larger variation in the female participation rate may be partly due to the total household income effect which tends to be larger in large households.

As far as social groups are concerned, the variation in adult participation rates is phenomenal for females. The female work participation is 45 per cent for STs and 38 per cent for the SCs in comparison with only 30 per cent for the rural population as a whole. Among the religious categories, Muslim women participate the least (only about 16 per cent) in the workforce in comparison with 31 per cent among Hindus and 37 per cent among Christians. Female WPRs do increase in accordance with the village development index, suggesting better work opportunities in developed villages (App. Table A.4.9).

WPRs with extended definition generally increase only among the population groups that are relatively well off. WPR reporting among the relatively poor and wage earning households increases only marginally, suggesting that women workers in these groups are regular workers whose contribution is essential for the household. Thus much of the extra work participation captured from our extended definition and the resultant probe could in fact be significant but it is marginal work. However, in this survey no effort has been made to expand the definition of work and productive employment so as to accord greater value to various types of domestic and outside work performed by women, including childbearing and rearing.

App. Tables A.4.10 and A.4.11 present male and female WPRs and adult WPRs respectively according to selected population groups cross-classified by states. The all India trend of male WPR increasing with income is true of practically all states excepting Bihar, and unlike the all India trend of a marginal increase in male WPR according to village development, the rates are relatively higher in less developed villages in Kerala, Punjab, Bihar, and Uttar Pradesh. Another pattern is that SCs and STs together have marginally higher male WPR across states.

The most interesting fact is that female WPRs are generally higher and substantial in all the four states of south India, Himachal Pradesh, Madhya

Female WPR is lower for Muslims across states but more so in West Bengal, UP, and Bihar.

TABLE 4.8

Average Household Size, Number of Workers, and Sex Ratio by States

Regions/States	Average Household Size			Usual Status					Usual and Subsidiary Status				
				Number of Workers			F/M	Non-worker –worker ratio	Number of Workers			F/M	Non-worker –worker ratio
	Total	Male	Female	Total	Male	Female			Total	Male	Female		
North													
Haryana	6.27	3.37	2.90	2.08	1.70	0.38	0.22	2.01	2.14	1.71	0.43	0.25	1.93
Himachal Pradesh	5.75	2.89	2.86	2.58	1.50	1.08	0.72	1.23	2.91	1.51	1.40	0.93	0.98
Upper Central													
Bihar	6.98	3.27	2.81	1.84	1.58	0.26	0.16	2.30	2.14	1.61	0.53	0.33	1.84
Uttar Pradesh	6.39	3.44	2.95	1.89	1.67	0.22	0.13	2.38	2.29	1.68	0.61	0.36	1.79
Lower Central													
Madhya Pradesh	6.08	3.19	2.89	2.53	1.72	0.81	0.47	1.40	2.54	1.72	0.82	0.47	1.39
Orissa	5.68	2.88	2.80	2.04	1.59	0.45	0.28	1.78	2.31	1.61	0.70	0.43	1.46
Rajasthan	6.43	3.40	3.03	1.94	1.62	0.32	0.20	2.31	2.41	1.63	0.78	0.48	1.67
East													
North-eastern Rg.	5.55	3.12	2.43	1.52	1.41	0.11	0.08	2.65	1.68	1.46	0.22	0.15	2.30
West Bengal	5.74	2.98	2.75	1.74	1.54	0.20	0.13	2.30	2.15	1.59	0.56	0.35	1.67
West													
Gujarat	5.55	2.89	2.67	2.20	1.62	0.58	0.35	1.52	2.42	1.63	0.79	0.48	1.29
Maharashtra	5.42	2.77	2.65	2.38	1.49	0.89	0.60	1.28	2.50	1.49	1.01	0.68	1.17
South													
Andhra Pradesh	4.91	2.54	2.37	2.35	1.48	0.87	0.59	1.09	2.37	1.48	0.89	0.60	1.07
Karnataka	5.74	2.97	2.77	2.51	1.62	0.86	0.53	1.29	2.53	1.63	0.90	0.55	1.27
Kerala	5.04	2.46	2.57	2.05	1.32	0.73	0.56	1.46	2.07	1.32	0.75	0.57	1.43
Tamil Nadu	4.54	2.51	2.23	1.93	1.33	0.60	0.45	1.35	2.00	1.35	0.65	0.48	1.27
All India	**5.72**	**3.00**	**2.72**	**2.06**	**1.56**	**0.50**	**0.32**	**1.78**	**2.28**	**1.57**	**0.71**	**0.45**	**1.51**
C.V.	9.00	10.90	7.90	14.37	7.60	54.60	56.80	28.47	12.08	7.40	34.50	36.50	23.16

Pradesh, Maharashtra, and Gujarat. Female WPR is extremely low in the North-eastern states, West Bengal, Uttar Pradesh, Bihar, Punjab, Orissa, and Rajasthan. The all India trend clearly indicates a decline in female WPR by income class. While this is true in all states, the decline is less steep in the four southern and North-eastern states. Generally speaking, female WPRs are lower for Muslim women across states but more so in West Bengal, Uttar Pradesh, and Bihar, and considerably lower than for other social groups in Kerala, West Bengal, Karnataka, and Andhra Pradesh.

Non-Worker–Worker Ratios

An average household in rural India consists of 5.7 members of which 3.0 are males and 2.7 females (Table 4.8). An average household includes 2.1 persons engaged in usual status productive activities of which 1.6 are males and 0.5 are females. Thus, the average household has 1.4 male and 2.2 female dependents. One earner, therefore, has to support 1.8 dependents of which 0.7 are males and 1.1 are females.

Household size and its composition varies across states and population groups. The household size is relatively large in the four central states of Bihar, Uttar Pradesh, Madhya Pradesh and Rajasthan, and also in Haryana. This could be due to the prevalence of the joint family system. However, the 'non-worker–worker ratios' (dependency ratios) are also relatively high among these states, suggesting a large younger population in these states. Another trend apparent in this data is in regard to work participation rates of women. On the whole the male participation rate is three times larger than that of females, but WPRs are around 50 per cent in the southern and western states and less than a quarter in the North-eastern region, Rajasthan, Bihar, Uttar Pradesh, Punjab, Haryana and West Bengal.

The non-worker–worker ratio, however, fell by about 18 per cent once the proportion of secondary status female participation was included in the estimates. As discussed earlier, the inclusion of secondary status work participation rate for females improved the earlier estimates in the central and northern states where the usual status employment reporting had been considerably low with the exception of Madhya Pradesh.

It is well known that large families normally stay together in the hope of keeping the family estate intact and to protect aggregate income from falling. Thus, there is a two-way relationship between household size and household income. Larger households have higher income mostly because of the presence of relatively more adult earning members.

Average household size increases consistently from a low of 5.03 in the lowest to 8.28 in the highest income category. In the above Rs 86,000 income group, the household size is about 40 per cent higher in comparison with the less than Rs 20,000 household income category. The sex ratio of workers falls as income increases. The proportion of male workers increases considerably and that of female workers falls slightly as household income increases. Thus, as the proportion of males increases, the dependency ratio increases. As income increases, females in the household are withdrawn from the workforce. These estimates are presented in App. Table A.4.12.

Larger households have higher income because of the presence of a larger number of adult earning members.

Household size decreases as per capita income increases, and most of the decline is caused by the relatively fewer women that are to be found in richer households.

Many among the marginal
population groups are at
risk of economic stress
which results in high work
participation as a coping
mechanism.

Child labour is an outcome
of extreme poverty and lack
of reasonable levels of adult
earnings.

The situation is reversed when per capita income is considered. Average household size falls as per capita income increases (data not presented). The richer households on an average are 20 per cent smaller in comparison with those who have low levels of per capita income. However, a surprising finding is that the sex ratio declines as per capita income increases. Although these figures need to be age-standardized, another method to assess this relationship is to investigate variation in sex ratio by household size itself; which in this case is not significant. To summarize, household size decreases as per capita income increases and most of this decline is caused by the relatively few women that are to be found in richer households. In fact, evidence points to the prevalence of either a gender bias among the richer households or of households being richer because of the presence of fewer women living in the household. Either of these arguments is gender discriminatory. However, the economic dependency ratio consistently falls as per capita income increases.

Household size has a positive association with the size of landholding. For example, while the household size is 20 per cent higher for landowners as a whole in comparison with the landless, large landowners live in 60 per cent larger households than the landless wage earners. This association again is mutual so far as it is true that large tracts of lands are consolidated and preserved within households mainly through the practice of living together in joint or large families.

Among the caste categories, the household size is found to be smallest for SCs. In the case of religious categories, Muslims have a household size of 6.2 members followed by Hindus with 5.7, and Christians 4.9 members. The household size also increases by poverty line group and decreases according to the level of village development.

While the dependency ratios are low among the relatively poor, they are very low among the landless wage earners, ST, and SC categories. The decline in dependency may be attributed to the higher participation of females in employment and income earning activities among these vulnerable population groups. This apparent paradox supports the hypothesis that many among the marginal population groups are at risk of economic stress which results in high work participation as a coping mechanism. The evidence also suggests that low economic dependency among the low income and vulnerable population groups is the result of poverty, and the data should be therefore interpreted accordingly.

Work Participation Among Children and the Elderly

It is clear from the discussion on alternative estimates of WPRs that usual status work participation is reported when individuals identify their work with regular employment and an occupation. Extending this definition to workers of different ages, it was found that about 4.4 per cent male and 3.5 per cent female children aged 6–14 reported working on a regular basis (Table 4.9). Most of these children work as wage earners and earn cash incomes. Although the extent of child labour could be many times higher, the proportion of children engaged in earning cash either through wage or

TABLE 4.9

Work Participation Rate (Usual Status) (Percentage) among Children and the Elderly by States

Regions/States	Child (6–14 years)			Elderly (60 years & above)		
	Male	Female	F/M	Male	Female	F/M
North						
Haryana	2.5	2.3	0.93	65.1	7.2	0.11
Himachal Pradesh	1.2	0.6	0.51	77.0	31.9	0.41
Punjab	5.7	3.0	0.53	54.8	6.6	0.12
Upper Central						
Bihar	4.0	1.2	0.29	68.9	8.3	0.12
Uttar Pradesh	2.2	0.8	0.34	74.1	4.9	0.07
Lower Central						
Madhya Pradesh	4.4	4.1	0.93	77.4	20.9	0.27
Orissa	4.9	4.2	0.86	71.7	12.1	0.17
Rajasthan	1.0	1.1	1.10	69.5	7.3	0.10
East						
North-eastern Rg.	1.9	1.0	0.54	68.7	7.9	0.11
West Bengal	4.9	2.3	0.48	54.3	3.2	0.06
West						
Gujarat	5.3	5.0	0.95	68.6	11.8	0.17
Maharashtra	6.9	5.8	0.84	69.1	21.9	0.32
South						
Andhra Pradesh	10.0	10.3	1.03	73.6	24.5	0.33
Karnataka	7.7	7.8	1.02	64.3	22.6	0.35
Kerala	1.3	0.5	0.42	71.9	33.2	0.46
Tamil Nadu	6.3	7.5	1.20	66.0	20.0	0.30
All India	**4.4**	**3.5**	**0.80**	**69.5**	**14.5**	**0.21**
C.V.	57.2	80.3	38.3	9.3	61.7	58.0

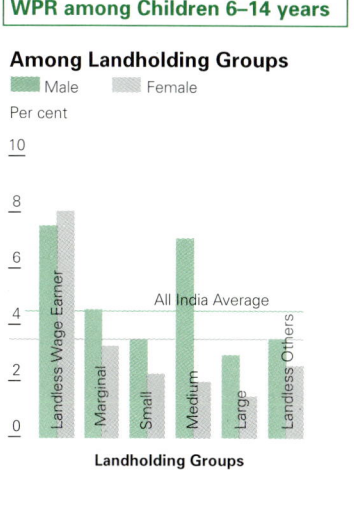

WPR among Children 6–14 years

Among Landholding Groups

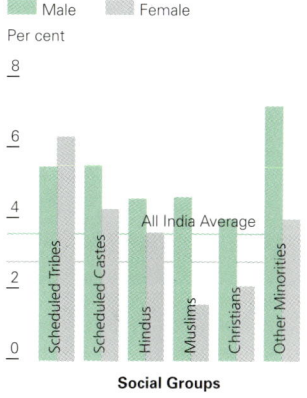

Among Social Groups

other forms of employment is of the order of about 10 m for rural India as a whole. The other category of child workers that is excluded from this estimate are those who work as unpaid family workers.

The incidence of child labour has been found to be relatively high in the rural areas of Andhra Pradesh, Karnataka, Maharashtra, Tamil Nadu, and Punjab. To what extent an association exists between the demand for child labour and the demand for adult labour, whether these types of labour are complementary or substitutable, and whether the incidence of child labour is due to high wage differentials needs further investigation.

In many respects child labour is an outcome of extreme poverty and lack of reasonable levels of adult earnings. Thus, one can see that the extent of child labour falls considerably as income increases, and as the placement in the poverty classification improves (App. Table A.4.13). An important point, however, is that participation rate for female children increases as income falls. Indeed, a larger proportion of female children work among the

TABLE 4.10

Percentage of Adult Wage Earners to All Adult Earners by States

Regions/States	Person	Male	Female	F/M
North				
Haryana	24.9	22.0	36.7	1.67
Himachal Pradesh	15.8	29.7	0.8	0.03
Punjab	19.9	23.7	12.0	0.51
Upper Central				
Bihar	32.6	31.1	37.3	1.20
Uttar Pradesh	22.2	24.1	16.7	0.69
Lower Central				
Madhya Pradesh	52.0	44.4	68.2	1.54
Orissa	40.3	40.9	38.6	0.94
Rajasthan	27.3	33.2	14.9	0.45
East				
North-eastern Rg.	18.6	19.4	12.5	0.64
West Bengal	29.6	34.8	14.0	0.40
West				
Gujarat	44.6	37.6	59.7	1.59
Maharashtra	50.5	43.5	61.2	1.41
South				
Andhra Pradesh	54.1	45.8	68.2	1.49
Karnataka	42.5	36.8	53.3	1.45
Kerala	41.0	44.2	35.4	0.80
Tamil Nadu	51.8	48.1	59.5	1.24
All India	**37.6**	**35.3**	**42.8**	**1.21**
C.V.	36.0	25.6	59.9	49.18

Feminization of wage labour is a reality across a large number of states. This phenomenon was found in states that registered low female work participation, and is indicative of a bias against women.

landless wage earner category and the STs. Female child labour is the lowest among the rich, large landowners, the salaried and professionals, Muslims, and households with literate males and females.

The WPR among those over 60 years of age are 70 per cent for males and only 15 per cent for females. Male participation in work among the elderly is only about 55 per cent in Punjab and West Bengal but as high as 77 per cent in Madhya Pradesh and Himachal Pradesh. There is wider variation among elderly female WPRs. It is extremely low in West Bengal, Uttar Pradesh, the North-east, Bihar, and Haryana, and high in Kerala, Himachal Pradesh, Madhya Pradesh, and all other states in southern and western India. These estimates across population groups are presented in App. Table A.4.13.

WPR among elderly males varies little across population groups. However, the variation among females is wider. Female work participation is lower among prosperous groups such as high household income, large farmers, the salaried, professionals, and the self-employed, and also among households with literate males and females. This perhaps confirms the observation made elsewhere that participation in economic activity by

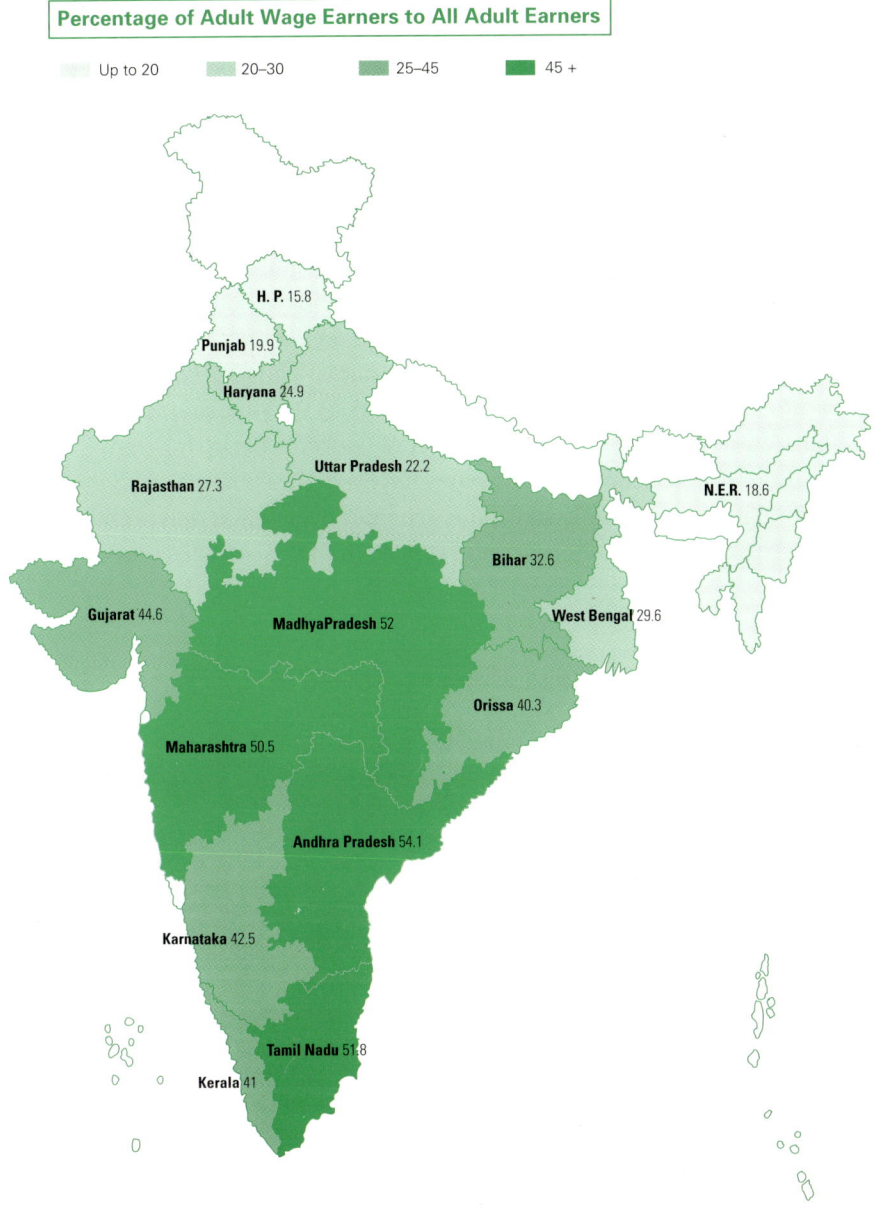

Up to 20   20–30   25–45   45 +

H. P. 15.8

Punjab 19.9

Haryana 24.9

Rajasthan 27.3

Uttar Pradesh 22.2

N.E.R. 18.6

Bihar 32.6

Gujarat 44.6

MadhyaPradesh 52

West Bengal 29.6

Orissa 40.3

Maharashtra 50.5

Andhra Pradesh 54.1

Karnataka 42.5

Tamil Nadu 51.8

Kerala 41

Macroeconomic development is not sensitive to the needs of the poor and vulnerable, and particularly to the needs of women.

women and children is the result of inadequacy of income earned by adult male members.

Employment Stability

The percentage of wage earners to total wage earners worked out to be 37.6 per cent for rural India as a whole (Table 4.10). This proportion is above 50 per cent in Andhra Pradesh, Tamil Nadu, Madhya Pradesh, and Maharashtra, above 40 per cent in Kerala, Karnataka, Gujarat, and Orissa, but below 25 per cent in Haryana, Punjab, Himachal Pradesh, Uttar Pradesh, and the North-east. It is likely that wage labour households in Uttar Pradesh and in Rajasthan might have migrated elsewhere in search of seasonal employment at the time of the survey. The qualitative village studies that form a sequel to this survey highlight this scenario but it is not the focus of the NCAER/HDI Survey, 1994.

The most interesting results emerge from an analysis of sex ratios of wage earners. Feminization of wage labour is a reality in India across a large number of states. The adverse sex ratio among wage earners is observed in states that registered low female work participation in the first place and is indicative of a bias against the female. This phenomenon is apparent in Haryana, Bihar, Gujarat, and Madhya Pradesh. For example, Haryana has a 13 per cent female WPR (15 per cent usual and subsidiary status), with a 0.26 f/m ratio. Similarly, Bihar recorded only 9.1 per cent of usual status female WPR (19 per cent usual and subsidiary status) with 0.19 f/m ratio. On the other hand, the f/m ratio of wage workers in Haryana and Bihar is 1.67 and 1.20 respectively. It is also a matter of concern that apart from Kerala, all the southern and western states have a higher proportion of females to males engaged in wage labour activities even when only usual status work participation is considered. Thus, even in the so-called

TABLE 4.11

Percentage of Adult Wage Earners by Population Groups and Gender

Population Groups	Person	Male	Female	F/M
Household Income Groups				
Up to 20,000	52.0	50.7	54.5	1.07
20,001–40,000	29.5	27.2	35.2	1.29
40,001–62,000	16.8	15.2	21.2	1.39
62,001–86,000	9.9	9.1	12.2	1.34
Above 86,000	4.7	4.2	6.2	1.48
Poverty Line Groups				
Lower segment below	52.5	51.6	54.5	1.06
Upper segment below	48.7	48.5	49.1	1.01
Lower segment above	37.8	34.8	44.3	1.27
Upper segment above	16.0	14.3	21.1	1.48
Landholding Groups				
Landless wage earner	91.7	97.3	82.8	0.85
Marginal	37.1	36.6	38.4	1.05
Small	22.1	19.2	29.8	1.55
Medium	14.7	12.7	20.5	1.61
Large	7.2	6.7	8.7	1.30
Landless	16.7	13.7	24.9	1.82
Landowners	26.6	24.7	31.2	1.26
Landless	60.5	59.1	63.4	1.07
Occupational Groups				
Cultivators	21.6	19.4	27.5	1.42
Salaried+Prof.+S.Empl.	7.9	6.1	13.0	2.13
Wage earners	87.9	93.3	79.2	0.85
All others	14.4	13.4	17.2	1.28

Contd.

Percentage of Adult Wage Earners

By Poverty Groups

Per cent

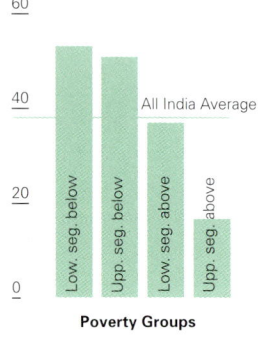

Poverty Groups

By Social Groups

Per cent

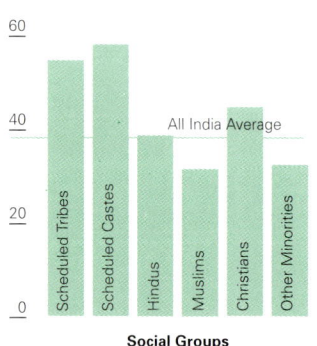

Social Groups

Social Groups				
Caste				
STs	54.9	49.3	65.4	1.33
SCs	58.0	57.6	58.7	1.02
Religion				
Hindus	38.2	35.6	44.3	1.24
Muslims	31.4	33.1	26.4	0.80
Christians	42.8	42.2	44.1	1.05
Other Minorities	33.3	31.6	36.5	1.16
Household Size Groups				
Up to 4	47.6	45.3	52.1	1.15
5–7	39.4	37.0	44.8	1.21
8 and above	26.2	24.9	29.4	1.18
Adult Literacy Groups				
None literate	59.8	59.0	61.1	1.04
Female literate	53.7	55.0	52.2	0.95
Male literate	36.6	34.8	41.2	1.18
Both literate	21.4	19.6	26.1	1.33
Village Development Groups				
Low	36.4	35.3	38.9	1.10
Medium	37.6	35.0	43.3	1.24
High	38.8	35.8	45.6	1.27
All India	**37.6**	**35.3**	**42.8**	**1.21**

One-fourth of the land-owning households also comprise wage workers.

developed states, the employment opportunities available for females are in manual wage employment. Wage employment is usually generated by state sponsored programmes such as the Jawahar Rozgar Yojana primarily targeted at STs, SCs, and other vulnerable groups. This is one sure piece of evidence to support the fact that macroeconomic development is not sensitive to the requirements of the poor and vulnerable, and particularly to the needs of women.

As expected, the proportion of wage earners falls drastically as household income increases; so does the f/m ratio, also suggesting higher wage participation of females among the poorer households. 97 per cent of males and 83 per cent of females are reported to be wage workers who belong to the landless wage earner category (Table 4.11). An important fact is however that one-fourth of all landowning households also comprised wage workers. This proportion is as high as 37 per cent among the marginal, 22 per cent among small, and 15 per cent among the medium farmers.

Participation in wage earning activities is high among SCs and STs : 58 and 55 per cent respectively. Wage earning households are lowest, only 31 per cent, among Muslims compared to 38 per cent among Hindus and 43 per cent among Christians. The female/male ratio was 1.24 among the Hindus and 0.80 among Muslims, suggesting a relatively high participation of Hindu women in wage labour employment. Poverty line classification also confirms the strong relationship of poverty with wage labour and feminization of wage labour.

TABLE 4.12
Average Days Worked per Adult Wage Earner by States (All India)

Regions/States	Agr. Wage Work			Non-agr. Work			All Wage Work		
	Male Days	Female Days	Total Days	Male Days	Female Days	Total Days	Male Days	Female Days	Total Days
North									
Haryana	91	53	75	163	88	157	159	60	131
Himachal Pradesh	84	45	77	200	98	199	195	65	192
Punjab	101	46	88	169	90	162	182	63	159
Upper Central									
Bihar	134	101	123	169	118	161	180	120	163
Uttar Pradesh	116	87	108	184	96	179	174	91	157
Lower Central									
Madhya Pradesh	104	84	95	114	97	108	135	109	124
Orissa	95	64	85	119	87	114	133	78	118
Rajasthan	63	40	53	153	89	146	148	75	135
East									
North-eastern Rg.	198	112	190	211	156	206	235	168	229
West Bengal	186	96	178	136	142	136	209	124	199
West									
Gujarat	161	139	151	140	962	126	169	142	158
Maharashtra	173	149	161	156	129	148	190	159	175
South									
Andhra Pradesh	184	182	183	145	205	169	185	192	188
Karnataka	155	135	146	174	175	174	165	145	156
Kerala	144	108	130	145	149	146	157	132	149
Tamil Nadu	129	105	119	189	184	188	166	126	151
All India	**145**	**124**	**137**	**157**	**133**	**152**	**172**	**137**	**160**

Wage Employment Stability

Inter-state Variations: Table 4.12 presents average person days of wage employment in agriculture and non-agricultural work. For rural India the overall duration of agricultural wage employment is 137 days per annum but it is substantially lower in Rajasthan, Haryana, Himachal Pradesh, Punjab, Orissa, Madhya Pradesh, and Uttar Pradesh. For example, the average duration of agricultural wage employment in Rajasthan is only 53 days per year which is only 39 per cent of the average for rural India. The average for Haryana, Himachal Pradesh, Orissa, and Punjab was 75, 76, 85 and 88 days respectively. Agricultural employment opportunities are relatively higher in Andhra Pradesh, Maharashtra, West Bengal, and Karnataka.

The average non-agricultural employment for rural India is 152 days per annum. Generally the number of non-agricultural employment days are higher in almost all states. The non-agricultural employment days are as high as 206 days in the North-east, 199 days in Himachal Pradesh, 188 days in Tamil Nadu, and 179 days in Uttar Pradesh. While the northern states had lower agricultural wage employment days they had relatively higher

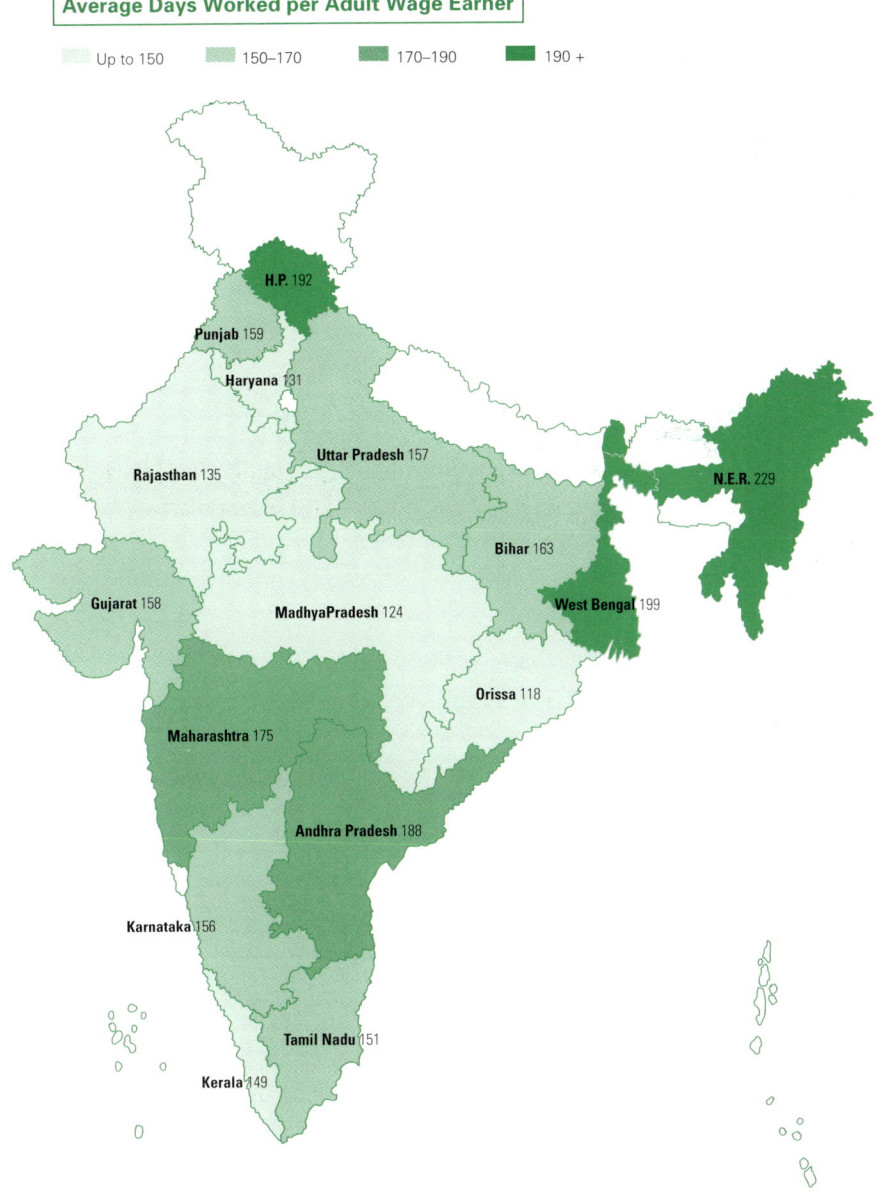

Up to 150   150–170   170–190   190 +

H.P. 192
Punjab 159
Haryana 131
Rajasthan 135
Uttar Pradesh 157
N.E.R. 229
Bihar 163
Gujarat 158
MadhyaPradesh 124
West Bengal 199
Orissa 118
Maharashtra 175
Andhra Pradesh 188
Karnataka 156
Tamil Nadu 151
Kerala 149

The number of employment days per worker increases as the level of village development improves.

number of non-agricultural employment days; the states of Madhya Pradesh, Orissa, and Rajasthan showed lower averages in both types of wage employment.

The average of days of wage employment for females is about 15 per cent less than that for males in agricultural and 18 per cent less in non-agricultural employment in rural India as a whole. Similarly, with regard to work participation rates, a parity is observed in the mean days of wage work in the southern, western, and upper central states, whereas among the other states averages for females are considerably lower for agricultural and other wage work. Male workers get 172 days and females get 137 days of all types of wage employment in rural India. Thus on the whole wage workers get 160 days wage employment a year in rural India.

Duration of wage employment increases as income increases at least in the first three income classes that participate in wage earning in relatively large numbers. The landless wage earners get 181 days of wage employment per annum followed by 147 days and 136 days for marginal and small farmers.

Access to wage employment is only 145 days for STs and 158 days for SCs respectively (App. Table A.4.14). Muslim wage workers work for 187 days a year as compared to 159 days for both Hindus and Christians, and 153 days for Other Minorities. The number of employment days increases as the level of village development improves, suggesting limited employment opportunities in remote villages. The relatively backward villages offer fewer days of wage employment in non-agricultural activities.

Duration of Wage Employment

Total person days of work for both agricultural and non-agricultural wage employment were disaggregated to find the distribution of duration of such employment. These estimates for males and females are presented separately in App. Table A.4.15. The duration of wage work intervals in days is below 91 days, 91 to 182 days, 183 to 274 days, and above 274 days

TABLE 4.13

Effective (Adult) Wage Rate for Agricultural and Non-Agricultural Wage Work by States (Rs per day)

Regions/States	Agricultural Wage Work				Non-agri. Wage Work				All Wage Work			
	All	Male Rate	Female Rate	F/M	All	Male Rate	Female Rate	F/M	All Rate	Male Rate	Female Rate	F/M
North												
Haryana	42.0	43.0	39.4	0.92	46.4	46.8	36.5	0.78	44.7	45.6	38.8	0.85
Himachal Pradesh	28.0	28.5	23.2	0.81	31.2	31.3	15.1	0.48	31.1	31.2	18.6	0.60
Punjab	34.7	35.7	27.9	0.78	40.7	41.6	23.4	0.56	38.4	39.4	26.2	0.66
Upper Central												
Bihar	22.5	23.7	19.4	0.82	25.6	26.2	21.1	0.81	24.6	25.0	19.9	0.80
Uttar Pradesh	20.3	21.0	18.0	0.86	30.8	31.2	19.1	0.61	25.3	27.4	18.2	0.66
Lower Central												
Madhya Pradesh	16.6	18.2	14.1	0.77	22.2	24.3	17.6	0.72	18.7	20.7	15.2	0.73
Orissa	17.5	18.3	15.0	0.82	21.4	22.5	14.5	0.64	19.5	20.6	14.8	0.72
Rajasthan	23.3	24.5	20.4	0.83	31.1	31.9	20.5	0.64	30.2	31.2	20.5	0.66
East												
North-eastern Rg.	25.0	25.3	20.1	0.79	32.2	33.3	16.1	0.48	28.7	29.4	17.8	0.61
West Bengal	22.9	23.0	21.7	0.94	21.3	22.5	13.2	0.59	22.5	22.9	17.4	0.76
West												
Gujarat	18.9	19.1	18.5	0.97	28.9	30.4	24.4	0.80	20.9	21.8	19.3	0.89
Maharashtra	15.5	19.3	11.2	0.58	21.5	24.3	13.9	0.57	16.5	20.4	11.5	0.56
South												
Andhra Pradesh	23.0	27.6	18.0	0.65	25.0	30.3	19.2	0.63	23.4	28.1	18.2	0.65
Karnataka	17.3	19.3	14.0	0.73	23.3	27.9	14.0	0.50	18.7	21.9	14.0	0.64
Kerala	40.8	44.4	31.4	0.71	39.9	51.3	27.6	0.54	43.0	48.0	30.0	0.63
Tamil Nadu	23.0	26.1	17.6	0.67	31.4	34.9	19.7	0.56	26.8	30.6	18.3	0.60
All India	**20.9**	**23.4**	**16.4**	**0.70**	**28.4**	**30.5**	**18.7**	**0.61**	**23.6**	**26.4**	**16.9**	**0.64**

a year. While women constitute only about 30 per cent of the total wage workers, 35 per cent of females as opposed to only 21 per cent of males worked for less than 91 days a year on wage employment. About the same proportions of males and females (36 to 37 per cent respectively) worked for durations between 91 to 182 days. The proportion of females in higher duration employment falls considerably. For example, while 30 and 13 per cent of males worked for 183–274 days, and over 274 days respectively, these percentages were only 22 and 7 for females. However, a consistent decline in female participation in wage employment according to duration of employment is generally less steep in the southern and western states in comparison with states in the north, central, and eastern areas of India. The stability of employment is relatively higher in the North-east, West Bengal, Maharashtra, and Himachal Pradesh; whereas it is much less so in Haryana, Rajasthan, Madhya Pradesh, Orissa, Kerala, and Karnataka. Employment stability in Uttar Pradesh, Bihar, and Gujarat is about average, but for

Public policy should aim at improving entitlement through creation of a larger number of employment days and then improve wage payments. Implementation of minimum wages alone will not benefit wage workers.

Wage Rate for Both Agricultural and Non-Agricultural Work (Rs)

Up to 20   20–30   30 +

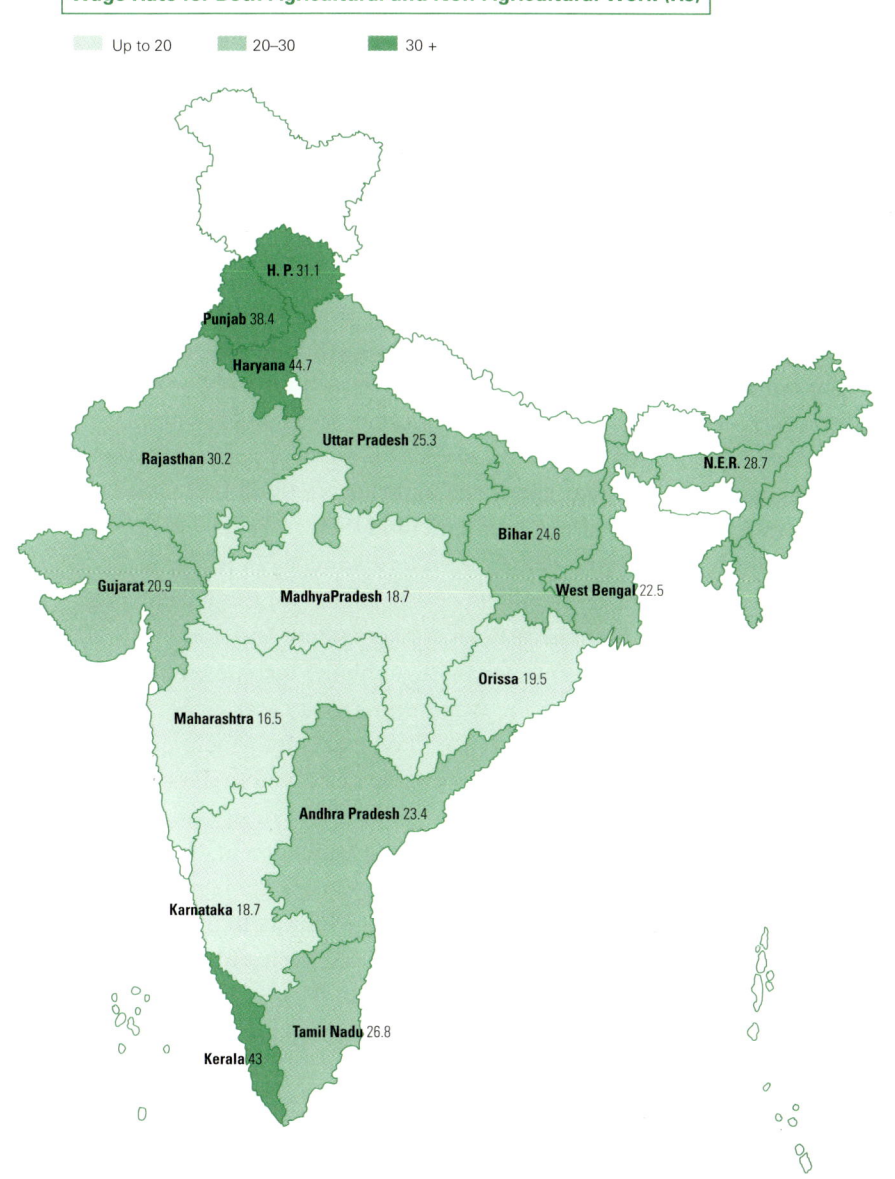

H. P. 31.1

Punjab 38.4

Haryana 44.7

Uttar Pradesh 25.3

Rajasthan 30.2

N.E.R. 28.7

Bihar 24.6

Gujarat 20.9

MadhyaPradesh 18.7

West Bengal 22.5

Orissa 19.5

Maharashtra 16.5

Andhra Pradesh 23.4

Karnataka 18.7

Tamil Nadu 26.8

Kerala 43

women it is worst in Himachal Pradesh, Uttar Pradesh, Rajasthan, West Bengal, and the North-east where women constitute less than 10 per cent of the workforce and have the least access to longer duration wage employment. In the context of abject poverty among the wage labour households, it is important to underscore that public policy should aim at improving entitlement through creation of more employment days and then improve wage payments. Just emphasizing the implementation of minimum wages in the rural areas does not help wage labourers. The percentage distribution of wage employment days according to population groups is presented in App. Table A.4.16.

The overall average daily wage rate for agricultural and non-agricultural work is Rs 21 and Rs 28 respectively in rural India (Table 4.13). The daily agricultural wage rate is high in Haryana (Rs 42), Kerala (Rs 41), and Punjab (Rs 35); and low in Madhya Pradesh (Rs 17), Orissa (Rs 18), Gujarat (Rs 19), Maharashtra (Rs 16), and Karnataka (Rs 17). The non-agricultural wage rates seem to be positively related to agricultural wage rates in most of these states. The non-agricultural wages are also higher in the same three states and low in the other five (Table 4.13).

The average daily wage rate for agricultural and non-agricultural wage work for rural India as a whole for males is Rs 23 and Rs 31, and for females Rs 16 and Rs 19 respectively. The combined wage rate is Rs 26 and Rs 17 for males and females respectively, which amounts to 36 per cent lower wages for females. This is another clear case of gender discrimination. The f/m ratio for wages is low in Maharashtra, and around 35 per cent in the southern states, and relatively higher in Gujarat, Haryana, and Bihar. The wages are more equitable in agriculture with a 0.7 f/m ratio compared with non-agricultural wages which have a female/male ratio of 0.61. It is clear that both types of wage days increase considerably as household income class increases, so also the wage rates. For example, households with an annual income of less than Rs 20,000 have 132 days or 13 per cent lower agricultural wage employment than those in the above Rs 86,000 category, and 141 days or 36 per cent lower non-agricultural wage employment. While the poorest household members earn Rs 20 and Rs 26 respectively, this wage income is 51 per cent and 49 per cent higher for those belonging to the highest household income category for agriculture and non-agriculture. It appears that persons belonging to higher income group households have a higher reservation wage, opportunity cost, and bargaining power as well as a wider choice of type of employment even in the labour market. Generally, both types of wage employment days fall as landholding size increases, as also wages, suggesting that those with land normally engage in marginal and peak time wage employment. Both agricultural and non-agricultural wage employment days are highest among Muslims followed by Hindus, but the average wage from both the sources is relatively low for Muslims. On the whole, Christians receive higher levels of wage rates in both agricultural and non-agricultural sectors. The employment and wages according to poverty class group present similar trends as those found in the case of income class.

TABLE 4.14

Agricultural and Non-Agricultural Wage Employment and Wages per Adult Wage Earner (Aged 15 + years) by States (All India)

Regions/States	Avg. Annual Wage Income per Household (Rs)		Avg. Annual Wage Income per Earner (Rs)			Average Person Days			Average Wage per Day (Rs)		
	Agricultural	Non-agri.	Agricultural	Non-agri.	ALL	Agricultural	Non-agri.	ALL	Agricultural	Non-agri.	ALL
North											
Haryana	7,012	11,614	3,152	7,295	5,824	75	157	130.3	42	46	45
Himachal Pradesh	2,828	8,468	2,147	6,210	5,962	77	199	191.7	28	31	31
Punjab	6,000	10,246	3,068	6,572	6,087	88	162	158.7	35	41	38
Upper Central											
Bihar	5,949	6,792	2,771	4,109	3,915	123	161	163.4	23	26	24
Uttar Pradesh	4,071	8,189	2,189	5,528	4,137	108	179	157.1	20	31	26
Lower Central											
Madhya Pradesh	4,168	5,159	1,577	2,403	2,312	95	108	123.8	17	22	19
Orissa	2,956	4,038	1,490	2,434	2,298	85	114	117.7	18	21	20
Rajasthan	2,279	7,278	1,241	4,546	4,074	53	146	134.9	23	31	30
East											
North-eastern Rg.	6,731	9,617	4,764	6,625	6,580	190	206	229.2	25	32	29
West Bengal	6,278	4,354	4,071	2,900	4,479	178	136	199.1	23	21	22
West											
Gujarat	7,545	7,295	2,348	3,633	3,292	151	126	157.9	16	29	21
Maharashtra	5,833	5,773	2,495	3,172	2,892	161	148	174.9	15	21	17
South											
Andhra Pradesh	9,900	9,287	4,208	4,221	4,405	183	169	188.3	23	25	23
Karnataka	5,892	8,489	2,530	4,049	2,923	146	174	156.2	17	23	19
Kerala	9,461	11,335	5,295	5,828	6,397	130	146	148.7	41	40	43
Tamil Nadu	7,745	14,796	2,725	5,898	4,059	119	188	151.2	23	31	27
All India	**6,341**	**7,844**	**2,848**	**4,313**	**3,768**	**137**	**152**	**159.8**	**21**	**28**	**24**

The poorest of the poor undertake 100 and 112 days of agricultural and non-agricultural wage employment respectively, which are 67 per cent and 76 per cent lower than those in the upper segment above the poverty group. The poorest of the poor also get 47 per cent lower agricultural wages and 97 per cent lower non-agricultural wages. The developed villages offer 23 per cent higher number of agricultural and 15 per cent higher number of non-agricultural employment days. Similarly, the wages are 12 per cent and 28 per cent lower in less developed villages in comparison with highly developed villages.

Wage Work and Household Income

The average annual income per wage worker from agricultural and non-agricultural work for rural India works out to Rs 2,848 and Rs 4,313 respectively (Table 4.14). This estimate is computed by multiplying actual number of wage employment days and actual wages received by all those who worked for wages during the previous year. The total per worker income from agricultural wage work was highest in Kerala with Rs 5,295 per annum followed by the North-east, Rs 4,764, and Andhra Pradesh with Rs 4, 208. Total income from agriculture was meagre in all the three lower central states of Rajasthan (Rs 1,241), Orissa (Rs 1,490), and Madhya Pradesh (Rs 1,577). The annual household income from agricultural wage work was Rs 6,341 for rural India. This was high for Andhra Pradesh and Kerala, and low in the lower central states and Uttar Pradesh. Household income is a cumulation of all wage earnings from all members of the household participating in wage work. There are wide variations in this income across states which is due to variations both in the number of days of employment and the average wage payment per day.

Non-agricultural income per wage worker is Rs 4,313 for rural India, and is high in Haryana, Punjab, and Himachal Pradesh, and low in Madhya Pradesh and Orissa. However, household income from non-agricultural sources is higher than agricultural wage work at Rs 7,844 for rural India; this income was high in Tamil Nadu, Kerala, Haryana, and Punjab.

Principal Findings

I   Ownership of Assets

1   About 63 per cent of rural households own land in India. Ownership is highest in Punjab, Haryana, Rajasthan, Gujarat, and Maharashtra, and lowest in Tamil Nadu, West Bengal, and Kerala. The average size of landholding is highest in Punjab—7.5 acres—and lowest in Kerala—0.9 acres

2   Ownership of land is highest among Hindus (70 per cent), followed by STs (69 per cent), and lowest among SCs (47 per cent) followed by Muslims (57 per cent). Hindus also have the largest average landholding size of 5.1 acres while Muslims have 3.6 acres, SCs 2.8 acres, and Christians 2.0 acres.

3   Ownership of durables such as television sets, radios, and bicycles is high in Punjab and Haryana and in the southern states of Kerala, Karnataka, and Andhra Pradesh. Bihar, West Bengal, Orissa, and Uttar Pradesh have the lowest record of electrified villages in the country. Only 25 per cent of households in rural India have access to piped water; a high proportion in Bihar, West Bengal, and Kerala have no access to tap water.

4   The highest values for indices of both productive and utility assets are found in Punjab and Haryana, reflecting the general level of prosperity in these states. Hindus have both a higher productive asset index as well as utility asset index in comparison to Muslims.

II   Work Participation

5   About 52 per cent of males and 18 per cent of females in rural India participate in some gainful economic activity. Variations across states are much wider for females (coefficient of variation 56 per cent) compared to those for males (coefficient of variation 6.8 per cent). Female WPR ranges from a low of 4.6

per cent in the North-east to a high of 37– 8 per cent in Andhra Pradesh and Himachal Pradesh.

6 Socio-cultural factors play a significant role in the work status of women. The female work participation rate is lowest among Muslims at about 10 per cent followed by Hindus (17 per cent), SCs (23 per cent), Christians (25 per cent), and STs (28 per cent).

7 The female participation rate falls with rising income and ownership of assets like land. Large farmers tend to employ hired labour to replace females who work in the family. Male participation rates are higher among poor households in lower income classes, poverty groups, and landless wage earners.

8 In an average household in rural India comprising 5.7 persons (3.0 males and 2.7 females), 2.1 persons are engaged in productive activities, that is 1.6 males and 0.5 females. In other words, every one earner has to support 0.7 male and 1.1 female non-earning members within each average household in rural India.

9 The dependency ratio is low among landless wage earners, SCs, and STs. This lower dependency ratio is largely due to a higher female work participation rate among these population groups.

III Child Labour And Work Participation of the Elderly

10 Child labour is prevalent where there is extreme poverty. About 4.4 per cent male children and 3.5 per cent female children are engaged in wage-earning activities on a regular basis. They number about 10 m in rural India. Participation of children, especially females, in gainful work falls as prosperity rises in terms of income, landholding, and also adult literacy.

11 Work participation among the elderly (over 60 years) is as high as 70 per cent for males and 15 per cent for females. Among the elderly, female work participation is lower in high income, landholding, salaried, and professional groups.

IV Wages

12 Wage earners in rural India constitute 37.6 per cent of total earners. This proportion is high in Andhra Pradesh, Tamil Nadu, Madhya Pradesh, and Maharashtra and low in Haryana, Punjab, Himachal Pradesh, Uttar Pradesh, and the North-eastern region. Except for Kerala, all the southern and western states have a high proportion of females engaged in wage employment. Employment opportunities available to females appear to be largely confined to wage employment even in the so-called developed states.

13 The proportion of wage earners to total earners falls with rising income and size of landholding as does the female to male (f/m) ratio. Participation in wage earning activities is high among SCs—over 58 per cent—and STs—55 per cent.

14 Average days of work available to a wage earner are 137 in agriculture and 152 in non-agricultural employment. Employment opportunities in agriculture are high in Andhra Pradesh, Maharashtra, West Bengal, and Karnataka and in non-agricultural wage employment in the North-eastern region, Himachal Pradesh, Tamil Nadu, and Uttar Pradesh.

5

Household Expenditure and Food Security

Targetting or limiting beneficiaries of the subsidized programme to the poor and nutritionally vulnerable has to be made administratively and politically feasible.

The objective of resource transfer to the needy through the supply of subsidized esential items has not really been achieved in India.

Household Expenditure on Minimum Needs

The survey collected disaggregated information on household expenditure on various types of day-to-day needs. Expenditure on cereals and foodgrains, other food items, expenditure on health care of all household members, and expenditure on children's education were separately collected. Expenditure on non-food items such as the purchase of household assets was not recorded although this would have provided complete information on household expenditure. In this discussion, however, the proportion of expenditure on non-food items (excluding expenditure on health and education) available from NSS 44th Round for 1988–9 is used for adjusting the estimates. A complete distribution of per capita expenditure per month on foodgrains, other food items, health care, children's education and other non-food items is discussed below.

Column 8 of App. Table A.5.1 presents estimated total expenditure per capita per month at current prices. Mean Per Capita per month Household Expenditure (MPCE) for rural India worked out to Rs 287. This expenditure ranged from a high of Rs 554 in Punjab, to a low of Rs 208 in Madhya Pradesh, and Rs 210 in Orissa. The actual expenditure in rupees on foodgrains, other food items, health, education, and non-food items was 87.5, 95.8, 21.3, 9.0, and 73.5 respectively. This amounts to 30.6, 33.4, 7.4, 3.1, and 25.6 per cent of total expenditure respectively for rural India.

Expenditure on foodgrains alone is about 31 per cent, but this proportion is low in Haryana, Punjab and Rajasthan. On the other hand, expenditure on this item is as high as 43.3 per cent and 42.7 per cent in Bihar and Orissa respectively. For Rajasthan, however, these proportions are in the expected direction. It is normally expected that the proportion of expenditure on basic food items will be relatively high in areas or population groups with low levels of income.

Since both expenditures on health and education are related to the respective state policies, facilities, and practices, it is not appropriate to make comparisons of the levels of expenditure between states; rather, one can look into the relative proportion of the total expenditure on these two items for a comparison. Expenditures on health and education are 7.4 and 3.1 per cent respectively for rural India (Table 5.1), and are presented separately for

TABLE 5.1

Estimated Per Capita Expenditure as a Percentage of Total Expenditure by States

Regions/States	Food Expenditure			Non-food Expenditure and CPI 1993-94				Total Expenditure
	Food-grains	Other Food	Total Food	Health	Education	Other Non-food	Total Non-food	
North								
Haryana	16.9	43.3	60.2	5.9	4.9	29.0	39.8	100.0
Himachal Pradesh	25.3	35.0	60.3	8.7	7.0	24.3	39.7	100.0
Punjab	15.8	41.9	57.8	5.8	3.2	33.2	42.2	100.0
Upper Central								
Bihar	43.3	26.2	69.5	10.2	3.4	16.9	30.5	100.0
Uttar Pradesh	29.5	33.4	62.9	6.6	2.7	2.8	37.1	100.0
Lower Central								
Madhya Pradesh	34.6	27.3	61.9	9.7	2.4	26.0	38.1	100.0
Orissa	42.5	26.4	68.9	5.9	3.0	22.2	31.1	100.0
Rajasthan	19.7	39.7	59.4	6.7	2.5	31.4	40.6	100.0
East								
North-eastern Rg.	39.9	32.4	71.7	6.3	4.5	17.4	28.3	100.0
West Bengal	38.9	31.5	70.4	8.5	2.9	18.2	29.6	100.0
West								
Gujarat	23.7	42.2	65.9	5.3	2.9	26.0	34.1	100.0
Maharashtra	26.8	34.3	61.1	7.5	3.2	28.2	38.9	100.0
South								
Andhra Pradesh	29.2	30.0	59.2	9.3	2.3	29.2	40.8	100.0
Karnataka	32.5	33.0	65.6	8.0	3.7	22.7	34.4	100.0
Kerala	22.5	39.7	62.2	6.5	5.3	26.0	37.8	100.0
Tamil Nadu	32.2	32.7	64.9	10.1	2.6	22.4	35.1	100.0
All India	**30.5**	**33.4**	**63.9**	**7.4**	**3.1**	**25.6**	**36.1**	**100.0**

Estimated Per Capita Expenditure Per Month

Expenditure on Total Food among States

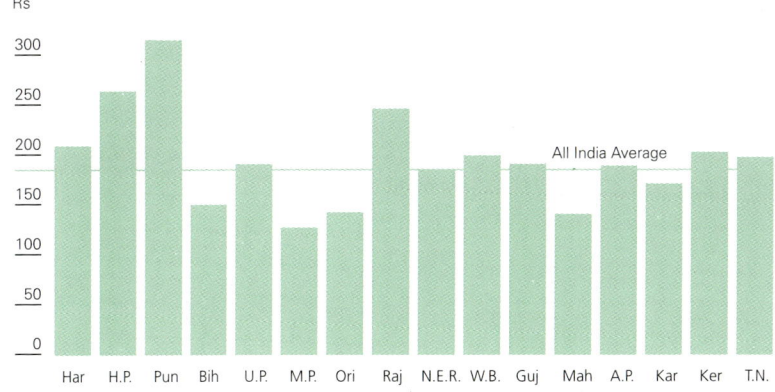

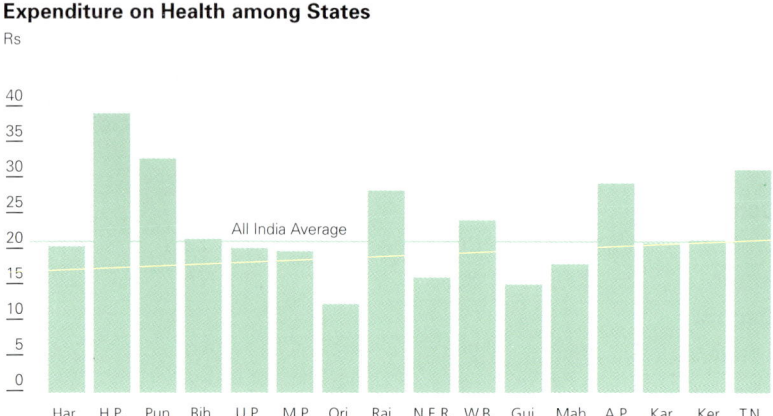

Expenditure on Health among States

Rs

All India Average

Har H.P. Pun Bih U.P. M.P. Ori Raj N.E.R. W.B. Guj Mah A.P. Kar Ker T.N.

TABLE 5.2

Estimated Per Capita Expenditure per Day (Rs) by States

Regions/States	Food Expenditure			Non-food Expenditure				Total Expenditure
	Food-grains	Other Food	Total Food	Health	Education	Other Non-food	Total Non-food	
North								
Haryana	1.96	5.05	7.01	0.67	0.57	3.38	4.62	11.64
Himachal Pradesh	3.71	5.12	8.84	1.28	1.03	3.52	5.83	14.68
Punjab	2.92	7.75	10.67	1.07	0.58	6.14	7.81	18.48
Upper Central								
Bihar	3.14	1.90	5.05	0.73	0.25	1.23	2.22	17.26
Uttar Pradesh	3.00	3.40	6.41	0.67	0.28	2.83	3.78	10.20
Lower Central								
Madhya Pradesh	2.39	1.88	4.28	0.66	0.16	1.81	2.65	6.93
Orissa	2.98	1.85	4.83	0.41	0.21	1.56	2.18	7.02
Rajasthan	2.68	5.42	8.11	0.91	0.34	4.30	5.56	13.68
East								
North-eastern Rg.	3.40	2.81	6.22	0.54	0.39	1.51	2.45	8.67
West Bengal	3.70	3.00	6.71	0.80	0.27	1.74	2.82	9.53
West								
Gujarat	2.30	4.07	6.41	0.51	0.28	2.53	3.32	9.70
Maharashtra	2.14	2.74	4.89	0.59	0.26	2.26	3.12	8.01
South								
Andhra Pradesh	3.04	3.12	6.17	0.96	0.24	3.05	4.25	10.43
Karnataka	2.89	2.94	5.84	0.71*	0.33	2.03	3.07	8.91
Kerala	2.50	4.41	6.92	0.72	0.59	2.90	4.22	11.14
Tamil Nadu	3.32	3.37	6.70	1.03	0.27	2.32	3.63	10.34
All India	**2.91**	**3.19**	**6.10**	**0.70**	**0.30**	**2.45**	**3.46**	**9.57**

* The figures are the same as the national average.

all states. Per capita proportion of expenditure on health care is high in Uttar Pradesh, Tamil Nadu, Madhya Pradesh, and Andhra Pradesh. Lower expenditures are found in Gujarat, Orissa, Haryana, and Punjab. Expenditure on education of children is high in Himachal Pradesh followed by Kerala and Haryana. It is low in Andhra Pradesh, Rajasthan, Uttar Pradesh, and Tamil Nadu.

Table 5.2 presents the expenditures on various items on a per capita per day (PCPDE) basis. Overall PCPDE is Rs 9.57 for rural India. It is as high as Rs 19 in Punjab, Rs 17 in Bihar, and Rs 14 in Rajasthan. The PCPDE is low in Madhya Pradesh, Orissa, Maharashtra, Karnataka, and Gujarat. Expenditure on foodgrains is Rs 2.91 per capita per day for rural India as a whole, but it was the lowest in Haryana and highest in Himachal Pradesh and West Bengal.

Consumption of Foodgrains and Food Security

In this survey detailed information regarding consumption of food items that are purchased and those that are home produced was collected for a reference period of one month prior to the date of survey. The data were collected between January and June 1994. The seasonal variations may not be important in estimating the consumption needs and actual consumption of foodgrains. The per capita consumption of foodgrains averages 14 kg per month for rural India as a whole, which corresponds to 467 g per day (App. Table A.5.2). This estimate is marginally less than the nutritional norm of intake for the rural population. Those who are below this average perhaps consume less than the nutritional requirement. There are some variations across states - around 10 kg in Kerala and Gujarat. On the other hand, average consumption in Himachal Pradesh and Rajasthan is over 17 kg per person per month. A part of this variation is explained by the difference in food habits. In Kerala, for example, nutritional requirements are met by consuming cereal substitutes such as tapioca and non-cereal items such as nuts, fruits, and vegetables. Similarly, Gujarati food habits favour greater use of edible oil, fruits, and vegetables which explains their relatively low cereal consumption. The climatic extremes and lack of cereal substitutes may account for the higher level of foodgrain consumption in Rajasthan and Himachal Pradesh.

The per capita consumption of foodgrains varies only marginally according to population groups. The consumption levels are lower for landless labourers, those living in the lower segment below the poverty line, and those living in larger households. The lower levels of consumption among all these groups appear to be due to lack of purchasing capacity or lack of resources. The consumption of cereals is also low among STs and Christians, which may be due to geographic and cultural reasons. Most of the Christians belong to Kerala which recorded lower levels of consumption of foodgrains. Since STs live in remote, possibly hilly and forest areas, their access to foodgrains is likely to be limited. The diet of STs may also contain low amounts of foodgrains and larger amounts of nuts, roots, leaves, fruits, and the like available from the common property resources (App. Table A 5.3).

The PDS, an income transfer programme aiming to provide food security to the masses, is found to be almost non-existent in states with high levels of poverty and under-nutrition.

The Public Distribution System in India

The most important food security policy in India today is the Public Distribution System (PDS). Due to lack of direct targeting, this system is being used by all, irrespective of their standard of living. Excepting in the case of sugar, jowar, and standard cloth (data not presented) supplied by the public distribution system, there is hardly any variation in the utilization of items supplied according to the levels of living. Rice and wheat, the two popular cereals, are purchased and consumed approximately by similar proportions of households within each monthly per capita expenditure class classified by the NSSO. A strong urban bias has also been found both in the supply and utilization of the PDS in all states excepting Kerala, Andhra Pradesh, Karnataka, and Tripura. Thus, the objective of resource transfer to the needy through the supply of subsidized essential items has not really been achieved in India. Targeting or limiting beneficiaries of the subsidized programme to the poor and nutritionally vulnerable, has to be made administratively and politically feasible. Targeting the subsidization of an inferior good, whose consumption falls as income rises, appears to be a good strategy. Direct distribution to most backward areas and vulnerable population groups such as those below the poverty line, landless wage earners, and other deprived social groups will be a cost-effective strategy.

The PDS in India has a network of over 4 lakh fair price shops (FPS) and serves about 160 m. families, and is perhaps, the largest such distribution network in the world. The system is intended to translate the macro level self-sufficiency in foodgrains to micro level by ensuring access to food and other essential items to poor families. Thus, the PDS has been an important constituent in the overall strategy for amelioration of poverty. However, the PDS, as it was being implemented, has been widely criticized for its

- Failure to reach the poor effectively,
- Urban bias, and
- Lack of transparency and accountability.

The Revamped Public Distribution System (RPDS) was started in 1992 in areas that had concentrations of poor families. The programme covered 1,775 Blocks under the Integrated Tribal Development Programme (ITDP), Draught Prone Area Programme (DPAP), Designated Hill Area (DHA), and Desert Development Programme (DDP). In these areas, foodgrains were released at a price held at a rupee per kilogramme lower than the Central Issue Price (CIP) to all families. Thus RPDS was targeted at all in poor areas irrespective of economic status. .

The issue of further streamlining the PDS was discussed in a conference of Chief Ministers on 4–5 July 1996 and another conference of State Food Ministers on 7 August 1996. On the basis of these discussions the target was changed to 'poor in all areas' from 'all in poor areas'. The new target of the PDS is the population below the poverty line (BPL) in all areas. This Targeted Public Distribution System (TPDS) has been implemented in all the states and union territories (barring Punjab, Delhi, Goa, and Lakshadweep) since May/June 1997.

In the light of the experience gained in the implementation of TPDS, and

Rice and wheat, the two popular cereals supplied through the PDS, are purchased and consumed approximately by similar proportions of households within each monthly per capita expenditure class.

the issues raised by the states in the Chief Minister's Conference on the subject in September 1997, a review of the progress and impact of the TPDS was proposed by the Ministry of Food and Consumer Affairs, Government. of India. Various aspects of the programme, such as identification of the beneficiaries, functioning of the Fair Price Shops, and effectiveness of the vigil by panchayats need to be scrutinized at the level of implementation to bring out their policy implications.

The PDS as a Social Safety Net

Public distribution of essential commodities is one way of transferring resources and providing the economically weaker sections of society with a minimum level of consumption. In relatively less developed countries such as India, availability and consumption of food by the masses is an important aspect of human life that needs to be investigated and monitored. Ever since India launched the Public Distribution System (PDS) in the early 1960s its aim has been to supply basic food items, such as the common grains, pulses, sugar, and oil through government approved stores both in rural and urban areas. Although, the PDS is a centrally sponsored programme it is implemented through the state machinery. The coverage and popularity of the PDS appears therefore dependent upon the demand, and the political, administrative, and infrastructural facilities available at the level of the states. The official statistics relating to the PDS do not present information on the number of users and the proportion of requirement met by the subsidized programme. The NSSO presents information on utilization of the PDS only by way of monthly per capita expenditure classes. This survey has made available for the first time nationally representative information on the actual size, location and extent of use of the PDS. The data are discussed below.

On the whole only 33 per cent of rural households in India reported use of the PDS on a regular basis (see Table 5.3). It is likely that this proportion may fall for short periods of time such as during the harvesting seasons. However, an increase depends upon the vibrancy of the programme and regularity of PDS supplies. Data indicate that the programme is working fairly efficiently in all the four southern states, two western states, and Himachal Pradesh, and at modest levels in Madhya Pradesh. The proportion of households using PDS is 82 per cent in Tamil Nadu, 78 per cent in Kerala, 70 per cent in Karnataka, and 66 per cent in Andhra Pradesh. On the other hand, only about 5 per cent of rural households have reported PDS utilization in Uttar Pradesh, Bihar, Orissa, and Punjab. With the exception of Punjab, the other three states have a very high level of undernutrition both among children and adult populations. Low PDS utilization in Punjab and Haryana is primarily a consequence of lack of demand since these are agriculturally prosperous states with substantial marketable surpluses. The programme is very weak in the states of Uttar Pradesh, Bihar, Orissa, and West Bengal. The proportion of users is very low and the proportion of requirement met by the PDS is also low in all the poorly performing PDS states. Overall, however, only 33 per cent of households utilized the PDS

The PDS programme has been found to function satisfactorily in all the four southern states, two western states, and in Himachal Pradesh.

TABLE 5.3

Consumption of Foodgrains and Utilization of the PDS in States

Regions/States	Household Income(Rs per year)	Per capita Income(Rs per year)	Per Capita Consumption of Foodgrain (kg/month)	Percentage of Households Met from PDS	Quantity of Cereals(kg) Using the PDS	Percentage of Requirement of Cereals Bought from PDS (per hh/month)	Met by PDS

Regions/States	Household Income(Rs per year)	Per capita Income(Rs per year)	Per Capita Consumption of Foodgrain Met from PDS	Percentage of Households Using the PDS	Quantity of Cereals(kg) Bought from PDS (per hh/month)	Percentage of Requirement of Cereals Met by PDS
North						
Haryana	39,956	6,368	12.8	9.0	18.1	32.4
Himachal Pradesh	23,973	4,168	17.4	75.6	43.8	41.4
Punjab	37,418	6,380	14.3	5.6	23.4	5.5
Upper Central						
Bihar	22,459	3,691	14.8	5.0	49.5	29.2
Uttar Pradesh	26,733	4,185	15.2	5.2	33.4	24.5
Lower Central						
Madhya Pradesh	25,319	4,166	13.5	34.2	15.7	20.4
Orissa	17,208	3,028	16.4	5.2	18.6	16.7
Rajasthan	27,184	4,229	17.6	23.6	33.1	14.7
East						
North-eastern Rg.	28,160	5,070	12.5	21.7	20.5	31.9
West Bengal	18,113	3,157	16.3	11.3	38.4	45.6
West						
Gujarat	29,356	5,288	10.1	47.6	17.3	18.1
Maharashtra	29,929	5,525	13.2	50.7	13.8	13.2
South						
Andhra Pradesh	24,776	5,046	14.3	66.4	18.6	30.6
Karnataka	27,372	4,769	15.1	70.1	15.0	22.8
Kerala	29,101	5,778	9.8	78.0	23.7	51.9
Tamil Nadu	23,271	5,122	12.6	82.4	12.0	21.6
All India	**25,653**	**4,485**	**14.3**	**33.2**	**19.0**	**23.5**
C.V.	21.25	20.70	15.66	78.24	44.87	45.84

Consumption of Foodgrains and Utilization of the PDS

Households Using the PDS in States

Per cent

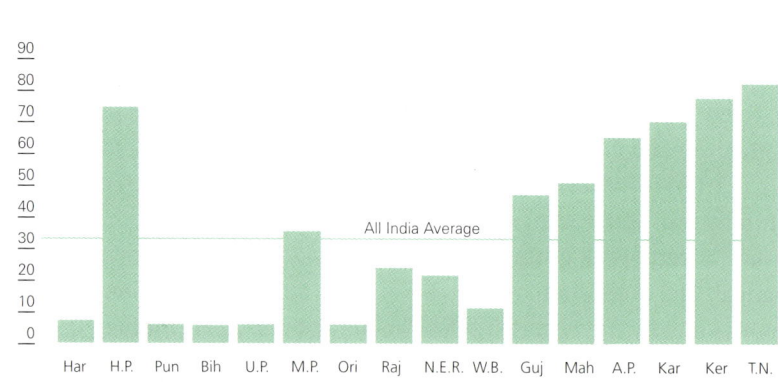

and only about 24 per cent of their requirements were met through this system. Thus the total PDS market as a proportion of the total cereal market in India worked out to be about 8 per cent only. Understanding this dimension is important to basically allay a number of misconceptions among academics and the common people alike that the issue prices of the PDS substantially affect the overall price levels and contribute to inflation. Such misconceptions can be dispensed with only when one takes a closer look at the data presented in this report.

BOX 5.1

Effective PDS Utilizers and Quantum of Food Distributed (All India Estimates based on Rural PDS Utilization Rates)

1 Number of Rural Households in India, 1991: 112 million

2 Number of Rural Households reporting PDS Utilization during 1993–4: (Estimate based on 36 per cent of rural households reporting PDS utilization in the NCAER/HDI Survey, 1994) 40 million

3 Total cereal and pulse requirements for the 40 m rural households reporting PDS utilization (Estimate based on reported rural per capita food consumption of 466 g per capita/day and a household size of 5.7 members in the NCAER/HDI Survey, 1994) 38 million tonnes per year

4 Estimated rural utilization of foodgrains by the 40 m. households reporting PDS purchases: (Estimated to be 24 per cent of the required supply. This matches well with the reported requirement of 23 per cent met by the PDS in the NCAER/HDI Survey, 1994) 9 million tonnes per year

5 Official offtake figures for foodstuffs both by Central and State governments for 1993–4 (rural and urban) 15 million tonnes per year

15 million tonnes–9 million tones = 6 million tonnes. or 40 per cent of the offtake appears to have been supplied to urban areas, while the proportion of urban population was only about 26 per cent.

Among Poverty Groups
Per cent

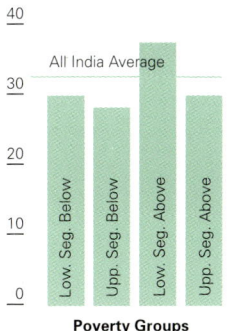

Poverty Groups

Among Social Groups
Per cent

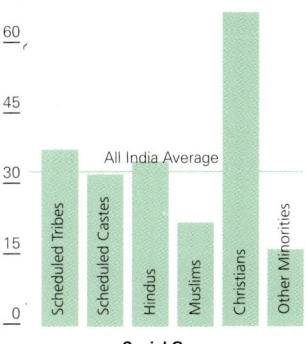

Social Groups

Among Village Development Groups
Per cent

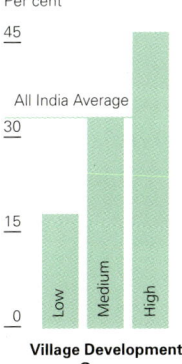

Village Development Groups

Although there are some differentials between various types of population groups, there are no noteworthy differentials either at the state level by poverty or by per capita income class (App. Table A.5.3). However, as expected it is the landless wage earners who constitute a large portion of those who use the PDS. About 43 per cent of wage earning households reported using the PDS. The other groups using PDS are the salaried, professional and trade category of occupation classification. These data suggest that 66 per cent of Christian households use the PDS, whereas the percentage is 38 for STs and as low as 22 per cent for Muslims. Most of the Christians surveyed for this study live in Kerala and Tamil Nadu where PDS utilization is relatively higher. Household size is closely related to the quantity of per capita food intake; it decreases as household size increases. Dependence on the PDS declines substantially as household size increases and only a small proportion of the household requirements is met by the PDS.

State specific distributions of PDS users according to key social groups are presented in App. Tables A.5.4 to A.5.5. Although there is a marginal decline in the proportion of rural households using the PDS for India as a whole, in Andhra Pradesh and Gujarat where the proportion of users is relatively high, a higher proportion of poorer households use the PDS. Similarly, in West Bengal the proportion of poorer households using the PDS is relatively large but at very low levels of utilization. On the other hand however, in Bihar and Orissa where the overall utilization is extremely low, it is those who are better off who utilize the PDS.

Child Malnutrition

Recent studies have documented the significant relationships between anthropometric measures and child health which are dependable indicators of child nutrition and cumulative health. The height-for-age is a measure of the long-term cumulative nutrition and health of surviving children. It is also used to highlight chronic under-nutrition among children and is identified as 'stunting'. This is a continuous variable expressed as a percentage or number of standard deviations away from the NCHS (National Council of Health Statistics) international reference median height-for-age. The height-for-age estimates—expressed as percentages falling (a) below −3 standard deviation which is considered to be an extreme degree of chronic undernutrition, and (b) between −3 and −2 standard deviations, which is considered to be a moderate degree of under-nutrition—are presented according to age and sex for 16 states and for selected population groups. The nutrition deprivation is considered chronic in the case of all children who fall in the less than −3 standard deviation category from the standard median.

In rural India about 37 per cent of children aged 0–4 years are second degree malnourished when compared to the international standard, and they fall below the −3 standard deviation. Another 21 per cent children are classified as moderately undernourished. All these children are identified as stunted. Gender differences in stunting are low but inter-state differentials are large. A high degree of stunting is found in Karnataka, Madhya Pradesh,

The PDS market as a proportion of the total cereal market in India works out to only 8 per cent.

Thirty-seven per cent of children aged 0–4 years have second degree malnourishment.

Gujarat, Andhra Pradesh, Bihar, Uttar Pradesh, the North-east, Haryana, and West Bengal. Kerala and Tamil Nadu recorded the lowest incidence of stunting among their 0–4 years child populations (Table 5.4).

About 29 per cent of children in the 5–12 years age group are found to be stunted. Boys are marginally more stunted in this age group. Inter-state differentials are large. A high degree of stunting is found in Karnataka, the North-east, Gujarat, Madhya Pradesh, Bihar, and West Bengal. It is lowest in Kerala and Punjab. Stunting is relatively insensitive to differentials in income, landholding, occupation, and social group, although one does recognize an expected pattern.

About 5 per cent of the children aged 0–4 years are wasted, i.e., below –3 standard deviation in the reference scale. Male children are relatively more wasted and inter-state differentials are wide. High levels of wasting are found in Uttar Pradesh, Gujarat (also high gender gaps), Karnataka, and Andhra Pradesh.

TABLE 5.4

Percentage of Children (Aged 0–12 Years) that are Stunted, Wasted, at Risk, and Gender Disparity by States

Regions /States	Percentage of 0–4 years Children						Percentage of 5–12 years Children					
	Height for Age		Weight for Hht		Bodymass Index		Height for Age		Weight for Hht		Bodymass Index	
	<–3	–3 to –2	<–3	–3 to –2	< 12	>=20	<–3	–3 to –2	< –3	–3 to –2	< 12	>= 20
North												
Haryana	40.2	22.2	4.2	10.4	11.6	16.2	26.6	29.7	1.0	4.3	5.5	3.9
Himachal Pradesh	34.0	28.7	3.0	4.2	5.2	18.3	28.7	33.8	0.7	3.1	3.7	5.3
Punjab	29.2	23.1	5.1	5.0	6.9	24.5	16.1	25.5	1.8	4.3	6.3	2.3
Upper Central												
Bihar	41.3	21.7	4.6	10.6	11.5	10.0	32.5	31.5	1.2	3.7	4.1	7.6
Uttar Pradesh	40.5	20.9	7.4	11.2	14.9	15.0	31.0	27.2	3.8	9.2	12.5	5.0
Lower Central												
Madhya Pradesh	43.7	20.7	3.9	10.0	8.9	27.3	32.6	24.9	1.0	7.3	10.2	9.0
Orissa	26.5	19.2	3.7	7.4	9.1	10.9	22.0	21.4	1.6	6.7	9.2	1.4
Rajasthan	36.7	21.5	4.8	8.4	9.9	16.5	23.6	28.9	1.8	5.3	6.7	2.1
East												
North-eastern Rg.	34.2	18.6	5.5	6.1	9.2	40.7	37.1	26.4	2.1	4.5	7.5	30.1
West Bengal	37.6	22.3	6.1	12.0	15.1	8.8	32.9	25.1	1.2	7.3	8.9	5.3
West												
Gujarat	38.1	24.0	7.2	13.1	16.1	12.7	33.3	29.0	3.0	10.4	14.6	9.6
Maharashtra	32.0	26.5	2.7	10.5	8.6	5.2	22.0	30.7	1.5	9.0	10.6	1.3
South												
Andhra Pradesh	35.8	17.1	7.0	9.8	14.7	16.4	23.2	24.7	2.7	10.2	16.5	5.7
Karnataka	43.4	16.8	7.0	7.9	11.4	28.7	38.7	28.1	3.0	9.8	15.2	15.6
Kerala	19.1	19.7	3.3	11.7	11.5	9.5	15.1	26.4	2.2	10.5	14.7	3.0
Tamil Nadu	28.4	20.9	2.4	8.3	7.0	11.4	26.5	30.6	0.8	5.4	6.9	2.6
All India												
Person	**37.2**	**21.4**	**5.2**	**10.0**	**11.6**	**15.9**	**29.0**	**27.7**	**2.1**	**7.3**	**9.9**	**6.8**
Gender Disparity	**0.97**	**0.90**	**0.89**	**0.86**	**1.07**	**0.96**	**0.98**	**1.00**	**0.67**	**0.73**	**1.13**	**0.88**

Distribution of Stunted and Wasted Children among States

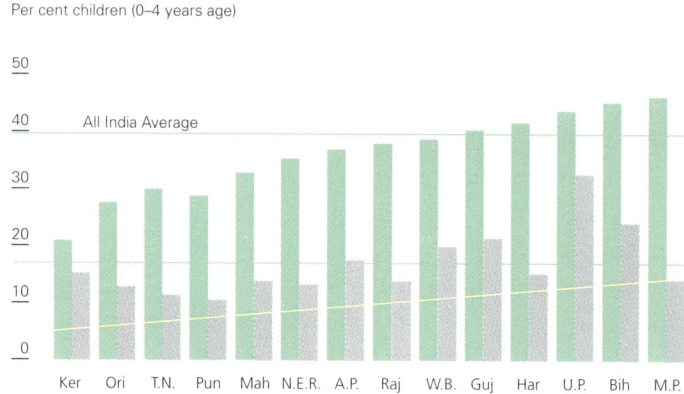

Dramatic differentials were found between states and gender even among children aged 5–12 years. High levels of wasting of children were found in Uttar Pradesh, Gujarat, Karnataka, Andhra Pradesh, all having high gender gaps favouring females as well. As was the trend in the case of stunting, even wasting is insensitive to economic, occupational, landholding, and social group difference.

It is apparent that the differentials in under-nutrition measured both in terms of height-for-age and weight-for height, were found to be related to age of children and to various states in India. The differentials, according to various population/social groups, are not substantial and apparent. One may argue that while the absolute deprivation in India is extremely high the relative differentials between social groups are low. There is scope therefore to undertake a comprehensive analysis of the determinants of under-nutrition among children in India.

Principal Findings

I Consumption of Foodgrains

1 The average per capita consumption of foodgrains in India is 14 kg per month which corresponds to 467 g per day. This varies from 9 kg in Kerala and 10 kg in Gujarat to 17 kg in Himachal Pradesh and Rajasthan.

2 Mean per capita per month household expenditure (MPCE) for rural India worked out to Rs 287, with very high inter-state variation ranging from Rs 555 for Punjab to Rs 208 for Madhya Pradesh.

3 About 31 per cent of total expenditure goes on food, but this proportion is relatively higher in Bihar and Orissa—about 43 per cent. Economically well-off states like Punjab and Haryana spend only about 16 per cent on food.

4 Per capita consumption of foodgrains varies only marginally according to population group. The consumption levels are lower for landless labourers, those living in the lower segment below the poverty line and those living in larger households.

5 Only 33 per cent of all rural households make use of the Public Distribution System on a regular basis. The PDS is most widely used in all the four southern states and is least used in Uttar Pradesh, Bihar, Orissa, and West Bengal.

6 There are some differentials between population groups. About 43 per cent of wage earning households reported use of the PDS. The other groups using the PDS are the salaried, professional and trade categories of the occupational classification.

II Undernutrition

5 About 37 per cent of children aged 0–4 years suffer from second degree malnourishment or 'stunting'. Stunting is higher in Karnataka, Madhya Pradesh, Gujarat, Andhra Pradesh, Bihar, Uttar Pradesh, the North–eastern region, Haryana, and West Bengal in comparison with Kerala and Tamil Nadu. About 29 per cent of children aged 5–12 are stunted. Boys have marginally higher rates of stunting. Stunting is insensitive to differentials in income, landholding, occupation, and social groups.

6 About 5 per cent of children aged 0–14 years suffer from wasting. Boys have higher levels of wasting than girls. Wasting is high in Uttar Pradesh, Gujarat, Karnataka, and Andhra Pradesh, and among children aged 5–12 years. Like stunting, wasting in also insensitive to economic, occupational, landholding, and social group differences.

6

Literacy and Education

Education-based knowledge and learning is one of the greatest gifts of mankind to its progeny. Today's store of knowledge is the collection of ideas and innovations since time immemorial. Every human being and every child has absolute right to access and use this knowledge to shape his/her personality and contribute to nation building. This chapter presents the level and structure of educational deprivation in India.

Introduction

Despite governmental efforts at universalization of elementary education, half the Indian adult population continues to be illiterate and two-thirds of women are illiterate. This chapter discusses the educational status of women, men, and children, and highlights gender disparities that are pertinent to development. The *Human Development Report 1995* identifies the different elements that contribute to women's well-being and empowerment. These include minimum levels of education, health, and material well-being. Empowerment, as distinct from well-being, also requires an assessment of their political, economic, and professional participation. Clearly, the issue of women's status, level of empowerment, and ability to respond to new opportunities or cope with adverse circumstances is a complex one, and cannot be adequately captured by any statistical profile. Yet, the ultimate concern of development professionals or policy-makers should be to devise policies that take these facts into consideration. It is hoped that the information contained in this chapter will be useful in assessing the impact of structural adjustment on women and in formulating gender sensitive policies that will facilitate their development.

The data presented here focus essentially on the levels of and variations in gender disparities that exist in the country as a whole and at state level by household income, land size, and social groups. Gender disparity is measured by the ratio of female to male (f/m) level or achievement in the respective categories.

The following indicators reflect literacy and education:

I **Ever Enrolment Rate (EER)**

Ever Enrolment Rate is defined as the proportion of children aged 6–14 years ever enrolled in school, at any level, at the time of survey.

II **Average Discontinuation Rate (ADR)**

Average Discontinuation Rate is estimated as the percentage of ever enrolled children who discontinued studies at any time in age-group 6–14 years. Since these rates are the average for an 8-year period, and the rate of discontinuation is higher in the early years, they are bound to be low. ADR multiplied by 8 can be compared with 1 minus the retention rate.

III Non-Attendance Rate (NAR)

Non-Attendance Rate refers to the percentage of students in the age-group 6–14 years not attending school for a period of more than 7 days in the working month preceding the date of survey. (The survey was conducted during January– July 1994.)

IV Quality of Education

This refers to the percentage of adults aged 15–34 years who had completed middle level schooling, which in most states is 8 years of schooling. This indicator has been used as a proxy for quality of education.

V Distribution by Type of School Management

Three types of school management were identified: (a) schools established and managed by Government and local bodies; (b) schools established by the community and aided by the Government; and (c) private schools.

VI Cost of Schooling

This refers to item-wise private expenditure on education by all households with children in age-group 6–14 years currently enrolled in schools, including expenditure on fees, books, stationery and uniforms, private coaching and transport; in other words, per household expenditure on primary and elementary education.

This section presents the differentials in elementary levels of schooling by major states and population groups. Population groups have been identified in terms of social, economic, household, and occupational characteristics. Education parameters include literacy rate, enrolment rate, dropout rate and private cost of elementary education.

Literacy Rate

Literacy rates across states for age-group 7 years and above are presented in Table 6.1. The literacy rate for rural India as a whole is 54 per cent: 66 per cent for males and 40 per cent for females with a gender disparity of about 40 per cent.[1] Literacy levels from this survey are compared with the literacy rates for rural India from the 1991 Census of India. On the whole, the estimates from this survey are relatively higher across states. The Census estimates an overall literacy rate of 45 per cent for 1991 which is nine percentage points lower than the survey estimates; a fact that may be attributed partly to a secular increase in mass education during the interim period (1991 to 1994), and partly due to better reporting of literacy levels in the survey. Both estimates are consistent as far as the relative ranking of states according to literacy is concerned. However, the Census appears to have underestimated the level of literacy in rural Andhra Pradesh. The survey also reveals higher f/m literacy ratios[1] consistent with the secular decline in gender disparity in education in India.

1 F/M ratio has been computed to highlight gender disparities in all educational parameters. This is the ratio of female levels to male levels. Thus, one minus the f/m ratio can be considered to be the level of gender disparity.

TABLE 6.1

Literacy Rates (Percentage) and Gender Disparity by States

| Regions/States | Literacy Rates (7 years & above) | | | | | F/M |
	1991[1] Person	1991 F/M	Person	Male	Female	
North						
Haryana	49.9	0.50	54.9	69.4	38.1	0.55
Himachal Pradesh	61.9	0.69	68.2	79.4	57.0	0.72
Punjab	52.8	0.72	60.2	68.2	51.2	0.75
Upper Central						
Bihar	33.8	0.37	43.8	56.6	28.8	0.51
Uttar Pradesh	36.7	0.36	46.7	62.0	28.3	0.46
Lower Central						
Madhya Pradesh	35.9	0.39	43.9	58.9	27.1	0.46
Orissa	45.5	0.52	54.5	67.8	40.7	0.60
Rajasthan	30.4	0.24	40.9	60.4	19.0	0.31
East						
North-eastern Rg.	49.3[2]	0.66	70.0	77.3	60.9	0.79
West Bengal	50.5	0.61	58.5	66.3	49.9	0.75
West						
Gujarat	53.1	0.58	59.4	71.3	46.7	0.65
Maharashtra	55.5	0.59	58.2	70.9	45.1	0.64
South						
Andhra Pradesh	35.7	0.51	50.2	60.6	39.1	0.65
Karnataka	47.7	0.58	54.9	65.1	43.9	0.67
Kerala	88.9	0.93	89.6	93.0	86.5	0.93
Tamil Nadu	54.6	0.63	64.1	74.6	53.2	0.71
All India	**44.7**	**0.53**	**53.5**	**65.6**	**40.1**	**0.61**
C.V.	-	-	20.4	12.9	34.9	23.1

1. GOI, *Census of India (1991)*, Series I, Part II-B(I), Primary
   Census Abstract. Office of the Registrar General, GOI, New Delhi,
2. Refers to Assam only.

It is well known that Kerala is the most literate state in India with the lowest gender disparity. States with above the national average of literacy such as the North-eastern region, Himachal Pradesh, Punjab, Tamil Nadu, Gujarat, Maharashtra, and West Bengal also display relatively lower levels of gender disparity. States with very low levels of literacy and high gender disparity are Rajasthan, Bihar, Madhya Pradesh, and Uttar Pradesh. While Madhya Pradesh has recorded substantial success in reducing gender disparities over time, Rajasthan shows slow progress. For example, in Rajasthan the literacy rate was only 40 per cent with a high disparity rate (f/m ratio equal to 0.31). The contrast between the low literacy rates recorded in the northern states and the high literacy rates in the south is both distinct and clearly identifiable except in the case of Punjab where relatively higher female literacy may be said to be income driven.

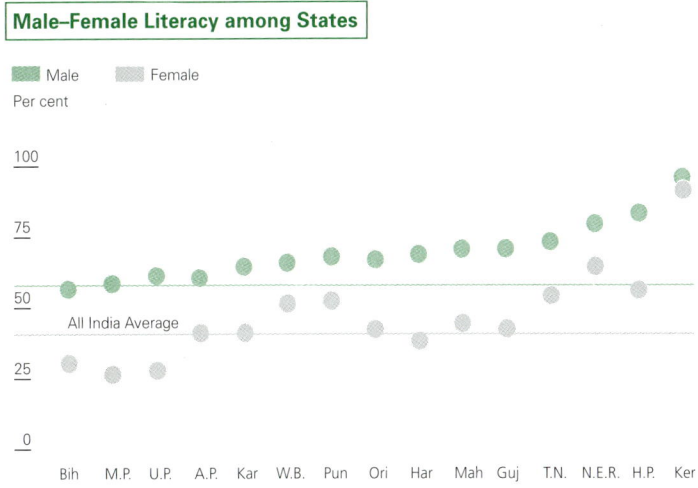

Male   Female
Per cent

100
75
50   All India Average
25
0

Bih M.P. U.P. A.P. Kar W.B. Pun Ori Har Mah Guj T.N. N.E.R. H.P. Ker

Literacy rates are similar for all land size groups; in contrast, only landless wage earners registered very low levels of literacy.

Household Income and Literacy: A cross-classification of literacy with household income suggests that literacy levels increase substantially as income increases (Table 6.2). Gender disparity also decreases as household income increases. However, it is interesting that when per capita income was used instead of household income, gender disparity was found to be roughly the same across per capita income classes.

While there is a positive association in all states between levels of household income and literacy, the trend is particularly strong in the relatively poorer states and moderate in Kerala, Haryana and Punjab (*see* App. Table A.6.1). The differential impact of income on literacy is an important one and there is a need to understand the dynamics of this differential. Quite often these associations can be traced to state-specific mass education inputs and programmes.

Land Size, Occupation, and Literacy: Since India is largely a rural society with two-thirds of its population still dependent upon land, it is useful to look into the impact of land on different social processes. Literacy rates are similar for all land size groups; in contrast, only landless wage earners registered very low levels of literacy (Table 6.2). Gender disparities are also significant and similar irrespective of land size category. Literacy is found to be highest among the salaried and lowest among wage earners. Gender disparity is high among wage earners and low among the salaried and professionals.

In spite of the above generalization, landownership is strongly associated with literacy in Uttar Pradesh, Bihar, and Punjab.[2] By contrast, landholding size has no association with literacy in Kerala, Rajasthan, and Himachal Pradesh. As with income, this differential also requires deeper probing.

Social Groups and Literacy: Religion and caste have an impact on many types of social behaviour in India, such as opting for a secular education normally imparted by public institutions. STs and SCs recorded a literacy level of about 40 per cent in comparison to an all India average of 54 per cent. Christians have the highest levels of literacy, of about 81 per cent. Muslims on the contrary have a literacy level of about 50 per cent.

2 Data not presented.

TABLE 6.2

Literacy Rates (Percentage) and Gender Disparity by Population Groups

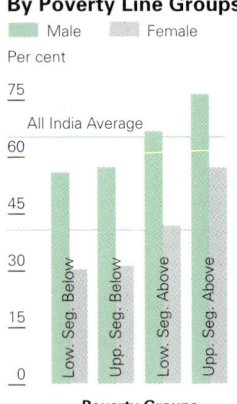

Literacy Rates and Gender Disparity

By Poverty Line Groups

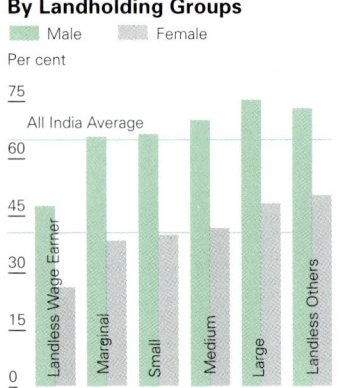

By Landholding Groups

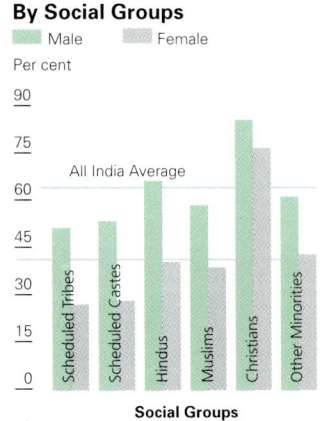

By Social Groups

Population Groups	Literacy Rates (aged 7 & above)			F/M
	Person	Male	Female	
Household Income Groups				
Up to 20,000	45.1	57.0	32.5	0.57
20,001–40,000	57.5	69.6	43.6	0.63
40,001–62,000	64.9	76.8	50.9	0.66
62,001–86,000	68.8	81.1	54.2	0.67
Above 86,000	74.9	86.4	62.2	0.72
Poverty Line Groups				
Lower segment below	43.5	55.5	31.1	0.56
Upper segment below	45.9	57.8	33.1	0.57
Lower segment above	54.4	66.6	40.7	0.61
Upper segment above	67.1	78.4	53.7	0.69
Landholding Groups				
Landless wage earner	36.9	47.0	26.0	0.55
Marginal	53.3	65.5	40.1	0.61
Small	55.2	67.4	41.2	0.61
Medium	58.0	71.6	42.6	0.59
Large	61.0	75.2	44.8	0.60
Landless others	62.4	74.2	49.6	0.67
Landowners	55.4	68.0	41.3	0.61
Landless	49.4	60.4	37.6	0.62
Occupational Groups				
Cultivators	53.9	66.7	39.6	0.59
Salaried+Prof.+S.Empl.	72.4	85.0	58.2	0.68
Wage earners	38.4	48.7	27.2	0.56
All others	58.3	70.3	45.3	0.64
Social Groups				
Caste				
STs	39.3	51.4	26.0	0.51
SCs	41.5	53.4	28.2	0.53
Religion				
Hindus	53.3	65.9	39.2	0.60
Muslims	49.4	59.5	38.0	0.64
Christians	80.8	85.0	76.5	0.90
Other Minorities	53.8	62.9	43.8	0.70
Household Size Groups				
Up to 4	48.7	60.5	35.5	0.59
5–7	54.5	66.0	41.6	0.63
8 and Above	55.0	68.3	40.5	0.59
Adult Literacy Groups				
None literate	12.2	15.4	8.7	0.57
Female literate	54.5	32.7	68.6	2.10
Male literate	48.7	74.5	16.0	0.21

Contd.

Both literate	82.3	89.5	74.7	0.83
Village Development Groups				
Low	42.3	56.1	26.5	0.47
Medium	53.7	66.0	40.0	0.61
High	63.9	74.4	52.7	0.71
All India	**53.5**	**65.6**	**40.1**	**0.61**

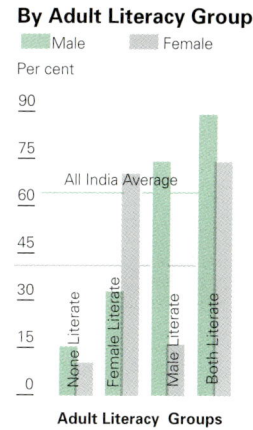

By Adult Literacy Groups

While female literacy is significantly low for all social groups, gender disparity is high among STs and SCs. For example, only about a fourth of ST and SC women and about 50 per cent of women in other social groups, are literate as opposed to about 50 per cent and 75 per cent of men respectively. Literacy levels are extremely low for STs and SCs in Bihar, Rajasthan, Uttar Pradesh, Madhya Pradesh, and Orissa. Gender disparities are also wide, especially among SCs and Muslims in Uttar Pradesh, Rajasthan, and Haryana in relation to others (App. Table A.6.2). SC women in the reproductive ages of 15 to 35 years recorded only 6 and 9 per cent of literacy in Bihar and Uttar Pradesh respectively.

Village Index: Village development has a strong association with level of literacy. Literacy in the relatively less developed villages was 42 per cent; the level rose to 54 per cent in moderately developed and to 64 per cent in developed villages. While male literacy rose to about 75 per cent in developed villages in comparison to the less developed ones, this rise was only 52 per cent in the case of females. The gender disparity decreased from 0.47 in the least developed to 0.71 in the developed villages.

On the whole, economic levels and levels of social well-being and village development may be seen to have a positive association with literacy. A cause for concern is that gender disparity is high among states and population groups that have lower levels of literacy.

Age-Specific Literacy Rates

Age- and sex-specific literacy rates for rural India and states are presented in the vairous figures (*see also* App. Table A.6.3). The following pattern emerges: (a) The literacy level increases considerably over the years for both sexes. For example, literacy for both sexes at about 43 per cent with a gender disparity of 0.39 for the 40–4 age group increased to about 70 per cent with a disparity of only 0.76 in the younger age group (15–19 years); (b) The pattern also suggests that over time there have been a considerable reduction in gender disparity in literacy levels. These findings can be corroborated by data from other sources such as The Census and NFHS surveys.

Low levels of literacy and high gender disparities are prevalent among the 25–34 age group in the five states categorized as Upper and Lower Central states. Illiteracy in this age group has implications not only for India's adult education programmes but also for the expected linkages between female literacy and the positive role it plays in reducing fertility and mortality levels, and in child survival.

Age-specific literacy according to population group highlights the very

SC and ST women in the reproductive age of 15–35 years recorded only 6 and 9 per cent literacy in Bihar and UP respectively.

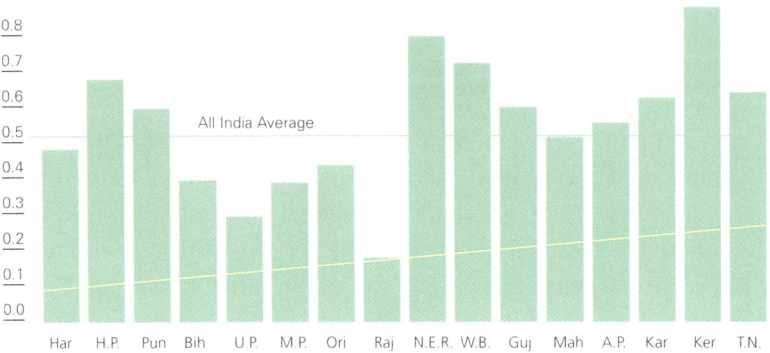

Gender Disparity in Literacy Rates in Age Group 7 and Above

Among Scheduled Tribes and Scheduled Castes

Low levels of literacy and high gender disparities are prevalent among the 25–34 year age group in five states, viz. UP, Bihar, MP, Rajasthan, and Orissa.

Literacy by Age

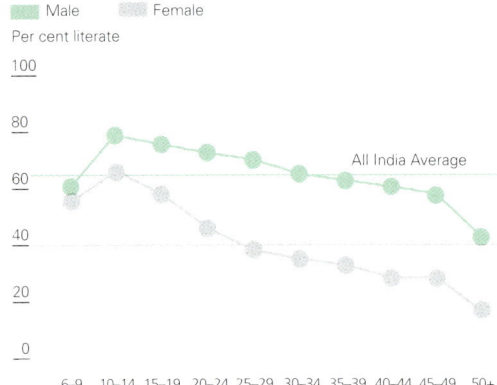

Age-specific Rural Literacy: India

low levels for older men and women belonging to households with low incomes, the landless, STs, SCs, Muslims, those in the lower segment of the poverty line, and those living in less developed villages (App. Table A.6.4). However, the positive side of this scenario is that literacy has increased considerably over the years among these very population groups in the 15–19 age group.

Enrolment Rates

According to the Constitution of India, primary and elementary schooling are required to be provided free of cost to all citizens, implying that neither school enrolment nor continuation rates should differ across states and by socio-economic groups. Table 6.3 summarizes enrolment rates (Panel I), discontinuation rates (Panel II), and non-attendance rates (Panel III), according to states.

The enrolment rate for rural India as a whole is 71 per cent with a gender disparity of 0.84 showing a deficit of 16 per cent for girls. As may be expected, enrolment rates are generally high in the southern and western states with low gender disparity. Although the lowest level of enrolment

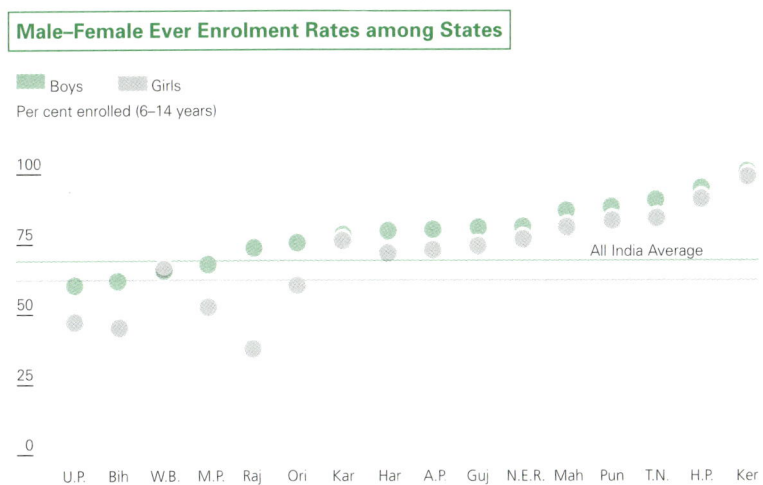

Male–Female Ever Enrolment Rates among States

Boys   Girls

Per cent enrolled (6–14 years)

All India Average

U.P.   Bih   W.B.   M.P.   Raj   Ori   Kar   Har   A.P.   Guj   N.E.R.   Mah   Pun   T.N.   H.P.   Ker

TABLE 6.3

Ever Enrolment, Discontinuation and Non-Attendance Rates (Percentage) for Children (aged 6–14 years) by States

Regions/States	Enrolment Rates Region/NSSO[1]		Panel I Ever Enrolment Rates				Panel II Discontinuation Rates				Panel III Non-attendance Rates			
	Person	F/M	Person	Male	Female	F/M	Person	Male	Female	F/M	Person	Male	Female	F/M
North														
Haryana	75.2	0.73	78.1	83.8	72.3	0.86	4.2	3.8	4.6	1.2	2.3	2.4	2.2	0.88
Himachal Pradesh	*	-	92.7	95.5	90.0	0.94	2.0	1.8	2.2	1.2	3.5	3.5	3.5	0.98
Punjab	71.6	0.87	86.8	89.0	84.4	0.95	5.4	4.8	6.1	1.28	2.1	1.6	2.7	1.71
Upper Central														
Bihar	38.3	0.53	58.8	64.7	51.2	0.79	3.2	2.6	4.1	1.58	11.6	11.1	12.4	1.12
Uttar Pradesh	48.5	0.48	64.2	73.2	53.4	0.73	4.2	3.3	5.6	1.7	6.8	6.9	6.6	0.96
Lower Central														
Madhya Pradesh	46.3	0.53	62.6	68.5	55.8	0.81	8.0	7.3	9.0	1.24	15.5	15.5	15.4	0.99
Orissa	47.2	0.72	70.9	78.5	63.4	0.81	7.6	6.2	9.3	1.5	11.7	12.1	11.1	0.91
Rajasthan	53.7	0.35	61.3	78.0	41.9	0.54	4.2	3.1	6.6	2.13	3.8	4.3	2.6	0.61
East														
North-eastern Rg.	65.6	0.86	81.3	84.6	76.3	0.90	3.3	2.9	4.1	1.44	9.1	7.8	11.2	1.43
West Bengal	54.2	0.77	66.1	67.0	65.1	0.97	6.2	5.9	6.5	1.1	8.9	9.4	8.3	0.88
West														
Gujarat	69.8	0.70	80.3	85.3	74.5	0.87	7.3	5.6	9.5	1.68	5.7	5.5	6.0	1.09
Maharashtra	77.6	0.83	85.2	88.1	82.3	0.93	7.1	5.9	8.4	1.41	4.1	3.6	4.6	1.27
South														
Andhra Pradesh	59.6	0.69	79.5	85.1	73.8	0.87	9.9	8.2	12.1	1.48	5.9	5.9	5.9	0.99
Karnataka	65.5	0.75	77.9	80.6	75.1	0.93	7.9	6.8	9.1	1.35	4.3	4.6	4.0	0.88
Kerala	97.4	0.99	98.6	99.2	98.0	0.99	1.7	1.5	2.0	1.32	3.7	3.9	3.5	0.91
Tamil Nadu	86.0	0.87	87.7	90.9	84.3	0.93	10.9	7.5	14.8	1.98	1.0	0.6	1.4	2.25
All India	**57.8**	**0.69**	**71.4**	**77.1**	**64.8**	**0.84**	**6.0**	**4.8**	**7.6**	**1.56**	**7.0**	**7.0**	**7.0**	**1.00**
C.V.	-	-	15.0	11.8	20.8	12.7	45.4	42.7	47.3	18.8	63.1	64.3	64.0	34.3

Note: 1. NSSO, 42nd Round (July 86 to June 87), Report No. 365 (Part II), Vol. I-II.

* Data not available

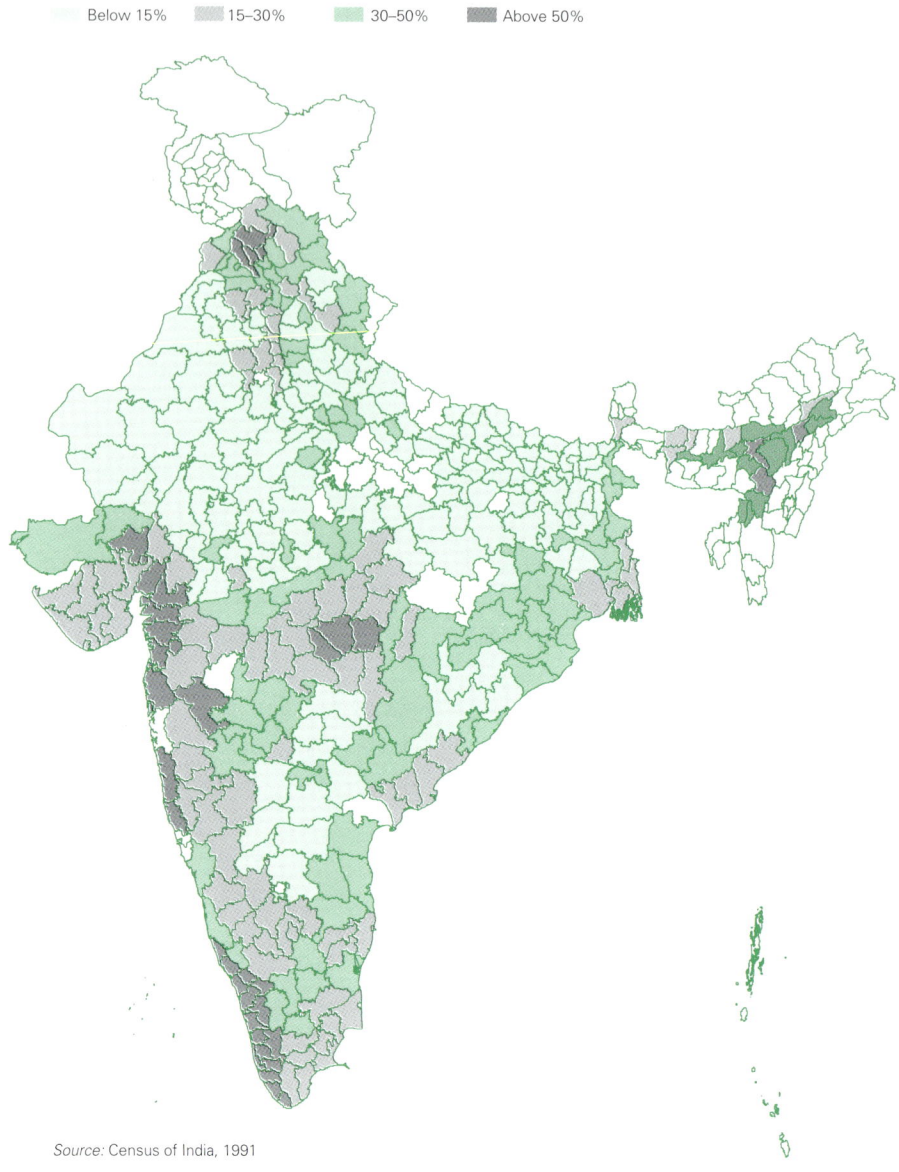

Below 15%   15–30%   30–50%   Above 50%

Enrolment rate for rural India as a whole is 71 per cent with a gender disparity of 0.84 showing a deficit of 16 per cent for girls.

Source: Census of India, 1991

was found in Bihar, 59 per cent, Rajasthan stands out both with regard to low levels of enrolment (61 per cent) and a high level of gender disparity (0.54 showing a deficit of 46 per cent).

School enrolment improves as household income increases and the increase is considerable among females (Table 6.4, Panel I). It appears that low school enrolment and gender disparity are manifestations of poverty and inaccessibility of the schooling system. Landless wage earners, STs, SCs, and Muslims, and villages with low development have very low levels of school enrolment.

While social group differentials are to be expected, interesting relationships also emerge between the current enrolment of children and

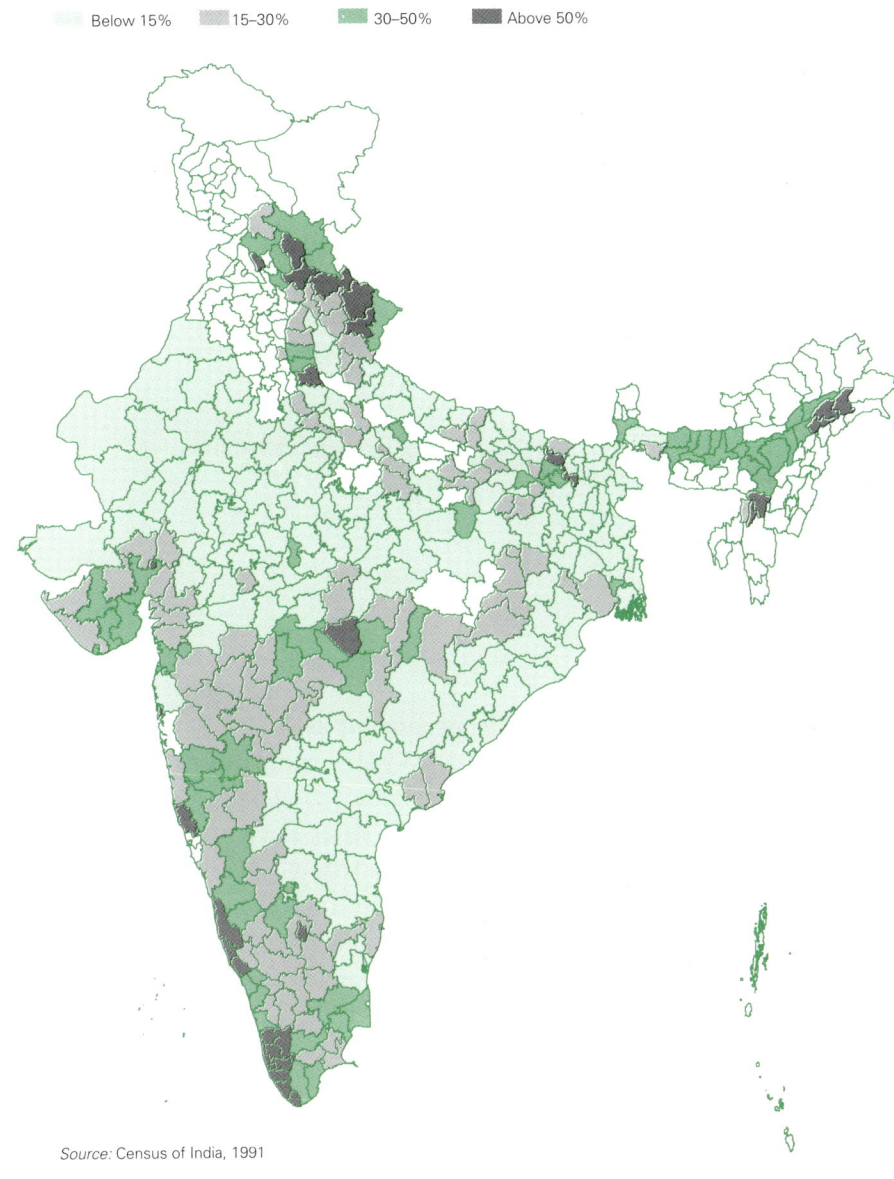

Female Literacy Rate among STs in Rural India

Below 15%   15–30%   30–50%   Above 50%

Landless wage earners, STs, SCs, Muslims and villages with low development have very low levels of school enrolment.

Source: Census of India, 1991

educational levels of adults (parents) in the household. For example, enrolment rates were lowest in households in which there was no adult literate male or female: 54 per cent for boys and 36 per cent for girls. The levels were so low that the disparity index on its own did not highlight the problem. The enrolment rate in households where both adult males and females were literate was as high as 92 per cent. Another interesting association was found between female education and enrolment. The enrolment rate was only 72 per cent in households in which no female was educated but in households where only the female was educated the rate was as high as 87 per cent. Female literacy also enhances gender equity in school enrolment, as is clearly evident by comparing f/m ratios in households consisting of only females and only males who are literate.

Another parameter that highlights a contrasting scenario in enrolment rates and underscores the importance of supply side factors is the level of village development. The enrolment rate which is 60 per cent in less developed villages, rises to 74 per cent in moderately developed ones, and to 81 per cent in developed villages. The gender disparity also decreases

Enrolment Ratio

Among States

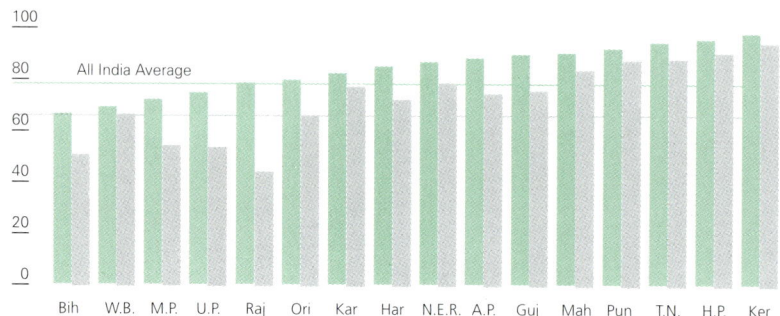

Among Poverty Groups
Per cent enrolled

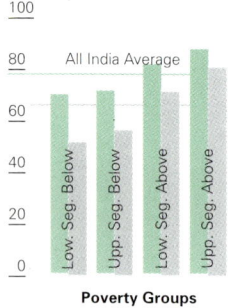

Poverty Groups

Among Village Development and Household Size Groups
Per cent enrolled

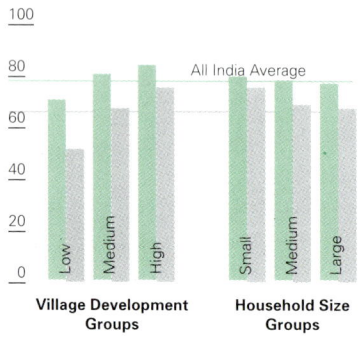

**Village Development   Household Size
Groups   Groups**

Among Social Groups
Per cent enrolled

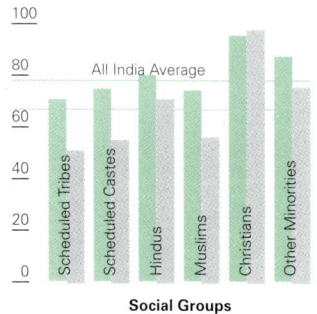

Social Groups

from 0.73, 0.84 to 0.93 as village development improves.

Enrolment rates show an interesting relationship with household income in different states (App. Table A.6.5). Kerala shows absolutely no variation in enrolment rate by income level unlike other states where the variation is quite high. Take for example Bihar, Madhya Pradesh, Rajasthan, and Uttar Pradesh where the enrolment rate is considerably lower among the last two income categories. Note that 82 per cent of the total households fall in the below Rs 40,000 annual income category and approximately the same proportion of children come from these income classes. The enrolment rates are as low as 50 per cent in Bihar, 54 per cent in Rajasthan, 55 per cent each in Madhya Pradesh, and Uttar Pradesh in the below Rs 20,000 income category. One very clear but unexpected result is with regard to West Bengal where the school enrolment rate is only 60 per cent in the below Rs 20,000 income category but increases to 93 per cent in the above Rs 62,000 income category showing a wide disparity by income. This is in total contrast with Kerala. However, the enrolment rates are fair in the states of Punjab and Himachal Pradesh. The question therefore arises as to why the enrolment rate is low among poor households when primary and elementary schooling is provided free of cost. The possible reasons are: (a) lack of demand for schooling; (b) inadequate facilities for schooling; and (c) high direct and indirect costs of schooling.

Considerable differences were evident with regard to the Ever Enrolment Rates (EERs) by social group between states. STs, SCs and Muslims recorded the lowest EER, just about 62 per cent (App. Table A.6.5). Christians had the highest levels (Table 6.4) followed by Hindus with 72 per cent.

TABLE 6.4

Ever Enrolment, Discontinuation, and Non-Attendance Rates (Percentage) for Children (aged 6–14 years) by Population Groups

Population Groups	Panel I Ever Enrolment Rates				Panel II Discontinuation Rates				Panel III Non-attendance Rates			
	Person	Male	Female	F/M	Person	Male	Female	F/M	Person	Male	Female	F/M
Household Income Groups												
Up to 20,000	65.3	72.3	57.5	0.80	7.2	5.9	9.0	1.52	7.1	7.1	7.1	0.99
20,001–40,000	75.1	79.9	69.6	0.87	5.7	4.4	7.4	1.67	6.7	7.0	6.3	0.90
40,001–62,000	80.9	85.4	75.6	0.89	4.3	3.1	5.9	1.91	7.5	6.9	8.4	1.22
62,001–86,000	84.1	88.3	79.3	0.90	2.6	2.8	2.3	0.83	5.7	6.7	4.5	0.68
Above 86,000	89.3	91.5	87.3	0.95	3.2	2.3	4.1	1.80	8.3	7.1	9.6	1.34
Poverty Line Groups												
Lower segment below	61.1	69.1	52.6	0.76	6.1	5.5	6.9	1.26	7.7	7.7	7.7	1.00
Upper segment below	64.3	70.5	57.2	0.81	7.2	5.8	9.0	1.55	7.4	7.7	7.0	0.91
Lower segment above	75.7	81.0	69.7	0.86	6.4	4.9	8.5	1.71	6.2	6.3	6.2	0.98
Upper segment above	83.8	86.6	80.4	0.93	3.6	2.9	4.6	1.56	8.0	7.6	8.4	1.10
Landholding Groups												
Landless wage earner	59.7	66.3	52.2	0.79	9.9	7.5	13.4	1.77	7.3	7.3	7.1	0.97
Marginal	71.0	77.8	63.6	0.82	5.3	4.5	6.4	1.44	6.4	6.3	6.4	1.01
Small	74.3	79.4	68.1	0.86	5.7	4.5	7.5	1.64	7.2	7.1	7.3	1.03
Medium	75.5	82.0	68.3	0.83	5.4	3.8	7.5	2.98	6.7	6.6	6.8	1.02
Large	77.8	83.4	71.7	0.86	4.4	3.5	5.5	1.56	8.9	8.7	9.2	1.05
Landless others	75.7	79.2	71.6	0.90	5.3	4.8	6.0	1.27	7.4	7.7	7.0	0.91
Landowners	73.3	79.4	66.4	0.84	5.4	4.3	6.8	1.58	6.9	6.8	7.0	1.03
Landless	67.4	72.5	61.7	0.85	7.4	6.1	9.2	1.51	7.3	7.5	7.1	0.94
Occupational Groups												
Cultivators	72.5	79.0	65.2	0.83	5.9	4.8	7.4	1.53	7.3	7.3	7.3	1.01
Salaried+Prof.+S.Empl.	85.9	88.2	83.2	0.94	2.1	1.8	2.4	1.36	6.0	6.0	6.0	1.00
Wage earners	60.4	67.3	52.6	0.78	9.4	7.1	12.9	1.82	7.0	6.9	7.0	1.01
All others	72.9	77.7	67.2	0.86	5.7	4.8	7.0	1.46	7.4	7.5	7.3	0.97
Social Groups												
Caste												
STs	60.3	67.6	51.5	0.76	7.2	6.6	8.0	1.20	10.1	9.3	11.5	1.24
SCs	62.5	69.6	54.7	0.79	7.0	5.7	8.8	1.54	7.0	7.1	7.0	1.00
Religion												
Hindus	72.0	78.1	65.1	0.83	5.9	4.7	7.6	1.62	7.2	7.1	7.3	1.04
Muslims	61.6	66.2	56.6	0.86	6.9	6.4	7.7	1.21	7.5	8.5	6.1	0.73
Christians	91.3	90.7	92.1	1.02	5.0	3.1	7.1	2.29	4.7	5.2	4.3	0.82
Other Minorities	78.5	83.2	73.6	0.88	5.3	4.9	5.7	1.16	4.0	3.4	4.8	1.41
Household Size Groups												
Up to 4	76.8	80.1	72.2	0.90	6.9	5.2	9.5	1.84	7.2	6.7	7.8	1.16
5–7	70.9	77.0	64.1	0.83	6.2	5.0	7.8	1.56	7.1	6.9	7.4	1.06
8 and above	70.2	76.3	63.9	0.84	5.4	4.4	6.5	1.47	6.9	7.4	6.2	0.84

Contd.

Adult Literacy Groups												
None literate	45.6	53.7	35.8	0.67	8.4	7.1	10.6	1.48	9.0	8.8	9.3	1.06
Female literate	87.2	87.4	86.9	1.99	8.8	6.1	11.8	1.93	4.2	2.9	5.7	1.95
Male literate	71.9	81.3	61.5	0.76	7.0	5.7	9.0	1.57	7.7	7.9	7.3	0.93
Both literate	91.7	93.0	90.3	1.97	3.9	2.8	5.2	1.87	6.0	5.8	6.2	1.07
Village Development Groups												
Low	59.9	68.4	50.0	0.73	5.8	4.6	7.6	1.64	8.0	8.0	8.1	1.01
Medium	73.8	79.6	67.1	0.84	6.1	4.8	8.0	1.68	7.1	7.2	7.1	1.00
High	80.9	83.9	77.8	0.93	6.0	5.2	7.0	1.35	6.1	5.9	6.2	1.04
All India	**71.4**	**77.1**	**64.8**	**0.84**	**6.0**	**4.8**	**7.6**	**1.58**	**7.0**	**7.0**	**7.0**	**1.00**

Ever Enrolment for Children (6–14 yrs)

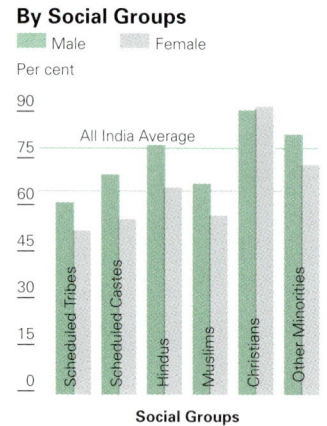

By Social Groups

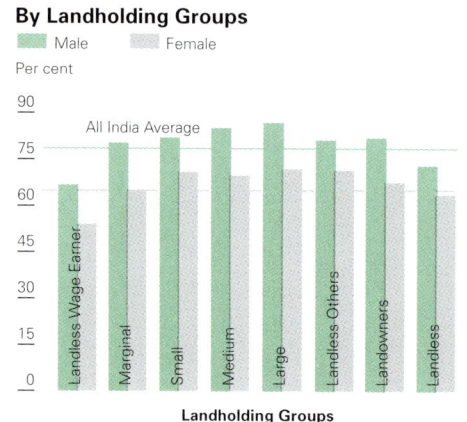

By Landholding Groups

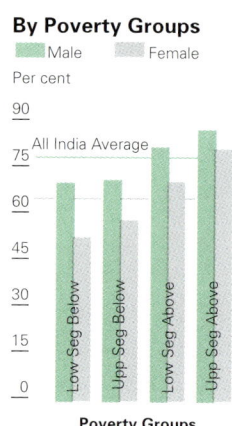

By Poverty Groups

Substantial variations however exist at the level of the states. STs were relevant only in 9 of the 16 major states, namely, Rajasthan, Madhya Pradesh, Bihar, Orissa, Gujarat, Maharashtra, Andhra Pradesh, and Karnataka. The combined EERs for STs and SCs in Bihar, Uttar Pradesh, Madhya Pradesh, and Rajasthan were low. Muslims in Rajasthan, Uttar Pradesh, Bihar, West Bengal, and Orissa recorded low levels of enrolment. On the whole, EERs are substantially low in the five major states, namely Rajasthan, Madhya Pradesh, Uttar Pradesh, Bihar, and Orissa. While the causes for this need further investigation, it is possible that low enrolment is due to inaccessibility of schools in these states, lack of quality education, and ineffective state intervention in implementing literacy policies.

Females have a 16 per cent lower EER for rural India (Table 6.3 and App. Table A.6.6) in comparison with males and considerable gender disparity exists between states. For example, Kerala and West Bengal are the most egalitarian states with lowest levels of gender disparity. In Kerala and West Bengal, almost all boys and girls between the ages of 6 and 14 were reported to be enrolled in schools. Other states where the gender disparity is around 5 to 7 per cent are Maharashtra, Karnataka, Tamil Nadu, Himachal Pradesh, and Punjab. States such as Andhra Pradesh, Gujarat, Orissa, Madhya

Pradesh, and Haryana have moderate levels of gender disparity ranging from 11 to 16 per cent. The states where gender disparity is highest are Uttar Pradesh with 20 and Rajasthan with 36 percentage points respectively. The female enrolment rate in Rajasthan is as low as 42 per cent. This is one of the most backward states in terms of education of women. It will be interesting to analyse how the enrolment rates are related to literacy levels in the respective states.

Factors responsible for non-enrolment of children in elementary schools by gender have been classified as follows: supply-related, demand-related, lack of interest, and customary factors. Supply-related factors are 'school too far' and 'dysfunctional school'; demand factors include 'financial constraints', 'domestic work', 'participation in household economic activity' and 'participation in paid economic activity outside the household'; lack of interest factors are 'parents did not feel it important' and 'child unwilling'; and customary factors include 'married off' and 'tradition'. Customary factors are cited more often in the case of female children and gender disparity is high in Haryana, Rajasthan, and Tamil Nadu. The percentages are computed based on multiple frequencies and, therefore, add up to over 100.

About 75 per cent of children were not enrolled in schools because of lack of interest on the part of parents and children, and also because of certain customary factors. Almost 50 per cent of the responses were demand-related and only 8 per cent were supply-related. Supply factors were relatively high in Orissa, Haryana, Uttar Pradesh, Punjab, and Madhya Pradesh. Lack of interest and customary factors were dominant in all the five central states of India, namely Uttar Pradesh, Bihar, Rajasthan, Madhya Pradesh, and Orissa.

Supply factors as reasons for non-enrolment were cited more often by the better-off, medium and large farmers, agriculturists, STs, and the least developed villages. Demand factors were predominant among the very poor, landless wage earners and households in which neither males nor females were literate.

Here we attempt a trend analysis of some of the important indicators pertaining to elementary education, such as the rate of non-enrolment, rate of discontinuation, distribution of students among schools by types of management and per pupil private expenditure on education. The observations are based on information relating to 16 major states of India. To observe trends in different indicators over time, findings of the studies conducted by various organizations at different points of time have been taken into account (App. Table A.6.7).

App. Table A.6.7 shows an increasing trend in EER between 1986 (NCERT Study), and 1994 (NCAER Survey), and also between 1986–7 (NSSO) and 1994. As may be observed, almost all the states, except Madhya Pradesh and Tamil Nadu, experienced a rise in the EER. The all India figure reflects the pattern prevalent in the major states. Increase in the EER in 1994 may be considered to be substantial, especially when it is compared with the other two studies. It may also be added that between 1986–7

Female education not only helps improve enrolment but also reduces gender disparity in school enrolment.

(NSSO) and 1994, increase in the EER was the highest in Punjab and the lowest in Haryana. When the EER is computed separately for boys and girls, the rate shows a rising trend for both segments in most states. However, an encouraging aspect is that the gender disparity decreased in most states during these periods, suggesting an improvement in enrolment of girls in elementary schools.

Average Discontinuation Rates

While EERs reflect the enrolment of children in schools, discontinuation rates reflect the proportion of pupils that continue their schooling after they are enrolled. It is useful to reiterate that 'average discontinuation rate' in this study is estimated as the percentage of ever enrolled children who discontinued studies at any time in the age bracket 6–14 years. Since these rates are the average for a 8 year period, the levels are bound to be low. The Average Discontinuation Rate multiplied by 8 can be compared with one minus the retention rate given by other sources. On an average about 6 per cent of children who have ever been enrolled discontinued (Table 6.3 Panel II). This estimate seems low because it is based on those children who confirmed their enrolment in schools during the household interviews. The school records, on the other hand, are based on a household census of children of school-going age and lists all eligible children even when they have not actively attended school. This practice leads to high and spurious drop-out rates which is what we were provided with as official estimates.

The average discontinuation rate is about 6 per cent for rural India (see Table 6.3, Panel II and App. Table A.6.8) but is fairly high in Tamil Nadu, Andhra Pradesh, Madhya Pradesh, Karnataka, and Orissa. The discontinuation rate is low in Bihar, Uttar Pradesh, Rajasthan, and Haryana. This appears contrary to expectation but a further disaggregation suggests that (a) drop-outs are positively related to enrolments, and (b) there are different thresholds at which the drop-outs are substantial. For example, the drop-outs are indeed almost negligible during the early years of schooling, which should be the case because of the factors discussed above. Discontinuation rate was just about one per cent among children in the age group 6–9 years which increased to 2.1 per cent among 6–11 year olds (App. Table A.6.9). However, the discontinuation rate among children of 12–14 years is 13 per cent for the country as a whole. This is contrary to what is generally believed that drop-outs are high in the early years after enrolment.

Thus higher discontinuation rates in Tamil Nadu and Andhra Pradesh may be explained by the fact that enrolments are fairly high to begin with and that practically all discontinuation occurs among children aged 12–14 years of age, especially females. A higher discontinuation rate is usually a manifestation of higher enrolment, at least in the rural parts of western and southern India.

Higher discontinuation rates in Orissa, Madhya Pradesh, and West Bengal are a cause of concern as enrolment rates are low even to begin with (Table 6.3). The same is true of Bihar, Rajasthan, and Uttar Pradesh. The causes for

Discontinuation Ratio

Among States

■ Male ■ Female

Per cent discontinued

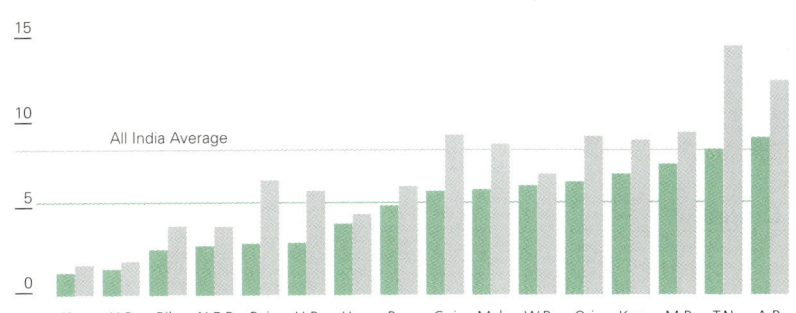

Among Poverty Groups

Per cent discontinued

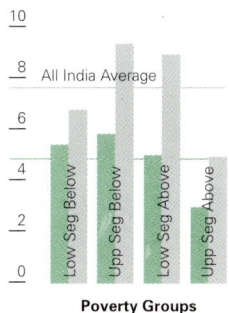

Poverty Groups

differentials in discontinuation rates between states needs further investigation to ascertain whether this phenomenon is due to inaccessibility of schools, lack of quality education, or low priority state intervention.

Discontinuation rates are relatively low among the higher income categories, the landed, professionals, males, and Hindus. Conversely, the discontinuation rates are substantially higher among the lower income categories, landless wage earners, females, and STs and SCs, that is those who have lower enrolment to begin with (Table 6.4, Panel II). For example, the discontinuation rates were only 4.8 per cent for boys but 7.6 per cent for girls with a gender disparity of 1.58. The discontinuation rate declined considerably for both girls and boys as income increased. However, disparity persists even among the better-off. The landless wage earners recorded very high levels of discontinuation: 7.5 per cent for boys and 13.4 per cent for girls. Discontinuation rates were relatively higher among STs, SCs, and Muslims, but gender disparity was high among Hindus.

Literacy status of adults in a household has a unique relationship with the discontinuation rate which is highest among children from households where there are no literate adults. This group of households has very low levels of enrolment to begin with. In education planning it may be necessary to identify such households on the basis of poverty criteria. Strangely enough, households having only literate females recorded very high discontinuation as well, although enrolment was high. These households are generally single parent or female headed households that generally face extreme forms of distress due to absence of other earning members.

Factors leading to discontinuation of education have been categorized in the same manner as for non-enrolment. The reasons worked out to be 17 per cent supply factors, 73 per cent demand-related factors and lack of interest, and 52 per cent customary factors. Demand factors were predominant in Bihar, Madhya Pradesh, Haryana, Uttar Pradesh, and Rajasthan. Gender disparity was as high as 5.4 in Punjab, 2.4 in Uttar Pradesh, and 5.5 in West Bengal (with a lower level of discontinuation).

Among Village Development and Household Size Groups

Per cent discontinued

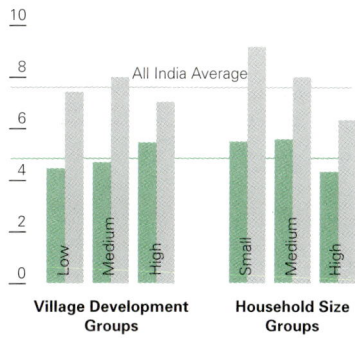

Village Development Groups   **Household Size Groups**

Among Social Groups

Per cent discontinued

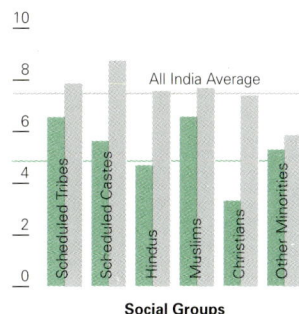

Social Groups

TABLE 6.5

Trends in Discontinuation Rates for Children (aged 6–14 years) (Percentage) by States

Regions/ States	1986[1]	1992[2]			1994		
	Person	Person	Boys	Girls	Person	Boys	Girls
North							
Haryana	6.3	4.0	4.4	3.4	4.2	3.6	4.6
Himachal Pradesh	3.6	-	-	-	2.0	1.9	2.2
Punjab	8.7	6.1	8.0	3.3	5.4	4.8	6.1
Upper Central							
Bihar	11.4	9.6	9.8	9.4	3.2	2.6	4.1
Uttar Pradesh	8.0	-	-	-	4.2	3.3	5.6
Lower Central							
Madhya Pradesh	8.0	8.4	3.7	17.5	8.0	7.3	9.0
Orissa	9.4	8.6	8.4	8.8	7.6	6.2	9.3
Rajasthan	9.4	7.4	5.6	11.0	4.2	3.1	6.6
East							
North-eastern Rg.	10.5	13.1	-	-	3.3	3.9	4.1
West Bengal	10.9	18.2	11.6	26.4	6.2	5.9	6.2
West							
Gujarat	8.6	6.7	3.2	11.3	7.3	5.6	9.5
Maharashtra	8.4	8.0	7.1	8.8	7.1	5.9	8.4
South							
Andhra Pradesh	10.4	8.7	8.9	10.7	10.0	8.2	12.1
Karnataka	9.7	12.2	18.5	6.8	7.9	6.8	9.1
Kerala	2.5	0.6	1.1	- 1.7	1.5	2.0	
Tamil Nadu	6.6	7.1	6.2	7.9	10.9	7.5	14.8
All India	**9.3**	**8.0**	**6.0**	**7.8**	**6.0**	**4.9**	**7.6**

1 *1986 Annual Report.* Department of Education, Ministry of Human Resource Development, Government of India, New Delhi, 1993.
2 NCAER, 'Non-Enrolment, Drop-Out and Private Expenditure on Elementary Education: A Comparison Across States, and Population Groups'. New Delhi, 1992.

Estimates available from various sources on changes in discontinuation rates between 1986 and 1994 (Table 6.5), indicate a declining trend in most of the major states and the country as a whole. However, there are states like Tamil Nadu and Kerala where discontinuation rates seemed to be increasing, while in a few others like West Bengal, Gujarat, Andhra Pradesh, and Karnataka the rate fluctuated during 1988–94. Bearing in mind the differences in conceptualization and methods of estimation caution should be exercised when comparing these estimates over time.

The proportion of children who had not attended school for a period of more than 7 days during the one month prior to the date of survey are given in Tables 6.3 and 6.4 (Panel III). Around 7 per cent of boys and girls reported not having attended schools for 7 and more days during the previous one month. Non-attendance was high in Bihar, Madhya Pradesh, and Orissa, and among STs.

Quality of Education

On the whole about 17 per cent of males aged 15 and above and about 9 per cent of females above the age of 15 complete elementary (middle) level schooling in rural India (Table 6.6). [3] There is a high level of gender disparity: only 52 girls for every 100 boys complete middle school education. Gender disparities are very high in Rajasthan, Uttar Pradesh, Madhya Pradesh, and Bihar. The disparities are low in the states of southern India.

The proportion of men aged 17 years and above who had completed matriculation was 12 per cent (Table 6.6). However, only 5 per cent of women fell in this category. This proportion is 20 per cent in Kerala, 15 per cent in Punjab, Haryana, Himachal Pradesh, and the North-east, and 11 per cent in Tamil Nadu. The proportion of matriculates is very low in Rajasthan, Madhya Pradesh, and West Bengal. Gender disparity is much higher among matriculates than at the elementary level: only about 40 women to every 100 men. The most gender egalitarian state in terms of education is Kerala; all other states fall far behind. Rajasthan has an f/m ratio of 0.12 and Madhya Pradesh, Uttar Pradesh, and Haryana have ratios between 0.21 and 0.23.

The proportion of the population that completes elementary and matriculation level education generally increases with an increase in income level — both household income and poverty level. Gender disparities persist, however. Gender disparity is very high among the low income categories, suggesting a preference for investing in the education of males across all states. The f/m ratio even among the richest is only 0.81 at elementary and 0.56 at matriculation levels of education and the respective estimates for the upper segment of the poverty line category are 0.74 and 0.54 respectively (Table 6.7).

It is important to note that only 2.6 per cent of all women aged 17 years and over complete matriculation in the up to Rs 20,000 income category. It is thus clear that understanding education transition only in terms of literacy rates is misleading and may even generate complacency in education planning in India. As expected, the levels of educational achievement are extremely low for landless wage earners, but land has a uniform and harmonious relationship with the levels of such achievement. Similarly, gender disparities persist in relatively developed villages that offer better opportunities for education, and this may be attributed to cultural and social factors.

STs and SCs have lower levels of literacy, especially at the level of matriculation and above; for example, only about 5 per cent of girls among these communities complete matriculation. The Christians had the highest percentage completing matriculation with 19 per cent followed by about 9 per cent among Hindus, and 6 per cent among Muslims. Christians are the most egalitarian religious group that believes in educating both boys and girls.

A finding that is relevant from the viewpoint of policy-makers is the linkage between the level of literacy among adult males and females, and

While 17 per cent of males and 9 per cent of females complete elementary-level schooling, only 12 per cent and 5 per cent respectively complete matriculation.

3 Middle and elementary level of schooling have been used synonymously as elementary education implies schooling up to class VIII (VII in some states) and middle level schooling means schooling between class VI (V in some states) and class VIII (VI in some states). Years of schooling up to the middle level are taken as a proxy for quality of education. A child who has completed the middle level of schooling is expected to have undergone on an average 8 years of schooling. In the absence of any specific measures, quality of education is related to the knowledge imparted in school. Hence the assumption that the greater the number of years of schooling, the greater the knowledge acquired and therefore a higher quality of education.

TABLE 6.6

Proportion of Population Completing Middle- and Matriculation-level Education and Gender Disparity by States

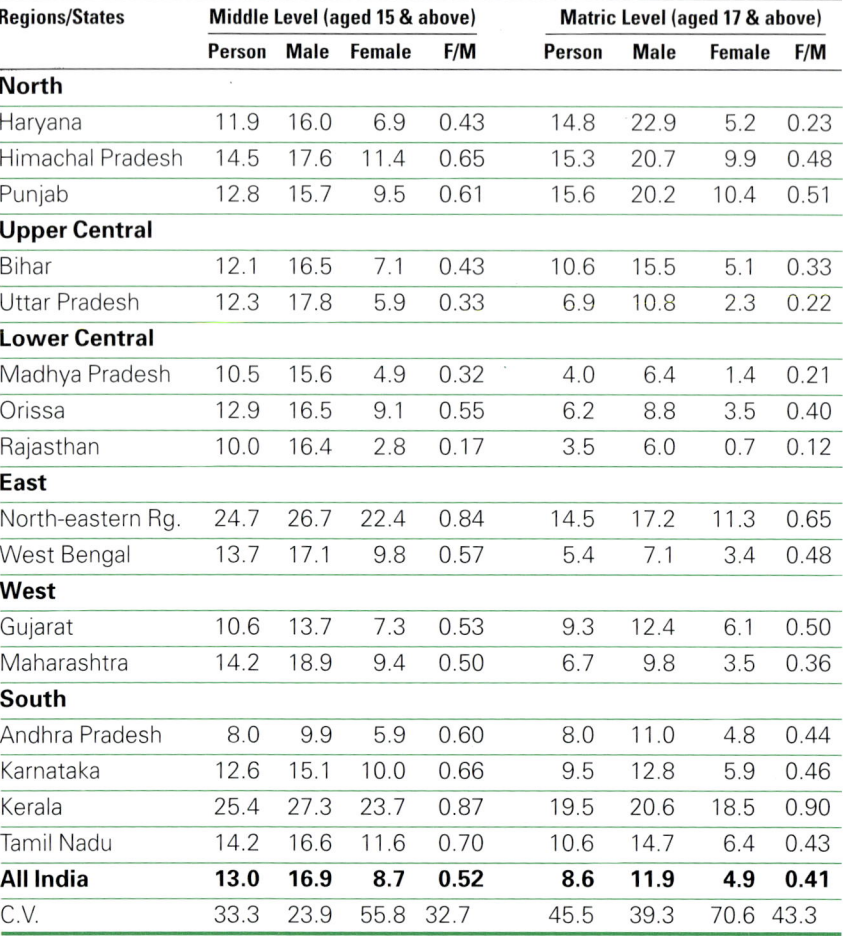

Regions/States	Middle Level (aged 15 & above)				Matric Level (aged 17 & above)			
	Person	Male	Female	F/M	Person	Male	Female	F/M
North								
Haryana	11.9	16.0	6.9	0.43	14.8	22.9	5.2	0.23
Himachal Pradesh	14.5	17.6	11.4	0.65	15.3	20.7	9.9	0.48
Punjab	12.8	15.7	9.5	0.61	15.6	20.2	10.4	0.51
Upper Central								
Bihar	12.1	16.5	7.1	0.43	10.6	15.5	5.1	0.33
Uttar Pradesh	12.3	17.8	5.9	0.33	6.9	10.8	2.3	0.22
Lower Central								
Madhya Pradesh	10.5	15.6	4.9	0.32	4.0	6.4	1.4	0.21
Orissa	12.9	16.5	9.1	0.55	6.2	8.8	3.5	0.40
Rajasthan	10.0	16.4	2.8	0.17	3.5	6.0	0.7	0.12
East								
North-eastern Rg.	24.7	26.7	22.4	0.84	14.5	17.2	11.3	0.65
West Bengal	13.7	17.1	9.8	0.57	5.4	7.1	3.4	0.48
West								
Gujarat	10.6	13.7	7.3	0.53	9.3	12.4	6.1	0.50
Maharashtra	14.2	18.9	9.4	0.50	6.7	9.8	3.5	0.36
South								
Andhra Pradesh	8.0	9.9	5.9	0.60	8.0	11.0	4.8	0.44
Karnataka	12.6	15.1	10.0	0.66	9.5	12.8	5.9	0.46
Kerala	25.4	27.3	23.7	0.87	19.5	20.6	18.5	0.90
Tamil Nadu	14.2	16.6	11.6	0.70	10.6	14.7	6.4	0.43
All India	**13.0**	**16.9**	**8.7**	**0.52**	**8.6**	**11.9**	**4.9**	**0.41**
C.V.	33.3	23.9	55.8	32.7	45.5	39.3	70.6	43.3

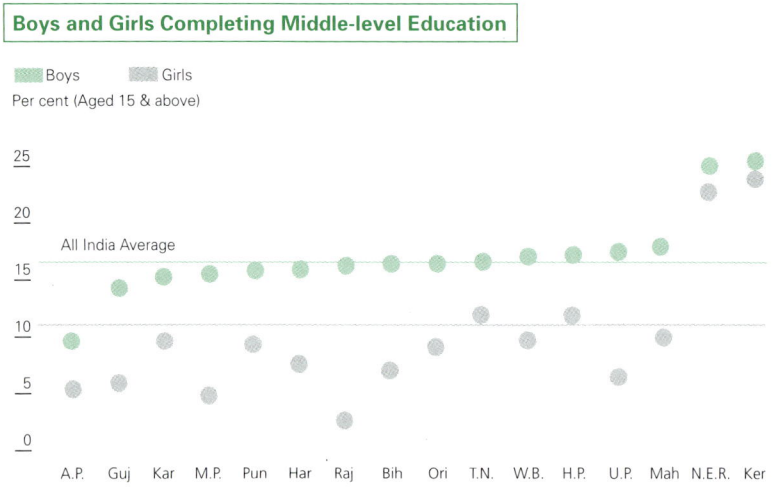

Boys and Girls Completing Middle-level Education

Boys   Girls
Per cent (Aged 15 & above)

A.P. Guj Kar M.P. Pun Har Raj Bih Ori T.N. W.B. H.P. U.P. Mah N.E.R. Ker

Among States

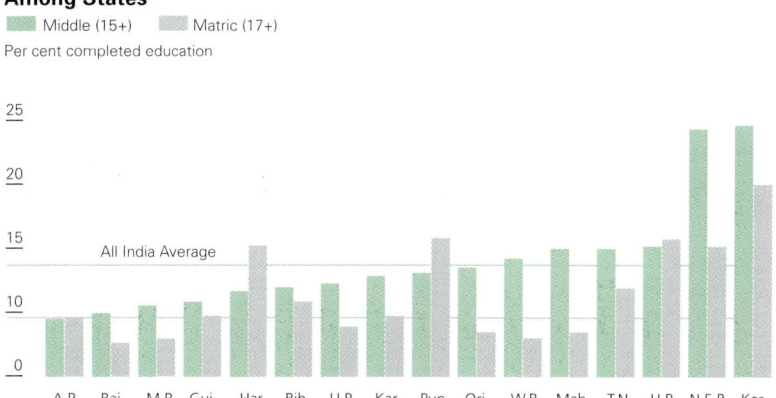

■ Middle (15+)   ■ Matric (17+)

Per cent completed education

Among Poverty Groups

Per cent completed education

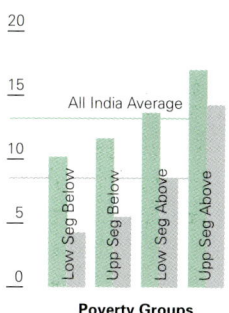

Poverty Groups

children aged 6–14 years. As we saw in Chapter 3, when there is no adult literate male or female in a household (which constitutes about 30 per cent of all rural households), the overall literacy and school enrolments are very low. The same is true in the case of elementary and matriculation levels of education. Indeed, the proportion who complete either of these levels is 'none' for the non-literate category (Table 6.7) for rural India as a whole. The rates are high only when both literate men and women are present in a household although gender disparity still persists.

Among Village Development and Household Size Groups

Per cent completed education

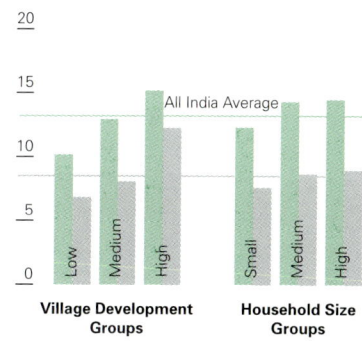

**Village Development   Household Size
Groups   Groups**

Private Schooling

Provision of mass education is a government responsibility in India. Primary and elementary education is imparted through innumerable village level schools largely run and managed by state governments and local bodies. There are also schools run by non-government organizations, private voluntary organizations, local associations, and religious trusts that receive grants from the government. These have been classified as government-aided schools. Of late, a number of private primary schools have come up in many states. While government schools and government-aided schools supplement each other's efforts, government and private schools complement one another and are often competitive.

On the whole, in rural India about 68 per cent of all school-going children attend government schools, 22 per cent go to government-aided schools, and 10 per cent to privately managed schools (Table 6.8). The sex ratio of students in government and government-aided schools is about the same, but private schooling exhibits highly discriminatory trends; for example, only 8 per cent of girls attend private schools compared to about 11 per cent boys.

Government-aided schools may be seen as a reflection of not only the government's commitment to education but also of the participation of the community in education. On the other hand, private schools are considered to be market oriented and not always interested in imparting quality education. Sometimes private schools are a response to poor quality services

Among Social Groups

Per cent completed education

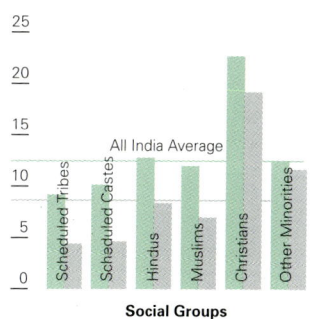

Social Groups

TABLE 6.7

Proportion of Population Completing Middle- and Matriculation-level Education by Population Groups

Population Groups	Middle Level (aged 15 & above)				Matric Level (aged 17 & above)			
	Person	Male	Female	F/M	Person	Male	Female	F/M
Household Income Groups								
Up to 20,000	10.7	15.0	6.1	0.41	5.3	7.8	2.6	0.34
20,001–40,000	14.9	19.0	10.2	0.54	10.1	13.9	5.8	0.42
40,001–62,000	15.7	18.3	12.6	0.69	13.6	17.5	9.0	0.51
62,001–86,000	15.0	17.7	11.9	0.67	13.2	17.4	8.1	0.47
Above 86,000	17.0	18.6	15.0	0.81	15.6	19.7	11.0	0.56
Poverty Line Groups								
Lower segment below	10.1	14.3	5.7	0.40	4.5	6.8	2.1	0.31
Upper segment below	11.5	16.3	6.4	0.39	5.4	8.0	2.6	0.32
Lower segment above	13.6	17.7	8.9	0.50	8.7	12.3	4.8	0.39
Upper segment above	15.4	17.5	12.9	0.74	13.9	17.6	9.5	0.54
Landholding Groups								
Landless wage earner	7.2	10.3	3.9	0.38	3.0	4.6	1.4	0.30
Marginal	13.3	17.4	8.8	0.50	8.6	11.7	5.2	0.45
Small	14.2	18.6	9.2	0.49	9.1	13.0	4.7	0.36
Medium	14.3	18.1	9.9	0.55	9.7	14.0	4.9	0.35
Large	14.9	18.8	10.4	0.55	10.0	13.6	5.8	0.42
Landless others	15.3	18.7	11.7	0.63	12.2	16.2	8.0	0.49
Landowners	13.9	18.0	9.2	0.51	9.1	12.6	5.1	0.40
Landless	11.2	14.5	7.7	0.53	7.5	10.3	4.6	0.45
Occupational Groups								
Cultivators	13.6	18.1	8.7	0.48	8.4	12.0	4.5	0.37
Salaried+Prof.+S.Empl.	17.2	19.3	14.8	0.77	16.4	21.2	11.0	0.52
Wage earners	8.0	11.3	4.5	0.40	3.3	4.9	1.7	0.35
All others	15.1	19.9	10.0	0.51	9.8	13.6	5.8	0.43
Social Groups								
Caste								
STs	9.2	12.7	5.4	0.43	4.9	7.3	2.3	0.31
SCs	10.1	14.6	5.1	0.35	4.9	7.3	2.3	0.31
Religion								
Hindus	13.0	16.9	8.6	0.51	8.5	12.0	4.7	0.39
Muslims	12.0	15.8	7.6	0.48	5.9	8.3	3.2	0.38
Christians	21.2	22.5	19.9	0.88	18.7	19.0	18.4	0.97
Other Minorities	12.3	15.7	8.6	0.55	11.5	15.3	7.3	0.48
Household Size Groups								
Up to 4	11.0	14.4	7.5	0.52	7.5	10.2	4.8	0.47
5–7	13.6	17.5	9.3	0.53	8.7	12.1	5.0	0.41
8 and above	13.6	17.8	8.9	0.50	9.1	12.8	5.0	0.39

Contd.

Households with no adult literate male or female (about 30 per cent of all households) do not have children who complete elementary- and matriculation-level education.

Adult Literacy Groups

None literate	0.1	0.1	–	0.40	–	–	–	–
Female literate	8.6	–	13.2	–	4.4	–	7.0	–
Male literate	12.1	21.2	–	–	6.0	10.9	–	–
Both literate	21.1	22.8	19.2	0.84	15.6	19.7	11.2	0.57
Village Development Groups								
Low	10.4	15.2	5.1	0.33	6.3	9.4	2.9	0.30
Medium	13.2	17.3	8.7	0.50	8.1	11.4	4.5	0.40
High	15.1	18.0	12.1	0.67	11.2	14.9	7.3	0.49
All India	**13.0**	**16.9**	**8.7**	**0.52**	**8.6**	**11.9**	**4.9**	**0.41**

Boys and Girls Completing Matriculation–level Education

■ Boys   ■ Girls

Per cent (Aged 17 & above)

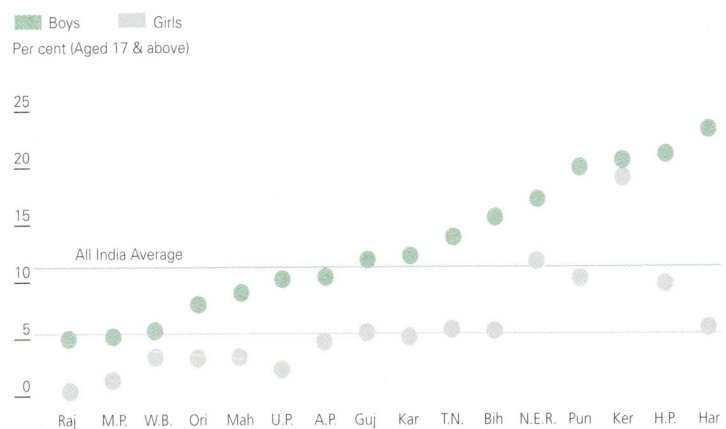

All India Average

Raj M.P. W.B. Ori Mah U.P. A.P. Guj Kar T.N. Bih N.E.R. Pun Ker H.P. Har

---

Proportion of Population Completing Matriculation–level Education

By Landholding Groups

■ Male   ■ Female

Per cent

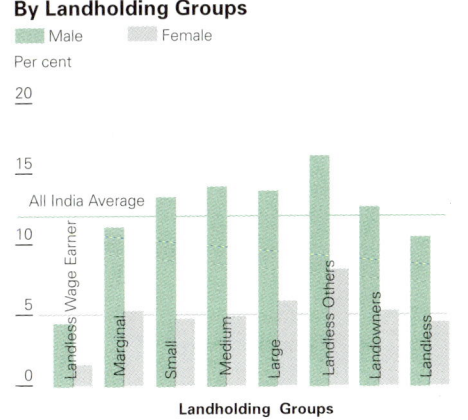

All India Average

Landless Wage Earner · Marginal · Small · Medium · Large · Landless Others · Landowners · Landless

Landholding Groups

By Poverty Groups

Per cent

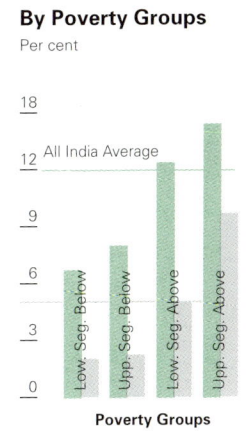

All India Average

Low. Seg. Below · Upp. Seg. Below · Low. Seg. Above · Upp. Seg. Above

Poverty Groups

By Social Groups

Per cent

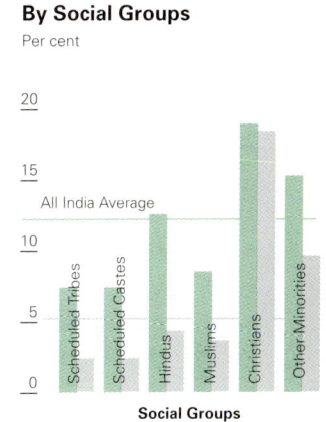

All India Average

Scheduled Tribes · Scheduled Castes · Hindus · Muslims · Christians · Other Minorities

Social Groups

in public schools and are also instituted to meet the needs of imparting education in the English language.

In the North-eastern states, West Bengal, and Kerala a significant number of people acquire primary and elementary schooling through government-aided schools. The proportion of students in the 6–14 age-group attending government-aided schools in these states was 91, 79, and 57 per cent respectively. Similarly, a relatively higher proportion of students attending private schools was seen in Uttar Pradesh (27 per cent), Punjab (20 per cent), and Haryana and Kerala (12 per cent).

According to the Fifth All India Education Survey,[4] only 2 per cent of students at primary level sought education in private schools in 1986. This increased to about 10 per cent by 1994 (Table 6.9). In Uttar Pradesh this proportion was 8.5 per cent in 1986, which increased substantially to 27 per cent in 1994. In Punjab it increased from a mere 0.5 per cent to 20 per cent,

4 All India Educational Surveys are conducted periodically and provide detailed educational statistics. The Sixth in the series has recently been carried out jointly by the National Council for Applied Education Research and Training (NCAERT), the National Informatics Centre (NIC), and the Department of Education

TABLE 6.8

Percentage Distribution of Students (aged 6–14 years) and Gender Disparity by States

Regions/States	Govt. Schools				Govt.-aided Schools				Private Schools			
	Person	Male	Female	F/M	Person	Male	Female	F/M	Person	Male	Female	F/M
North												
Haryana	85.1	82.6	88.1	1.07	1.8	2.1	1.4	0.69	12.8	15.2	10.0	0.66
Himachal Pradesh	94.6	93.7	95.5	1.02	0.4	0.3	0.4	1.29	4.8	5.6	3.9	0.70
Punjab	78.6	75.7	82.2	1.09	1.6	2.3	0.7	0.29	19.5	21.8	16.8	0.77
Upper Central												
Bihar	79.2	78.0	81.2	1.04	11.4	11.1	11.8	1.07	8.6	10.1	6.3	0.62
Uttar Pradesh	56.3	55.9	56.9	1.02	16.5	16.4	16.6	1.01	27.2	27.6	26.4	0.96
Lower Central												
Madhya Pradesh	84.0	83.1	85.3	1.03	12.1	12.8	11.2	0.88	3.8	4.1	3.4	0.84
Orissa	74.5	72.4	77.2	1.07	21.2	23.3	18.6	0.80	4.1	4.2	3.9	0.91
Rajasthan	93.0	93.3	92.4	0.99	3.5	3.0	4.5	1.49	3.4	3.7	2.9	0.77
East												
North-eastern Rg.	8.6	8.8	8.2	0.93	90.6	90.5	90.8	1.00	0.8	0.7	0.9	1.28
West Bengal	20.5	20.7	20.2	0.98	78.5	77.8	79.1	1.02	1.0	1.4	0.6	0.41
West												
Gujarat	78.2	77.0	79.9	1.04	19.7	20.6	18.6	0.91	2.0	2.4	1.5	0.60
Maharashtra	80.4	78.9	82.2	1.04	17.9	19.1	16.5	0.86	1.5	1.9	1.0	0.51
South												
Andhra Pradesh	88.4	88.0	88.9	1.01	1.3	1.3	1.5	1.15	10.2	10.7	9.4	0.88
Karnataka	86.0	84.4	87.8	1.04	4.2	4.6	3.8	0.82	9.6	10.8	8.1	0.75
Kerala	30.9	30.7	31.1	1.01	57.1	54.2	60.3	1.11	12.0	15.2	8.6	0.57
Tamil Nadu	83.8	83.2	84.6	1.02	9.1	8.8	9.6	1.09	7.0	8.0	5.8	0.73
All India	**67.9**	**67.4**	**68.7**	**1.02**	**22.1**	**21.6**	**22.8**	**1.05**	**9.8**	**10.8**	**8.3**	**0.77**
C.V.	36.8	36.7	37.0	3.5	126.0	123.9	128.5	26.7	87.8	83.7	95.9	26.5

Distribution of Students in Various Schools: Rural India

■ Govt. School   ■ Govt.-aided Schools   ▨ Pvt. Schools
Per cent students

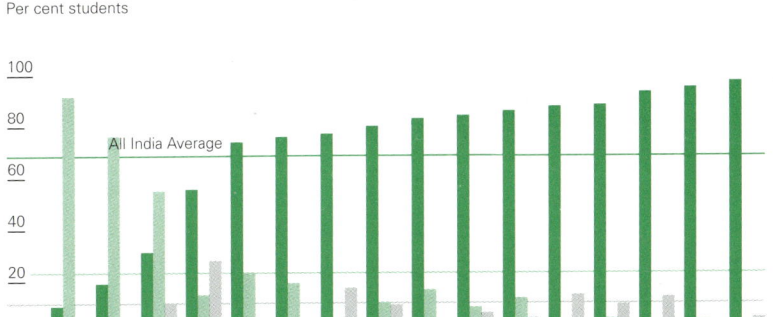

Among Poverty Groups
Per cent students

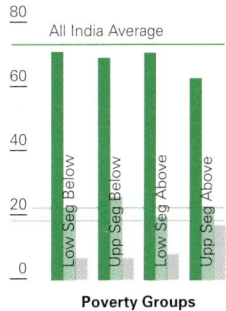

Poverty Groups

and in Haryana from a negligible proportion to 13 per cent. Private schooling is also catching up in the south, including Kerala.

The culture of government-aided schools is widespread in West Bengal, where more than 75 per cent of students go to such schools, followed by Kerala. About 50 per cent of students in the North-east go to aided schools. Some interesting questions that the above data throw up in the context of India's education transition are: Is universal education dependent upon community participation in education? Are today's private schools the government-aided schools of tomorrow and the government schools of the future? What are the reasons for the phenomenon of growth in private education in India?

All findings point to an increase in demand for private schooling; parents too appear to prefer to send boys to private schools. The proportion of children going to private schools is highest among the high income households, those in the top segment of poverty classification, those who are salaried and professionals, as well as among Muslims (App. Table A.6.11). It is interesting that over 70 per cent of children from ST and SC households study in government schools. Only about 43 per cent of Christian and 49 per cent of Muslim children attend government schools. While most of the remaining Christian children go to government-aided schools, Muslim children go both to government-aided and private schools. This scenario suggests that government facilities cater to the requirements of the majority community in rural India. Lower participation of Muslim and Christian children in public schools may be related both to the medium of instruction and the content of the school curricula.

Data also indicate that private schools bridge the gap when there is a dearth of government schools in remote areas. For example, it was seen that 13 per cent of students living in less developed villages went to private schools during 1993–4 as opposed to only 9 and 8 per cent in moderately developed and developed villages (App. Table A.6.11) (also *see* App. Table A.6.12 to A.6.14).

Between 1986 and 1994, the share of government schools went down in

Among Village Development and Household Size Groups
Per cent students

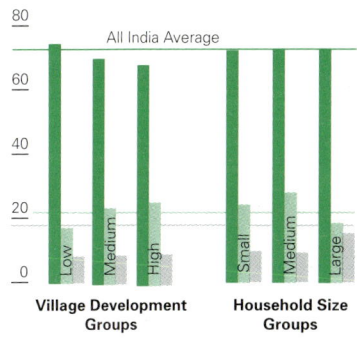

Village Development   Household Size
Groups   Groups

Among Social Groups
Per cent completed education

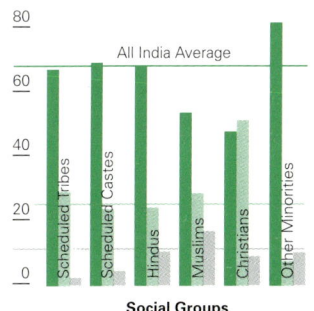

Social Groups

TABLE 6.9

Trends in Percentage Distribution of Students (aged 6–14 years) by States

Regions/States	Govt. Schools		Aided Schools		Private Schools		All Schools	
	NCERT[1] 1986	NCAER 1994	NCERT 1986	NCAER 1994	NCERT 1986	NCAER 1994	NCERT 1986	NCAER 1994
North								
Haryana	99.2	85.3	0.6	1.8	0.2	12.9	100	100
Himachal Pradesh	99.1	94.8	0.4	0.4	0.5	4.8	100	100
Punjab	98.2	78.8	1.4	1.6	0.5	19.6	100	100
Upper Central								
Uttar Pradesh	83.7	56.3	7.8	16.5	8.5	27.2	100	100
Bihar	98.6	79.9	1.3	11.5	0.1	8.7	100	100
Lower Central								
Madhya Pradesh	97.1	84.1	1.7	12.1	1.2	3.8	100	100
Orissa	74.7	74.4	23.9	21.3	1.7	4.1	100	100
Rajasthan	95.8	93.1	1.9	3.5	2.4	3.4	100	100
East								
West Bengal	71.5	20.5	28.5	78.5	–	1.0	100	100
West								
Gujarat	94.9	78.2	5.0	19.7	0.6	2.0	100	100
Maharashtra	82.2	80.5	15.9	17.9	2.0	1.5	100	100
South								
Andhra Pradesh	92.7	88.5	5.6	1.4	1.7	10.2	100	100
Karnataka	92.5	86.2	6.0	4.2	1.4	9.6	100	100
Kerala	40.2	30.9	58.6	57.1	1.2	12.0	100	100
Tamil Nadu	78.5	83.8	21.3	9.1	0.2	7.0	100	100
All India	**85.9**	**68.0**	**12.0**	**22.2**	**2.1**	**9.8**	**100**	**100**

1 *Fifth All-India Education Survey.* NCERT, New Delhi 1992.

*Data on North-Eastern Region not available

Percentage of Students in Private Schools

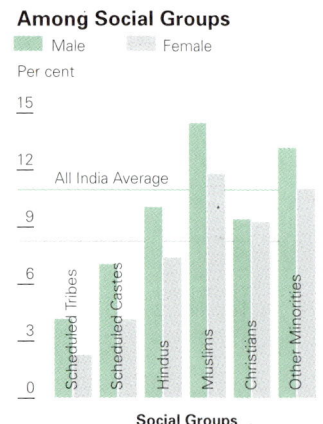

Among Social Groups

■ Male   ▨ Female

Per cent

All India Average

Social Groups

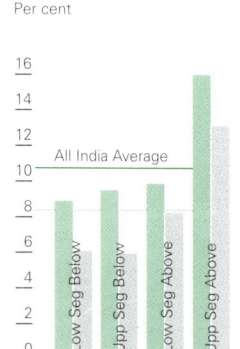

Among Poverty Groups

Per cent

All India Average

Poverty Groups

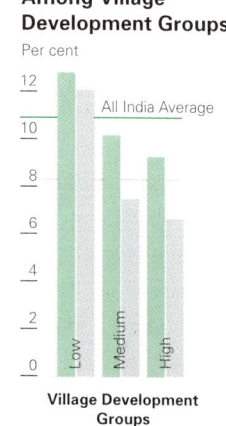

Among Village Development Groups

Per cent

All India Average

Village Development Groups

all the states under consideration and in India as a whole (Table 6.9). As a result, the shares of both government-aided and private schools went up. When the increases in the share of aided and private schools are compared, they are found to be generally higher in the case of private schools than in the case of aided schools. It may therefore be concluded that the growth in enrolment in private schools has been higher than in aided schools, possibly at the cost of government schools. This may be due to the availability of better facilities and teaching standards in private schools at the elementary level of education. When the distribution of students is considered separately for boys and girls, a similar trend is observed in the case of the major states and for all India.

Cost of Schooling

Disaggregated data on per household expenditure on elementary education and gender disparity for all types of schools—government, aided, and private—is discussed under five categories, namely: (1) examination and other fees; (2) books, stationery, and uniforms; (3) private coaching; (4) transport; and (5) boarding and lodging (see Table 6.10).

The total per household expenditure on educating children aged 6–14 years in rural India was estimated to be Rs 680 per household or Rs 378 per pupil per year. Expenditure on schooling for girls was about 68 per cent that spent on boys. A large proportion of this expenditure was incurred on books, stationery, and school uniforms followed by private coaching and fees. This expenditure increased or decreased with the annual fluctuations in the cost of books, stationery, and uniforms. Another NCAER survey of over 20,000 households in 1992 estimated the total cost per student per year to be Rs 464.[5]

Only about 75 girls for every 100 boys go to private schools. The expenditure on girls is much lower, especially in regard to private schooling whereas parents do not think twice about spending large sums of money on educating boys in private schools. There is an increasing dependence on private schooling in recent years that has affected female education more than male education. The household expenditure on education was found to be higher among the large landowners, relatively rich and salaried persons.

Private coaching accounts for about 10 per cent of total household expenditure (App. Table A.6.15) the reported costs of private coaching were about Rs 350 per reporting child. About 10 per cent more funds were spent on boys than on girls on private coaching. The differential is large among STs followed by Hindus. The expenditure was very low for girls in the states of Uttar Pradesh, Madhya Pradesh, Karnataka, and Punjab.

The expenditure on government schooling is Rs 539 per annum (App. Table A.6.16), Rs 665 for government-aided schooling, and Rs 1,262 for private schooling (App. Table A.6.19). Given an average of about 1.8 children per household, the expenditure per pupil would be Rs 317, Rs 391, and Rs 742 per annum in the respective school categories. There is considerable gender disparity in patterns of expenditure on schooling. The f/m

This research points to an increase in demand for private elementary schooling especially in Punjab, UP and Haryana.

5 'Non-Enrolment, Dropout and Private Expenditure on Elementary Education—A Comparison across States and Population Groups' NCAER (mimeo), Sept. 1994.

TABLE 6.10

Percentage Distribution of Annual Household Expenditure on Schooling (all schools) of Children (aged 6–14 years) by States

When it is a matter of household allocation of funds or out of pocket expenditure, it is males who receive a disproportionately higher share.

Regions/States	Exam. & Other Fees	Books, Station., & Uniform	Coaching	Transpt.	Boarding & Lodging	Total	Av. No. of Stds per Household
North							
Haryana							
Person	21.3	71.3	4.2	2.7	0.5	1360	1.9
Gender disparity	0.88	1.07	0.76	0.97	-	0.73	0.83
Himachal Pradesh							
Person	11.8	84.7	0.8	1.3	1.5	1667	1.9
Gender disparity	0.93	1.03	0.69	0.75	0.50	0.84	0.92
Punjab							
Person	27.3	63.9	5.3	3.5	-	1333	1.9
Gender disparity	0.89	1.09	0.88	0.63	0.89	0.68	0.81
Upper Central							
Bihar							
Person	19.9	54.1	2.0	1.0	5.1	676	1.8
Gender disparity	0.94	1.17	0.98	1.39	-	0.52	0.60
Uttar Pradesh							
Person	24.6	67.6	5.6	1.3	1.0	689	1.9
Gender disparity	1.02	1.04	0.39	0.89	2.77	0.55	0.59
Lower Central							
Madhya Pradesh							
Person	13.5	80.4	3.0	1.5	1.7	480	1.8
Gender disparity	0.88	1.04	0.55	0.48	2.17	0.68	0.70
Orissa							
Person	16.1	62.6	20.4	0.9	-	426	1.7
Gender disparity	1.04	0.99	1.09	-7	-	0.82	0.80
Rajasthan							
Person	10.3	82.3	5.8	1.0	0.6	820	1.8
Gender disparity	1.10	1.03	0.67	0.48	-	0.43	0.44
East							
North-eastern Rg.							
Person	21.8	55.5	8.6	14.1	-	733	1.8
Gender disparity	1.07	0.93	1.49	0.91	-	0.57	0.60
West Bengal							
Person	8.7	53.6	36.0	1.2	0.6	549	1.8
Gender disparity	0.78	0.99	1.04	1.31	3.51	0.99	0.97
West							
Gujarat							
Person	9.4	67.4	5.6	4.9	12.7	545	1.9
Gender disparity	0.84	0.99	0.59	1.11	1.45	0.72	0.73
Maharashtra							
Person	8.6	87.1	2.4	1.7	0.2	586	1.9

Contd.

Gender disparity	0.61	1.06	0.82	0.57	1.71	0.79	0.87
South							
Andhra Pradesh							
Person	23.1	57.1	11.4	5.2	3.1	493	1.7
Gender disparity	0.84	1.00	1.11	1.30	1.75	0.87	0.81
Karnataka							
Person	17.7	67.6	4.2	3.2	7.3	705	1.8
Gender disparity	0.87	1.08	0.44	0.74	1.22	0.82	0.87
Kerala							
Person	9.0	71.5	12.5	6.2	0.8	1091	1.7
Gender disparity	0.84	1.07	0.88	0.91	-	0.85	0.93
Tamil Nadu							
Person	26.3	62.7	5.3	4.7	0.9	593	1.6
Gender disparity	1.32	0.94	0.72	0.62	1.88	0.84	0.81
All India							
Person	**17.8**	**67.2**	**9.8**	**3.1**	**2.1**	**680**	**1.8**
Gender disparity	**0.93**	**1.04**	**0.93**	**0.90**	**0.86**	**0.68**	**0.72**
C.V.Person	38.9	15.5	93.6	95.7	149.0	44.7	5.3

ratio was 0.73 in government and aided schools and 0.52 in private schools. Thus when it comes to allocation of funds or out of pocket expenditures, it is males that receive a disproportionately higher share. Gender disparity is the highest in Rajasthan, the North-east, Bihar, and Uttar Pradesh.

Private elementary schooling is 230 per cent more expensive than schooling in government schools. Expenditure on fees as a percentage of total expenditure was estimated to be 13 per cent in government, 15 per cent in aided, and 34 per cent in private schools. Major heads of expenditure in both government and aided schools were books, stationery, and uniforms.

Household expenditure on elementary education in government schools was very high (about double the national average) in Himachal Pradesh

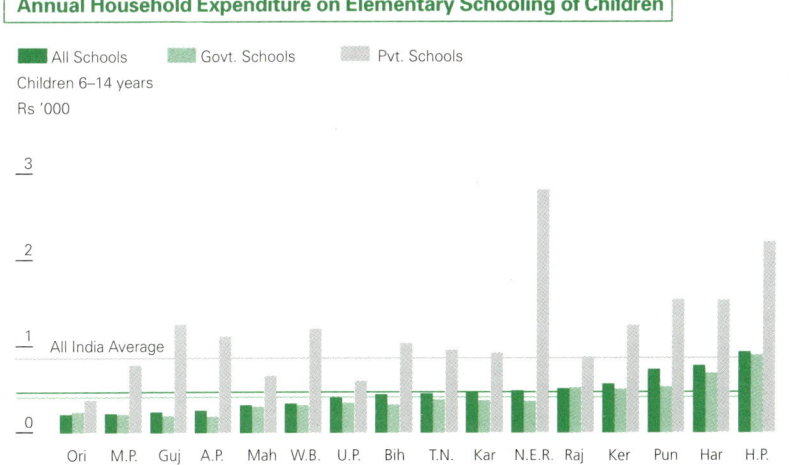

Annual Household Expenditure on Elementary Schooling of Children

All Schools   Govt. Schools   Pvt. Schools
Children 6–14 years
Rs '000

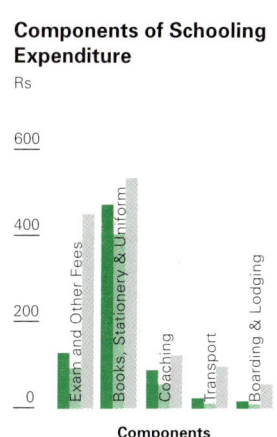

Components of Schooling Expenditure
Rs

(Rs 1,548) followed by Haryana (Rs 1,094), Kerala (Rs 852), and Rajasthan (Rs 777) (App. Table A.6.17). Cost of public schooling was the least in Andhra Pradesh (Rs 329), Orissa (Rs 420), and Madhya Pradesh (Rs 438). The lowest costs for elementary schooling were recorded in the states of Orissa, Madhya Pradesh, Gujarat, Maharashtra, Andhra Pradesh, and West Bengal. Cost of both government and private schooling were relatively high in Punjab, Haryana, Himachal Pradesh, and Kerala in comparison with other states. However, reported household expenditure on fees in government schools is as high as 30 per cent of the total in the North-eastern states, followed by 20 per cent in both Tamil Nadu and Uttar Pradesh. While transportation costs were high in Gujarat, the North-east, and Karnataka, expenditure on private coaching was found to be 41 per cent of education expenditure on government schooling in West Bengal, followed by about 20 per cent in Orissa and Bihar, and 15 per cent in Andhra Pradesh and Kerala.

As discussed earlier, the importance of aided schools is evident only in Kerala and West Bengal, and the cost of education thereof is only somewhat higher than the cost incurred in government schools. The culture of sending children to private schools is widespread in Uttar Pradesh, Punjab, and Haryana. The household expenditure incurred on elementary education in private schools was two to three times that incurred in government schools in these states. The cost of private schooling is very high in the North-east, Haryana, Himachal Pradesh, and Punjab. It should, however be noted that, with a few noteworthy exceptions, the majority of children in rural India study in government schools for which parents spend considerable sums in any case.

Disaggregated information on household expenditure on elementary education and gender disparity according to various population groups is presented in App. Tables A.6.15 to A.6.21.

Overall household expenditure on primary education increases considerably as household income increases. For example, those in the lowest income category spend about Rs 512 per annum which increases to Rs 1399 per annum in the highest income category. In terms of per pupil cost it works out to Rs 300 and Rs 600 respectively (App. Table 6.15). Gender disparity in expenditures does not really fall as income increases except in the highest income category. A similar contrast is apparent between the landless wage earners and the large landholders. The expenditure is relatively low among STs, SCs, and Muslims at about 3 per cent of household income for the respective social groups.

Between 1992 and 1994, only 4 out of 16 states (Punjab, Bihar, Rajasthan, and Tamil Nadu) recorded a rise in the per pupil private expenditure (PPPE) on elementary education (App. Table A.6.22). In the case of India, the PPPE dropped from Rs 464 in 1992 to Rs 378 in 1994. Similarly, the share of examination and other fees in total expenditure fell substantially in 10 out of 16 states, the highest reduction having been observed in Kerala, that is, from 23.6 per cent in 1992 to 8.8 per cent in 1994.

Private elementary schooling is 230 per cent more expensive than that in government schools.

Expenditure on fees as a percentage of total expenditure works out to 13 per cent in government, 15 per cent in aided, and 34 per cent in private schools.

Participation in Non-formal Literacy Programmes

The participation of children aged 6–14 years in non-formal literacy programmes that fall outside the formal school system is highest in Himachal Pradesh and lowest in Uttar Pradesh. App. Table A.6.23 presents the state-wise participation rates under the categories 'cannot read or write' (level 1), 'can read but cannot write' (level 2), 'can read and write with difficulty' (level 3), and 'can read and write fluently' (level 4). Himachal Pradesh recorded about 20 per cent of children not enrolled in the school system but participating in non-formal literacy programmes while Uttar Pradesh recorded only 0.3 per cent of children attending non-formal literacy programmes. The average estimate for rural India as a whole is 1.5 per cent with both the upper and lower central states as well as Tamil Nadu showing very low rates of participation ranging from 0.3 to 1.5 per cent.

In Karnataka, Himachal Pradesh, and Madhya Pradesh relatively large numbers of girls were reported to be attending non-formal schooling, that is 2.31, 1.95, and 1.29 respectively. The f/m ratios were 2.3, 2.0, and 1.3 respectively in favour of girls. In the other states, a substantial bias against girl children is evident in non-formal literacy programmes. The gender disparity was low (f/m ratio being less than 1) in case of positive levels of achievement (levels 2, 3, and 4) across most population groups, indicating thereby the prevalence of a gender bias against the girl child.

What is significant with regard to achievement levels is that none of the participants could read and write fluently after attending non-formal schooling in almost all the major states, except in West Bengal (3.8 per cent) and Tamil Nadu (9.0). However, 91 per cent of the participants could read and also write with some difficulty in Tamil Nadu. The figures as regards reading and writing skills for children in non-formal schooling in other states range from 47.4 per cent in Madhya Pradesh to 5.5 per cent in Andhra Pradesh.

Both participation rate and level of achievement of children in non-formal literacy programmes were highest in the highest household income class (App. Table A.6.24). Participation across landholding and occupation groups does not show any substantial differentials. SCs among the caste groups and Christians among the religious groups have the highest participation rates. The rates are also high among small size households, households in the lower segment of the poverty line, households with both male and female literate members, and in highly developed villages.

Thus it can be said that in order to keep all children aged 6–14 years in school in India at the existing level of quality, a total of Rs 249,690 m., i.e., about 3.5 per cent of GNP is required. This works out to 57 per cent of the estimated total national plan budget expenditure of Rs 436,620 m. for 1993–4. Currently, however, public expenditure is only about 42 per cent (Rs 105,922 m.) of the total requirement and about 1.5 per cent of GNP. GNP at current prices for 1993–4 was Rs 720,5310 m.

It is, therefore, of vital importance to provide mass education, particularly to the clearly identified vulnerable sections of the population such as STs, SCs, Muslims, and women in India. Given the limited resources available,

A meagre 1.5 per cent of children aged 6–14 years and not enrolled in the school system have been reported to be participating in non-formal literacy programmes.

especially for social sector activities such as education, it is imperative that education services be targeted to the most needy and backward. This survey should help not only in placing the population groups in a relative perspective but also in estimating absolute numbers so necessary for resource allocation.

Overall, analysis of data on education suggests that:

1 Level of income has substantial and differential impacts on literacy and net enrolment rates in the five central states.
2 Privatization of education is likely to lead to greater gender disparity.
3 Policies to reduce gender disparity cannot be uniform across social and occupational groups; there is need to address the special needs and constraints of different population groups.

These findings support what is already known about schooling and enrolment patterns from other studies. As regards monitoring of the gender-differentiated impact, the focus should be on drop-out rates rather than non-attendance. However, the latter is also crucial in an assessment of the quality of education or commitment to it.

Given the differences in absolute levels, there is some basis to conclude that privatization of schooling will most affect expenditure on schooling for girls. At the state level, the difference between the two types of schools is low in the case of Haryana, Uttar Pradesh, Orissa, the North-east, Gujarat, Andhra Pradesh, and Kerala.

None of the participants in the non-formal literacy programmes could read and write fluently after completing such schooling.

BOX 6.1

Cost to Universalize Elementary Education in India

	Total	Rural	Urban
• Estimated 6–14 years old as on March 1995 (millions)	205	152	53

Deflators:
Rural: 30 per cent non-enrolment in rural areas evidence from NCAER, 1994.
Urban: 15 per cent of 70 per cent urban children are not enrolled and 50 per cent of the remaining 30 per cent of urban children are not enrolled.

	Total	Rural	Urban
• Estimated number of children attending schools (millions)	146	106	40
• Estimated number of children not attending schools (millions)	59	46	13

Expenditures:
- Household expenditure per pupil / year @ Rs 378 — Rs 55,188 million
- Public, Community, and Private sector expenditure per pupil/year @ Rs 840 — Rs 122,640 million
- @ Rs 1,218/- per pupil total expenditure per year — Rs 177,828 million

a Total expenditure on those children who are attending school as on March 1995 is Rs 177,828 million
b @ Rs 1,218/- per pupil/year it requires Rs 71,862 million to enrol 59 million children who are outside school.
c To impart universal elementary education it costs a total of (a+b) Rs 249,690 million

Additionally
d Should mid-day meals continue to be an integral part of the elementary education programme, it would cost an additional Rs 61,500 million
e To provide bare minimum infrastructure to the 59 million non-enrolled children it requires about 19,70,000 classrooms and @ Rs 25,000 per classroom it is a total one time capital cost of Rs 49,250 million.
f Escalate annual expenditure @ at least 2 per cent over and above the rate of inflation to account for additional increase in pupils.

Principal Findings

I Literacy Rate

1 Literacy levels are lowest in Rajasthan, Bihar, Uttar Pradesh, and Madhya Pradesh and high in Kerala, the North-eastern states, Tamil Nadu, Maharashtra, Gujarat, and West Bengal. Rajasthan has the highest gender differential among states.

2 The literacy rates rise considerably with income but this is not true of gender disparity. Literacy rates are similar across land size groups; landless wage earners, SCs and STs have low levels of literacy. Literacy is high and the gender gap low among the salaried, but female literacy is relatively low among all social groups.

3 About 17 per cent of adult males and 9 per cent of adult females complete middle school in rural India, that is, on an average, 52 girls for every 100 boys. Gender disparity is high in Rajasthan, Uttar Pradesh, and Madhya Pradesh, and among lower income levels in most states.

II Enrolment Rate

4 The enrolment rate rises with size of landholding and income. Enrolment rates are high among the salaried and professionals, and low among wage earners in almost all states. Punjab shows high enrolment rates in comparison with Rajasthan, Madhya Pradesh, Uttar Pradesh, Bihar, and Orissa. While STs have the lowest enrolment rate (60 per cent), Hindus have an enrolment rate of 78 per cent. Gender disparity is highest in Uttar Pradesh and Rajasthan. Increase in enrolments over the years has been highest in Punjab and Haryana.

III Discontinuation Rate

5 The average discontinuation rate is about 6 per cent for rural India. It is high in Tamil Nadu, Andhra Pradesh, Madhya Pradesh, Karnataka, and Orissa, and low in Himachal Pradesh and Kerala.

6 Contrary to general belief, drop-outs are negligible (about 1 per cent) among children aged 6–9 years; they increase to 2.1 per cent among 6–11 year olds and to 13 per cent among 12 year olds.

7 Discontinuation rates are lower among high income groups, the landed, professionals, males, and Hindus. The discontinuation rate while decreasing for the country as a whole, appears to be rising in states like Tamil Nadu and Kerala and fluctuating in West Bengal, Gujarat, Andhra Pradesh, and Karnataka.

IV Private Schooling

8 About 68 per cent of all children go to government schools while another 22 per cent attend government-aided schools. While 11 per cent of boys go to private schools, only 8 per cent of girls do so. The proportion of children seeking education in private schools has increased from 2 per cent in 1986 to about 10 per cent in 1994. This increase is substantial in Uttar Pradesh, Punjab, and Haryana. More than three-fourths of students attend aided schools in West Bengal.

V Expenditure on Schooling

9   Total household expenditure on elementary schooling is Rs 378 per student per year. In 1992 the corresponding figure was Rs 464. The cost of schooling is Rs 300 per child in government schools, Rs 380 per child in aided schools, and Rs 735 per child in private schools.

10 To impart elementary education to all children in India at the prevailing level of quality involves an expenditure of Rs 236,348 million which is equal to about 3.3 per cent of GDP. The current expenditure is only 1.7 per cent of GDP.

7

Health, Morbidity, and Disability

The enjoyment of the highest attainable standard of health is one of the fundamental rights of every human being without distinction of race, religion, political belief, economic, or social condition.

[Preamble to the Constitution of the World Health Organization]

Introduction

The treatment of sickness and containment of disease is basically the realm of the medical and epidemiological sciences. Yet social scientists have a role to play in tracking morbidity and health patterns and in explaining health-seeking behaviour in order to devise appropriate policies to protect and maintain human health.

In the recent past, the measurement of 'morbidity' or 'state of ill health' is being used increasingly as an indicator of the level of well-being of the population in place of conventional indices like death and infant mortality rates that were used to measure social development and personal well being. Since morbidity is relatively more common than death and infant mortality, it can also be measured cost-effectively.

The study of morbidity patterns becomes imperative in a subcontinent like India with substantial regional, rural–urban and social group differentials in the standard and quality of life. Health is an indicator of well-being that has direct implications not only for the quality of life but also indirect implications for the production of economic goods and services. 'Health for All by the year 2000' was a national goal set by Indian policy-makers over 20 years ago in Alma Ata.[1] Since then a lot of planning, effort and public expenditure have gone into improving human health both in rural and urban India. The spread of and accessibility to modern medicine have improved substantially across the country. Despite concerted efforts, however, India continues to be among the many developing countries of the world with high levels of morbidity, especially among infants, children, women, and the elderly. There is also a high incidence of communicable diseases normally associated with low levels of sanitation and public hygiene, poor quality of drinking water and under-nutrition.

Data on morbidity are currently being used to construct a Disability-Adjusted Life Year (DALY) index for international comparisons. DALY is 'a measure which combines healthy life years lost because of premature mortality with those lost as a result of disability'.[2] The data available from this survey make it possible to estimate disease-specific DALYs at state level and for the country as a whole. It is clear that to objectively evaluate the disease burden of a country and its many regions, community level

1. A global initiative towards health-related research and action was taken at an international conference on Primary Health Care held in Alma Ata (in the erstwhile USSR) in 1978. In its Declaration, the conference spelt out the goal of the signatory nations which was to ensure 'Health for All by the Year 2000' with primary health care as its top priority.

2. World Bank, *World Development Report, 1993.* Oxford University Press, 1993.

estimates of morbidity are essential. Information on short duration morbidity and major morbidity under treatment at the time of survey were collected separately. Accordingly, two separate prevalence rates, Short Duration Morbidity Prevalence Rate (MPR–SD) and Point Prevalence Rate of Major Morbidity (PPR–MM), are discussed in this chapter. The former has a reference period of 30 days and is estimated per thousand population, and the latter is measured in terms of the point prevalence rate at the time of survey per lakh population. Both these rates are presented for major states and according to selected population groups in Tables 7.1 and 7.2. Data collected on all types of morbidity as reported by the respondents are categorized as episodes:

- Starting before the first day of the reference period and terminating within the reference period;
- Starting and terminating within the reference period;
- Starting within the reference period and continuing at the time of the interview;
- Starting before the reference period and continuing on the date of survey.

It would, however, be misleading to compute the annual Morbidity Prevalence Rates (MPRs) using the two sets of data together.

Nature and Type of Illness

The illnesses reported in the survey do not necessarily constitute clinically confirmed diseases. Under MPR–SD, information was collected on different types of diarrhoea, respiratory infections, fevers and other episodes of acute illness. Direct enquiries were made to find out the PPR–MM of eight clearly identifiable diseases, namely epilepsy, hypertension, diabetes mellitus, heart disease, mental illness, tuberculosis, leprosy, and cancer. The diseases reported are those for which patients were under medication at the time of survey and about which other household members had knowledge either from doctors or paramedical personnel. Thus the reporting of diseases by respondents may be perceived as a combination of lay reporting of symptoms and clinically identified illnesses.

Reporting of Morbidity

The reporting of clinically identified illnesses is subject to recall and reporting errors. No effort was made in this survey to establish the authenticity of clinically identified illnesses. The symptoms and names of diseases thus collected were labelled using the lay reporting of illness technique developed by the World Health Organization.[3]

Before undertaking inter-state and inter-group comparisons of morbidity rates, it is useful to note how morbidity reporting can vary among the survey population. Besides actual occurrence, on the whole, reporting of morbidity depends upon perceptions regarding ill health, sickness, and disease. The following assumptions and observations remain unavoidable issues while explaining inter-state and inter-group morbidity differentials.

- Many types of simple, common and frequently experienced sickness

Despite concerted efforts, India continues to record high levels of morbidity, especially among infants, children, the elderly, and women.

3. World Health Organization, *Lay Reporting of Health Information*. Geneva, 1978.

may not be reported, for example, aches, wounds, diarrhoea, cold and cough, and so on.

- Morbidity reporting may improve with level of household education levels, especially if females are literate. A case in point is the high incidence of morbidity in the state of Kerala.
- Many types of sicknesses in India are culturally sensitive due to the unique association between life and death, origins of sicknesses, etc. People may be reluctant to report sicknesses such as tuberculosis, leprosy, leucoderma, sexually transmitted diseases (STDs), psychiatric and gynaecological disorders.
- In a survey situation, the respondent may not be fully aware of the sickness suffered by other family members. This may be especially so in large households and joint families.
- Sickness suffered by infants and children may be under-reported if the respondent is not the biological mother or someone who normally cares for the child.
- Many types of sicknesses suffered by teenaged unmarried girls may not be reported due to cultural reasons.
- Proximity and exposure to medical care institutions may increase the reporting of morbidity.
- Treated and hospitalized episodes may be better reported.
- Reporting of sickness of the dead before the survey may be low.

Morbidity reporting depends upon perceptions regarding ill health, sickness, and disease, normally governed and regulated by cultural practices.

Short Duration Morbidity Prevalence Rate (MPR–SD)

Incidences of diarrhoea, cough and cold, and unspecified fevers during a 30-day reference period preceding the date of survey were considered as constituting short duration morbidity. Since there are a number of factors, such as perceptions and non-sampling/reporting errors that affect the reporting of morbidity, inter-state and inter-group comparisons should be used only in understanding broad trends and comparisons.

The MPR–SD for all India worked out to 122 per 1000 population for the 30-day reference period. Females reported slightly higher MPRs (127) than males (117) and the gender disparity worked out to 1.08 (Table 7.1). The annual MPR–SD which can be computed by multiplying monthly MPR–SD by 12, worked out to 1464 per 1000 population.

Notwithstanding the various factors affecting the reporting of morbidity, MPR–SD was high in Madhya Pradesh, West Bengal, Tamil Nadu, Punjab, Haryana, Orissa and Andhra Pradesh, and low in Gujarat, Maharashtra, Kerala, Uttar Pradesh and Rajasthan. Very high female morbidity in comparison with male morbidity was reported in Tamil Nadu followed by Punjab, Haryana, and Orissa (Table 7.1).

For all India, the incidence of diarrhoea was 31, cold and cough 72, and fevers 25 per thousand population. At state level, the incidence of diarrhoea was very high in Madhya Pradesh, Orissa, and West Bengal, and very low in Kerala, Gujarat, Maharashtra, and Punjab. While the incidence of diarrhoea was generally low among females, possibly due to reporting problems, it appeared to be high for females in Punjab.

Reported incidences of cold and cough were high in West Bengal and Tamil Nadu but low in Gujarat and Maharashtra. Fevers were high in Haryana and Madhya Pradesh.

App. Table A.7.1 shows that the MPR–SD declined with an increase in levels of household income. For example, in the lower income group the

Short Duration Morbidity

Distribution of Short Duration Morbidity (SDM) among States

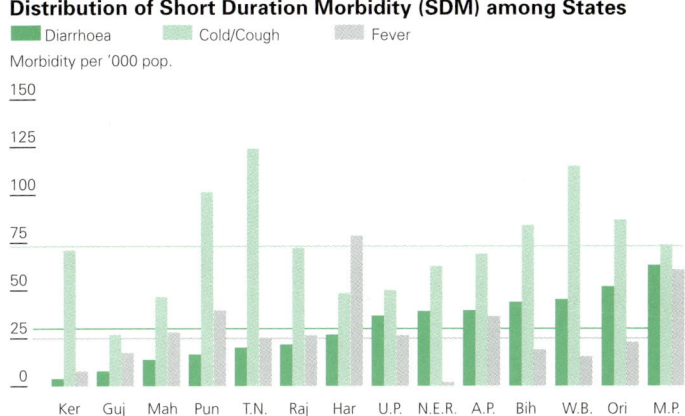

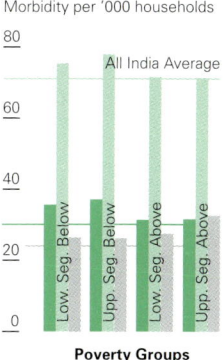

SDM Rates among Poverty Groups

MPR was 129 per thousand, while it was 91 per thousand population in the higher income group. This pattern was found in cases of diarrhoea and cold and cough; however, the incidence of fever showed no association with income levels.

The MPR did not show any association with landholding and occupational characteristics of households. However, among the salaried and self-employed a higher MPR may be associated with better reporting due to better awareness.

The MPR was considerably higher among STs than SCs, possibly due to the higher incidence of diarrhoea and fever among STs. However, the reported MPR was highest among other minorities followed by Christians with 128 per thousand population. Contrary to expectation, morbidity was seen to decline as household size increased. This may be attributed to under-reporting among larger households. Morbidity also generally falls as the level of village development increases.

The prevalence of diarrhoea is marginally higher among households with no literate adults. There is a clear association between level of village development and prevalence of diarrhoea; prevalence is very high among the less developed villages and considerably lower in the developed villages. Overall, the prevalence of diarrhoea is lower among women; it decreases with an increase in income, literacy level of adults in the household, and with the level of development of villages.

The prevalence of cough and cold is high among children; it falls in the middle years and again rises sharply among the elderly. The pattern with respect population groups is similar to the case of diarrhoea. Prevalence of fever is considerably uniform across all ages; it is only marginally lower among the middle-aged. It, however, does not vary much across population

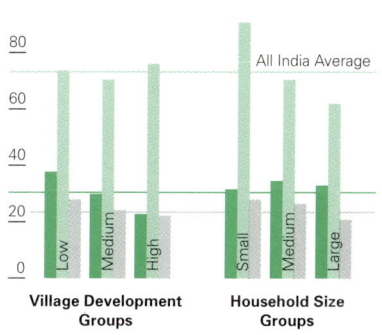

Among Village Development and Household Size Groups

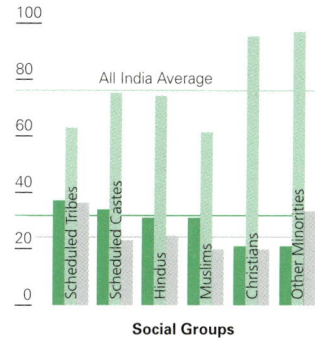

Among Social Groups

TABLE 7.1

Prevalence Rates of Short Duration and Major Morbidity by States

Regions/States	Short Duration Morbidity per Thousand Population				Major Morbidity (per lakh pop.)
	Diarrhoea	Cold/Cough	Fever	Total	
North					
Haryana					
Person	29	48	84	153	6,697
Gender disparity	-	-	-	1.20	1.21
Punjab					
Person	16	104	36	154	6,692
Gender disparity				1.17	1.25
Upper Central					
Bihar					
Person	39	83	19	132	3,817
Gender disparity				1.05	0.75
Uttar Pradesh					
Person	31	51	26	97	3,523
Gender disparity				1.02	1.21
Lower Central					
Madhya Pradesh					
Person	63	79	60	195	4,801
Gender disparity				1.09	0.95
Orissa					
Person	54	85	22	143	5,011
Gender disparity				1.10	0.93
Rajasthan					
Person	19	72	26	113	3,150
Gender disparity				0.94	1.10
East					
North-eastern Rg.					
Person	35	60	3	94	3,076
Gender disparity				0.94	0.77
West Bengal					
Person	45	114	11	164	6,168
Gender disparity				1.08	0.96
West					
Gujarat					
Person	9	33	18	57	2,551
Gender disparity				1.02	0.74
Maharashtra					
Person	14	48	26	85	3,487
Gender disparity				1.03	1.05
South					
Andhra Pradesh					
Person	36	68	31	132	7,684
Gender disparity				1.09	0.88

Contd.

Kerala					
Person	6	75	8	89	7,319
Gender disparity				0.99	1.17
Tamil Nadu					
Person	19	125	27	168	6,775
Gender disparity				1.29	1.10
All India					
Person	**31**	**72**	**25**	**122**	**4,578**
Gender disparity	**0.92**	**1.08**	**1.17**	**1.08**	**1.00**

groups. The prevalence of cold and cough, and especially fevers is high among women (App. Table A.7.1). A more disaggregated picture for population groups at the level of the states is presented in App. Table A.7.2.

The MPR–SD has an inverted 'J' type relationship with age, that is, it decreases from a high level and then rises again. MPR is highest among the 0–4 years age group and lowest among the 15–34 years age group (App. Table A.7.3). Morbidity is very high among children below age 4 in Haryana and Madhya Pradesh. Short duration morbidity among the aged was high in Madhya Pradesh, Tamil Nadu, and Orissa. Gender disparity in short duration morbidity is very high among the 15–34 years age group in comparison with the 35–59 and 60 and over age groups. It is likely that such morbidity is related to pregnancy and childbirth related problems.

Diarrhoea is generally a childhood sickness. The MPR for diarrhoea among children aged 0–4 years worked out to 108 per thousand, followed by 22 per thousand population among the 5–14 years age group, 15 among 15–34 years age group, 25 among 35–59 years age group, and 26 among the elderly (*see* App. Tables A.7.4, A.7.5 and A.7.6 for details).

Point Prevalence Rate of Major Morbidity (PPR–MM)

An attempt was made to establish if any of the family members in a household were on medication for chronic or major illnesses such as epilepsy, heart disease, hypertension, tuberculosis, diabetes, mental disorders, and leprosy at the time of the survey. Such an investigation enables estimation of the all India Point Prevalence Rate (PPR) for all ages and all types of major morbidity and worked out to 4,578 per lakh population. PPR–MM was high in Andhra Pradesh, Kerala, Tamil Nadu, Haryana, and Punjab. It was considerably higher among adults and the older population. For example, the PPR was only 966 per lakh population among the 0–4 years age group, followed by 1138 among the 5–14 age group, 2,578 among the15–34 age group, 7,933 among the 35–59 age group, and 22,317 among the 60 and above population. Age-specific prevalence clearly suggests that point prevalence increases sharply as age increases: it is about 23 times higher among the elderly (60 years and above) in comparison with the 0–4 years age group. Thus it is only to be expected that the point prevalence will be higher among states which have higher life expectancy such as Kerala, Tamil Nadu, Haryana, and Punjab (App. Table A.7.7).

The prevalence of major morbidity among the poor could be low because the severely affected would already have been dead.

Incidence of leprosy among STs is three times higher than the national average.

Diarrhoea among Poverty Groups

Short Duration Morbidity ('000 pop.)

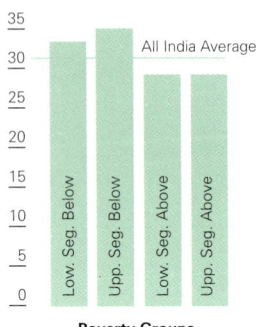

Cough among Poverty Groups

Short Duration Morbidity ('000 pop.)

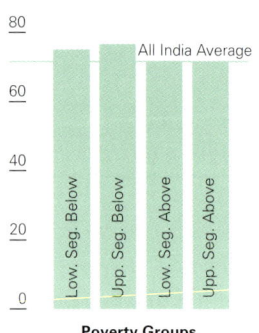

Fever among Poverty Groups

Short Duration Morbidity ('000 pop.)

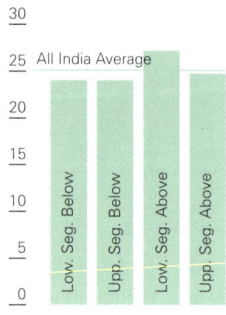

Total among Poverty Groups

Short Duration Morbidity ('000 pop.)

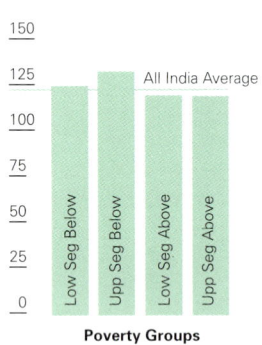

Diarrhoea among Social Groups

Short Duration Morbidity ('000 pop.)

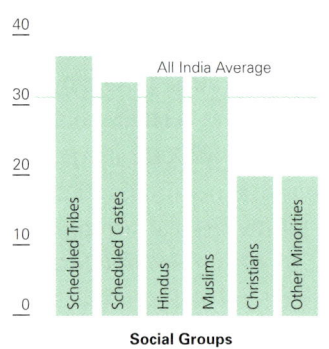

Cough among Social Groups

Short Duration Morbidity ('000 pop.)

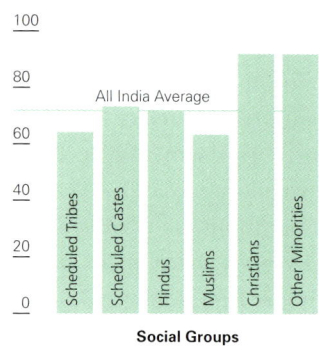

Fever among Social Groups

Short Duration Morbidity ('000 pop.)

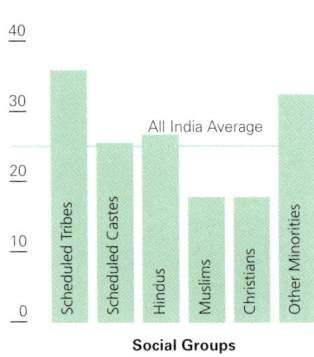

Total among Social Groups

Short Duration Morbidity ('000 pop.)

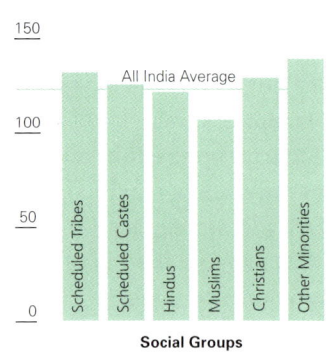

Diarrohea among Age Groups

Short Duration Morbidity ('000 pop.)

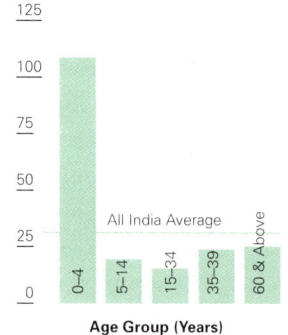

Cough among Age Groups
Short Duration Morbidity ('000 pop.)

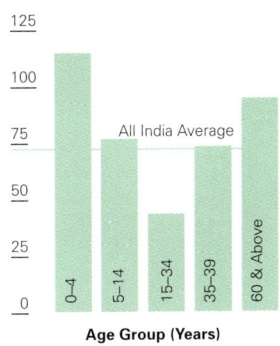

Age Group (Years)

Fever among Age Groups
Short Duration Morbidity ('000 pop.)

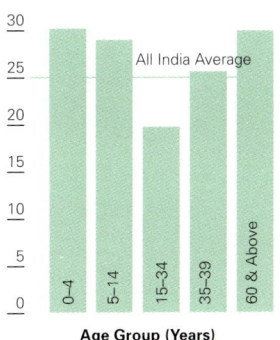

Age Group (Years)

Total among Age Groups
Short Duration Morbidity ('000 pop.)

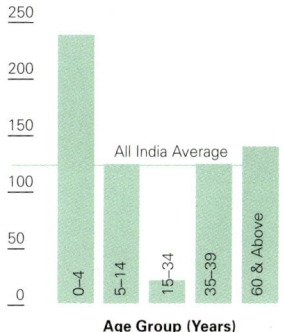

Age Group (Years)

Prevalence Rates of Major Morbidity

Among Poverty Groups
(Per lakh pop.)

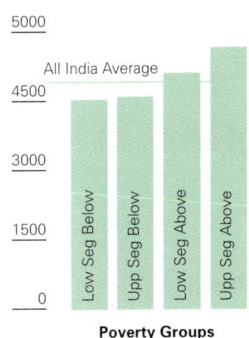

Poverty Groups

Among Social Groups
(Per lakh pop.)

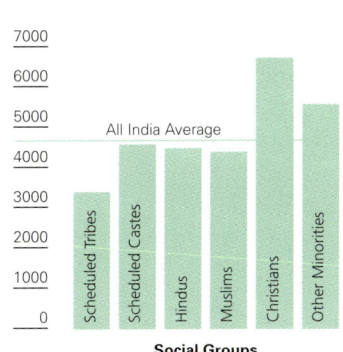

Social Groups

Among Age Groups
(Per lakh pop.)

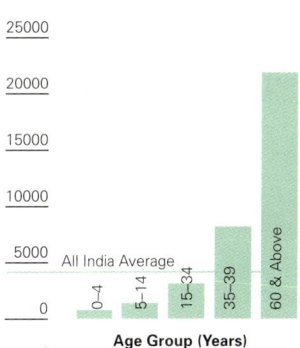

Age Group (Years)

The PPR has no noteworthy association with population groups except that it rises according to the level of village development. It is likely that due to availability of hospital care and diagnostic services, people in developed villages avail of these facilities and also report better. PPR estimates for population groups at the level of states can be found in App. Tables A.7.8 to A.7.11.

Disease-specific prevalence of morbidity for states is presented in Table 7.2. and Box 7.1 summarizes these rates and presents the population size affected by the listed sicknesses.

As presented in Box 7.1, an estimated 41 m. individuals receive medication for major illnesses at a given point in time in India as a whole. The highest prevalence, however, has been recorded for hypertension (589 per lakh population) followed by tuberculosis (423 per lakh population).

There are a number of inter-state variations in PPRs. The general pattern is that PPRs are higher in the southern states and in Uttar Pradesh, Bihar, and Rajasthan. These variations are all the more complex since the type of diseases have a geographic and seasonal pattern which requires further investigation. Nonetheless, higher prevalence in the southern states appears

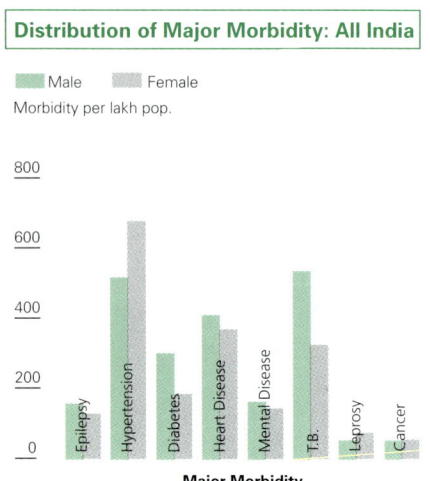

Distribution of Major Morbidity: All India

■ Male ■ Female
Morbidity per lakh pop.

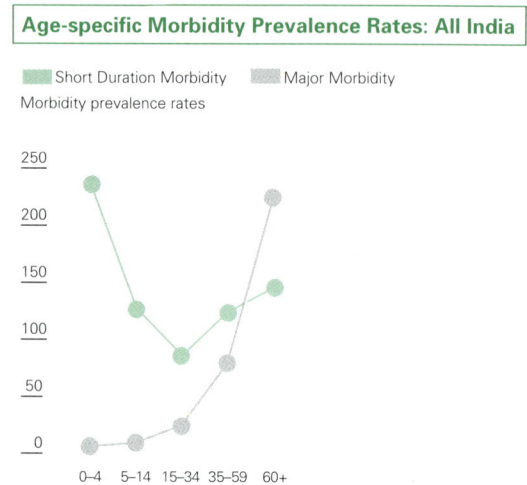

Age-specific Morbidity Prevalence Rates: All India

■ Short Duration Morbidity ■ Major Morbidity
Morbidity prevalence rates

BOX 7.1

Point Prevalence and Population Estimates for Major Morbidity under Treatment– All India

Disease	Point Prevalence (per lakh)	No. Suffering (millions)	States with High Prevalence
Hypertension	589	5.5	Punjab, Kerala, Andhra Pradesh, Tamil Nadu, and West Bengal
Heart disease	385	3.5	Tamil Nadu, Kerala, West Bengal, Andhra Pradesh, Bihar
Tuberculosis	423	3.8	Madhya Pradesh, West Bengal, Tamil Nadu, Andhra Pradesh, and Kerala.
Diabetes	221	2.0	Southern states, the North-east and Gujarat
Epilepsy	120	1.1	Orissa, Tamil Nadu, Maharashtra, West Bengal
Mental disorder	133	1.2	Kerala, Punjab, Andhra Pradesh, and West Bengal
Leprosy	57	0.5	Madhya Pradesh, Tamil Nadu (none in Kerala, Punjab, Haryana)
Cancer	43	0.4	Orissa, Andhra Pradesh, Maharashtra, Madhya Pradesh
All major morbidity	4,578	41.0	High in Andhra Pradesh, Kerala, Tamil Nadu, Haryana, Punjab, West Bengal, Haryana; Low in Gujarat, the North-east, Rajasthan, Uttar Pradesh, Bihar, Maharashtra.

Note: A total of 38 illnesses were reported in this category including the seven listed above.
The prevalence rates derived from this survey for rural areas have been applied for the total population to arrive at the above estimates.

to be due to better reporting of sickness and treatment. The high prevalence in other parts reflects the low level of the health in the respective states.

The prevalence rate generally increases with household income, and this increase is specially marked in cases of hypertension and diabetes. However, the prevalence of tuberculosis, leprosy, and cancer falls as household income increases. The prevalence of hypertension and heart disease has been reported to be high for the salaried and professional class even in the rural areas. The MPR of major illnesses is highest among the Christians (the most literate group) with evidence of a high incidence of hypertension—about twice the national average—as also of diabetes and mental disorders.

TABLE 7.2
Prevalence Rates of Major Morbidity by States

| Regions/States | Major Morbidity (per lakh pop.) | | | | | | | | Major Morbidity |
	Epilepsy	Hyper-tension	Diabetes	Heart Disease	Mental Disease	TB	Leprosy	Cancer	
North									
Haryana	103	372	100	230	143	322	-	34	6,697
Punjab	103	1,475	196	166	268	230	-	28	6,692
Upper Central									
Bihar	78	481	143	443	169	496	29	19	3,817
Uttar Pradesh	120	221	158	231	120	370	27	34	3,523
Lower Central									
Madhya Pradesh	74	366	138	160	136	686	313	57	4,801
Orissa	369	863	116	245	99	206	31	74	5,011
Rajasthan	60	64	55	84	79	303	-	37	3,150
East									
North-eastern Rg.	50	732	226	502	105	189	74	127	3,076
West Bengal	133	1,049	207	795	151	636	22	32	6,168
West									
Gujarat	103	381	215	188	160	276	30	7	2,551
Maharashtra	147	241	130	151	84	282	65	62	3,487
South									
Andhra Pradesh	129	1,295	545	676	163	580	63	66	7,684
Kerala	81	1,433	980	914	283	504	-	39	7,319
Tamil Nadu	205	1,191	377	949	80	583	83	15	6,775
All India									
Person	**120**	**589**	**221**	**385**	**132**	**423**	**57**	**43**	**4,578**
Gender disparity	**0.71**	**1.31**	**0.65**	**0.86**	**0.75**	**0.59**	**1.64**	**0.95**	**1.00**

The prevalence of tuberculosis was high among STs and SCs, and might be related to their low levels of living and consequent malnutrition. Prevalence of tuberculosis decreases as poverty decreases, suggesting that this disease is closely related to poverty. A surprising fact, however, is the higher incidence of tuberculosis among Christians (475 per lakh population). This finding needs further investigation and corroboration. The incidence of leprosy among STs is three times higher than the national average. Prevalence rates for hypertension, diabetes, heart disease, and cancer increase with the level of development of the village. Tuberculosis and leprosy, on the other hand, decrease with village development. The incidence of tuberculosis is 32 per cent higher in the less developed villages whereas leprosy is 200 per cent

Short Duration Morbidity Prevalence Rate Per '000 Population

Up to 100   100–125   125–150   150 +

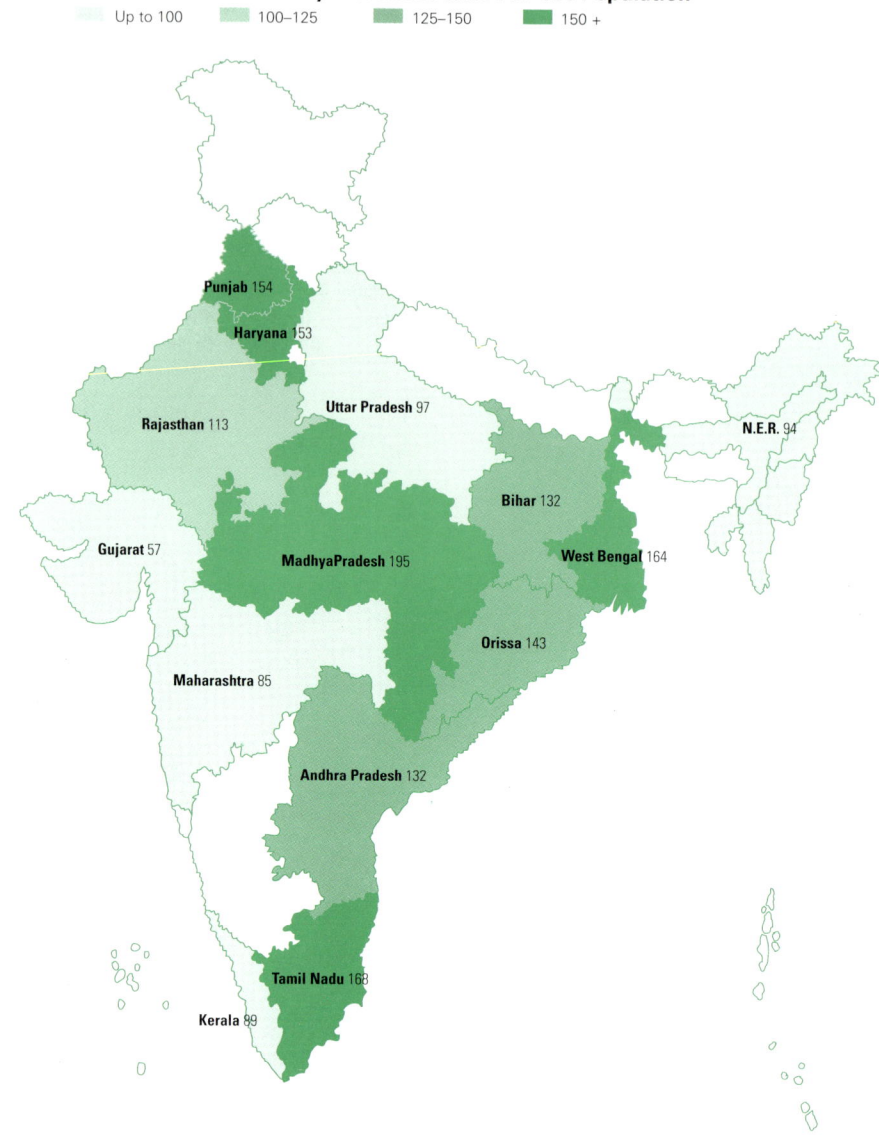

Punjab 154
Haryana 153
Rajasthan 113
Uttar Pradesh 97
N.E.R. 94
Bihar 132
Gujarat 57
MadhyaPradesh 195
West Bengal 164
Orissa 143
Maharashtra 85
Andhra Pradesh 132
Tamil Nadu 168
Kerala 89

Morbidity Prevalence Rates

Short Duration and Major Morbidity Prevalence Rates: Rural India

Short Duration   Major Morbidity

Morbidity per '000 pop.

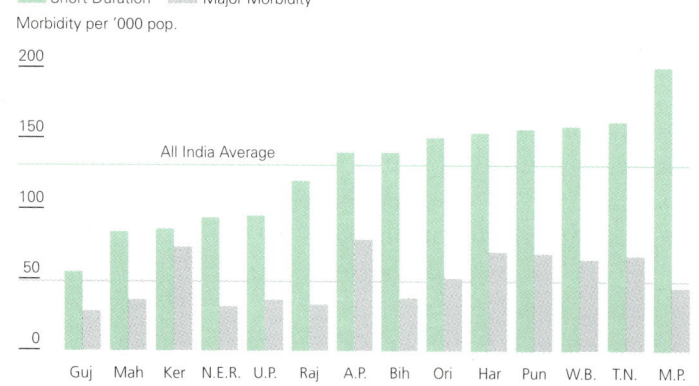

All India Average

Guj Mah Ker N.E.R. U.P. Raj A.P. Bih Ori Har Pun W.B. T.N. M.P.

Among Poverty Groups

Short Duration   Major Morbidity

Major morbidity per '000 pop.

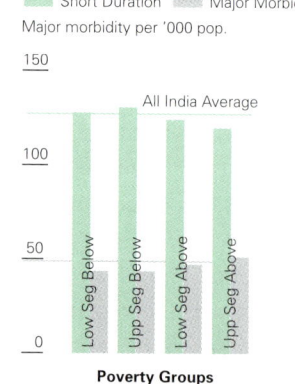

All India Average

Low Seg Below   Upp Seg Below   Low Seg Above   Upp Seg Above

Poverty Groups

Major Morbidity Prevalence Rate Per Lakh Population

Up to 4,000   4,000–6,000   6,000–7,000   7,000 +

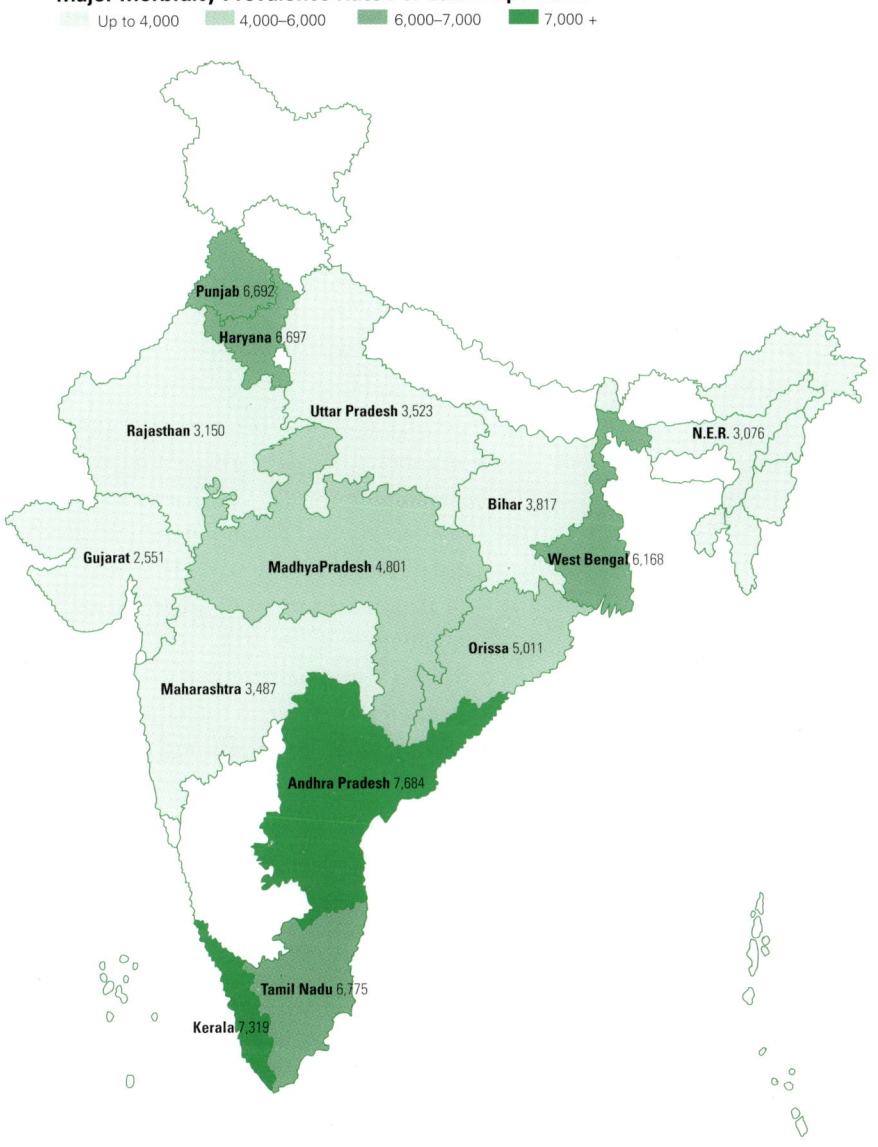

Punjab 6,692

Haryana 6,697

Uttar Pradesh 3,523

Rajasthan 3,150

N.E.R. 3,076

Bihar 3,817

Gujarat 2,551

MadhyaPradesh 4,801

West Bengal 6,168

Orissa 5,011

Maharashtra 3,487

Andhra Pradesh 7,684

Tamil Nadu 6,775

Kerala 7,319

Among Development and Household Size Groups

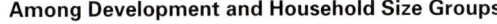

Short Duration   Major Morbidity

Major morbidity per '000 pop.

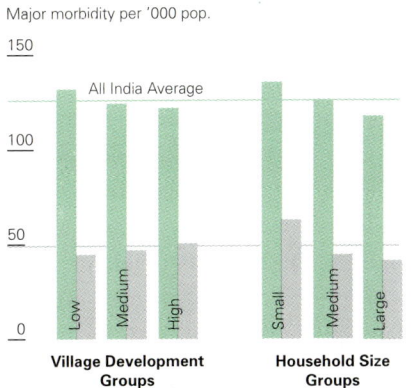

All India Average

150

100

50

0

Low   Medium   High

Small   Medium   Large

Village Development Groups

Household Size Groups

Among Social Groups

Short Duration   Major Morbidity

Major morbidity per '000 pop.

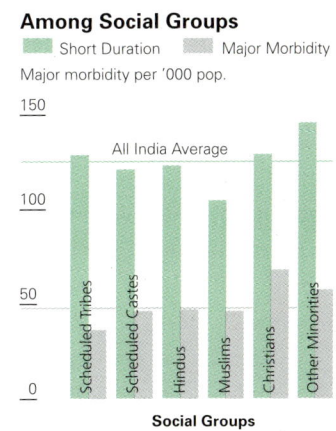

All India Average

150

100

50

0

Scheduled Tribes   Scheduled Castes   Hindus   Muslims   Christians   Other Minorities

Social Groups

higher. Age clearly is a factor that influences the prevalence of all types of major morbidity which is seen to increase with age.

Tuberculosis: A Special Focus

An effective public programme has been launched recently to tackle the management of this disease. There is paucity of dependable data for its planning. Survey estimates suggest that there were over 3.8 m individuals under treatment for tuberculosis across India during 1994. Indeed, the actual number of cases may be many times higher. A recent study estimated that over 13 m individuals suffer from tuberculosis in India, which may actually be closer to the truth.

The point prevalence of tuberculosis is high in Kerala, Andhra Pradesh, Tamil Nadu, Madhya Pradesh, West Bengal, and Bihar. In Kerala this estimate may partly be due to better reporting as well as better accessibility to health care services. The prevalence of tuberculosis is relatively low in the western states of Gujarat and Maharashtra, and in the North-east.

Tuberculosis has been found to be considerably higher among men in all states except Andhra Pradesh. The gender disparity is only 0.59. This may be largely due to under-reporting as well as non-treatment of tuberculosis among women.

Point prevalence of tuberculosis decreases substantially with a rise in household income but practically all the difference is due to the differential incidence among males. The incidence among women across household income classes remains unchanged. This pattern of gender differentials with regard to the incidence of tuberculosis is similar across other population group classifications as well. The prevalence of tuberculosis is higher among villages categorized as relatively less developed.

Household Expenditure on Treatment of Morbidiy

Average annual household (direct) expenditure on treating short duration morbidity per person and major illness per person, per sick person, and per reporting person is given in Table 7.3. Direct costs include expenditures only on doctor's fees and medicines, while total cost includes expenditure on travel and diet. Here only direct expenditures are discussed. Expenditure on short duration morbidity and major sickness worked out to Rs 121 and Rs 49 per person respectively. The cost per sick person and per reporting person in the case of major sickness was Rs 1,071 and Rs 1,217 respectively for rural India as a whole. Thus, a total of Rs 170 per person annually (per person expenditure on short duration and per person expenditure on major morbidity are additive) is spent on seeking treatment during a year. This amounts to an annual expenditure of Rs 969 per annum per household, which is about 3.4 per cent of average household income (Rs 25,653). The direct cost worked out to be about 75 per cent of all reported costs which included travel, board, and lodging expenses. Other expenditures were relatively high in Andhra Pradesh, Gujarat, and Madhya Pradesh, but least in Punjab.

While per person expenditure on Short Duration Morbidity (MPR–SD) was high in Himachal Pradesh, Punjab, Tamil Nadu, Andhra Pradesh, and

Incidence of tuberculosis is 32 per cent higher in the less developed villages whereas leprosy is 200 per cent higher.

The poorest of the poor (about 20 per cent of all households) spend about 20 per cent of their annual income on health care alone.

TABLE 7.3

Per Person Household Expenditure for Treatment of Illness and Gender Disparity by States

Regions/States	Cost of Short Illness		Cost of Long Illness			
	Fees and Medicines	Proportion of Total Cost	Fees and Medicines	Proportion of Total Cost	Per Sick	Per Reporting
North						
Haryana						
Person	105	0.76	57	0.66	861	884
Gender disparity	1.14	-	1.17	-	0.96	0.97
Punjab						
Person	203	0.92	114	0.73	1,703	1,847
Gender disparity	0.75	-	1.10	-	0.88	0.86
Upper Central						
Bihar						
Person	125	0.71	38	0.59	998	1,029
Gender disparity	1.15	-	0.64	-	0.85	0.83
Uttar Pradesh						
Person	127	0.81	62	0.68	1,775	1,917
Gender disparity	1.01	-	1.09	-	0.90	0.89
Lower Central						
Madhya Pradesh						
Person	121	0.68	29	0.60	622	689
Gender disparity	1.06	-	0.72	-	0.76	0.80
Orissa						
Person	75	0.76	15	0.48	311	569
Gender disparity	1.00	-	0.80	-	0.86	0.86
Rajasthan						
Person	156	0.83	50	0.57	1,593	1,735
Gender disparity	0.71	-	1.16	-	1.05	1.04
East						
North-eastern Rg.						
Person	107	0.68	22	0.65	741	768
Gender disparity	0.89	-	0.68	-	0.88	0.86
West Bengal						
Person	117	0.84	62	0.75	1,016	1,053
Gender disparity	0.98	-	0.82	-	0.86	0.86
West						
Gujarat						
Person	84	0.69	28	0.55	1,124	1,461
Gender disparity	1.05	-	0.50	-	0.68	0.68
Maharashtra						
Person	89	0.71	38	0.62	1,116	1,261
Gender disparity	0.93	-	1.01	-	0.96	0.96

(Contd.)

The cost of treatment is disproportionately high for children under the age of 5 and persons above 60 years of age.

South						
Andhra Pradesh						
Person	152	0.61	52	0.53	678	890
Gender disparity	0.89	-	0.82	-	0.93	1.01
Kerala						
Person	111	0.80	87	0.74	1,194	1,240
Gender disparity	0.90	-	1.05	-	0.90	0.87
Tamil Nadu						
Person	166	0.73	76	0.65	1,122	1,385
Gender disparity	0.85	-	0.97	-	0.89	0.90
All India						
Person	**121**	**0.75**	**49**	**0.65**	**1,071**	**1,217**
Gender disparity	**0.95**	**-**	**0.93**	**-**	**0.92**	**0.93**

Note: Estimates for the states of Himachal Pradesh and Karnataka are not presented here due to deficiency in data.

Health Expenditure

Household Expenditure for Treatment of Illness: Rural India

Short Illness   Long Illness

Expenditure (Rs) per person

All India Average

Ori   Guj   Mah   Har   N.E.R.   Ker   W.B.   M.P.   Bih   U.P.   A.P.   Raj   T.N.   Pun

Per Person Household Expenditure for Treatment of Long Illness

Cost Per Sick Person

Rs

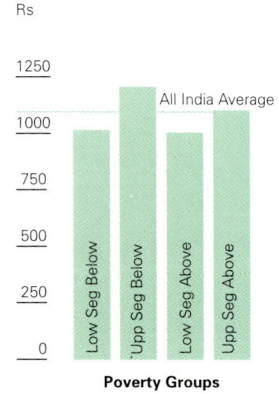

All India Average

Low Seg Below | Upp Seg Below | Low Seg Above | Upp Seg Above

Poverty Groups

Fees and Medicine

Rs

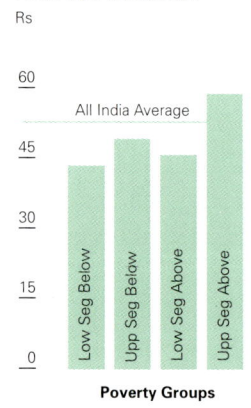

All India Average

Low Seg Below | Upp Seg Below | Low Seg Above | Upp Seg Above

Poverty Groups

Fees and Medicine

Rs

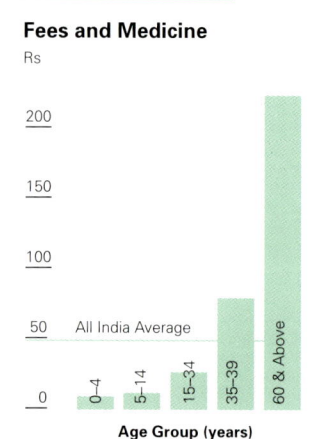

All India Average

0-4 | 5-14 | 15-34 | 35-39 | 60 & Above

Age Group (years)

Rajasthan, costs as well as gender disparity were high in Rajasthan, Punjab, and Andhra Pradesh.

Per person expenditure does not alter much according to household income or by land-holding category. However, the salaried and professionals spend larger amounts in comparison to wage earners, and expenditures are low among STs and high among Christians. While there is gender parity at lower levels of expenditure, higher expenditures are normally associated with high gender disparity, as in the case of Christians with a f/m ratio of 0.51. Expenditure is also higher among households having literate men and women. The level of expenditure does not show an association with level of village development. Cost of treatment, however, was disproportionately high for children under the age of 5 years and persons above 60 years of age (App. Table A.7.12).

There are noteworthy gender disparities in expenditure on health care. Household expenditure on health care is higher for males in the early ages which subsequently falls and increases again as age increases. While 10 per cent higher expenditure is incurred on males in the age group 0–4 years, it declines to less than 5 per cent in the middle years and increases to 11 per cent in the 60 and above age group.

Although the richer classes spend more in absolute terms, they spend an insignificant proportion in relation to their household income. For example, households having an annual income of above Rs 86,000 spend only 0.6 per cent; those who have an income between Rs 62,000 and Rs 82,000 and between Rs 40,000 and Rs 62,000 spend just about 1.6 per cent; and those in the income group of Rs 20,000 to 40,000 spend 3.7 per cent. The less than Rs 20,000 income category households spend 8.3 per cent of their household income on treatment of illnesses. This clearly underscores the importance and need for public health services for the poorer sections of the population (App. Table A.7.12).

Treatment costs per person for major morbidity were found to be Rs 65 for rural India as a whole. This is because of the lower prevalence of morbidity rather than cheaper cost of health care. However, cost of treatment was considerably higher in West Bengal, Punjab, and Kerala, but low in Orissa, Rajasthan, Andhra Pradesh and Madhya Pradesh. The low cost of treatment may be due to poor quality of services available in these states. The cost of treatment per sick person and per reporting person worked out to Rs 1,071 and Rs 1,217 respectively. Costs per reporting person were as high as Rs 1,847, Rs 1,735, and Rs 1,461 in Punjab, Rajasthan, and Gujarat respectively. The high cost of treatment could be due to both the extended duration of illness and the high cost of medication.

The cost of treatment of major morbidity increases substantially as household income increases; this is true of all types of cost estimates presented in App. Table A.7.12. Landholding does not generally have an association with expenditure, and those from salaried and professional services spend relatively larger sums on medication. Christians spend considerably larger amounts followed by Muslims for treating major morbidity. Since morbidity prevalence rates are low among the younger age

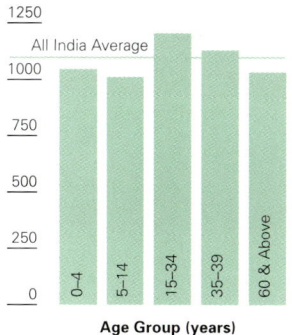

Cost Per Sick Person

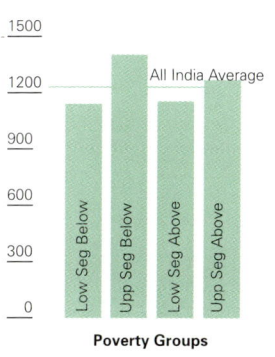

Cost Per Reporting

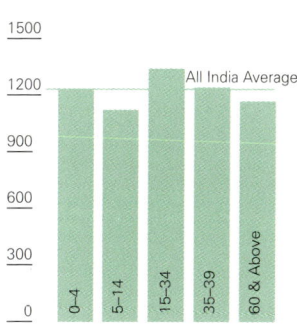

Cost Per Reporting

Fees and Medicine

Rs

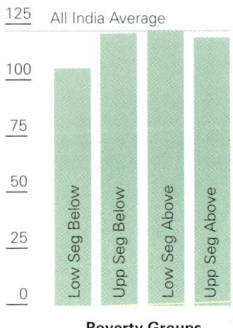

Poverty Groups

Fees and Medicine

Rs

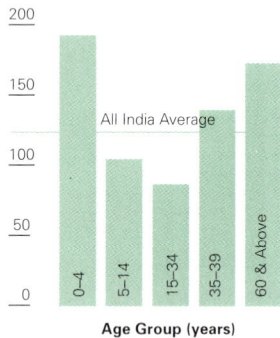

Age Group (years)

The results of this survey show high gender disparities in the incidence of sickness, cost of treatment, and incidence of disabilities.

groups, per person expenditure is also low with high levels for treatment of the aged. However, the expenditure per sick person or per reporting person shows that cost of treatment increases up to the age of about 35 years and then falls. Expenditure is high among men and women in the working age group and gender disparity is relatively low. On the other hand, cost of treatment for infants and the very old is relatively low with high levels of gender disparity.

The proportion of expenditure on doctor's fees and medicines alone works out to about 75 per cent of the total reported cost in the case of short duration morbidity and 65 per cent in the case of major morbidity (Table 7.3). Given the above pattern of expenditure, it is estimated that about Rs 1,20,000 m out of pocket expenditure is incurred towards medical care in rural India alone. Suffice it to say that in spite of the health care services in India, the household expenditure on treatment of sickness is substantial. A large private market for health care is therefore thriving. Cuts in public expenditure as a result of structural adjustment and privatization of health care will adversely affect the relatively poor and vulnerable. This points to the urgent need to regulate the private health care market in India.

It can be inferred from the above findings that in India the burden of both short duration and major morbidity falls on the vulnerable sections of the population, including wage labourers, minorities, and the low income groups. Inter-state variations are complex while geographic and seasonal patterns of morbidity further complicate the overall picture and require deeper investigation.

Prevalence of Physical Disability

In this survey the incidence of various types of physical disability, such as bitot spot, night blindness, and impairments related to the visual, auditory, vocal and locomotor systems, are presented for children up to the age of 12 years. The incidence of any type of physical disability (excluding bitot spot) worked out to 2,042 per lakh among the 0–4 years age group and 2,896 per lakh children among the 5–12 years age group (App. A.7.13). The prevalence of physical disabilities among the young is over 70 per cent that in older age groups. This suggests that most physical disabilities are genetic, biological, and even birth defects, and future research must focus on the causes of such disabilities among the very young population in India.

There are wide variations across states as regards the prevalence of physical disability. Disability estimates are low in Kerala and Gujarat among the 0–4 years age group but high in Bihar and West Bengal. The apparently low prevalence in Orissa may be due to reporting errors. Among the 5–12 years age-group the prevalence was as high as 6,779 per lakh in West Bengal, 4,670 in Himachal Pradesh, and 4,519 in Tamil Nadu. This rate was considerably lower in Haryana, the North-eastern states, Gujarat, Karnataka, and Kerala. On the whole, the reporting of physical disability was higher for boys; under-reporting in the case of girls may be due to cultural factors.

Bitot spot in the eyes is a manifestation of extreme malnutrition due to

Among Poverty Groups

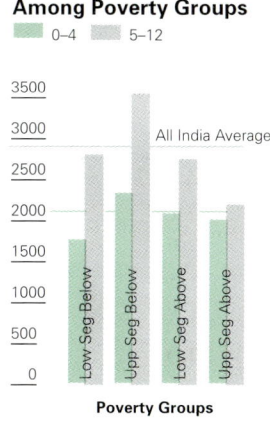

Poverty Groups

Among Social Groups

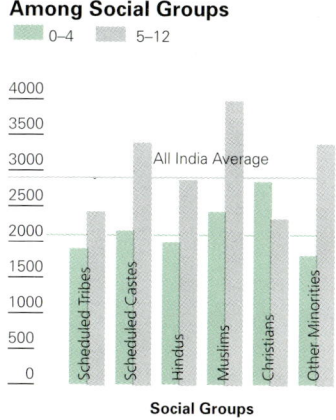

Social Groups

Among Village Development Groups

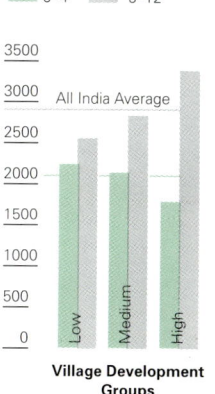

Village Development
Groups

calorie and protein deficiencies. For rural India as a whole the prevalence of bitot spot is 1,136 and 2,090 per lakh population in the 0–4 and 5–12 years age group respectively. The prevalence of bitot spots was high in Madhya Pradesh and Rajasthan among the 0–4 years age group; and in Rajasthan, Himachal Pradesh, and Tamil Nadu among the 5–12 years age group. There have been almost no incidences of bitot spots in Kerala and Punjab in either of the age groups mentioned above, reflecting both the availability of food and also the food habits of both adults and children in these two states. Crude estimates of the size of population suffering from physical impairments and disabilities are presented in Box 7.2.

No clear association seems to exist between physical disability and most of the population groups. What appears to be the only trend is the somewhat higher incidence among the non-landowning classes, especially wage earners. The incidence of different kinds of physical disability is presented in App. Table A.7.14 which shows some association with the caste affiliation of households. Physical disability is much higher among SCs in the 0–4 years and the 5–12 years age groups, i.e. 2,058 and 3,325 disabled children per lakh children respectively. As far as religion is concerned, one finds a relatively high incidence among Christians (2,711), followed by Muslims (2,409) in the 0–4 years age group. However, in the higher age group (5 to 12 years), the incidence is much higher (3,792 per lakh children) among Muslims. The reasons for this need further investigation. The prevalence of bitot has a very clear association with income. It is 162 per cent higher among the less than Rs 20,000 income category and 140 per cent higher in the 0–4 and 5–12 years age groups respectively. Prevalence of bitot is high among the landless, the wage earners, and SCs.

All India (Age 0–12 years)

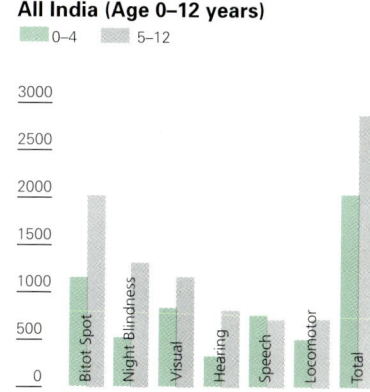

Disabilities

BOX 7.2

Crude Estimates of the Size of Population Suffering from Various Forms of Disabilities in India

	0–4 Years Old (millions)	5–12 Years Old (millions)	All Children up to 12 years (millions)
Bitot Spot	2.3	4.2	6.5
Physical disability	3.6	5.1	8.7
Visual impairment	0.9	2.3	3.2
Hearing impairment	0.3	1.5	1.8
Speech impediment	0.6	0.8	1.4
Locomotor disability	0.4	1.0	1.4
Total	**8.1**	**14.9**	**23.0**

Note: Disability estimates are arrived at by applying the survey rates to the total projected population in the respective ages. [Children in age group 0–4 years and 5–12 years numbered about 110 m and 200 m respectively in 1993–4.]

Principal Findings

I Morbidity

1   Short duration morbidity for rural India is 122 per '000 population. STs have the highest prevalence of diarrhoea and fever. Diarrhoea is low among women and decreases with rising income, literacy rate of adults in the household, and level of development of the village. Prevalence of coughs and colds is highest among children and the elderly while prevalence of fever is more or less the same across all ages.

2   About 41 m people suffer from major morbidity at a given point of time in rural India. The prevalence ratio is highest for hypertension (589 per lakh persons) followed by tuberculosis (423 per lakh population). By state, it is higher in the southern states, Uttar Pradesh, Bihar, and Rajasthan. Both short-term morbidity and major morbidity are disproportionately higher among the vulnerable population groups including wage labourers, minorities, and those with low levels of income.

3   On an average, rural households spend 4 per cent of household income on treatment of common ailments but the poor spend about 9 per cent of their income. This is despite the delivery of free health care services by the government. Over 3.8 m people are under treatment for tuberculosis (1994) across India. The prevalence of tuberculosis is high in Kerala, Andhra Pradesh, Tamil Nadu, Madhya Pradesh, West Bengal, and Bihar, and low in Gujarat, Maharashtra, and the North-eastern states.

II Disability

4   About 2,042 per lakh children in the 0–4 year age group and about 2,896 per lakh children in the 5–12 year age group suffer from physical disabilities in India. Children from families of wage earners and minorities have a higher incidence of disability.

Demographic Parameters and Reproductive Health Care

This chapter deals with demographic parameters such as fertility and mortality, maternal and child health care services, and the use of family planning methods. The parameters discussed in this section can be termed as enabling factors to achieve higher levels of human development. The survey results bring to the fore very low levels of reproductive health care in India.

Fertility

This survey collected information from women in the reproductive age groups regarding number of births and deaths in households in the course of one year from the date of commencement of the survey. The data were used to compute crude birth rate, total fertility rate, and crude death rate using the standard definitions.

A widely used fertility measure is crude birth rate (CBR) which is defined as the number of live births in a given period for a total population of one thousand. For rural India as a whole, the CBR worked out to be 32 live births per thousand population per year (Table 8.1). The CBR varies considerably among states. The rate is highest in Rajasthan at 44 per thousand population and ranges between 32 and 38 per thousand population in Uttar Pradesh, Bihar, West Bengal, the North-eastern states, and Madhya Pradesh. The CBR in the southern states is relatively low ranging from 21 in Kerala to 28 per thousand in Tamil Nadu, compared to the Upper and Lower Central states. This low CBR among the southern

Crude Birth and Death Rates

Among Poverty Groups
Births/Deaths per '000 pop.

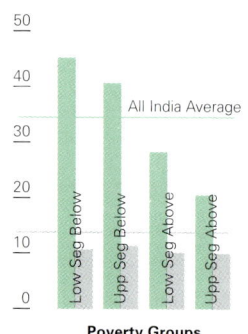

Poverty Groups

Among States: All India
■ CBR ■ CDR
Births and deaths per '000 pop.

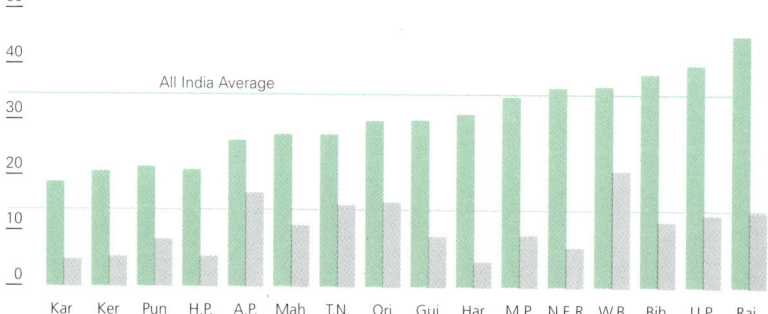

TABLE 8.1

Fertility Rates by States

Regions/ States	CBR			TFR(15-49)		Ave. Children Ever Born: EMW			EMW 40-9
	HDI (1994)	NFHS1 (1990–2)	SRS2 (1991–2)	HDI (1994)	NFHS (1990–2)	HDI (1994) Boys	(All) Girls	All	All
North									
Haryana	30	35	33	4.2	4.3	1.6	1.4	3.0	4.7
Himachal Pradesh	22	29	-	2.7	3.1	1.5	1.4	2.8	4.8
Punjab	22	24	28	3.1	3.1	1.6	1.4	3.0	4.9
Upper Central									
Bihar	37	31	31	5.3	4.1	1.7	1.3	3.0	4.5
Uttar Pradesh	38	38	36	5.9	5.2	1.7	1.5	3.1	5.1
Lower Central									
Madhya Pradesh	32	33	36	4.3	4.1	1.5	1.4	2.9	4.8
Orissa	29	27	29	3.7	3.0	1.5	1.4	2.9	4.2
Rajasthan	44	28	35	6.8	3.9	1.6	1.4	3.0	5.5
East									
North-eastern Rg.	34	-	-	3.9	3.4	1.7	1.1	2.8	4.1
West Bengal	34	28	27	4.3	3.3	1.6	1.5	3.1	5.5
West									
Gujarat	29	28	28	3.7	3.2	1.4	1.2	2.7	3.6
Maharashtra	28	26	26	3.7	3.1	1.5	1.4	2.9	4.4
South									
Andhra Pradesh	26	25	26	3.1	2.7	1.3	1.2	2.5	4.0
Karnataka	25	28	27	2.4	3.1	1.5	1.4	2.8	4.5
Kerala	21	20	18	2.2	2.1	1.2	1.1	2.3	3.8
Tamil Nadu	28	24	21	3.0	2.5	1.3	1.2	2.5	4.2
All India	**32**	**30**	**30**	**4.3**	**3.7**	**1.5**	**1.3**	**2.9**	**4.6**

Notes:
1. National Family Health Survey, *India Report, 1992–3* (figures are averages of a three year period).IIPS, Bombay, 1995.
2. Registrar General, Sample Registration System, 1991–2.
3. Average of three other southern states.

Among Village Development and Household Size Groups
Births/Deaths per '000 pop.

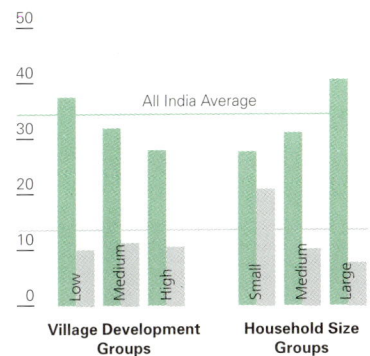

Among Social Groups
Births/Deaths per '000 pop.

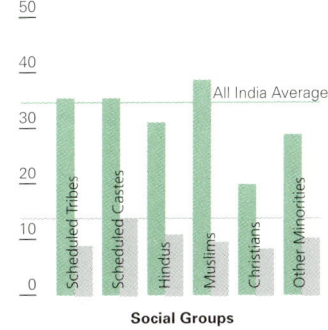

states may be due to higher age at marriage, higher levels of female literacy, and the wider use of contraception among the population. CBRs estimated in this survey are somewhat higher than those provided by the National Family Health Survey (NFHS) in 1990–2 and the Sample Registration System (SRS) in 1991–2, both of which give 30 as the CBR. The NFHS estimate of the CBR in Rajasthan appears to be particularly low. However, all sources are united in suggesting that the fertility rates in the central states are high and continue to be at levels prevailing in the south during the 1960s. There are substantial demographic lags in the backward states situated in central India.

CBR has the advantage of being easy to calculate, but is inadequate for depicting underlying fertility patterns associated with the age of women. Hence, more sophisticated measures, namely, total fertility rates (TFRs) were computed. The TFR is obtained by calculating age-specific fertility levels using current data. Thus TFR is an age-adjusted measure that represents the total number of children a woman would have borne during her reproductive span, assuming that the age-specific fertility rates (ASFRs) computed from current data are given. The estimated TFR was 4.3, which is slightly higher than the TFR (3.99) provided by the SRS. The differences in TFR estimates between states and population groups could partly be due to differences in the age profiles of eligible women.

There are significant inter-state variations in the total fertility rate (TFR). As in the case of CBR, all the southern states and Punjab and Himachal Pradesh have lower TFRs. The average for rural India as a whole is 4.3. Maharashtra and Gujarat have fertility rates that are much lower than the national average, while the TFR is as high as 6.8 in Rajasthan, 5.9 in Uttar Pradesh, 5.3 in Bihar. As in the case of CBR, it is likely that the variations in the TFR are associated with levels of female education, age at marriage, and use of family planning measures, besides age structure of women in the reproductive age group.

TFR appears to be underestimated in Rajasthan by the NFHS. The NCAER/HDI survey estimated were CBR 44 per thousand, and TFR as 6.8

Fertility rates in the central parts of India encompassing UP, Bihar, Rajasthan, and Madhya Pradesh are high and continue to be at levels prevailing in the south during the 1960s.

Total Fertility Rate

Among States: All India

Children per Woman (15–49 age group)

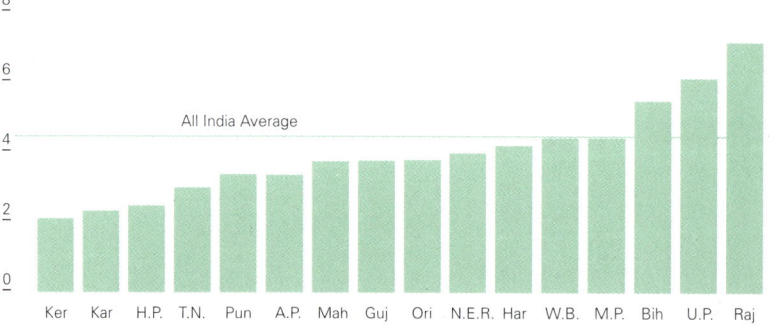

All India Average

Ker Kar H.P. T.N. Pun A.P. Mah Guj Ori N.E.R. Har W.B. M.P. Bih U.P. Raj

BOX 8.1

Distribution of Major States according to Levels of Fertility Transition

CBR - 21–28 per thousand population:

NCAER   Kerala, Karnataka, Andhra Pradesh, Tamil Nadu, Maharashtra, Himachal Pradesh, and Punjab.

NFHS   Kerala, Karnataka, Andhra Pradesh, Tamil Nadu, Maharashtra, Gujarat, Orissa, Rajasthan, West Bengal, and Punjab.

SRS   Kerala, Karnataka, Andhra Pradesh, Tamil Nadu, Maharashtra, West Bengal, Gujarat, and Punjab

CBR - 29–33 per thousand population:

NCAER   Madhya Pradesh, Orissa, Gujarat, and Haryana

NFHS   Bihar, Madhya Pradesh, and Himachal Pradesh

SRS   Orissa, Bihar, and Haryana.

CBR - 34–44 per thousand population:

NCAER   Rajasthan, Uttar Pradesh, Bihar, the North-east, and West Bengal

NFHS   Uttar Pradesh and Haryana

SRS   Rajasthan, Uttar Pradesh, and Madhya Pradesh

Among Poverty Groups
Children per Woman (15–49 age group)

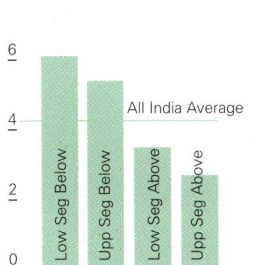

Poverty Groups

Among Village Development and Household Size Groups
Children per woman (15–49 age group)

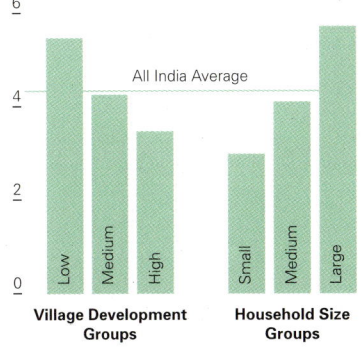

Village Development Groups   Household Size Groups

Among Social Groups
Children per woman (15–49 age group)

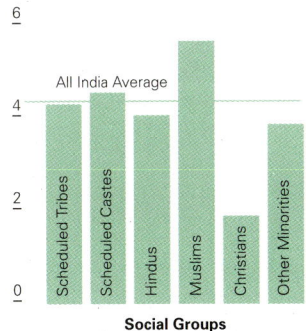

Social Groups

per thousand children, as compared to a CBR of 28 and TFR of 3.9 by the NFHS. The survey had problems arriving at fertility estimates for the state of Karnataka. Although the imputed average of three other states, Andhra Pradesh, Kerala, and Tamil Nadu, are included in the CBR values, the TFRs are unadjusted and therefore underestimated in Karnataka.

Data on lifetime births for all currently married women interviewed during the survey were collected. One way of validating TFRs is by comparing the mean number of children ever born (MCEB). This average for all the ever married women is about 3 children and for women aged 40–9 it is 4.3 children for rural India as a whole which compares well with the TFR for rural India (*see* Table 8.1). The MCEB for 40–9-year-olds can be compared with the TFR although the latter is based on current data, whereas the MCEB is based on lifetime experience.

Thus all the three indicators of fertility (two based on current and the other on cumulative fertility) point to various levels of demographic transition among the states. Box 8.1 presents states in various levels of fertility transition.

Crude Birth Rate: Table 8.2 presents the CBR and TFR for the eight population groups created in this survey. The CBR declines considerably as household income increases. For example, the CBR is as high as 37 per thousand for the low income group and decreases to 28, 27, 25, and 24 per thousand population respectively in the four subsequent income groups.

TABLE 8.2

Fertility Rates by Population Groups in Rural India

A high crude birth rate can be associated with low levels of living and low levels of literacy among social groups.

Population Groups	CBR per '000	TFR (15–49)	Ave. Children Ever Born to Ever Married Women		
			Boys	Girls	Total
Household Income Groups					
Up to 20,000	37	4.9	1.5	1.4	2.9
20001–40,000	28	3.8	1.6	1.3	2.8
40001–62,000	27	3.5	1.5	1.3	2.8
62001–86,000	25	3.2	1.4	1.2	2.6
Above 86,000	24	3.2	1.4	1.3	2.7
Landholding Groups					
Landless wage earner	35	4.4	1.5	1.3	2.8
Marginal	33	4.4	1.5	1.4	2.9
Small	30	4.2	1.6	1.3	2.9
Medium	31	4.3	1.5	1.3	2.8
Large	31	4.2	1.5	1.3	2.8
Landless others	31	4.1	1.6	1.4	2.9
Landowners	32	4.3	1.5	1.3	2.9
Landless	33	4.2	1.5	1.3	2.9
Occupational Groups					
Cultivators	30	4.2	1.5	1.3	2.9
Salaried+Prof.+S.Empl.	31	4.0	1.5	1.3	2.8
Wage earners	35	4.4	1.5	1.3	2.8
All others	33	4.5	1.6	1.4	3.0
Social Groups					
Caste					
STs	35	4.4	1.6	1.4	3.0
SCs	35	4.7	1.6	1.4	2.9
Religion					
Hindus	32	4.2	1.5	1.3	2.8
Muslims	39	5.8	1.8	1.5	3.4
Christians	20	2.1	1.2	1.1	2.4
Other Minorities	28	3.9	1.6	1.4	3.0
Household Size Groups					
Up to 4	27	2.9	1.1	0.9	2.0
5–7	29	4.1	1.7	1.5	3.2
8 and above	40	5.6	1.6	1.4	3.0
Poverty Line Groups					
Lower segment below	45	6.4	1.7	1.6	3.3
Upper segment below	41	5.5	1.6	1.4	3.1
Lower segment above	28	3.6	1.5	1.2	2.7
Upper segment above	21	2.7	1.4	1.1	2.5
Adult Literacy Groups					
None literate	38	5.3	1.6	1.4	3.0
Female literate	25	2.9	1.3	1.6	2.9

Contd.

Male literate	32	5.0	1.7	1.4	3.0
Both literate	29	3.3	1.4	1.3	2.6
Village Development Groups					
Low	37	5.3	1.6	1.4	3.0
Medium	31	4.2	1.5	1.3	2.9
High	28	3.5	1.5	1.3	2.8
All India	**32**	**4.3**	**1.5**	**1.3**	**2.9**

Landed households irrespective of their land size, with an exception of marginal landholding, have similar levels of fertility. The real differential appears to be between the landless wage earners and the landed. For example, the landless have a CBR of 35 per thousand and all landowners together (including marginal farmers) have a birth rate of 32 per thousand.

Information on social groups has been disaggregated at two levels: by caste affiliation of the head of the household among Hindus; and by religious affiliation of the head of the household. The CBR among STs and SCs is high at 35 per thousand population. Among religious groups, Hindus have a CBR of 32, Muslims a high 39, whereas among Christians it is 20 per thousand population. A high CBR may be associated with low levels of living and low levels of literacy among these social categories.

This is vindicated when one studies CBRs according to poverty and adult literacy categories. Very high CBRs exist among households categorized as lower segment below the poverty line with 45 per thousand population and 41 per thousand population among the higher segment below the poverty line. This indicates that either the child survival rate is low or the belief that the more children the better is still considered an asset. This relationship demands further investigation, especially the impact of poverty on fertility and demographic transition.

The CBR also varies according to the level of village development and household size. The CBR falls as village development increases, and is relatively high among the large households. The relationship between household size and CBR is well understood after controlling age structure of Ever Married Women (EMW).

A more detailed picture may be obtained from App. Tables A.8.1 and A.8.2 which present inter-group variations by state in TFR and CBR. At the all India level, there is not much change in CBR as household income increases. However, there are wide inter-state variations. In almost all the southern states except Kerala, and also in Maharashtra, the North-east, and Haryana, we find that the CBR decreases with an increase in household income whereas in Kerala and Gujarat, it increases with household income. It may also be noted that in other central Indian states, the CBR seems to be indifferent to an increase in household income. The state-wise analysis of CBR vis-à-vis social categories and village development category shows a picture broadly similar to the all India level.

It is a well known biological fact that fertility increases up to a certain age and then starts to decline. An estimation of this trend is found in the age-specific fertility rate. The ASFR increases steeply in the early years and

Crude birth rate falls as village development increases and is relatively high among large households.

TABLE 8.3
Age-specific Fertility Rates in Rural India

Age Groups	Fertility Rates						
	SRS (1971–5)	SRS (1976–80)	SRS (1986)	SRS (1990)	SRS (1990–2)	NFHS (1990–2)	HDI (1994)
15–19	0.107	0.096	0.100	0.093	0.087	0.131	0.065
20–24	0.260	0.257	0.265	0.250	0.248	0.243	0.271
25–29	0.258	0.244	0.229	0.210	0.204	0.177	0.245
30–34	0.204	0.180	0.154	0.135	0.130	0.108	0.146
35–39	0.136	0.112	0.089	0.082	0.078	0.051	0.082
40–44	0.063	0.052	0.044	0.036	0.036	0.019	0.028
45–49	0.026	0.019	0.018	0.015	0.014	0.012	0.018
TFR	5.2*	4.6**	4.5	4.1	4.00	3.7	4.3
GFR	159*	137**	166	133	129	133	132
CBR	37.2	34.7	34.2	31.7	32.2	29.6	32.0

Note: NFHS and SRS figures are averages for the respective periods.
* refers to 1974 ** refers to 1978
Source for 1974 and 1978: RGCC, *Levels, Trends and Differentials in Fertility*, 1979, Vital Statistics Division, Registrar General, New Delhi.

The pattern of early child-bearing is consistent in all of rural India.

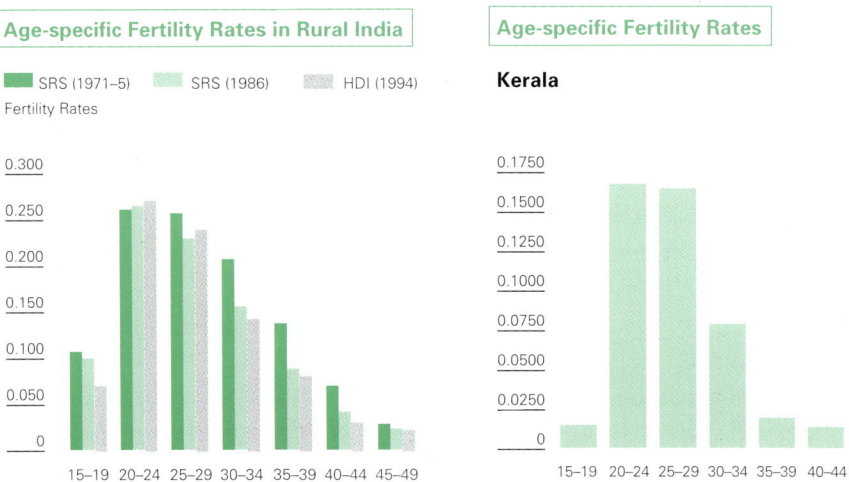

Age-specific Fertility Rates in Rural India

■ SRS (1971–5)   ▨ SRS (1986)   ▨ HDI (1994)

Age-specific Fertility Rates

Kerala

then begins to fall usually in the 20–24 age group, and declines sharply in the late 30s age group. This suggests a pattern of early childbearing which is consistent in all of rural India. One may obtain a temporal trend in age-specific fertility rates from 1971 to 1994 from Table 8.3, although the shape of the curve has remained almost unchanged with only a marginal decline over a period of three decades.

App. Table A.8.4 presents inter-state variations in age-specific fertility rates (*see* Table 8.3). It is apparent that in spite of differentials in levels of fertility, the fertility schedule (slope) is similar in almost all states as is the trend for rural India as a whole. The levels of age-specific fertility are lower for Kerala, Andhra Pradesh, and Tamil Nadu as compared to Bihar, Rajasthan, and Haryana. This reinforces the differential fertility pattern across the country discussed above.

Age-specific Fertility Rates by Population Groups

Age in Completed Years 15–19

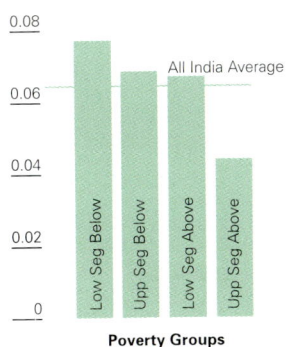

Poverty Groups

Age in Completed Years 20–24

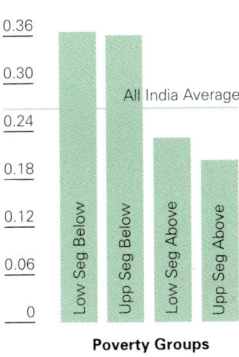

Poverty Groups

Age in Completed Years 25–29

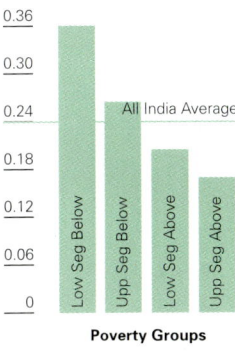

Poverty Groups

Age in Completed Years 30–34

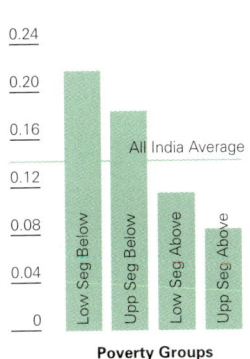

Poverty Groups

Age in Completed Years 35–39

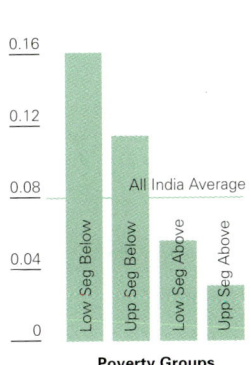

Poverty Groups

Age in Completed Years 40–44

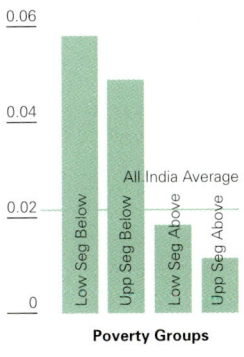

Poverty Groups

Age-specific fertility rates by population group are presented in App. Table A.8.5. The fertility rate is high for younger women in low income categories. This may be partly due to early age at marriage and also non-use of contraception in these early years of the reproductive cycle. Significant variations exist in the landholding categories where landless households show much higher levels of childbearing during the early years in comparison with the landed households.

Data by caste reveal that the ASFRs are high in the younger age groups among SCs in comparison with STs. According to religious groups, however, ASFRs are high among Muslims, and low among Christians, indicating births at relatively later ages due to the higher age at marriage among them.

Mortality

Table 8.4 depicts various indicators of mortality, namely crude death rate (CDR), infant mortality rate (IMR), and mortality of children under 5 years of age (U5 mortality), for the country as a whole and also for different states. While the CDR has been calculated using the standard definition during the one year reference period, the IMR and U5 mortality have been

Age in Completed Years 45–49

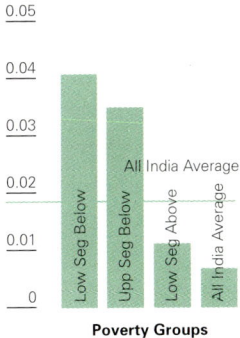

Poverty Groups

Age in Completed Years 15–19

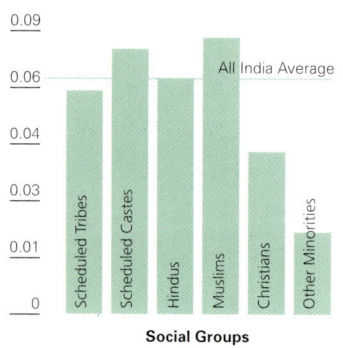

Age in Completed Years 20–24

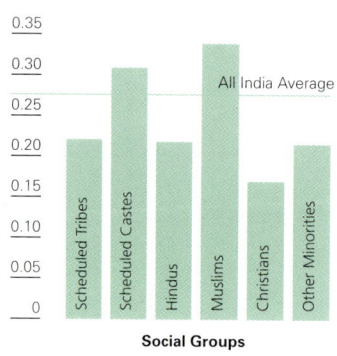

Age in Completed Years 25–29

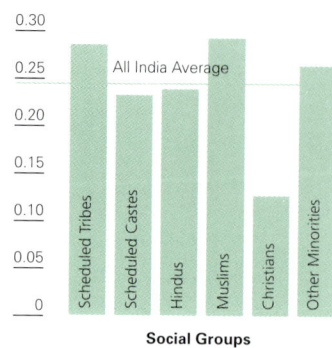

Age in Completed Years 30–34

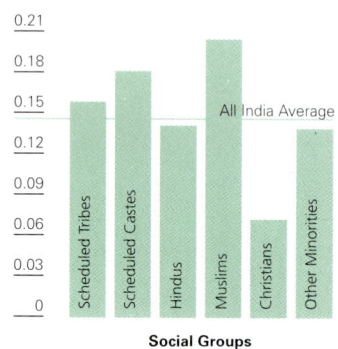

Age in Completed Years 35–39

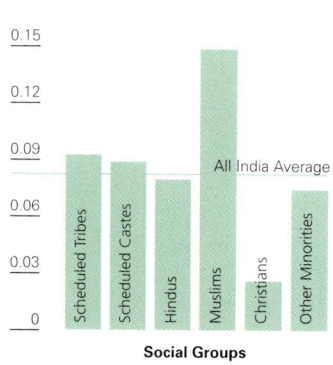

Age in Completed Years 40–44

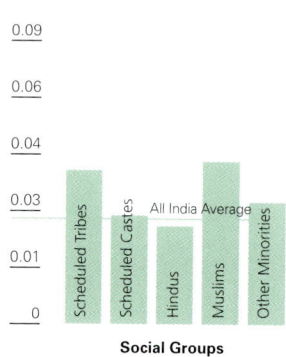

Age in Completed Years 45–49

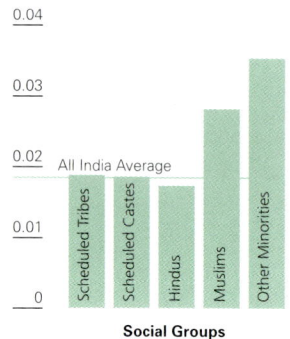

estimated using the lifetime experience of ever married women (EMW) with children who died before completing infancy and 5 years respectively. This, lifetime IMR and U5 mortality is presented according to the marital duration of ever married women. Thus while death rates are based on current data, the IMR and U5 mortality are useful only to understand the time trend rather than the actual levels of the respective parameters. As this survey was a multipurpose one, it was not designed exclusively to estimate sensitive and difficult parameters such as infant mortality and U5 mortality.

The CDR for rural India worked out to 11.1 per thousand population (according to this survey) which is the same as the SRS estimates (11 for the year 1991–2). The estimated CDR for the state of West Bengal was unreasonably high and is therefore suppressed in the estimates presented in Table 8.4. A low CDR was recorded in the states of Kerala, Karnataka, Haryana, and Himachal Pradesh whereas the CDR was as high as 16 in Andhra Pradesh, 13 in Orissa, and 12 in Tamil Nadu and Rajasthan.

The CDR is strongly related to level of household income. For example, the rich have a CDR of 7 per thousand compared with 13 per thousand for low income households. Similarly, landowners have lower levels of CDR in comparison with landless wage earners who recorded a higher level of CDR (14 per thousand population). The CDR is high among SCs and low among Christians. Surprisingly, the death rate is high among small households in

TABLE 8.4

Mortality Rates by States

Regions/States	HDI[1] (1994)	CDR SRS (1991–2)	CDR NFHS (1991–2)	Infant Mortality Marital Duration of EMW (0–9)	(10–19)	(20+)	All	SRS (19–92)	NFHS[2] (19–92)	U5 Mortality Marital Duration Of EMW (0–9)	(10–19)	(20+)	All	NFHS (19–92)
North														
Haryana	5	9	9	50	63	69	63	73	73	73	90	114	97	99
Himachal Pradesh	6	-	9	65	66	74	70	78	56	78	97	115	101	69
Punjab	9	9	7	67	68	79	71	58	54	81	97	120	102	68
Upper Central														
Bihar	10	11	12	54	63	76	67	71	89	88	113	128	115	127
Uttar Pradesh	11	14	13	87	88	112	99	102	99	108	122	157	137	141
Lower Central														
Madhya Pradesh	9	14	11	111	118	131	122	125	85	132	157	176	160	130
Orissa	13	12	12	86	91	122	105	129	112	105	117	159	135	131
Rajasthan	12	11	8	66	99	127	107	84	72	92	128	158	136	102
East														
North-eastern Rg.	7	11	12	25	42	52	39	83	-	34	54	69	51	-
West Bengal	21*	9	10	76	84	133	106	76	75	104	108	175	139	99
West														
Gujarat	8	10	10	61	62	50	57	73	69	77	78	73	76	104
Maharashtra	11	9	8	76	75	97	85	69	51	88	95	137	112	70
South														
Andhra Pradesh	16	10	9	58	62	72	66	77	70	66	91	111	96	91
Karnataka	5	9	8	50	55	57	55	87	65	61	74	81	75	87
Kerala	5	6	6	24	20	35	26	17	24	33	33	54	40	32
Tamil Nadu	12	9	11	62	92	104	91	65	68	66	117	148	119	87
All India	**11**	**11**	**10**	**67**	**77**	**97**	**84**	**87**	**79**	**85**	**108**	**138**	**117**	**109**
C.V.	38.5	-	-	33.2	31.4	35.2	33.4	-	-	31.1	29.2	30	30.1	-

Notes:
1. HDI, IMR and U5 mortality rates are according to marital duration of ever married women (in years).
2. NFHS figures are averages for the respective periods.
3. * Shows that the estimates are not reliable.

comparison with large ones comprising eight members and above. This may be due to the relatively larger number of children found in smaller households. The CDR does not vary by poverty group categorization. However, literacy of adults, both males and females, contributes to a low CDR. It may be noted that the village development categories do not show any consistent relationship with the CDR (App. Table A.8.6).

Infant mortality rate in this survey refers to all deaths that take place during the lifetime of EMW before a child has completed one year. These estimates are useful in support of a secular decline in IMR over the past 2–3 decades. These figures do not present the levels of the IMR and should therefore not be used as the estimates for the survey year 1994.

This estimate takes into account all births during the lifetime of a woman and computes rates according to marital duration. The rates for women

BOX 8.2

Distribution of Major States by Levels of Mortality Transition

CDR - from 5–8 per thousand population:

NCAER   Kerala, Karnataka, Gujarat, N.E.R, Himachal Pradesh, and Haryana

NFHS   Kerala, Karnataka, Maharashtra, Rajasthan, Himachal Pradesh and Punjab

SRS   Kerala

CDR - from 9–12 per thousand population:

NCAER   Uttar Pradesh, Bihar, Rajasthan, Punjab, Maharashtra, Tamil Nadu, and Madhya Pradesh.

NFHS   Andhra Pradesh, Bihar, Madhya Pradesh, Orissa, Haryana, North-eastern region, West Bengal, Gujarat, and Tamil Nadu

SRS   Bihar, Rajasthan, Orissa, North eastern region, Gujarat, Andhra Pradesh, Haryana, Punjab, West Bengal, Maharashtra, Tamil Nadu, and Karnataka

CDR - 13 per thousand population and above:

NCAER   Andhra Pradesh, Orissa, and West Bengal

NFHS   Uttar Pradesh

SRS   Madhya Pradesh and Uttar Pradesh.

Crude death rate does not vary by poverty group. Literacy of adults, both men and women, contributes to low CDR.

with a marital duration of 10 to 19 years and 20 years and above have been discussed. However, IMRs thus estimated in Table 8.4 are presented along with the rates available from the SRS and NFHS for 1991–92 and 1987–92 respectively. The purpose is not to compare or highlight declines in IMR but to only point out a temporal trend and discuss the relative position of states in terms of mortality transition.

Overall, IMRs thus collected are 97 and 77 per thousand live births respectively. Although these figures appear to be underestimates, what is consistent is a decline in both the IMR and U5 mortality over the past two decades or so. Actual IMRs from the SRS are about 87 and 79 respectively during the late 80s and early 90s. The pattern is similar for U5 mortality.

Contraceptive Prevalence Rate (CPR)

Prevailing trends and patterns of 'ever use' of modern contraceptives among all currently married women aged 13–49 years were collected in this survey. CPRs estimated using these data are discussed below.

Overall, 36 per cent of eligible women reported having used some method of contraception (Table 8.5). This compares well with the NFHS estimates. A disaggregation according to methods used suggested that about

30 per cent of married women were using terminal methods such as tubectomy and laparoscopy or their husbands had undergone vasectomy. The proportion of males who had undergone vasectomy to those who had used permanent methods was about 8 per cent. The CPR for spacing through the use of IUDs, oral pills, and conventional contraceptives was 6 per cent. This survey gives a relatively higher CPR for spacing methods as compared with NFHS estimates.

There are wide variations in CPRs between states. The CPR is generally higher than the national average in all the southern and western states, and in the northern states of Haryana, Himachal Pradesh, and Punjab. The use of family planning methods is extremely low in Bihar (20 per cent), Uttar Pradesh (18 per cent), and Rajasthan (28 per cent).

India's family planning programme has consistently been criticized for excessive dependence on terminal methods. This is evident across states and states that exhibit relatively higher use of spacing methods such as Kerala and Punjab. States with a higher proportion of spacing methods even when the prevalence rates are low are Uttar Pradesh and Madhya Pradesh. The estimates of this survey generally confirm the NFHS estimates and NSSO (1986–7) results with a few exceptions.[1]

The use of family planning methods (Table 8.6) shows little association with household income. CPR is higher among the salaried categories as compared to wage earners and the agricultural community. As far as religious groups are concerned, contraception is practiced least among Muslims (CPR of 25 per cent). Among Christians, the CPR is 50 while Hindus have lower CPRs. The use of family planning measures shows a positive and significant association with adult literacy and village development. A more detailed picture, however, emerges in App. Tables A.8.7 to A.8.9.

The proportion of non-users along with dominant reasons for non-use of contraceptives are presented in App. Table A.8.10. The most frequent reasons are demand related and include current pregnancy and desire for children of unspecified sex. However, 14 per cent of all non-users expressed

Among Social Groups

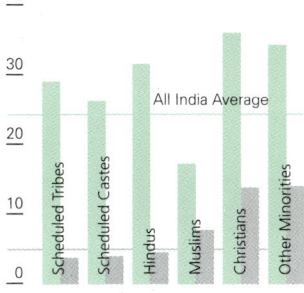

CPR among eligible ever married women
Per cent

Among Village Development and Household Size Groups

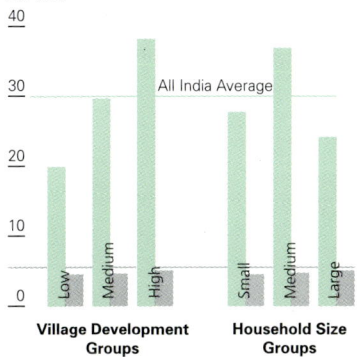

CPR among eligible ever married women
Per cent

Among Poverty and Literacy Groups

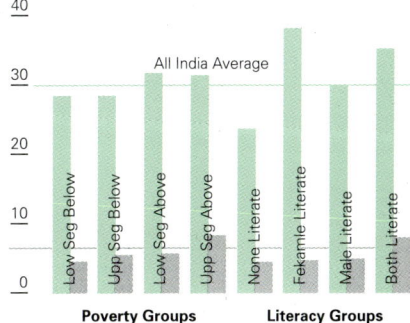

CPR among eligible ever married women
Per cent

Contraceptive Prevalence Rates

Among States

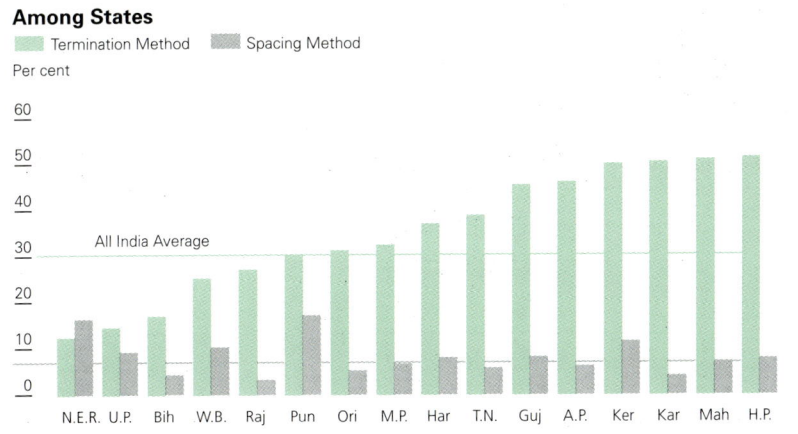

1. NSSO, 1986–7 reveals that there were about 107.1 m. eligible couples in rural India of whom about 25 per cent were protected, i.e. they had either undergone sterilization or were currently practicing any one family planning method. (See NSSO, *Sarvekshana*, vol. XVI, no.1, July–Sept. 1992, Department of Statistics, Ministry of Planning, GOI, pp.1–11.

TABLE 8.5

Contraception Prevalence Rates (Percentage) for Ever Married Women by States

| Regions/States | Termination Method | | | | Spacing Method | | | | All Methods | |
| | All | | Vasectomy as % of All | | All | | Loop/Copper T as % of All | | | |
	(HDI) (1993–4)	(NFHS) (1992–3)	(HDI) (1993–4)	(NFHS) (1992–3)	(HDI) (1993–4)	(NFHS) (1992–3)	(HDI) (1993–4)	(NFHS) (1992–3)	(HDI) (1993–4)	(NFHS) (1992–3)
North										
Haryana	36.3	37.0	4.2	13.5	6.9	5.8	20.7	41.4	43.3	46.7
Himachal Pradesh	50.5	46.6	27.3	29.2	5.4	6.9	29.7	30.0	55.9	57.1
Punjab	30.1	35.4	8.6	6.8	15.4	14.8	39.6	38.5	45.5	57.2
Upper Central										
Bihar	15.6	16.6	1.5	6.0	2.2	2.0	13.0	20.0	17.8	19.8
Uttar Pradesh	13.7	12.4	9.5	9.7	8.6	3.4	25.8	17.6	22.3	16.7
Lower Central										
Madhya Pradesh	32.0	30.7	10.2	17.3	4.9	1.8	11.1	22.2	36.0	33.4
Orissa	31.4	30.6	13.5	10.8	2.4	2.1	33.8	57.1	33.8	34.2
Rajasthan	24.4	25.1	1.9	8.4	1.9	2.0	37.5	45.0	26.4	28.2
East										
North-eastern Rg.	12.1	15.6	18.2	7.9	15.5	6.5	18.7	43.0	27.6	31.9
West Bengal	23.2	32.5	5.7	15.7	9.6	5.0	29.0	22.0	32.5	55.7
West										
Gujarat	44.3	42.6	3.3	8.7	6.2	3.2	33.0	53.1	50.6	47.5
Maharashtra	50.1	50.8	10.5	16.7	4.1	2.9	27.3	37.9	54.2	54.3
South										
Andhra Pradesh	44.9	42.4	14.2	15.1	3.3	0.9	31.3	44.4	48.2	43.6
Karnataka	49.5	43.5	1.3	4.1	2.2	2.9	63.6	79.3	51.7	47.7
Kerala	49.3	47.5	14.5	12.6	9.2	5.8	48.4	50.0	58.5	61.4
Tamil Nadu	38.8	42.2	3.5	5.5	2.6	3.4	56.0	64.7	41.4	49.2
All India	**30.1**	**29.8**	**8.3**	**11.7**	**5.6**	**3.4**	**28.5**	**35.3**	**35.7**	**36.9**

TABLE 8.6

Contraception Prevalence Rates for Ever Married Women by Population Groups

| Population Groups | Termination Method | | Spacing Method | | % EMW Using Methods |
	% EMW Users	Vasectomy % to All	% EMW Users	Loop/CopT % to All	
Household Income Groups					
Upto 20,000	30.3	8.9	4.8	30.1	35.0
20,001–40,000	29.4	9.3	5.8	26.3	35.2
40,001–62,000	28.7	6.0	7.2	25.8	35.9
62,001–86,000	28.5	2.9	9.3	27.7	37.7
Above 86,000	37.7	3.6	10.0	32.4	47.6

Contd.

Poverty Line Groups					
Lower segment below	28.4	7.4	4.6	31.1	33.0
Upper segment below	28.4	8.3	5.2	27.4	33.6
Lower segment above	31.4	9.0	5.5	28.5	36.9
Upper segment above	31.2	7.7	7.7	28.1	38.9
Landholding Groups					
Landless wage earner	32.0	8.3	3.9	25.2	35.9
Marginal	28.3	9.7	5.1	27.9	33.3
Small	30.0	8.8	5.7	31.0	35.7
Medium	30.3	5.4	6.4	25.0	36.7
Large	34.8	3.6	6.2	28.2	41.0
Landless others	29.6	9.4	7.7	31.1	37.3
Landowners	29.7	8.1	5.6	28.3	35.3
Landless	30.9	8.8	5.7	29.0	36.6
Occupational Groups					
Cultivators	30.5	7.3	5.5	29.2	36.1
Salaried+Prof.+S.Empl.	30.9	10.2	8.3	31.6	39.2
Wage earners	31.6	9.0	3.9	27.3	35.5
All others	25.7	8.4	6.3	24.5	31.9
Social Groups					
Caste					
STs	29.5	13.5	4.4	35.5	33.9
SCs	26.7	9.6	4.7	19.1	31.4
Religion					
Hindus	31.4	8.2	4.9	29.2	36.3
Muslims	16.5	7.4	8.2	18.7	24.7
Christians	35.1	11.1	13.0	33.3	48.1
Other Minorities	32.7	12.6	13.7	38.9	46.5
Household Size Groups					
Up to 4	27.2	11.6	5.1	27.3	32.3
5–7	35.7	7.9	5.6	30.2	41.3
8 and above	23.5	6.4	6.0	26.9	29.5
Adult Literacy Groups					
None literate	23.9	9.2	4.1	24.4	28.0
Female literate	38.0	7.7	4.7	29.8	42.8
Male literate	30.3	8.0	4.8	25.7	35.1
Both literate	33.4	8.2	7.3	31.5	40.8
Village Development Groups					
Low	20.4	9.2	5.5	24.4	25.8
Medium	31.1	8.7	5.4	27.4	36.5
High	38.4	7.4	6.1	33.7	44.4
All India	**30.1**	**8.3**	**5.6**	**28.5**	**35.7**

Contraception has been found to be significantly associated with adult literacy and village development.

Innovative information, education, communication strategies, and improved supply of quality contraceptives will help in promoting practice among Muslims.

Health Factors

Per cent

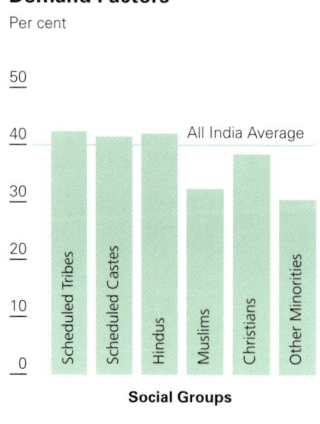

Demand Factors

Per cent

Desire for Son

Per cent

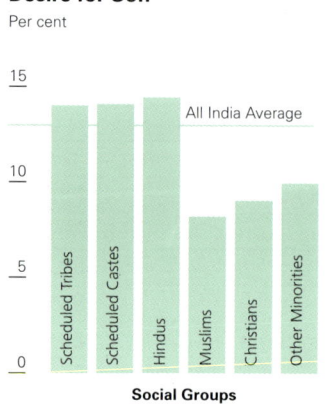

Supply Factors

Per cent

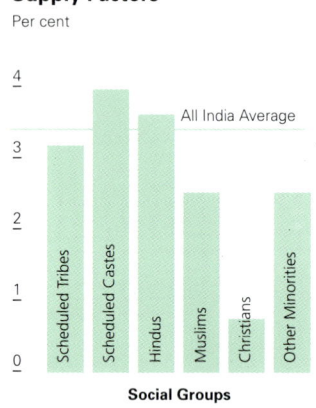

Household Factors

Per cent

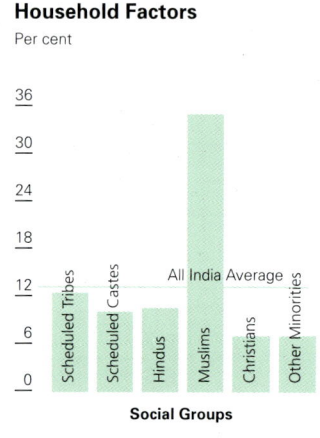

Lack of Knowledge Factors

Per cent

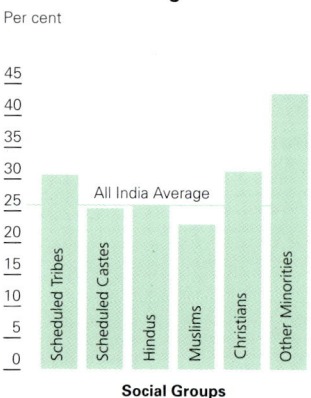

a desire for more sons. Thus, the demand factor accounts for 54 per cent of total responses. One-fourth of non-users expressed lack of knowledge of contraceptives, another 14 per cent gave cultural reasons including opposition from family members as reasons for non-use. The non-availability of contraceptives or supply factors do not appear to be dominant reasons for non-adoption of family planning methods.

It is important to reiterate that the reasons for non-adoption of family planning methods should be standardized according to duration of marriage and number of surviving children. In the absence of such data, the analysis here presents only the frequency distribution for various states. States that cited demand factors were Andhra Pradesh, Madhya Pradesh, and Karnataka. The desire for another son was mentioned in Karnataka, Rajasthan, Haryana, Maharashtra, and Orissa. Supply factors were higher in Bihar, Himachal Pradesh, Rajasthan, and the North-eastern states.

It is surprising to find that in Kerala, of the non-users, comprising 39 per cent (possibly in the younger age group), 41.3 per cent expressed lack of knowledge. In Punjab, too, lack of knowledge as a reason for non-acceptance was high (39.5 per cent), as also in Bihar (34.1 per cent), and

Karnataka (31.0 per cent) (see App. Table A.8.10).

The cross-classification of data according to population groups (App. Table A.8.11) indicates that there is hardly any variation according to household income, landholding, occupation, poverty groups and village index. But there is variation in the case of desire for another son. For example, this is a common reason among the high income category, large landholders, and among the illiterates. However, there are variations according to social groups and household size. It is noteworthy, notwithstanding the need for standardization, that desire for a son is relatively less common among the Muslims. The reasons cited by about 36 per cent of the Muslim respondents were related to household factors such as elders and husband's approval, and religious reasons. Appropriate information, education and communication strategies could help in promoting contraception among the Muslims.

Maternal Care

The present survey collected data on ante-natal care (ANC), medical interventions during birth and post-natal care for all women in the sample who were either currently pregnant and/or had delivered a child during the year preceding the date of the survey.

The percentage of women who had received antenatal services is given in App. Table A.8.12. For rural India as a whole about 7 per cent of EMW were pregnant during the reference period. This rate was low in the southern states but high in the North-eastern region and states falling in the northern and lower central regions of the country.

On the whole only about 10 per cent of all those who reported pregnancies had received ANC in rural India. This information was collected from those who were pregnant on the date of survey (irrespective of duration of pregnancy). Normally the percentage of women who receive ANC is computed from women who have already delivered.

Nevertheless, ANC received by currently pregnant women varies remarkably among the different states (with a coefficient of variation of 89.7 per cent). The proportions are as high as 46.8 per cent in Tamil Nadu, 22.5 per cent in Himachal Pradesh, 20.5 per cent in Karnataka, 18 per cent Punjab, and 17 per cent in West Bengal. However, in developed states such as Haryana, Gujarat, and Maharashtra, where health care infrastructure is generally expected to be better, only a very small percentage of expectant mothers had been beneficiaries of ANC services. The percentage of those who had received these services was also very low in the upper and lower central regions. Further information on type of ANC received reveals that about 90 per cent of beneficiaries were immunized against tetanus, but few had had check-ups for blood pressure.

Inter-population group comparisons (App. Table A.8.13) do not correspond with poverty line groups and household income groups for mothers who receive ANC. However, adult literacy groups more specifically female literacy groups, and also groups where both partners were literate, had more expectant mothers who had received ANC. A much more

Desire for another son is common among the high income category, large landholders, and among the illiterates.

TABLE 8.7

Mothers Immunized (EMW that delivered in the previous year) by States

Regions/States	Received Type of ANC	Type of ANC		
		TT Immunztn.	Iron Tablets	BP Check-up
North				
Haryana	73.6	71.6	59.0	18.9
Himachal Pradesh	67.1	66.2	39.3	34.3
Punjab	76.2	72.0	45.8	41.3
Upper Central				
Bihar	53.1	46.1	16.6	14.9
Uttar Pradesh	42.6	35.6	21.4	9.3
Lower Central				
Madhya Pradesh	39.4	35.1	25.0	13.8
Orissa	58.9	54.2	30.5	19.8
Rajasthan	32.0	30.3	19.6	17.3
East				
North-eastern Rg.	47.6	46.7	24.1	15.4
West Bengal	60.3	53.9	28.3	15.4
West				
Gujarat	73.7	69.1	56.0	45.5
Maharashtra	80.4	79.1	63.4	37.6
South				
Andhra Pradesh	79.0	76.3	56.0	66.4
Karnataka	78.0	75.5	39.8	54.8
Kerala	94.4	93.8	76.7	93.2
Tamil Nadu	89.8	88.2	75.2	72.4
All India	**57.5**	**53.0**	**34.2**	**26.6**
C.V.	27.3	30.3	45.7	68.0

This survey makes available for the first time data on BP checks by pregnant women. In all, about 27 per cent of expectant women had undergone BP checks.

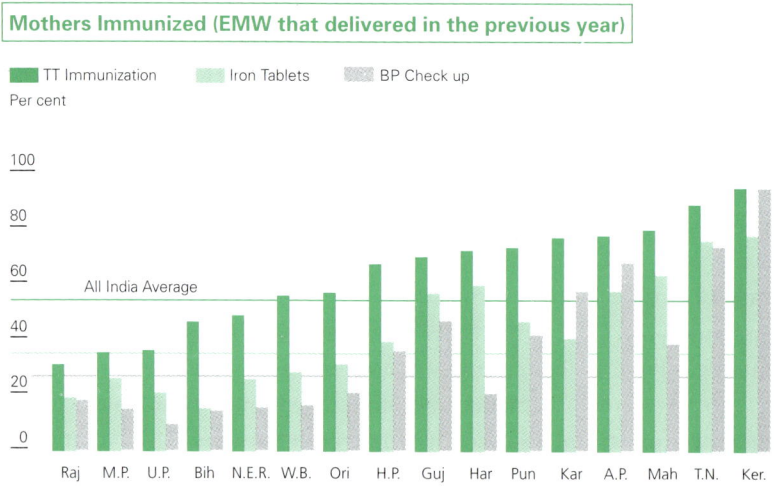

Mothers Immunized (EMW that delivered in the previous year)

TT Immunization   Iron Tablets   BP Check up
Per cent

Among States: All India
Per cent women received ANC

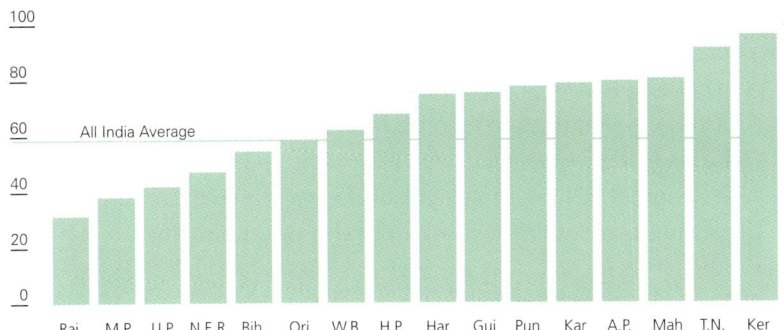

Among Social Groups
Per cent women received ANC (15–49 age)

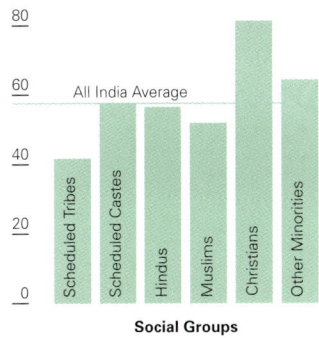

Among Poverty and Literacy Groups
Per cent women received ANC

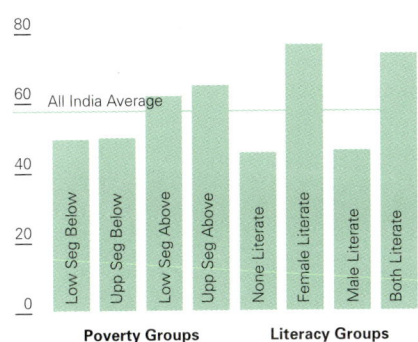

Among Village Development and Household Size Groups
Per cent women received ANC

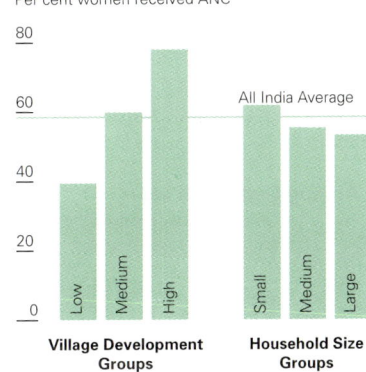

significant association is seen with village development categories. In better developed villages, expectant mothers who had received ANC were about three times higher than in poorly developed villages. In developed villages, the quality of ANC was better with periodic checks to monitor intake of iron tablets and blood pressure.

Table 8.7 presents three types of ANC services, namely, tetanus toxoid immunization, prophylaxis through iron and folic acid tablets, and blood pressure check-up. Overall, 57 per cent of women who had delivered during the year preceding the survey had received some type of ANC. The majority of women had been immunized for tetanus. There were high inter-state variations, with almost all women receiving services in Kerala and Tamil Nadu but very few in Rajasthan (33 per cent), Madhya Pradesh (37 per cent), and the North-east, Bihar, and Uttar Pradesh (45–55 per cent). The utilization of iron and folic acid tablets was relatively lower.

The data on blood pressure checks is interesting in that it was available for the first time through a nationally representative sample survey. Overall, about 27 per cent of all women had undergone such checks, with 93 per cent of these in Kerala, 72 per cent in Tamil Nadu, 66 per cent in Andhra

Pradesh. However, the percentages are very low in all the five Upper Central and Lower Central states (App. Table A.8.14).

App. Table A.8.15 shows a clear association of ANC services with levels of household income. Landholding categories and occupational groups did not however show such association. The level of ANC services among STs (42.2 per cent) and among Muslims (51.7 per cent) was relatively low, while it was 82 per cent among Christians. The wide variation may be related to differences in levels of education among these categories. Expectant mothers who were literate also received better ante-natal care. A similar positive association of ANC with village development was evident in the survey, suggesting that better provision of health care infrastructure has a bearing on the levels of ANC.

Table 8.8 presents data regarding total deliveries, institutional care (i.e., births conducted by trained *dais* or other trained medical/ paramedical staff), and problems encountered. At the all India level, about 17 per cent of ever married women gave birth to a child during the one year reference period. Since the fertility rate is high in the states of Rajasthan, Bihar, and Uttar Pradesh the proportion of mothers who delivered a child was also high.

Institutional Deliveries Conducted by Trained Personnel

Among States: All India
Per cent delivered by trained personnel

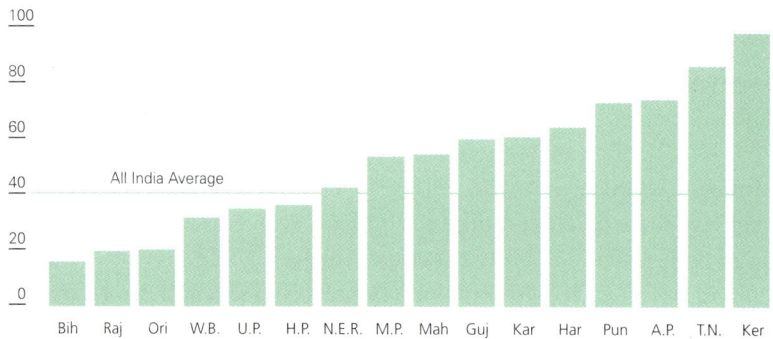

Among Social Groups
Per cent delivered by trained personnel

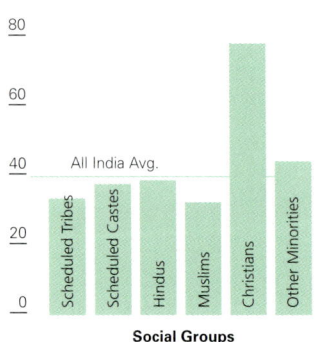

Among Poverty and Literacy Groups
Per cent delivered by trained personnel

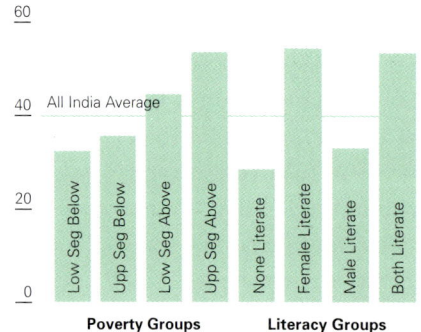

Among Village Development and Household Size Groups
Per cent delivered by trained personnel

TABLE 8.8

Distribution of Ever Married Women (EMW) (Percentage) who Delivered in the Year Prior to Survey by States

| Regions/States | Attended by Trained Person | Place of Delivery | | |
		Hospital	CHC/PHC	Home
North				
Haryana	61.7	8.7	5.2	86.2
Himachal Pradesh	31.6	12.5	1.5	86.0
Punjab	71.3	15.3	6.3	78.5
Upper Central				
Bihar	15.7	6.7	8.8	84.5
Uttar Pradesh	30.4	8.1	6.0	85.9
Lower Central				
Madhya Pradesh	47.8	3.0	3.0	94.1
Orissa	20.5	8.2	3.6	88.2
Rajasthan	20.3	4.3	2.9	92.8
East				
North-eastern Rg.	41.5	16.4	3.7	79.8
West Bengal	28.1	19.9	4.6	75.4
West				
Gujarat	55.9	23.2	5.5	71.4
Maharashtra	48.2	23.0	5.3	71.7
South				
Andhra Pradesh	71.9	37.8	8.5	53.7
Karnataka	56.8	28.1	6.4	65.5
Kerala	96.5	92.4	0.7	6.9
Tamil Nadu	82.6	69.7	4.9	25.4
All India	**40.0**	**17.9**	**5.5**	**76.6**
C.V.	47.4	101.2	44.7	34.1

Sixty per cent of all births are attended by untrained persons in rural India.

Distribution of Currently Pregnant Women Receiving ANC

Type of ANC among Social Groups

Per cent

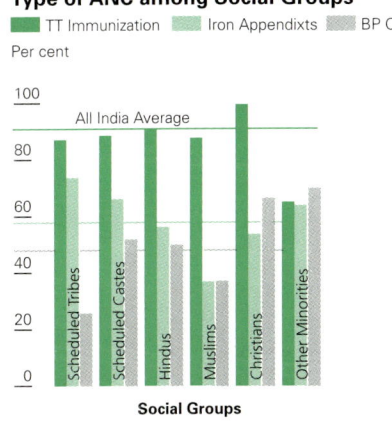

Social Groups

Among Village Development Groups

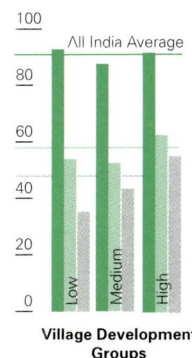

Village Development Groups

TABLE 8.9

Women Undergoing Complicated Deliveries and Nature of Complications by States

Regions/States	% of EMW having Delivery Last Yr	% Attended by Untrained Personnel	% of Complicated Delivery Last Yr	Caesarean		Forceps		Bleeding		Prolonged Delv.		Convulsion/Fever	
				% to Total	% to Complc.	% to Total	% to Complc.	% to total	% to Complc.	% to Total	% to Complc.	% to Total	% to Complc.
North													
Haryana	17.0	38.3	9.0	2.0	22.4	0.5	5.9	0.4	4.9	5.0	54.8	1.1	12.1
Himachal Pradesh	13.5	68.1	6.8	5.4	32.1	0.9	5.2	2.5	14.8	7.7	46.1	0.3	1.8
Punjab	14.3	28.2	8.0	6.2	77.9	-	-	0.2	2.9	1.4	17.3	0.2	1.9
Upper Central													
Bihar	19.7	84.3	11.9	0.6	4.8	0.4	3.4	1.3	11.0	·6.8	57.4	2.8	23.3
Uttar Pradesh	21.6	69.5	4.3	0.9	21.2	-	-	0.5	11.1	2.1	49.5	0.8	18.2
Lower Central													
Madhya Pradesh	16.9	52.3	7.8	0.5	6.7	-	-	2.0	25.9	2.8	35.6	2.5	31.9
Orissa	16.1	79.4	10.7	1.3	12.2	1.1	10.6	2.9	27.1	3.9	36.7	1.4	13.4
Rajasthan	24.5	79.7	8.4	0.2	2.4	0.6	6.9	1.3	15.1	3.1	36.7	3.3	38.9
East													
North-eastern Rg.	19.0	58.6	21.8	1.7	7.8	3.6	16.4	14.3	65.6	0.9	3.9	1.4	6.4
West Bengal	18.5	72.0	13.1	1.5	11.7	0.6	4.3	4.1	31.2	5.3	40.0	1.7	12.8
West													
Gujarat	15.5	44.1	11.8	2.6	22.5	1.6	13.2	3.5	29.6	2.6	22.3	1.4	12.3
Maharashtra	14.9	51.8	8.3	1.9	22.8	0.7	8.5	1.3	15.2	3.0	36.0	1.4	17.5
South													
Andhra Pradesh	12.6	28.1	23.7	7.8	32.9	0.6	2.5	3.3	14.1	11.5	48.4	0.5	2.1
Karnataka	10.4	42.9	7.7	1.3	17.6	-	-	1.2	15.5	4.6	59.7	0.6	7.3
Kerala	11.3	3.5	15.4	14.8	96.2	0.1	0.9	0.1	0.9	0.3	1.9	-	0.0
Tamil Nadu	13.9	17.5	14.5	7.4	51.0	1.8	12.3	3.5	24.1	1.4	9.9	0.4	2.8
All India	**17.3**	**59.8**	**10.7**	**2.2**	**21.1**	**0.6**	**5.7**	**2.3**	**21.9**	**3.9**	**37.0**	**1.5**	**14.3**
C.V.	22.5	100	42.6	107.9	92.8	114.6	90.7	122.8	77.2	72.1	51.9	75.7	86.0

Table 8.8 also shows that 60 per cent of total births are attended by untrained personnel in rural India. These percentages were high in Bihar (85 per cent), Orissa, and Rajasthan (about 80 per cent). In Uttar Pradesh and West Bengal about four-fifths of the total deliveries were conducted by untrained *dais* or family members. The situation was relatively better in the states of Gujarat and Maharashtra. In the economically developed states of Punjab and Haryana about one-fourth to one-third of births were not attended by trained health personnel. In Kerala a very negligible percentage were delivered by untrained personnel. One may conclude that it is both better availability of health care and better education, especially in the form of health care awareness programmes, which have a bearing on maternal health care.

Table 8.9 indicates that about 11 per cent of all deliveries reported had complications; this incidence was high in Andhra Pradesh (24 per cent), in the North-east (22 per cent), and in Himachal Pradesh, Kerala, and Tamil Nadu (15 per cent). All complicated deliveries are presented according to the nature of the complication. Only 2.2 per cent of all births or 22 per cent of complicated births were by Caesarean section. The highest number of so-called complicated births were in Kerala (78 per cent), and 51 per cent of all

Post-Natal Care

Among States: All India
Per cent eligible women received PNC

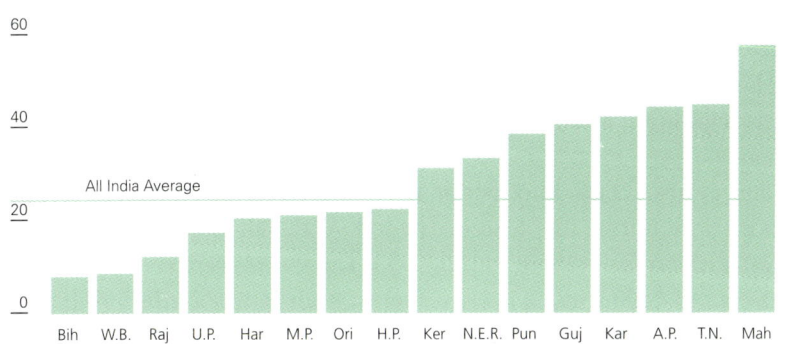

PNC among Social Groups
Per cent women received PNC

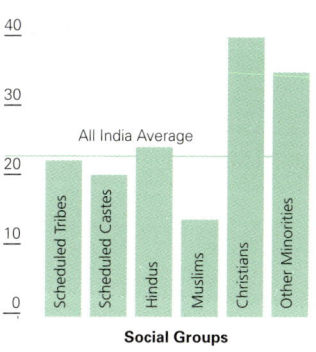

PNC among Poverty and Literacy Groups
Per cent women received PNC

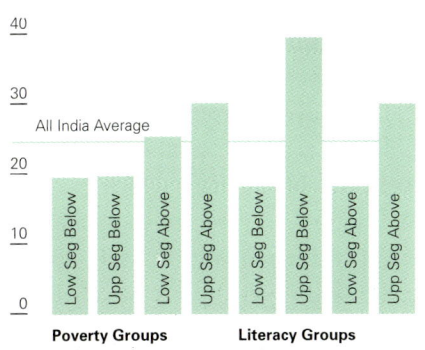

PNC among Village Development and Household Size Groups
Per cent women received PNC

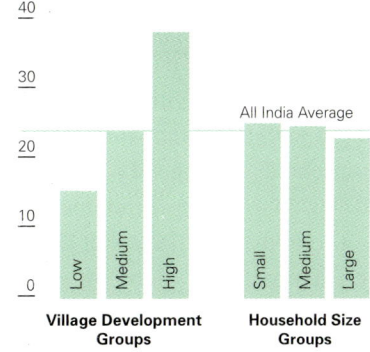

Caesarean births were in Punjab and Tamil Nadu. An equal number of births classified as 'bleeding' were high in the North-east, West Bengal, Gujarat, and Orissa. About 4 per cent of all and 37 per cent of complicated deliveries were reported to have taken place after prolonged labour and 1.5 and 14 per cent reported convulsions and fever during deliveries. Less than one per cent of all births were with the aid of forceps.

The study broadly indicates that literacy, economic conditions, and religion or cultural norms have a role to play in total fertility levels, as can be seen from the high proportion of mothers who gave birth during 1993 who were illiterate and fell in the lower segment of the poverty line. However, the nature of complications or the percentage of complicated births to total births do not show any striking association with the socio-economic background of households (see App. Tables A.8.16).

App. Tables A.8.17 and A.8.18 provide information about post-natal care (PNC) and type of post-natal care among women who had delivered a child during the year preceding the survey. It shows that about one-fourth of rural women had received post-natal care. Such care was highest in Maharashtra followed by the southern states of Tamil Nadu, Andhra Pradesh, Karnataka, Punjab, and Gujarat. Such care was almost absent in Bihar (7.6 per cent), West Bengal (8 per cent), Rajasthan (11 per cent), and Uttar Pradesh (16 per cent). App. Table A.8.18 shows that utilization of post-natal care facilities was lowest (14 per cent) among Muslims and highest (39 per cent) among Christians. The utilization of preventive care has a strong relationship with village development and levels of adult literacy, and ranges from 15 per cent in the less developed to 37 per cent in the developed villages.

The above analysis clearly shows that literacy, especially female literacy, has a very significant and positive role to play in improving the health status of women.

This survey also carries information regarding 'stillbirths' identified as the babies born dead during the reference period. At the all India level 5.5 per cent of all births were stillborn during 1993. These rates vary remarkably across the states. Stillbirths comprised about 15 per cent of births in Bihar and West Bengal, and about 8.4 and 7 per cent in Orissa and Himachal Pradesh respectively. Such high rates of stillborns are usually associated with low age of mother, poor nutritional level of women, and low utilization of primary health care in these particular states.

Stillbirths are also associated with income, household size, poverty line groups, and social groups (App. Table A.8.18). Although the stillbirth rate was only 4.8 in the up to Rs 20,000 household income category, the rate was as high as 6.5 in the lower segment of the poverty group. However, larger variations appeared in the household size category: smaller households having very low levels (2.9 per cent) of stillbirths which increased to 4 in 5–7 member households and to 8.3 in the above 8 member households. It is likely that the age profile of women in large households is much lower than in the other two types. Stillbirths were also relatively high among the Muslims and STs.

Both better availability of health care and better education, especially in the form of health care awareness programmes, have a bearing on maternal and child health care.

Breastfeeding is an important component of health care of newborn babies. It helps to maintain and strengthen their natural immunity against many types of sicknesses. This survey presents breastfeeding data for women who had delivered a child during a one year reference period (App. Table A.8.19). In India, breastfeeding is almost an universal practice except in Bihar and West Bengal. Whether this latter fact is due to cultural factors or due to the influence of the supplementary food industry needs to be established. Among those who breastfed their children, about 50 per cent initiated feeding about two days after birth. This practice was prevalent in the states of Punjab, Rajasthan, Uttar Pradesh, and Karnataka, where about two-thirds to three-fourths of women follow it. The healthy trend of universal breastfeeding and early initiation is found in the state of Kerala. We may therefore conclude that better educational levels and health awareness do play an important role in developing the child's immunity at birth.

Population group differentials are almost non-existent except for the fact that early initiation into breastfeeding is more prevalent among STs and Christians. Some studies have shown relatively shorter durations of breastfeeding among Muslims and Christians in comparison with Hindus. SC mothers were found to breastfeed for a longer duration than mothers among the other caste groups.

As far as education of mothers is concerned, data clearly indicate that mothers who were literate, breastfed their children within two days of delivery as compared to the non-literate household groups. Similarly, an association was found to exist between mothers from more developed villages and early initiation of breastfeeding.

Immunization

Immunization of infants and children against infectious and degenerative diseases is one of the most effective strategies for ensuring child survival and child health. Recommended vaccinations for children during the first year of their lives are against BCG, Polio, Diphtheria–Pertussis–Tetanus (DPT), and Measles. Booster doses are then administered at different stages of childhood.

Child Immunization

Among Children: All India
Per cent immunized children (1–2 years)

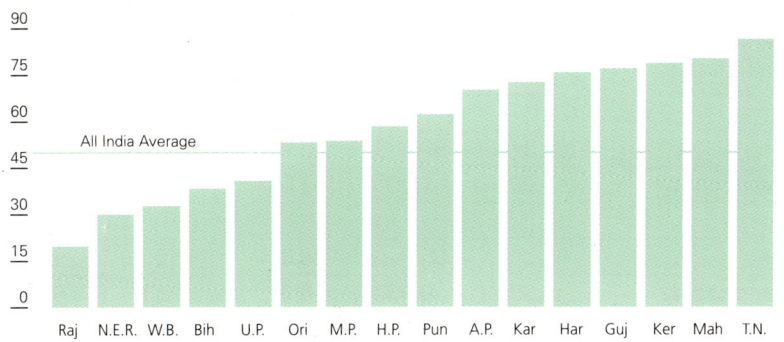

Among Social Groups
Per cent immunized children (1–2 years)

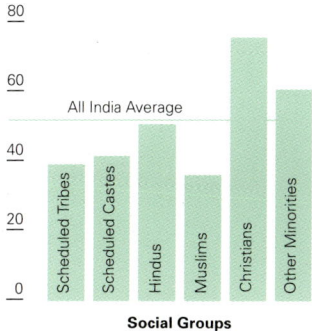

Among Village Development and Household Size Groups
Per cent immunized children (1–2 years)

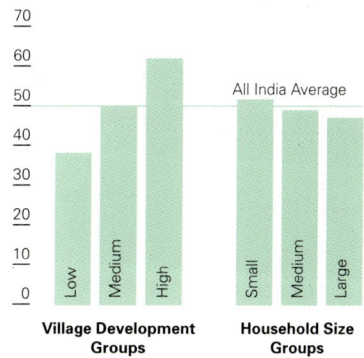

Among Poverty and Literacy Groups
Per cent immunized children (1–2 years)

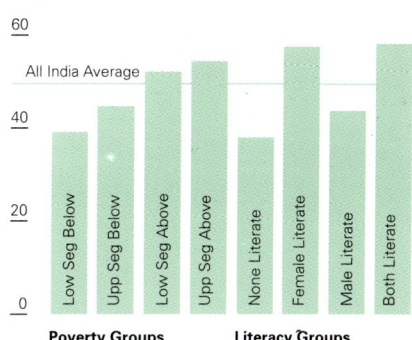

TABLE 8.10

Percentage of Children (aged 12–23 months) who were Immunized by States

Regions/ States	DPT 3 Doses	POLIO 3 Doses	BCG 1 Dose	MEASLES 1 Dose	ALL 8 Doses
North					
Haryana					
Person	79.1	78.2	83.9	77.0	73.9
Gender disparity	0.86	0.86	0.91	0.89	0.85
Himachal Pradesh					
Person	70.9	69.8	77.8	66.7	57.2
Gender disparity	0.78	0.89	0.91	0.88	0.81
Punjab					
Person	73.2	70.2	74.1	67.5	62.0
Gender disparity	0.91	0.88	0.97	0.96	1.00
Upper Central					
Bihar					
Person	47.2	48.1	53.3	41.4	37.5
Gender disparity	1.21	1.17	1.04	1.21	1.27
Uttar Pradesh					
Person	51.6	53.3	61.3	49.0	41.3
Gender disparity	0.94	0.93	0.98	0.92	0.95
Lower Central					
Madhya Pradesh					
Person	61.2	60.9	67.1	56.1	53.2
Gender disparity	0.92	0.92	0.90	0.92	0.92
Orissa					
Person	64.2	63.1	68.7	54.1	52.7
Gender disparity	0.84	0.83	0.87	0.91	0.89
Rajasthan					
Person	28.4	28.8	39.6	30.3	20.3
Gender disparity	0.89	0.82	0.86	0.73	0.75
East					
North-eastern Rg.					
Person	37.8	36.2	45.4	30.5	28.4
Gender disparity	0.82	0.79	0.98	0.96	0.82
West Bengal					
Person	43.3	44.9	49.0	33.5	31.2
Gender disparity	0.96	0.98	0.97	1.12	1.03
West					
Gujarat					
Person	80.3	80.6	83.8	75.9	74.6
Gender disparity	1.00	1.00	1.03	1.01	1.05
Maharashtra					
Person	85.3	85.7	88.3	81.2	79.0
Gender disparity	0.95	0.95	0.94	0.93	0.92

Contd.

South					
Andhra Pradesh					
Person	76.5	78.0	84.1	71.5	69.6
Gender disparity	0.97	1.02	1.09	1.08	1.02
Karnataka					
Person	78.1	78.3	84.5	76.0	73.0
Gender disparity	0.99	0.98	0.95	0.96	0.95
Kerala					
Person	93.6	92.3	95.2	79.5	78.6
Gender disparity	0.96	0.95	1.00	0.96	0.94
Tamil Nadu					
Person	87.2	89.6	93.3	87.7	82.8
Gender disparity	0.96	0.98	1.02	0.93	0.88
All India					
Person	**57.5**	**58.1**	**64.3**	**52.9**	**48.5**
Gender disparity	**0.96**	**0.95**	**0.97**	**0.96**	**0.96**

Levels of child immunization are lowest among Muslims, followed by STs.

This survey provides information regarding the percentage of immunized children in the 1 to 2 years age group and 0 to 2 years age group against DPT, Polio, BCG, and Measles, and also regarding those who were immunized against all possible diseases (Table 8.10). About 50 per cent of the children (1 to 2 years of age) were fully immunized in rural India although the proportion of partly immunized children (i.e., immunization against Polio or BCG or Measles) was relatively higher at 64 per cent. The proportion of both fully immunized and partly immunized children was higher among the economically developed states of Haryana, Gujarat, Maharashtra, and Punjab, and among the southern states of Kerala, Tamil Nadu, and Andhra Pradesh. Immunization (full and part) was low in Rajasthan (only 21 per cent of the total children) followed by the states in the North-eastern region and Bihar. This may be attributed to the better availability of health care infrastructure that plays a dominant role in higher levels of immunization among children. However, gender disparities persist and are high in Haryana, Rajasthan, and the North-eastern region.

Although immunization improves marginally by income category and is high among the salaried, professionals, self-employed, and the better educated, variation is found only among social groups and between villages at different levels of development.

The data indicate clearly that the percentage of fully immunized and partly immunized children is higher among households where both males and females are literate, as compared to households with illiterates. The percentage of fully immunized children was about 44 where only male members were literate; while it was about 60 in households where females were literate. Similarly, the village development index also shows a significant association with levels of immunization or health care of children. In developed villages, about two-thirds of the children in the referred age-group were fully immunized and about 75 per cent were partly immunized as compared to less developed villages where only one-third received

Only about 50 per cent of all eligible children have been vaccinated for all the 8 doses of relevant immunizations.

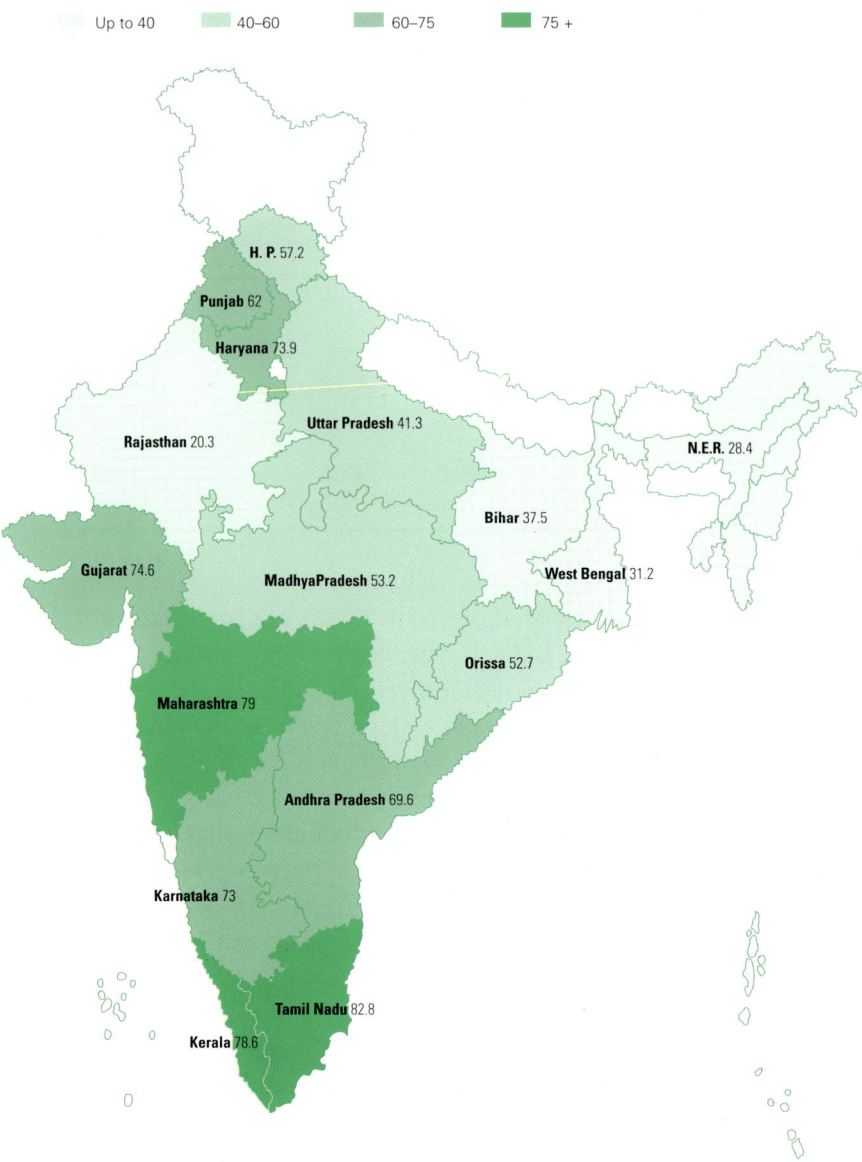

Percentage of Children (aged 12–23 months) who were Immunized (all 8 doses)

Up to 40   40–60   60–75   75 +

H. P. 57.2

Punjab 62

Haryana 73.9

Uttar Pradesh 41.3

Rajasthan 20.3

N.E.R. 28.4

Bihar 37.5

Gujarat 74.6

MadhyaPradesh 53.2

West Bengal 31.2

Orissa 52.7

Maharashtra 79

Andhra Pradesh 69.6

Karnataka 73

Tamil Nadu 82.8

Kerala 78.6

Public/government facilities are the dominant source of immunization in rural India.

vaccinations for all major infectious diseases.

As far as caste and religion are concerned, the data indicate that the levels of immunization were low among Muslims, followed by ST households but were highest among Christians. Better education levels among Christians appears to be a contributory factor in this. About 50 per cent of all Hindu children were immunized (App. Table A.8.20).

Public facilities are the dominant source of immunization in India. About 85 per cent of all DPT and 83 per cent of measles immunizations were conducted through government facilities located at either the village centre, sub-centre, primary health centre (PHC), or other government dispensaries. It can be inferred that easy availability through the extension approach of the government primary health care services has played an important role

Sources of Immunization among States: All India

■ Govt. Facility   ■ Pvt. Hospital   ▨ NGO Camp
Per cent utilizing health care facilities

In developing countries, non-availability of health care facilities and lack of awareness are the main reasons for non-immunization of children.

in determining levels of immunization. Kerala is the only exception, where about one-third of total immunized children had received vaccination from private sources. It might be noted that in Kerala levels of immunization were also quite high. Hence, it could be said that better awareness impels people to get their children immunized even if they have to go to private clinics.

Levels of immunization show a clear association with household income; the higher the income of the household the better is the level of children's immunization. Similar patterns exist among different poverty groups where significant development in the levels of children's health care was evident with better economic status. Adult literacy and village development too show a correspondence with levels of children's immunization. One can therefore say that the villages which are relatively developed, and where the levels of literacy are high or if both males and females are educated, children's health is better cared for. Occupational and social categories do not however show any association with children's immunization.

Overall, it may be said that levels of immunization were relatively low among Muslims and relatively high among Christians, and both tended to depend more on private sources for immunization. Almost all the categories preferred public health care services for immunization of children; however, among high income groups there was a tendency to go to private sources/ doctors as well.

Immunization for measles is about 37 per cent that of DPT immunization which was around 65 per cent. Overall, the gender disparity in measles immunizations is lower, and was evident across states and population groups when immunization services were received from a private source.

The survey reveals that on the whole government health care facilities were more frequently used for preventive medical care.[2]

App. Table A.8.21 presents reasons for non-immunization of children against DPT and measles. In developing countries, non-availability of health care facilities and lack of awareness are the main reasons for non-immunization of children. The statistics presented here show that in the

2 This is true of this survey as much as of the NSSO survey results (*Sarvekshana*, 1992). It is true also only in the case of preventive measures, that is in immunization, and ante-natal care. In the case of illness, both sources reveal that private clinics were visited more frequently.

For DPT (3 doses)
Among Poverty Groups

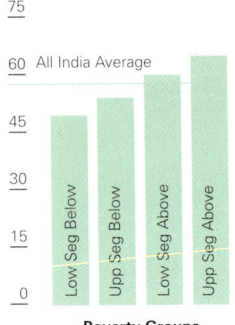

For DPT (3 doses)
Among Social Groups

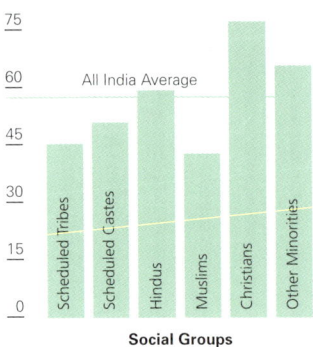

For DPT (3 doses)
Among Vill. Dev. Groups

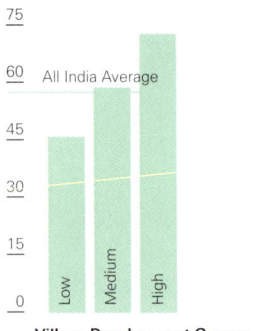

For Polio (3 doses)
Among Poverty Groups

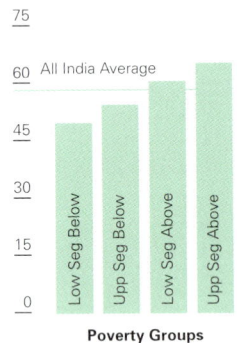

For Polio (3 doses)
Among Social Groups

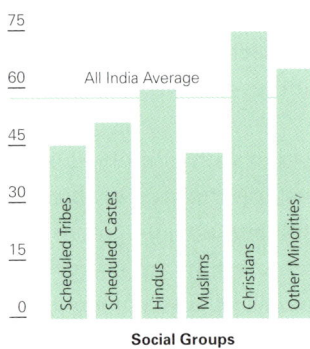

For Polio (3 doses)
Among Village
Development Groups

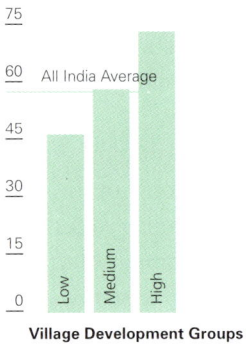

For BCG (1 dose)
Among Poverty Groups

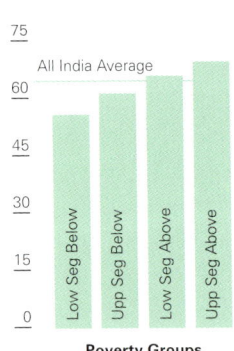

For BCG (1 dose)
Among Social Groups

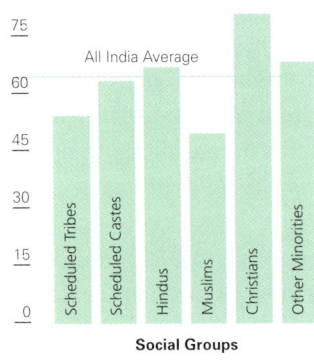

For BCG (1 dose)
Among Village
Development Groups

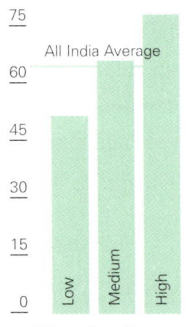

case of both DPT and measles vaccinations, about 50 per cent of respondents stated non-availability of vaccinations as the main reason for non-immunization. Another important reason appears to be wrong beliefs, i.e., lack of awareness about its effects and existing cultural norms or practices. About 7 to 10 per cent of non-users despite a positive attitude towards immunization stated they had taken the child/children for vaccination, but

**For Measles (1 dose)
Among Poverty Groups**

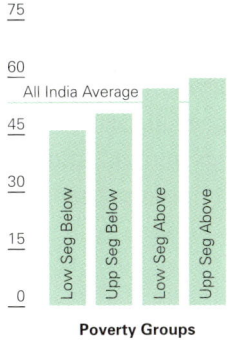

Poverty Groups

**For Measles (1 dose)
Among Social Groups**

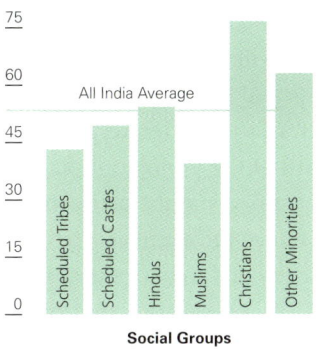

Social Groups

**For Measles (1 dose)
Among Village
Development Groups**

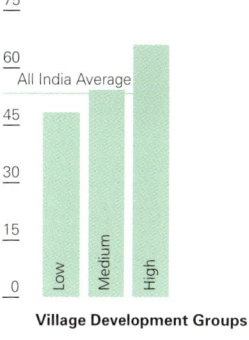

Village Development Groups

**All 8 Doses
Among Poverty Groups**

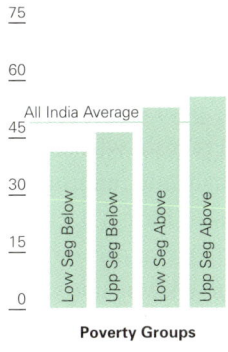

Poverty Groups

**All 8 Doses
Among Social Groups**

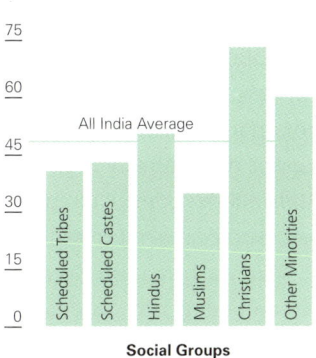

Social Groups

**All 8 Doses
Among Village
Development Groups**

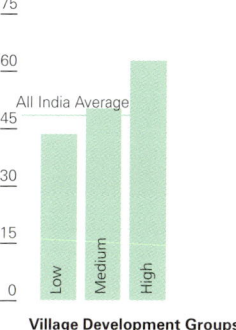

Village Development Groups

did not receive it because the child was ill at the time of vaccination. Hence, levels of immunization could be increased with better supply of vaccines and health awareness programmes.

There are wide inter-state variations among non-users. In the case of the developed states such as Haryana, Punjab, Himachal Pradesh, Karnataka, and Kerala, the major reason for non-immunization seems to be erroneous beliefs. Though Gujarat and Maharashtra are among the better provided states in terms of availability of health care facilities, they still experience wide gaps in the rural areas. In the central states of India, namely Bihar, Rajasthan, Madhya Pradesh, Orissa, Himachal Pradesh, and Tamil Nadu, non-availability of vaccines was a major reason for not immunizing children against DPT and Measles, and lack of target oriented camps in these states. Thus the goal of 'immunization for all' by 2000 still appears a distant dream as non-availability of vaccines and erroneous beliefs dominate 25 per cent of households in the country.

The proportion of immunized children is higher among households that have higher income levels (i.e., above Rs 86,000). As expected, non-availability is not a major reason among such households for non-immunization of children, because they can choose to access health care facilities even outside the village due to their better economic status. However, erroneous beliefs and existing social norms emerged as major reasons for non-immunization. Since household income groups overlap the poverty line categories, the picture is similar in both categories. Better developed villages generally enjoy better infrastructure to deal with health problems and therefore have a lower percentage of non-immunized children. In the moderately developed and better developed villages about one-tenth of the population had a positive attitude towards immunization; the rest quoted supply factors or non-availability of health facilities that tended to decline significantly (from 52.8 to 37.7 per cent) from underdeveloped to better developed villages.

Erroneous beliefs and existing social norms emerged as major reasons for non-immunization

Incidence of Diarrhoea

It is generally observed that the burden of communicable diseases is much higher in developing countries. Among communicable diseases, the incidence of intestinal infections is very high. This survey presents data regarding diarrhoeal diseases among children (up to 3 years of age) found to be responsible for a large number of deaths among children.

The survey revealed that about 60 per cent of children (below 3 years), in rural India had suffered from diarrhoea during the survey period. This proportion is dramatically high in Haryana and Madhya Pradesh, where about 90 to 95 per cent of children (in the referred age) had suffered from diarrhoea. Such cases were reportedly fewer in West Bengal, Karnataka, Gujarat, Maharashtra, and Kerala. This points to the existence of preventive measures and adequate water supply and sanitation in these states unlike in the north and central Indian states.

App. Table A.8.22 presents state-wise information regarding the quantity of liquid and solid food given during diarrhoeal episodes. At the all India level, about 22 per cent of the population (i.e., parents whose children had suffered from diarrhoea) had no knowledge of the kinds of food or liquids that were to be administered during this illness. A similar number had administered less than the required quantity of liquids to counter this condition. State-wise patterns show that lack of awareness was more glaring in Rajasthan, Bihar, and Madhya Pradesh where the cases of diarrhoea were also quite high. This may further be related to the social and economic characteristics of the households. A comparison among occupational categories reveals that the proportion of children who suffered from diarrhoea was lower among the salaried, professionals, and self-employed as compared to wage earners and those whose principal occupation was agriculture.

As far as caste and religion are concerned, better health status of children was evident among Christians which may be associated with their higher levels of education. The percentage of diarrhoeal cases was reportedly high (about 65 per cent) among STs which may be due to poor availability of safe drinking water and lack of other preventive measures and health awareness among this group. A clearer and more distinct association of diarrhoeal episodes is seen with the level of village development. Better developed villages not only showed better infrastructural facilities for health care as compared to the underdeveloped ones, but also improved health status and better awareness and knowledge of preventive measures (App. Table A.8.23)

App. Table A.8.24 provides information regarding medical intervention during diarrhoea and the stage at which medical attention was sought. For one-third of total diarrhoeal patients (children) in rural India no medical attention was sought. For another two-thirds, in the majority of cases medical attention was sought only after repeated vomiting by the children. This shows that only in an emergency was medical attention sought. The state-wise pattern shows that lack of medical attention was very high (about 50 per cent) in Uttar Pradesh, Orissa, Rajasthan, and Bihar, even when the proportion of children who suffered from diarrhoea was high in these states. Medical intervention was more satisfactory in south Indian states and also in the economically developed states of Haryana and Maharashtra. The easy availability of health care facilities may be the reason for this situation in these states.

The source of treatment used during diarrhoeal episodes also reveals an interesting pattern. At the all India level, government facilities were used more frequently in comparison with private ones. State-wise patterns show that in the north-eastern region, in Karnataka, Gujarat, Himachal Pradesh, and Andhra Pradesh, government facilities were being used more frequently in the treatment of diarrhoeal cases. In economically developed states, e.g. in Haryana, Maharashtra, and Punjab, private facilities were used quite frequently, possibly due to the higher purchasing power of the people. In the case of Kerala, however, both sources, i.e., private and public were used almost equally. In West Bengal, private facilities were more popular for almost any illness, perhaps due to the poor availability and the poor quality of government facilities. In all central Indian states government facilities were used more than private ones even when the proportion of total users was relatively low.

As far as the socio-economic conditions of households vis-a-vis source of treatment in diarrhoea is concerned, data (App. Table A.8.25) indicate that among the better educated households (especially where females were literate), medical attention was sought more frequently and preferably from government facilities. The level of village development also shows a significant association with the proportion of diarrhoeal cases that were medically examined. A large percentage of these had availed of government facilities while private doctors were also consulted. The economic background of the households does not appear to influence the source of treatment in the case of diarrhoeal episodes among children.

App. Table A.8.26 presents information regarding knowledge and use of the Oral Rehydration Scheme (ORS) for treating cases of diarrhoea. State-wise patterns show that such knowledge was higher among the southern states, West Bengal, and in the north in the state of Himachal Pradesh. Knowledge of easy and home based curative measures for diarrhoea was practically absent in Madhya Pradesh, Rajasthan, and Punjab where only 25

It has been found that medical attention is sought only after children experience repeated and recurrent diarrhoea and vomiting.

per cent of the women had reported its incidence. In Madhya Pradesh this was the case despite a very high incidence of diarrhoea.

Knowledge and use of ORS by population groups (presented in App. Table A.8.27), shows a positive association with income group, adult literacy group, and village index group. It may be said that with an increase in income, literacy, and overall development of the village, the incidence of diarrhoeal cases become fewer and when they occur, parents have knowledge of curative and preventive measures. In caste and religious groups, such knowledge was least among STs and SCs, while it was quite high (about two-thirds of mothers had such knowledge) among Christians.

In rural India, about 59 per cent of total ORS packets used were made available from government sources, showing that government policies have played a major role in combating the infection. By state, procurement from government sources was highest in the North-eastern region, Madhya Pradesh (87 per cent), followed by Himachal Pradesh, Gujarat, and Andhra Pradesh. Procurement of ORS packages from government sources was lowest in Bihar (22 per cent) and West Bengal (30 per cent). In the southern states, private sources were also frequently utilized for procurement of ORS packets in cases of diarrhoea (App. Tables A.8.28 and A.8.29).

Principal Findings

I Demographic Rates

1 CBR is high among the poorest households and among Muslims and lowest among Christians.

2 CDR is high among landless labourers and shows an association with household income.

II Health Care Utilization

3 In terms of health care parameters and service utilization, ANC is widespread in Kerala and Tamil Nadu whereas only one-third of mothers receive this service in Rajasthan, Madhya Pradesh, and Bihar. Not more than one-fourth of mothers receive PNC in rural India.

4 About 60 per cent of total births are conducted by untrained health personnel in rural India, especially in Bihar, Orissa, and Rajasthan (more than four-fifths of all births). Safe motherhood shows correspondence with literacy and the economic status of households.

5 Immunization of infants and children also shows an association with literacy and village development. Immunization levels are low among Muslims and also STs.

6 In general, village development categories and adult-literacy groups have a significant relationship with demographic advancement. Overall, government health care facilities are utilized more frequently than private clinics in almost all states and also across population groups in India.

9

Village-level Infrastructure and Human Development

This chapter attempts to capture the impact of village-level infrastructure on human development indicators by constructing a composite index of village development using certain parameters that reflect the economic prosperity of a village, such as access to land and irrigation, and education and health facilities. The survey was conducted in 1,765 villages spread over 195 districts across the whole of rural India. A comprehensive survey instrument was administered to selected village elders and functionaries.

About one half of all villages do not have any source of 'protected' drinking water.

Village development is used as one of eight population group categories in the NCAER/HDI Survey, 1994, to cross-tabulate data on human development. This category is divided into three sub-categories, namely, less developed, moderately developed, and developed villages. This classification established some important associations between the levels of village development and human development indicators. In what follows, selected parameters that highlight the level of village development and infrastructure, such as availability of all-weather roads, telephones, schools, health sub-centres, and access to potable water, are linked to selected human development indicators such as level of literacy, school enrolment, level of household income, health and nutritional status.

The presence or absence of a certain indicator has been defined in terms of distance. For example, existence of a bus stop, post office, and telephone within the village or within a distance of 2 km is considered reasonable, whereas an *anganwadi* centre or primary school should exist within the village. A distance of 5 km is considered reasonable to evaluate access to a railway station. It is important to note that most of the parameters discussed below only highlight the availability of certain infrastructure and do not reflect access or actual utilization.

Profile of Villages Surveyed

Thirty-seven per cent of villages surveyed were connected with *pucca* or all weather roads and 65 per cent had a bus stop within a distance of 2 km (Table 9.1). The highest proportion of villages connected by *pucca* roads was found in Kerala (85 per cent) followed by Punjab (81 per cent), and Haryana (61 per cent). The lowest percentage was found in West Bengal (14 per cent), Orissa (16 per cent), Bihar (19 per cent), and Madhya Pradesh, and in the North-eastern states (21 per cent each). The highest proportion of villages (above 80 per cent) that had a bus stop within 2 km were found in Kerala, Tamil Nadu, Andhra Pradesh, Karnataka, Gujarat, and Maharashtra; less than 50 per cent of villages in Uttar Pradesh, Orissa, Madhya Pradesh, and Bihar were connected to a bus stop.

Over 22 per cent of all villages in Orissa (63 per cent), followed by Bihar (33 per cent), Gujarat, Kerala, and Haryana had access to a railway station, indicating a well developed railway network in these states. States with the least developed rail links were Himachal Pradesh, Madhya Pradesh, Karnataka, Rajasthan, and the North-eastern states.

Seventy per cent of villages in rural India reported the existence of a post office within a distance of 2 km while 51 per cent reported the availability of a telephone indicating a well developed post and telecommunication system. The two states that stand out by virtue of having 50 per cent or less such villages are Orissa and Madhya Pradesh. Tamil Nadu reported 85 per cent villages with telephone connections, Kerala (80 per cent), Gujarat (68 per cent), and Punjab, Karnataka, and Maharashtra over 60 per cent. The least number of telephone connections were found in the North-east (29 per cent), Bihar, Orissa, and Madhya Pradesh (around 36–38 per cent) and Rajasthan and West Bengal around 45 per cent each.

Only about 35 per cent of all villages in rural India reported over 50 per cent of gross cropped area under irrigation. Irrigation infrastructure was most developed in Haryana (85 per cent villages), Punjab (75 per cent), Uttar Pradesh (68 per cent), and Andhra Pradesh (50 per cent). The lowest levels (less than 10 per cent) of irrigated land were found in the North-eastern states, Kerala, Himachal Pradesh, and Maharashtra. Irrigated land in Bihar, Orissa, and Madhya Pradesh ranged between 20 and 25 per cent.

The existence of sources of drinking water in rural areas is one of the most important indicators of development. It was seen that people used multiple sources, and sources also varied according to the season. In the following, however, source of drinking water for the selected villages has been categorized as pipe/tap, hand pump, protected wells/tanker truck, and other unprotected sources.

Only about 17 per cent of villages reported piped water as the dominant source of drinking water; another 18 per cent reported using hand pumps, and 13 per cent had other sources of protected water. This points to the startling fact that about one half of all villages in India do not have any source of protected drinking water. Sources of piped water were highest in Himachal Pradesh (62 per cent), followed by Tamil Nadu (53 per cent), and lowest in the North-eastern states, West Bengal, Orissa, and Madhya Pradesh (all with less than 3 per cent). Hand pumps were popular in West Bengal, Punjab, and Karnataka. States with any one protected source of drinking water were Tamil Nadu, Gujarat, Punjab, and Kerala. Orissa, Bihar, Madhya Pradesh, the North-east and Uttar Pradesh did not draw drinking water from any protected source in a majority of their villages.

All villages in India are expected to have at least one primary school (up to class 4), and, depending upon the size of the village, a middle school

The existence of sources of drinking water in rural areas is one of the most important indicators of development.

TABLE 9.1

Percentage of Villages and Availability of Different Facilities by States

Regions/States	Transportation			Communication		Irrigation	Major Sources of Drinking Water			
	Connected with *Pucca* Road	Bus Stop Within 2 km	Railway Station Within 5 km	Post Office Within 2 km	Telephone Within 2 km	50% of Gross Crop Area Irrigated	Piped Water	Hand Pump	Other Protected Water	Unprot. Source of Water
North										
Haryana	61.1	76.7	25.6	77.8	55.6	84.4	32.2	12.2	13.3	42.2
Himachal Pradesh	23.8	61.9	4.8	68.3	54.0	7.9	61.9	0.0	1.6	36.5
Punjab	81.4	68.6	21.4	78.6	65.7	75.7	34.3	48.6	0.0	17.1
Upper Central										
Bihar	19.0	42.2	32.8	74.1	37.9	22.4	0.0	32.8	3.5	63.8
Uttar Pradesh	34.3	44.4	23.6	65.3	35.2	68.5	6.0	20.4	13.0	60.7
Lower Central										
Madhya Pradesh	21.2	40.1	11.5	41.9	37.8	23.5	2.8	3.2	6.9	87.1
Orissa	15.7	44.1	62.8	53.9	36.3	20.6	0.0	5.9	0.0	94.1
Rajasthan	40.6	53.8	13.2	68.9	42.5	20.8	9.4	13.2	2.8	74.5
East										
North-eastern Rg.	21.2	63.6	15.2	63.6	28.8	6.1	3.0	3.0	3.0	90.9
West Bengal	14.1	56.4	35.9	79.5	47.4	26.9	2.6	59.0	0.0	38.5
West										
Gujarat	54.6	85.2	27.3	79.6	68.2	38.6	47.7	5.7	33.0	13.6
Maharashtra	45.0	81.5	15.2	64.2	60.9	10.6	24.5	6.6	35.8	33.1
South										
Andhra Pradesh	44.3	92.0	15.0	94.7	58.4	50.4	8.9	15.0	17.7	58.4
Karnataka	25.9	85.9	11.9	76.3	62.2	28.2	22.2	51.9	3.7	22.2
Kerala	85.3	94.7	26.7	94.7	80.0	6.7	10.7	0.0	62.7	26.7
Tamil Nadu	40.8	93.4	30.3	92.1	85.5	46.1	52.6	26.3	11.8	9.2
All India	**36.8**	**64.5**	**22.4**	**70.2**	**50.9**	**34.7**	**16.6**	**18.4**	**13.0**	**52.0**

(normally classes 5–7) as well. Overall, 88 per cent of all villages in rural India have a primary school within the village. About a quarter of villages in Uttar Pradesh, Himachal Pradesh, and Orissa do not have even primary schools. Given the relatively poor transport network in these states, implementing the goal of universal primary education in these states also seems remote. Surprisingly, only 50 per cent of the villages in Kerala reported having primary schools. This may be to be due to the problem of defining village boundaries in a uniquely continuous domiciliary pattern in that state. Kerala has a fairly well developed transportation network which partly resolves the problem of distance in primary education.

On the other hand, only 41 per cent of villages across India have a middle school within the village. The existence of middle schools was highest in Karnataka (60 per cent), Punjab, Haryana, and Orissa (about 55 per cent each). Kerala had middle schools within only 20 per cent of villages, but over 62 per cent of villages reported a middle school within a distance of 5 km. West Bengal, Uttar Pradesh, and Madhya Pradesh reported

Table 9.1 Contd.

Regions/States	Education			Health			Anganwadi Centre	Govt. Programme Only	Govt.+ NGO Programme	Village Size	
	Primary School	Middle School Within Village	Middle School Within 5 km	Sub-centres	No Sub-centre/ Hospital Beyond 5 km	Pharmacy				Above	Below
North											
Haryana	97.8	54.4	26.7	32.2	45.6	21.1	82.2	81.1	7.8	12.2	87.8
Himachal Pradesh	74.6	36.5	50.8	20.6	31.8	22.2	46.0	92.1	6.4	71.4	28.6
Punjab	95.7	55.7	31.4	5.7	18.6	31.4	35.7	81.4	11.4	21.4	78.6
Upper Central											
Bihar	92.2	41.4	39.7	6.0	23.3	29.3	19.8	16.4	0.9	12.9	87.1
Uttar Pradesh	73.6	25.5	24.5	13.0	37.0	33.3	30.1	74.1	3.7	20.4	79.6
Lower Central											
Madhya Pradesh	94.0	31.8	28.1	16.1	24.0	12.9	33.2	69.6	2.8	28.6	71.4
Orissa	77.5	54.9	23.5	7.8	25.5	31.4	45.1	73.5	7.8	45.1	54.9
Rajasthan	92.5	47.2	32.1	30.2	42.5	17.0	44.3	90.6	4.7	24.5	75.5
East											
West Bengal	100.0	25.6	51.3	25.6	51.3	37.2	53.9	75.6	7.7	7.7	92.3
North-eastern Rg.	92.4	39.4	34.9	36.4	47.0	34.9	37.9	83.3	1.5	25.8	74.2
West											
Gujarat	96.6	46.6	28.4	12.5	26.1	12.5	79.6	87.5	10.2	18.2	81.8
Maharashtra	97.4	52.3	31.8	35.8	51.0	19.9	78.8	64.9	34.4	21.9	78.2
South											
Andhara Pradesh	92.9	35.4	23.9	26.6	47.8	48.7	62.8	70.8	21.2	6.2	93.8
Karnataka	91.1	59.3	17.8	26.7	58.5	28.2	83.7	78.5	14.1	11.9	88.2
Kerala	49.3	20.0	62.7	26.7	73.3	53.3	70.7	14.7	6.7	0.0	100.0
Tamil Nadu	89.5	38.2	31.6	51.3	82.9	48.7	75.0	82.9	13.2	2.6	97.4
All India	**88.1**	**40.8**	**31.4**	**22.1**	**41.2**	**28.5**	**52.8**	**70.3**	**9.8**	**20.5**	**79.5**

less than 30 per cent of villages with a middle school. The percentage of villages in these states with middle schools within a 5 km range was as low as 50 per cent in Uttar Pradesh and 60 per cent in Madhya Pradesh. West Bengal, however, had about 75 per cent of villages that had a middle school within a 5 km range.

Primary health care in rural areas is provided through a number of sub-centres, primary health centres (PHCs), and hospitals. The target of the national health programme is to set up sub-centres to serve a population of about 5,000 each (3,000 in tribal and hilly areas). Two types of measures are discussed in this context: first the number of villages that have a sub-centre within the village, and proportion of villages that have either a sub-centre within the village or access to a PHC/ hospital within a 5 km range.

Only about 22 per cent of all villages had a sub-centre within the village according to the population criteria. In states like Bihar, Orissa, and Punjab only 5–6 per cent of villages have sub-centres. Less than 30 per cent of villages have access to a PHC/hospital in Bihar, Gujarat, Madhya Pradesh, Orissa, and Punjab. States with relatively better coverage in terms of sub-centres are Tamil Nadu (50 per cent), Maharashtra, Haryana, and the north-eastern states with about 30–36 per cent of villages covered by this facility. In terms of access to a hospital within a 5 km range, the better endowed states were Tamil Nadu, Kerala and Karnataka.

The response to a general enquiry as to whether there were any non-government organizations (NGOs) implementing development programmes in the area of education, health, nutrition, employment, and poverty alleviation, just about 10 per cent of all villages reported an NGO presence. NGO presence was reported to be high in the villages of Maharashtra (34 per cent), Andhra Pradesh (21 per cent), and Tamil Nadu (13 per cent). NGO presence ranged between 0 and 5 per cent in Bihar, the North-eastern states, Madhya Pradesh, Rajasthan, and Uttar Pradesh.

The government launched a massive programme of establishing one *anganwadi* centre per 1000 rural population across India. This survey estimated that 52 per cent of all villages had an *anganwadi* centre within the village. The percentage of these centres was high (above 70 per cent) in the villages of Karnataka, Haryana, Gujarat, Maharashtra, Tamil Nadu, and Kerala. Only about 20 per cent of villages in Bihar, 30–33 per cent in Uttar Pradesh and Madhya Pradesh reported having an *anganwadi* centre within the village.

Relationship between Village Development and HDIs

This section reviews the extent of the relationship between village level infrastructure and selected human development indicators developed from household level data. Most of these associations are mutual and the causality of this association is not easy to establish. This becomes all the more difficult if information on how long such infrastructural facilities have been in existence is not available. The following discussion should be understood in this perspective. Besides, these associations are only discussed at the aggregate all India level.

Table 9.2 presents in matrix form the link between the village level variable and human development indicators. The relationships between some of these variables are not necessarily important, but because the analysis has been undertaken on the basis of a standardized format, this information is also available. For example, the existence of a sub-centre and level of average agricultural wage may not actually have a relevant association. On the other hand, the existence of a sub-centre and the value of health indicators is expected to be positively related.

Transport and communication infrastructure appears to have a strong association with most human development indicators. Villages connected with all weather roads and villages with bus stops generally show higher levels of human development and have 16 and 17 per cent higher household income respectively than villages without these facilities. This translates itself into 18 and 25 per cent higher per capita income respectively. Similarly villages with access to a post office and telephone have 6–8 per cent higher household incomes. As a result, in these villages the mean income for those below the poverty line is also higher. For example, the 'head count ratio' (HCR) for villages with roads is only 33 per cent in comparison with those not connected by road which is 40 per cent. The HCRs for villages with and without a bus stop are 34 and 43 per cent respectively. Villages with relatively better transportation facilities also have a lower proportion of wage workers but relatively higher wage levels.

Villages connected by *pucca* roads and bus stops showed consistently high literacy rates and enrolment rates for both males and females. They also had high child immunization rates, substantially high contraceptive prevalence, low birthrates, low short duration morbidity, and relatively low child under-nutrition. The associations are similar in villages with post offices and telephones. It was also found that villages with better infrastructure have relatively lower expenditure on foodgrains and health but higher expenditure on education. The utilization of the public distribution system (PDS) is considerably higher among the well-endowed villages that have better transportation and communication.

Although the causality is not established, the substantial and consistent positive association between transport and communication infrastructure and human development indicators needs to be recognized. Rail links, however, do not show any consistent association with human development indicators.

Availability of potable water has a direct relationship with health related indicators. In rural areas children and women spend substantial time fetching water for their household needs. If water sources were located within the village, e.g., taps and hand pumps, it could alter lifestyles, result in better health, higher productivity and income, and lead to improvements in school enrolments as well.

As expected, villages with piped water supply had higher levels of household and per capita income, low levels of HCR, and relatively higher wage rates. Conversely, this relationship can be viewed as the reason why better off villages invest in expensive piped water supply schemes. Villages in which hand pumps are the dominant source of water supply do not show a positive association between levels of income and poverty as appears to be the case in relatively backward villages.

This contrast is more evident in the case of the association with educational and health utilization indicators. For example, villages with piped water have a very high level of literacy, enrolment rates, immunization, and contraceptive prevalence rate. Birth rates are also the lowest in these villages. The expenditure on food is relatively low and PDS utilization is considerably higher in villages with piped water supply. This association can also be viewed from the reverse perspective where piped water supply is the dominant source of water in relatively better off villages while hand pumps are the dominant source in backward villages. It should also be highlighted that about 52 per cent of villages still use unprotected sources as the major source of drinking water. Indeed, the direct link between availability of potable water and health indicators is strong at least

Villages connected by pucca *roads and bus stops showed high literacy and enrolment rates for both males and females. They also had high immunization and low child undernutrition.*

TABLE 9.2

Relationship between Village Development Variables and Selected HDIs
(a) Levels of Income

Village Variable		Household Income (Rs)	Per Capita Income (Rs)	Pop. Below Poverty (%)	PCI Below Poverty (Rs)	Wage Workers as % Worker	Average Wage Agri. (Rs)	Average Wage Non-Agri. (Rs)
Pucca road		28,131	4,971	33.0	1,607	40.2	25	34
		24,323	4,227	40.1	1,583	42.0	22	31
Bus stop	< 2 km	27,056	4,848	34.4	1,597	42.8	24	34
	2+ km	23,147	3,877	43.2	1,581	38.8	21	29
Railway station	< 5 km	25,411	4,368	39.9	1,615	39.2	24	32
	5+ km	25,735	4,524	36.9	1,581	42.0	23	32
Post Office	< 2 km	26,221	4,627	36.4	1,603	41.0	24	33
	2+ km	24,148	4,118	40.9	1,560	42.3	19	28
Telephone	< 2 km	26,403	4,732	36.3	1,596	42.7	25	35
	2+ km	24,914	4,252	39.0	1,585	40.0	22	29
Piped water		30,099	5,442	30.8	1,593	43.8	24	38
Hand pump		24,998	4,336	39.2	1,643	37.7	24	34
Prot. water		25,659	4,827	35.5	1,613	48.4	23	35
Unprotected water		24,758	4,230	39.2	1,566	40.4	22	29
Primary school	Within vill.	25,756	4,504	37.4	1,598	41.5	23	32
	Not in vill.	24,931	4,348	39.8	1,537	40.0	25	32
Middle school	Within vill.	27,061	4,694	36.5	1,592	40.3	23	33
	Not in vill.	24,133	4,274	38.2	1,625	44.3	23	32
Sub-centre		26,841	4,885	32.4	1,648	42.9	25	36
No sub/no hosp.	Upto 5 km	25,526	4,380	39.0	1,574	41.1	22	29
Anganwadi centre	within vill.	26,001	4,676	35.8	1,586	44.5	23	34
	not in vill.	25,316	4,308	39.4	1,594	38.2	24	30
Govt.		26,018	4,496	37.6	1,579	41.5	22	32
Govt.+NGO		27,197	5,152	31.5	1,557	49.3	22	30
Irrigated land	> 50 %	27,091	4,689	36.5	1,598	38.7	25	34
	< 50 %	24,875	4,373	38.3	1,586	42.8	22	31
Village size	< 750	22,714	3,971	42.5	1,514	41.2	18	28
	> 750	26,289	4,596	36.6	1,609	41.4	24	33
All India		**25,653**	**4,485**	**37.7**	**1,590**	**41.3**	**23**	**32**

in this analysis. However, such an association is better understood in the micro-analysis of household data, which often accords greater importance to actual use rather than to just availability.

A positive association is evident between education and health infrastructure and levels of literacy, enrolment, and health indicators. The estimates however suggest that such an association is not necessarily straightforward.

Although villages that have primary and middle schools do have relatively higher levels of income, this does not appear to directly affect

TABLE 9.2
(b) Education, Health, and Demographic Parameters

Village Variable		Literacy		Enrolment Rate		Immuni-zation Rate	Contra-ception Rate	Birth Rate ('000)	Morbidity Rate		Height for Age	
		Male	Female	Male	Female				Short Duration ('000)	Major Morbidity ('0000)	<-3 (%)	–3to–2 (%)
Pucca road		70.1	46.1	82.3	70.9	55.2	40.9	31	115	4,887	35.9	22.0
		63.2	36.8	74.5	61.7	45.1	33.0	33	125	4,412	37.9	21.2
Bus stop	< 2 km	69.0	44.9	81.1	70.7	55.4	40.3	30	118	4,754	36.2	21.8
	2+ km	59.8	31.4	71.1	55.1	39.5	27.9	36	128	4,279	38.5	21.0
Railway station	< 5 km	69.8	43.7	78.4	66.0	47.4	33.6	32	123	4,719	37.0	20.1
	5+ km	64.2	38.9	76.7	64.4	48.8	36.4	32	121	4,530	37.3	21.9
Post office	< 2 km	68.0	43.3	79.1	68.2	50.9	37.2	31	119	4,711	37.0	22.3
	2+ km	59.3	31.4	72.4	56.6	43.2	31.9	35	128	4,232	37.7	19.6
Telephone	< 2 km	69.3	45.9	80.6	69.7	54.7	40.3	29	122	4,856	37.1	22.2
	2+ km	62.0	34.2	74.1	60.4	43.6	31.4	35	122	4,313	37.3	20.9
Piped water		74.8	52.2	88.0	81.1	71.2	49.3	27	121	4,984	33.1	22.5
Hand pump		64.5	41.0	74.4	64.3	44.8	31.9	31	114	4,778	41.1	20.9
Protected water		69.9	47.3	84.0	73.8	67.0	43.2	31	115	4,934	31.7	23.7
Unprotected water		62.8	34.8	74.5	59.5	42.3	32.1	34	126	4,323	37.8	20.9
Primary school	within vill.	65.6	39.9	77.4	65.7	48.7	36.4	32	122	4,564	37.6	21.7
	not in vill.	65.7	41.2	75.1	58.8	46.6	30.9	33	118	4,667	34.6	20.0
Middle school	within vill.	68.4	42.6	79.5	67.5	49.7	38.0	32	113	4,488	38.0	23.0
	not in vill.	65.7	42.0	77.2	66.7	52.9	36.0	31	132	5,154	35.8	21.2
Sub-centre		71.4	46.5	83.3	71.7	54.4	42.8	29	122	4,843	39.4	24.0
No sub/ no hosp.	upto 5 km	62.2	35.7	74.5	61.4	45.7	32.9	33	123	4,396	37.1	20.7
Anganwadi centre	within vill.	68.7	44.9	81.3	71.2	56.9	41.6	30	115	4,681	35.6	21.6
	not in vill.	62.7	35.3	73.5	59.0	42.1	30.2	34	128	4,480	38.5	21.3
Govt.		66.0	39.4	78.4	65.3	47.6	36.7	32	119	4,503	36.8	21.8
Govt.+NGO		68.1	45.4	84.5	75.8	65.2	46.9	27	112	4,619	34.5	23.8
Irrigated land	> 50 %	65.5	38.5	77.7	64.0	51.9	34.4	33	110	4,556	38.8	21.1
	< 50 %	65.6	40.9	76.8	65.3	46.6	36.4	32	128	4,588	36.4	21.6
Village size	< 750	62.2	34.2	75.1	60.3	43.6	33.8	35	129	3,876	36.6	20.6
	> 750	66.3	41.3	77.6	65.8	49.7	36.1	31	120	4,727	37.4	21.6
All India		**65.6**	**40.1**	**77.1**	**64.8**	**48.5**	**35.7**	**32**	**122**	**4,578**	**37.2**	**21.4**

literacy, and affects enrolment rates only marginally and that too in the case of females only. Literacy and education have become more a matter of attitudes and values rather than just a matter of proximity to schools. This evidence, however, does not undermine the important role that schooling infrastructure and the quality of education play in achievement of higher levels of literacy and enrolment rates.

The existence of a health sub-centre and an *anganwadi* centre have shown a substantial association with health output measures, such as the immunization, contraceptive prevalence, and birth rates. The existence of

TABLE 9.2

(c) Structure of Household Expenditure

Village Variable		Percentages of Total Household Income				
		Expenditure on Food Grain	Expenditure on Other Foods	Expenditure on Education	Expenditure on Health	% of House-holds Using PDS
Pucca road		20.4	24.0	2.6	5.5	40.0
		25.2	22.8	2.2	5.9	29.5
Bus stop	< 2 km	21.6	22.8	2.4	5.4	42.0
	2+ km	27.6	25.2	2.2	6.3	17.4
Railway station	< 5 km	25.2	22.8	2.6	5.9	26.0
	5+ km	22.8	24.0	2.3	5.7	35.5
Post office	< 2 km	22.8	24.0	2.5	5.8	36.5
	2+ km	24.0	22.8	2.0	5.5	24.4
Telephone	< 2 km	21.6	24.0	2.6	5.8	43.7
	2+ km	25.2	22.8	2.2	5.6	22.7
Piped water		18.0	25.2	2.6	5.1	55.9
Hand pump		26.4	22.8	2.4	6.5	28.7
Protected water		20.4	24.0	2.2	5.9	46.3
Unprotected water		25.2	22.8	2.2	5.9	25.8
Primary school within vill.		22.8	22.8	2.3	5.6	33.7
	not in vill.	25.2	24.0	2.6	5.7	29.8
Middle school within vill.		21.6	22.8	2.5	5.4	33.3
	not in vill.	25.2	24.0	2.4	6.2	33.9
Sub centre		21.6	22.8	2.6	5.3	45.0
No sub/ no hosp.	upto 5 km	24.0	24.0	2.2	5.8	26.2
Anganwadi centre	within vill.	21.6	22.8	2.4	5.2	44.2
	not in vill.	25.2	24.0	2.3	6.2	22.4
Govt.		22.8	24.0	2.4	5.9	33.6
Govt.+NGO		19.2	21.6	2.1	4.6	47.7
Irrigated land	> 50 %	22.8	24.0	2.3	5.6	27.6
	< 50 %	24.0	22.8	2.4	5.8	36.2
Village size	< 750	25.2	25.2	2.5	5.7	25.8
	> 750	22.8	22.8	2.4	5.7	34.8
All India		**22.8**	**22.8**	**2.4**	**5.7**	**33.2**

an *anganwadi* centre has shown additionally a low incidence of short duration morbidity and low levels of child undernutrition. Further, villages with sub-centers and *anganwadis* have recorded lower expenditures on foodgrains and on health as a proportion to total household income.

About 10 per cent of villages reported having NGOs engaged in the implementation of development programmes. The relative levels of human development indicators are better in these villages. For example, household and per capita incomes were about 5 and 14 per cent higher, and consequently the poverty ratio was substantially lower, only 31.5 per cent

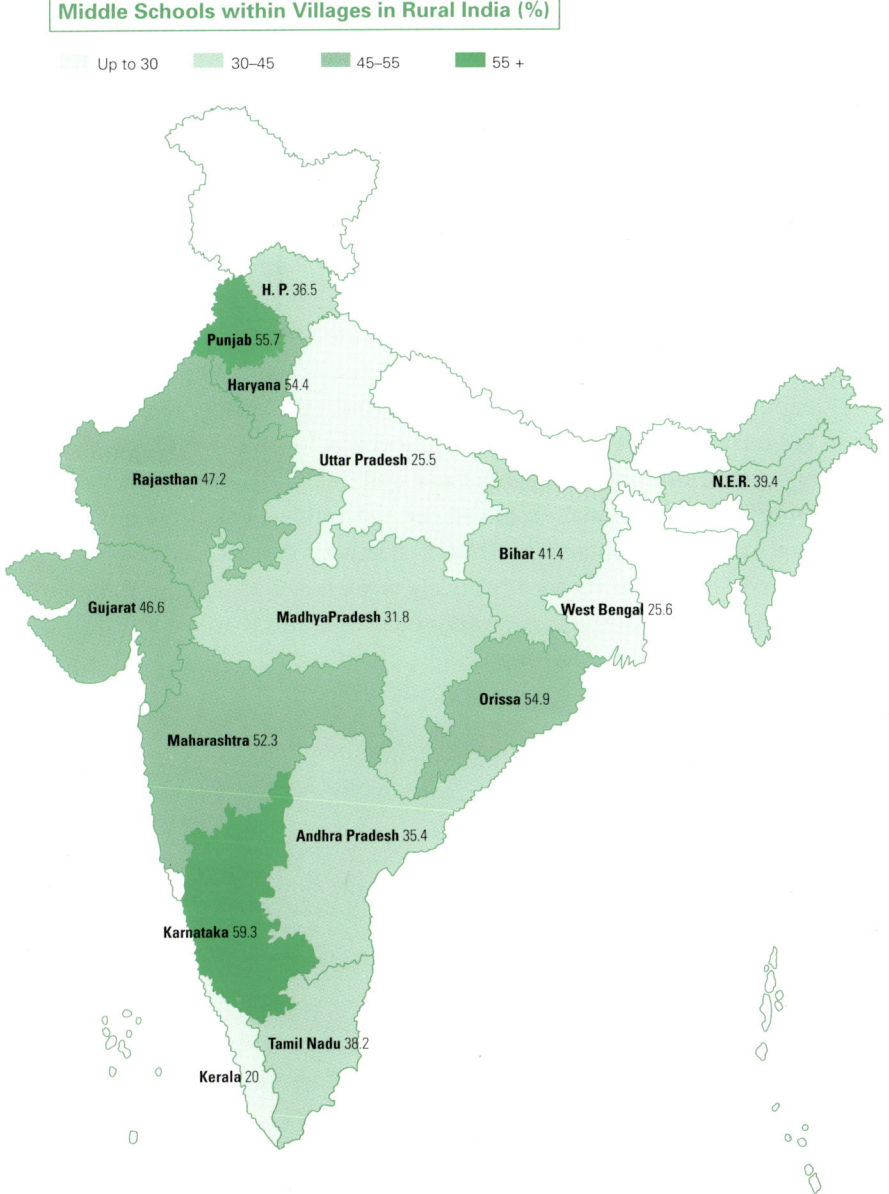

H. P. 36.5

Punjab 55.7

Haryana 54.4

Rajasthan 47.2

Uttar Pradesh 25.5

N.E.R. 39.4

Bihar 41.4

Gujarat 46.6

MadhyaPradesh 31.8

West Bengal 25.6

Orissa 54.9

Maharashtra 52.3

Andhra Pradesh 35.4

Karnataka 59.3

Tamil Nadu 38.2

Kerala 20

Small-sized villages are relatively backward, have lower levels of income, and higher levels of poverty.

when compared with villages where only government programmes were operating. In other words, poverty levels were about 20 per cent lower in villages where NGO programmes were in operation. This is the third most prominent variable associated with poverty after motorable roads and bus stops. Although this is an important finding, it is not a conclusive one that suggests that NGO programmes are always successful in India. Such a conclusion would require a case by case and micro-evaluation of NGO activities.

Similarly, education and health output indicators have a positive association with an NGO's presence. Literacy and enrolment, especially of females are better, as is immunization and contraceptive prevalence, and birth rates are substantially lower. Short duration morbidity and extreme undernutrition are also relatively lower in villages with NGO activity. While expenditure on foodgrains is lower, household expenditure on education and health is also lower suggesting considerable success of NGO programmes. The use of PDS is also substantially higher among these villages.

Villages with over 50 per cent of gross cropped area under irrigation showed marginally higher levels of income and only marginally lower levels of poverty. The levels of other human development indicators were also only marginally different. However, only in the case of PDS utilization is there a substantial difference. For example, PDS use is about 30 per cent higher among the less irrigated villages. As expected, the smaller-sized villages are relatively backward, have lower levels of income, with higher levels of poverty. However, both agricultural and non-agricultural wages are considerably lower in the small sized villages, suggesting a link between these villages and their remoteness. Thus, in comparison with roads and communication, irrigation shows a relatively weak link with income and human development. However, as mentioned earlier, this is only a broad association and not a conclusive one.

Principal Findings

1   Thirty-seven per cent of villages surveyed were connected by *pucca* or all weather roads and 65 per cent had a bus stop within a distance of 2 km.

2   Over 22 per cent of all villages in Orissa (63 per cent), followed by Bihar (33 per cent), Gujarat, Kerala, and Haryana had access to a railway station indicating a well-developed railway network in these states. States with the least developed rail links were Himachal Pradesh, Madhya Pradesh, Karnataka, Rajasthan, and, the North-eastern states.

3   Seventy per cent of villages in rural India reported the presence of a post office within a distance of 2 km while 51 per cent reported the presence of a telephone indicating the existence of a well-developed postal and telecommunication system.

4   About one-half of all villages in India do not have any source of protected drinking water.

5   Overall, 88 per cent of all villages in rural India have a primary school within the village.

6   Only 41 per cent of villages across India have a middle school within the village.

7   About 22 per cent of all vilages have a sub-centre within the village according to the population criteria.

8   Overall 52 per cent of all vilages had an *anganwadi* centre within the village.

10

Synthesis of the Village Studies

To supplement the survey, broad research on human development in a series of village studies was undertaken across India. In all, 135 focus group discussions were conducted in 28 selected villages in 14 states. Besides, a number of semi- and unstructured interviews were conducted by the principal investigators who stayed in the villages for the duration of the study.

Introduction

Investigations following the methodology of large-scale surveys like the NCAER/HDI Survey, 1994, coupled with a time constraint, are limited in their use as they fail to capture details such as the complex social, economic, and infrastructural fabric that are an inseparable part of the respondents' lives. The two indicators of human development, health and economic well-being, are influenced by a number of factors and returns on them are not always explicit nor tangible within the socio-economic environment. Over time, interesting new approaches to study human development have evolved. One such is the 'participatory appraisal method', where the principal investigator with a team of trained personnel undertakes field studies on predetermined topics and issues. The NCAER launched 28 such village studies during 1994–5 to support and complement the findings of the main NCAER/HDI survey. The quantitative data generated by the latter were set against 'qualitative data' gathered in the village studies that reflect the social, cultural, and economic environment of the village.

The series of village studies was based on the premise that many crucial aspects remain hidden or camouflaged in analyses of quantitative information. This assumption underlies the issues examined in each of these village reports. The reports emphasize the significant bearing that qualitative parameters have on the attitudinal, perceptional, and behavioural patterns of villagers in India, besides linking them to supply side aspects such as lack of access and utilization of publically provided services. Although it is well accepted that the provision of schools, health services, and other infrastructural facilities is essential for the well-being of the local people, mere provision does not ensure access to all. The structural and functional aspects of these services also play a role in the formation of perceptions among the rural population as well as in the choices they make.

Levels of poverty, income inequalities, and asset ownership have a crucial impact on the ability of the masses to avail of services, be it education, health, drinking water, or even transport. There is no doubt that the state or district has some bearing on human development indicators,

The qualitative findings provide a number of explanations for the quantitative estimates and data which are presented in earlier chapters.

especially education, health status, and other amenities provided by the government. However, the class and caste composition of a village over and above that in districts or states plays a significant role in determining behavioural patterns as well as perceptions.

Additionally, the location of a village, the infrastructural facilities that are available such as transport, electricity, accessibility of the village, and extent of mobility among villagers both to and from the village, all have a bearing on the nature and extent of development in the area. Exposure to the media and the degree of government intervention increase levels of awareness among the people, thereby enabling them to recognize their status and rights as citizens. Such a knowledge backed by support from family and society can lead to a positive trend in the actual delivery of public goods and services, as it increases the accountability of the executing authorities vis-à-vis the demands of the rural population. An elaboration of these issues and the dynamics they encompass help to place the picture of rural India in proper perspective. The synthesis of the village surveys brings out these aspects by taking into consideration the processes influencing the development of India's villages.

The methodology evolved for the qualitative studies is discussed below. The human development indicators specifically chosen for this study, i.e., education, health and old age security and factors affecting them such as social structure and caste composition, location of the village, physical mobility, extent of exposure to media and government intervention are then discussed taking into account methodological limitations.

Qualitative techniques offered flexibility in approaching the objectives of the study in an in-depth manner.

Methodology

Since qualitative research offers flexibility in using different approaches, a combination of techniques that suited the objectives of the study was selected. To that extent, this qualitative research is unique to NCAER. The specific research techniques used were as follows:

(i)   Transects;
(ii)   Social and infrastructural mappings;
(iii)   Time line charts;
(iv)   Collecting information relating to the social, economic, and political structure of the village with special reference to the infrastructural facilities related to health and education;
(v)   Focus group discussions;
(vi)   Free listing of illnesses;
(vii)   Interviewing school drop-out children;
(viii) Revisits to the households selected for the sample survey.

The effectiveness of these techniques depends not only on the competence of the investigators but also on the sequence in which the techniques were administered. The sequence followed in the present study was similar to the one given above. However, the techniques of focus group discussions, free listing of diseases, children's interviews, household interviews were applied simultaneously.

Three issues, namely health, education, and social security, were chosen as the focus of the study. The study is different from other participatory research approaches in two respects: (a) the 'emics' or insiders did not play any role in deciding the problems to be investigated and instead acted only as facilitators in making the outsiders understand their perceptions and practices; and (b) the study was not oriented for action.

The qualitative study was planned in two villages in each of the 15 major states of India except Andhra Pradesh during November 1994 and July 1995.[1] The villages selected were part of the sample for the NCAER/HDI household survey. First, two districts were shortlisted from each of the states using the following criteria: (a) each district had to belong to a distinct agro-climatic zone of the state; (b) the districts were to be physically distant from each other; and (c) within the state, the districts were to have wide economic disparities. The rationale was to compare the cultural and behavioural differences or similarities among those population groups that were not mutually influential. The village selection was based on:

(i)   Village size (villages with about 200 to 300 households);
(ii) Ethnic composition (multi-caste and multi-religion villages were preferred);
(iii) Of the two villages, one was to belong to the interior of the district.

The size of the villages was the most important criterion and almost all the villages met this requirement.[2] Some of the villages were however spread over a vast area making the coverage difficult. This was true of one village in Madhya Pradesh, located in the tribal districts of Sarguja, Himachal Pradesh (district Kulu), Orissa (district Puri), and both villages of Kerala (districts Mallapuram and Kottayam).

The research team comprised four to five members: the principal investigator, i.e., the team leader, regional staff of NCAER, and three investigators of which two were often female postgraduates and were recruited locally.[3] All the four investigators were given intensive training by the principal investigator at the regional headquarters. The training was important for two reasons:

(i) The methods were required to be used with reference to the objectives;
(ii) In some cases the team leader was not conversant with the local language and therefore making the interviewers understand the content of each of the methods was essential.

The transects in the villages led to some observations of the general surroundings—hygiene, sanitation, sewage, pattern of housing, kind of houses, spread of the village, any distinct characteristic relating to the location of houses, water sources, etc. These transects were also useful in informally introducing the team to the respondents, i.e., in affecting the process of rapport building.

1 The list of the villages selected for this purpose (their names and population, their districts, states, number of focus group discussions conducted, number of primary school dropouts interviewed, number of 'free listing' cases canvassed) is given in Annexe III.
2 We adhered to the small size village criterion because the efficacy of intensive studies falls with large populations or large villages when an attempt is made to study multiple issues.
3 One of the implied preconditions for selection of the staff was that they should be well versed with the vernacular languages.

The transects were followed by social mapping of the village which provided up-to-date household listing along with caste, location of the household with caste/religious identities, sites of infrastructural facilities related to health, education, water sources, any other private health facility, location of government or cooperative society offices: *anganwadi, balwadi,* fair price shop, *panchayat bhawan*, etc. Such mapping not only gave an insight into the ethnic composition and its significance in the lives of people, but also the role of government and the community in the development of the village. Time line charts drawn with the co-operation of the villagers recorded chronologies of major remembered events with approximate dates.

A detailed profile of the village was drawn on topics decided on earlier, namely health, education, society, occupational structure. This work was started on the second and third day of the field work. The key informants (identified during the process of mapping and/or by observation), government officials, health and education personnel were interviewed to gather information on the location of the village, ethnic composition, social mores and customs of the various groups, occupation, employment opportunities, and social and economic interaction amongst the groups. Visits to the school, health centres—private, government, traditional and faith healers, *anganwadi, balwadi,* night school centres, fair price shops— were made where open interviews were conducted to collect information.[4]

Focus group discussions formed the pivotal part of the study. It was through this process of group dynamics that the investigators were able to capture data on perceptions and behaviour regarding health, education, treatment patterns, social security issues. Four to five group discussions were arranged in each village. A sincere attempt was made to represent all the major socio-economic groups.

The characteristics of the participants were predetermined to the extent that there was one group discussion for young men, one for old men and for women, and the remaining two or three for married women with infants. The selection of the candidates for focus groups was done bearing in mind the existing compatibility across the various socio-economic groups. In all, 135 discussions were conducted across the country and the average number of participants per group discussion was 8.4.

The discussions followed a definite set of guidelines on all the three issues (health, education, social security). The sequence of discussion was flexible depending on the interest and enthusiasm of the participants.

The group discussions proved to be extremely useful in eliciting a range of information and insights that are inaccessible in more traditional methods. The transcripts of all the individual focus group discussions conducted in all villages were analyzed for three topics separately: health, education, and social security. A note containing the analysis as well as a comment on the quality of discussion appeared in the final report of all the villages.

Another technique used to exclusively capture the knowledge and awareness levels of women about diseases was 'free listing'. Open-ended proformas were used to collect information on the nature of illnesses with

Focus group discussions provided an excellent opportunity to study group dynamics and capture data on perceptions and behaviours regulating human development.

4 Open interviews followed a checklist for reference but not a pre-set sequence of questions

their associated symptoms and causes. In all, 530 women were contacted with an average of 17.7 women per village. A distinction between diseases was made on the basis of the quickness of response, namely spontaneous or probed. A frequency table using the number of responses was prepared for each village. In cases where the diseases were mentioned in the local language, the corresponding names in English were reported on the basis of symptoms, causes and/or consultation with the health experts.

Background information such as age, caste educational level attained was also noted with the objective of establishing a possible link between the above mentioned characteristics and the names of diseases. A conscious attempt was made to include interviews with women belonging to all castes/religions.

Semi-structured interview schedules were canvassed among children (both boys and girls) selected randomly in the age-group 10–14 years who had dropped out of school before completing elementary education. In all, 225 interviews were conducted. There were five villages where no drop-out children in the relevant age group could be traced.[5] The answers provide some very interesting insights as far as demand side constraints and perceptions are concerned. These micro level investigations can play a crucial role in the formulation of policies and programmes.

The households selected for the sample survey were revisited during this fieldwork to cross-check the information collected as well as to update it. The above work agenda called for a long stay of 10 to 12 days in each village which all the research teams accomplished.

Common Characteristics of Villages and Village Infrastructure

A typical Indian village is usually made up of a combination of thatched roof habitations interspersed with a few *pucca* buildings. Official buildings usually comprise the local government school, post office, or primary health centre. Places of worship like a temple, mosque or gurdwara are generally located at the entrance of the village. The residential area is contiguous and cluttered in most villages with pastoral lands on the periphery.

Facilities for water include community hand pumps/tube-wells generally located in the central section of the village while roads are by and large *kutcha*.

Village homes are semi-*pucca* or *kutcha,* made up of mud or brick walls with thatched, mud-tiled or asbestos roofs. There is no uniformity across communities or within caste groups regarding the type of houses they live in. They differ depending on the status of the family and the household income. Most rural homes are small and have only one or two rooms per dwelling Regional influences may lead to the use of different building materials. For instance, the Sikh houses in Rajasthan use red stone slabs for their roofs and have rock walls that are mud layered forming semi-*pucca* dwellings, while the economically weaker sections of the people live in houses made from clay mud with thatched roofs. Some of the better-off Sikh households had built concrete structures with modern finishes. In Bihar the lower castes all live in *kutcha* houses with thatched roofs and mud walls. Rajputs/Yadavas usually own *pucca* or semi-*pucca* houses.

A conscious attempt was made to include interviews with women belonging to all castes/religions.

5 The districts in which such villages were located are Ludhiana and Hoshiarpur (Punjab), Kottayam (Kerala), and Kamrup (Assam).

In a majority of the villages, caste groups were seen living together in clusters. Most often the locality is named after the community that resides there. In West Bengal's Belpur village there were two prominent clusters: Das *para* and Mohammedan *para* named after the Hindus (largely belonging to the Das community) and Muslims who inhabited these *para*s. Although apparently segregated, there was no visible untouchability between the two communities. Scheduled castes are usually located in a cluster on the periphery of most villages.

Toilets within or near dwellings are a rarity in rural areas. Defecation in the open is common among villagers, not only because there is no alternative, but also because it is a preference. Even among the upper caste households that have a latrine constructed within, only the women use it while men continue to go to the fields. In very few villages was there any reference to public latrines. In village Nathupur in Uttar Pradesh, 40 latrines were built under the JRY scheme. These latrines, however, had no proper side walls and roofs. Water scarcity in some villages is another factor for dysfunctional latrines. While garbage disposal was managed well in a few cases, no collective initiative was evidenced in the organization of an efficient waste disposal system in the majority of villages. One case of community level action was recorded in Panitema in Assam where frequent floods had caused widespread destruction.

Almost all the villages surveyed did not have motorable roads. In most, roads were either *kutcha* or semi-*pucca* given to waterlogging during rains as a result of bad drainage. Apart from a few instances where the villagers used tractors to travel to nearby towns, most villages had an utter lack of public or private transport services. The villages that had brick-laid roads reported that they were built due to the initiative of either the local leaders or because of the various government employment generation schemes.

Most of the villages surveyed had provision for electricity, although the year in which this became operational varied from the 1960s right up to 1994 (the year in which the survey was carried out). There were villages in Raghunathpur district of Bihar where electricity was not meant for domestic use and only authorized for agricultural purposes. A few unauthorized connections were found in some well-to-do upper caste households that possessed television sets and tape-recorders.

Irrespective of whether the village was totally electrified as in Nathupur (UP) where almost 90 per cent of the households had electric connections or where lines had been unauthorizedly tapped, the supply of electric power was highly erratic in all cases. What is of concern, however, is the fact that even under circumstances where electric supply is not dependable, it is only the well-off households that can access it. The case of Indwas in Bihar is a case in point, where only two of the four hamlets were electrified. These two hamlets consisted of Brahmin and Kayastha households while the other two comprised SC and Muslim households. In the SC hamlet, to which electric connections had been provided under the scheme, 'one electric lamp per household' remained in darkness due to theft of wire. In another hamlet, despite the provision of electric poles, access to power supply was denied due to the absence of wired connections.

Further, in Alampur village in Alwar district (Rajasthan), the 'main' village where the Sikh community resides was electrified in 1986–7, while the vast part of the village inhabited by Scheduled Castes and Muslims was electrified only in 1994. Whether this was due to practical or operational reasons or an act of discrimination could not be clearly identified.

The availability and accessibility of potable water in rural areas has social, political as well as economic implications on households in addition to affecting the health and sanitation of villagers. The available sources of water in rural areas range from protected sources such as pipe/tap, hand pumps, protected wells/tanker trucks to unprotected sources such as ponds, open wells, rivers, etc. In many villages open wells continue to be used even when tube-wells have been provided near dwellings as the water is softer and is preferred for drinking purposes.

Hand pumps are preferred to open wells by some women. In Nathupur (UP), powerful households owned outlets of water while some of the upper caste households had appropriated public hand pumps and located these near their own homes and the homes of persons close to the *pradhan*. The single hand pump provided for the harijan *basti* proved inadequate as Harijans (Untouchables) who constitute the second largest caste group of the village were not allowed to draw water from the privately owned open wells.

In Rattangarh in Haryana, water is made available through pipes at community level. However, about 20–5 households had extended the line illegally to their houses at personal cost. In Indwas where only two of the hand pumps were working, these were used by Rajputs and Yadavas, while the lower caste women had to travel distances of half to one kilometre to fetch water.

Some of the reports suggest that cleanliness and a hygienic lifestyle are a matter of culture and habits rather than economic status. In Alampur village (Rajasthan) it was reported that:

Sikh houses were very clean compared to Muslim and Scheduled Caste households irrespective of their economic well-being; and Sikhs built separate shelters for their livestock while Muslims tied them inside their houses.

Even in areas where pump-sets were used along with open wells, the well-off households resorted to diesel pumps to overcome the problem of erratic electric supply and fluctuating water levels in open wells. This is an illustration of how even a commodity that is free of cost has differential access across income class categories in rural India.

In dry areas like Rajasthan time and resources are required to access water. The summer months accentuate the problem of scarce water, involving long walks to the nearest accessible source located one to five kilometres away. The time spent in collecting water can be linked to the issue of education. Poor enrolment or attendance in schools is related to the preoccupation with household chores, including fetching water, especially in the case of females.

Poor enrolment or attendance in schools is related to preoccupation with household chores, especially in the case of females.

Water requirements of households vary with occupation. For example, a Yadava family selling milk, and owning three buffaloes and a cow, requires an average of about 50 buckets of water per day. By contrast, a Vishwakarma household that comprises blacksmiths requires only 30 buckets per day. As it took as long as eight and half hours per day to collect water for the daily requirements of the Yadava household, the eldest son had to drop out of school in the tenth year of schooling. His sisters who were married by then used to do this task during the summer months when their open well dried up.

Some of the implications of such a scenario of accessing potable water in the surveyed villages can be related to the evolving social relations. Even the Viswakarma household whose requirement was only 30 buckets per day faced problems during summer when their own well dried up. Belonging to a minority caste, they had little choice as other communities denied them access to their wells. Such relations create constraints and restrictions among caste groups and subservience among the weaker sections of society.

Human Development Indicators

Education

The positive association between education and development is well known. Although mass education is an essential input, the quality and levels of literacy also matter substantially for development and growth. However, differences in levels of educational attainment are common across countries, states, districts, households, and even within a household. Often, there may be pockets with high or low levels of schooling/literacy in districts that have been categorized as backward or developed respectively. This may be caused by a number of factors that vary from distribution of schools across villages to levels of deprivation among certain sections of the village population. Quantitative data reveal inequitable patterns in availability of schools within any given district. For example, even within a particular village with schooling facilities, a certain number of children belonging to certain population groups may not get enrolled, while another set drops out post-enrolment. One of the objectives of this research has been to explore and explain such unusual exclusions, if any, and to identify the population characteristics so that they become amenable to policy-planning and interventions. These were the basic tenets under which this qualitative study was carried out.

The village level documentation of the time-line for public institutions such as schools and school grades provided useful linkages to explain the differentials in literacy levels between villages. It was noticed that villages in which schools had been in existence for the previous three to four decades had achieved a relatively higher educational status in terms of number of children enrolled and those that were continuing their studies. The existence of schools also appears to be instrumental in reducing gender disparity and enhancing school enrolment of children belonging to the backward sections of society. Thus one can establish a direct relationship between the existence of an educational institution, it duration in a village and the utilization of such a facility. However, it was found that mere availability did not necessarily influence enrolment in all villages.

The awareness that education is important for human development as it increases the opportunities of acquiring regular or better paid jobs is accepted by most rural populations. Parents, however, favour educating only sons who are expected to take care of them in their old age. Wherever girls were also being enrolled the primary reasons for doing so were different. For example, one of the reasons given was the aspiration for a better placed groom if their daughter was educated. Education, especially of sons, is also considered a means to non-agricultural and urban jobs, so that pressure on land is reduced and subdividing the land can be avoided. While such a view was very common, it was particularly stated by the tribal women in Rajasthan.

Other recurrent reasons advanced by parents for disallowing children, especially sons, from continuing in schools up to senior levels were that it could endanger or propagate alienation among the younger generation to family professions, trades and occupations. This view normally emanates from that fact even if an individual is educated, the likelihood of getting a decent job is low and that it forces children to leave their homes and move over to towns and cities both within the state and other distant places. The other explanation is that education fosters resistance to the cultivation strategy of using own or family labour adopted by the landed farmers. Some of the villages in the agriculturally commercial belts reveal a clear tendency to revert to self-cultivation. Even high caste farmers who depended on hired hands now resort to self-cultivation to avoid entanglements in the new land reforms in a few states. Such an attitude creates a negative impact on the education even of sons as parents feel that children should be educated only up to elementary level so as to enable them to read and write only but ensures that they return to work on the land. This was clearly the case in the state of Karnataka.

By and large, however, male children are educated up to the level they can reach without failure, subject to the availability and accessibility of schooling facilities. Many of the students enrolled in schools find it extremely difficult to pass the board examinations for their matriculation due to the limited inputs and poor teaching methods they are exposed to in rural areas. Despite the numerous difficulties, there are still a few matriculates and even occasionally graduates in the villages. In some villages, local educated members become teachers in the village school. This was found to be a very positive factor in enhancing the educational status of children in a village. Among girls, however, one rarely located a graduate.

Primary schools were found in the vicinity of all villages, although Raghunandapur (Bihar) and Nathupur (U.P.) had no schools within the village (see Box 10.1). Only 8 of the 28 villages appeared to have satisfactory levels of enrolment among students in local schools. Availability of schools, therefore, is an essential but not a sufficient condition for higher enrolment and continuance of schooling. In the villages that were close to

BOX 10.1

Education: Availability and Standards

States	Villages	Availability of (in the village)	Level of Schooling	Access by Lower Strata	Standards
Assam	Panitema	Yes	High School	Yes	Satisfactory
	Bongaligaon	Yes	Primary	No	Substandard
Bihar	Indwas	Yes	Primary	No	Substandard
	Raghunandapur	No	-	-	N.A.
Haryana	Rattangarh	Yes	Primary	Yes	N.A.
	B. Hoshnak	Yes	High School	No	N.A.
H.P.	Bhullang	Yes	High School		Good
	Batran	Yes			Backward
Karnataka	Madapura	Yes	High School	Yes	Good
	Jalwadgi	Yes		No	N.A.
Kerala	V. Kannu	Yes	Primary School	Yes	N.A.
	Pathiricode	Yes	Primary	Yes	N.A.
M.P.	Golwa	Yes	Primary	Yes	Satisfactory
	Digma	Yes	Primary	No	Lacking
Maharashtra	Gharalwadi	Yes	Middle VIII Class		Unsatisfactory
	Chachkheda	Yes	Middle VII Class		Unsatisfactory
Orissa	Churiana	Yes	Primary	No	N.A.
	Katabaga	Yes	Primary	No	N.A.
Punjab	Bowani	Yes	High School	Yes	Unsatisfactory
	Barohi	Yes		Yes	N.A.
Rajasthan	Alampur	Yes	High School		N.A.
	Suker	Yes	Primary	No	N.A.
Tamil Nadu	Thervarki	Yes	Middle	Yes	N.A.
	Kannur	Yes	Middle	No	N.A.
U.P.	Rehri Mustakam		-	-	N.A.
	Nathupur	No	-	-	N.A.
W.B.	Belpur	Yes	Primary	No	Unsatisfactory
	Shahpur	Yes	Primary	No	Unsatisfactory

N.A.: Not applicable as assessment not made.

The affluent and high caste may even send their offspring to other states for education in the hope of better job prospects.

urban locales, households with resources and motivation to educate their children, sent them to private or urban schools outside the village. In fact, Raghunandapur, due to its location adjacent with villages that had schools up to the high school level, had a relatively better educational status in comparison with Indwas which is situated in the interior requiring a three-kilometre trek to the nearest high school. Sometimes, as in the case of village Bongaligaon in Assam, the affluent high caste Hindus and some Muslims send their offspring to other states for education in the hope of better job prospects. Indeed, most of the upper caste households exhibit a higher literacy level, comparable across villages and states especially in those areas that are relatively more accessible due to the provision of transport facilities.

Of the 28 villages, 9 were found to have levels of schooling beyond elementary level (*see* Box 10.1). However, in only about five villages did the parents find the availability, in terms of level of schooling, satisfactory. Given this scenario, rural children who are keen to continue schooling have to cross a number of hurdles before they get an opportunity to join the mainstream of education.

Only a third of all villages studied were found to encourage children belonging to the weaker sections of society to access schooling facilities (*see* Box 10.1). The reason for this lies elsewhere—in the ethnic and caste composition of the village, level of economic development, and the concessions/incentives provided to the students belonging to the lower strata of village societies. The response of the community in a few villages to public schemes such as the exemption of fees, provision of mid-day meals, books and uniforms to students belonging to the weaker sections of the society was positive and appears to have acted as an incentive for school enrolments. In some of the villages, a stipend was also given to students belonging to SCs/STs. For example, in B. Hoshnak in Haryana, a monthly stipend of Rs 10 to 15 was given as an incentive to the properly dressed and regular attenders. Monetary incentives, such as an annual sum of Rs 100, were given to students belonging to the weaker sections of the community even in Kerala's Pathiricode village. While such incentives motivate enrolment, they do not ensure continuation of education up to a certain threshold. For instance, in Alampur in Rajasthan, despite governmental assistance of about Rs 180–250 per annum, it was noted that only tuition fee expenses were covered while other expenses on books and stationery remained a burden for the economically backward households.

This is not to say that parents of SC/ST households are not interested in educating their children. Instances of some households expending additional amounts on tutoring their children in order to enable them to fare better in their studies was noted. The treatment meted out to SC/ST students in some schools either due to the social attitudes or as a result of the teacher's bias against them causes disinterest among such students in pursuing education. Alternatively, where there exists either a possibility of gainful employment or even a helping hand in the family enterprise, discontinuation of studies results. Such a practice is more prevalent in the case of girls.

Many a social factor restricts the education of girl children in rural areas, as a result of which female literacy levels are far lower. There are many social, cultural, and economic factors for such practices. Although, the social taboo attached to sending girls out of the house is not as strong a factor, parents still hesitate to send daughters outside the village, especially when this entails traversing open fields or deserted paths. Thus, the absence of a school in the village acts as a deterrent to girls' education. This was found to be the case in Raghunandapur and Nathupur villages in the states of Bihar and U.P. respectively.

Weaker sections of the community in a few villages had a positive attitude towards public schemes such as exemption of fees and mid-day meals which acted as incentives for school enrolment.

While incentives did help enrolment, they did not ensure continuation of education at higher levels.

There exist many other reasons for not utilizing the educational facilities even where such services are in existence, especially in the case of girls. The sociocultural practices that are still prevalent among villagers, such as curtailing girls' mobility post-puberty and the differences of opinion among parents regarding inter-caste and across-gender interaction constrain female education. In fact, the investigators came across a constant demand from parents interested in educating their daughters, for separate girls' schools or at least separate classes for girls, preferably with female teachers in the states of Rajasthan, Punjab, Karnataka, and Tamil Nadu among others.

Among the labour classes, parents expressed difficulty in looking after girl children after they returned from school in the absence of an adult member at home. Such households usually resort to the practice of retaining older girl children in the house to look after the younger siblings and manage other household chores which prevents enrolment and attendance in schools. Even in villages where these factors are not prominent, girls education suffers as parents assign greater importance to sons' education. In consequence, in times of resource constraints, the axe falls first on the girl child's aspirations to study. These village studies highlight and reconfirm that many parents, who otherwise claim to be unbiased in terms of providing education to both boys and girls, in fact do discriminate on one pretext or another in educating girls.

Resource constraint is the most prominent cause for dropping out among rural children. The manner in which this may occur varies from case to case. Inadequate cash flow compels rural households to withdraw their children from school. Girls are the first to be pulled out on these grounds. In villages where alternative avenues of earning through gainful employment exist, as in the tea gardens in Bongaligaon in Assam, cotton seed separation in Jalwadgi in Karnataka, which fetches a child Rs 40 as weekly wage, or collection of prawn seedings in Churiana village in Orissa, parents are motivated to discontinue their children's education.

The seasonal requirements for agricultural activities of the family also result in discontinuation among some children of resource poor households. The inability of rural schools to accommodate such requirements limits the scope of literacy attainment in villages. Unfortunately, in some villages, such as Rattangarh in Haryana, re-enrolment fees of Rs 25 to Rs 50 are charged, acting as a deterrent to readmission of even the very keen students.

Indeed, what is referred to as free primary education is not actually so, as the cost of stationery and maintenance requirements of a school-going child adds to the household expenditure. This is often the reason even for the pre-primary level drop-out of children, especially among households of wage-earning parents with poor resources. Only in four of the 28 villages surveyed was there no mention of children dropping out. In both villages of Punjab, in Panitema in Assam, and V. Kannu in Kerala, no child was reported to discontinue studies up to the level available within the village. Pathiricode reported only two instances. Both of these boys belonged to exceptional households, one with a separated mother and the other a motherless child with a not very active father. These drop-outs were

This study highlights and reconfirms that many parents, who otherwise claim to be unbiased in terms of providing education to both boys and girls, in fact do discriminate on one pretext or another in educating girls.

BOX 10.2

Health Services: Availability and Standards

States	Villages	Services Available	Access by Lower Strata	Standards
Assam	Panitema	No	-	-
	Bongaligaon	No	-	-
Bihar	Indwas	No	-	-
	Raghunandapur	No	-	-
Haryana	Rattangarh	Yes	Poor	Lacking
	B. Hoshnak	No	-	-
H.P.	Bhullang	Yes	Those in	Relatively poor
	Batran	Yes	service	Well managed
Karnataka	Madapura	No	-	-
	Jalwadgi	Yes	Poor	Lacking
Kerala	V. Kannu	Yes	Yes	Better facilities
	Pathiricode	Yes	-	Lacking somewhat
M.P.	Golwa	No	-	-
	Digma	Yes	-	-
Maharashtra	Gharalwadi	No	-	-
	Chachkheda	No	-	-
Orissa	Churiana	No	-	-
	Katabaga	No	-	-
Punjab	Bowani	No	-	-
	Barohi	No	-	-
Rajasthan	Alampur	No	-	-
	Suker	Yes	No	Unsatisfactory
Tamil Nadu	Thervarki	Yes	Partly	Good facilities
	Kannur	No	-	-
U.P.	Rehri Mustakam	-	-	-
	Nathupur	-	-	-
W.B.	Belpur	No	-	-
	Shahpur	No	-	-

obviously working towards earning a livelihood to support their respective households. There exist other instances of villages belonging to districts known to be fully literate such as in Birbhum (West Bengal) among others, which reported drop-outs. These drop-out cases mostly occurred among the deprived sections of the people.

Educational levels are lower in rural areas. The reasons for this lie in the attitudes of villagers. The lack of infrastructural facilities, poor teaching methods, and disinterested or biased teachers are some of the major reasons pointed out by the respondents for the poor standards of education and their resultant lack of motivation to educate their children. The village schools lack proper buildings, seating equipment, toilets or, in some cases, even water. Often all the classes are clubbed together and held in a single room. Absenteeism among teachers is another problem that results in lack of seriousness among students. The teachers in most cases reside elsewhere and have to commute long distances daily, which causes them to be irregular.

The use of students to sweep, clear, drain out water, and the like, is strongly objected to by the parents, especially when the students belonging to certain sections of the community are made use of in such activities by the teachers. Verbal and physical abuse of children is also another deterrent to children's education. Poor resource allocation and lack of educational equipment in the rural schools constrain the teachers' motivation efforts. The methods of teaching are substandard. In consequence, when students, after completion of studies in local schools, seek admission elsewhere, they fail miserably. Most of the rural schools work under the directive of state governments to promote as many children as possible and minimize detention.

However, the case of Golwa in Madhya Pradesh, where a tap for drinking water was installed to prevent children from leaving school on the pretext of being thirsty, and the case of Bhullang village in Himachal Pradesh, where teachers visited every household to motivate parents and enthuse children to study, are examples that could be replicated in other villages.

Health

A majority of the rural areas (among the villages surveyed) do not have provision for primary health care services. Only 12 of the 28 villages surveyed had some sort of health facilities in the village (see Table 10.2). Of these 12, except for three villages—Batran in H.P., Varikkam Kunnu in Kerala and Thervazhi in Tamil Nadu—all the other village level health facilities were unsatisfactory, where villagers expressed the need for provision of good quality and low cost health services from the government.

The level of hygiene and sanitation and availability of certain infrastructural facilities also affect the health status of villagers. For instance, lack of clean drinking water to certain sections of the population due to a variety of factors (described in the section discussing common characteristics of village and village infrastructure) can lead to epidemics among the deprived groups. The appropriation of public water supplies by the better-off and dominant households is one of the reasons. For example, the Choupals in Bihar, who used pond water for washing utensils, were faced with an epidemic of gastroenteritis and diarrhoea that claimed a dozen lives.

The common ailments affecting most villagers are fever, cold, cough, stomach disorders; and various aches affecting vital parts of the body such as back, leg, hand, ear, eye, and head, and other infections. On the health aspect the focus group discussions (FGDs) were targeted to assess the awareness levels among the participants. As FGDs were conducted among persons belonging to different castes and classes it was possible to note differences in the knowledge and perception levels regarding health status. The causes of ailments varied considerably among different groups. While the upper castes mentioned status-related diseases, the lower castes

While the upper castes mentioned status-related diseases, the lower castes identified general weakness as a major constraint for their livelihood.

identified weakness as the reason for the lack of ability to protect themselves. Additionally, external influences such as interaction with semi-urban or urbanized groups of persons, access to other informational channels, be it radio or television, also appeared to affect the understanding of villagers in this area.

The higher the level of awareness regarding health status, ailments, symptoms and their causes, the greater the need to seek assistance from medical or other health personnel. However, even this health-seeking behaviour differed considerably across the population groups. Variations were witnessed in and across households, communities, and regions. The attitudinal differences among population groups appear to be influenced less by the presence or absence of heath care institutions within the village. Such differences were however well defined with regard to the resource position of households while gender differentials were not so clear. Needless to say, it was the resourceful well-off households that sought treatment whenever available.

The perceived value of seeking health services is not as clear as compared to that of education precisely because of the levels of awareness about medical ailments and their treatment. Low awareness levels or misinformed villagers who ascribed non-medical causes as symptoms of their ailment were quite a few. The simple fact that fever is a symptom and not an illness to be cured is known to very few villagers. Sheer lack of knowledge or awareness about ailments, symptoms, causes, and cures, or prevention, is the reason for a high degree of suffering due to low health status. The situation is worse when such ignorance of ailments leads to subsequent treatment for a wrong cause.

Thus, mere awareness of an ailment, was not seen as a sufficient condition for seeking medical aid. Where villagers perceived the ailment to be caused by supernatural powers or any other cause (other than the medical), their health-seeking behaviour also varied accordingly. For instance, in Assam, patients and members of their families take permission of the *devta* to seek medical assistance, while in Karnataka's Jalwadgi village *ane* (foot corns) are not seen as a medically curable ailment. In consequence, no villager sought medical help for this problem which makes walking painful. Some considered tobacco consumption to be the cause of corns, while they overlooked the practice of walking barefoot on harsh terrain in all weather conditions.

There are many instances of diseases that are area-specific. Leprosy was reported in two of the villages, Katabaga in Orissa and Madapura in Karnataka. Although it is a climate-influenced, germ-caused disease, it is considered to be hereditary by many of the villagers. Interestingly, unlike in urban areas, villagers do not restrict the movement and interaction of leprosy affected persons. Gharalwadi in Maharashtra is a hilly region where villagers are prone to arthritic problems, while Bhullang in H.P. has incidences of respiratory diseases and joint pains due to the extreme cold climate and hilly terrain in the area.

Even in areas where health services are available, the reasons for their

Low levels of awareness about ailments and sheer ignorance cause villagers to ascribe their ailments to non-medical causes.

falling short are commonly lack of infrastructural facilities such as proper buildings or medicines. The low-lying location of the sub-centre is also a problem in many cases where waterlogging causes the health centre to be cut off. Absenteeism or irregular attendance by medical staff is another cause mentioned by many villagers in FGDs. Medical staff, on the other hand, complain of lack of residential facilities in the village and poor transportation leading to problems of commuting on a regular basis.

In some cases, fees are charged by government health workers that the villagers cannot afford. Those who can afford them prefer to avail of better quality services in nearby towns or from private practitioners. This perception of quality health services and the behaviour of villagers is closely linked to the cost incurred of availing of such services. One illustration is of Suker village in Rajasthan where it was common for patients visiting a government hospital to spend money to purchase medicines costing on an average Rs 20 to Rs 40 (in 1994) even for common ailments. However, the private practitioners who charge as little as Rs 15 were reported to provide free medication for a period of three to four days, by which time the patient would be cured of the sickness. This demonstrates that private practitioners tend to be a more practical and economic choice for villagers.

Whatever the nature of health services sought by rural households, it is the male, generally the head of the household or the major income earning member, who decides on the requirements of any sick member. This situation has many implications for women and their health status. Gender differentiation in seeking medical assistance is worse as a consequence of the lack of awareness among men of women's ailments. This was the perception among a set of persons who were included in the focus group discussions.

Regarding different attitudes vis-a-vis women's ailments and their health-seeking behaviour in comparison to that of men, most of the survey based information does not find any obvious gender bias. However, to the extent the awareness levels are low or women do not themselves reveal their diseases either due to shyness or out of fear that it may cause undue expense to the households' fragile income balances, there does exist some bias. This is evident in that women in most cases tend to be more concerned about the well-being of the household and the next generation at the expense of their own care and comfort.

Pregnant women in many of the villages do not have any special diet; in fact they reduce their food intake! This is done in the belief that pregnant women cannot digest heavy food. A similar lack of awareness or superstitious beliefs makes women throw away the first milk post-delivery as it is considered harmful to the child. They are obviously unaware of the fact that mother's milk contains many protective elements that enhance the child's resistance to common ailments.

The shortage of money and easily available tradition-based home remedies curtails the growth of modern medication. Given the prevalence of corrupt practices, with few dedicated medical practitioners available, it is difficult for villagers to reject or ignore the traditional practices followed in

While absenteeism and irregular attendance of medical staff have been emphasized by the people, medical staff on the other hand complain of lack of residential and transportation facilities.

The best choice would be a sagacious blending by dedicated health workers of traditional values and practices and modern medicine.

rural areas. The best choice would be a sagacious blending by dedicated, sincere auxiliary nurses and midwives (ANMs) and VHNs of traditional values and practices and modern medication.

There is no doubt that, if health services are free, dependable, and easily accessible, the incidence of use of such services will improve. Such a need is more openly and insistently expressed in the case of children's illnesses by parents, especially mothers.

Social Security

In the village surveys, the study of social security was limited to the care of the elderly and old age benefit schemes of the government. The questions posed were: Are the aging population of rural villages taken care of? If so, who looks after them? And more importantly, what do the older folk think about the care they receive and who is responsible for such service. Only in a few of the villages did the older generation point out in the Focus Group Discussions that the government should be concerned about them and give them some benefits (in cases where there was no reference to any pension scheme) or a higher amount (where some amount was being released to them).

The problem of social security has necessarily to be linked to societal norms in India and prevalent family structures. As social norms are undergoing change, more and more families are moving away from the joint or extended family system to nuclear families. Erosion of family values has also taken place with growing urbanization and exposure to the media and break-up of families due to migration of villagers. However, a large number of households still continue to have linkages and binding relationships with their kith and kin.

Care of the elderly is a major problem facing rural people in India. Often the family members do not know what course of action to take. The treatment of the elderly and terminally sick entails costs in terms of time, personal care and attention, provision of food and medicine, as well as the upkeep and maintenance of hygiene.

Under these circumstances the possibility of community endorsement for locating the sick outside the regular domiciliary space may occur. For example, a daughter-in-law who purchased a buffalo impounded it within the living space of the household and a terminally sick mother-in-law was kept out in a temporary shed where she died even as the observer was conducting his interview. In other cases, a family may perceive an economic asset or a person with future earning capacity as gainful in contrast to an aged person in the household. However, aged persons who own assets are more likely to be well looked after.

A majority of the villagers above the age of 60 feel insecure as their capacity to earn decreases and their meagre earnings do not provide for saving. They are inevitably faced with the prospect of total dependence on their wards and kin. The survey sought to elicit their responses regarding the kind of support and security they expected or considered important.

This perception among the elderly that sons are the only source of security is an age-old tradition in India which allows parents to depend on

There are a number of circumstances in rural areas that allow the possibility of community endorsement for locating the old and sick outside the regular domiciliary space.

their male offspring while daughters are given away in marriage to another family. This is also the root of the preference for the boy child in Indian families which has led to abortion the female foetus in areas where modern tests to identify sex through amniocentesis are available, as in the states of Haryana and Punjab. A son's birth is cause for celebration while the household laments the birth of a girl child.

Interestingly, some of the FGDs brought out that landownership was the preferred social security for the future. This is probably due to failure of expectations from sons either because of their changing attitudes and responsibilities or due to the increasing economic pressure on families. Many old parents or single parents are forced to live separately with little support from their children. Under these circumstances, it is hardly surprising that parents feel asset ownership will take care of their future when they can no longer earn their living.

Many old and single parents are forced to live separately with little support from their sons and/or daughters.

Apart from a few households who belonged to the landowning castes of the village and the salaried employee households, not many others managed to save. In a majority of cases, households had to resort to borrowing from moneylenders at steep rates of interest in the times of distress. Such practices of usurious moneylending continue because the demand for credit encourages such borrowing practices. Realizing this, one or two of the villages had set up their own cooperatives to lend money, as an alternative to other formal credit institutions, to serve their so-called 'unproductive' requirements like marriage and maternity costs, as in the case of Rajasthan's Chidwa Village Cooperative Samiti Limited.

Government programmes for the elderly were not in evidence. One of the investigators who had a camera proved to be very popular among the elderly because they needed photographs in order to be able to apply for the old age pensions amounting to Rs 50–75 per month. When asked what they would do with the pension, the most frequent response was that they would give it to their sons with whom they normally resided.

Conclusion

A review of the overall findings of the village studies on three major issues of education, health, and old age security reveals that dichotomies prevail in Indian social structures. For instance, while education is considered important, lack of a healthy attitude towards the dignity of labour results in alienation of the educated from traditional family occupations, and eventually curtails educational attainment itself. Beliefs and superstitions delimit entry of modern, scientific medical practices, on the one hand, while on the other, lack of adequate health facilities promote the acceptance and dependence upon traditional health practices. Assistance from government authorities strengthens the informal and personalized relations among children and parents within the folds of family structures. Within these dichotomies, variations cut across caste, region, and degrees of intervention. These variations influence the level of development as revealed in the qualitative study on HDIs.

Factors Affecting HDIs

In this section various parameters that are found to have a significant bearing on the human development indicators are discussed with a few illustrative examples. These parameters can be divided into three categories: (a) economic dominance and caste composition; (b) location of the village and population mobility; and (c) media exposure and various government interventions.

Economic Dominance and Caste Composition

The composition of the village based on ethnicity, religion, caste, and class factors has a significant impact on the outlook of villagers and their behavioural patterns. The influence of these factors is specific to each particular village and is unrelated by and large to district or state policies, unless the intervention is widespread with the support and involvement of all the villagers, as in the case of Kerala's educational attainment.

Certain specific occurrences in history and the level of development attained as a result of natural resources in a particular region can influence the composition of caste and class in a village. In Bhoda Hoshnak village of Haryana, the Other Backward Castes (OBCs)—potters (Kumhars) and carpenters (Khatis)—have become the dominant landowning class as a result of two major changes affecting the village. The two groups however played no role in bringing about such changes. The external factors that resulted in this were, first, the partition of India, when Muslims sold their land and moved out of the country; and second, when the state of Haryana was formed and many of the Punjabi households migrated from their villages selling off their lands which were then acquired by these two groups. As a result of such shifts in landownership patterns, potters and carpenters left their traditional occupations and began to depend on cultivation alone.

Another instance where development of the region has provided better avenues to even the weaker and poor sections of the people is Punjab's village Bowani. With agricultural advancement the need for transport facilities rose. Subsequently, the small landowning and peasant communities who found agriculture unprofitable switched to other occupations, thus leading to the harmonious coexistence of people belonging to different communities. On the other hand, areas where such avenues are absent the dependence of SCs on the higher castes continues, as in Rattangarh of Haryana where contracted bonded labour practices are common. However, in another area, Golwa village of Madhya Pradesh where bonded labour practices are found, an interesting incident was noted. The SCs, as a consequence of their increasing consciousness, dared to dishonour labour contracts after taking an advance from the employer. This became possible largely due to the active propaganda both from government sources and many other NGOs working towards abolition of bonded labour practices.

Another instance of villagers' increasing levels of awareness was witnessed in village Raghunandapur of Bihar, where the lower caste

Choupals and Kouris, who leased land from the Brahmins for share cultivation, demanded legal documents from Brahmin households to prove their ownership of the land. They subsequently claimed the land as their own and stopped giving the Brahmins a share of the produce when the latter failed to produce the ownership documents. The Choupals had migrated from Bihar to Punjab, Haryana, and Delhi, and the exposure and knowledge of legalities together with political backing gave them the courage to rebel against the age-old exploiting classes.

It is interesting to note how village Belpur and Shahpur of West Bengal, inhabited both by Muslims and Hindus, recorded different incidences of communal violence. While the Muslim dominated village Belpur belonging to the relatively developed district of North 24-Parganas did not report any violent instances, Sahaopur village with 50 per cent Hindu landowning classes in the relatively less developed Birbhum district reported communal violence.

Location of Village and Mobility

Villages with transport facilities to towns and cities have a distinct advantage in that the physical linkage and proximity promotes awareness of programmes and linkages for the attainment of higher levels of development. They provide the opportunity to migrate and enlarge the market demand for products or services supplied by the villagers. As already described above, in the case of Bihar, migration to Punjab and Haryana and the resultant rebellion against local oppression had been successful. The possibility of earning or gainful employment provides the essential income support which in turn facilitates access to education or health services.

An interesting incident of inter-state migration for a different purpose was noted in Orissa's village Katabaga. It was found in Orissa that migrants from Andhra Pradesh sold irrigated land for high values in the developed market of West Godavari and bought eight times more land in the village of their origin. The local Oriya people were employed as labourers by these migrant settlers.

Government Intervention and Media Exposure

The process of urbanization, increased interaction with developed regions both facilitated by modern media in the form of newspapers, radio, or television can effect significant changes in behavioural patterns of a population. Many forms of public broadcasts relating to education, health, savings schemes, and the like, do significantly influence the rural populace. For example, villages where family planning methods are actively adopted are found to have significant exposure to such media broadcasts.

As is to be expected, an increase in the awareness level of villagers enables them to recognize their status as citizens, their rights and also duties towards the community and the state. Such an enlightened approach supported by both family and society can be a catalytic factor in improving the actual delivery and use of public goods and services. This also results in transparency and accountability in public discourse among the rural people.

An increase in awareness enables villagers to recognize their status and identity as citizens, their rights and also duties towards the community and state. This will help improve the delivery and use of public services.

Otherwise the government takes decisions on behalf of the public without the public ever being aware of what is happening or its consequences, till it is too late. For instance, the Government of India in 1957 and 1971 rehabilitated Bangladesh refugees in the tribal village of Digma in Madhya Pradesh. Nearly 80 per cent of the village's population is made up of rehabilitated Bengalis who have been provided plots of land. The tribals fear the shrinking land share and natural resources and naturally grudge the control of 'their' resources by the government which they fear may go as donations to others. Most often existing facilities in education and health are utilized by the rehabilted familes while excluding the erstwhile local tribal population. Such a drastic shift in composition has led a social crisis among the original tribal population who have been marginalized.

There is also evidence of positive government intervention through various credit, poverty alleviation, and employment generation schemes. For these schemes to have the required impact, the support of dominant sections of the village and/or active political groups is required. Additionally, there is a need for more sustained efforts in this direction.

Principal Findings

It needs to be emphasized that none of the factors in the qualitative studies conducted by NCAER can be meaningfully analysed in isolation. The human development indicators discussed above are only an indication of the nature of influences that have a bearing on the behavioural and attitudinal patterns of villagers. To understand why a particular phenomenon is prevalent in one village and not in another, we need to look at its social, political, as well as economic indicators before giving reasons for such occurrences.

In addition to infrastructural, educational, and health-related institutions in the surveyed villages, the reports throw light on occupational aspects, resource endowments, religion and caste diversity, and interrelated social and structural issues. Since the design was to achieve uniformity of method in eliciting information so as to, as far as possible, retain spontaneity, the task of synthesizing these studies was a difficult one.

The technique of free listing of diseases in particular seems not to have added rigour to understanding the dynamics of health. The methdology does not make an effort to document the prevalence and magnitude of a reported ailment. Some of the reported diseases could only have been heard of but not experienced while some others that actually occurred in the village may not have come to the notice of the selected group. One of the demerits of the technique of interviewing school drop-outs is that children are not reliable respondents. However, since the exercise was meant to draw out the reasons for discontinuation, the method used served the intended purpose.

This qualitative study succeeded in eliciting village-level details that make the reports unique and interesting. The cost of inconsistencies is low, given the objective of attempting to understand the socio-cultural diversity that influences the human development profile of rural India.

ANNEXE I Allocation of Sample Households in States

S. No.	Religion/Caste	Stratum Occupation	Haryana	Himachal Pradesh	Punjab	Bihar	Uttar Pradesh	Madhya Pradesh	Orissa	Rajasthan	NER	West Bengal	Gujarat	Maharashtra	Andhra Pradesh	Karnataka	Kerala	Tamil Nadu
								Selected Sample Households in States										
1	Households with at least one pregnant woman		301	113	251	301	290	379	242	306	286	293	204	302	306	301	225	313
2	Households with at least one child aged less than 12 months but no pregnant women		305	166	360	301	594	662	362	295	282	304	269	495	326	380	230	333
3	Muslim	Marginal farmer	—	—	—	23	170	—	—	—	—	61	—	—	—	20	43	—
4	Muslim	Small farmer	—	—	—	18	114	—	—	—	—	29	—	—	—	45	9	—
5	Muslim	Large farmer	—	—	—	14	46	—	—	—	—	7	—	—	—	49	1	—
6	Muslim	Agricultural lab.	—	—	—	123	149	—	—	—	—	74	—	—	—	122	55	—
7	Muslim	Other	—	—	—	171	289	—	—	—	—	71	—	—	—	92	120	—
8	Christian	Marginal farmer	—	—	—	—	—	—	—	—	87	—	—	—	—	—	77	—
9	Christian	Small farmer	—	—	—	—	—	—	—	—	8	—	—	—	—	—	29	—
10	Christian	Large farmer	—	—	—	—	—	—	—	—	2	—	—	—	—	—	24	—
11	Christian	Agricultural lab.	—	—	—	—	—	—	—	—	21	—	—	—	—	—	79	—
12	Christian	Other	—	—	—	—	—	—	—	—	30	—	—	—	—	—	99	—
13	SCs	Marginal farmer	51	88	8	45	244	90	69	102	30	48	—	—	97	78	—	96
14	SCs	Small farmer	46	25	14	24	155	116	18	101	15	28	—	—	95	52	—	23
15	SCs	Large farmer	40	0	20	6	30	57	3	102	4	6	—	—	27	18	—	4
16	SCs	Agricultural lab.	151	87	126	181	313	218	145	91	13	125	—	—	227	240	—	128
17	SCs	Other	154	81	116	124	253	169	57	101	36	104	—	—	94	103	—	108
18	STs	Marginal farmer	—	—	—	96	—	106	95	50	—	—	86	—	—	—	—	—
19	STs	Small farmer	—	—	—	107	—	215	84	46	—	—	79	—	—	—	—	—
20	STs	Large farmer	—	—	—	38	—	127	18	43	—	—	84	—	—	—	—	—
21	STs	Agricultural lab.	—	—	—	121	—	240	149	48	—	—	111	—	—	—	—	—
22	STs	Other	—	—	—	43	—	189	36	55	—	—	107	—	—	—	—	—
23	Others	Marginal farmer	151	251	76	163	382	186	185	163	100	80	102	384	194	208	75	118
24	Others	Small farmer	144	85	79	72	372	364	163	164	94	38	110	485	212	218	38	55
25	Others	Large farmer	94	44	115	41	249	438	72	166	28	20	205	428	162	296	41	63
26	Others	Agricultural lab.	108	104	98	172	295	328	148	102	87	93	208	498	253	266	175	154
27	Others	Other	263	216	110	154	306	436	194	167	153	179	203	406	251	259	180	150
	Total		1,808	1,260	1,373	2,338	4,251	4,320	2,040	2,102	1,276	1,560	1,768	2,998	2,244	2,747	1,500	1,545

Note: — denotes not applicable. NER = North-eastern region

ANNEXE II Estimated Parameters for States and Standard Errors

States	Annual Income Of the HouseHold	Esti-mated Standard Error	Per Capita Income (Rs Per year)	Esti-mated Standard Error	Literacy Rate 7+ (%)	Esti-mated Standard Error	Enrolment Rate 6-14 (%)	Esti-mated Standard Error	Exp. on Edu. (per capita Per year)	Esti-mated Standard Error
North										
Haryana	39,956	1,749	6,368	274	54.9	1.40	78.1	2.87	1,360	128.00
Himachal Pradesh	23,973	2,014	4,168	305	68.2	2.06	92.7	0.97	1,667	152.00
Punjab	37,418	115	6,380	120	60.2	1.22	86.8	2.83	1,333	97.68
Upper Central										
Bihar	22,459	867	3,691	113	43.8	3.22	58.8	4.34	676	76.70
Uttar Pradesh	26,733	1,193	4,185	185	46.7	1.50	64.2	2.37	689	40.95
Lower Central										
Madhya Pradesh	25,319	1,955	4,166	284	43.9	2.42	62.6	2.44	484	39.22
Orissa	17,208	1,110	3,028	210	54.5	1.75	70.9	2.73	426	28.11
Rajasthan	27,184	2,594	4,229	351	40.9	2.57	61.3	2.45	820	113.29
East										
North-eastern Rg.	28,160	3,421	5,075	557	70.0	4.10	81.3	4.72	733	151.34
West Bengal	18,113	1,359	3,157	172	58.5	3.95	66.1	3.17	549	56.96
West										
Gujarat	29,356	3,675	5,288	548	59.4	2.35	80.3	2.17	545	110.40
Maharashtra	29,929	1,987	5,525	298	58.2	1.45	85.2	1.24	586	64.23
South										
Andhra Pradesh	24,776	1,635	5,046	333	50.2	1.86	79.5	3.69	493	43.00
Karnataka	27,372	2,446	4,769	531	54.9	7.27	77.9	4.29	705	104.00
Kerala	29,101	1,519	5,778	511	89.6	1.20	98.6	0.41	1,091	89.59
Tamil Nadu	23,271	2,856	5,122	754	64.1	2.74	87.7	0.79	593	108.35

Contd.

ANNEXE II Estimated Parameters for States and Standard Errors

States	Short Duration Morbidity Prevalence (per '000)	Estimated Standard Error	Long Duration Morbidity Prevalence (per '000)	Estimated Standard Error	Work Parti-cipation Rate Including Family Worker All	Estimated Standard Error (All)	Work Parti-cipation Rate Including Family Worker Male	Estimated Standard Error (Male)	Work Parti-cipation Rate Including Family Worker Female	Estimated Standard Error (Female)
North										
Haryana	153	1.33	6,697	57	0.34	0.0085	0.51	0.0105	0.15	0.0126
Himachal Pradesh	313	2.68	—	—	0.52	0.0078	0.52	0.0131	0.45	0.0171
Punjab	154	1.60	6,692	70	0.42	0.0201	0.53	0.0059	0.29	0.0378
Upper Central										
Bihar	133	1.08	3,817	52	0.35	0.0085	0.49	0.0077	0.19	0.0141
Uttar Pradesh	97	0.93	3,523	24	0.36	0.0121	0.49	0.0075	0.21	0.0211
Lower Central										
Madhya Pradesh	195	0.94	4,801	36	0.42	0.0166	0.54	0.0087	0.28	0.0297
Orissa	143	1.21	5,011	93	0.41	0.0164	0.56	0.0148	0.25	0.0277
Rajasthan	113	1.79	3,150	46	0.37	0.0258	0.48	0.0099	0.26	0.0473
East										
North-eastern Rg.	94	0.87	3,076	39	0.30	0.0172	0.47	0.0229	0.09	0.0281
West Bengal	164	6.06	6,168	117	0.38	0.0110	0.53	0.0112	0.20	0.0269
West										
Gujarat	57	0.94	2,551	41	0.43	0.0084	0.56	0.0074	0.29	0.0135
Maharashtra	85	1.04	3,487	57	0.46	0.0126	0.54	0.0060	0.38	0.0256
South										
Andhra Pradesh	132	2.81	7,684	96	0.48	0.0218	0.58	0.0143	0.38	0.0366
Karnataka	23	0.49			0.44	0.0164	0.55	0.0151	0.32	0.0207
Kerala	59	2.21	7,319	71	0.41	0.0196	0.54	0.0175	0.29	0.0209
Tamil Nadu	168	2.67	6,775	26	0.44	0.0149	0.58	0.0178	0.29	0.0176

Contd.

ANNEXE II Estimated Parameters for States and Standard Errors

States	Agricultural Wage Rate (All)	Estimated Standard Error (All)	Agricultural Wage Rate (Male)	Estimated Standard Error (Male)	Agricultural Wage Rate (Female)	Estimated Standard Error (Female)	Non-Agricultural Wage Rate (All)	Estimated Standard Error (All)	Non-Agricultural Wage Rate (Male)	Estimated Standard Error (Male)	Non-Agricultural Cultural Wage Rate (Female)	Estimated Standard Error (Female)
North												
Haryana	42	0.76	43	0.44	39	1.70	46	1.51	47	1.48	37	1.73
Himachal Pradesh	28	1.48	29	1.53	23	1.57	31	0.57	31	0.57	15	9.75
Punjab	35	1.38	36	2.12	28	0.34	41	1.47	42	1.39	23	2.05
Upper Central												
Bihar	23	1.21	24	1.23	19	1.22	26	1.72	26	1.77	21	1.25
Uttar Pradesh	20	0.82	21	0.92	18	0.74	31	1.40	31	1.45	19	2.38
Lower Central												
Madhya Pradesh	17	0.75	18	0.80	14	0.58	22	1.94	24	1.40	18	2.06
Orissa	18	0.53	18	0.61	15	0.67	21	1.26	23	1.13	15	1.55
Rajasthan	23	0.95	25	1.15	20	0.66	31	1.93	32	1.93	21	0.79
East												
North-eastern Rg.	25	1.23	25	1.59	20	2.41	32	2.57	33	2.62	16	2.62
West Bengal	23	0.84	23	0.85	22	0.84	21	1.12	23	1.07	13	1.33
West												
Gujarat	19	1.49	19	1.44	19	1.58	29	2.17	30	2.29	24	2.43
Maharashtra	16	0.54	19	0.87	11	0.39	22	1.44	24	1.44	14	1.15
South												
Andhra Pradesh	23	0.84	28	0.92	18	0.57	25	1.50	30	1.45	19	0.97
Karnataka	17	0.91	20	1.03	14	0.92	23	2.84	28	2.27	14	1.91
Kerala	41	3.79	44	4.01	31	1.31	40	2.52	51	2.31	28	1.52
Tamil Nadu	23	3.03	26	3.21	18	2.40	31	3.20	35	2.78	20	2.17

Contd.

ANNEXE II Estimated Parameters for States and Standard Errors

States	Crude Birth Rate ('000)	Esti-mated Standard Error	Crude Death Rate ('000)	Esti-mated Standard Error	Children Immunity Rate (All 8 dozes) (%)	Esti-mated Standard Error	Contraceptive Prevalence Rate (Any Method) (%)	Esti-mated Standard Error	Percent of Popul-ation below Poverty Line*	Esti-mated Standard Error
North										
Haryana	31	1.4	5	1.4	73.9	4.32	43.3	2.12	24.4	2.22
Himachal Pradesh	22	1.4	6	2.0	57.2	4.20	55.9	2.32	42.1	5.71
Punjab	22	1.0	9	2.8	62.0	3.83	45.5	2.55	29.4	2.65
Upper Central										
Bihar	37	1.7	10	1.4	37.5	6.70	17.8	1.93	43.6	2.82
Uttar Pradesh	38	1.7	11	1.0	41.3	5.84	22.3	2.08	41.3	3.27
Lower Central										
Madhya Pradesh	32	1.7	9	1.0	53.2	4.88	36.0	1.86	36.1	3.26
Orissa	29	1.4	13	1.4	52.7	5.90	33.8	1.97	52.0	2.95
Rajasthan	44	2.2	12	2.0	20.3	5.98	26.4	3.39	42.2	4.88
East										
North-eastern Rg.	34	8.2	7	2.4	28.4	10.53	27.6	7.39	30.5	7.14
West Bengal	34	2.2	21	4.9	31.2	5.15	32.5	4.82	55.7	2.94
West										
Gujarat	29	2.6	8	1.0	74.6	2.76	50.6	5.78	35.7	2.75
Maharashtra	28	1.7	11	1.0	79.0	3.45	54.2	1.45	29.7	3.43
South										
Andhra Pradesh	26	2.8	16	5.0	69.6	6.91	48.2	3.41	19.7	1.62
Karnataka	25	2.0	5	1.0	73.0	4.38	51.7	2.22	37.6	3.34
Kerala	21	1.4	5	1.0	78.6	4.42	58.5	4.30	28.7	3.63
Tamil Nadu	28	2.0	12	3.2	82.8	2.96	41.4	3.53	30.7	8.82

* State-specific Poverty Line estimated by the Planning Commission for 1973–4 have been updated using state-specific CPIAL as deflator.

These estimated parameters have been obtained from ungrouped data and are therefore marginally different from those presented in Table 3.6 derived from grouped data.

Statistical Appendix

List of Appendix Tables

Percentage Distribution of Households by States

Regions/States	Income Groups (Rs per year)					Poverty Groups				All Groups
	Up to 20,000	20,001– 40,000	40,001– 62,000	62,001– 86,000	Above 86,000	Lower Seg. Below Poverty	Upper Seg. Below Poverty	Lower Seg. Above Poverty	Upper Seg. Above Poverty	
North										
Haryana	33.5	32.8	16.2	9.4	8.1	10.1	13.0	48.7	28.2	100.0
Himachal Pradesh	53.6	30.9	11.2	2.9	1.4	18.5	20.1	37.9	23.4	100.0
Punjab	41.8	29.6	13.7	6.9	7.9	13.6	14.6	47.7	24.1	100.0
Upper Central										
Bihar	59.5	30.5	6.2	1.8	1.9	17.1	22.2	41.4	19.3	100.0
Uttar Pradesh	54.9	27.2	10.4	3.9	3.6	18.8	20.6	40.2	20.3	100.0
Lower Central										
Madhya Pradesh	59.2	24.8	9.3	3.3	3.4	14.9	18.6	45.3	21.1	100.0
Orissa	73.8	18.0	5.5	1.6	1.0	23.8	25.3	33.4	17.5	100.0
Rajasthan	55.5	26.6	9.8	4.3	3.7	18.2	21.3	40.3	20.2	100.0
East										
North-eastern Rg.	43.5	34.0	16.9	3.7	1.9	13.5	15.5	41.8	29.1	100.0
West Bengal	71.2	21.1	5.0	1.9	0.7	23.7	29.3	30.3	16.7	100.0
West										
Gujarat	56.3	25.9	9.4	3.3	5.2	15.1	17.5	48.8	18.6	100.0
Maharashtra	56.3	24.8	9.1	4.1	5.7	13.1	15.5	50.3	21.2	100.0
South										
Andhra Pradesh	58.1	28.4	8.1	2.3	3.2	7.4	9.9	56.7	26.0	100.0
Karnataka	59.7	23.4	8.4	3.7	4.8	16.3	18.8	45.1	19.8	100.0
Kerala	49.7	33.2	8.9	3.9	4.3	11.8	14.2	50.5	23.5	100.0
Tamil Nadu	59.4	27.1	7.8	2.9	2.8	13.0	14.6	45.3	27.1	100.0
All India	**57.6**	**26.8**	**8.9**	**3.3**	**3.4**	**15.9**	**18.8**	**43.8**	**21.6**	**100.0**

Percentage Distribution of Households by Population Groups

Population Groups	Household Income Groups (Rs per year)					Poverty Groups				All Groups
	Up to 20,000	20,001– 40,000	40,001– 62,000	62,001– 86,000	Above 86,000	Lower Seg. Below Poverty	Upper Seg. Below Poverty	Lower Seg. Above Poverty	Upper Seg. Above Poverty	
Household Income Groups										
Up to 20,000	–	–	–	–	–	27.3	29.6	39.6	3.5	100.0
20,001–40,000	–	–	–	–	–	0.7	6.2	65.9	27.3	100.0
40,001–62,000	–	–	–	–	–	0.1	0.5	29.9	69.5	100.0
62,001–86,000	–	–	–	–	–	–	–	15.6	84.3	100.0
Above 86,000	–	–	–	–	–	–	–	3.4	96.6	100.0
Poverty Line Groups										
Lower segment below	98.8	1.1	–	–	–	–	–	–	–	100.0
Upper segment below	90.9	8.9	0.2	–	–	–	–	–	–	100.0
Lower segment above	52.1	40.4	6.1	1.2	0.3	–	–	–	–	100.0
Upper segment above	9.3	33.9	28.7	12.9	15.1	–	–	–	–	100.0
Landholding Groups										
Landless wage earner	89.7	9.1	0.9	0.2	0.1	32.0	28.2	35.4	4.4	100.0
Marginal	64.7	27.1	6.1	1.4	0.7	17.5	21.9	45.7	14.9	100.0
Small	39.7	39.5	14.2	4.1	2.4	7.9	13.1	50.2	28.8	100.0
Medium	19.5	37.3	22.7	10.8	9.6	5.0	7.2	41.9	45.9	100.0
Large	9.8	19.9	20.9	15.9	33.4	3.8	4.0	28.5	63.8	100.0
Landless others	60.6	29.7	6.9	1.8	1.0	12.2	18.5	48.6	20.8	100.0
Landowners	46.9	31.5	11.9	4.6	5.0	12.0	15.9	45.0	27.1	100.0
Landless	76.0	18.8	3.7	1.0	0.5	22.7	23.6	41.6	12.1	100.0
Occupational Groups										
Cultivators	46.9	31.1	11.2	4.7	6.0	12.6	14.8	44.0	28.6	100.0
Salaried+Prof.+S.Empl.	28.4	41.5	19.5	6.5	4.1	4.8	9.3	45.6	40.3	100.0
Wage earners	85.8	12.4	1.4	0.3	0.1	28.8	28.3	38.1	4.8	100.0
All others	62.9	27.5	6.8	1.8	0.9	12.1	21.3	51.3	15.3	100.0
Social Groups										
Caste										
STs	70.5	19.5	6.8	2.0	1.1	20.2	24.3	41.6	14.0	100.0
SCs	72.0	21.3	4.7	1.4	0.7	22.1	23.6	42.4	12.0	100.0
Religion										
Hindus										
Muslims	59.4	28.6	7.3	2.6	2.0	17.5	23.7	42.6	16.3	100.0
Christians	51.5	29.6	9.8	4.5	4.6	12.9	11.8	46.7	28.7	100.0
Other Minorities	55.7	24.8	9.6	4.3	5.6	18.9	18.0	42.8	20.3	100.0
Household Size Groups										
Up to 4	72.0	19.5	5.3	1.7	1.5	9.7	14.6	46.3	29.4	100.0
5–7	56.7	29.0	8.8	2.8	2.7	18.2	20.6	43.1	18.2	100.0
8 and above	33.4	34.6	16.0	7.6	8.5	21.1	21.7	40.9	16.3	100.0
Adult Literacy Groups										
None literate	78.7	16.5	3.5	0.9	0.5	22.2	23.4	41.6	12.7	100.0

(Contd.)

Female literate	68.7	21.0	7.5	1.9	0.9	17.5	19.9	45.2	17.4	100.0
Male literate	56.4	30.0	8.2	3.0	2.4	15.8	19.2	45.1	19.8	100.0
Both literate	39.8	33.2	14.3	5.7	7.0	10.4	14.3	44.3	31.0	100.0
Village Development Groups										
Low	60.8	25.1	8.4	2.9	2.8	19.0	20.6	41.1	19.3	100.0
Medium	57.6	27.0	8.9	3.2	3.2	16.0	18.9	44.1	20.9	100.0
High	54.5	28.2	9.4	3.8	4.1	12.8	16.8	45.8	24.5	100.0
All India	**57.6**	**26.8**	**8.9**	**3.3**	**3.4**	**15.9**	**18.8**	**43.8**	**21.6**	**100.0**

APPENDIX A.3.3

Average (Annual) Income by Source (Rs) Across States

Regions/States	Average Income per Reporting Household from										All Sources
	Agr+Alld. Activity	Artisan/ Ind.Work	Petty Trd. Small Bus.	Orgnd Trd. Business	Salaried Employmt.	Qualified Professn.	Rent/Int. Dividend	Agrl. Wage	Non-agrl. Wage	Other Sources	
North											
Haryana	34,046	16,408	18,663	29,467	28,354	33,422	16,722	7,012	11,614	11,196	39,956
Himachal Pradesh	9,747	13,886	14,492	28,978	21,942	17,901	8,271	2,828	8,468	13,285	23,973
Punjab	42,639	17,179	19,838	17,960	29,037	24,551	18,783	6,000	10,246	14,251	37,418
Upper Central											
Bihar	18,937	10,831	13,282	22,347	26,507	13,072	8,163	5,949	6,792	8,572	22,459
Uttar Pradesh	18,643	13,667	12,362	31,859	27,682	19,901	9,121	4,071	8,189	12,264	26,733
Lower Central											
Madhya Pradesh	21,675	4,847	11,186	22,376	22,937	8,730	5,272	4,168	5,159	4,213	25,319
Orissa	12,368	8,588	10,328	33,915	22,451	10,555	7,618	2,956	4,038	5,176	17,208
Rajasthan	17,209	15,603	19,343	39,245	31,512	12,243	11,681	2,279	7,278	8,758	27,184
East											
North-eastern Rg.	16,548	13,270	16,126	30,566	33,858	33,516	5,622	6,731	9,617	6,187	28,160
West Bengal	11,692	10,732	13,617	19,601	19,110	12,204	4,453	6,278	4,354	6,750	18,113
West											
Gujarat	28,160	14,160	20,068	30,762	26,966	18,425	11,517	7,545	7,295	10,103	29,356
Maharashtra	28,390	9,721	12,100	24,916	21,108	21,177	9,234	5,833	5,773	9,179	29,929
South											
Andhra Pradesh	23,878	8,188	8,444	19,334	21,038	13,991	5,970	9,900	9,287	6,170	24,776
Karnataka	27,615	13,257	13,129	20,790	22,313	10,852	8,308	5,892	8,489	7,055	27,372
Kerala	16,321	9,201	9,840	17,317	23,808	17,810	12,282	9,461	11,335	12,299	29,101
Tamil Nadu	20,563	15,184	11,755	24,022	28,569	10,196	6,962	7,745	14,796	9,077	23,271
All India	**20,701**	**11,044**	**13,109**	**25,985**	**25,789**	**16,381**	**8,981**	**6,341**	**7,844**	**9,262**	**25,653**
C.V.	38.8	27.3	25.7	24.1	16.0	42.8	41.4	36.5	33.5	32.3	21.3

Average (Annual) Income (Rs) by Source Across Population Groups

Population Groups	Agr.+Alld. Activity	Artisan/ Ind.Work	Petty Trd. Small Bus.	Orgnd. Trd. Business	Salaried Employmt.	Qualified Professn.	Rent/Int. Dividend	Agrl. Wage	Non-agrl. Wage	Other Sources	All Sources
Household Income Groups											
Up to 20,000	7,459	7,509	9,030	10,810	10,330	7,986	5,482	5,485	6,028	5,164	11,027
20,001–40,000	18,203	13,189	15,540	20,381	21,935	15,554	9,030	9,126	11,267	10,586	28,141
40,001–62,000	32,013	19,026	19,436	30,112	33,358	29,251	10,490	10,083	16,375	15,201	49,072
62,001–86,000	50,731	23,570	21,563	37,938	41,993	35,178	16,874	10,936	21,478	19,906	72,178
Above 86,000	1,19,487	37,899	27,934	63,739	62,696	32,149	20,861	10,847	25,275	21,590	1,47,855
Poverty Line Groups											
Lower segment below	5,148	4,829	5,866	9,572	6,733	3,670	2,943	3,776	4,189	3,005	6,950
Upper segment below	7,907	7,843	9,727	13,947	10,728	8,532	5,484	5,824	6,506	4848	12,379
Lower segment above	15,084	11,249	13,276	18,533	19,652	11,629	7,882	7,516	9,175	9,012	22,138
Upper segment above	46,357	19,835	19,470	38,154	37,713	27,377	12,827	9,385	14,464	14,420	58,100
Landholding Groups											
Landless wage warner	2,320	4,117	4,837	5,211	7,286	6,854	3,732	7,496	9,149	4,007	11,313
Marginal	9,410	9,940	11,299	20,643	23,068	15,001	9,172	5,648	6,868	10,427	19,586
Small	21,127	9,900	12,331	30,690	29,558	17,827	8,653	5,327	6,266	10,196	29,377
Medium	36,737	10,827	12,668	33,499	31,144	28,936	10,444	5,495	7,007	10,431	44,695
Large	77,571	13,915	18,430	35,612	34,547	17,714	13,255	4,691	7,883	12,224	85,969
Landless others	5,575	13,646	15,061	25,642	25,595	16,745	8,754	3,734	6,054	8,377	21,574
Landowners	21,978	10,204	12,111	26,782	26,636	17,213	9,742	5,546	6,778	10,481	31,154
Landless	3,757	11,802	14,151	24,904	24,679	15,357	8,216	7,009	8,778	7,372	16,141
Occupational Groups											
Cultivators	28,518	7,368	9,275	16,413	18,140	13,702	7,740	4,219	4,627	6,994	32,374
Salaried+Prof.+S.Empl.	9,941	10,630	11,214	17,022	28,926	19,198	7,086	3,617	5,946	7,551	35,760
Wage earners	3,956	4,061	4,868	8,153	7,059	6,185	3,557	7,623	9,150	4,077	12,580
All others	6,486	14,087	15,321	29,642	11,415	7,706	10,921	3,687	6,291	12,044	21,010
Social Groups											
Caste											
STs	14,612	6,033	12,544	23,959	22,912	20,758	5,018	5,243	5,332	4,927	19,556
SCs	12,301	9,839	12,666	20,012	21,739	13,973	8,290	6,617	7,484	6,863	17,465
Religion											
Hindus	20,828	10,806	13,125	26,761	25,663	15,965	8,563	6,312	7,708	8,598	25,712
Muslims	16,388	12,260	12,624	22,591	25,728	17,444	8,082	6,417	8,233	12,963	22,807
Christians	20,697	13,336	13,412	23,053	28,819	14,319	10,097		8,573	10,850	8,326	28,860
Other Minorities	30,315	11,169	16,159	21,326	26,063	24,624	16,918		5,162	8,178	13,347	30,330
Household Size Groups											
Up to 4	15,872	9,017	11,002	20,055	22,534	14,737	8,511	5,895	6,883	7,965	18,399
5–7	19,767	10,991	12,965	25,896	25,187	17,782	8,557	6,371	7,597	8,909	25,060
8 and above	29,233	13,784	15,446	30,150	30,058	15,740	10,813	7,552	10,255	12,429	40,449
Adult Literacy Groups											
None literate	13,434	8,281	9,482	12,975	12,767	7,675	6,982	6,086	6,513	6,223	15,271

(Contd.)

Female literate	16,680	9,299	10,197	18,147	19,035	35,263	9,900	6,596	9,098	13,699	19,060
Male literate	19,288	11,559	12,427	22,806	21,422	13,452	8,532	6,164	8,104	8,769	24,367
Both literate	27,321	13,207	14,852	28,903	29,822	19,911	9,937	7,180	9,829	11,024	36,187
Village Development Groups											
Low	18,743	10,112	11,205	25,439	26,308	13,861	8,467	5,139	6,619	8,320	24,149
Medium	20,721	10,956	13,312	25,976	24,313	15,973	8,303	6,541	7,467	9,171	25,173
High	23,093	12,057	13,938	26,214	27,000	18,475	9,952	7,039	9,681	10,055	27,628
All India	**20,701**	**11,044**	**13,109**	**25,985**	**25,789**	**16,381**	**8,981**	**6,341**	**7,844**	**9,262**	**25,653**

APPENDIX A.4.1

Land and Livestock Owned by Households by Population Groups

Population Groups	Landholdings			Draught Animals			Milch Animals		
	% Rep Household	Average per Reporting Household (acres)	Average per Household (acres)	% Rep Household	Average per Reporting Household (number)	Average per Household (Number)	% Rep Household	Average per Reporting Household (number)	Average per Household (number)
Household Income Groups									
Up to 20,000	51.6	2.5	1.3	26.0	2.7	0.7	38.1	2.0	0.8
20,001–40,000	74.3	4.2	3.1	38.9	2.7	1.1	56.8	2.4	1.4
40,001–62,000	84.7	6.2	5.3	47.1	3.0	1.4	67.4	2.6	1.7
62,001–86,000	89.2	9.2	8.2	48.0	3.2	1.5	73.6	2.8	2.1
Above 86,000	94.3	16.6	15.6	55.1	2.9	1.6	79.2	3.5	2.8
Poverty Line Groups									
Lower segment below	47.7	2.4	1.1	27.1	2.6	0.7	38.7	2.0	0.8
Upper segment below	53.8	2.6	1.4	29.1	2.8	0.8	42.9	2.1	0.9
Lower segment above	65.2	3.9	2.5	33.2	2.7	0.9	49.0	2.3	1.1
Upper segment above	79.5	7.6	6.0	40.7	2.9	1.2	58.5	2.6	1.5
Landholding Groups									
Landless wage earner	–	–	–	7.0	2.6	0.2	23.7	1.9	0.5
Marginal	100.0	1.3	1.3	35.6	2.5	0.9	51.6	2.0	1.0
Small	100.0	3.8	3.8	57.1	2.8	1.6	66.5	2.4	1.6
Medium	100.0	7.5	7.5	64.2	2.9	1.9	77.9	2.7	2.1
Large	100.0	21.8	21.8	68.9	3.1	2.1	86.1	3.4	2.9
Landless others	–	–	–	6.1	4.0	0.2	24.5	2.3	0.6
Landowners	100.0	4.5	4.5	48.4	2.7	1.3	62.2	2.4	1.5
Landless	–	–	–	6.6	3.2	0.2	24.1	2.1	0.5
Occupational Groups									
Cultivators	98.5	5.6	5.5	54.6	2.7	1.5	66.2	2.5	1.7
Salaried+Prof.+S.Empl.	48.8	2.9	1.4	20.4	3.1	0.6	44.2	2.0	0.9
Wage earners	28.2	1.3	0.4	14.0	2.5	0.3	29.1	1.9	0.5
All others	37.8	2.3	0.9	16.2	3.4	0.6	34.4	2.3	0.8
Social Groups									
Caste									
STs	69.0	4.3	2.9	51.6	3.2	1.6	44.9	2.5	1.1
SCs	46.6	2.8	1.3	22.8	2.7	0.6	38.1	2.0	0.7
Religion									
Hindus	64.5	4.6	3.0	34.3	2.7	0.9	49.6	2.3	1.1
Muslims	56.5	3.6	2.0	28.0	3.9	1.1	38.0	2.7	1.0
Christians	58.2	2.0	1.1	12.0	4.3	0.5	30.3	2.3	0.7
Other Minorities	55.8	5.5	3.1	31.0	2.4	0.7	54.5	2.5	1.4
Household Size Groups									
Up to 4	53.9	3.3	1.8	21.9	2.6	0.6	34.5	2.0	0.7
5–7	64.5	4.2	2.7	35.0	2.9	1.0	51.0	2.4	1.2
8 and above	77.5	6.6	5.1	48.3	2.6	1.3	66.2	2.6	1.7

(Contd.)

Adult Literacy Groups									
None literate	53.6	3.4	1.9	28.7	2.5	0.7	38.6	2.2	0.8
Female literate	54.2	3.2	1.7	22.8	2.7	0.6	35.8	2.0	0.7
Male literate	67.0	4.5	3.0	35.5	2.6	0.9	53.4	2.2	1.2
Both literate	69.1	5.2	3.6	35.5	3.1	1.1	52.8	2.6	1.4
Village Development Groups									
Low	76.2	4.6	3.5	41.4	2.6	1.1	56.8	2.3	1.3
Medium	62.5	4.4	2.7	33.2	2.9	1.0	48.7	2.4	1.2
High	52.6	4.4	2.3	25.3	2.9	0.7	39.9	2.3	0.9
All India	**63.4**	**4.5**	**2.8**	**33.1**	**2.8**	**0.9**	**48.3**	**2.3**	**1.1**

APPENDIX A.4.2

Percentage of Households Having a *Kutcha* House by States

Regions/States	Household Income Groups (Rs per year)				Social Groups				Village Development Groups			All Groups
	Up to 20,000	20,001– 40,000	40,001– 62,000	Above 62,000	STs and SCs	Hindus	Muslims	Other Minorities	Low	Medium	High	
North												
Haryana	22.0	13.3	9.0	2.7	24.4	13.2	29.2	2.9	18.0	13.4	13.0	13.7
Himachal Pradesh	63.1	52.7	37.5	36.8	67.3	58.3	39.7	15.9	63.3	52.0	53.2	55.9
Punjab	25.7	16.5	9.5	4.5	26.7	24.0	26.0	15.2	40.3	15.8	16.9	17.6
Upper Central												
Bihar	81.5	58.1	54.9	27.7	86.1	70.0	71.8	95.3	81.7	63.6	59.9	70.7
Uttar Pradesh	67.4	50.9	38.3	26.9	67.5	57.8	59.6	19.3	63.2	48.3	46.2	56.8
Lower Central												
Madhya Pradesh	66.6	55.8	40.8	35.4	67.2	61.3	44.2	29.2	66.0	52.1	48.6	59.4
Orissa	83.2	66.1	51.5	33.5	86.6	80.8	62.8	47.1	85.5	74.7	66.5	77.1
Rajasthan	54.6	37.5	22.0	15.5	62.5	44.0	52.1	26.7	50.5	38.3	17.5	43.7
East												
North-eastern Rg.	84.3	61.4	31.3	41.7	63.6	66.5	76.4	30.4	86.3	67.2	52.0	65.2
West Bengal	80.6	68.3	48.6	53.7	81.1	79.9	87.6	39.1	97.8	70.6	76.1	75.7
West												
Gujarat	47.4	21.5	13.8	18.5	43.5	37.3	34.5	34.6	35.7	42.6	25.4	35.1
Maharashtra	59.8	50.2	40.3	20.2	68.9	54.3	47.7	68.4	71.8	57.2	46.1	51.8
South												
Andhra Pradesh	49.8	35.3	27.0	18.5	49.9	43.3	44.9	74.9	35.3	45.0	42.5	42.2
Karnataka	75.2	66.5	57.6	48.7	80.7	74.3	66.7	58.8	77.5	65.9	72.5	69.4
Kerala	34.6	15.9	6.5	6.4	49.0	30.2	12.7	20.3	29.4	21.2	24.2	23.6
Tamil Nadu	25.2	14.0	10.7	6.4	35.5	22.7	26.5	15.1	–	26.7	17.8	20.0
All India	**62.9**	**45.3**	**33.1**	**23.3**	**66.2**	**55.2**	**63.6**	**36.8**	**65.1**	**51.9**	**42.9**	**52.9**
C.V.	36.4	46.7	54.5	62.1	32.2	40.2	41.1	66.6	47.6	40.4	47.8	42.6

Percentage of Households Having Separate Kitchen by States

Regions/States	Household Income Groups (Rs per year)				Social Groups				Village Development Groups			All Groups
	Up to 20,000	20,001–40,000	40,001–62,000	Above 62,000	STs and SCs	Hindus	Muslims	Other Minorities	Low	Medium	High	
North												
Haryana	22.9	46.9	58.8	72.4	28.0	46.2	17.0	74.7	48.5	46.2	44.1	45.3
Himachal Pradesh	71.6	91.6	90.0	95.0	73.9	81.3	61.5	100.0	78.5	80.3	85.8	80.9
Punjab	34.6	50.3	64.6	70.1	38.1	42.7	28.0	51.6	27.2	49.9	50.3	48.8
Upper Central												
Bihar	9.4	20.5	32.6	53.1	9.0	16.1	17.5	8.0	15.8	14.4	20.9	15.9
Uttar Pradesh	12.7	19.3	30.4	37.0	11.2	17.7	20.0	75.2	15.1	20.5	31.1	18.1
Lower Central												
Madhya Pradesh	22.8	38.4	54.8	62.9	22.0	32.1	42.7	30.3	25.3	38.2	51.2	32.3
Orissa	38.8	59.1	72.6	76.5	30.2	45.8	36.7	24.6	37.4	51.5	46.6	45.3
Rajasthan	25.1	43.2	68.7	81.4	21.5	39.0	38.9	14.1	37.3	37.4	56.3	38.8
East												
North-eastern Rg.	58.6	81.2	92.3	92.2	68.4	71.0	82.1	81.1	65.4	76.0	75.2	74.0
West Bengal	52.6	76.7	88.6	95.5	52.6	63.3	55.6	61.9	64.9	60.2	61.0	61.1
West												
Gujarat	35.7	56.5	72.3	82.3	41.6	48.8	44.2	48.4	59.3	48.8	44.2	48.5
Maharashtra	43.4	57.5	61.0	74.8	43.4	52.3	55.3	43.5	43.6	42.1	58.3	51.7
South												
Andhra Pradesh	31.2	44.6	64.6	77.0	21.8	40.9	44.8	13.3	37.8	37.0	45.5	40.3
Karnataka	58.8	72.8	80.6	88.1	56.1	67.3	57.6	68.2	72.1	66.0	66.5	66.5
Kerala	83.4	93.0	98.1	97.5	70.8	86.7	94.7	91.3	90.0	88.9	89.1	89.1
Tamil Nadu	46.0	61.8	82.2	84.7	42.6	55.1	60.1	64.8	52.1	44.0	60.2	55.7
All India	**33.5**	**47.8**	**61.9**	**70.1**	**31.5**	**41.5**	**44.7**	**54.2**	**28.2**	**42.7**	**55.7**	**42.4**
C.V.	49.4	37.5	27.3	20.4	50.6	34.6	44.9	52.4	44.8	39.3	31.6	38.9

Percentage of Households Having Electric Connection by States

Regions/States	Household Income Groups (Rs per year)				Social Groups				Village Development Groups			All Groups
	Up to 20,000	20,001–40,000	40,001–62,000	Above 62,000	STs and SCs	Hindus	Muslims	Other Minorities	Low	Medium	High	
North												
Haryana	69.5	83.6	89.3	95.5	71.8	83.1	53.4	96.4	78.7	80.5	83.5	81.9
Himachal Pradesh	82.8	93.1	96.9	92.0	84.4	88.1	77.7	100.0	82.7	89.1	93.4	88.0
Punjab	72.5	88.0	94.1	96.1	67.6	82.4	75.2	84.2	73.8	82.9	85.7	83.5
Upper Central												
Bihar	4.3	14.0	18.4	48.4	4.1	10.3	8.4	5.9	5.3	11.1	19.2	9.8
Uttar Pradesh	14.4	20.4	30.6	46.2	12.5	20.0	20.0	77.8	16.0	22.0	42.8	20.1
Lower Central												
Madhya Pradesh	38.1	61.3	75.2	84.0	42.4	50.0	65.7	58.3	43.5	54.6	72.1	50.4
Orissa	11.3	33.7	49.9	62.2	6.5	18.7	16.5	25.7	6.5	21.6	35.5	18.8
Rajasthan	38.3	53.6	72.5	79.7	32.5	48.7	54.8	52.6	42.8	55.6	66.7	49.1
East												
North-eastern Rg.	25.3	51.2	71.5	64.7	46.2	46.1	27.0	75.5	14.2	43.7	59.1	44.1
West Bengal	10.9	22.8	40.1	39.5	10.8	17.4	9.4	30.2	6.5	15.7	17.7	15.6
West												
Gujarat	60.4	83.6	89.3	93.3	54.7	71.9	70.2	85.9	61.9	64.2	85.3	71.9
Maharashtra	47.8	69.4	75.5	88.3	37.8	60.7	67.0	44.7	44.3	53.1	65.3	59.7
South												
Andhra Pradesh	53.5	71.4	80.8	96.2	47.4	63.4	70.5	40.1	64.1	60.0	66.0	63.1
Karnataka	53.3	70.3	86.1	87.5	49.2	62.6	64.9	77.8	42.2	62.5	65.6	63.0
Kerala	47.1	70.3	80.5	87.7	41.1	59.2	61.7	65.3	41.0	61.5	65.6	61.1
Tamil Nadu	54.6	70.6	84.3	85.7	47.2	62.6	75.2	68.4	3.5	58.0	65.5	63.0
All India	**32.6**	**49.8**	**63.4**	**75.8**	**30.4**	**43.2**	**30.0**	**60.2**	**26.6**	**42.2**	**58.6**	**42.9**
C.V.	54.1	40.5	32.1	24.0	55.4	45.3	48.2	42.0	68.6	44.1	35.3	45.9

APPENDIX A.4.5

Percentage of Households Having Access to Protected Water by States

Regions/States	Household Income Groups (Rs per year)				Social Groups				Village Development Groups			All Groups
	Up to 20,000	20,001– 40,000	40,001– 62,000	Above 62,000	STs and SCs	Hindus	Muslims	Other Minorities	Low	Medium	High	
North												
Haryana	81.3	83.0	87.9	87.2	82.1	84.3	76.4	87.3	73.3	85.8	84.8	84.0
Himachal Pradesh	72.3	78.5	69.9	69.6	74.5	73.9	66.6	91.5	72.4	69.7	84.5	73.9
Punjab	95.0	95.0	99.7	98.2	92.8	93.9	98.8	97.0	94.4	94.9	97.9	96.1
Upper Central												
Bihar	65.4	73.0	73.7	79.6	68.1	70.5	62.6	54.3	62.3	77.7	60.5	68.8
Uttar Pradesh	67.3	71.3	74.3	79.1	69.1	68.1	83.1	100.0	66.2	74.2	80.2	70.0
Lower Central												
Madhya Pradesh	64.6	68.5	66.4	66.9	60.1	65.7	70.1	77.5	67.7	61.0	71.4	65.9
Orissa	46.6	54.0	52.2	61.8	44.4	47.9	76.5	67.9	47.8	45.4	57.1	48.6
Rajasthan	41.8	50.1	55.5	59.3	47.3	48.0	24.8	48.6	42.3	46.1	81.5	46.8
East												
North-eastern Rg.	51.1	64.3	77.8	83.6	52.5	59.9	58.9	92.4	70.3	57.7	64.2	61.9
West Bengal	74.4	84.4	90.4	82.6	75.9	75.4	88.6	21.4	77.2	70.8	85.1	77.5
West												
Gujarat	85.2	91.4	89.6	91.7	79.6	87.2	94.2	100.0	73.0	88.2	92.6	87.8
Maharashtra	80.3	80.0	71.4	78.8	81.4	78.9	86.0	88.5	70.9	70.2	85.3	79.3
South												
Andhra Pradesh	79.4	84.0	73.6	68.7	78.1	80.0	90.9	46.5	83.1	72.7	85.6	79.6
Karnataka	81.4	80.3	80.1	72.1	81.3	79.6	85.3	96.6	69.4	81.3	80.2	80.2
Kerala	76.2	80.0	88.0	84.9	73.2	79.8	88.5	72.9	68.2	82.5	79.2	79.2
Tamil Nadu	71.6	72.5	65.8	74.0	82.9	73.9	78.3	27.4	100.0	63.7	74.0	71.6
All India	**69.6**	**74.8**	**74.9**	**77.7**	**69.2**	**71.1**	**78.1**	**75.0**	**64.4**	**71.3**	**79.7**	**72.0**
C.V.	19.7	15.6	16.5	13.4	18.7	17.0	22.6	34.5	19.5	19.1	13.7	17.3

Percentage of Households Having Access to Piped Water by States

Regions/States	Household Income Groups (Rs per year)				Social Groups				Village Development Groups			All Groups
	Up to 20,000	20,001– 40,000	40,001– 62,000	Above 62,000	STs and SCs	Hindus	Muslims	Other Minorities	Low	Medium	High	
North												
Haryana	38.9	46.1	49.0	46.9	39.6	44.3	46.3	41.8	23.8	49.1	45.0	44.3
Himachal Pradesh	68.6	76.2	66.6	65.6	72.3	71.5	30.7	82.1	71.6	65.0	80.5	70.6
Punjab	22.7	20.2	22.2	16.6	33.8	36.0	20.8	15.0	46.1	19.0	20.1	21.0
Upper Central												
Bihar	2.7	3.2	7.2	14.7	2.8	2.6	11.3	0.6	3.8	4.3	0.9	3.6
Uttar Pradesh	14.5	14.9	14.7	15.2	12.4	14.6	14.9	11.2	10.7	18.5	28.0	14.7
Lower Central												
Madhya Pradesh	9.5	12.6	12.1	16.0	8.5	10.8	17.8	18.3	9.0	6.8	33.0	11.0
Orissa	22.2	31.5	31.5	21.4	23.1	24.1	19.5	38.3	25.8	21.2	28.8	24.4
Rajasthan	24.6	30.7	37.5	36.1	23.1	29.1	16.0	36.8	24.1	26.5	67.9	28.4
East												
North-eastern Rg.	4.3	9.8	13.0	22.6	4.0	3.9	1.8	79.3	–	6.6	16.0	8.7
West Bengal	9.5	8.0	7.3	9.9	6.9	7.1	15.1	1.8	12.3	12.9	4.1	9.1
West												
Gujarat	56.3	63.4	64.3	66.0	46.0	59.6	57.1	100.0	30.8	50.7	81.6	59.7
Maharashtra	41.5	45.4	41.8	49.8	38.7	42.2	62.4	49.1	25.2	31.2	52.3	43.3
South												
Andhra Pradesh	31.1	31.1	31.1	33.0	24.9	30.7	41.3	25.8	24.7	25.4	41.0	31.2
Karnataka	46.6	48.1	49.4	38.5	37.8	46.2	48.5	54.4	4.8	40.5	57.5	46.5
Kerala	16.7	17.2	17.4	14.0	24.5	17.9	11.6	16.8	0.9	23.9	14.7	16.7
Tamil Nadu	48.2	51.8	52.2	56.0	50.3	51.7	38.1	21.7	90.3	41.4	52.5	49.9
All India	**23.4**	**25.5**	**27.2**	**31.0**	**20.8**	**25.3**	**19.4**	**23.8**	**13.7**	**22.2**	**38.3**	**24.8**
C.V.	66.4	65.1	59.6	57.0	66.2	65.3	62.5	77.2	97.1	61.3	62.5	64.4

Percentage of Households Having a Toilet by States

Regions/States	Household Income Groups (Rs per year)				Social Groups				Village Development Groups			All Groups
	Up to 20,000	20,001–40,000	40,001–62,000	Above 62,000	STs and SCs	Hindus	Muslims	Other Minorities	Low	Medium	High	
North												
Haryana	3.5	7.5	10.3	15.7	3.6	8.0	1.3	22.8	6.8	8.3	8.1	8.0
Himachal Pradesh	11.9	17.4	28.0	30.3	15.3	15.8	18.2	45.3	9.0	15.5	28.3	16.2
Punjab	11.8	19.9	24.9	37.4	8.0	16.5	3.5	21.5	2.2	17.2	25.5	19.8
Upper Central												
Bihar	3.1	11.3	13.1	32.6	2.9	6.9	12.6	1.8	4.6	7.2	15.9	7.3
Uttar Pradesh	8.6	11.2	14.8	18.2	5.2	7.5	33.3	5.4	8.2	11.4	26.2	10.7
Lower Central												
Madhya Pradesh	2.1	6.2	13.3	21.6	2.3	5.3	8.1	19.8	3.1	5.4	17.2	5.5
Orissa	1.4	7.8	15.1	18.3	0.7	3.7	13.1	6.1	0.9	4.1	8.6	3.8
Rajasthan	2.4	3.0	9.0	11.9	2.1	3.9	5.9	0.0	2.2	5.1	11.5	4.0
East												
North-eastern Rg.	55.5	74.3	81.0	86.7	67.3	67.5	60.9	93.4	53.5	66.5	77.2	68.0
West Bengal	15.5	31.1	61.7	56.6	17.6	24.5	13.1	52.7	12.5	20.4	26.4	22.2
West												
Gujarat	13.3	25.3	42.2	46.8	8.7	21.4	28.7	21.9	21.1	15.4	30.5	21.9
Maharashtra	2.8	5.3	9.8	16.9	3.0	5.6	7.6	2.6	2.4	1.5	7.9	5.4
South												
Andhra Pradesh	10.1	17.5	25.0	42.7	7.9	14.6	28.7	8.8	18.1	10.3	19.1	15.2
Karnataka	7.6	13.5	16.4	17.8	8.3	9.7	18.6	22.7	12.1	8.6	12.7	10.6
Kerala	51.4	69.6	83.4	85.2	41.0	59.8	71.4	66.0	36.1	65.8	67.2	63.1
Tamil Nadu	6.5	14.2	20.4	31.4	5.1	10.0	26.6	26.2	0.0	4.5	13.6	11.1
All India	**10.0**	**19.1**	**26.8**	**30.9**	**9.6**	**13.2**	**26.7**	**30.3**	**8.2**	**14.9**	**22.4**	**15.3**
C.V.	122.6	98.4	81.9	63.4	137.0	105.2	87.4	97.1	116.5	116.1	78.5	102.8

Ownership of House and Selected Consumer Durables by Population Groups

Population Groups	Percentage of Households Owning						
	House	Bicycle	Tele-vision	Radio/ Transistor	Electric Fan	Motorcycle/ Scooter	Sewing Machine
Household Income Groups							
Up to 20,000	94.6	44.3	4.3	27.0	10.5	0.8	5.3
20,001–40,000	96.3	64.5	14.6	47.1	25.6	3.8	11.7
40,001–62,000	96.3	70.8	29.0	56.9	40.7	10.7	19.3
62,001–86,000	97.9	74.1	35.9	64.2	51.2	16.5	25.1
Above 86,000	98.6	76.9	47.3	70.9	59.9	26.8	28.7
Poverty Line Groups							
Lower segment below	94.8	42.1	3.6	21.3	7.7	1.1	5.7
Upper segment below	94.9	48.3	4.7	27.3	10.2	0.6	5.9
Lower segment above	95.8	55.2	10.7	39.1	20.4	2.6	9.9
Upper segment above	95.9	66.0	26.1	56.1	38.1	11.3	15.7
Landholding Groups							
Landless wage earner	93.2	34.9	2.0	22.0	7.0	0.2	3.0
Marginal	98.0	2.4	8.6	32.9	15.1	2.4	8.4
Small	98.4	65.5	12.4	44.4	22.8	3.9	9.8
Medium	98.0	67.9	17.8	49.9	31.1	7.6	14.8
Large	98.9	64.1	27.7	53.8	41.7	15.1	19.3
Landless others	88.2	57.1	20.3	46.3	30.3	5.6	14.4
Land owners	98.2	59.2	12.5	40.2	21.6	4.6	10.5
Landless	90.8	45.3	10.6	33.4	17.9	2.7	8.4
Occupational Groups							
Cultivators	98.2	59.6	11.1	40.0	21.3	4.2	9.7
Salaried+Prof.+S.Empl.	88.4	65.8	31.6	55.8	40.1	10.1	19.1
Wage earners	94.5	6.4	2.1	22.2	6.9	0.2	3.2
All others	95.3	59.7	14.2	43.1	24.1	4.1	13.3
Social Groups							
Caste							
STs	95.0	3.2	6.5	27.1	10.5	3.3	2.9
SCs	96.5	48.1	5.6	29.4	10.7	1.2	5.9
Religion							
Hindus	95.4	54.1	11.5	37.7	19.6	3.7	8.5
Muslims	96.5	57.2	8.2	36.9	16.5	3.1	12.1
Christians	93.0	3.7	20.1	54.4	26.9	6.9	7.4
Other Minorities	95.2	60.9	25.3	29.3	45.3	8.8	39.9
Household Size Groups							
Up to 4	93.5	42.5	8.2	32.4	17.0	2.5	6.1
5–7	96.0	56.6	12.1	39.3	20.6	3.9	9.9
8 and above	97.7	68.9	17.6	43.3	25.3	6.5	16.0
Adult Literacy Groups							
None literate	95.8	37.6	1.4	18.0	5.4	0.3	3.2

(Contd.)

Female literate	92.2	36.5	8.0	34.0	18.9	0.8	9.7
Male literate	96.2	60.2	7.3	35.1	15.9	1.9	8.7
Both literate	94.9	64.1	25.0	57.2	36.9	9.0	16.2
Village Development Groups							
Low	97.8	55.3	5.9	28.7	10.8	2.2	8.0
Medium	95.4	54.5	11.2	38.5	20.2	3.6	9.9
High	93.5	52.6	18.0	45.1	29.0	5.7	11.2
All India	**95.5**	**54.1**	**11.8**	**37.7**	**20.3**	**3.9**	**9.7**

Work Participation Rate (%) among All Persons and Adults by Population Groups

Population Groups	Usual Status						Usual And Subsidiary Status					
	All Persons			(Adults (15–59 years)			All Persons			(Adults (15–59 years)		
	Male	Female	F/M	Male	Female	F/M	Male	Female	F/M	Male	Female	F/M
Household Income Groups												
Up to 20,000	51.1	21.7	0.42	85.3	35.5	0.42	51.6	28.5	0.55	85.7	45.4	0.53
20,001–40,000	52.7	16.6	0.31	81.3	26.1	0.32	53.3	24.6	0.46	81.8	38.0	0.46
40,001–62,000	52.1	13.3	0.25	79.3	20.7	0.26	52.6	22.2	0.42	79.7	33.9	0.43
62,001–86,000	52.9	11.7	0.22	78.5	18.9	0.24	53.3	21.2	0.40	79.0	33.0	0.42
Above 86,000	53.2	11.9	0.22	78.9	19.5	0.25	53.5	19.5	0.36	79.2	31.0	0.39
Poverty Line Groups												
Lower segment below	45.1	16.8	0.37	83.0	31.0	0.37	45.6	23.7	0.52	83.5	41.7	0.50
Upper segment below	48.8	17.8	0.36	84.6	30.3	0.36	49.5	25.8	0.52	85.3	42.5	0.50
Lower segment above	53.7	20.2	0.38	83.0	31.4	0.38	54.2	27.8	0.51	83.4	42.5	0.51
Upper segment above	56.9	16.4	0.29	80.2	23.7	0.30	57.3	24.2	0.42	80.5	34.5	0.43
Landholding Groups												
Landless wage earner	54.0	32.6	0.60	88.5	52.4	0.59	54.4	37.7	0.69	88.9	59.2	0.67
Marginal	53.0	19.2	0.36	84.2	30.9	0.37	53.5	27.3	0.51	84.6	43.1	0.51
Small	52.4	15.0	0.29	82.6	24.0	0.29	52.9	23.1	0.44	83.0	35.9	0.43
Medium	52.9	14.0	0.27	81.1	22.4	0.28	53.3	21.9	0.41	81.5	34.1	0.42
Large	51.7	12.8	0.25	79.6	21.2	0.27	52.2	20.0	0.38	80.1	32.1	0.40
Landless others	46.3	11.2	0.24	76.3	17.8	0.23	47.0	19.7	0.42	77.0	30.5	0.40
Land owners	52.7	16.5	0.31	82.8	26.6	0.32	53.2	24.5	0.46	83.2	38.5	0.46
Landless	50.2	22.2	0.44	82.5	35.6	0.43	50.8	29.0	0.57	83.0	45.3	0.55
Occupational Groups												
Cultivators	52.7	15.6	0.30	82.7	25.0	0.30	53.2	22.8	0.43	83.1	35.6	0.43
Salaried+Prof.+S.Empl.	47.9	10.0	0.21	74.9	16.0	0.21	48.5	20.1	0.42	75.3	31.4	0.42
Wage earners	55.3	33.0	0.60	89.1	52.9	0.59	55.7	37.9	0.68	89.3	59.4	0.66
All others	47.8	11.3	0.24	80.1	18.3	0.23	48.5	21.8	0.45	80.9	34.5	0.43
Social Groups												
Caste												
STs	51.6	27.7	0.54	87.2	45.3	0.52	52.4	32.1	0.61	88.0	51.4	0.58
SCs	52.8	23.0	0.44	85.0	37.9	0.45	53.2	30.4	0.57	85.4	48.8	0.57
Religion												
Hindus	52.3	19.3	0.37	82.8	30.8	0.37	52.7	26.5	0.50	83.2	41.4	0.50
Muslims	48.0	9.6	0.20	82.6	16.3	0.20	48.8	19.3	0.40	83.4	32.0	0.38
Christians	52.8	25.5	0.48	78.0	37.1	0.48	53.3	27.8	0.52	78.7	40.2	0.51
Other Minorities	53.3	17.1	0.32	83.6	27.5	0.33	53.7	30.9	0.58	84.2	48.1	0.57
Household Size Groups												
Up to 4	64.5	30.7	0.48	87.4	40.3	0.46	64.9	36.9	0.57	87.6	47.7	0.55
5–7	49.2	18.1	0.37	81.9	30.1	0.37	49.8	25.2	0.51	82.4	40.6	0.49
8 and above	48.5	11.7	0.24	80.5	20.5	0.25	49.0	20.9	0.43	81.1	35.5	0.44
Adult Literacy Groups												
None literate	53.0	25.7	0.48	95.2	43.7	0.46	53.5	32.2	0.60	95.5	53.2	0.56
Female literate	47.4	30.1	0.64	96.5	43.2	0.45	47.9	34.3	0.72	97.0	48.8	0.50

(Contd.)

Male literate	52.0	17.0	0.33	80.7	29.2	0.36	52.4	26.0	0.50	81.2	43.5	0.54
Both literate	51.3	13.9	0.27	77.4	21.0	0.27	51.9	21.3	0.41	77.9	31.4	0.40
Village Development Groups												
Low	51.0	15.4	0.30	84.7	26.0	0.31	51.5	24.7	0.48	85.1	40.6	0.48
Medium	51.3	18.9	0.37	82.3	30.2	0.37	51.9	26.3	0.51	82.8	41.4	0.50
High	53.6	20.8	0.39	81.3	31.9	0.39	54.0	26.8	0.50	81.7	40.0	0.49
All India	**51.9**	**18.4**	**0.35**	**82.7**	**29.6**	**0.36**	**52.4**	**26.0**	**0.5**	**83.1**	**40.7**	**0.49**

Adult Male Work Participation Rate (Usual and Subsidiary Status) (%) by States

Regions/States	Household Income Groups (Rs per year)				Social Groups				Village Development Groups			All Groups
	Up to 20,000	20,001–40,000	40,001–62,000	Above 62,000	STs and SCs	Hindus	Muslims	Other Minorities	Low	Medium	High	
North												
Haryana	83.1	83.2	81.4	85.3	83.3	82.8	90.2	90.9	81.7	85.4	82.2	83.3
Himachal Pradesh	82.1	78.1	76.6	75.7	82.6	77.6	81.6	72.0	80.8	80.3	76.4	79.6
Punjab	82.3	78.7	87.2	85.5	86.7	80.6	76.8	83.7	89.2	82.2	82.6	82.7
Upper Central												
Bihar	86.5	79.4	73.1	75.7	84.4	82.3	79.3	89.9	84.0	80.6	82.1	82.3
Uttar Pradesh	85.1	81.5	76.5	75.4	86.4	81.2	85.8	87.7	82.4	81.1	79.3	81.7
Lower Central												
Madhya Pradesh	89.1	86.0	83.4	82.2	89.5	86.9	86.2	81.0	88.0	86.1	83.3	86.8
Orissa	87.6	78.2	76.8	81.6	90.3	84.4	90.7	83.4	87.7	84.4	79.4	84.4
Rajasthan	86.7	82.1	78.1	78.7	86.9	83.4	80.5	72.9	85.9	80.4	76.8	83.2
East												
North-eastern Rg	84.0	79.8	80.8	74.7	83.1	78.5	88.6	87.8	88.0	81.9	77.1	81.1
West Bengal	84.4	81.1	75.6	76.0	85.1	81.9	86.5	56.1	89.0	80.4	83.2	82.4
West												
Gujarat	87.9	82.8	81.4	85.3	87.1	85.0	91.0	70.5	86.2	87.3	82.8	85.4
Maharashtra	87.4	83.8	85.0	80.5	87.6	84.9	84.0	87.4	90.8	89.4	82.2	85.0
South												
Andhra Pradesh	85.8	86.9	83.1	78.0	86.7	86.0	75.3	82.7	89.1	85.3	83.6	85.3
Karnataka	84.6	81.1	83.0	74.8	85.7	82.4	82.8	74.0	96.6	81.5	82.0	82.3
Kerala	77.6	75.3	80.4	74.8	77.7	77.9	73.2	76.1	79.6	76.4	76.3	76.7
Tamil Nadu	84.4	82.8	80.2	85.5	84.1	84.2	61.4	83.3	100.0	86.2	82.6	83.6
All India	**85.7**	**81.8**	**79.7**	**79.1**	**86.2**	**83.2**	**83.4**	**82.0**	**85.1**	**82.8**	**81.7**	**83.2**
C.V.	3.2	3.6	4.6	5.3	3.4	3.4	9.2	11.1	6.0	3.9	3.2	2.9

Adult Female Work Participation Rate (Usual and Subsidiary Status) (%)by States

Regions/States	Household Income Groups (Rs per year)				Social Groups				Village Development Groups			All Groups
	Up to 20,000	20,001–40,000	40,001–62,000	Above 62,000	STs and SCs	Hindus	Muslims	Other Minorities	Low	Medium	High	
North												
Haryana	35.7	25.5	19.9	20.0	36.0	25.9	30.6	21.2	21.1	26.6	26.5	26.0
Himachal Pradesh	70.0	81.0	75.2	72.8	72.6	74.6	70.8	76.9	76.2	75.4	70.4	74.6
Punjab	40.8	42.4	52.7	47.6	53.1	45.2	57.3	43.8	24.2	45.7	45.5	44.5
Upper Central												
Bihar	38.2	22.3	23.4	15.6	37.3	30.5	29.2	34.7	35.9	24.3	33.3	30.5
Uttar Pradesh	34.4	36.4	36.4	36.0	42.6	35.1	37.7	59.4	33.7	37.8	37.3	35.5
Lower Central												
Madhya Pradesh	59.4	44.2	29.7	18.2	56.9	47.6	35.4	49.3	51.0	44.9	37.2	47.3
Orissa	42.3	24.6	22.4	25.7	49.4	36.9	20.5	20.2	39.0	35.7	33.5	36.4
Rajasthan	44.2	47.8	49.4	45.6	52.4	46.9	29.8	60.2	46.4	46.2	43.5	46.0
East												
North-eastern Rg.	12.6	12.3	8.4	9.5	11.9	12.8	7.4	8.2	8.9	13.0	10.4	11.5
West Bengal	31.8	28.3	18.8	28.4	33.6	30.1	27.7	44.8	38.2	31.9	25.8	29.9
West												
Gujarat	58.6	31.0	25.9	23.8	60.4	42.7	52.3	35.2	46.8	48.3	36.2	43.3
Maharashtra	70.8	56.7	46.2	35.8	73.8	59.2	47.0	67.8	59.5	70.5	53.8	59.4
South												
Andhra Pradesh	60.2	56.1	46.8	38.3	75.7	55.9	40.5	90.9	54.7	59.8	52.7	56.0
Karnataka	56.7	44.7	35.2	34.2	59.9	49.5	44.4	50.6	65.8	49.1	47.6	49.1
Kerala	43.1	40.6	34.8	39.1	59.7	45.8	29.7	37.0	41.0	39.8	41.7	40.9
Tamil Nadu	41.5	42.2	38.7	37.7	54.0	41.0	30.4	45.7	13.7	51.5	37.9	41.1
All India	**45.4**	**38.0**	**33.9**	**32.0**	**49.7**	**41.4**	**32.0**	**44.6**	**40.6**	**41.4**	**40.1**	**40.7**
C.V.	32.1	40.2	45.0	44.6	31.3	33.0	39.7	44.5	43.5	36.0	33.2	33.7

Average Household Size, Number of Workers and Sex Ratio by Population Groups

Population Groups	Average Household Size			Usual Status					Usual and Subsidiary Status				
	Total	Male	Female	Number of Workers			Non-worker F/M–worker Ratio		Number of Workers			Non-worker F/M–worker Ratio	
				Total	Male	Female			Total	Male	Female		
Household Income Groups													
Up to 20,000	5.03	2.60	2.42	1.86	1.33	0.53	0.39	1.70	2.03	1.34	0.69	0.51	1.48
20,001–40,000	6.24	3.32	2.92	2.23	1.75	0.48	0.28	1.80	2.49	1.77	0.72	0.41	1.51
40,001–62,000	6.88	3.70	3.18	2.35	1.93	0.42	2.20	1.93	2.66	1.95	0.71	0.36	1.59
62,001–86,000	7.75	4.17	3.58	2.62	2.20	0.42	0.19	1.96	2.98	2.22	0.76	0.34	1.60
Above 86000	8.28	4.34	3.94	2.78	2.31	0.47	0.20	1.98	3.09	2.32	0.77	0.33	1.68
Poverty Line Groups													
Lower segment below	6.35	3.23	3.12	1.99	1.46	0.53	0.36	2.19	2.21	1.47	0.74	0.50	1.87
Upper segment below	6.11	3.18	2.93	2.07	1.55	0.52	0.34	1.95	2.38	1.57	0.76	0.48	1.62
Lower segment above	5.63	2.97	2.66	2.13	1.59	0.54	0.34	1.64	2.35	1.61	0.74	0.46	1.40
Upper segment above	5.10	2.76	2.34	1.95	1.57	0.38	0.24	1.62	2.15	1.58	0.57	0.36	1.37
Landholding Groups													
Landless wage earner	4.90	2.54	2.36	2.14	1.37	0.77	0.56	1.29	2.27	1.38	0.89	0.64	1.16
Marginal	5.59	2.91	2.68	2.06	1.55	0.51	0.33	1.71	2.29	1.56	0.73	0.47	1.44
Small	6.12	3.27	2.85	2.14	1.71	0.43	0.25	1.86	2.39	1.73	0.66	0.38	1.56
Medium	6.86	3.63	3.21	2.38	1.93	0.45	0.23	1.88	2.65	1.95	0.70	0.36	1.59
Large	7.86	4.15	3.71	2.68	2.15	0.48	0.22	1.99	2.91	2.17	0.74	0.34	1.70
Landless others	6.25	2.74	2.50	1.35	1.27	0.28	0.28	2.39	1.78	1.29	0.49	0.38	1.95
Land owners	6.10	3.22	2.88	2.17	1.69	0.48	0.28	1.81	2.42	1.71	0.71	0.41	1.52
Landless	5.06	2.64	2.43	1.86	1.32	0.54	0.41	1.72	2.04	1.34	0.70	0.52	1.48
Occupational Groups													
Cultivators	5.99	3.16	2.83	2.11	1.67	0.44	0.26	1.84	2.32	1.68	0.64	0.38	1.58
Salaried+Prof.+S.Empl.	6.10	3.24	2.87	1.84	1.55	0.29	0.18	2.32	2.15	1.57	0.58	0.37	1.84
Wage earners	5.13	2.67	2.47	2.29	1.47	0.82	0.55	1.24	2.41	1.48	0.93	0.63	1.13
All others	5.66	2.96	2.70	1.72	1.42	0.30	0.21	2.29	2.03	1.44	0.59	0.41	1.79
Social Groups													
Caste													
STs	5.58	2.92	2.66	2.25	1.51	0.74	0.49	1.48	2.38	1.53	0.85	0.56	1.34
SCs	5.39	2.83	2.56	2.09	1.50	0.59	0.39	1.38	2.29	1.51	0.78	0.52	1.35
Religion													
Hindus	5.70	2.99	2.70	2.09	1.56	0.52	0.33	2.29	1.58	0.72	0.45	–	–
Muslims	6.20	3.28	2.92	1.85	1.57	0.28	0.18	2.35	2.16	1.60	0.56	0.35	1.87
Christians	4.87	2.47	2.40	1.91	1.30	0.61	0.47	1.56	1.99	1.32	0.67	0.51	1.45
Other Minorities	5.59	2.92	2.67	2.02	1.56	0.46	0.29	1.77	2.39	1.57	0.82	0.52	1.34
Household Size Groups													
Up to 4	3.24	1.71	1.53	1.57	1.10	0.47	0.43	1.06	1.67	1.11	0.56	0.51	0.94
5–7	5.79	3.06	2.74	2.00	1.50	0.50	0.33	1.89	2.21	1.52	0.69	0.45	1.62
8 and above	10.06	5.24	4.82	3.10	2.54	0.56	0.22	2.25	3.58	2.57	1.01	0.39	1.81
Adult Literacy Groups													
None literate	4.87	2.52	2.35	1.94	1.34	0.60	0.45	1.51	2.10	1.35	0.75	0.56	1.32

(Contd.)

Female literate	4.78	1.99	2.79	1.78	0.94	0.84	0.89	1.69	1.91	0.95	0.96	1.00	1.50
Male literate	5.89	3.24	2.65	2.13	1.68	0.45	0.27	1.77	2.39	1.70	0.69	0.41	1.45
Both literate	6.37	3.29	3.08	2.12	1.69	0.43	0.25	2.00	2.36	1.70	0.66	0.38	1.70
Village Development Groups													
Low	5.97	3.17	2.80	2.05	1.62	0.43	0.27	1.91	2.32	1.63	0.69	0.42	1.57
Medium	5.76	3.03	2.73	2.07	1.56	0.51	0.33	1.78	2.29	1.57	0.72	0.46	1.52
High	5.44	2.82	2.62	2.05	1.51	0.54	0.36	1.65	2.22	1.52	0.70	0.46	1.45
All India	**5.72**	**3.00**	**2.72**	**2.06**	**1.56**	**0.50**	**0.32**	**1.78**	**2.28**	**1.57**	**0.71**	**0.45**	**1.51**

Work Participation Rate (Usual Status) (%) among Children and the Elderly by Population Groups

Population Groups	Child (6–14 years)			Old (60 years and above)		
	Male	**Female**	**F/M**	**Male**	**Female**	**F/M**
Household Income Groups						
Up to 20,000	5.2	4.3	0.82	67.9	18.0	0.27
20,001–40,000	4.2	3.4	0.82	71.7	13.4	0.19
40,001–62,000	2.5	1.9	0.75	69.4	9.9	0.14
62,001–86,000	2.3	0.9	0.40	71.0	6.0	0.08
Above 86,000	1.1	0.6	0.56	69.6	7.4	0.11
Poverty Line Groups						
Lower segment below	4.3	3.2	0.74	59.3	11.0	0.18
Upper segment below	4.5	3.4	0.75	66.4	12.8	0.19
Lower segment above	4.9	4.4	0.90	70.5	16.1	0.23
Upper segment above	2.7	1.6	0.57	76.0	15.4	0.20
Landholding Groups						
Landless wage earner	7.6	8.1	1.06	65.3	25.8	0.40
Marginal	4.5	3.2	0.70	75.8	17.9	0.24
Small	3.5	2.2	0.64	72.7	10.5	0.14
Medium	2.5	2.0	0.81	74.7	11.8	0.16
Large	2.7	1.5	0.55	72.3	8.1	0.11
Landless others	3.5	2.5	0.71	48.3	9.3	0.19
Land owners	3.7	2.6	0.69	74.3	13.6	0.18
Landless	5.7	5.4	0.95	56.6	16.6	0.29
Occupational Groups						
Cultivators	3.8	2.5	0.67	74.2	13.6	0.18
Salaried+Prof.+S.Empl.	1.4	0.9	0.63	61.4	6.7	0.11
Wage earners	7.5	7.7	1.02	69.4	25.9	0.37
All others	3.8	2.2	0.58	60.0	9.8	0.16
Social Groups						
Caste						
STs	5.6	6.2	1.10	69.8	19.4	0.28
SCs	5.7	4.2	0.74	67.9	17.9	0.26
Religion						
Hindus	4.3	3.8	0.88	69.3	14.4	0.21
Muslims	4.5	1.7	0.37	72.8	13.0	0.18
Christians	4.0	2.1	0.52	75.0	29.3	0.39
Other Minorities	7.0	4.0	0.57	61.2	10.7	0.17
Household Size Groups						
Up to 4	7.1	5.4	0.76	80.1	29.5	0.37
5–7	4.4	4.0	0.91	65.9	11.1	0.17
8 and above	3.1	2.1	0.67	66.1	7.7	0.12
Adult Literacy Groups						
None literate	7.8	6.0	0.76	74.3	24.0	0.32

(Contd.)

Female literate	4.0	5.0	1.25	70.2	36.8	0.52
Male literate	3.9	3.4	0.87	70.1	10.5	0.15
Both literate	1.8	1.4	0.81	65.9	9.7	0.15
Village Development Groups						
Low	3.6	2.5	0.68	74.4	11.8	0.16
Medium	4.6	4.0	0.86	68.1	14.3	0.21
High	4.8	3.9	0.81	66.7	17.0	0.26
All India	**4.4**	**3.5**	**0.80**	**69.5**	**14.5**	**0.21**

Average Days Worked Per Adult Wage Earner by Population Groups

Population Groups	Agr. Wage Work			Non-agr. Wage Work			All Wage Work		
	Male Days	Female Days	Total Days	Male Days	Female Days	Total Days	Male Days	Female Days	Total Days
Household Income Groups									
Up to 20,000	140	118	132	146	121	141	166	130	153
20,001–40,000	156	140	150	178	144	171	185	152	174
40,001–62,000	165	145	157	196	180	192	190	165	182
62,001–86,000	150	129	142	197	241	206	181	173	179
Above 86,000	155	147	152	226	206	222	190	164	182
Poverty Line Groups									
Lower segment below	109	85	100	119	87	112	135	94	122
Upper segment below	147	112	134	155	114	148	175	124	158
Lower segment above	157	143	151	169	146	164	183	155	172
Upper segment above	176	156	168	198	197	198	197	177	190
Landholding Groups									
Landless wage earner	162	134	151	172	147	167	198	150	181
Marginal	134	116	127	150	116	144	157	126	147
Small	124	118	121	131	111	127	140	128	137
Medium	117	106	113	137	106	129	135	118	129
Large	121	94	110	135	97	129	134	105	125
Landless others	122	116	119	133	154	140	136	135	136
Land owners	130	115	124	145	113	138	151	125	142
Landless	158	132	148	168	148	164	191	148	176
Occupational Groups									
Cultivators	112	102	108	119	97	115	125	109	120
Salaried+Prof.+S.Empl.	109	115	112	130	157	138	126	131	128
Wage earners	160	135	151	171	142	165	194	150	179
All others	118	104	112	143	139	142	139	122	133
Social Groups									
Caste									
STs	133	115	125	131	95	120	157	128	145
SCs	143	119	133	155	127	149	172	130	158
Religion									
Hindus	143	123	135	154	129	149	169	136	157
Muslims	167	131	158	178	166	177	197	148	187
Christians	137	130	134	157	166	159	164	146	158
Other Minorities	124	120	122	164	127	157	167	129	153
Household Size Groups									
Up to 4	154	135	146	150	151	150	175	149	166
5–7	144	123	136	158	123	151	174	135	160
8 and above	130	107	122	165	128	158	163	122	150
Adult Literacy Groups									
None literate	146	126	138	154	122	147	174	138	161
Female literate	156	126	141	133	184	152	166	150	158

(Contd.)

Male literate	140	122	133	159	122	153	168	133	157
Both literate	149	124	139	162	156	161	175	140	163
Village Development Groups									
Low	129	108	121	153	106	144	163	122	150
Medium	148	125	139	155	127	150	172	134	158
High	155	136	147	164	165	165	180	153	170
All India	**145**	**124**	**137**	**157**	**133**	**152**	**172**	**137**	**160**

Percentage Distribution by Gender of Adult Wage Earners over Different Durations of Employment by States

Regions/ States	Below 91 Days				91–182 Days				183–274 Days				Above 274 Days			
	Person	Male	Female	F/M Ratio	Person	Male	Female	F/M Ratio	Person	Male	Female	F/M Ratio	Person	Male	Female	F/M Ratio
North																
Haryana	38.3	19.3	84.8	4.39	34.6	43.7	12.1	0.28	22.1	30.2	2.2	0.07	5.1	6.8	0.9	0.13
Himachal Pradesh	17.8	16.6	70.1	4.22	31.4	31.8	14.7	0.46	27.9	28.2	15.3	0.54	22.9	23.5	–	–
Punjab	32.7	20.7	81.2	3.92	22.6	25.2	12.2	0.48	32.4	39.3	4.2	0.11	12.4	14.9	2.5	0.17
Upper Central																
Bihar	24.7	17.7	42.7	2.41	34.6	35.0	33.6	0.96	29.8	33.2	21.2	0.64	10.8	14.1	2.5	0.18
Uttar Pradesh	31.6	23.4	64.4	2.75	31.5	33.6	23.0	0.68	22.3	25.6	9.2	0.36	14.7	17.5	3.4	0.19
Lower Central																
Madhya Pradesh	41.2	35.2	49.6	1.41	38.7	39.2	38.0	0.97	16.3	21.0	9.7	0.46	3.8	4.6	2.7	0.59
Orissa	42.9	33.5	66.9	2.00	39.1	44.5	25.0	0.56	12.6	15.2	5.9	0.39	5.5	6.8	2.2	0.32
Rajasthan	33.3	25.2	71.5	2.84	45.3	49.7	24.6	0.49	15.8	18.4	3.4	0.18	5.6	6.7	0.6	0.09
East																
North-eastern Rg.	11.8	8.6	47.4	5.51	21.7	22.6	11.5	0.51	29.7	31.1	14.2	0.46	36.7	37.6	26.9	0.72
West Bengal	16.4	12.1	48.7	4.02	30.0	31.0	22.6	0.73	28.3	29.9	16.2	0.54	25.3	27.1	12.4	0.46
West																
Gujarat	18.8	15.6	23.3	1.49	46.4	42.1	52.2	1.24	23.7	29.5	15.7	0.53	11.1	12.8	8.8	0.69
Maharashtra	16.9	14.3	19.8	1.38	38.3	32.4	44.7	1.38	31.7	35.4	27.7	0.78	13.1	17.9	7.7	0.43
South																
Andhra Pradesh	12.6	13.1	11.9	0.91	31.1	30.5	31.8	1.04	46.4	48.2	44.4	0.92	9.9	8.1	11.9	1.47
Karnataka	21.4	18.8	24.7	1.31	46.2	43.1	50.2	1.16	25.1	29.1	20.0	0.69	7.2	8.9	5.1	0.57
Kerala	23.6	15.7	40.8	2.60	42.9	48.9	29.8	0.61	26.9	28.7	23.1	0.80	6.6	6.7	6.4	0.96
Tamil Nadu	32.4	25.9	43.6	1.68	31.9	30.5	34.4	1.13	25.0	31.7	13.5	0.43	10.7	11.9	8.5	0.71
All India	**25.6**	**20.6**	**35.2**	**1.71**	**36.2**	**36.1**	**36.5**	**1.01**	**27.2**	**30.2**	**21.7**	**0.72**	**10.9**	**13.1**	**6.7**	**0.51**
C. V.	37.7	36.2	43.6	49.34	20.8	21.7	44.0	40.58	29.5	25.6	67.4	47.61	68.0	61.7	101.7	76.95

Effective (Adult) Wage Rate for Agricultural and Non-Agricultural Wage Work by Population Groups

Population Groups	Agriculture Wage Work				Other Wage Work				All Wage Work			
	All	Male Rate	Female Rate	F/M	All	Male Rate	Female Rate	F/M	All	Male Rate	Female Rate	F/M
Household Income Groups												
Up to 20,000	20.0	22.3	15.8	0.71	25.7	27.6	17.1	0.62	21.9	24.4	16.1	0.66
20,001–40,000	22.6	25.8	17.4	0.67	31.0	33.2	20.6	0.62	26.0	29.3	18.2	0.62
40,001–62,000	23.0	26.1	17.3	0.66	36.4	40.7	22.5	0.55	43.0	33.3	19.1	0.57
62,001–86,000	24.5	27.9	18.6	0.67	39.3	44.0	23.9	0.54	31.9	36.8	20.6	0.56
Above 86,000	41.1	29.4	31.2	1.06	50.3	58.1	16.0	0.28	39.0	44.0	26.9	0.61
Poverty Line Groups												
Lower segment below	18.1	19.8	14.5	0.73	22.6	23.9	15.0	0.63	19.7	21.5	14.6	0.68
Upper segment below	20.0	22.0	15.6	0.71	26.2	27.7	17.0	0.61	22.3	24.4	15.9	0.65
Lower segment above	21.3	24.4	16.6	0.68	29.5	32.1	19.1	0.60	24.2	27.6	17.1	0.62
Upper segment above	25.3	28.6	19.8	0.69	35.9	40.0	22.4	0.56	29.7	33.9	20.5	0.60
Landholding Groups												
Landless wage earner	21.8	24.1	17.4	0.72	28.8	31.0	19.0	0.61	24.3	26.9	17.7	0.66
Marginal	20.9	23.5	16.3	0.69	28.7	30.3	19.6	0.65	23.8	26.5	16.9	0.64
Small	13.0	21.2	14.2	0.67	26.8	29.1	17.4	0.60	21.0	24.3	14.8	0.61
Medium	17.6	20.1	13.7	0.68	29.6	32.0	20.6	0.64	21.7	24.9	15.2	0.61
Large	16.1	18.9	10.9	0.58	30.7	32.5	18.5	0.57	22.2	25.5	12.5	0.49
Landless others	18.8	21.7	15.3	0.71	23.8	27.8	15.5	0.56	20.8	24.5	15.3	0.62
Land owners	20.0	22.7	15.4	0.68	28.4	30.2	19.1	0.63	23.0	25.9	16.1	0.62
LandLess	21.5	23.9	17.1	0.72	28.3	30.7	18.4	0.60	24.0	26.7	17.5	0.66
Occupational Groups												
Cultivators	18.1	20.7	13.8	0.67	24.4	26.3	15.7	0.60	20.0	22.8	14.1	0.62
Salaried+Prof.+Self Empl.	18.7	22.0	15.9	0.72	25.0	28.8	17.1	0.59	21.5	25.7	16.3	0.63
Wage earners	21.8	24.2	17.3	0.71	29.4	31.5	19.7	0.63	24.6	27.5	17.8	0.65
All others	19.4	22.0	15.3	0.70	26.3	29.5	15.2	0.52	22.5	25.8	15.2	0.59
Social Groups												
Caste												
STs	16.8	18.6	14.5	0.78	23.0	24.6	18.1	0.74	18.9	21.0	15.3	0.73
SCs	21.8	23.9	17.8	0.74	28.6	30.5	18.5	0.61	24.2	26.6	17.9	0.67
Religion												
Hindus	20.5	23.0	16.3	0.71	28.0	30.2	18.6	0.62	23.2	26.1	16.8	0.64
Muslims	22.5	23.9	17.0	0.71	29.0	30.2	20.3	0.67	25.2	26.7	18.1	0.68
Christians	29.9	33.5	23.8	0.71	34.0	39.1	18.7	0.48	31.5	35.9	22.2	0.62
Other Minorities	18.8	23.2	12.5	0.54	31.6	34.0	17.1	0.50	23.5	28.1	13.3	0.47
Household Size Groups												
Up to 4	21.2	23.9	16.7	0.70	27.5	30.1	18.6	0.62	23.2	26.2	17.1	0.65
5–7	20.9	23.4	16.4	0.70	28.5	30.5	18.5	0.61	23.5	26.3	16.8	0.64
8 and above	20.0	22.2	15.7	0.71	29.3	31.1	19.3	0.62	24.2	26.7	16.7	0.63
Adult Literacy Groups												
None literate	20.3	22.6	16.3	0.72	25.7	27.4	18.1	0.66	22.1	24.5	16.6	0.68
Female literate	21.7	25.0	17.9	0.72	27.6	31.9	22.4	0.70	23.5	27.2	19.2	0.71

(Contd.)

Male literate	20.4	22.8	15.8	0.69	29.2	30.9	18.8	0.61	23.7	26.4	16.4	0.62
Both literate	22.7	25.6	17.2	0.67	31.8	35.1	18.4	0.52	26.3	29.9	17.5	0.59
Village Development Groups												
Low	19.2	21.0	15.8	0.75	26.4	27.8	18.2	0.65	22.4	24.4	16.4	0.67
Medium	21.2	23.7	16.7	0.70	28.9	30.8	19.5	0.63	23.6	26.4	17.2	0.65
High	21.6	24.7	16.4	0.66	29.7	33.1	18.4	0.56	24.4	28.1	16.9	0.60
All India	**20.9**	**23.4**	**16.4**	**0.70**	**28.4**	**30.5**	**18.7**	**0.61**	**23.6**	**26.4**	**16.9**	**0.64**

Estimated Per Capita Expenditure (Rs) Per Month by States

Regions/ States	Food Expen.			Non-food				Total Expenditure	CPI 1993–94 (BASE 1960–6) = 100
	Food-grains	Other Food	Total Food	Health	Education	Other Non-food	Total Non-food		
North									
Haryana	58.9	152.0	210.5	20.3	17.0	101.5	138.8	349.3	939
Himachal Pradesh	111.5	153.9	265.4	38.5	30.9	105.6	175.0	440.4	1,173
Punjab	87.7	232.6	320.3	32.4	17.5	184.3	234.2	554.5	1,258
Upper Central									
Bihar	94.4	57.2	151.6	22.2	7.4	36.9	66.5	218.1	1,183
Uttar Pradesh	90.3	102.2	192.5	20.2	8.4	84.8	113.4	305.9	1,250
Lower Central									
Madhya Pradesh	71.9	56.7	128.6	20.1	4.9	54.4	79.4	208.0	1,133
Orissa	89.6	55.6	145.2	12.4	6.3	46.7	65.4	210.6	1,118
Rajasthan	80.7	162.8	243.5	27.5	10.2	129.1	166.8	410.3	1,170
East									
North-eastern Rg.	102.3	84.4	186.7	16.5	11.8	45.3	73.6	260.3	
West Bengal	111.3	90.1	201.4	24.2	8.2	52.1	84.5	285.9	1,074
West									
Gujarat	69.2	122.3	191.5	15.4	8.4	75.8	99.6	291.1	1,012
Maharashtra	64.5	82.4	146.9	18.0	7.8	67.7	93.5	240.4	1,033
South									
Andhra Pradesh	91.3	93.9	185.2	29.0	7.2	91.4	127.6	312.8	939
Karnataka	87.0	88.3	175.3	21.3*	9.9	76.5	60.8	236.1	1,093
Kerala	75.1	132.6	207.7	21.7	17.8	87.0	126.5	334.2	1,274
Tamil Nadu	99.9	101.4	201.3	31.2	8.1	69.6	108.9	310.2	1,039
All India	**87.5**	**95.8**	**183.3**	**21.3**	**9.0**	**73.5**	**103.8**	**287.1**	**1,114**

* The figures match the national average.

Per Capita Consumption of Foodgrains (kg per month) by States

Regions/States	Household Income Groups (Rs per year)				Social Groups				Village Development Groups			All Groups
	Up to 20,000	20,001–40,000	40,001–62,000	Above 62,000	STs and SCs	Hindus	Muslims	Other Minorities	Up to 30	31–45	Above 45	
North												
Haryana	12.3	12.3	13.2	14.0	12.6	12.9	11.6	14.3	13.0	12.9	12.7	12.8
Himachal Pradesh	17.6	17.4	17.0	16.2	17.4	17.4	16.2	18.2	16.9	17.1	18.6	17.4
Punjab	13.4	14.1	15.1	15.4	13.1	13.8	13.8	14.5	15.1	13.7	14.8	14.3
Upper Central												
Bihar	14.4	14.9	16.3	16.4	15.0	15.0	14.8	11.9	14.6	15.3	14.1	14.8
Uttar Pradesh	15.1	14.9	15.6	15.2	14.7	15.3	14.3	14.4	15.2	15.2	14.6	15.2
Lower Central												
Madhya Pradesh	13.7	13.4	13.0	13.0	13.3	13.5	12.4	16.2	13.8	13.3	12.7	13.5
Orissa	16.5	16.4	15.7	15.6	15.8	16.3	13.7	18.7	16.4	16.5	16.0	16.4
Rajasthan	18.4	17.5	15.8	16.1	17.5	17.6	17.2	22.2	17.5	18.2	15.7	17.6
East												
North-eastern Rg.	11.8	12.9	12.5	13.7	11.4	12.2	13.2	12.6	13.4	12.1	12.5	12.5
West Bengal	15.8	17.2	17.3	17.1	16.1	16.4	16.1	16.0	15.2	16.6	16.3	16.3
West												
Gujarat	9.7	10.1	10.5	12.2	9.8	10.2	9.7	12.6	10.9	9.8	10.3	10.1
Maharashtra	12.8	13.4	13.3	13.8	13.4	13.3	11.1	12.6	14.0	13.8	12.7	13.2
South												
Andhra Pradesh	13.9	14.4	14.5	15.9	14.6	14.3	12.6	16.3	14.3	14.5	14.0	14.3
Karnataka	14.6	15.6	15.6	16.1	14.9	15.3	14.0	14.2	17.8	15.1	14.9	15.1
Kerala	9.4	10.1	9.5	10.5	9.4	9.7	8.9	10.6	10.2	9.5	9.9	9.8
Tamil Nadu	12.5	12.7	13.2	12.4	12.9	12.6	12.6	11.5	9.7	12.5	12.7	12.6
All India	**14.2**	**14.3**	**14.4**	**14.7**	**14.4**	**14.4**	**14.0**	**13.3**	**14.9**	**14.5**	**13.5**	**14.3**
C.V.	17.6	15.8	15.1	12.4	16.5	15.8	16.5	20.0	16.4	16.8	15.5	15.6

Consumption of Foodgrains and Utilization of PDS by Population Groups

Population Groups	Average Hhold Income	Per Capita Income	P capita Consmpt. of Foodgrn	% Hhold Using PDS	Average Cereals bght from PDS	% Requirm. from PDS
Household Income Groups						
Up to 20,000	11,027	2,192	14.2	34.3	19.0	26.3
20,001–40,000	28,141	4,506	14.3	32.4	19.0	22.0
40,001–62,000	49,072	7,132	14.4	31.9	19.8	20.5
62,001–86,000	72,178	9,309	14.6	28.1	18.7	16.4
Above 86,000	1,47,855	17,865	14.7	28.0	17.6	13.0
Poverty Line Groups						
Lower segment below	6,950	1,095	13.7	30.1	23.0	26.3
Upper segment below	12,379	2,026	14.1	29.5	19.7	22.7
Lower segment above	22,138	3,931	14.2	37.1	18.7	23.9
Upper segment above	58,100	11,396	15.4	30.6	16.6	21.0
Landholding Groups						
Landless wage earner	11,313	2,308	13.5	44.3	17.5	25.8
Marginal	19,586	3,502	14.4	31.4	21.1	28.0
Small	29,377	4,803	14.7	27.0	17.1	18.7
Medium	44,695	6,516	15.0	25.7	17.3	14.7
Large	85,969	10,930	15.1	29.7	20.1	13.6
Landless others	21,574	4,111	13.6	35.2	19.8	28.1
Land owners	31,154	5,108	14.7	29.2	19.5	21.5
Landless	16,141	3,187	13.6	40.0	18.4	26.8
Occupational Groups						
Cultivators	32,374	5,408	14.8	28.0	18.3	19.5
Salaried+Prof.+S.Empl.	35,760	5,857	14.0	33.8	23.0	28.3
Wage earners	12,580	2,450	13.8	43.0	18.3	26.0
All others	21,010	3,709	13.9	30.3	19.1	25.9
Social Groups						
Caste						
STs	19,556	3,504	13.7	37.5	21.6	25.7
SCs	17,465	3,237	14.4	32.1	17.3	22.5
Religion						
Hindus	25,712	4,514	14.4	34.1	18.6	22.9
Muslims	22,807	3,678	14.0	21.8	23.6	28.8
Christians	28,860	5,920	12.5	66.1	22.0	38.3
Other Minorities	30,330	5,427	13.8	15.7	18.1	11.4
Household Size Groups						
Up to 4	18,399	5,687	15.5	37.9	16.7	31.1
5–7	25,060	4,326	14.2	33.0	19.3	23.0
8 and above	40,449	4,019	13.8	24.9	24.9	16.8

(Contd.)

Adult Literacy Groups

None literate	15,271	3,138	14.5	29.0	18.1	23.6
Female literate	19,060	3,987	13.7	50.7	16.3	27.2
Male literate	24,367	4,137	14.7	29.9	18.2	20.4
Both literate	36,187	5,683	13.9	38.2	20.6	25.6
Village Development Groups						
Low	24,149	4,045	14.9	18.0	22.2	20.8
Medium	25,173	4,369	14.5	33.4	20.2	24.6
High	27,628	5,079	13.5	46.8	16.8	23.8
All India	**25,653**	**4,485**	**14.3**	**33.2**	**19.0**	**23.5**

Percentage of Households Using PDS by States

Regions/States	Household Income Groups (Rs per year)				Social Groups				Village Development Groups			All Groups
	Up to 20,000	20,001–40,000	40,001–62,000	Above 62,000	STs and SCs	Hindus	Muslims	Other Minorities	Up to 30	31–45	Above 45	
North												
Haryana	8.8	8.2	11.4	8.6	11.1	9.2	8.9	3.6	12.6	8.1	8.9	9.0
Himachal Pradesh	73.8	78.9	77.4	69.7	79.3	75.7	63.0	100.0	76.2	74.5	77.1	75.6
Punjab	6.6	5.0	5.3	4.3	10.5	9.1	–	4.3	4.5	1.7	10.8	5.6
Upper Central												
Bihar	3.1	5.9	15.3	9.3	9.4	5.1	5.5	1.8	4.3	5.0	6.6	5.0
Uttar Pradesh	5.8	5.0	5.0	2.0	6.1	5.9	0.5	–	5.1	5.1	6.7	5.2
Lower Central												
Madhya Pradesh	32.2	37.4	37.1	34.8	34.7	34.1	35.3	34.4	29.3	38.7	44.4	34.2
Orissa	4.2	6.5	12.4	10.4	5.1	4.7	31.9	19.6	4.5	4.4	8.4	5.2
Rajasthan	25.6	22.8	19.7	17.5	25.5	24.5	10.4	–	21.9	25.3	29.3	23.6
East												
North-eastern Rg.	23.6	20.4	25.0	4.1	29.2	24.3	11.4	25.2	16.6	23.8	20.8	·21.7
West Bengal	14.2	2.8	7.3	7.7	12.0	12.2	4.4	56.5	4.9	18.5	4.7	11.3
West												
Gujarat	53.4	44.4	37.9	30.2	52.8	46.7	57.5	67.6	45.2	51.2	43.9	47.6
Maharashtra	50.9	50.2	56.1	45.4	56.5	51.0	49.0	47.0	51.8	51.7	50.0	50.7
South												
Andhra Pradesh	74.0	61.4	46.9	40.0	71.7	65.0	78.2	88.5	56.6	67.5	70.2	66.4
Karnataka	72.5	71.4	63.2	56.6	71.2	69.0	80.7	83.9	46.6	69.0	73.9	70.1
Kerala	80.8	77.1	75.4	67.1	74.5	77.2	82.6	77.2	83.6	75.7	78.5	78.0
Tamil Nadu	83.8	80.9	82.4	75.5	88.9	82.3	94.0	81.6	100.0	83.6	81.8	82.4
All India	**34.3**	**32.4**	**31.9**	**28.0**	**33.8**	**34.1**	**21.8**	**38.2**	**18.0**	**33.4**	**46.8**	**33.2**
C.V.	78.0	81.0	73.9	83.3	73.3	75.9	85.3	81.5	86.7	76.3	75.6	78.3

Percentage Requirement of Cereals Met from PDS by States

Regions/States	Household Income Groups (Rs per year)				Social Groups				Village Development Groups			All Groups
	Up to 20,000	20,001–40,000	40,001–62,000	Above 62,000	STs and SCS	Hindus	Muslims	Other Minorities	Up to 30	31–45	Above 45	
North												
Haryana	34.0	41.3	21.4	22.8	31.0	32.1	37.5	100.0	21.8	39.1	33.0	32.4
Himachal Pradesh	40.6	42.4	44.1	35.5	44.0	41.5	28.4	59.7	35.9	41.3	50.8	41.4
Punjab	12.2	4.0	1.0	2.1	5.6	4.2	0.0	6.4	91.0	2.0	8.4	5.5
Upper Central												
Bihar	49.5	15.3	11.7	9.8	21.8	34.0	11.4	16.1	25.7	11.6	68.5	29.2
Uttar Pradesh	20.1	30.8	46.2	14.9	21.8	25.3	2.0	0.0	22.4	25.1	40.4	24.5
Lower Central												
Madhya Pradesh	22.5	21.9	15.8	12.5	20.4	20.3	27.0	22.2	19.7	19.6	24.5	20.4
Orissa	19.8	10.2	10.9	27.9	18.0	16.6	34.2	8.6	16.3	16.9	16.8	16.7
Rajasthan	13.7	15.9	17.1	14.3	15.2	14.7	14.2	0.0	13.5	14.6	24.4	14.7
East												
North-eastern Rg.	39.2	26.3	26.5	33.3	37.6	33.3	15.3	41.3	15.6	35.6	32.2	31.9
West Bengal	47.7	41.0	20.5	13.8	42.5	43.0	38.6	67.9	56.5	50.3	19.4	45.6
West												
Gujarat	23.2	17.5	9.8	6.0	21.7	17.7	22.0	16.3	14.0	21.9	15.0	18.1
Maharashtra	16.1	10.6	12.3	8.4	17.2	12.6	40.0	8.8	12.6	16.4	11.3	13.2
South												
Andhra Pradesh	32.2	28.3	30.1	24.6	30.6	30.5	31.6	29.7	28.8	30.6	31.4	30.6
Karnataka	24.5	18.7	25.2	22.0	24.2	22.7	23.2	23.5	21.3	20.0	25.9	22.8
Kerala	56.7	48.7	49.8	42.9	55.2	52.4	56.4	47.8	49.4	53.8	50.9	51.9
Tamil Nadu	23.3	20.2	19.1	17.1	20.8	21.7	20.6	20.8	23.1	20.8	21.9	21.6
All India	**26.3**	**22.0**	**20.5**	**14.5**	**23.7**	**22.9**	**28.8**	**26.2**	**20.8**	**24.6**	**23.8**	**23.5**
C.V.	44.3	51.9	59.8	57.3	45.9	46.4	56.9	91.4	68.6	53.0	52.9	45.8

Literacy Rates (%) in the Age Group of 7 Years and Above by States

Regions/States	Household Income Groups (Rs per year)				Social Groups				Village Development Groups			All
	Up to 20,000	20,001– 40,000	40,001– 62,000	Above 62,000	STs and SCs	Hindus	Muslims	Other Minorities	Low	Medium	High	Groups
North												
Haryana	45.3	54.7	62.4	61.3	46.0	55.9	29.7	71.0	59.6	50.7	57.0	54.9
Himachal Pradesh	62.8	71.9	74.7	76.0	63.2	68.3	57.9	84.6	62.3	69.4	74.5	68.2
Punjab	51.3	62.0	64.1	70.5	46.5	61.7	32.7	60.2	57.0	59.3	61.8	60.2
Upper Central												
Bihar	32.7	53.0	56.1	72.4	28.2	44.5	43.2	31.8	39.4	46.9	47.0	43.8
Uttar Pradesh	36.7	48.0	58.9	69.4	32.5	48.2	35.0	65.8	43.9	49.2	55.9	46.7
Lower Central												
Madhya Pradesh	34.5	48.5	55.0	62.9	31.6	43.6	48.9	59.1	39.2	46.5	57.5	43.9
Orissa	46.5	66.0	76.0	80.6	35.1	54.4	53.9	59.6	45.3	56.2	65.9	54.5
Rajasthan	31.4	41.2	53.8	63.7	29.9	41.7	27.8	33.4	35.6	45.3	57.5	40.9
East												
North-eastern Rg.	65.2	68.0	81.9	77.7	74.5	45.8	46.0	86.2	42.3	71.1	80.9	70.0
West Bengal	49.9	67.9	83.1	84.9	53.9	61.0	52.1	55.4	43.9	56.2	64.2	58.5
West												
Gujarat	51.5	65.4	69.8	70.6	46.6	59.2	59.4	91.3	41.3	58.2	68.0	59.4
Maharashtra	50.1	60.7	64.8	75.3	43.1	58.4	63.7	53.1	44.6	51.0	63.8	58.2
South												
Andhra Pradesh	45.1	50.0	59.6	77.1	38.5	49.4	60.5	54.6	40.8	49.7	55.4	50.2
Karnataka	49.4	58.9	62.5	65.9	43.7	54.4	58.6	75.5	45.2	54.5	56.4	54.9
Kerala	87.0	90.2	91.9	96.7	77.5	88.2	86.9	94.8	91.8	87.4	91.0	89.6
Tamil Nadu	57.2	68.7	75.9	80.8	47.6	63.0	79.7	75.6	0.7	53.3	68.7	64.1
All India	**45.1**	**57.5**	**64.9**	**72.0**	**40.8**	**53.3**	**49.4**	**65.2**	**42.3**	**53.7**	**63.9**	**53.5**
C.V.	27.2	18.9	16.1	11.9	31.2	20.0	31.0	27.4	38.5	18.9	16.5	20.4

Gender Disparity in Literacy Rates (%) in the Age Group of 7 Years and Above by States

Regions/States	Household Income Groups (Rs per year)				Social Groups				Village Development Groups			All Groups
	Up to 20,000	20,001– 40,000	40,001– 62,000	Above 62,000	STs and SCs	Hindus	Muslims	Other Minorities	Low	Medium	High	
North												
Haryana	0.51	0.52	0.58	0.61	0.48	0.56	0.15	0.70	0.59	0.52	0.56	0.55
Himachal Pradesh	0.69	0.73	0.73	0.81	0.68	0.72	0.74	0.72	0.69	0.73	0.74	0.72
Punjab	0.71	0.75	0.80	0.82	0.60	0.71	0.38	0.77	0.87	0.73	0.76	0.75
Upper Central												
Bihar	0.44	0.55	0.49	0.70	0.40	0.50	0.53	0.55	0.45	0.54	0.59	0.51
Uttar Pradesh	0.37	0.44	0.55	0.61	0.29	0.46	0.43	0.68	0.43	0.46	0.59	0.46
Lower Central												
Madhya Pradesh	0.40	0.48	0.48	0.59	0.38	0.46	0.45	0.69	0.42	0.49	0.55	0.46
Orissa	0.53	0.71	0.68	0.77	0.44	0.60	0.60	0.55	0.58	0.57	0.68	0.60
Rajasthan	0.21	0.29	0.44	0.50	0.18	0.32	0.17	0.26	0.27	0.32	0.50	0.31
East												
North-eastern Rg.	0.72	0.80	0.89	0.84	0.81	0.81	0.63	0.96	0.65	0.78	0.85	0.79
West Bengal	0.71	0.77	0.93	0.86	0.73	0.75	0.75	0.71	0.71	0.72	0.78	0.75
West												
Gujarat	0.58	0.70	0.74	0.74	0.61	0.66	0.56	0.88	0.66	0.63	0.68	0.65
Maharashtra	0.60	0.64	0.65	0.72	0.52	0.64	0.69	0.61	0.58	0.60	0.66	0.64
South												
Andhra Pradesh	0.64	0.62	0.71	0.76	0.56	0.65	0.56	0.84	0.60	0.64	0.67	0.65
Karnataka	0.66	0.71	0.68	0.68	0.63	0.66	0.74	0.94	0.70	0.68	0.67	0.67
Kerala	0.92	0.93	0.93	0.97	0.89	0.91	0.93	0.97	0.98	0.92	0.93	0.93
Tamil Nadu	0.67	0.75	0.78	0.83	0.65	0.70	0.68	0.83	–	0.62	0.74	0.71
All India	**0.57**	**0.63**	**0.66**	**0.70**	**0.52**	**0.60**	**0.64**	**0.81**	**0.47**	**0.61**	**0.71**	**0.61**
C.V.	27.20	18.90	16.10	11.90	31.20	22.5	31.00	27.40	38.50	18.90	16.50	20.4

Age-Specific Literacy Rates (%) and Gender Disparity by States

Regions/States	Age in Completed Years										All
	6–9	10–14	15–19	20–24	25–29	30–34	35–39	40–44	45–49	50+	Ages
North											
Haryana											
Person	53.7	82.0	79.0	64.9	55.8	46.2	44.2	35.2	38.5	17.5	54.0
Gender disparity	0.88	0.85	0.76	0.51	0.39	0.35	0.30	0.19	0.15	0.15	0.55
Himachal Pradesh											
Person	85.6	94.4	91.6	83.4	72.4	72.5	61.9	59.3	48.4	24.5	68.4
Gender disparity	0.89	0.97	0.92	0.80	0.70	0.67	0.50	0.42	0.40	0.23	0.72
Punjab											
Person	74.2	86.4	78.8	77.1	67.1	58.0	46.5	45.5	39.3	25.5	60.1
Gender disparity	1.06	0.92	0.92	0.85	0.70	0.62	0.60	0.59	0.59	0.28	0.76
Upper Central											
Bihar											
Person	49.7	64.2	58.3	46.8	38.3	35.6	37.5	36.1	30.5	20.4	43.3
Gender disparity	0.76	0.79	0.67	0.40	0.37	0.46	0.41	0.31	0.28	0.12	0.52
Uttar Pradesh											
Person	48.4	66.2	63.8	53.2	46.0	41.6	38.6	35.5	35.7	21.6	46.1
Gender disparity	0.76	0.71	0.61	0.41	0.32	0.32	0.23	0.25	0.24	0.17	0.46
Lower Central											
Madhya Pradesh											
Person	43.6	66.7	63.9	50.4	43.2	33.9	34.0	33.8	31.1	19.5	43.2
Gender disparity	0.86	0.78	0.60	0.42	0.32	0.26	0.28	0.22	0.26	0.13	0.47
Orissa											
Person	60.7	75.8	68.0	63.4	54.3	50.1	49.4	41.8	41.4	29.0	54.0
Gender disparity	0.81	0.80	0.73	0.61	0.54	0.53	0.48	0.42	0.30	0.25	0.61
Rajasthan											
Person	57.4	82.1	76.9	69.5	58.0	52.3	53.2	50.2	50.1	32.4	58.5
Gender disparity	0.92	0.86	0.83	0.72	0.54	0.57	0.64	0.51	0.46	0.34	0.66
East											
North-eastern Rg.											
Person	62.1	82.9	83.1	76.8	73.6	76.2	74.3	70.9	61.6	34.7	69.0
Gender disparity	0.90	0.92	0.93	0.90	0.80	0.73	0.64	0.50	0.76	0.38	0.79
West Bengal											
Person	59.9	72.8	70.4	65.3	59.1	55.4	51.6	48.0	47.5	35.6	57.9
Gender disparity	0.97	0.95	0.90	0.82	0.67	0.64	0.61	0.57	0.39	0.39	0.76
West											
Gujarat											
Person	57.4	82.1	76.9	69.5	58.0	52.3	53.2	50.2	50.1	32.4	58.5
Gender disparity	0.92	0.86	0.83	0.72	0.54	0.57	0.64	0.51	0.46	0.34	0.66
Maharashtra											
Person	62.6	84.8	79.1	70.1	58.1	53.3	52.4	48.4	45.7	24.0	57.2
Gender disparity	1.04	0.88	0.84	0.66	0.59	0.54	0.45	0.38	0.42	0.19	0.64

(Contd.)

South

Andhra Pradesh											
Person	77.0	77.3	66.7	56.1	48.3	40.2	40.8	36.1	32.6	21.9	50.7
Gender disparity	0.82	0.88	0.78	0.54	0.56	0.52	0.59	0.35	0.42	0.32	0.65
Karnataka											
Person	73.5	79.1	72.9	61.6	52.0	45.7	40.3	40.6	40.9	25.2	54.8
Gender disparity	0.95	0.92	0.85	0.68	0.62	0.48	0.49	0.34	0.49	0.22	0.68
Kerala											
Person	92.3	99.3	98.3	98.5	96.3	94.0	91.3	90.0	83.6	68.3	89.3
Gender disparity	0.96	1.01	0.99	0.98	0.97	1.02	0.94	0.89	0.79	0.78	0.93
Tamil Nadu											
Person	79.2	89.7	82.5	69.9	63.4	65.6	57.0	51.8	52.9	35.3	63.7
Gender disparity	0.90	0.93	0.84	0.79	0.73	0.70	0.51	0.42	0.53	0.42	0.72
All India											
Person	**58.0**	**74.1**	**70.0**	**60.9**	**53.5**	**49.0**	**46.3**	**43.4**	**41.1**	**26.5**	**53.0**
Gender disparity	**0.86**	**0.83**	**0.76**	**0.60**	**0.55**	**0.53**	**0.46**	**0.39**	**0.40**	**0.30**	**0.62**
C.V. Person	22.5	13.0	14.8	20.5	24.3	30.6	30.4	31.5	30.6	43.3	20.6

Age-Specific Literacy Rates (%) and Gender Disparity by Population Groups

Population Groups	Age in Completed Years										All Ages
	6–9	10–14	15–19	20–24	25–29	30–34	35–39	40–44	45–49	50+	
Household Income Groups											
Up to 20,000											
Person	52.1	68.4	62.7	49.6	42.3	37.5	35.7	34.4	31.6	19.5	44.6
Gender disparity	0.83	0.78	0.72	0.51	0.48	0.46	0.37	0.31	0.38	0.25	0.58
20,001–40,000											
Person	62.4	77.0	72.0	64.3	59.5	56.6	54.4	47.3	45.7	28.2	57.0
Gender disparity	0.87	0.86	0.76	0.64	0.58	0.54	0.50	0.37	0.40	0.31	0.63
40,001–62,000											
Person	66.8	83.4	78.2	73.9	67.1	67.4	63.4	58.9	52.2	35.0	64.3
Gender disparity	0.86	0.90	0.83	0.70	0.65	0.64	0.60	0.44	0.38	0.33	0.67
62,001–86,000											
Person	69.3	86.5	83.6	75.7	73.3	69.6	63.9	58.9	58.8	41.7	68.0
Gender disparity	0.95	0.92	0.81	0.75	0.65	0.67	0.53	0.51	0.33	0.35	0.67
Above 86,000											
Person	76.3	91.7	89.7	83.9	80.9	77.7	71.5	69.6	65.0	46.0	74.3
Gender disparity	0.95	0.95	0.86	0.76	0.75	0.67	0.56	0.62	0.56	0.37	0.72
Poverty Line Groups											
Lower segment below											
Person	49.1	64.3	60.4	47.1	39.5	33.7	34.6	31.2	29.8	16.5	42.9
Gender disparity	0.80	0.74	0.70	0.54	0.35	0.43	0.29	0.32	0.35	0.21	0.57
Upper segment below											
Person	51.4	66.8	60.7	50.0	44.6	40.4	35.4	34.4	29.3	20.6	45.3
Gender disparity	0.86	0.78	0.71	0.50	0.51	0.45	0.35	0.28	0.28	0.27	0.58
Lower segment above											
Person	61.8	78.0	71.1	60.3	54.0	50.3	48.4	44.1	41.0	25.2	54.0
Gender disparity	0.86	0.86	0.76	0.60	0.56	0.52	0.46	0.34	0.42	0.28	0.62
Upper segment above											
Person	71.3	85.7	82.5	78.4	73.0	70.3	64.7	58.3	55.8	39.3	66.7
Gender disparity	0.91	0.94	0.84	0.76	0.71	0.68	0.62	0.49	0.42	0.38	0.69
Landholding Groups											
Landless wage earner											
Person	48.6	61.5	54.1	39.1	33.2	26.7	25.5	25.4	21.2	11.0	36.6
Gender disparity	0.82	0.76	0.63	0.47	0.48	0.49	0.32	0.18	0.29	0.24	0.56
Marginal											
Person	58.0	74.2	69.0	60.8	52.3	49.3	46.8	42.6	39.8	28.0	52.8
Gender disparity	0.82	0.82	0.77	0.60	0.51	0.53	0.47	0.38	0.39	0.35	0.62
Small											
Person	60.8	76.3	71.3	64.3	57.4	52.6	48.8	45.4	41.1	26.1	54.7
Gender disparity	0.90	0.84	0.74	0.64	0.56	0.53	0.43	0.36	0.39	0.26	0.62
Medium											
Person	60.4	77.8	75.7	67.2	60.4	56.4	53.2	47.6	47.6	28.7	57.5
Gender disparity	0.87	0.83	0.78	0.64	0.55	0.51	0.45	0.37	0.36	0.24	0.60

(Contd.)

Large											
Person	63.2	80.5	77.3	69.5	64.6	60.6	58.4	51.7	48.2	31.7	60.3
Gender disparity	0.86	0.85	0.73	0.58	0.59	0.51	0.49	0.42	0.45	0.25	0.60
Landless others											
Person	61.3	79.3	78.2	69.8	65.0	59.3	56.8	55.4	54.9	34.7	61.7
Gender disparity	0.91	0.89	0.85	0.67	0.64	0.57	0.57	0.52	0.47	0.33	0.68
Land owners											
Person	59.7	76.0	71.7	63.9	56.3	52.4	49.4	45.0	42.2	27.9	54.9
Gender disparity	0.85	0.83	0.76	0.61	0.54	0.52	0.46	0.38	0.39	0.29	0.61
Landless											
Person	54.6	70.2	66.4	54.4	48.1	42.6	40.5	40.2	38.7	22.9	48.9
Gender disparity	0.87	0.83	0.76	0.58	0.57	0.54	0.48	0.41	0.41	0.31	0.63

Occupational Groups

Cultivators											
Person	57.8	75.3	71.7	63.5	54.8	49.8	47.6	43.7	40.1	25.9	53.4
Gender disparity	0.85	0.82	0.74	0.60	0.51	0.50	0.44	0.38	0.37	0.28	0.60
Salaried+Prof.+S.Empl.											
Person	71.9	89.4	85.6	80.2	76.2	70.5	68.5	65.1	65.8	44.2	71.8
Gender disparity	0.96	0.94	0.85	0.74	0.65	0.58	0.59	0.52	0.44	0.33	0.69
Wage earners											
Person	49.4	62.1	53.6	42.2	35.1	29.6	28.3	25.5	23.7	13.5	38.1
Gender disparity	0.80	0.77	0.66	0.50	0.46	0.47	0.36	0.21	0.32	0.25	0.56
All others											
Person	60.7	75.7	74.8	63.7	60.7	58.6	51.0	49.3	45.5	31.9	57.7
Gender disparity	0.87	0.84	0.83	0.62	0.64	0.57	0.47	0.42	0.48	0.35	0.65

Social Groups

Caste											
STs											
Person	46.9	60.2	55.1	42.1	35.0	38.0	34.3	27.8	23.4	14.2	38.7
Gender disparity	0.83	0.72	0.63	0.43	0.43	0.46	0.30	0.17	0.20	0.13	0.51
SCs											
Person	49.0	65.5	59.2	48.2	40.3	32.3	31.4	27.3	26.0	14.7	41.1
Gender disparity	0.83	0.77	0.67	0.44	0.40	0.40	0.36	0.20	0.24	0.19	0.53
Religion											
Hindus											
Person	58.9	74.7	70.6	60.7	52.8	48.7	46.1	42.8	40.8	25.8	52.8
Gender disparity	0.85	0.82	0.75	0.58	0.52	0.51	0.46	0.37	0.38	0.28	0.60
Muslims											
Person	46.8	65.1	62.9	55.2	50.8	44.2	41.0	42.5	37.1	25.1	48.6
Gender disparity	0.90	0.85	0.70	0.62	0.62	0.57	0.43	0.38	0.52	0.30	0.65
Christians											
Person	79.3	95.9	89.4	85.9	84.0	79.8	80.8	80.4	71.0	61.2	80.0
Gender disparity	1.03	1.03	0.98	0.88	0.88	0.80	0.87	0.94	0.57	0.84	0.90
Other Minorities											
Person	66.9	77.9	68.3	68.6	56.0	48.5	42.3	37.8	39.2	23.4	53.6
Gender disparity	0.94	0.85	0.87	0.79	0.61	0.61	0.43	0.54	0.45	0.24	0.70

(Contd.)

Household Size Groups

Up to 4

Person	64.7	78.5	70.3	55.3	48.5	46.6	44.8	41.7	41.1	25.7	48.6
Gender disparity	0.86	0.93	0.77	0.55	0.59	0.60	0.58	0.46	0.43	0.34	0.59

Village Development Groups

Low

Person	45.7	62.2	57.4	47.9	40.7	35.8	35.2	32.9	29.6	18.6	41.8
Gender disparity	0.77	0.70	0.58	0.40	0.39	0.36	0.32	0.26	0.23	0.17	0.48

Medium

Person	60.2	76.6	70.9	60.1	53.1	48.3	45.1	43.9	40.3	25.0	53.2
Gender disparity	0.86	0.84	0.76	0.61	0.51	0.52	0.43	0.38	0.39	0.27	0.61

High

Person	69.5	83.4	80.5	73.7	65.6	62.6	58.5	52.6	52.2	35.4	63.4
Gender disparity	0.94	0.91	0.87	0.74	0.68	0.65	0.60	0.48	0.50	0.38	0.71

All India

Person	**58.0**	**74.1**	**70.0**	**60.9**	**53.5**	**49.0**	**46.3**	**43.4**	**41.1**	**26.5**	**53.0**
Gender disparity	**0.86**	**0.83**	**0.76**	**0.60**	**0.55**	**0.53**	**0.46**	**0.39**	**0.40**	**0.30**	**0.62**

Ever Enrolment Rates (%) in Age Group 6–14 Years by States

Regions/States	Household Income Groups (Rs per year)				Social Groups				Village Development Groups			All
	Up to 20,000	20,001–40,000	40,001–62,000	Above 62,000	STs and SCs	Hindus	Muslims	Other Minorities	Low	Medium	High	Groups
North												
Haryana	69.2	78.5	86.2	86.4	68.5	80.7	41.4	88.1	83.6	75.1	79.2	78.1
Himachal Pradesh	90.6	96.0	94.7	90.1	87.7	93.1	80.2	94.4	88.4	94.4	96.7	92.7
Punjab	83.3	85.8	88.9	96.4	72.9	85.3	65.4	87.9	88.9	86.5	86.9	86.8
Upper Central												
Bihar	49.8	66.5	70.9	83.6	44.7	59.9	54.5	50.6	52.6	64.4	59.7	58.8
Uttar Pradesh	54.7	67.7	75.5	85.3	53.4	66.4	49.7	96.0	60.5	68.3	72.7	64.2
Lower Central												
Madhya Pradesh	54.6	67.7	73.2	79.4	51.4	62.3	64.8	87.9	57.8	67.0	73.0	62.6
Orissa	65.2	81.6	83.9	90.7	52.6	70.7	58.7	88.0	62.3	75.0	78.8	70.9
Rajasthan	53.9	61.9	75.4	79.2	48.9	62.4	42.7	56.9	59.4	61.8	71.8	61.3
East												
North-eastern Rg.	78.3	80.1	90.1	84.5	88.5	88.6	61.9	87.9	56.5	85.4	89.3	81.3
West Bengal	59.9	77.1	80.0	92.5	63.9	69.8	57.9	66.2	56.7	65.3	69.2	66.1
West												
Gujarat	74.0	89.1	82.8	91.5	73.7	80.9	71.9	100.0	63.6	83.2	84.6	80.3
Maharashtra	82.8	84.8	90.9	92.4	76.5	85.3	89.2	82.4	70.5	84.1	88.4	85.2
South												
Andhra Pradesh	77.4	77.9	88.5	99.8	75.5	79.0	82.1	86.8	67.1	80.5	84.4	79.5
Karnataka	75.9	79.7	82.0	81.1	69.7	77.4	81.9	83.0	67.9	80.5	76.0	77.9
Kerala	98.6	98.7	97.9	98.9	97.2	98.7	97.7	99.4	99.1	98.3	98.8	98.6
Tamil Nadu	86.0	89.0	93.4	94.7	84.7	87.2	97.9	91.7	18.8	84.5	90.7	87.7
All India	**65.3**	**75.1**	**80.9**	**86.9**	**61.8**	**72.0**	**61.6**	**83.5**	**59.9**	**73.8**	**80.9**	**71.4**
C.V.	19.6	12.7	9.3	7.2	22.1	14.5	25.5	16.4	27.4	13.4	12.6	15.0

Gender Disparity in Ever Enrolment Rates in Age Group 6–14 Years by States

Regions/States	Household Income Groups (Rs per year)				Social Groups				Village Development Groups			All Groups
	Up to 20,000	20,001– 40,000	40,001– 62,000	Above 62,000	STs and SCs	Hindus	Muslims	Other Minorities	Low	Medium	High	
North												
Haryana	0.83	0.82	0.95	0.93	0.85	0.88	0.28	0.96	0.93	0.84	0.86	0.86
Himachal Pradesh	0.94	0.93	0.94	1.06	0.93	0.94	0.91	0.87	0.90	0.97	0.97	0.94
Punjab	0.92	0.95	0.98	0.99	0.79	0.88	0.46	0.98	1.11	0.93	0.95	0.95
Upper Central												
Bihar	0.73	0.81	0.87	0.90	0.72	0.89	0.81	0.72	0.69	0.85	0.93	0.79
Uttar Pradesh	0.61	0.78	0.79	0.94	0.57	0.73	0.73	0.94	0.71	0.74	0.78	0.73
Lower Central												
Madhya Pradesh	0.76	0.81	0.88	0.99	0.77	0.81	0.81	0.91	0.75	0.86	0.96	0.81
Orissa	0.74	0.95	0.86	1.00	0.65	0.80	0.73	1.05	0.78	0.81	0.88	0.81
Rajasthan	0.41	0.58	0.69	0.70	0.39	0.55	0.30	0.33	0.53	0.49	0.67	0.54
East												
North-eastern Rg.	0.87	0.88	1.01	0.92	0.99	0.96	0.79	0.96	0.74	0.91	0.99	0.90
West Bengal	0.95	1.03	1.08	0.93	0.98	0.96	1.03	0.95	0.80	0.97	1.01	0.97
West												
Gujarat	0.81	0.94	0.88	0.96	0.90	0.89	0.65	1.00	0.86	0.87	0.88	0.87
Maharashtra	0.94	0.92	0.89	0.98	0.89	0.94	1.03	0.86	0.94	0.90	0.95	0.93
South												
Andhra Pradesh	0.84	0.88	0.93	1.00	0.84	0.86	0.85	1.02	0.90	0.82	0.90	0.87
Karnataka	0.90	1.00	0.91	0.97	0.89	0.94	0.88	1.09	0.87	0.97	0.88	0.93
Kerala	1.00	0.98	0.96	0.98	1.00	0.98	0.97	1.01	1.03	0.99	0.98	0.99
Tamil Nadu	0.89	0.98	1.07	1.01	0.85	0.93	1.03	0.90	1.52	0.82	0.96	0.93
All India	**0.80**	**0.87**	**0.89**	**0.93**	**0.78**	**0.83**	**0.86**	**0.94**	**0.73**	**0.84**	**0.93**	**0.84**
C.V.	19.6	12.7	9.3	7.2	22.1	12.1	25.5	16.4	27.4	13.4	12.6	15.0

Trends in Enrolment Rates in Age Group 6–14 Years and Gender Disparity by States

Regions/States	NCERT (1986)[1]			NSSO (1986–87)[2]			NCAER (1994)		
	Percentage		Gender	Percentage		Gender	Percentage		Gender
	Boys	Girls	Disp.	Boys	Girls	Disp.	Boys	Girls	Disp.
North									
Haryana	83	56	0.67	85	62	0.73	84	72	0.86
Himachal Pradesh	84	69	0.82	–	–	–	95	90	0.95
Punjab	87	78	0.90	76	66	0.87	89	84	0.94
Upper Central									
Bihar	75	35	0.47	47	25	0.53	65	51	0.78
Uttar Pradesh	64	32	0.50	63	30	0.48	73	53	0.73
Lower Central									
Madhya Pradesh	84	45	0.54	60	32	0.53	69	56	0.81
Orissa	70	47	0.67	61	44	0.72	79	63	0.80
Rajasthan	76	26	0.34	65	23	0.35	78	42	0.54
East									
North-eastern Rg.	75	61	0.81	70	60	0.86	85	76	0.89
West Bengal	74	56	0.76	61	47	0.77	67	65	0.97
West									
Gujarat	82	61	0.74	77	54	0.70	85	74	0.87
Maharashtra	84	78	0.93	84	70	0.83	88	82	0.93
South									
Andhra Pradesh	67	44	0.66	71	49	0.69	85	74	0.87
Karnataka	76	57	0.75	75	56	0.75	81	75	0.93
Kerala	86	85	0.99	98	97	0.99	99	98	0.99
Tamil Nadu	98	83	0.85	92	80	0.87	91	84	0.92
All India	**76**	**50**	**0.66**	**68**	**47**	**0.69**	**77**	**65**	**0.84**

1. *Fifth All India Education Survey.* NCERT, New Delhi, 1992.
2. NSSO, *42nd Round (July 1986–June 1987)* Report No. 365, part II, vol. I-II.

Discontinuation Rates (%) in Age Group 6–14 Years by States

Regions/States	Household Income Groups (Rs per year)				Social Groups				Village Development Groups			All Groups
	Up to 20,000	20,001–40,000	40,001–62,000	Above 62,000	STs and SCs	Hindus	Muslims	Other Minorities	Up to 30	31–45	Above 45	
North												
Haryana	6.1	3.0	3.5	3.9	6.0	3.5	22.6	4.0	3.7	5.0	3.7	4.2
Himachal Pradesh	2.9	1.7	–	–	3.4	2.0	2.9	–	2.7	2.4	0.4	2.0
Punjab	6.6	5.0	5.4	3.3	10.1	6.1	5.2	5.1	5.9	5.0	5.8	5.4
Upper Central												
Bihar	3.4	3.4	3.7	0.5	1.9	7.4	5.4	0.9	4.6	2.7	1.3	3.2
Uttar Pradesh	4.4	4.9	3.1	3.2	4.3	3.8	7.0	6.3	4.0	4.4	4.4	4.2
Lower Central												
Madhya Pradesh	9.8	7.2	7.1	4.0	9.8	7.9	12.5	2.9	10.3	6.0	4.4	8.0
Orissa	9.7	4.6	4.4	–	9.7	7.6	7.6	5.2	5.3	10.0	6.0	7.6
Rajasthan	4.3	6.7	2.8	0.9	3.3	4.1	7.9	–	5.5	3.0	1.2	4.2
East												
North-eastern Rg.	3.5	4.5	0.5	5.6	0.7	2.1	8.1	2.2	9.0	3.1	1.7	3.3
West Bengal	6.3	7.0	4.0	2.2	6.0	5.6	7.5	9.5	10.4	6.3	5.2	6.2
West												
Gujarat	8.7	6.8	5.0	3.7	10.7	7.4	6.4	–	4.4	9.3	5.8	7.3
Maharashtra	8.3	6.2	6.2	5.0	8.7	7.0	6.9	8.0	7.6	8.9	6.0	7.1
South												
Andhra Pradesh	11.9	7.4	9.6	3.7	12.9	10.1	6.3	16.1	5.6	10.3	11.2	9.9
Karnataka	9.4	7.3	5.1	3.8	9.4	7.6	10.6	3.4	15.1	7.9	7.1	7.9
Kerala	1.7	2.2	1.3	–	5.2	2.7	0.9	0.5	4.1	1.7	1.2	1.7
Tamil Nadu	12.3	11.0	6.8	–	12.7	11.0	16.9	8.3	–	12.9	10.2	10.9
All India	**7.2**	**5.7**	**4.3**	**2.9**	**7.1**	**5.9**	**6.9**	**5.2**	**5.8**	**6.1**	**6.0**	**6.0**
C.V.	46.6	41.5	57.0	76.2	51.8	44.2	60.7	93.7	57.2	52.8	64.7	45.4

Age-Specific Ever Enrolment, Discontinuation and Non-Attendance Rates (%) in Age Group 6–14 Years and Gender Disparity by States

Regions/States	Ever Enrolment Rates				Discontinuation Rates				Non-attendance Rates			
	6–9	6–11	12–14	6–14	6–9	6–11	12–14	6–14	6–9	6–11	12–14	6–14
North												
Haryana												
Person	70.0	75.2	83.6	78.1	0.7	1.1	9.6	4.2	2.5	2.7	1.5	2.3
Gender disparity	0.85	0.85	0.87	0.86	0.34	0.31	1.34	1.20	1.11	0.96	0.71	0.88
Himachal Pradesh												
Person	89.4	92.0	94.1	92.7	0.3	0.9	3.9	2.0	3.7	4.2	2.2	3.5
Gender disparity	0.92	0.93	0.96	0.94	0.85	1.03	1.35	1.20	0.85	0.99	0.84	0.98
Punjab												
Person	84.6	86.5	87.4	86.8	0.6	1.5	11.7	5.4	2.6	2.4	1.5	2.1
Gender disparity	1.01	0.97	0.92	0.95	5.56	0.59	1.60	1.28	0.95	1.43	2.64	1.71
Upper Central												
Bihar												
Person	51.7	55.9	64.8	58.8	0.5	1.1	7.0	3.2	14.7	12.6	9.7	11.6
Gender disparity	0.77	0.78	0.80	0.79	0.37	1.24	1.59	1.58	0.79	1.03	1.36	1.12
Uttar Pradesh												
Person	58.8	62.4	68.0	64.2	0.5	1.3	9.7	4.2	7.8	7.4	5.4	6.8
Gender disparity	0.75	0.75	0.70	0.73	1.78	1.68	1.83	1.70	0.89	0.90	1.09	0.96
Lower Central												
Madhya Pradesh												
Person	53.4	59.4	69.9	62.6	1.5	3.3	17.1	8.0	17.5	16.6	13.1	15.5
Gender disparity	0.87	0.85	0.77	0.81	1.61	1.45	1.40	1.24	1.13	0.96	1.04	0.99
Orissa												
Person	64.7	68.6	75.6	70.9	0.7	2.3	17.5	7.6	12.7	12.0	10.9	11.7
Gender disparity	0.83	0.82	0.80	0.81	2.76	1.32	1.65	1.50	1.09	0.88	0.98	0.91
Rajasthan												
Person	56.4	59.4	65.7	61.3	0.8	1.5	9.6	4.2	5.0	4.0	3.2	3.8
Gender disparity	0.57	0.55	0.51	0.54	4.92	2.70	2.14	2.13	0.75	0.66	0.44	0.61
East												
North-eastern Rg.												
Person	75.1	79.0	87.2	81.3	0.2	0.5	10.2	3.3	8.2	8.7	9.9	9.1
Gender disparity	0.88	0.88	0.93	0.90	1.16	1.17	1.30	1.44	1.10	1.01	3.22	1.43
West Bengal												
Person	59.2	63.5	71.3	66.1	0.4	1.5	14.7	6.2	8.0	8.2	10.2	8.9
Gender disparity	0.95	0.96	1.00	0.97	0.19	0.60	1.20	1.10	0.72	0.95	0.78	0.88
West												
Gujarat												
Person	73.7	78.8	83.0	80.3	0.3	2.3	16.3	7.3	5.9	5.9	5.4	5.7
Gender disparity	0.89	0.89	0.85	0.87	–	1.11	1.95	1.68	0.79	1.25	0.79	1.09

(Contd.).

Maharashtra												
Person	81.2	83.9	88.1	85.2	1.0	3.1	15.4	7.1	4.9	4.4	3.4	4.1
Gender disparity	0.99	0.94	0.92	0.93	1.09	2.04	1.37	1.41	1.56	1.36	1.00	1.27
South												
Andhra Pradesh												
Person	81.9	81.0	76.2	79.5	2.1	4.9	21.7	9.9	6.4	6.1	5.5	5.9
Gender disparity	0.84	0.86	0.88	0.87	2.66	2.01	1.31	1.48	1.03	1.07	0.76	0.99
Karnataka												
Person	75.7	78.1	77.4	77.9	1.6	3.3	16.5	7.9	4.6	4.5	4.0	4.3
Gender disparity	0.94	0.95	0.90	0.93	0.24	0.91	1.63	1.35	1.17	1.03	0.57	0.88
Kerala												
Person	97.2	97.9	99.7	98.6	–	–	4.4	1.7	4.4	4.5	2.3	3.7
Gender disparity	0.95	0.97	1.01	0.99	–	–	1.15	1.32	0.99	0.95	0.92	0.91
Tamil Nadu												
Person	84.3	87.5	88.1	87.7	1.1	2.8	25.7	10.9	1.4	1.3	0.2	1.0
Gender disparity	0.89	0.94	0.91	0.93	1.28	2.47	1.58	1.98	2.38	2.73	–	2.25
All India												
Person	**66.1**	**69.6**	**75.1**	**71.4**	**0.8**	**2.1**	**13.5**	**6.0**	**7.8**	**7.4**	**6.2**	**7.0**
Gender disparity	**0.85**	**0.85**	**0.83**	**0.84**	**1.41**	**1.60**	**1.58**	**1.56**	**0.95**	**0.98**	**1.03**	**1.00**
C.V. Person	18.5	16.3	12.7	15.0	72.1	62.7	44.2	45.4	63.9	61.0	70.1	63.1

Age-Specific Ever Enrolment, Discontinuation and Non-Attendance Rates (%) in Age Group 6–14 Years and Gender Disparity by Population Groups

Population Groups	Ever Enrolment Rates				Discontinuation Rates				Non-Attendance Rates			
	6–9	6–11	12–14	6–14	6–9	6–11	12–14	6–14	6–9	6–11	12–14	6–14
North												
Household Income Groups												
Upto 20,000												
Person	59.8	63.4	69.5	65.3	1.1	2.9	15.8	7.2	8.0	7.5	6.3	7.1
Gender disparity	0.81	0.81	0.77	0.80	1.57	1.61	1.56	1.52	0.94	1.01	0.92	0.99
20,001–40,000												
Person	70.2	73.7	77.8	75.1	0.6	1.5	13.4	5.7	7.0	6.9	6.4	6.7
Gender disparity	0.87	0.87	0.87	0.87	1.23	1.69	1.61	1.67	0.83	0.81	1.16	0.90
40,001–62,000												
Person	76.4	79.2	84.3	80.9	0.6	1.4	9.6	4.3	8.5	7.7	7.0	7.5
Gender disparity	0.87	0.89	0.89	0.89	2.03	2.57	1.92	1.91	1.13	1.15	1.35	1.22
62,001–86,000												
Person	80.6	83.8	84.7	84.1	0.1	0.4	6.8	2.6	5.8	6.5	4.1	5.7
Gender disparity	0.89	0.88	0.93	0.90	–	0.93	0.76	0.83	0.77	0.70	0.65	0.68
Above 86,000												
Person	84.8	87.4	93.1	89.3	0.3	1.0	7.1	3.2	10.7	9.9	5.2	8.3
Gender disparity	0.97	0.96	0.95	0.95	0.23	0.56	2.69	1.80	1.14	1.39	1.05	1.34
Poverty Line Groups												
Lower segment below												
Person	55.5	59.3	65.2	61.1	0.9	2.3	14.0	6.1	8.5	8.3	6.2	7.7
Gender disparity	0.79	0.78	0.73	0.76	0.78	1.14	1.33	1.26	0.89	0.97	1.09	1.00
Upper segment below												
Person	59.5	62.6	68.1	64.3	1.2	2.9	16.0	7.2	8.0	7.6	6.9	7.4
Gender disparity	0.84	0.82	0.79	0.81	2.28	2.05	1.43	1.55	0.84	0.97	0.77	0.91
Lower segment above												
Person	70.8	74.3	78.6	75.7	0.9	2.1	14.6	6.4	6.7	6.4	5.8	6.2
Gender disparity	0.86	0.87	0.85	0.86	1.63	1.56	1.81	1.71	0.97	0.95	1.05	0.98
Upper segment above												
Person	79.6	82.3	86.4	83.8	0.4	1.1	8.0	3.6	9.8	8.8	6.5	8.0
Gender disparity	0.92	0.92	0.95	0.93	0.52	2.02	1.47	1.56	1.05	1.05	1.24	1.10
Landholding Groups												
Landless wage earner												
Person	55.8	59.1	61.2	59.7	1.9	4.1	22.2	9.9	8.1	7.7	6.0	7.3
Gender disparity	0.82	0.81	0.74	0.79	2.02	2.16	1.71	1.77	0.94	1.02	0.76	0.97
Marginal												
Person	65.4	69.0	75.2	71.0	0.9	2.0	11.7	5.3	7.3	6.8	5.5	6.4
Gender disparity	0.81	0.82	0.82	0.82	1.35	1.00	1.62	1.44	1.00	0.97	1.12	1.01
Small												
Person	69.3	72.7	77.7	74.3	0.8	1.8	13.5	5.7	7.7	7.6	6.1	7.2
Gender disparity	0.87	0.86	0.85	0.86	1.53	2.12	1.54	1.64	0.89	0.93	1.34	1.03

(Contd.)

Medium												
Person	70.2	73.5	79.3	75.5	0.3	1.5	12.2	5.4	6.8	6.4	7.3	6.7
Gender disparity	0.84	0.84	0.83	0.83	1.10	1.82	2.19	1.98	1.32	1.12	0.89	1.02
Large												
Person	72.3	75.9	81.6	77.8	0.3	1.4	10.0	4.4	10.8	10.5	5.7	8.9
Gender disparity	0.88	0.86	0.86	0.86	0.40	2.94	1.38	1.56	1.13	1.16	0.69	1.05
Landless others												
Person	69.8	73.2	80.8	75.7	0.5	1.7	12.1	5.3	8.1	7.4	7.3	7.4
Gender disparity	0.91	0.91	0.89	0.90	0.89	1.40	1.26	1.27	0.70	0.85	1.05	0.91
Land owners												
Person	67.9	71.4	77.2	73.3	0.7	1.8	12.1	5.4	7.7	7.4	6.0	6.9
Gender disparity	0.84	0.84	0.84	0.84	1.30	1.47	1.65	1.58	1.03	1.01	1.07	1.03
Landless												
Person	62.5	65.9	70.8	67.4	1.2	2.8	16.5	7.4	8.1	7.6	6.8	7.3
Gender disparity	0.87	0.87	0.82	0.85	1.56	1.80	1.46	1.51	0.80	0.93	0.96	0.94
Occupational Groups												
Cultivators												
Person	66.4	70.4	76.5	72.5	0.6	1.8	13.4	5.9	8.0	7.8	6.4	7.3
Gender disparity	0.83	0.83	0.82	0.83	1.06	1.45	1.57	1.53	0.99	0.99	1.03	1.01
Salaried+Prof.+S.Empl.												
Person	80.6	83.8	90.0	85.9	0.5	0.8	4.5	2.1	7.4	6.2	5.5	6.0
Gender disparity	0.94	0.94	0.95	0.94	1.03	0.74	1.66	1.36	0.85	0.87	1.34	1.00
Wage earners												
Person	56.6	59.5	62.4	60.4	1.8	3.9	20.9	9.4	7.6	7.4	6.0	7.0
Gender disparity	0.80	0.80	0.75	0.78	2.19	2.16	1.73	1.82	0.97	1.04	0.90	1.01
All others												
Person	68.0	70.9	77.4	72.9	0.6	1.9	13.7	5.7	8.0	7.7	6.8	7.4
Gender disparity	0.87	0.87	0.85	0.86	0.91	1.56	1.51	1.46	0.90	0.97	0.95	0.97
Social Groups												
Caste												
STs												
Person	56.6	59.4	62.7	60.3	1.1	3.1	16.8	7.2	10.5	10.2	9.8	10.1
Gender disparity	0.79	0.78	0.72	0.76	0.81	1.10	1.37	1.20	1.25	1.27	1.12	1.24
SCs												
Person	56.8	60.7	66.5	62.5	1.2	2.9	15.2	7.0	7.3	7.4	6.3	7.0
Gender disparity	0.81	0.81	0.74	0.79	1.32	2.00	1.51	1.54	0.74	0.92	1.21	1.00
Religion												
Hindus												
Person	66.9	70.3	75.6	72.0	0.9	2.2	13.1	5.9	8.0	7.5	6.3	7.2
Gender disparity	0.84	0.84	0.81	0.83	1.47	1.78	1.61	1.62	1.00	1.01	1.09	1.04
Muslims												
Person	55.6	59.3	66.8	61.6	0.4	1.4	17.7	6.9	7.8	7.6	7.1	7.5
Gender disparity	0.86	0.83	0.91	0.86	1.60	0.55	1.34	1.21	0.59	0.77	0.62	0.73
Christians												
Person	85.2	88.6	96.2	91.3	0.3	0.6	12.4	5.0	5.5	6.2	2.0	4.7
Gender disparity	0.98	1.00	1.01	1.02	–	1.24	1.80	2.29	0.99	0.77	2.10	0.82

(Contd.)

Other Minorities												
Person	76.5	77.8	79.7	78.5	1.1	1.8	11.6	5.3	3.8	4.2	3.7	4.0
Gender disparity	0.94	0.91	0.85	0.88	0.84	0.64	1.57	1.16	1.07	1.38	1.45	1.41
Household Size Groups												
Up to 4												
Person	73.0	76.0	78.2	76.8	0.8	2.5	14.5	6.9	7.5	7.6	6.4	7.2
Gender disparity	0.86	0.88	0.94	0.90	2.20	2.80	1.50	1.84	1.35	1.28	0.94	1.16
5–7												
Person	65.2	68.8	75.4	70.9	1.0	2.3	13.5	6.2	8.0	7.4	6.5	7.1
Gender disparity	0.84	0.84	0.83	0.83	1.63	1.53	1.61	1.56	0.94	0.99	1.25	1.06
8 and above												
Person	65.4	68.8	73.4	70.2	0.6	1.6	13.0	5.4	7.8	7.4	5.7	6.9
Gender disparity	0.87	0.86	0.80	0.84	0.83	1.40	1.56	1.47	0.85	0.88	0.72	0.84
Adult Literacy Groups												
None literate												
Person	43.4	46.1	44.4	45.6	1.3	3.6	21.0	8.4	9.1	8.6	10.1	9.0
Gender disparity	0.71	0.69	0.60	0.67	1.00	1.46	1.78	1.48	1.01	1.05	1.16	1.06
Female literate												
Person	82.4	85.7	89.3	87.2	3.1	4.9	14.3	8.8	3.0	3.9	4.7	4.2
Gender disparity	1.03	1.02	0.96	0.99	5.16	2.48	1.77	1.93	2.79	2.50	1.46	1.95
Male literate												
Person	66.2	70.3	75.1	71.9	1.0	2.4	15.9	7.0	8.7	8.2	6.4	7.7
Gender disparity	0.78	0.78	0.71	0.76	1.92	1.82	1.61	1.57	1.01	0.92	0.91	0.93
Both literate												
Person	87.1	90.0	95.0	91.7	0.4	1.0	9.1	3.9	6.9	6.5	5.1	6.0
Gender disparity	0.97	0.97	0.97	0.97	0.81	1.72	1.84	1.87	0.87	1.00	1.25	1.07
Village Development Groups												
Low												
Person	54.4	57.9	64.4	59.9	0.7	2.1	12.9	5.8	9.2	8.3	7.4	8.0
Gender disparity	0.77	0.75	0.70	0.73	0.99	1.56	1.79	1.64	0.96	1.00	1.02	1.01
Medium												
Person	68.6	72.1	77.2	73.8	1.0	2.2	13.5	6.1	8.2	7.7	6.1	7.1
Gender disparity	0.84	0.84	0.84	0.84	1.97	1.54	1.73	1.68	0.98	0.99	1.01	1.00
High												
Person	76.5	79.6	83.6	80.9	0.8	2.0	13.8	6.0	6.3	6.4	5.4	6.1
Gender disparity	0.93	0.93	0.91	0.93	1.05	1.78	1.26	1.35	0.92	0.99	1.15	1.04
All India												
Person	**66.1**	**69.6**	**75.1**	**71.4**	**0.8**	**2.1**	**13.5**	**6.0**	**7.8**	**7.4**	**6.2**	**7.0**
Gender disparity	**0.85**	**0.85**	**0.83**	**0.84**	**1.41**	**1.60**	**1.58**	**1.56**	**0.95**	**0.98**	**1.03**	**1.00**

Percentage Distribution of Students in the Age Group of 6–14 years and Gender Disparity by States

Population Groups	Govt. School				Govt.-aided Schools				Private Schools			
	Person	Male	Female	F/M	Person	Male	Female	F/M	Person	Male	Female	F/M
Household Income Groups												
Upto 20,000	70.2	69.8	70.7	1.01	22.4	21.8	23.3	1.07	7.2	8.2	5.7	0.70
20,001–40,000	66.3	65.9	66.8	1.01	23.0	22.1	24.1	1.09	10.5	11.8	8.8	0.75
40,001–62,000	63.8	62.3	66.0	1.06	23.2	23.5	22.8	0.97	12.8	14.1	11.0	0.78
62,001–86,000	66.8	64.6	69.7	1.08	19.7	19.5	19.9	1.02	13.5	15.9	10.4	0.65
Above 86,000	66.0	66.1	66.0	1.00	14.8	14.4	15.2	1.06	19.1	19.6	18.6	0.95
Poverty Line Groups												
Lower segment below	69.5	69.6	69.4	1.00	22.4	21.2	24.1	1.14	7.6	8.7	6.1	0.69
Upper segment below	67.4	67.3	67.4	1.00	24.5	23.1	26.5	1.15	8.1	9.5	6.0	0.63
Lower segment above	70.1	69.4	71.1	1.02	20.5	20.5	20.5	1.00	9.3	10.0	8.2	0.82
Upper segment above	61.9	60.4	63.8	1.06	23.1	23.2	23.1	0.99	14.9	16.3	13.0	0.80
Landholding Groups												
Landless wage earner	77.5	76.5	79.1	1.03	17.9	17.9	18.0	1.00	4.4	5.6	2.5	0.44
Marginal	62.0	61.8	62.2	1.01	26.8	25.4	28.7	1.13	11.1	12.6	9.0	0.71
Small	69.2	68.9	69.6	1.01	21.6	21.0	22.5	1.07	9.1	10.0	7.8	0.78
Medium	72.9	72.4	73.6	1.02	17.1	17.5	16.5	0.94	9.4	9.5	9.2	0.97
Large	74.4	74.3	74.5	1.00	13.9	13.7	14.2	1.04	11.6	11.9	11.1	0.94
Landless others	63.6	61.6	66.0	1.07	24.2	24.7	23.7	0.96	12.1	13.6	10.3	0.75
Land owners	67.1	66.9	67.4	1.01	22.4	21.7	23.5	1.08	10.3	11.3	8.9	0.79
Landless	69.8	68.6	71.4	1.04	21.4	21.5	21.3	0.99	8.7	9.9	7.1	0.72
Occupational Groups												
Cultivators	70.6	70.2	71.3	1.01	20.3	19.8	21.0	1.06	8.8	9.7	7.6	0.78
Salaried+Prof.+S.Empl.	58.0	56.5	59.8	1.06	25.8	25.6	26.0	1.02	16.2	17.8	14.1	0.79
Wage earners	75.0	75.0	75.0	1.00	19.6	18.4	21.5	1.17	5.3	6.6	3.1	0.46
All others	61.7	60.2	63.9	1.06	26.6	27.0	26.0	0.96	11.7	12.8	10.1	0.79
Social Groups												
Caste												
STs	67.1	64.0	72.2	1.13	29.2	31.7	25.2	0.79	3.2	3.8	2.3	0.62
SCs	71.5	71.2	71.8	1.01	22.6	21.7	23.8	1.10	5.8	6.9	4.2	0.61
Religion												
Hindus	70.3	69.4	71.5	1.03	20.2	20.0	20.5	1.02	9.3	10.4	7.7	0.75
Muslims	49.4	51.4	46.9	0.91	37.3	34.2	41.3	1.21	13.3	14.4	11.9	0.82
Christians	42.9	41.6	44.3	1.07	47.5	48.7	46.2	0.95	9.6	9.6	9.5	0.98
Other Minorities	80.4	78.4	82.8	1.06	6.6	7.5	5.5	0.74	12.3	13.1	11.3	0.86
Household Size Groups												
Upto 4	67.2	66.5	68.5	1.03	23.1	22.7	23.8	1.05	9.5	10.7	7.5	0.70
5–7	67.9	67.2	68.8	1.02	23.7	23.4	24.1	1.03	8.3	9.3	7.0	0.75
8 and above	68.3	68.1	68.5	1.01	19.1	18.1	20.4	1.13	12.3	13.6	10.7	0.79
Adult Literacy Groups												
None literate	78.9	77.6	81.3	1.05	13.9	14.3	13.0	0.91	7.0	7.9	5.4	0.68
Female literate	68.8	67.2	70.6	1.05	24.2	23.4	25.1	1.07	7.0	9.4	4.1	0.44

(Contd.)

Male literate	72.4	71.9	73.1	1.02	18.0	17.5	18.8	1.08	9.6	10.6	7.9	0.75
Both literate	59.9	58.4	61.6	1.06	28.6	28.8	28.3	0.98	11.3	12.6	9.9	0.78
Village Development Groups												
Low	71.1	71.4	70.6	0.99	15.8	15.0	17.0	1.13	12.8	13.2	12.1	0.91
Medium	67.4	66.6	68.6	1.03	23.4	23.2	23.6	1.02	9.1	10.2	7.6	0.75
High	65.9	64.6	67.4	1.04	25.8	25.9	25.8	1.00	8.1	9.4	6.6	0.69
All India	**67.9**	**67.4**	**68.7**	**1.02**	**22.1**	**21.6**	**22.8**	**1.05**	**9.8**	**10.8**	**8.3**	**0.77**

Percentage of Students in the Age Group of 6–14 Years in Government Schools by States

Regions/States	Household Income Groups (Rs per year)				Social Groups				Village Development Groups			All Groups
	Up to 20,000	20,001– 40,000	40,001– 62,000	Above 62,000	STs and SCs	Hindus	Muslims	Other Minorities	Low	Medium	High	
North												
Haryana	92.3	86.0	78.5	79.6	93.3	85.0	85.9	87.2	89.4	85.6	83.8	85.1
Himachal Pradesh	97.0	92.7	93.5	84.0	97.7	94.5	100.0	94.1	94.9	95.8	91.7	94.6
Punjab	87.3	80.1	68.5	63.2	88.1	76.5	61.8	79.6	75.7	81.8	75.0	78.6
Upper Central												
Bihar	85.3	74.6	76.1	70.0	79.0	79.1	76.3	90.8	82.5	75.5	83.3	79.2
Uttar Pradesh	60.5	54.7	53.7	50.0	65.8	58.5	36.4	54.4	58.8	56.5	38.9	56.3
Lower Central												
Madhya Pradesh	84.2	85.1	81.0	83.8	90.1	84.2	82.3	65.9	78.6	89.5	89.4	84.0
Orissa	78.8	69.5	60.4	77.8	78.0	75.3	86.0	41.7	77.6	67.3	84.3	74.5
Rajasthan	93.9	92.5	93.7	90.8	95.8	92.8	97.7	100.0	95.5	91.4	85.5	93.0
East												
North-eastern Rg.	7.9	13.8	2.9	–	0.9	10.1	3.8	2.9	–	7.7	12.6	8.6
West Bengal	19.4	19.3	40.4	19.9	21.1	18.6	27.0	–	8.5	19.9	23.4	20.5
West												
Gujarat	74.4	77.8	87.7	89.0	77.3	79.2	67.2	63.8	75.1	83.0	73.6	78.2
Maharashtra	83.9	80.1	74.7	72.4	89.0	80.4	76.9	82.2	91.6	86.2	75.8	80.4
South												
Andhra Pradesh	90.3	90.1	85.3	67.3	92.8	88.2	87.7	96.3	93.6	90.0	84.4	88.4
Karnataka	88.3	81.2	83.0	88.3	88.5	86.1	84.9	89.1	97.1	84.1	87.3	86.0
Kerala	32.5	33.2	24.5	16.7	31.1	29.3	41.3	23.4	13.3	31.4	34.0	30.9
Tamil Nadu	83.9	84.3	75.3	86.9	96.5	86.5	32.3	66.0	100.0	96.9	78.8	83.8
All India	**70.2**	**66.3**	**63.8**	**66.4**	**70.1**	**70.3**	**49.4**	**64.3**	**71.1**	**67.4**	**65.9**	**67.9**
C.V.	37.1	35.6	36.7	42.6	38.9	36.9	42.3	48.4	45.6	37.9	36.4	36.8

Percentage of Students in the Age Group 6–14 Years in Government-Aided Schools by States

Regions/States	Household Income Groups (Rs per year)				Social Groups				Village Development Groups			All Groups
	Up to 20,000	20,001–40,000	40,001–62,000	Above 62,000	STs and SCs	Hindus	Muslims	Other Minorities	Low	Medium	High	
North												
Haryana	0.4	2.3	4.8	0.4	0.6	2.2	–	2.7	1.7	3.3	0.7	1.8
Himachal Pradesh	–	0.3	1.2	2.7	0.3	0.4	–	–	0.1	0.4	0.7	0.4
Punjab	0.9	0.1	7.5	1.7	–	0.5	–	2.0	–	0.1	3.6	1.6
Upper Central												
Bihar	9.3	13.4	12.4	12.3	15.9	11.6	11.6	4.6	11.1	12.8	7.4	11.4
Uttar Pradesh	14.8	18.3	17.6	16.3	16.2	16.5	16.4	13.2	12.8	17.6	34.7	16.5
Lower Central												
Madhya Pradesh	13.7	10.3	13.3	9.6	7.4	12.1	15.0	3.5	17.2	8.4	2.7	12.1
Orissa	18.6	24.8	28.1	20.6	20.0	20.6	14.0	48.4	15.9	30.1	11.9	21.2
Rajasthan	4.0	2.1	1.9	5.3	1.9	3.6	–	–	2.8	3.2	7.5	3.5
East												
North-eastern Rg.	92.0	85.9	93.8	100.0	98.7	89.0	95.8	96.9	95.1	92.3	86.8	90.6
West Bengal	80.0	79.4	58.6	74.7	77.9	80.2	72.8	90.7	91.5	79.2	75.2	78.5
West												
Gujarat	23.8	18.8	11.4	10.3	20.5	18.6	32.8	36.2	14.7	16.9	25.2	19.7
Maharashtra	14.6	17.8	24.0	25.7	9.2	17.8	19.5	17.8	7.9	12.5	22.2	17.9
South												
Andhra Pradesh	0.9	1.4	–	6.7	2.4	1.5	–	–	0.8	1.2	1.7	1.3
Karnataka	3.7	5.8	5.7	1.9	3.9	4.4	3.4	–	–	4.7	4.1	4.2
Kerala	59.4	53.5	56.0	61.8	65.5	55.0	52.1	66.7	82.4	59.4	50.0	57.1
Tamil Nadu	9.4	9.0	13.0	4.6	2.9	7.7	40.0	17.7	–	0.9	12.3	9.1
All India	**22.4**	**23.0**	**23.2**	**17.0**	**24.7**	**20.2**	**37.3**	**24.1**	**15.8**	**23.4**	**25.8**	**22.1**
C.V.	130.3	123.4	115.4	130.4	139.2	127.3	119.1	128.5	149.4	132.4	120.8	126.0

Percentage of Students in the Age Group 6–14 Years in Private Schools by States

Regions/States	Household Income Groups (Rs per year)				Social Groups				Village Development Groups			All Groups
	Up to 20,000	20,001–40,000	40,001–62,000	Above 62,000	STs and SCs	Hindus	Muslims	Other Minorities	Low	Medium	High	
North												
Haryana	7.1	11.4	16.3	20.0	5.8	15.3	14.1	10.1	8.3	10.7	15.4	12.8
Himachal Pradesh	2.9	6.6	5.3	13.3	1.8	4.9	–	5.9	4.5	3.6	7.7	4.8
Punjab	11.5	19.3	23.9	34.8	11.8	23.0	38.2	18.0	24.1	18.1	20.6	19.5
Upper Central												
Bihar	4.6	10.8	11.5	17.7	4.4	8.4	12.1	1.9	4.6	11.5	9.3	8.6
Uttar Pradesh	24.6	27.0	28.5	33.7	17.9	24.9	47.1	32.4	28.2	25.9	26.4	27.2
Lower Central												
Madhya Pradesh	2.0	4.6	5.7	6.6	2.5	3.6	2.7	30.6	4.1	2.0	7.9	3.8
Orissa	2.4	5.5	11.5	1.6	2.0	4.0	–	10.0	6.6	2.5	3.4	4.1
Rajasthan	2.0	5.3	4.4	3.9	1.9	3.5	2.3	–	1.6	5.2	7.0	3.4
East												
North-eastern Rg.	0.1	0.1	3.3	–	0.4	0.9	0.4	–	4.9	–	0.4	0.8
West Bengal	0.6	1.3	–	5.4	1.0	1.0	0.2	9.3	–	0.9	1.3	1.0
West												
Gujarat	1.8	3.4	0.9	0.7	2.3	2.2	–	–	10.2	0.2	1.2	2.0
Maharashtra	1.3	2.0	0.9	1.4	1.3	1.5	3.6	–	–	1.3	1.8	1.5
South												
Andhra Pradesh	8.5	8.4	14.7	26.0	4.7	10.1	12.3	3.7	5.6	8.8	13.5	10.2
Karnataka	7.9	12.8	10.5	9.7	7.4	9.3	11.7	8.2	2.9	11.1	8.4	9.6
Kerala	8.1	13.3	19.5	21.6	3.5	15.6	6.6	9.9	4.2	9.3	16.0	12.0
Tamil Nadu	6.6	6.7	11.3	8.5	0.5	5.7	27.7	16.3	–	2.1	8.9	7.0
All India	**7.2**	**10.5**	**12.8**	**16.5**	**5.0**	**9.3**	**13.3**	**11.1**	**12.8**	**9.1**	**8.1**	**9.8**
C.V.	102.4	78.8	77.8	87.5	104.9	88.2	125.4	100.9	114.1	99.3	77.5	87.5

Percentage Distribution of Annual Household Expenditure on Schooling (All Schools) of Children in Age Group 6–14 Years by Population Groups

Population Groups	Exam. & Other Fees	Books, Staion. & Uniform	Coaching	Transpt.	Board-ing & Lodging	Total	Av. No. of Stds per Household
Household Income Groups							
Up to 20,000	16.8	71.8	8.0	2.1	1.4	512	1.7
20,001–40,000	17.1	66.9	10.9	2.6	2.6	731	1.8
40,001–62,000	18.0	61.8	11.8	6.2	2.2	938	1.9
62,001–86,000	20.3	64.8	9.3	3.0	2.6	1,008	2.1
Above 86,000	23.3	58.5	11.2	4.2	2.8	1,399	2.3
Poverty Line Groups							
Lower segment below	16.8	73.6	6.9	1.5	1.3	510	1.8
Upper segment below	17.6	71.4	8.2	1.8	1.1	548	1.8
Lower segment above	16.3	69.6	9.2	2.7	2.0	667	1.8
Upper segment above	20.8	58.1	13.0	5.0	3.1	1,003	1.8
Landholding Groups							
Landless wage earner	16.6	74.3	6.3	0.9	1.8	429	1.6
Marginal	16.1	69.5	9.9	2.9	1.6	653	1.8
Small	18.1	67.0	9.9	3.5	1.4	683	1.8
Medium	18.4	68.0	8.2	3.5	1.9	774	2.0
Large	19.2	65.1	9.6	2.2	3.9	1,047	2.2
Landless others	2.0	60.9	12.4	4.0	2.7	762	1.8
Landowners	17.4	68.0	9.6	3.1	1.9	715	1.8
Landless	18.8	65.4	10.4	3.0	2.4	606	1.7
Occupational Groups							
Cultivators	17.9	69.5	8.6	2.5	1.5	657	1.8
Salaried+Prof.+S.Empl.	19.4	60.7	11.3	4.9	3.7	1,022	1.9
Wage earners	15.0	76.1	6.3	1.1	1.5	446	1.6
All others	18.0	62.6	13.9	3.7	1.8	735	1.8
Social Groups							
Caste							
STs	13.1	71.2	5.2	6.0	4.5	511	1.7
SCs	15.1	72.3	9.5	1.4	1.6	514	1.7
Religion							
Hindus	17.5	67.4	10.1	2.8	2.2	667	1.8
Muslim	19.1	65.3	9.5	3.8	2.3	625	1.9
Christians	15.4	68.2	10.6	5.8	–	885	1.7
Other Minorities	23.8	65.8	5.4	3.7	1.3	1,069	1.9
Household Size Groups							
Up to 4	18.9	64.9	10.2	4.3	1.7	569	1.3
5–7	17.1	67.5	10.0	3.1	2.3	652	1.7
8 and above	18.7	67.7	9.3	2.4	1.8	808	2.2

(Contd.)

Adult Literacy Groups							
None literate	16.3	75.6	5.2	1.1	1.7	413	1.6
Female literate	16.9	69.1	7.8	5.6	0.6	676	1.8
Male literate	17.4	71.9	7.5	1.7	1.5	581	1.8
Both literate	18.5	62.6	12.3	4.0	2.6	891	1.9
Village Development Groups							
Low	17.9	70.2	7.1	2.8	2.0	601	1.8
Medium	17.5	67.4	9.9	2.8	2.4	680	1.8
High	18.2	65.0	11.6	3.5	1.7	746	1.8
All India							
Person	**17.8**	**67.2**	**9.8**	**3.1**	**2.1**	**680**	**1.8**
Gender Disparity	**0.93**	**1.04**	**0.93**	**0.90**	**0.86**	**0.68**	**0.72**

Percentage Distribution of Annual Household Expenditure on Schooling (Government Schools) of Children in Age Group 6–14 Years and Gender Disparity by States

Regions/States	Exam. & Other Fees	Books, Station. & Uniform	Coaching	Transpt.	Board-ing & Lodging	Total	Av. No. of Stds per Household
North							
Haryana							
Person	14.6	80.7	2.8	1.8	–	1,094	1.8
Gender disparity	0.96	1.02	0.86	0.81	–	0.84	0.89
Himachal Pradesh							
Person	9.3	88.2	0.7	0.9	0.8	1,548	1.9
Gender disparity	1.02	1.00	0.85	0.62	1.65	0.90	0.94
Punjab							
Person	15.9	76.2	5.5	2.4	–	911	1.9
Gender disparity	1.01	1.06	0.56	0.52	–	0.83	0.88
Upper Central							
Bihar							
Person	14.7	63.1	19.0	0.2	3.0	529	1.7
Gender disparity	1.11	1.10	0.88	0.89	–	0.62	0.63
Uttar Pradesh							
Person	19.6	77.2	2.6	0.6	–	492	1.7
Gender disparity	1.07	1.03	0.35	–7	–	0.60	0.60
Lower Central							
Madhya Pradesh							
Person	9.9	84.8	2.1	1.2	2.0	438	1.8
Gender disparity	0.94	1.00	0.83	0.51	2.15	0.72	0.72
Orissa							
Person	15.8	63.1	21.0	0.2	–	420	1.7
Gender disparity	1.06	0.98	1.03	0.32	–	0.85	0.85
Rajasthan							
Person	7.1	85.1	6.1	1.1	0.6	777	1.8
Gender disparity	0.95	1.05	0.65	0.52	–	0.41	0.44
East							
North-eastern Rg.							
Person	29.9	60.4	2.1	7.6	–	488	1.7
Gender disparity	1.15	0.88	–	0.65	–	0.50	0.56
West Bengal							
Person	9.0	47.6	41.0	0.9	1.5	516	1.8
Gender disparity	0.86	0.85	1.18	0.02	–	0.83	0.95
West							
Gujarat							
Person	5.9	76.8	4.0	3.0	10.4	431	1.9
Gender disparity	1.30	0.96	0.48	1.10	1.45	0.77	0.76

(Contd.)

Maharashtra							
Person	7.9	89.6	1.4	0.9	0.2	507	1.8
Gender disparity	0.49	1.08	0.39	0.38	2.21	0.84	0.90
South							
Andhra Pradesh							
Person	9.3	71.3	15.7	2.4	1.4	329	1.6
Gender disparity	0.87	0.98	1.14	0.51	6.56	0.94	0.82
Karnataka							
Person	12.1	74.9	3.2	2.3	7.6	504	1.7
Gender disparity	0.98	1.03	0.27	0.77	1.36	0.98	0.91
Kerala							
Person	4.2	78.3	15.0	2.5	–	852	1.6
Gender disparity	1.26	1.04	0.65	2.79	–	1.00	0.94
Tamil Nadu							
Person	20.2	70.4	4.9	3.8	0.7	470	1.5
Gender disparity	1.55	0.95	0.54	0.61	0.55	0.83	0.82
All India							
Person	**12.6**	**76.3**	**7.9**	**1.5**	**1.7**	**539**	**1.7**
Gender disparity	**1.02**	**1.02**	**0.83**	**0.68**	**1.02**	**0.73**	**0.73**
C.V Person	49.5	14.7	113.7	88.9	162.8	48.1	6.1

Household Expenditure (Rs) on Education of Children in Age Group 6–14 Years in Government Schools by States

Regions/States	Household Income Groups (Rs per year)				Social Groups				Village Development Groups			All
	Up to 20,000	20,001–40,000	40,001–62,000	Above 62,000	STs and SCs	Hindus	Muslims	Other Minorities	Low	Medium	High	Groups
North												
Haryana	945	1,053	1,101	1,440	1,017	1,090	679	1,762	1,276	1,022	1,103	1,094
Himachal Pradesh	1,381	1,597	2,088	1,822	1,444	1,550	1,441	1,520	1,588	1,522	1,543	1,548
Punjab	819	985	881	1,069	644	884	300	934	1,254	812	1,000	911
Upper Central												
Bihar	433	553	834	877	397	523	609	448	520	505	624	529
Uttar Pradesh	430	532	518	636	401	493	496	367	475	487	691	492
Lower Central												
Madhya Pradesh	353	516	444	601	388	430	703	634	374	506	480	438
Orissa	354	596	515	444	272	421	309	482	347	405	548	420
Rajasthan	594	706	987	1518	585	793	469	556	718	850	872	777
East												
North-eastern Rg.	397	462	1,433	–	549	445	853	627	–	329	634	488
West Bengal	412	481	912	1,546	401	488	568	–	506	536	499	516
West												
Gujarat	316	534	507	576	368	434	356	772	370	439	441	431
Maharashtra	414	512	599	878	450	518	385	421	640	544	462	507
South												
Andhra Pradesh	293	379	285	501	231	–	318	467	262	315	372	329
Karnataka	475	597	540	422	421	500	525	705	203	538	497	504
Kerala	827	922	786	774	701	856	687	1093	918	985	755	852
Tamil Nadu	420	452	1107	577	436	481	71	361	67	562	432	470
All India	**448**	**577**	**674**	**816**	**434**	**619**	**515**	**719**	**514**	**550**	**547**	**539**
C.V.	51.5	44.8	51.3	56.4	54.2	54.9	46.5	62.1	73.8	47.4	44.0	48.1

Gender Disparity in Household Expenditure on Education of Children in Age Group 6–14 Years in Government Schools by States

Regions/States	Household Income Groups (Rs per year)				Social Groups				Village Development Groups			All Groups
	Up to 20,000	20,001–40,000	40,001–62,000	Above 62,000	STs and SCs	Hindus	Muslims	Other Minorities	Low	Medium	High	
North												
Haryana	0.81	0.73	0.79	1.11	0.93	0.84	0.26	1.37	0.53	1.00	0.84	0.84
Himachal Pradesh	0.84	0.81	1.09	2.38	0.86	0.99	0.53	0.84	0.92	0.95	0.78	0.90
Punjab	0.89	0.65	1.03	0.90	0.58	0.78	0.31	0.85	0.91	0.83	0.80	0.83
Upper Central												
Bihar	0.50	0.65	0.82	0.91	0.53	0.60	0.67	0.74	0.44	0.70	0.85	0.62
Uttar Pradesh	0.49	0.65	0.76	0.77	0.44	0.61	0.49	0.67	0.52	0.73	0.66	0.60
Lower Central												
Madhya Pradesh	0.70	0.74	0.56	0.93	0.63	0.72	0.73	0.73	0.59	0.81	0.91	0.72
Orissa	0.74	0.97	1.27	0.91	0.63	0.83	0.82	3.99	0.97	0.79	0.82	0.85
Rajasthan	0.28	0.43	0.50	0.60	0.29	0.42	0.06	0.68	0.42	0.31	0.84	0.41
East												
North-eastern Rg.	0.49	0.46	0.65	–	8.62	0.42	0.86	1.44	–	0.40	0.55	0.50
West Bengal	0.67	0.63	2.32	0.81	1.54	1.03	0.58	–	0.27	0.80	0.93	0.83
West												
Gujarat	0.59	0.91	0.73	1.00	0.70	0.84	0.16	0.07	0.83	0.87	0.64	0.77
Maharashtra	0.71	0.86	0.86	1.18	0.81	0.83	1.10	0.93	0.80	0.66	1.01	0.84
South												
Andhra Pradesh	0.88	0.98	1.04	1.03	0.85	–	0.92	0.93	0.70	0.98	0.98	0.94
Karnataka	0.92	1.30	0.77	0.82	1.04	1.00	0.69	3.02	0.67	1.30	0.68	0.98
Kerala	0.90	1.10	1.30	1.13	0.69	0.86	1.41	1.01	3.46	0.99	0.90	1.00
Tamil Nadu	0.93	0.76	0.70	0.68	0.93	0.81	0.85	1.53	0.82	0.40	1.25	0.83
All India	**0.66**	**0.75**	**0.79**	**0.87**	**0.67**	**0.72**	**0.64**	**0.92**	**0.55**	**0.74**	**0.89**	**0.73**
C.V.	51.50	44.80	51.30	56.40	54.20	35.5	54.40	62.10	73.80	47.40	44.00	48.10

Percentage Distribution of Annual Household Expenditure on Schooling (Private Schools) of Children in the Age Group of 6–14 Years and Gender Disparity by States

Regions/States	Exam. & Other Fees	Books, Station. & Uniform	Coaching	Transpt.	Board- ing & Lodging	Total	Av. No. of Stds per Household
North							
Haryana							
Person	37.8	51.8	5.6	4.7	0.1	2,235	1.6
Gender disparity	0.97	0.97	1.10	1.50	–	0.56	0.55
Himachal Pradesh							
Person	30.5	57.5	1.1	4.1	6.7	2,766	1.4
Gender disparity	1.02	1.16	–	1.67	–	0.47	0.64
Punjab							
Person	40.8	50.1	4.9	4.2	–	2,098	1.5
Gender disparity	0.93	1.02	1.84	0.79	–	0.60	0.63
Upper Central							
Bihar							
Person	33.4	31.1	20.6	3.0	11.9	1,652	1.5
Gender disparity	0.94	1.09	1.64	2.36	–	0.29	0.38
Uttar Pradesh							
Person	31.6	56.0	8.0	2.2	2.3	852	1.6
Gender disparity	0.97	1.02	0.58	1.26	3.92	0.53	0.56
Lower Central							
Madhya Pradesh							
Person	38.9	51.2	6.7	3.2	–	1,114	1.5
Gender disparity	0.89	1.22	0.39	0.83	–	0.60	0.59
Orissa							
Person	15.6	53.5	26.8	4.1	–	560	1.6
Gender disparity	0.85	1.00	1.49	–	–	0.92	0.73
Rajasthan							
Person	43.9	50.4	5.1	0.5	–	1,289	1.7
Gender disparity	0.99	0.94	2.06	–	–	0.42	0.34
East							
North-eastern Rg.							
Person	25.7	13.1	–	61.1	–	4,533	1.6
Gender disparity	0.50	0.73	–	1.40	–	0.84	0.76
West Bengal							
Person	34.1	33.6	27.8	4.5	–	1,380	1.1
Gender disparity	0.68	3.04	–	–	–	0.21	0.40
West							
Gujarat							
Person	36.5	32.3	9.0	10.7	11.5	2,042	1.6
Gender disparity	0.68	0.99	0.72	1.17	3.30	0.55	0.44

(Contd.)

Maharashtra							
Person	23.2	66.3	0.5	9.9	–	816	1.4
Gender disparity	1.03	1.07	0.49	0.55	–	0.38	0.45
South							
Andhra Pradesh							
Person	46.0	33.9	4.4	1-	5.8	1,692	1.5
Gender disparity	0.95	0.90	0.51	2.05	1.28	0.74	0.71
Karnataka							
Person	29.0	59.6	6.1	4.7	0.6	1,391	1.5
Gender disparity	0.91	1.17	0.50	0.32	10.88	0.62	0.66
Kerala							
Person	23.5	45.0	15.6	15.9	–	1,714	1.5
Gender disparity	0.98	1.03	1.51	0.60	–	0.57	0.53
Tamil Nadu							
Person	41.2	42.0	5.4	11.4	–	1,502	1.6
Gender disparity	0.98	0.95	2.32	0.82	–	0.49	0.59
All India							
Person	**34.5**	**47.0**	**9.2**	**6.0**	**3.3**	**1,262**	**1.6**
Gender disparity	**0.95**	**1.05**	**0.89**	**1.24**	**0.79**	**0.52**	**0.55**
C.V. Person	24.4	29.0	92.1	144.1	167.1	52.7	8.5

Household Expenditure(Rs) on Education of Children in the Age Group 6–14 Years in Schools by States

| Regions/States | Household Income Groups (Rs per year) | | | | Social Groups | | | | Village Development Groups | | | All |
	Up to 20,000	20,001– 40,000	40,001– 62,000	Above 62,000	STs and SCs	Hindus	Muslims	Other Minorities	Low	Medium	High	Groups
North												
Haryana	1,794	1,854	2,561	2,624	1,351	2,179	2,327	4,321	3,112	1,983	2,269	2,235
Himachal Pradesh	2,251	1,930	4,086	5,734	2,657	2,760	–	2,960	2,056	3,527	2,623	2,766
Punjab	1,330	2,202	2,008	2,752	1,371	1,702	2,618	2,260	1,434	2,171	2,161	2,098
Upper Central												
Bihar	877	1,632	920	3,790	1,191	1,781	1,062	2,034	1,164	1,675	2,103	1,652
Uttar Pradesh	589	790	1,094	1,481	573	926	501	672	757	991	855	852
Lower Central												
Madhya Pradesh	596	1,300	1,264	1,452	932	1,051	2,480	1,827	1,186	1,122	986	1,114
Orissa	180	957	835	350	79	596	–	138	553	486	737	560
Rajasthan	1,086	1,517	923	1,535	1,305	1,225	450	–	898	1,194	2,316	1,289
East												
North-eastern Rg.	280	30	5,362	–	534	5,362	155	–	6,337	–	534	4,533
West Bengal	1,569	774	–	2,013	1,672	1,469	1,345	710	–	1,341	1,403	1,380
West												
Gujarat	1,973	2,083	3,270	570	1,988	2,042	–	–	2,719	1,900	585	2,042
Maharashtra	581	1,078	456	1,111	677	834	616	–	–	745	855	816
South												
Andhra Pradesh	1,074	707	2,888	4,641	468	1,547	4,808	600	1,608	1,072	2,208	1,692
Karnataka	1,150	1,683	1,150	2,028	1,376	1,285	2,677	551	10,400	1,247	1,403	1,391
Kerala	1,155	2,081	2,021	1,824	2,362	1,666	2,047	1,661	2,247	1,851	1,612	1,714
Tamil Nadu	1,062	1,773	1,169	3,572	1,139	1,233	2,900	2,282	–	2,730	1,372	1,502
All India	**814**	**1,239**	**1,469**	**2,250**	**840**	**1,728**	**968**	**1,990**	**946**	**1,294**	**1,603**	**1,262**
C.V.	52.0	42.9	74.2	68.7	55.2	62.3	90.0	99.1	121.4	55.8	45.0	52.7

Gender Disparity in Household Expenditure on Education of Children in Age Group 6–14 Years in Private Schools by States

Regions/States	Household Income Groups (Rs per year)				Social Groups				Village Development Groups			All Groups
	Up to 20,000	20,001–40,000	40,001–62,000	Above 62,000	STs and SCs	Hindus	Muslims	Other Minorities	Low	Medium	High	
North												
Haryana	0.52	0.70	0.54	0.50	0.39	0.52	0.63	2.21	1.05	0.49	0.55	0.56
Himachal Pradesh	0.84	0.81	0.29	0.10	0.16	0.49	–	–	0.54	0.33	0.62	0.47
Punjab	0.53	0.58	0.66	0.61	0.08	0.46	–	0.68	0.06	0.38	1.11	0.60
Upper Central												
Bihar	0.20	0.35	0.24	0.25	0.21	0.27	0.32	2.75	0.34	0.24	0.40	0.29
Uttar Pradesh	0.45	0.48	0.41	0.85	0.40	0.51	0.72	–	0.59	0.46	0.60	0.53
Lower Central												
Madhya Pradesh	0.38	0.87	0.37	0.62	0.28	0.51	1.00	2.10	0.57	0.45	0.85	0.60
Orissa	1.82	0.82	0.75	–	0.58	0.96	–	–	0.46	1.14	3.00	0.92
Rajasthan	0.04	0.67	0.36	0.66	0.38	0.43	–	–	0.16	0.42	0.72	0.42
East												
North-eastern Rg.	–	–	0.84	–	–	0.84	9.33	–	0.90	–	–	0.84
West Bengal	0.16	0.04	–	0.37	0.32	0.16	0.50	1.00	–	0.19	0.22	0.21
West												
Gujarat	0.23	0.52	–	–	1.89	0.55	–	–	0.70	–	0.07	0.55
Maharashtra	0.19	0.95	–	–	0.03	0.36	0.65	–	–	0.11	0.55	0.38
South												
Andhra Pradesh	1.04	0.27	0.75	0.76	0.67	0.72	0.99	–	0.32	1.17	0.69	0.74
Karnataka	0.54	0.44	0.81	1.36	0.24	0.66	0.41	0.90	1.12	0.49	0.76	0.62
Kerala	0.66	0.67	0.27	0.61	1.01	0.41	0.26	1.76	2.56	0.29	0.68	0.57
Tamil Nadu	0.64	0.28	6.22	0.41	0.06	0.65	1.00	0.11	–	0.19	0.58	0.49
All India	**0.50**	**0.48**	**0.52**	**0.61**	**0.35**	**0.53**	**0.56**	**0.75**	**0.57**	**0.41**	**0.65**	**0.52**
C.V.	52.00	42.90	74.20	68.70	55.20	36.8	90.00	99.10	121.40	55.80	45.00	52.70

Per Student Annual Household Expenditure on Elementary Education by States

Regions/States	NCAER 1992[1]		NCAER/HDI 1994	
	Total Expenditure (Rupees)	Share of Exam. and Other Fees (percentage)	Total expenditure (Rupees)	Share of Exam. and Other Fees (percentage)
North				
Haryana	801	29.1	696	22.5
Himachal Pradesh	–	–	842	12.2
Punjab	612	20.9	670	28.5
Upper Central				
Uttar Pradesh	–	–	351	26.1
Bihar	246	24.3	375	20.2
Lower Central				
Madhya Pradesh	281	17.4	258	13.8
Orissa	309	17.4	253	15.6
Rajasthan	364	14.6	428	10.9
East				
North-eastern Rg.	587	12.4	404	22.0
West Bengal	504	10.5	316	8.5
West				
Gujarat	342	13.4	278	9.6
Maharashtra	329	15.5	302	7.2
South				
Andhra Pradesh	378	20.4	295	23.1
Karnataka	448	20.3	383	17.3
Kerala	754	23.6	586	8.8
Tamil Nadu	349	17.2	379	26.3
All India	**464**	**18.7**	**378**	**18.2**

1. *Non-Enrolment, Drop-out and Expenditure on Elementary Education: A Comparison Across States and Population Groups.* NCAER, New Delhi, 1992.

Participation (%) in Literacy Programmes and Achievement of Non-Enrolled Children in the Age Group of 6–14 Years and Gender Disparity by States

Regions/States	Participation Rate	Level of Achievement (%)			
		1	2	3	4
North					
Himachal Pradesh					
Person	19.7	80.5	4.8	14.6	-
Gender disparity	1.95	1.10	–	–	–
Upper Central					
Uttar Pradesh					
Person	0.3	65.8	23.3	10.9	–
Gender disparity	0.48	1.21	–	–	–
Lower Central					
Madhya Pradesh					
Person	0.4	21.4	31.2	47.4	–
Gender disparity	1.29	–	0.81	0.56	–
Orissa					
Person	1.4	85.6	14.4	–	–
Gender disparity	0.63	1.43	–	–	–
Rajasthan					
Person	1.4	79.5	12.9	7.6	–
Gender disparity	0.85	1.04	–	–	–
East					
West Bengal					
Person	4.5	20.8	31.7	43.7	3.8
Gender disparity	0.47	4.90	1.02	0.21	–
South					
Andhra Pradesh					
Person	7.3	90.8	3.7	5.5	-
Gender disparity	0.89	1.24	–	0.15	–
Karnataka					
Person	5.8	41.4	16.2	42.4	–
Gender disparity	2.31	0.69	0.59	2.13	–
Tamil Nadu					
Person	1.6	9.0	–	91.0	-
Gender disparity	0.13	–	–	0.50	–
All India					
Person	**1.5**	**53.1**	**18.0**	**27.3**	**1.7**
Gender disparity	**0.84**	**1.72**	**0.60**	**0.44**	**–**
C.V.	183.1	114.6	131.3	154.5	354.7

Notes: (1)Level 1 refers to cannot read or write; Level 2 refers to can read cannot write; Level 3 refers to can read and write with difficulty; and Level 4 refers to can read and write fluently.
(2)Data are not available for States such as Haryana, Kerala, Punjab, Bihar, Gujarat, and the North-eastern Rg.

Participation Rate (%) in Literacy Programmes and Achievement of Non-Enrolled Children in Age Group 6–14 Years by Population Groups

Population Groups	Participation Rate	Level of Achievement (%)			
		1	2	3	4
Household Income Groups					
Upto 20,000	1.4	54.9	18.4	24.8	1.9
20,001–40,000	1.7	51.9	20.5	25.6	1.9
40,001–62,000	1.3	37.6	13.5	48.9	-
62,001–86,000	2.4	47.4	–	52.6	–
Poverty Line Groups					
Lower segment below	1.3	45.5	13.2	36.8	4.5
Upper segment below	1.0	43.9	34.4	21.7	–
Lower segment above	1.9	63.0	16.8	19.0	1.2
Upper segment above	1.3	42.0	–	58.0	–
Landholding Groups					
Landless wage earner	1.5	61.7	16.7	21.6	–
Marginal	1.8	41.8	23.3	34.9	–
Small	1.2	66.7	9.5	19.9	3.9
Medium	1.1	62.3	18.4	19.2	–
Large	1.4	100.0	–	–	–
Landless others	1.1	27.1	21.4	40.7	10.8
Land Owners	1.5	54.0	17.9	27.2	0.9
Landless	1.4	51.4	18.1	27.3	3.2
Occupational Groups					
Cultivators	1.3	56.1	13.1	30.8	-
Salaried+Prof.+S.Empl.	0.6	100.0	–	–	-
Wage earners	1.6	63.7	12.6	22.2	1.5
All others	2.0	21.6	39.3	33.5	5.6
Social Groups					
Caste					
STs	1.3	74.0	18.5	2.6	4.9
SCs	1.6	47.2	11.2	41.6	–
Religion					
Hindus	1.4	57.7	17.6	24.0	0.7
Muslims	1.6	33.3	18.8	41.1	6.8
Christians	2.2	25.9	–	74.1	–
Household Size Groups					
Up to 4	1.8	55.7	16.3	27.9	–
5–7	1.6	53.1	17.3	28.8	0.9
8 and above	1.1	51.9	20.3	23.5	4.3
Adult Literacy Groups					
None literate	1.3	58.6	22.3	19.1	–
Male literate	1.6	54.6	15.7	28.2	1.5

(Contd.)

Both literate	2.2	33.2	10.0	48.9	7.9
Village Development Groups					
Low	1.0	63.3	27.5	7.4	1.8
Medium	1.8	49.9	15.5	31.9	2.6
High	2.0	46.5	11.2	42.3	–
All India					
Person	**1.5**	**53.1**	**18.0**	**27.3**	**1.7**
Gender Disparity	**0.84**	**1.72**	**0.60**	**0.44**	**–**

Prevalence Rates of Short Duration and Major Morbidity and Gender Disparity by Population Groups

Population Groups	Short Duration Morbidity('000 pop.)				Major Morbid. (per lakh pop.)
	Diarr.	Cold/ Cough	Fever	Total	
Household Income Groups					
Upto 20,000					
Person	33	77	26	129	4,466
Gender disparity	–	–	–	1.08	0.97
20,001–40,000					
Person	31	71	25	121	4,790
Gender disparity	–	–	–	1.10	1.00
40,001–62,000					
Person	27	62	22	107	4,529
Gender disparity	–	–	–	0.97	1.06
62,001–86,000					
Person	29	58	28	111	4,751
Gender disparity	–	–	–	1.06	1.10
Above 86,000					
Person	20	50	25	91	4,408
Gender disparity	–	–	–	1.19	1.13
Poverty Line Groups					
Lower segment below					
Person	33	74	24	125	4,183
Gender disparity	–	–	–	1.10	0.92
Upper segment below					
Person	35	77	24	128	4,216
Gender disparity	–	–	–	1.05	0.95
Lower segment above					
Person	29	69	27	120	4,615
Gender disparity	–	–	–	1.09	1.04
Upper segment above					
Person	29	69	25	117	5,231
Gender disparity	–	–	–	1.05	1.04
Landholding Groups					
Landless wage earner					
Person	27	73	25	121	4,598
Gender disparity	–	–	–	1.09	0.97
Marginal					
Person	32	72	25	121	4,658
Gender disparity	–	–	–	1.10	1.03
Small					
Person	33	69	26	122	4,489
Gender disparity	–	–	–	1.06	1.05

(Contd.)

Medium					
Person	31	60	26	112	3,870
Gender disparity	–	–	–	1.04	0.96
Large					
Person	29	60	27	112	4,431
Gender disparity	–	–	–	1.07	1.09
Landless others					
Person	33	87	23	136	5,044
Gender disparity				1.07	0.92
Land Owners					
Person	32	68	26	119	4,463
Gender disparity	–	–	-	1.08	1.03
Landless					
Person	30	80	24	128	4,816
Gender disparity	–	–	–	1.08	0.94
Occupational Groups					
Cultivators					
Person	33	67	26	118	4,407
Gender disparity	-	–	–	1.06	1.04
Salaried+Prof.+S.Empl.					
Person	31	84	27	135	4,457
Gender disparity	–	–	–	1.14	1.09
Wage Earners					
Person	29	72	26	121	4,699
Gender disparity	–	–	–	1.11	0.97
All Others					
Person	30	75	22	120	4,996
Gender disparity	-	–	–	1.03	0.90
Social Groups					
Caste					
STs					
Person	38	64	37	130	3,377
Gender disparity	–	–	–	1.08	0.89
SCs					
Person	34	72	25	124	4,527
Gender disparity	–	–	–	1.04	1.08
Religion					
Hindus					
Person	32	71	26	123	4,503
Gender disparity	–	–	–	1.08	0.99
Muslims					
Person	32	63	18	106	4,441
Gender disparity	–	–	–	1.02	1.01
Christians					
Person	20	93	18	128	6,773
Gender disparity	–	–	–	1.27	0.96

(Contd.)

Other Minorities					
Person	20	93	32	143	5,748
Gender disparity	–	–	–	1.17	1.29
Household Size Groups					
Up to 4					
Person	31	84	28	136	5,899
Gender disparity	–	–	–	1.10	1.05
5–7					
Person	32	74	26	124	4,405
Gender disparity	–	–	–	1.08	0.98
8 and above					
Person	31	61	23	109	4,063
Gender disparity	–	–	–	1.05	1.00
Adult Literacy Groups					
None literate					
Person	36	76	26	130	4,394
Gender disparity	–	–	–	1.05	0.98
Female literate					
Person	28	82	27	134	5,317
Gender disparity	–	–	–	1.01	0.81
Male literate					
Person	33	69	29	124	4,214
Gender disparity	–	–	–	1.09	1.01
Both literate					
Person	27	70	22	114	4,956
Gender disparity	–	–	–	1.09	1.02
Village Development Groups					
Low					
Person	39	73	29	131	4,301
Gender disparity	–	–	–	1.07	1.01
Medium					
Person	31	68	24	118	4,466
Gender disparity	–	–	–	1.08	0.99
High					
Person	24	75	23	117	5,002
Gender disparity	–	–	–	1.09	1.01
Age Groups (Years)					
0–4					
Person	108	114	31	237	966
Gender disparity	–	–	–	0.92	0.59
5–14					
Person	22	76	28	122	1,138
Gender disparity	–	–	–	1.01	0.67
15–34					
Person	15	47	20	79	2,578
Gender disparity	–	–	–	1.31	1.27

(Contd.)

35–59					
Person	25	73	26	117	7,933
Gender disparity	–	–	–	1.18	1.17
60 & Above					
Person	26	94	30	140	22,317
Gender disparity	–	–	–	0.98	0.89
All India					
Person	**31**	**72**	**25**	**122**	**4,578**
Gender disparity	**0.92**	**1.08**	**1.17**	**1.08**	**1.00**

Prevalence Rate (Per Thousand Population) of Short Duration Morbidity by States

Regions/States	Household Income Groups (Rs per year)				Social Groups				Village Development Groups			All Groups
	Up to 20,000	20,001–40,000	40,001–62,000	Above 62,000	STs and SCs	Hindus	Muslims	Other Minorities	Low	Medium	High	
North												
Haryana												
Person	176	165	135	122	157	150	161	259	155	160	148	153
Gender disparity	1.24	1.18	1.23	1.14	1.31	1.19	1.35	1.25	1.12	1.24	1.19	1.20
Himachal Pradesh												
Person	348	287	290	225	326	309	439	291	332	287	339	313
Gender disparity	1.25	1.24	1.30	1.08	1.33	1.26	1.19	0.58	1.26	1.19	1.34	1.25
Punjab												
Person	143	167	152	157	125	131	222	161	121	148	165	154
Gender disparity	1.25	1.08	1.21	1.16	1.22	1.16	1.77	1.15	1.83	1.08	1.21	1.17
Upper Central												
Bihar												
Person	139	131	104	116	121	132	137	122	128	128	156	132
Gender disparity	1.08	1.03	0.82	1.17	0.92	1.05	1.17	0.89	1.02	1.13	0.93	1.05
Uttar Pradesh												
Person	99	103	90	81	107	96	101	120	94	97	118	97
Gender disparity	0.97	1.08	0.90	1.27	0.90	1.00	1.15	1.58	1.06	0.95	1.08	1.02
Lower Central												
Madhya Pradesh												
Person	199	192	184	192	210	195	178	164	196	190	204	195
Gender disparity	1.11	1.17	0.92	1.03	1.09	1.10	1.03	1.27	1.11	1.04	1.16	1.09
Orissa												
Person	149	142	109	109	162	195	120	170	163	131	133	143
Gender disparity	1.09	1.07	1.47	0.83	1.06	1.10	0.91	1.46	1.12	1.02	1.19	1.10
Rajasthan												
Person	118	108	102	112	108	115	73	38	123	100	94	113
Gender disparity	0.92	0.93	1.03	0.98	0.94	0.94	1.00	–	0.87	1.19	0.71	0.94
East												
North-eastern Rg.												
Person	90	96	100	89	89	102	76	66	78	97	97	94
Gender disparity	0.81	1.17	0.85	0.98	0.96	0.97	0.88	0.80	1.01	0.99	0.85	0.94
West Bengal												
Person	185	136	122	100	154	172	124	428	214	186	128	164
Gender disparity	1.11	0.99	1.09	0.84	1.12	1.10	0.96	1.12	1.13	1.15	0.95	1.08
West												
Gujarat												
Person	63	54	53	41	56	59	39	48	57	56	59	57
Gender disparity	1.06	1.09	0.86	0.73	1.19	0.99	1.55	1.98	1.01	1.07	0.96	1.02
Maharashtra												
Person	97	74	73	70	91	85	120	64	112	92	77	85
Gender disparity	1.14	0.85	0.91	1.00	0.96	0.99	0.97	2.00	1.06	1.09	0.98	1.03

(Contd.)

South

Andhra Pradesh												
Person	135	130	133	119	142	135	115	86	207	105	123	132
Gender disparity	1.06	1.12	0.97	1.34	1.06	1.11	0.85	0.89	1.11	1.09	1.08	1.09
Karnataka												
Person	27	22	15	14	24	23	19	17	32	19	26	23
Gender disparity	0.98	1.42	0.90	0.91	1.61	1.11	0.69	0.49	0.64	1.22	1.03	1.07
Kerala												
Person	115	86	51	32	99	101	74	74	67	104	82	89
Gender disparity	0.90	1.22	0.63	0.92	0.91	0.96	0.85	1.22	1.13	0.92	1.04	0.99
Tamil Nadu												
Person	161	190	149	162	133	165	106	243	32	147	178	168
Gender disparity	1.24	1.43	1.03	1.42	1.40	1.28	0.43	1.47	–	1.25	1.30	1.29
All India												
Person	**129**	**121**	**107**	**101**	**126**	**123**	**106**	**137**	**131**	**118**	**117**	**122**
Gender disparity	**1.08**	**1.10**	**0.97**	**1.12**	**1.06**	**1.08**	**1.02**	**1.21**	**1.07**	**1.08**	**1.09**	**1.08**
C.V. Person	49.1	46.8	52.1	50.2	49.9	51.8	70.7	72.8	57.4	46.2	52.0	48.0

Short Duration Morbidity Prevalence Rates and Gender Disparity by States

Regions/States	Short Duration Morbidity ('000 pop) Age Groups(completed years)					All Ages
	0–4	5–14	15–34	35–59	60 +	
North						
Haryana						
Person	422	164	64	119	137	153
Gender disparity	0.91	0.97	1.52	2.30	1.70	1.20
Punjab						
Person	253	156	137	131	134	154
Gender disparity	0.88	0.93	1.44	1.38	1.22	1.17
Upper Central						
Bihar						
Person	299	144	73	102	134	132
Gender disparity	0.89	1.02	1.29	1.26	0.76	1.05
Uttar Pradesh						
Person	215	97	53	78	132	97
Gender disparity	0.94	1.10	1.11	0.92	0.97	1.02
Lower Central						
Madhya Pradesh						
Person	444	210	117	151	198	195
Gender disparity	0.99	1.05	1.28	1.13	0.96	1.09
Orissa						
Person	307	143	91	128	176	143
Gender disparity	0.95	1.03	1.19	1.20	1.25	1.10
Rajasthan						
Person	231	92	69	116	130	113
Gender disparity	0.86	0.82	1.09	1.08	0.82	0.94
East						
North-eastern Rg.						
Person	81	88	79	126	142	94
Gender disparity	0.87	0.91	1.01	1.14	0.79	0.94
West Bengal						
Person	233	168	119	200	146	164
Gender disparity	0.95	0.91	1.45	1.00	1.27	1.08
West						
Gujarat						
Person	86	46	36	59	151	57
Gender disparity	0.93	0.80	0.91	1.37	0.99	1.02
Maharashtra						
Person	143	76	54	97	107	85
Gender disparity	0.81	0.94	1.12	1.42	0.81	1.03

(Contd.)

South

Andhra Pradesh						
Person	241	108	90	165	151	132
Gender disparity	0.99	0.99	1.38	1.06	1.05	1.09
Kerala						
Person	216	143	41	74	84	89
Gender disparity	0.87	0.88	1.70	1.42	0.53	0.99
Tamil Nadu						
Person	243	171	135	172	184	168
Gender disparity	0.76	1.22	1.70	1.54	1.32	1.29
All India						
Person	**237**	**122**	**79**	**117**	**140**	**122**
Gender disparity	**0.92**	**1.01**	**1.31**	**1.18**	**0.98**	**1.08**

Prevalence Rate (Per Thousand Population) among Age Group 15–34 Years of Short Duration Morbidity by States

Regions/States	Household Income Groups (Rs per year)				Social Groups				Village Development Groups			All Groups
	Up to 20,000	20,001– 40,000	40,001– 62,000	Above 62,000	STs and SCs	Hindus	Muslims	Other Minorities	Low	Medium	High	
North												
Haryana												
Person	83	64	60	48	60	64	43	125	76	69	59	64
Gender disparity	1.28	2.36	1.24	1.16	1.66	1.56	2.49	0.61	0.68	1.59	1.78	1.52
Himachal Pradesh												
Person	293	229	229	196	274	254	334	254	268	236	283	256
Gender disparity	1.45	1.27	1.21	1.08	1.41	1.37	1.37	–	1.24	1.23	1.79	1.34
Punjab												
Person	130	167	122	117	84	86	323	153	105	132	147	137
Gender disparity	1.33	1.15	1.60	2.74	1.05	0.97	2.96	1.49	2.93	1.21	1.63	1.44
Upper Central												
Bihar												
Person	78	71	55	67	74	74	64	72	79	65	76	73
Gender disparity	1.16	1.62	0.56	2.20	1.06	1.30	1.29	1.08	1.05	1.64	1.28	1.29
Uttar Pradesh												
Person	57	50	52	43	58	53	50	88	51	51	72	53
Gender disparity	1.06	1.16	0.75	2.11	1.03	1.10	1.25	0.36	1.32	0.81	1.17	1.11
Lower Central												
Madhya Pradesh												
Person	124	115	108	100	130	117	122	126	113	120	125	117
Gender disparity	1.29	1.44	1.02	1.08	1.21	1.29	1.06	0.94	1.35	1.04	1.89	1.28
Orissa												
Person	94	90	75	76	107	91	13	109	100	90	76	91
Gender disparity	1.13	1.49	1.85	0.32	1.09	1.19	–	1.50	1.25	0.99	1.63	1.19
Rajasthan												
Person	76	65	65	54	75	69	57	84	74	59	70	69
Gender disparity	1.02	1.17	1.65	0.77	1.08	1.09	1.24	–	0.92	1.66	0.89	1.09
East												
North-eastern Rg.												
Person	70	92	88	43	95	94	37	42	46	88	81	79
Gender disparity	0.61	1.75	0.86	0.73	0.80	1.00	1.32	0.79	1.30	1.01	0.95	1.01
West Bengal												
Person	139	92	85	55	113	124	71	475	172	136	87	119
Gender disparity	1.47	1.55	0.81	0.78	1.49	1.53	1.21	1.04	1.56	1.65	1.16	1.45
West												
Gujarat												
Person	43	28	23	37	36	37	23	–	26	37	37	36
Gender disparity	1.22	0.60	0.61	0.55	1.38	0.87	2.46	-	0.95	0.95	0.85	0.91

(Contd.)

Maharashtra												
Person	65	42	45	48	53	55	68	36	52	68	48	54
Gender disparity	1.38	0.92	0.50	1.03	0.98	1.06	1.34	2.59	0.39	1.18	1.23	1.12
South												
Andhra Pradesh												
Person	109	75	60	80	101	92	68	54	153	65	85	90
Gender disparity	1.28	1.59	1.29	1.23	1.32	1.40	1.29	0.71	1.64	1.33	1.18	1.38
Karnataka												
Person	19	11	9	3	17	15	5	-	16	12	15	14
Gender disparity	0.92	1.25	1.28	-	2.11	1.06		-	0.15	1.70	0.73	1.00
Kerala												
Person	56	42	6	14	47	50	27	29	44	50	31	41
Gender disparity	1.43	2.22	7.15	0.40	0.50	2.36	0.82	0.89	1.16	1.84	1.75	1.70
Tamil Nadu												
Person	134	141	113	136	101	133	98	185	-	116	143	135
Gender disparity	1.49	1.93	2.02	2.37	2.10	1.74	0.27	1.82	-	2.24	1.61	1.70
All India												
Person	**88**	**75**	**65**	**60**	**84**	**88**	**57**	**113**	**81**	**77**	**79**	**79**
Gender disparity	**1.26**	**1.48**	**1.03**	**1.35**	**1.22**	-	**1.18**	**1.35**	**1.26**	**1.31**	**1.37**	**1.31**
C.V. Person	61.4	62.2	68.9	66.6	62.7	60.0	108.4	99.2	75.7	58.2	68.0	61.6

Prevalence Rate (Per Thousand Population) among Age Group 35–59 Years of Short Duration Morbidity by States

Regions/States	Household Income Groups (Rs per year)				Social Groups				Village Development Groups			All Groups
	Up to 20,000	20,001–40,000	40,001–62,000	Above 62,000	STs and SCs	Hindus	Muslims	Other Minorities	Low	Medium	High	
North												
Haryana												
Person	134	118	100	114	119	117	72	239	110	141	105	119
Gender disparity	2.72	1.48	2.59	3.69	2.39	2.11	5.31	12.24	3.37	1.93	2.55	2.30
Himachal Pradesh												
Person	377	299	297	211	356	325	508	384	345	313	346	330
Gender disparity	1.66	1.90	2.45	1.92	1.95	1.81	2.32	1.94	2.06	1.68	1.79	1.82
Punjab												
Person	96	141	141	163	113	108	122	140	55	126	148	131
Gender disparity	1.91	1.26	1.28	1.23	1.85	1.70	9.53	1.25	–	1.36	1.29	1.38
Upper Central												
Bihar												
Person	97	118	79	84	91	100	124	68	96	101	122	102
Gender disparity	1.36	1.08	1.50	1.88	1.31	1.13	2.55	0.94	1.03	1.47	1.36	1.26
Uttar Pradesh												
Person	76	81	76	82	88	79	72	139	84	73	56	78
Gender disparity	0.92	0.83	0.87	1.22	0.71	0.92	0.83	–	1.00	0.74	1.17	0.92
Lower Central												
Madhya Pradesh												
Person	155	150	140	150	162	152	134	94	157	141	156	151
Gender disparity	1.14	1.10	1.14	1.22	1.06	1.14	1.29	0.46	1.19	0.99	1.32	1.13
Orissa												
Person	138	119	87	83	141	127	93	188	133	113	152	128
Gender disparity	1.23	0.91	1.99	1.90	1.08	1.18	1.58	1.97	1.32	1.08	1.23	1.20
Rajasthan												
Person	120	113	114	109	112	118	94	–	127	107	80	116
Gender disparity	1.01	1.05	1.07	1.65	1.30	1.10	0.70	–	1.06	1.07	1.42	1.08
East												
North-eastern Rg.												
Person	120	128	131	140	74	122	163	33	140	116	135	126
Gender disparity	1.41	0.84	1.43	0.88	1.28	0.97	1.58	4.37	1.49	1.19	0.95	1.14
West Bengal												
Person	228	161	163	101	175	221	105	533	273	244	136	200
Gender disparity	0.99	1.02	1.11	0.96	0.87	0.98	0.94	1.38	0.98	1.01	0.98	1.00
West												
Gujarat												
Person	72	49	50	34	65	61	46	–	63	60	58	59
Gender disparity	1.64	1.77	0.30	0.71	1.78	1.32	2.82	–	0.85	1.69	1.26	1.37

(Contd.)

Maharashtra												
Person	113	86	83	73	108	96	129	97	171	95	88	97
Gender disparity	1.43	1.40	1.44	1.35	1.28	1.37	1.72	2.07	2.05	1.19	1.41	1.42
South												
Andhra Pradesh												
Person	172	170	135	129	188	164	195	125	238	126	172	165
Gender disparity	1.05	1.09	0.83	1.31	1.20	1.09	0.98	0.50	1.05	1.20	0.97	1.06
Karnataka												
Person	30	25	17	15	31	26	20	26	17	24	29	26
Gender disparity	1.50	1.60	0.49	2.53	3.36	1.48	1.84	–	–	1.60	1.24	1.47
Kerala												
Person	87	82	40	20	111	81	60	67	100	101	47	74
Gender disparity	1.38	1.39	1.03	–	2.02	1.19	0.97	3.43	1.50	1.51	1.30	1.42
Tamil Nadu												
Person	148	223	173	171	130	·174	69	190	–	156	181	172
Gender disparity	1.42	1.53	1.64	2.26	1.18	1.54	–	1.48	–	1.32	1.60	1.54
All India												
Person	**123**	**119**	**102**	**96**	**118**	**129**	**103**	**126**	**120**	**114**	**117**	**117**
Gender disparity	**1.18**	**1.12**	**1.16**	**1.43**	**1.13**	**–**	**1.28**	**1.47**	**1.14**	**1.15**	**1.27**	**1.18**
C.V. Person	56.4	49.3	55.6	50.8	54.5	52.3	85.6	95.1	66.9	52.0	57.7	51.6

Prevalence Rate (Per Thousand Population) among Age Group 60 and Above of Short Duration Morbidity by States

Regions/States	Household Income Groups (Rs per year)				Social Groups				Village Development Groups			All Groups
	Up to 20,000	20,001–40,000	40,001–62,000	Above 62,000	STs and SCs	Hindus	Muslims	Other Minorities	Low	Medium	High	
North												
Haryana												
Person	146	177	45	140	149	138	92	212	156	147	126	137
Gender disparity	1.86	1.41	30.27	1.37	2.02	1.76	3.18	–	0.52	1.67	2.30	1.70
Himachal Pradesh												
Person	344	316	273	262	329	314	499	422	306	327	324	320
Gender disparity	1.55	1.41	1.14	0.69	1.66	1.44	1.33	–	1.54	1.46	1.02	1.38
Punjab												
Person	130	160	149	90	113	123	77	138	139	114	157	134
Gender disparity	1.78	1.93	0.51	0.22	5.38	1.82	–	1.09	1.84	0.85	1.57	1.22
Upper Central												
Bihar												
Person	141	149	64	77	132	129	161	176	128	99	247	134
Gender disparity	0.63	0.79	2.28	1.92	0.49	0.73	0.72	1.31	0.84	1.04	0.39	0.76
Uttar Pradesh												
Person	145	140	107	89	143	133	125	111	118	154	119	132
Gender disparity	0.90	0.96	0.62	2.71	0.85	0.98	0.81	–	0.96	0.98	0.93	0.97
Lower Central												
Madhya Pradesh												
Person	193	193	211	218	205	200	80	308	201	189	215	198
Gender disparity	0.96	1.15	0.69	0.84	0.95	0.93	3.09	–	0.99	0.93	0.89	0.96
Orissa												
Person	188	161	113	198	184	176	198	170	214	129	218	176
Gender disparity	1.25	1.41	1.03	0.85	1.55	1.26	0.55	1.56	1.74	1.25	0.86	1.25
Rajasthan												
Person	131	120	173	115	124	135	47	–	148	96	142	130
Gender disparity	0.62	0.90	0.96	1.50	0.60	0.81	1.03	–	0.77	1.07	0.52	0.82
East												
North-eastern Rg.												
Person	129	136	188	116	190	134	196	17	116	148	143	142
Gender disparity	0.32	0.87	1.10	4.97	1.01	0.82	0.72	–	1.48	0.74	0.72	0.79
West Bengal												
Person	173	103	152	20	151	150	128	244	262	172	91	146
Gender disparity	1.50	0.35	3.47	–	1.79	1.13	2.02	0.74	1.48	1.56	0.89	1.27
West												
Gujarat												
Person	149	182	146	92	153	155	85	233	137	169	135	151
Gender disparity	0.73	1.57	1.85	0.37	1.07	0.99	0.50	–	1.56	0.78	1.22	0.99

(Contd.)

Maharashtra												
Person	115	107	94	95	145	108	177	74	150	98	108	107
Gender disparity	1.05	0.37	0.94	1.05	0.85	0.79	0.67	1.55	1.10	0.86	0.74	0.81
South												
Andhra Pradesh												
Person	177	123	138	105	198	155	137	55	179	127	163	151
Gender disparity	1.13	0.88	0.92	0.85	1.16	1.11	–	3.55	1.00	0.94	1.20	1.05
Karnataka												
Person	70	79	56	49	37	69	74	–	208	54	73	68
Gender disparity	0.58	1.14	1.26	0.87	0.83	0.85	0.35	–	0.35	0.69	1.03	0.79
Kerala												
Person	105	101	15	33	136	95	67	68	53	89	86	84
Gender disparity	0.46	0.47	1.35	2.08	0.52	0.55	0.26	0.55	0.79	0.58	0.46	0.53
Tamil Nadu												
Person	172	246	93	135	197	179	30	302	–	105	214	184
Gender disparity	1.17	1.73	0.36	1.14	1.72	1.29	1.15	1.23	–	1.56	1.30	1.32
All India												
Person	**149**	**145**	**118**	**103**	**155**	**149**	**123**	**125**	**149**	**130**	**143**	**140**
Gender disparity	**0.94**	**0.99**	**0.96**	**1.23**	**1.02**	**–**	**0.79**	**1.21**	**1.01**	**1.00**	**0.93**	**0.98**
C.V. Person	36.6	37.0	51.1	54.9	36.4	35.2	77.9	75.3	45.4	43.0	40.8	36.2

Prevalence Rates of Major Morbidity and Gender Disparity by States

Regions/States	Major Morbidity Age Groups (completed years)					All Ages
	0–4	5–14	15–34	35–59	60+	
North						
Haryana						
Person	1,359	1,715	3,052	11,179	36,590	6,697
Gender disparity	0.33	0.75	1.98	1.33	1.07	1.21
Punjab						
Person	966	1,501	3,168	12,826	25,502	6,692
Gender disparity	0.85	0.22	1.55	1.73	0.99	1.25
Upper Central						
Bihar						
Person	469	1,173	2,452	6,623	21,236	3,817
Gender disparity	0.27	0.22	1.22	0.76	0.84	0.75
Uttar Pradesh						
Person	483	774	2,489	6,733	14,009	3,523
Gender disparity	0.85	0.81	2.39	1.26	0.82	1.21
Lower Central						
Madhya Pradesh						
Person	888	1,048	2,479	8,639	27,627	4,801
Gender disparity	0.70	0.62	0.99	1.12	0.83	0.95
Orissa						
Person	2,296	1,859	3,012	7,980	19,832	5,011
Gender disparity	0.74	0.80	1.04	1.14	0.85	0.93
Rajasthan						
Person	1,554	1,371	2,026	5,129	11,998	3,150
Gender disparity	0.76	0.71	1.42	1.45	0.83	1.10
East						
North-eastern Rg.						
Person	560	576	1,706	5,726	23,817	3,076
Gender disparity	0.34	1.09	0.96	1.04	0.75	0.77
West Bengal						
Person	1,849	1,506	3,821	11,666	33,748	6,168
Gender disparity	0.19	1.16	1.25	1.15	0.87	0.96
West						
Gujarat						
Person	28	725	1,017	4,439	13,253	2,551
Gender disparity	–	0.90	1.39	0.75	0.51	0.74
Maharashtra						
Person	709	364	1,917	5,863	17,089	3,487
Gender disparity	0.95	0.88	0.89	1.25	0.94	1.05
South						
Andhra Pradesh						
Person	2,141	1,796	3,600	13,690	34,577	7,684
Gender disparity	0.85	0.40	1.07	1.06	0.91	0.88

(Contd.)

Kerala						
Person	1,395	1,509	2,610	9,257	34,194	7,319
Gender disparity	0.93	0.51	1.51	1.45	0.99	1.17
Tamil Nadu						
Person	1,061	2,025	3,611	9,992	36,048	6,775
Gender disparity	0.67	0.97	0.89	1.61	1.08	1.10
All India						
Person	**966**	**1,138**	**2,578**	**7,933**	**22,317**	**4,578**
Gender disparity	**0.59**	**0.67**	**1.27**	**1.17**	**0.89**	**1.00**

Prevalence Rate (Per Lakh Population) of Major Morbidity by States

Regions/States	Household Income Groups (Rs per year)				Social Groups				Village Development Groups			All Groups
	Up to 20,000	20,001– 40,000	40,001– 62,000	Above 62,000	STs and SCs	Hindus	Muslims	Other Minorities	Low	Medium	High	
North												
Haryana												
Person	7,448	6,815	6,504	5,729	7,242	6,813	6,215	3,367	6,456	7,258	6,334	6,697
Gender disparity	1.06	1.42	1.23	1.13	1.10	1.19	1.34	4.81	1.78	1.27	1.07	1.21
Himachal Pradesh												
Person	10,867	11,910	10,382	9,024	10,521	10,985	11,298	13,718	12,222	9,604	12,332	11,024
Gender disparity	1.26	1.21	1.18	1.94	1.28	1.28	0.96	0.87	1.27	1.41	1.05	1.26
Punjab												
Person	6,941	6,812	6,766	5,972	6,105	4,823	5,303	7,432	7,841	6,986	6,184	6,692
Gender disparity	1.26	1.12	1.36	1.34	0.60	1.21	1.75	1.24	1.71	1.34	1.09	1.25
Upper Central												
Bihar												
Person	3,832	4,032	2,523	4,165	3,783	3,745	4,555	3,004	4,026	3,956	2,784	3,817
Gender disparity	0.78	0.72	0.39	0.96	0.74	0.72	0.88	1.07	0.68	0.71	1.37	0.75
Uttar Pradesh												
Person	3,317	3,774	3,835	3,365	3,284	3,415	4,297	3,179	3,619	3,407	3,338	3,523
Gender disparity	1.18	1.26	1.09	1.35	1.39	1.21	1.22	1.40	1.28	1.10	1.28	1.21
Lower Central												
Madhya Pradesh												
Person	4,679	5,019	4,657	4,973	4,496	4,801	4,155	7,342	4,590	4,827	5,729	4,801
Gender disparity	0.98	0.89	1.07	0.83	0.87	0.95	1.38	0.08	1.05	0.92	0.67	0.95
Orissa												
Person	4,885	5,554	3,835	6,692	4,547	4,801	8,925	8,989	5,348	4,731	5,005	5,010
Gender disparity	0.94	0.87	1.23	0.80	0.98	0.95	0.30	0.68	0.88	1.07	0.78	0.93
Rajasthan												
Person	3,349	2,199	2,717	4,951	3,303	3,162	2,692	5,909	3,140	3,270	2,774	3,150
Gender disparity	0.88	1.34	1.44	1.41	1.25	1.09	1.69	0.46	1.05	1.20	1.10	1.10
East												
North-eastern Rg.												
Person	2,776	3,085	4,159	1,918	2,726	3,215	3,228	770	2,376	3,510	2,734	3,076
Gender disparity	0.68	0.64	1.02	1.76	0.86	0.80	0.70	0.06	1.27	0.80	0.56	0.77
West Bengal												
Person	5,975	6,340	6,916	6,828	6,042	6,776	4,648	6,798	6,542	6,123	6,132	6,168
Gender disparity	0.89	0.99	1.22	1.47	0.99	0.98	0.90	0.80	0.79	0.99	0.97	0.96
West												
Gujarat												
Person	2,431	2,315	2,621	3,684	1,776	2,504	2,375	13,682	1,795	2,592	2,796	2,551
Gender disparity	0.64	0.85	0.82	0.93	0.92	0.76	0.46	1.55	0.83	0.57	0.96	0.74
Maharashtra												
Person	3,669	3,276	3,078	3,561	3,338	3,528	2,889	3,256	2,821	4,110	3,254	3,487
Gender disparity	0.92	1.34	0.98	1.14	0.98	1.00	1.38	1.68	0.62	1.07	1.10	1.05

(Contd.)

South

Andhra Pradesh

Person	6,917	8,584	8,482	8,307	6,681	7,605	8,382	8,594	9,989	6,715	7,572	7,684
Gender disparity	0.95	0.86	0.75	0.81	0.96	0.89	0.93	0.73	0.84	0.88	0.92	0.88

Karnataka

Person	1,060	1,264	1,074	1,111	898	1,099	1,116	3,117	900	1,149	1,107	1,119
Gender disparity	0.60	0.96	1.09	0.83	0.77	0.73	0.90	0.95	1.20	0.61	0.91	0.75

Kerala

Person	7,475	7,127	7,505	7,127	5,423	7,648	5,689	7,770	6,239	7,014	7,808	7,319
Gender disparity	1.04	1.37	1.46	0.90	1.33	1.25	1.11	1.07	1.15	1.23	1.13	1.17

Tamil Nadu

Person	6,291	7,464	7,849	6,481	6,142	6,700	9,354	7,163	3,738	5,149	7,400	6,775
Gender disparity	1.14	0.97	1.28	1.23	1.22	1.05	2.90	1.46	5.42	1.58	0.99	1.10

All India

Person	**4,466**	**4,790**	**4,529**	**4,572**	**4,147**	**4,503**	**4,441**	**6,171**	**4,301**	**4,466**	**5,002**	**4,577**
Gender disparity	**0.97**	**1.00**	**1.06**	**1.12**	**1.02**	**0.99**	**1.01**	**1.13**	**1.01**	**0.99**	**1.01**	**1.00**
C.V. Person	46.9	50.3	49.1	40.6	48.1	48.9	52.0	55.2	57.5	41.3	52.4	46.5

Prevalence Rate (Per Lakh Population) among Age Group 15–34 Years of Major Morbidity by States

Regions/States	Household Income Groups (Rs per year)				Social Groups				Village Development Groups			All Groups
	Up to 20,000	20,001–40,000	40,001–62,000	Above 62,000	STs and SCs	Hindus	Muslims	Other Minorities	Low	Medium	High	
North												
Haryana												
Person	4,412	3,223	3,258	1,320	3,068	3,095	3,138	1,124	3,167	3,502	2,705	3,052
Gender disparity	1.27	4.56	1.43	1.64	2.49	2.01	1.17	–	5.20	2.68	1.25	1.98
Himachal Pradesh												
Person	7,819	8,093	7,705	2,941	7,537	3,095	5,845	5,311	8,840	5,736	9,630	7,555
Gender disparity	1.37	0.94	1.23	1.14	1.05	1.13	2.91	–	1.08	1.68	0.94	1.18
Punjab												
Person	2,828	4,275	3,139	2,064	1,888	2,060	5,150	3,549	5,054	3,012	3,117	3,168
Gender disparity	1.31	1.66	1.88	1.42	0.18	2.05	4.14	1.40	0.93	2.15	1.21	1.55
Upper Central												
Bihar												
Person	2,857	2,549	128	1,942	1,930	2,371	2,866	2,879	2,295	2,595	2,490	2,452
Gender disparity	1.18	1.10	1.45	2.28	1.11	1.12	1.52	2.76	1.47	0.91	1.97	1.22
Uttar Pradesh												
Person	2,004	2,920	2,946	2,892	2,281	2,517	2,351	–	2,822	2,342	720	2,489
Gender Disparity	2.48	1.88	2.19	4.94	2.60	1.13	2.64	–	2.27	2.46	21.39	2.39
Lower Central												
Madhya Pradesh												
Person	2,309	2,927	2,138	2,463	2,352	2,449	2,149	8,956	2,588	2,149	2,968	2,479
Gender Disparity	1.24	0.79	0.97	0.72	0.77	1.02	1.77	–	1.08	0.94	0.76	0.99
Orissa												
Person	2,829	3,520	2,661	4,031	3,313	2,947	5,936	4,219	3,534	2,700	2,765	3,012
Gender Disparity	1.22	0.71	2.15	0.45	1.21	1.03	0.93	1.14	0.88	1.20	1.11	1.04
Rajasthan												
Person	1,732	1,613	2,365	3,761	1,917	1,851	5,402	–	2,306	1,871	847	2,026
Gender Disparity	0.82	1.45	2.64	2.74	1.34	1.25	3.42	–	1.15	1.80	9.37	1.42
East												
North-eastern Rg.												
Person	1,373	1,942	2,585	–	1,755	1,521	2,815	681	2,924	1,616	1,296	1,706
Gender Disparity	0.78	0.84	1.52	–	0.91	1.08	0.84	–	2.31	0.95	0.39	0.96
West Bengal												
Person	3,552	4,404	4,342	3,267	4,803	4,058	3,585	402	5,074	3.37	3,753	3,821
Gender Disparity	0.95	1.50	6.07	1.34	1.31	1.30	1.15	–	1.00	1.56	1.06	1.25
West												
Gujarat												
Person	1,165	1,028	547	865	1,060	3,095	328	1,996	1,104	954	1,059	1,017
Gender disparity	2.22	0.49	7.34	1.01	1.79	2.01	–	–	1.52	0.98	1.96	1.39
Maharashtra												
Person	2,591	945	1,694	1,735	1,923	1,883	234	3,132	1,125	2,250	1,855	1,917
Gender disparity	0.84	1.05	0.60	1.13	0.70	0.81	–	1.67	0.27	1.14	0.83	0.89

(Contd.)

South

Andhra Pradesh												
Person	3,947	3,952	1,111	3,456	3,152	3,446	6,615	2,244	4,872	2,714	3,889	3,600
Gender disparity	1.10	1.13	0.58	0.69	1.02	1.02	1.32	–	1.02	1.18	0.99	1.07
Karnataka												
Person	445	293	183	175	393	3,826	–	–	915	358	276	345
Gender disparity	0.10	0.96	–	–	–	0.21	–	–	0.90	0.11	0.20	0.21
Kerala												
Person	3,681	2,536	1,008	566	2,340	3,269	1,051	2,189	1,594	2,562	2,891	2,610
Gender disparity	0.98	2.94	1.12	1.63	3.04	1.71	1.20	1.16	4.43	2.10	1.06	1.51
Tamil Nadu												
Person	3,330	4,188	4,311	2,567	4,357	3,468	–	7,299	–	4,604	3,303	3,611
Gender disparity	0.81	0.85	7.23	0.19	0.86	0.82	–	1.72	–	1.38	0.72	0.89
All India												
Person	**2,622**	**2,781**	**2,171**	**2,187**	**2,573**	**2,809**	**2,740**	**3,075**	**2,811**	**2,454**	**2,520**	**2,578**
Gender disparity	**1.16**	**1.25**	**1.92**	**1.45**	**1.19**	**–**	**1.44**	**1.47**	**1.45**	**1.39**	**1.00**	**1.27**
C.V. Person	55.8	59.0	73.8	57.7	59.5	25.7	74.6	93.2	69.4	47.4	76.7	54.5

Prevalence Rate (Per Lakh Population) among Age Group 35–59 Years of Major Morbidity by States

Regions/States	Household Income Groups (Rs per year)				Social Groups				Village Development Groups			All
	Up to 20,000	20,001–40,000	40,001–62,000	Above 62,000	STs and SCs	Hindus	Muslims	Other Minorities	Low	Medium	High	Groups
North												
Haryana												
Person	11,533	12,835	10,997	8,425	13,932	11,332	12,032	4,665	11,181	13,763	9,360	11,179
Gender disparity	1.25	1.21	1.50	1.72	1.30	1.35	1.07	0.98	1.32	1.78	1.00	1.33
Himachal Pradesh												
Person	16,918	17,296	15,858	20,988	17,123	11,332	21,913	21,372	18,965	15,650	17,796	17,141
Gender disparity	1.33	1.92	1.42	4.15	2.21	0.76	0.68	1.47	1.81	1.58	1.43	1.62
Punjab												
Person	14,110	13,157	9,542	12,991	13,033	10,339	7,183	14,015	12,857	12,899	12,721	12,826
Gender disparity	1.57	1.94	3.77	1.21	1.15	1.54	0.95	1.82	2.33	1.68	1.74	1.73
Upper Central												
Bihar												
Person	6,856	5,923	6,345	9,157	6,561	6,537	8,320	3,249	7,638	6,533	4,068	6,623
Gender disparity	0.73	0.98	0.29	0.90	0.88	0.80	0.63	0.53	0.66	0.79	1.34	0.76
Uttar Pradesh												
Person	6,639	7,421	6,914	5,098	7,064	6,484	8,652	–	6,755	6,308	8,528	6,733
Gender disparity	1.40	1.26	1.12	0.90	1.40	0.76	1.42	–	1.28	1.13	1.71	1.26
Lower Central												
Madhya Pradesh												
Person	8,691	9,221	8,005	7,433	9,341	8,651	6,844	12,181	8,126	8,603	11,051	8,639
Gender disparity	1.10	1.13	1.12	1.22	1.01	1.13	3.15	–	1.18	1.23	0.78	1.12
Orissa												
Person	8,192	7,724	6,430	8,765	7,674	8,024	10,040	5,056	9,535	7,134	7,357	7,980
Gender disparity	1.06	1.31	2.55	0.63	1.13	1.16	–	2.10	1.20	1.15	1.07	1.14
Rajasthan												
Person	5,828	2,739	4,516	8,503	6,525	5,270	2,922	–	4,628	5,825	5,620	5,129
Gender disparity	1.49	1.44	2.27	1.08	1.85	1.46	1.25	–	1.58	1.41	1.07	1.45
East												
North-eastern Rg.												
Person	5,640	5,018	7,954	4,271	5,662	5,973	5,563	2,314	4,466	6,510	5,104	5,726
Gender disparity	1.29	0.47	1.21	7.46	0.93	1.15	0.64	0.31	0.88	1.21	0.85	1.04
West Bengal												
Person	11,717	11,512	9,737	14,499	11,887	12,394	8,921	16,677	14,265	11,289	11,537	11,666
Gender disparity	1.07	1.00	1.83	2.88	0.91	1.10	1.49	0.78	1.42	1.09	1.15	1.15
West												
Gujarat												
Person	3,734	5,487	4,044	5,473	2,796	11,332	4,229	31,601	2,409	5,091	4,329	4,439
Gender disparity	0.53	0.95	0.64	1.36	0.94	1.35	0.49	1.94	0.43	0.66	0.99	0.75
Maharashtra												
Person	5,844	5,998	5,757	5,754	5,442	5,841	5,125	6,507	5,733	7,207	5,180	5,863
Gender disparity	1.03	1.40	1.40	1.90	1.04	1.18	5.61	1.57	0.63	1.21	1.43	1.25

(Contd.)

South

Andhra Pradesh												
Person	11,718	15,748	17,705	12,337	12,029	13,418	16,332	16,284	16,328	12,731	13,486	13,690
Gender disparity	1.21	1.00	0.78	0.96	1.37	1.02	1.40	1.31	1.31	1.10	0.90	1.06
Karnataka												
Person	1,913	1,643	1,677	1,697	1,568	1,807	1,910	–	1,624	2,051	1,543	1,800
Gender disparity	0.61	0.65	0.25	1.07	0.79	0.63	0.47	–	2.29	0.59	0.57	0.61
Kerala												
Person	9,250	9,442	11,470	5,882	9,925	9,928	10,276	7,040	7,782	9,983	9,002	9,257
Gender disparity	1.40	1.29	2.82	1.02	1.41	1.43	1.47	1.53	1.68	1.51	1.35	1.45
Tamil Nadu												
Person	9,581	11,219	8,907	9,862	7,351	9,929	23,066	5,462	13,624	6,061	11,270	9,992
Gender disparity	1.91	1.20	1.40	1.92	1.68	1.53	1.36	9.20	16.68	1.65	1.52	1.61
All India												
Person	**7,815**	**8,261**	**7,977**	**7,496**	**7,625**	**8,661**	**8,484**	**9,512**	**7,716**	**7,796**	**8,316**	**7,933**
Gender disparity	**1.15**	**1.15**	**1.17**	**1.31**	**1.17**	**–**	**1.23**	**1.59**	**1.15**	**1.14**	**1.21**	**1.17**
C.V. Person	43.8	48.8	47.3	51.3	46.8	35.0	62.3	94.2	53.4	41.9	47.7	44.1

Prevalence Rate (Per Lakh Population) among Age Group 60 and Above of Major Morbidity by States

Regions/States	Household Income Groups (Rs per year)				Social Groups				Village Development Groups			All Groups
	Up to 20,000	20,001– 40,000	40,001– 62,000	Above 62,000	STs and SCs	Hindus	Muslims	Other Minorities	Low	Medium	High	
North												
Haryana												
Person	43,746	32,729	31,969	36,747	37,840	36,566	39,708	24,079	44,992	36,030	35,617	36,590
Gender disparity	0.86	1.25	1.21	1.07	0.96	1.04	1.49	–	1.74	1.03	1.00	1.07
Himachal Pradesh												
Person	32,981	39,218	31,162	28,077	31,810	36,566	49,340	70,216	35,572	31,415	39,198	34,365
Gender disparity	1.48	0.98	1.29	1.25	0.95	0.68	1.73	0.35	1.32	1.36	0.96	1.24
Punjab												
Person	29,609	20,861	34,262	19,668	32,250	19,593	19,277	27,179	33,478	29,903	19,790	25,502
Gender disparity	1.11	0.54	1.04	1.76	0.52	0.63	2.03	1.07	1.02	1.04	0.93	0.99
Upper Central												
Bihar												
Person	18,944	25,744	15,660	20,697	20,976	20,063	30,685	21,614	21,915	21,742	17,853	21,236
Gender disparity	1.05	0.65	0.71	1.11	0.83	0.73	1.08	3.80	0.72	0.86	1.35	0.84
Uttar Pradesh												
Person	14,007	14,026	14,741	13,218	14,151	13,035	21,092	23,355	13,908	14,069	14,477	14,009
Gender disparity	0.71	0.93	0.91	0.89	0.97	0.68	0.93	1.00	0.90	0.78	0.51	0.82
Lower Central												
Madhya Pradesh												
Person	26,965	25,394	31,258	32,591	25,745	27,719	29,592	9,081	26,911	27,579	31,486	27,627
Gender disparity	0.97	0.70	0.91	0.65	0.93	0.83	0.75	–	1.02	0.69	0.59	0.83
Orissa												
Person	20,627	18,766	18,100	17,195	16,595	19,230	22,513	48,413	21,067	18,041	21,690	19,832
Gender disparity	0.91	0.70	0.64	1.10	0.89	0.89	0.77	0.36	0.80	0.93	0.81	0.85
Rajasthan												
Person	14,292	10,747	7,784	10,444	15,322	12,150	2,592	59,561	12,132	12,369	9,984	11,998
Gender disparity	0.76	1.10	0.57	0.86	0.96	0.85	–	0.32	0.83	0.81	0.87	0.83
East												
North-eastern Rg.												
Person	23,689	21,196	27,499	28,604	20,864	24,562	22,295	7,319	11,076	28,269	21,153	23,817
Gender disparity	0.55	0.70	1.06	1.46	1.24	0.79	0.68	–	3.15	0.60	0.86	0.75
West Bengal												
Person	32,377	34,383	39,951	38,871	28,484	34,210	29,738	71,334	37,406	32,982	33,651	33,748
Gender disparity	0.91	0.94	0.43	1.23	1.56	1.03	0.42	0.74	0.49	0.75	1.16	0.87
West												
Gujarat												
Person	14,734	6,553	18,408	18,811	10,091	36,566	15,987	18,937	7,542	12,486	16,355	13,253
Gender disparity	0.45	0.77	0.37	0.68	0.77	1.04	0.47	–	0.65	0.41	0.57	0.51
Maharashtra												
Person	17,610	18,257	12,476	16,622	15,526	17,460	27,429	7,646	12,205	18,665	16,840	17,089
Gender disparity	0.82	1.34	0.88	0.81	1.18	0.94	0.71	1.57	0.77	1.01	0.94	0.94

(Contd.)

South

Andhra Pradesh												
Person	33,504	32,290	48,053	37,481	31,682	35,614	15,319	44,627	48,040	29,842	33,039	34,577
Gender disparity	1.01	0.76	0.85	0.80	0.86	0.91	1.20	0.30	0.86	0.74	1.18	0.91
Karnataka												
Person	5,516	7,306	8,147	8,052	4,175	6,072	8,282	27,959	4,539	6,211	7,116	6,564
Gender disparity	0.93	0.89	3.08	0.93	1.09	1.04	1.20	1.20	0.76	0.98	1.18	1.06
Kerala												
Person	32,422	34,419	37,137	36,637	20,229	31,747	42,403	36,012	38,038	30,808	36,202	34,194
Gender disparity	0.79	1.35	0.90	0.93	1.00	0.95	1.10	1.02	1.19	0.93	1.00	0.99
Tamil Nadu												
Person	34,509	38,720	43,750	28,244	35,602	36,648	23,568	32,522	2,530	25,846	40,118	36,048
Gender disparity	1.08	0.90	1.30	2.78	1.06	1.07	16.75	0.96	–	1.49	1.02	1.08
All India												
Person	**22,133**	**22,582**	**23,315**	**21,439**	**20,357**	**25,488**	**24,362**	**29,366**	**20,045**	**21,459**	**25,458**	**22,317**
Gender disparity	**0.90**	**0.86**	**0.90**	**0.95**	**1.00**	**–**	**0.89**	**0.959**	**0.86**	**0.83**	**0.98**	**0.89**
C.V. Person	39.7	44.0	47.3	40.3	41.8	40.4	47.1	60.3	61.8	36.5	42.4	39.3

Per Person Household Expenditure on Treatment of Illness and Gender Disparity by Population Groups

Population Groups	Cost of Short Illness		Cost of Long Illness		Per Sick Person	Per Reporting
	Fees and Medicines	Proportion of Total Cost	Fees and Medicines	Proportion of Total Cost		
Household Income Groups						
Upto 20,000	116	0.74	44	0.63	997	1,150
20,001–40,000	129	0.74	52	0.66	1,092	1,229
40,001–62,000	108	0.73	51	0.69	1,141	1,285
62,001–86,000	152	0.85	56	0.61	1,196	1,332
Above 86,000	112	0.71	62	0.67	1,424	1,552
Poverty Line Groups						
Lower segment below	107	0.75	43	0.65	1,030	1,161
Upper segment below	123	0.74	51	0.62	1,220	1,383
Lower segment above	124	0.75	46	0.65	1,006	1,149
Upper segment above	122	0.73	57	0.65	1,104	1,253
Landholding Groups						
Landless wage earner	112	0.73	44	0.56	972	1,180
Marginal	119	0.76	52	0.68	1,123	1,254
Small	111	0.71	46	0.65	1,041	1,154
Medium	120	0.76	45	0.65	1,166	1,340
Large	120	0.75	47	0.65	1,065	1,203
Landless others	146	0.76	53	0.64	1,059	1,195
Landowners	117	0.74	49	0.67	1,099	1,231
Landless	129	0.75	48	0.60	1,016	1,188
Occupational Groups						
Cultivators	118	0.73	46	0.67	1,044	1,175
Salaried+Prof.+S.Empl.	146	0.81	55	0.62	1,235	1,365
Wage earners	113	0.73	46	0.61	984	1,175
All others	118	0.75	56	0.69	1,138	1,266
Social Groups						
Caste						
STs	96	0.69	22	0.65	655	778
SCs	119	0.73	43	0.68	963	1,094
Religion						
Hindus	118	0.74	46	0.64	1,037	1,190
Muslims	116	0.74	57	0.67	1,287	1,378
Christians	179	0.76	73	0.70	1,084	1,191
Other Minorities	163	0.89	72	0.70	1,260	1,403
Household Size Groups						
Up to 4	126	0.73	52	0.62	896	1,052
5–7	123	0.73	46	0.64	1,062	1,203
8 and above	114	0.78	50	0.67	1,236	1,372
Adult Literacy Groups						
None literate	109	0.72	41	0.65	946	1,114

(Contd.)

Female literate	113	0.73	59	0.72	1,123	1,301
Male literate	128	0.74	45	0.59	1,084	1,215
Both literate	122	0.76	55	0.67	1,129	1,269
Village Development Groups						
Low	126	0.74	46	0.66	1,079	1,227
Medium	116	0.74	49	0.63	1,097	1,237
High	120	0.74	51	0.64	1,033	1,184
Age Groups (years)						
0–4	196	0.77	10	0.71	1,038	1,205
5–14	103	0.77	11	0.58	1,005	1,113
15–34	83	0.74	30	0.60	1,187	1,333
35–59	139	0.73	85	0.63	1,080	1,223
60 & Above	168	0.68	225	0.70	1,010	1,164
All India						
Person	**121**	**0.75**	**49**	**0.65**	**1,071**	**1,217**
Gender disparity	**0.95**	–	**0.93**	–	**0.92**	**0.93**

Incidence of Disabilities among Children in Age Group 0–12 Years and Gender Disparity by States

Regions/States	Bitot Spot		Night Blindness		Visual		Hearing		Speech		Locomotor		Total	
	0–4	5–12	0–4	5–12	0–4	5–12	0–4	5–12	0–4	5–12	0–4	5–12	0–4	5–12
North														
Haryana	492	461	440	85	891	273	170	121	312	297	516	879	1,322	1,396
Himachal Pradesh	1,829	6,800	551	732	2,118	2,674	147	1,712	1,088	1,454	277	809	2,930	4,670
Punjab	79	–	109	50	437	539	138	340	727	765	711	2,022	1,557	3,565
Upper Central														
Bihar	355	967	477	408	589	595	406	941	2,192	429	581	539	3,577	2,059
Uttar Pradesh	734	1,055	397	1,169	915	1,181	128	190	596	404	335	411	1,771	2,004
Lower Central														
Madhya Pradesh	2,456	3,510	1,709	2,570	984	1,626	190	303	303	434	562	921	1,857	3,040
Orissa	267	627	589	1351	257	599	270	859	350	520	114	468	820	2,146
Rajasthan	2,248	7,579	1,103	4,206	1,217	1,918	56	281	175	866	820	1,034	2,092	3,711
East														
North-eastern Rg.	883	874	927	786	1,725	1,165	353	409	546	280	465	140	2,418	1,816
West Bengal	1,222	2,678	108	2,299	393	2,015	1,128	3,474	1,163	1,219	730	1,075	325	6,779
West														
Gujarat	1,509	1,920	236	100	332	682	–	100	80	250	132	544	545	1,576
Maharashtra	1,722	2,648	310	1,262	817	1,397	270	742	325	966	478	605	1,592	3,278
South														
Andhra Pradesh	1,790	992	24	551	1,081	1,032	95	821	408	727	1,074	1,122	2,244	3,134
Karnataka	703	1,037	698	642	761	590	666	629	824	1,040	517	570	1,680	1,964
Kerala	34	–	34	200	–	467	34	567	423	701	105	757	494	1,697
Tamil Nadu	1,455	5,297	179	890	89	1,481	64	672	503	1,808	831	1,839	1,088	4,519
All India														
Person	1,136	2,090	532	1,273	782	1,160	279	763	735	678	536	751	2,042	2,896
Gender disparity	0.91	0.95	1.01	1.07	0.92	1.09	1.05	0.87	0.74	0.74	0.74	0.73	0.87	0.86

Incidence of Disabilities among Children in Age Group 0–12 years and Gender Disparity by Population Groups

Population Groups	Bitot Spot		Night Blindness		Visual		Disabilities Hearing		Speech		Locomotor		Total	
	0–4	5–12	0–4	5–12	0–4	5–12	0–4	5–12	0–4	5–12	0–4	5–12	0–4	5–12
Household Income Groups														
Upto 20,000	1,129	2,460	550	1,523	665	1,289	298	922	673	734	538	839	1,946	3,211
20,001–40,000	1,223	1,992	469	1,140	868	1,182	274	639	945	563	525	669	2,332	2,688
40,001–62,000	1,290	1,363	717	729	1,092	832	255	530	355	268	732	544	2,021	1,974
62,001–86,000	1,043	793	419	851	717	1,060	203	496	967	1,807	440	1,021	1,598	3,955
Above 86,000	430	725	394	502	978	162	206	295	829	615	220	382	1,841	1,293
Poverty Line Groups														
Lower segment below	1,280	3,038	626	1,774	760	1,199	282	859	479	653	521	690	1,836	2,861
Upper segment below	1,160	2,302	477	1,281	681	1,403	348	1,010	815	731	665	945	2,258	3,521
Lower segment above	1,187	1,907	435	1,170	717	1,093	244	660	887	728	499	720	2,045	2,823
Upper segment above	751	860	751	801	1,151	916	264	531	566	493	461	632	2,000	2,195
Landholding Groups														
Landless wage earner	1,252	2,439	488	1,013	627	1,187	136	1,030	935	1,064	646	1,014	2,014	3,530
Marginal	805	2,121	476	1,486	621	1,203	374	978	434	655	388	553	1,636	2,875
Small	1,450	2,126	731	1,510	1,058	1,174	359	630	1,032	393	508	609	2,559	2,518
Medium	1,303	1,886	482	1,187	679	1,070	167	469	774	509	513	655	2,089	2,312
Large	1,254	1,436	488	841	693	1,000	113	172	628	1,057	356	832	1,364	2,845
Landless others	1,139	1,994	512	1,083	1,057	1,149	298	637	777	596	821	1,046	2,522	3,080
Landowners	1,104	2,022	549	1,387	758	1,156	312	724	671	596	437	611	1,933	2,686
Landless	1,199	2,225	500	1,046	830	1,168	212	841	860	839	729	1,029	2,253	3,314
Occupational Groups														
Cultivators	1,121	2,170	544	1,348	686	1,143	296	686	806	570	455	689	1,996	2,735
Salaried+Prof.+S.Empl	968	1,658	307	621	913	733	188	537	339	515	352	791	1,509	2,196
Wage earners	1,219	2,382	575	1,295	599	1,114	263	1,049	698	996	553	908	1,850	3,301
All others	1,181	1,779	611	1,547	1,212	1,611	328	727	-914	626	863	657	2,866	3,285
Social Groups														
Caste														
STs	2,153	2,277	1,028	1,668	890	1,063	158	576	725	413	307	746	1,881	2,406
SCs	1,084	2,757	552	1,497	638	1,088	385	1,272	843	693	564	803	2,058	3,325

(Contd.)

Religion														
Hindus	1,195	2,112	566	1,283	796	1,119	264	689	717	663	508	737	1,983	2,771
Muslims	1,067	2,312	167	1,409	571	1,435	324	1,328	944	823	781	830	2,409	3,792
Christians	108	944	2,064	674	2064	1,612	295	590	52	559	351	298	2,711	2,200
Other Minorities	307	1,111	154	700	492	972	501	764	785	573	451	1,153	1,831	3,386
Household Size Groups														
Up to 4	969	1,996	571	1,181	993	1,381	233	965	417	825	649	1,053	2,005	3,410
5–7	1,138	2,155	547	1,312	729	1,171	274	911	936	726	468	755	2,125	3,070
8 and above	1,200	2,015	499	1,239	764	1,069	303	456	615	550	574	646	1,953	2,444
Adult Literacy Groups														
None literate	1,158	2,376	591	1,317	694	1,041	219	883	499	784	525	876	1,844	3,036
Female literate	772	2,029	860	2,108	1,165	1,447	329	1,596	267	720	280	357	1,547	3,049
Male literate	1,235	2,239	485	1,315	846	1,166	309	618	826	661	463	876	2,125	2,831
Both literate	1,051	1,671	506	1,116	775	1,240	298	735	878	593	627	535	2,160	2,823
Village Development Groups														
Low	1,179	2,207	621	1,451	783	1,111	287	510	856	633	515	672	2,199	2,541
Medium	1,200	2,008	483	1,214	811	1,188	224	788	682	625	574	765	2129	2,877
High	991	2,071	496	1,146	738	1,177	348	1,030	665	808	505	826	1,720	3,349
All India														
Person	**1,136**	**2,090**	**532**	**1,273**	**782**	**1,160**	**279**	**763**	**735**	**678**	**536**	**751**	**2,042**	**2,896**
Gender disparity	**0.91**	**0.95**	**1.01**	**1.07**	**0.92**	**1.09**	**1.05**	**0.87**	**0.74**	**0.74**	**0.74**	**0.73**	**0.87**	**0.86**

Crude Birth Rates (Per Thousand Population) by States

Regions/States	Household Income Groups (Rs per year)				Social Groups				Village Development Groups			All Groups
	Up to 20,000	20,001– 40,000	40,001– 62,000	Above 62,000	STs and SCs	Hindus	Muslims	Other Minorities	Low	Medium	High	
North												
Haryana	34	30	25	30	36	31	35	13	29	27	33	30
Himachal Pradesh	20	26	22	24	21	22	39	12	21	26	17	22
Punjab	24	22	21	19	27	20	35	23	22	22	22	22
Upper Central												
Bihar	40	33	32	41	40	37	39	46	36	38	39	37
Uttar Pradesh	39	34	41	36	41	37	41	28	40	36	29	38
Lower Central												
Madhya Pradesh	32	33	33	32	33	32	34	15	33	31	30	32
Orissa	30	28	26	18	32	29	46	30	32	25	30	29
Rajasthan	42	49	44	40	47	44	45	46	46	40	42	44
East												
North-eastern Rg.	42	28	35	23	44	35	36	26	45	39	22	34
West Bengal	36	33	29	34	31	29	50	6	41	34	34	34
West												
Gujarat	29	27	30	32	33	29	28	–	27	28	30	29
Maharashtra	30	25	22	31	32	28	28	29	32	28	27	28
South												
Andhra Pradesh	27	28	20	23	25	26	28	32	31	25	25	26
Karnataka	19	19	16	18	20	18	26	21	18	18	19	19
Kerala	19	18	26	33	27	19	31	18	19	20	22	21
Tamil Nadu	31	26	21	22	28	29	34	12	54	25	28	28
All India	**33**	**30**	**31**	**31**	**35**	**32**	**39**	**24**	**37**	**31**	**28**	**32**
C.V.	23.8	23.5	26.9	25.3	23.0	23.8	18.4	55.4	30.1	22.1	22.9	21.9

Total Fertility Rates for Ever Married Women by States

Regions/States	Household Income Groups (Rs per year)				Social Groups				Village Development Groups			All Groups
	Up to 20,000	20,001–40,000	40,001–62,000	Above 62,000	STs and SCs	Hindus	Muslims	Other Minorities	Low	Medium	High	
North												
Haryana	5.2	4.4	3.1	3.3	5.3	4.1	7.2	1.7	3.8	3.8	4.6	4.2
Himachal Pradesh	2.5	3.3	2.4	2.4	2.7	2.7	4.3	1.0	2.7	3.0	2.1	2.7
Punjab	3.6	3.5	2.4	2.3	4.5	3.0	3.8	3.1	3.5	3.2	2.9	3.1
Upper Central												
Bihar	5.7	4.8	4.2	6.4	5.4	5.1	6.0	6.0	5.0	5.5	5.8	5.3
Uttar Pradesh	6.1	5.5	6.5	5.3	6.1	5.7	7.0	5.0	6.2	5.7	4.7	5.9
Lower Central												
Madhya Pradesh	4.3	4.5	4.1	3.7	4.5	4.3	4.8	1.7	4.5	4.1	3.9	4.3
Orissa	3.9	3.5	3.4	1.8	4.2	3.6	6.1	3.7	4.1	3.2	3.7	3.7
Rajasthan	6.7	7.3	6.4	5.8	7.3	6.7	7.0	7.6	7.1	6.3	6.7	6.8
East												
North-eastern Rg.	5.0	3.2	3.8	2.9	4.8	3.9	4.5	1.9	5.7	4.4	2.4	3.9
West Bengal	4.4	4.1	3.5	4.5	3.6	3.4	7.0	1.3	6.2	4.2	4.0	4.3
West												
Gujarat	3.8	3.3	3.5	3.6	4.0	3.7	3.8	2.1	3.7	3.6	3.8	3.7
Maharashtra	4.1	3.2	2.5	3.9	4.6	3.6	3.8	4.1	4.4	3.9	3.4	3.7
South												
Andhra Pradesh	3.3	3.2	2.1	2.6	2.9	3.0	4.9	3.7	3.8	3.1	2.9	3.1
Karnataka	2.5	2.6	2.1	2.2	2.6	2.3	3.9	5.9	2.5	2.4	2.4	2.4
Kerala	2.1	1.9	3.0	3.2	2.6	1.9	3.5	2.1	2.2	2.2	2.3	2.2
Tamil Nadu	3.2	3.1	2.2	2.5	3.1	3.1	3.1	1.2	13.1	2.7	3.0	3.0
All India	**4.5**	**4.1**	**4.0**	**4.0**	**4.6**	**4.2**	**5.8**	**3.1**	**5.3**	**4.2**	**3.4**	**4.3**
C.V.	31.2	32.2	38.2	36.8	30.7	32.0	27.8	66.5	51.1	29.7	33.8	30.9

Average Children Ever Born to Ever Married Women by States

Regions/States	Household Income Groups				Social Groups				Village Development Groups			All Groups
	Up to 20,000	20,001– 40,000	40,001– 62,000	Above 62,000	STs and SCs	Hindus	Muslims	Other Minorities	Low	Medium	High	
North												
Haryana	3.2	3.1	2.8	2.6	3.2	2.4	3.8	3.1	3.1	3.0	2.9	3.0
Himachal Pradesh	3.0	2.8	2.7	2.5	2.8	2.8	3.1	3.7	2.9	2.8	2.9	2.8
Punjab	3.3	3.1	2.3	2.5	3.3	3.0	2.9	2.9	3.2	3.0	2.8	3.0
Upper Central												
Bihar	3.0	3.0	3.1	3.2	2.9	2.9	3.5	3.2	3.0	2.9	3.2	3.0
Uttar Pradesh	3.2	3.2	2.9	2.9	3.2	3.1	3.5	4.3	3.1	3.1	3.4	3.1
Lower Central												
Madhya Pradesh	3.1	2.9	2.7	2.7	3.0	2.9	3.2	3.0	2.9	2.9	2.8	2.9
Orissa	2.9	3.1	2.7	2.2	2.8	2.9	3.4	2.9	2.9	2.9	3.0	2.9
Rajasthan	3.3	2.8	2.9	2.7	3.2	3.0	3.1	3.8	3.0	3.1	3.1	3.0
East												
North-eastern Rg.	2.9	2.7	2.8	2.3	2.8	2.7	3.1	2.0	3.2	2.8	2.6	2.8
West Bengal	3.1	3.0	2.8	3.0	3.1	2.9	3.6	3.1	3.3	3.0	3.1	3.1
West												
Gujarat	2.7	2.7	2.8	2.5	2.8	2.7	3.1	2.1	2.9	2.7	2.6	2.7
Maharashtra	3.0	2.8	2.7	2.7	3.2	2.9	3.3	3.0	3.0	3.0	2.8	2.9
South												
Andhra Pradesh	2.6	2.4	2.4	2.4	2.5	2.5	3.2	2.5	2.4	2.6	2.4	2.5
Karnataka	2.8	3.0	3.0	2.6	2.9	2.8	3.2	3.5	3.1	2.9	2.8	2.8
Kerala	2.3	2.3	2.3	1.8	2.3	2.1	2.7	2.1	2.3	2.4	2.2	2.3
Tamil Nadu	2.5	2.7	2.0	2.2	2.5	2.5	2.9	2.5	3.0	2.5	2.5	2.5
All India	**3.0**	**2.9**	**2.7**	**2.7**	**2.9**	**2.8**	**3.4**	**2.7**	**3.0**	**2.9**	**2.8**	**2.9**
C.V.	9.6	8.7	10.5	12.7	9.5	9.2	8.5	21.2	8.7	7.5	11.0	8.1

Age-Specific Fertility Rates by States

| Regions/States | Age in Completed Years | | | | | | | TFR |
	15–19	20–24	25–29	30–34	35–39	40–44	45–49	15–49
North								
Haryana	0.0691	0.3080	0.2733	0.0929	0.0497	0.0316	0.0136	4.2
Himachal Pradesh	0.0301	0.2113	0.1822	0.0776	0.0349	–	0.0101	2.7
Punjab	0.0163	0.2052	0.2577	0.0880	0.0262	0.0142	0.0125	3.1
Upper Central								
Bihar	0.1022	0.3279	0.2773	0.2048	0.0742	0.0364	0.0343	5.3
Uttar Pradesh	0.0686	0.3221	0.3003	0.2335	0.1671	0.0587	0.0279	5.9
Lower Central								
Madhya Pradesh	0.0603	0.2982	0.2405	0.1510	0.0699	0.0248	0.0106	4.3
Orissa	0.0280	0.1957	0.2649	0.1261	0.0922	0.0153	0.0091	3.7
Rajasthan	0.0823	0.3812	0.3274	0.2710	0.1759	0.0574	0.0592	6.8
East								
North-eastern Rg.	0.0317	0.1728	0.2938	0.1680	0.0622	0.0193	0.0414	3.9
West Bengal	0.1085	0.3006	0.2229	0.1109	0.0747	0.0217	0.0174	4.3
West								
Gujarat	0.0141	0.2479	0.2905	0.1089	0.0374	0.0296	0.0034	3.6
Maharashtra	0.0592	0.2951	0.2129	0.0877	0.0453	0.0211	0.0120	3.7
South								
Andhra Pradesh	0.1084	0.2216	0.1746	0.0593	0.0507	0.0027	0.0098	3.1
Karnataka	0.0416	0.1678	0.1362	0.0819	0.0335	0.0110	0.0099	2.4
Kerala	0.0115	0.1669	0.1630	0.0762	0.0188	0.0106	–	2.2
Tamil Nadu	0.0299	0.2310	0.2245	0.0647	0.0423	0.0025	0.0028	3.0
All India	**0.0645**	**0.2714**	**0.2446**	**0.1456**	**0.0820**	**0.0282**	**0.0181**	**4.3**
C.V.	60.2	25.3	22.3	49.2	67.1	75.7	89.8	30.9

Age-Specific Fertility Rates by Population Groups

Population Groups	Age in Completed Years							TFR
	15–19	20–24	25–29	30–34	35–39	40–44	45–49	15–49
Household Income Groups								
Upto 20,000	0.0745	0.3124	0.2680	0.1627	0.1021	0.0381	0.0249	4.9
20,001–40,000	0.0567	0.2496	0.2233	0.1395	0.0671	0.0143	0.0047	3.8
40,001–62,000	0.0686	0.2012	0.2357	0.0942	0.0426	0.0329	0.0317	3.5
62,001–86,000	0.0372	0.2437	0.1764	0.1290	0.0430	0.0053	0.0069	3.2
Above 86,000	0.0377	0.2237	0.1872	0.0985	0.0566	0.0301	0.0057	3.2
Poverty Line Groups								
Lower segment below	0.0792	0.3652	0.3614	0.2170	0.1609	0.0582	0.0405	6.4
Upper segment below	0.0693	0.3648	0.2880	0.1858	0.1132	0.0471	0.0341	5.5
Lower segment above	0.0679	0.2354	0.2073	0.1187	0.0595	0.0188	0.0108	3.6
Upper segment above	0.0414	0.1967	0.1681	0.0873	0.0332	0.0131	0.0073	2.7
Landholding Groups								
Landless wage earner	0.0961	0.2930	0.2395	0.1314	0.0692	0.0283	0.0203	4.4
Marginal	0.0644	0.2626	0.2530	0.1525	0.1077	0.0292	0.0121	4.5
Small	0.0557	0.2509	0.2487	0.1598	0.0730	0.0303	0.0158	4.2
Medium	0.0607	0.2801	0.2385	0.1564	0.0769	0.0223	0.0210	4.3
Large	0.0510	0.2955	0.2384	0.1448	0.0670	0.0307	0.0087	4.2
Landless others	0.0540	0.2725	0.2364	0.1274	0.0670	0.0269	0.0319	4.1
Landowners	0.0599	0.2659	0.2482	0.1544	0.0894	0.0285	0.0144	4.3
Landless	0.0748	0.2831	0.2381	0.1295	0.0681	0.0276	0.0261	4.2
Occupational Groups								
Cultivators	0.0574	0.2590	0.2430	0.1553	0.0860	0.0237	0.0132	4.2
Salaried+Prof.+S.Empl.	0.0455	0.2685	0.2721	0.1209	0.0681	0.0297	0.0048	4.0
Wage earners	0.0928	0.2895	0.2413	0.1350	0.0784	0.0330	0.0177	4.4
All others	0.0614	0.2804	0.2321	0.1566	0.0895	0.0335	0.0501	4.5
Social Groups								
Caste								
STs	0.0597	0.2321	0.2850	0.1587	0.0909	0.0385	0.0187	4.4
SCs	0.0770	0.3081	0.2302	0.1803	0.0898	0.0291	0.0185	4.7
Religion								
Hindus	0.0639	0.2681	0.2423	0.1409	0.0763	0.0273	0.0171	4.2
Muslims	0.0888	0.3430	0.2972	0.2089	0.1495	0.0418	0.0289	5.8
Christians	0.0403	0.1656	0.1233	0.0701	0.0253	–	–	2.1
Other Minorities	0.0210	0.2303	0.2586	0.1396	0.0727	0.0312	0.0342	3.9
Household Size Groups								
Up to 4	0.0779	0.2409	0.1611	0.0675	0.0223	0.0025	0.0081	2.9
5–7	0.0470	0.2635	0.2589	0.1495	0.0692	0.0284	0.0131	4.1
8 and above	0.0821	0.3002	0.2900	0.1967	0.1690	0.0559	0.0379	5.6
Adult Literacy Groups								
None literate	0.0987	0.3158	0.2541	0.1789	0.1296	0.0532	0.0363	5.3
Female literate	0.0319	0.1891	0.1915	0.0911	0.0341	0.0377	–	2.9

(Contd.)

Male literate	0.1050	0.3157	0.2707	0.1715	0.0947	0.0256	0.0227	5.0
Both literate	0.0447	0.2325	0.2231	0.1012	0.0431	0.0153	0.0067	3.3
Village Development Groups								
Low	0.0755	0.2907	0.2779	0.2054	0.1320	0.0482	0.0300	5.3
Medium	0.0647	0.2705	0.2384	0.1476	0.0748	0.0237	0.0149	4.2
High	0.0547	0.2548	0.2232	0.0850	0.0445	0.0161	0.0116	3.4
All India	**0.0645**	**0.2714**	**0.2446**	**0.1456**	**0.0820**	**0.0282**	**0.0181**	**4.3**

Mortality Rates by Population Groups

Population Groups	Crude Death Rate'000	Infant Mortality Marital Duration of EMW				U5 Mortality Marital Duration of EMW			
		(0–9)	(10–19)	(20+)	All	(0–9)	(10–19)	(20+)	All
Household Income Groups									
Up to 20,000	13	80	87	115	97	101	121	159	133
20,001–40,000	10	60	71	85	76	76	99	124	107
40,001–62,000	8	47	58	80	66	68	76	119	95
62,001–86,000	8	36	53	63	54	45	78	84	74
Above 86,000	7	38	47	67	54	48	65	87	71
Poverty Line Groups									
Lower segment below	11	73	77	107	88	90	107	146	120
Upper segment below	12	69	86	115	95	92	117	158	129
Lower segment above	11	70	78	93	83	89	108	135	116
Upper segment above	11	50	65	81	70	62	93	117	100
Landholding Groups									
Landless wage earner	14	84	97	108	99	112	129	153	135
Marginal	11	73	81	103	89	92	111	147	124
Small	10	64	70	99	82	80	100	138	114
Medium	9	55	68	82	72	68	101	124	106
Large	7	53	65	73	66	70	84	99	88
Landless others	13	53	67	93	76	66	97	128	105
Land owners	10	66	74	96	83	82	104	137	115
Landless	13	70	83	100	88	91	114	140	121
Occupational Groups									
Cultivators	10	63	75	93	81	80	106	132	113
Salaried+Prof.+S.Empl.	10	38	57	85	67	55	81	119	94
Wage earners	13	88	93	111	100	112	127	158	137
All others	11	65	75	101	84	80	103	140	115
Social Groups									
Caste									
STs	9	75	91	119	98	96	120	157	129
SCs	13	88	95	107	99	113	133	157	140
Religion									
Hindus	11	69	79	99	86	88	110	139	119
Muslims	10	52	65	93	75	69	97	136	110
Christians	8	32	56	88	61	36	67	103	71
Other Minorities	11	83	79	82	81	92	114	112	109
Household Size Groups									
Up to 4	20	108	134	131	126	130	183	190	173
5–7	10	52	74	97	81	68	104	139	114
8 and above	7	58	59	80	68	77	82	108	92
Adult Literacy Groups									
None literate	14	86	99	117	104	112	138	172	146
Female literate	12	46	49	115	76	68	78	158	110
Male literate	11	83	80	103	91	103	110	145	126

(Contd.)

Both literate	9	47	56	79	64	59	77	108	87

Village Development Groups

Low	10	85	84	110	96	109	118	156	133
Medium	12	59	78	92	81	80	111	131	115
High	11	60	69	92	77	70	91	127	103
All India	**11**	**67**	**77**	**97**	**84**	**85**	**108**	**138**	**117**

Percentage of Ever Married Women Using Termination Methods by States

Regions/States	Household Income Groups (Rs per year)				Social Groups				Village Development Groups			All Groups
	Up to 20,000	20,001–40,000	40,001–62,000	Above 62,000	STs and SCs	Hindus	Muslims	Other Minorities	Low	Medium	High	
North												
Haryana	32.0	37.5	43.1	35.2	34.0	38.1	3.8	37.3	44.6	35.7	35.1	36.3
Himachal Pradesh	52.2	51.0	43.7	48.0	53.2	50.4	47.8	64.6	49.4	47.8	58.9	50.5
Punjab	31.3	35.2	21.3	27.2	29.9	29.1	43.2	30.1	37.1	30.7	28.4	30.1
Upper Central												
Bihar	12.8	18.7	15.6	24.8	13.6	16.5	10.7	10.3	13.2	17.9	15.2	15.6
Uttar Pradesh	13.0	14.7	15.0	12.8	12.2	14.9	4.9	10.0	12.7	15.1	15.4	13.7
Lower Central												
Madhya Pradesh	30.9	31.6	32.6	38.1	27.3	32.1	27.5	36.2	28.1	35.7	40.2	32.0
Orissa	31.2	33.2	32.1	24.0	27.0	31.6	26.6	24.2	28.8	34.5	29.4	31.4
Rajasthan	23.6	19.7	27.2	36.2	15.1	25.2	11.2	0.0	23.1	24.0	35.1	24.4
East												
North-eastern Rg.	10.9	11.0	18.9	6.4	20.3	14.4	7.7	1.9	5.5	13.2	13.5	12.1
West Bengal	23.5	22.7	23.1	21.0	27.6	26.9	13.1	25.1	17.1	21.8	26.2	23.2
West												
Gujarat	44.6	44.1	39.2	48.6	43.8	45.1	32.3	50.3	37.4	44.4	46.7	44.3
Maharashtra	50.1	50.0	52.5	48.4	46.0	49.6	53.3	55.3	36.9	47.3	53.5	50.1
South												
Andhra Pradesh	45.1	43.7	43.5	50.3	38.9	45.0	38.1	55.0	29.2	49.6	47.9	44.9
Karnataka	49.7	48.2	52.9	47.7	49.5	51.2	31.7	52.5	44.2	51.7	47.6	49.5
Kerala	56.6	49.9	34.6	29.9	54.0	55.6	32.7	48.6	55.1	44.8	51.8	49.3
Tamil Nadu	40.5	38.6	30.9	36.2	37.0	39.2	41.2	32.0	19.8	42.1	37.9	38.8
All India	**29.9**	**29.9**	**29.7**	**32.2**	**27.6**	**31.4**	**16.5**	**33.8**	**20.4**	**31.1**	**38.4**	**30.1**
C.V.	41.9	37.8	36.0	39.0	40.4	37.1	58.7	58.9	46.0	36.1	37.9	38.2

Percentage of Ever Married Women Using Spacing Methods by States

Regions/States	Household Income Groups (Rs per year)				Social Groups				Village Development Groups			All Groups
	Up to 20,000	20,001– 40,000	40,001– 62,000	Above 62,000	STs and SCs	Hindus	Muslims	Other Minorities	Low	Medium	High	
North												
Haryana	6.3	7.0	4.7	9.1	4.9	6.4	7.4	25.5	9.3	6.0	7.2	6.9
Himachal Pradesh	4.1	6.7	6.8	5.1	4.0	5.3	3.0	19.4	4.5	5.5	6.5	5.4
Punjab	11.6	10.9	21.5	23.9	5.0	9.1	12.7	17.7	8.4	12.9	19.3	15.4
Upper Central												
Bihar	2.1	2.4	2.1	2.5	1.8	2.0	2.5	5.8	2.7	1.9	1.7	2.2
Uttar Pradesh	7.2	8.8	9.3	13.4	8.4	8.2	11.6	25.7	8.4	8.7	9.5	8.6
Lower Central												
Madhya Pradesh	3.2	4.5	3.3	7.2	3.7	4.0	2.3	0.0	3.3	4.6	5.2	4.0
Orissa	1.8	3.1	2.7	9.7	1.4	2.3	20.0	1.4	1.6	2.4	3.9	2.4
Rajasthan	1.7	1.5	2.7	2.7	1.2	1.9	2.1	17.2	1.8	1.5	4.4	1.9
East												
North-eastern Rg.	13.1	14.1	20.2	25.0	12.4	9.9	25.2	41.7	27.6	13.7	12.5	15.5
West Bengal	9.7	8.5	8.0	16.2	9.1	10.4	5.0	36.2	9.0	11.6	7.4	9.6
West												
Gujarat	4.3	6.4	11.5	9.5	4.1	6.3	5.8	0.0	2.0	5.8	8.3	6.2
Maharashtra	4.5	3.6	2.7	4.6	3.5	4.0	1.9	6.7	1.7	2.7	5.2	4.1
South												
Andhra Pradesh	3.0	3.7	1.8	6.2	2.5	3.0	9.7	0.0	4.9	1.0	5.1	3.3
Karnataka	1.7	3.0	1.6	4.1	0.9	2.0	4.3	4.0	5.0	1.5	2.8	2.2
Kerala	7.8	6.2	13.6	22.0	4.0	9.4	8.1	9.6	7.9	8.7	9.8	9.2
Tamil Nadu	3.1	1.8	1.2	2.9	1.1	2.5	0.0	4.0	0.0	1.4	3.0	2.6
All India	**4.8**	**5.4**	**6.7**	**9.3**	**4.6**	**4.9**	**8.2**	**13.4**	**5.5**	**5.4**	**6.1**	**5.6**
C.V.	66.0	59.1	89.2	72.3	73.8	56.1	88.7	96.1	102.4	74.8	60.5	68.9

Percentage of Users of Spacing Methods (Loop/Copper T) by States

Regions/States	Household Income Groups (Rs per year)				Social Groups				Village Development Groups			All Groups
	Up to 20,000	20,001– 40,000	40,001– 62,000	Above 62,000	STs and SCs	Hindus	Muslims	Other Minorities	Low	Medium	High	
North												
Haryana	0.0	22.0	28.5	33.5	4.6	18.4	0.0	51.8	32.7	13.6	21.9	20.7
Himachal Pradesh	30.8	40.1	10.4	0.0	37.1	29.5	0.0	47.3	40.2	18.7	40.1	29.7
Punjab	24.3	30.8	56.1	47.2	16.9	16.2	0.0	44.6	0.0	47.1	35.3	39.6
Upper Central												
Bihar	14.3	16.1	0.0	0.0	33.2	17.2	0.0	0.0	16.6	3.5	29.9	13.0
Uttar Pradesh	24.4	26.1	26.6	27.8	15.9	24.6	30.9	68.1	27.6	23.4	23.2	25.8
Lower Central												
Madhya Pradesh	8.4	9.6	11.3	20.0	12.4	11.3	0.0	0.0	5.2	11.2	28.9	11.1
Orissa	19.6	40.7	72.5	46.4	23.7	34.3	33.3	0.0	30.7	36.2	33.0	33.8
Rajasthan	34.7	51.8	32.2	29.9	59.5	31.9	100.0	100.0	34.1	26.0	61.5	37.5
East												
North-eastern Rg.	29.1	10.8	19.8	6.2	40.1	31.1	8.4	8.4	3.1	31.0	14.2	18.7
West Bengal	37.6	17.1	8.4	0.0	20.6	30.5	9.6	45.4	35.2	28.3	28.5	29.0
West												
Gujarat	46.6	24.3	23.9	29.9	29.3	35.1	0.0	0.0	79.5	29.9	31.5	33.0
Maharashtra	24.2	31.9	0.0	43.8	31.2	29.5	0.0	13.5	0.0	17.8	31.1	27.3
South												
Andhra Pradesh	16.2	52.0	34.3	26.9	36.2	34.8	13.7	0.0	45.5	0.0	30.7	31.3
Karnataka	74.8	75.3	11.1	37.2	46.5	63.5	61.3	100.0	74.1	57.5	65.1	63.6
Kerala	54.8	35.4	38.6	58.8	37.1	49.5	34.6	56.0	47.7	50.0	47.3	48.4
Tamil Nadu	57.8	49.3	28.6	70.0	45.7	54.7	0.0	70.1	0.0	51.9	56.7	56.0
All India	**30.1**	**26.3**	**25.8**	**30.4**	**24.2**	**29.2**	**18.7**	**36.5**	**24.4**	**27.4**	**33.7**	**28.5**
C.V.	60.9	51.5	75.2	68.2	45.4	42.7	150.4	91.1	81.8	59.9	38.7	43.0

APPENDIX A.8.10

Reasons for Non-Adoption (%) of Birth Control Measures by States

Regions/States	Non-adoption	Reasons for Not Using Birth Control Measures					
		Demand Factors	Want Son	Health Factors	Supply Factors	Hhold Factors	Lack of Knowledge Factors
North							
Haryana	56.4	43.7	16.6	5.6	2.0	14.6	25.8
Himachal Pradesh	45.5	39.9	11.2	9.5	5.6	9.1	18.1
Punjab	56.7	29.4	4.9	9.1	0.5	8.7	39.5
Upper Central							
Bihar	82.0	32.2	12.8	8.7	8.0	13.1	34.1
Uttar Pradesh	78.0	38.0	15.2	12.5	1.3	11.7	19.8
Lower Central							
Madhya Pradesh	64.2	53.4	13.6	7.8	1.8	13.0	21.9
Orissa	66.0	45.7	17.4	18.4	3.9	8.3	18.4
Rajasthan	74.2	44.5	21.6	8.3	4.2	9.0	21.0
East							
North-eastern Rg.	71.6	21.5	4.0	10.5	4.0	13.4	44.6
West Bengal	66.5	29.2	7.7	15.8	3.9	21.7	29.1
West							
Gujarat	50.8	42.4	21.3	4.9	2.1	28.5	23.6
Maharashtra	44.4	44.3	19.5	5.0	1.3	4.6	27.7
South							
Andhra Pradesh	51.6	59.8	8.1	8.0	3.2	12.0	19.8
Karnataka	47.5	50.1	24.4	12.6	3.8	21.7	31.0
Kerala	38.8	37.3	6.2	5.9	–	10.7	41.3
Tamil Nadu	58.2	44.4	8.4	21.2	3.1	13.2	20.0
All India	**64.3**	**40.4**	**13.6**	**10.9**	**3.4**	**13.2**	**26.1**
C.V.	20.9	22.9	46.8	45.2	64.3	43.6	30.7

Note: Percentage might not add to 100 because more than one reason exists for not adopting birth control measures.

Reasons for Non-Adoption (%) of Birth Control Measures by Population Groups

Population Groups	Reasons for Not Using Birth Control Measures					
	Demand Factors	Want Son	Health Factors	Supply Factors	Hhold Factors	Lack of Knowledge Factors
Household Income Groups						
Up to 20,000	39.2	13.9	11.9	3.6	13.0	27.3
20,001–40,000	41.4	12.5	9.8	3.7	14.2	25.2
40,001–62,000	42.0	12.7	9.4	2.3	13.6	24.3
62,001–86,000	44.7	13.5	9.5	2.1	10.6	21.7
Above 86,000	44.8	18.9	5.9	2.0	12.3	21.8
Poverty Line Groups						
Lower segment below	35.3	13.7	12.6	3.8	14.6	27.4
Upper segment below	38.2	14.9	11.4	3.6	13.8	26.4
Lower segment above	43.2	13.2	10.4	3.2	12.3	25.6
Upper segment above	43.3	12.6	8.9	2.9	12.8	25.0
Landholding Groups						
Landless wage earner	43.7	13.7	11.1	3.9	13.7	25.6
Marginal	38.3	13.6	11.3	3.0	12.1	27.2
Small	42.1	12.8	10.3	4.2	13.2	25.7
Medium	42.1	15.2	9.9	2.2	14.6	23.8
Large	46.4	18.1	7.9	2.5	11.1	22.0
Landless others	35.6	11.3	12.2	3.8	15.1	27.9
Land owners	40.7	14.1	10.5	3.2	12.7	25.8
Landless	39.9	12.6	11.6	3.8	14.4	26.6
Occupational Groups						
Cultivators	40.6	13.6	11.1	3.5	13.1	25.8
Salaried+Prof.+S.Empl.	38.2	13.7	11.2	3.1	11.1	26.6
Wage earners	43.6	13.9	10.5	3.6	13.3	26.3
All others	36.7	12.9	10.6	3.0	15.3	26.1
Social Groups						
Caste						
STs	42.6	14.0	9.2	3.2	12.4	30.6
SCs	41.3	14.1	13.1	4.0	10.1	25.5
Religion						
Hindus	41.7	14.5	11.2	3.6	10.6	25.9
Muslims	32.7	7.9	9.3	2.5	35.8	23.5
Christians	39.1	9.2	11.3	0.9	7.3	31.5
Other Minorities	30.8	10.0	7.4	2.5	7.3	43.1
Household Size Groups						
Up to 4	48.6	13.2	9.2	2.4	9.4	26.5
5–7	34.0	13.3	12.8	4.3	15.2	28.4
8 and above	42.7	14.2	9.6	3.0	13.6	22.7

(Contd.)

Adult Literacy Groups

None literate	40.5	15.2	11.5	3.8	13.2	26.3
Female literate	30.9	10.0	10.5	3.2	11.9	38.7
Male literate	40.8	13.5	11.0	3.3	13.1	25.0
Both literate	40.7	12.5	10.2	3.2	13.5	26.0
Village Development Groups						
Low	40.6	13.9	10.5	2.5	11.9	25.3
Medium	40.5	13.6	11.2	4.2	13.7	25.9
High	40.1	13.1	10.9	3.3	14.4	27.3
All India	**40.4**	**13.6**	**10.9**	**3.4**	**13.2**	**26.1**

Percentage Distribution of Currently Pregnant Women Receiving Ante-Natal Care(ANC) by States

Regions/States	EMW Currently Pregnant	Received ANC	Type of ANC		
			TT Immu–nization	Iron Supplements	BP Check–ups
North					
Haryana	6.3	4.0	100.0	62.0	–
Himachal Pradesh	6.3	22.5	88.7	39.4	25.3
Punjab	8.3	18.4	82.5	42.5	49.7
Upper Central					
Bihar	6.3	6.9	94.5	58.5	38.0
Uttar Pradesh	7.6	5.1	82.4	52.3	19.9
Lower Central					
Madhya Pradesh	7.8	2.0	100.0	40.7	31.8
Orissa	7.0	3.3	78.0	48.8	40.1
Rajasthan	7.7	5.8	96.4	96.4	52.8
East					
North-eastern Rg.	8.6	8.1	81.8	54.7	4.9
West Bengal	7.6	17.0	79.2	44.5	37.9
West					
Gujarat	5.4	4.2	100.0	74.9	76.5
Maharashtra	7.9	4.5	100.0	81.7	35.5
South					
Andhra Pradesh	6.4	11.3	90.3	62.1	88.3
Karnataka	5.3	20.5	94.7	39.6	65.2
Kerala	4.6	18.1	77.3	64.7	100.0
Tamil Nadu	5.0	46.8	94.8	63.1	45.1
All India	**6.9**	**9.8**	**89.1**	**56.9**	**46.8**
C.V.	17.8	89.7	9.3	27.2	60.1

Percentage Distribution of Currently Pregnant Women Receiving ANC by Population Groups

Population Groups	EMW Currently Pregnant	Received ANC	Type of ANC		
			TT Immu-nization	Iron Supplements	BP Check-ups
Household Income Groups					
Up to 20,000	7.2	10.2	87.8	52.2	45.0
20,001–40,000	6.9	9.0	90.7	64.2	50.5
40,001–62,000	6.2	10.2	96.1	53.6	45.6
62,001–86,000	6.5	10.0	79.5	80.7	66.8
Above 86,000	4.8	8.3	96.3	79.7	29.0
Poverty Line Groups					
Lower segment below	7.2	10.7	82.3	44.6	49.9
Upper segment below	6.9	10.2	96.1	61.6	43.2
Lower segment above	7.1	9.3	89.5	57.9	48.1
Upper segment above	6.1	9.6	87.8	66.3	44.0
Landholding Groups					
Landless wage earners	7.3	11.7	89.9	61.2	52.5
Marginal	7.2	10.8	92.7	50.3	40.9
Small	7.0	6.5	98.1	72.5	44.7
Medium	6.7	7.9	84.5	65.3	52.6
Large	6.5	5.6	94.2	71.1	58.6
Landless others	6.1	13.0	76.2	47.0	48.0
Land owners	7.0	8.6	92.8	58.3	44.4
Landless	6.7	12.3	83.7	54.8	50.4
Occupational Groups					
Cultivators	6.9	8.2	93.3	57.6	45.2
Salaried+Prof.+Empl.	5.9	11.2	89.7	68.1	42.7
Wage earners	7.2	10.6	89.8	56.8	54.6
All others	7.3	12.0	79.9	48.2	41.3
Social Groups					
Caste					
STs	8.3	5.7	88.4	77.3	22.9
SCs	7.7	11.6	89.4	63.9	47.5
Religion					
Hindus	6.8	9.9	90.1	58.7	46.4
Muslims	7.9	8.0	89.3	37.4	37.5
Christians	4.2	12.3	100.0	52.7	64.0
Other Minorities	7.5	14.6	63.2	61.2	68.5
Household Size Groups					
Up to 4	8.0	11.4	88.8	53.9	36.5
5–7	6.3	9.3	86.3	55.1	51.9
8 and above	7.0	9.2	93.5	62.8	50.9
Adult Literacy Groups					
None literate	7.7	6.7	80.7	61.6	41.6

(Contd.)

Female literate	4.9	11.6	96.5	32.6	12.1
Male literate	6.8	8.5	89.8	58.6	34.9
Both literate	6.6	13.3	91.6	55.2	56.9
Village Development Groups					
Low	7.5	5.4	93.0	53.7	33.2
Medium	7.0	9.9	84.2	53.2	41.5
High	6.2	15.1	92.2	61.7	57.8
All India	**6.9**	**9.8**	**89.1**	**56.9**	**46.8**

Percentage of Ever Married Women who Delivered Last Year and Received Blood Pressure Check-ups by States

Regions/States	Household Income Groups (Rs per year)				Social Groups				Village Development Groups			All Groups
	Up to 20,000	20,001– 40,000	40,001– 62,000	Above 62,000	STs and SCs	Hindus	Muslims	Other Minorities	Low	Medium	High	
North												
Haryana	15.6	20.2	9.6	27.3	15.9	18.5	19.3	44.1	18.0	17.6	19.8	18.9
Himachal Pradesh	28.7	31.6	49.8	54.8	42.8	35.8	11.0	0.0	21.5	39.2	41.7	34.3
Punjab	30.3	39.1	53.1	60.9	27.2	30.4	22.5	45.6	29.2	39.9	44.5	41.3
Upper Central												
Bihar	10.8	18.1	10.4	41.1	8.8	15.6	15.1	2.4	12.2	16.4	17.8	14.9
Uttar Pradesh	6.9	11.0	6.6	19.3	7.7	9.6	7.4	0.0	8.4	8.2	24.7	9.3
Lower Central												
Madhya Pradesh	9.8	16.8	18.1	20.1	7.5	13.8	18.7	0.0	9.6	16.2	28.8	13.8
Orissa	16.0	29.9	26.7	25.6	11.1	19.3	37.5	26.2	8.8	23.5	33.3	19.8
Rajasthan	14.9	18.1	24.4	16.5	17.8	17.8	10.1	0.0	14.5	18.5	31.9	17.3
East												
North-eastern Rg.	14.4	7.3	24.2	40.2	6.3	16.3	3.8	60.4	6.2	17.4	19.5	15.4
West Bengal	13.3	15.0	42.6	16.0	13.1	16.0	14.6	0.0	10.6	14.9	17.3	15.4
West												
Gujarat	36.0	57.4	61.2	45.3	42.1	47.0	26.9	0.0	37.5	47.5	46.0	45.5
Maharashtra	33.6	37.2	38.9	51.2	27.0	35.8	41.8	57.0	7.7	32.5	45.3	37.6
South												
Andhra Pradesh	62.4	66.8	80.8	81.6	67.2	66.9	60.4	66.6	52.0	69.3	72.3	66.4
Karnataka	56.0	48.1	58.0	62.8	53.1	54.2	58.8	55.6	34.6	53.1	58.5	54.8
Kerala	91.4	92.4	94.8	98.1	91.8	94.0	95.7	88.3	100.0	91.8	93.0	93.2
Tamil Nadu	67.9	82.9	71.5	69.2	72.4	72.0	79.2	80.5	0.0	76.1	73.3	72.4
All India	**23.3**	**29.0**	**28.2**	**36.9**	**20.5**	**26.7**	**20.8**	**45.6**	**13.1**	**26.8**	**44.3**	**26.6**
C.V.	76.3	68.0	61.7	52.3	81.3	68.9	81.3	96.3	103.2	66.8	52.4	68.0

Mothers Immunized by Population Groups

Population Groups	Received ANC	Type of ANC		
		TT Immunztn.	Iron Supplements	BP Check-ups
Household Income Groups				
Up to 20,000	55.9	51.5	33.4	24.5
20,001–40,000	57.9	53.5	34.3	27.9
40,001–62,000	61.4	57.3	34.5	27.2
62,001–86,000	60.1	55.4	39.8	34.4
Above 86,000	68.1	60.1	39.8	42.8
Poverty Line Groups				
Lower segment below	52.2	47.8	29.8	19.9
Upper segment below	54.3	50.6	32.0	23.4
Lower segment above	60.9	55.7	37.2	30.2
Upper segment above	63.9	60.1	38.1	35.6
Landholding Groups				
Landless wage earner	61.5	57.5	41.1	30.6
Marginal	56.5	51.4	32.0	24.0
Small	54.9	51.0	31.7	22.8
Medium	51.5	46.5	31.7	24.8
Large	55.8	51.4	36.0	27.9
Landless others	62.6	58.5	34.5	32.8
Landowners	55.3	50.5	32.2	24.2
Landless	62.0	58.0	38.1	31.6
Occupational Groups				
Cultivators	55.8	50.9	32.3	23.3
Salaried+Prof.+S.Empl.	61.2	57.5	37.6	31.0
Wage earners	58.7	54.8	38.5	29.7
All others	57.1	52.1	29.5	26.9
Social Groups				
Caste				
STs	42.2	39.4	29.6	12.8
SCs	57.6	52.5	35.0	24.3
Religion				
Hindus	57.8	53.3	35.1	26.7
Muslims	51.7	46.4	24.5	20.8
Christians	81.9	81.3	54.6	68.0
Other Minorities	65.4	60.3	39.6	34.2
Household Size Groups				
Up to 4	63.8	59.9	41.8	35.8
5–7	57.6	54.0	35.2	24.9
8 and above	54.9	49.2	30.0	24.8
Adult Literacy Groups				
None literate	47.3	42.4	24.5	16.3
Female literate	75.6	73.0	55.1	46.6

(Contd.)

Male literate	49.0	44.1	28.6	18.7
Both literate	72.9	69.1	46.3	41.6
Village Development Groups				
Low	40.6	36.0	21.0	13.1
Medium	59.6	54.9	33.0	26.8
High	76.8	72.8	53.5	44.3
All India	**57.5**	**53.0**	**34.2**	**26.6**

Women who had Complicated Deliveries and Nature of Complication by Population Groups

Population Groups	% of EMW Delivering Last Yr.	% Attended by Untrained - Personnel	% Compli-cated delivery Last Yr.	Caesarean		Forcep's		Bleeding		Prolonged Del.		Convulsion/ Fever	
				% to Total	% to Complc.	% to Total	% to Complc	% to Total	% to Complc.	% to Total	% to Complc.	% to Total	% to Complc.
Household Income Groups													
Up to 20,000	17.6	62.5	10.0	1.9	18.7	0.6	6.2	2.6	25.5	3.3	32.9	1.7	16.7
20,001–40,000	16.7	58.4	11.3	2.0	17.4	0.3	2.9	1.9	16.5	5.4	48.1	1.7	15.1
40,001–62,000	16.9	58.3	10.6	3.3	31.1	1.2	11.0	2.7	25.2	3.3	31.6	0.1	1.0
62,001–86,000	16.9	52.9	14.5	4.7	32.3	0.9	6.2	1.9	13.4	5.2	35.6	1.8	12.5
Above 86,000	17.5	43.4	14.0	5.3	37.8	0.9	6.2	1.9	13.8	4.5	32.2	1.4	10.1
Poverty Line Groups													
Lower segment below	20.8	67.6	9.1	1.4	15.3	0.6	6.3	3.0	33.0	2.7	30.0	1.4	15.4
Upper segment below	20.1	64.8	9.4	1.4	14.5	0.5	5.6	2.3	24.7	3.5	37.9	1.6	17.3
Lower segment above	15.6	56.3	11.7	2.6	22.2	0.5	4.2	1.6	13.7	5.3	45.2	1.7	14.8
Upper segment above	13.4	46.9	13.5	4.7	34.8	1.2	9.2	3.3	24.6	3.2	23.7	1.0	7.7
Landholding Groups													
Landless wage earner	17.7	54.7	11.1	2.4	21.8	0.6	5.5	2.0	17.7	3.9	35.0	2.2	20.0
Marginal	17.7	64.3	9.4	2.2	22.9	0.4	4.7	2.6	27.3	3.5	37.4	0.7	7.6
Small	16.6	62.1	12.1	1.6	12.9	0.6	4.7	3.4	28.4	5.4	45.0	1.1	9.0
Medium	17.4	60.7	11.3	3.2	28.4	0.7	6.5	2.2	19.3	4.2	36.6	1.0	9.2
Large	17.3	57.2	12.7	2.3	18.3	0.6	4.4	1.2	9.7	5.4	42.3	3.2	25.3
Landless others	16.7	55.8	9.8	2.4	24.0	0.9	9.7	1.6	16.4	2.4	24.3	2.5	25.7
Land owners	17.3	62.4	10.8	2.2	20.2	0.5	5.0	2.6	24.2	4.3	40.2	1.1	10.4
Landless	17.2	55.2	10.5	2.4	22.8	0.8	7.3	1.8	17.1	3.2	30.4	2.3	22.4
Occupational Groups													
Cultivators	16.7	62.4	10.0	1.8	18.5	0.7	6.6	2.4	24.3	4.0	40.0	1.1	10.6
Salaried+Prof.+S.Empl.	16.7	56.8	12.1	3.5	28.6	1.1	9.3	2.8	23.0	3.3	27.5	1.4	11.5
Wage earners	18.0	56.8	11.8	2.7	23.0	0.5	3.9	2.5	21.0	4.2	35.5	2.0	16.6
All others	18.4	61.5	9.4	1.6	16.4	0.3	3.1	1.5	15.9	3.9	41.5	2.2	23.1
Social Groups													
Caste													
STs	18.7	68.1	13.0	0.9	6.6	0.7	5.2	5.6	43.5	4.1	31.4	1.7	13.3
SCs	18.2	62.4	10.2	2.3	22.3	0.5	4.4	2.1	20.2	4.0	38.9	1.4	14.1
Religion													
Hindus	16.9	–	10.8	2.3	20.8	0.6	5.7	2.4	22.5	3.9	36.2	1.6	14.8
Muslims	22.6	68.5	8.9	0.7	8.4	0.3	3.1	2.2	24.7	4.3	48.8	1.3	15.0
Christians	10.6	24.5	23.6	15.3	64.8	4.2	17.7	1.5	6.2	2.7	11.3	–	0.0
Other Minorities	16.5	53.2	7.8	2.9	37.8	0.5	6.3	0.1	1.9	3.5	45.2	0.7	8.8
Household Size Groups													
Up to 4	12.0	51.3	13.4	3.7	27.2	1.1	7.8	2.7	20.0	4.0	30.0	2.0	14.9
5–7	16.1	59.7	11.2	2.0	17.5	0.5	4.9	3.0	26.8	4.1	36.5	1.6	14.4
8 and above	23.2	63.9	9.0	2.0	22.1	0.5	5.7	1.5	16.3	3.8	42.0	1.2	13.9

(Contd.)

Adult Literacy Groups													
None literacy	19.9	70.5	9.5	1.2	13.1	0.2	1.7	1.6	17. 1	4.1	43.4	2.3	24.7
Female literate	12.9	45.2	9.0	2.6	28.9	0.9	9.6	2.0	22.2	2.8	31.0	0.8	8.3
Male literate	17.6	66.3	10.1	0.9	9.0	0.6	6.2	2.4	24.1	4.8	47.6	1.3	13.1
Both literate	15.5	46.3	12.3	4.3	35.1	1.0	7.8	2.9	23.3	3.1	25.0	1.1	8.8
Village Development Groups													
Low	20.2	72.0	8.7	1.0	11.9	0.3	3.1	1.6	18.2	4.1	47.5	1.7	19.3
Medium	16.7	61.0	11.4	2.5	21.9	0.7	6.3	2.9	25.6	3.6	31.8	1.6	14.4
High	15.1	42.8	12.3	3.5	28.5	0.9	7.5	2.5	20.5	4.2	34.1	1.2	9.6
All India	**17.3**	**60.0**	**0.7**	**2.2**	**21.1**	**0.6**	**5.7**	**2.3**	**21.9**	**3.9**	**37.0**	**1.5**	**14.3**

Post-Natal Care Received by Women who Delivered in the Previous Year (%) by States

Regions/States	EMW Delivery Last Year	Still-births	Received Post-Natal Care	One Check-up	Two and more Check-ups
North					
Haryana	17.0	0.3	20.5	53.9	46.1
Himachal Pradesh	13.5	6.6	22.3	43.2	56.8
Punjab	14.3	1.9	37.4	51.1	47.7
Upper Central					
Bihar	19.7	13.7	7.6	72.9	19.8
Uttar Pradesh	21.6	3.4	16.4	81.5	13.9
Lower Central					
Madhya Pradesh	16.9	1.9	21.3	61.1	38.5
Orissa	16.1	8.4	21.9	55.3	33.4*
Rajasthan	24.5	2.6	11.4	58.3	41.7
East					
North-eastern Rg.	19.0	4.2	31.5	35.1	64.9
West Bengal	18.5	14.6	8.0	70.1	27.0
West					
Gujarat	15.5	2.1	39.7	47.1	52.9
Maharashtra	14.9	2.0	56.7	41.7	58.0
South					
Andhra Pradesh	12.6	2.1	44.9	46.1	52.3
Karnataka	10.4	4.7	40.8	55.4	43.9
Kerala	11.3	1.5	29.8	51.1	48.9
Tamil Nadu	13.9	2.7	45.6	53.9	44.8
All India	**17.3**	**5.5**	**23.8**	**55.4**	**42.7**
C.V.	22.5	91.1	49.8	21.3	31.2

*In the case of Orissa, the type of post-natal care might not add up to 100 per cent as about 12 per cent had received unspecified post-natal care.

Post-Natal Care Received by Women who Delivered in the Previous Year (%) by Population Groups

Population Groups	EMW Delivery Last Year	Still Births	Received Post-natal Care	One Check-up	Two + Check-ups
Household Income Groups					
Up to 20,000	17.6	4.8	22.0	56.5	41.1
20,001–40,000	16.7	6.1	26.5	53.8	44.9
40,001–62,000	16.9	8.4	24.5	56.4	40.6
62,001–86,000	16.9	7.6	36.1	50.5	48.8
Above 86,000	17.5	4.1	30.7	54.1	45.7
Poverty Line Groups					
Lower segment below	20.8	6.5	20.4	58.8	37.5
Upper segment below	20.1	5.7	20.7	58.5	40.1
Lower segment above	15.6	5.2	25.9	53.9	44.5
Upper segment above	13.4	4.4	30.4	50.4	48.3
Landholding Groups					
Landless wage earner	17.7	4.2	26.3	57.2	40.9
Marginal	17.7	6.2	21.1	61.3	36.9
Small	16.6	5.3	23.8	51.7	46.0
Medium	17.4	8.1	23.8	57.3	40.9
Large	17.3	4.1	26.2	43.4	56.0
Landless other	16.7	4.9	25.5	51.4	46.0
Land owners	17.3	6.0	22.8	55.8	42.4
Land less	17.2	4.5	25.9	54.6	43.2
Occupational Groups					
Cultivators	16.7	6.4	21.9	54.5	43.0
Salaried+Prof.+Empl.	16.7	5.5	27.9	51.8	47.0
Wage earners	18.0	4.2	25.8	58.7	40.0
All others	18.4	5.3	22.3	55.2	42.5
Social Groups					
Caste					
STs	18.7	6.0	23.3	43.0	57.0
SCs	18.2	4.6	21.3	61.2	36.0
Religion					
Hindus	16.9	5.2	24.8	56.3	41.7
Muslims	22.6	7.7	13.5	50.4	47.2
Christians	10.6	3.3	39.3	57.8	39.4
Other Minorities	16.5	6.5	34.6	41.1	58.1
Household Size Groups					
Up to 4	12.0	2.9	25.8	61.2	37.4
5–7	16.1	4.0	24.9	51.3	46.8
8 and above	23.2	8.3	21.8	57.6	40.0
Adult Literacy Groups					
None literate	19.9	4.2	17.5	64.1	33.8

(Contd.)

Female literate	12.9	3.3	39.4	62.1	37.9
Male literate	17.6	5.3	18.2	58.6	38.6
Both literate	15.5	7.0	33.4	49.5	48.9
Village Development Groups					
Low	20.2	4.5	14.5	65.4	32.8
Medium	16.7	7.0	23.1	55.9	42.4
High	15.1	4.7	37.2	49.7	48.0
All India	**17.3**	**5.5**	**23.8**	**55.4**	**42.7**

APPENDIX A.8.19

Women (who Delivered in the Previous Year) who were Breastfeeding and Duration (%) by States

Regions/States	Breast Feeding	Women Started Breastfeeding		
		< Than 2 Hrs	2 Days	> Than 2 Days
North				
Haryana	99.0	3.7	47.9	48.4
Himachal Pradesh	89.9	22.9	21.3	55.8
Punjab	95.2	2.0	21.0	77.0
Upper Central				
Bihar	82.2	3.9	52.9	43.2
Uttar Pradesh	93.6	5.9	29.7	64.4
Lower Central				
Madhya Pradesh	95.7	34.0	33.5	32.5
Orissa	89.8	44.3	39.5	16.2
Rajasthan	93.3	3.8	29.5	66.8
East				
North-eastern Rg.	94.0	14.9	63.6	21.5
West Bengal	81.3	18.1	52.1	29.8
West				
Gujarat	96.3	29.0	39.0	32.0
Maharashtra	93.2	13.7	46.0	40.3
South				
Andhra Pradesh	94.6	9.6	45.3	45.1
Karnataka	92.7	8.3	31.6	60.1
Kerala	96.9	45.6	53.4	1.1
Tamil Nadu	94.0	31.9	49.6	18.5
All India	**91.2**	**14.9**	**41.1**	**44.0**
C.V.	5.0	78.2	29.2	49.6

Percentage of Children in the Age Group of 12–23 Months that were Immunized and Gender Disparity by Population Groups

Population Groups	DPT 3 Doses	POLIO 3 Doses	BCG 1 Dose	MEASLES 1 Dose	All 8 Doses
Household Income Groups					
Up to 20,000					
Person	54.2	55.8	61.9	50.0	45.6
Gender disparity	0.98	0.97	0.99	0.98	0.96
20,001–40,000					
Person	58.1	57.6	64.7	54.0	49.7
Gender disparity	0.92	0.92	0.91	0.89	0.92
40,001–62,000					
Person	61.8	61.4	66.1	55.8	52.1
Gender disparity	1.00	0.99	1.04	1.06	1.06
62,001–86,000					
Person	59.6	58.8	65.4	52.2	47.3
Gender disparity	0.90	0.85	0.98	0.94	0.91
Above 86,000					
Person	77.1	77.7	81.8	73.1	66.3
Gender disparity	0.92	0.93	0.92	1.01	0.98
Poverty Line Groups					
Lower segment below					
Person	50.0	51.1	57.5	45.2	40.8
Gender disparity	0.89	0.88	0.93	0.89	0.87
Upper segment below					
Person	54.0	55.7	61.6	49.7	45.4
Gender disparity	1.02	1.03	1.00	1.01	1.01
Lower segment above					
Person	60.2	60.3	67.6	56.3	52.0
Gender disparity	0.96	0.95	0.96	0.96	0.97
Upper segment above					
Person	65.6	65.4	70.1	59.5	54.6
Gender disparity	0.97	0.98	0.99	1.01	1.01
Landholding Groups					
Landless wage earner					
Person	58.4	59.2	65.5	53.1	49.0
Gender disparity	0.98	0.97	0.93	0.96	0.99
Marginal					
Person	55.3	56.7	62.1	51.4	47.0
Gender disparity	0.98	0.97	1.02	1.00	0.98
Small					
Person	54.8	54.8	61.6	50.8	46.3
Gender disparity	0.88	0.86	0.88	0.81	0.84
Medium					
Person	56.3	57.1	64.2	49.9	44.6
Gender disparity	0.86	0.87	0.91	0.97	0.88

(Contd.)

Large					
Person	63.8	63.8	68.5	59.2	55.3
Gender disparity	0.94	0.94	0.96	0.94	0.97
Landless others					
Person	62.1	61.8	68.9	57.6	53.1
Gender disparity	1.04	1.06	1.06	1.09	1.08
Land owners					
Person	56.1	56.9	62.9	51.8	47.3
Gender disparity	0.93	0.92	0.95	0.93	0.92
Landless					
Person	60.2	60.5	67.2	55.3	51.0
Gender disparity	1.01	1.02	0.99	1.02	1.03
Occupational Groups					
Cultivators					
Person	56.1	56.9	62.8	51.3	47.4
Gender disparity	0.94	0.93	0.96	0.95	0.93
Salaried+Prof.+S.Empl.					
Person	64.6	64.1	70.7	59.9	53.6
Gender disparity	0.92	0.92	0.93	0.89	0.90
Wage earners					
Person	56.7	57.6	63.6	51.9	47.7
Gender disparity	0.98	0.97	0.95	0.95	0.98
All others					
Person	56.4	57.1	63.9	53.2	48.6
Gender disparity 1.00	1.00	1.03	1.08	1.06	
Social Groups					
Caste					
STs					
Person	46.4	46.6	54.2	42.1	39.5
Gender disparity 1.02	1.01	1.03	1.00	0.98	
SCs					
Person	53.6	54.6	62.6	48.9	42.6
Gender disparity	0.98	0.97	0.96	0.95	0.98
Religion					
Hindus					
Person	58.8	59.6	66.1	54.3	49.7
Gender disparity	0.97	0.96	0.97	0.96	0.96
Muslims					
Person	43.6	44.0	49.7	38.9	34.5
Gender disparity	0.94	0.97	0.98	1.03	1.04
Christians					
Person	77.8	74.9	80.0	75.8	72.8
Gender disparity	1.08	1.02	1.15	1.12	1.07
Other Minorities					
Person	65.6	64.3	66.4	62.9	60.0
Gender disparity	0.82	0.79	0.82	0.83	0.84

(Contd.)

Household Size Groups

Up to 4

Person	59.8	61.6	68.0	55.4	51.5
Gender disparity	0.93	0.96	0.96	0.94	0.94

5–7

Person	57.5	57.7	64.4	53.5	48.6
Gender disparity	1.01	0.99	0.99	0.97	0.98

8 and above

Person	56.4	57.1	62.6	51.2	47.1
Gender disparity	0.91	0.90	0.94	0.96	0.95

Adult Literacy Groups

None literate

Person	46.5	46.7	52.9	42.5	38.1
Gender disparity	1.00	0.98	0.95	0.96	1.02

Female literate

Person	68.4	68.5	74.0	60.6	57.1
Gender disparity 0.87	0.92	0.90	0.80	0.79	

Male literate

Person	52.0	53.2	60.1	49.4	43.8
Gender disparity	0.94	0.93	0.97	0.94	0.91

Both literate

Person	70.4	70.9	76.6	64.0	60.4
Gender disparity	0.95	0.95	0.97	0.98	0.97

Village Development Groups

Low

Person	46.1	47.5	53.5	43.3	38.1
Gender disparity	0.94	0.93	0.95	0.93	0.98

Medium

Person	58.6	58.2	65.6	53.5	49.1
Gender disparity	0.95	0.95	0.98	1.00	0.97

High

Person	72.0	73.1	77.7	65.9	62.6
Gender disparity	0.98	0.98	0.97	0.94	0.94

All India

Person	**57.5**	**58.1**	**64.3**	**52.9**	**48.5**
Gender disparity	**0.96**	**0.95**	**0.97**	**0.96**	**0.96**

Principal Reasons for DPT Non-Immunization (%) among Children in Age Group 0–24 Months and Gender Disparity by States

Regions/States	Children Not Immunized	Reasons for Non-immunization			
		Child Unwell	Time Constraint	Supply Constraint	Wrong Beliefs
North					
Haryana					
Person	16.7	6.7	13.2	19.3	60.8
Gender disparity	1.49	0.38	1.95	1.01	0.97
Himachal Pradesh					
Person	7.5	9.6	8.9	44.2	37.3
Gender disparity	1.66	–	2.08	6.61	0.35
Punjab					
Person	15.9	16.5	33.9	28.6	21.0
Gender disparity	1.51	1.64	1.09	0.72	0.94
Upper Central					
Bihar					
Person	38.8	7.1	8.7	64.6	19.6
Gender disparity	0.95	0.74	0.77	1.15	0.79
Uttar Pradesh					
Person	26.9	5.4	16.5	35.8	42.3
Gender disparity	1.22	0.88	1.45	1.21	0.75
Lower Central					
Madhya Pradesh					
Person	31.2	1.6	14.9	56.8	26.8
Gender disparity	1.00	1.07	1.05	0.97	1.03
Orissa					
Person	24.5	6.6	26.7	37.1	29.5
Gender disparity	1.44	0.72	1.15	0.89	1.10
Rajasthan					
Person	40.1	3.0	15.1	64.9	17.0
Gender disparity	1.17	4.07	1.34	0.85	1.15
East					
North-eastern Rg.					
Person	28.2	3.9	6.6	53.4	36.2
Gender disparity	0.90	1.86	0.43	0.98	1.11
West Bengal					
Person	33.0	10.6	17.1	29.1	43.1
Gender disparity	0.96	1.43	0.90	0.88	1.04
West					
Gujarat					
Person	11.5	8.2	28.9	36.9	25.9
Gender disparity	0.55	0.49	0.79	1.59	0.77

(Contd.)

Maharashtra					
Person	7.2	12.8	26.0	32.4	28.9
Gender disparity	1.43	2.45	1.04	1.09	0.62
South					
Andhra Pradesh					
Person	9.1	20.9	7.2	39.6	32.3
Gender disparity	0.58	1.48	2.35	0.96	0.64
Karnataka					
Person	13.7	18.3	17.0	10.7	54.1
Gender disparity	0.84	0.78	0.46	1.54	1.24
Kerala					
Person	7.2	27.8	8.0	25.0	39.2
Gender disparity	0.52	0.67	1.08	0.76	1.48
Tamil Nadu					
Person	2.9	12.2	25.2	52.5	10.0
Gender disparity	0.51	1.74	2.14	0.62	0.56
All India					
Person	**24.9**	**6.7**	**14.7**	**47.6**	**31.0**
Gender disparity	**1.06**	**1.01**	**1.11**	**1.04**	**0.90**
C.V. Person	60.0	64.6	48.7	38.6	39.7

APPENDIX A.8.22

Children Under 3 Years who had Diarrhoea in the Last Year and Quantity of Fluid and Food Administered (%) by States

Regions/States	Child Having Diarr.	Fluid			Food		
		No Knowldg.	< Than Requid.	> Than Requid.	No Knowldg.	< Than Requid.	> Than Requid.
North							
Haryana	94.5	15.5	51.0	33.5	16.3	58.5	25.3
Himachal Pradesh	71.4	4.6	72.5	22.9	10.0	79.9	10.1
Punjab	53.2	16.3	34.6	49.1	26.2	34.2	39.6
Upper Central							
Bihar	68.4	35.1	40.7	24.2	35.7	41.7	22.6
Uttar Pradesh	54.9	19.6	61.6	18.9	28.1	59.5	12.4
Lower Central							
Madhya Pradesh	91.4	25.2	49.9	24.9	26.5	52.7	20.8
Orissa	70.9	19.4	47.2	33.5	14.8	71.4	13.8
Rajasthan	61.2	36.5	33.4	30.1	34.5	39.0	26.5
East							
North-eastern Rg.	57.4	10.7	38.0	51.3	16.6	36.6	46.8
West Bengal	31.7	5.5	50.9	43.6	12.7	68.9	18.4
West							
Gujarat	43.6	17.1	55.7	27.2	11.8	67.9	20.3
Maharashtra	48.7	10.8	62.3	26.9	11.0	74.5	14.5
South							
Andhra Pradesh	64.3	16.1	53.5	30.3	16.4	68.2	15.3
Karnataka	38.9	37.9	45.0	17.1	32.6	50.6	16.8
Kerala	45.6	8.2	35.7	56.2	6.9	82.7	10.4
Tamil Nadu	62.0	16.3	53.6	30.1	8.4	67.8	23.7
All India	**59.5**	**21.8**	**49.8**	**28.4**	**23.4**	**56.5**	**20.1**
C.V.	27.8	54.9	21.7	34.7	48.9	25.3	46.3

Children (Under 3 Years) who had Diarrhoea in the Last Year and the Quantity of Fluid and Food Administered (%) by Population Groups

Population Groups	Child Having Diarr.	Fluid			Food		
		No Knowldg.	< Than Requid	> Than Requid	No Knowldg.	< Than Requid	> Than Requid
Household Income Groups							
Up to 20,000	59.6	22.9	49.5	27.6	22.6	57.7	19.7
20,001–40,000	61.4	22.3	49.7	28.0	26.2	54.0	19.7
40,001–62,000	58.2	16.9	52.6	30.5	19.7	57.6	22.7
62,001–86,000	53.8	15.1	49.6	35.3	20.4	58.5	21.2
Above 86,000	54.7	18.7	49.1	32.1	27.2	50.4	22.4
Poverty Line Groups							
Lower segment below	58.0	23.0	48.2	28.8	24.1	54.9	20.9
Upper segment below	60.6	23.8	50.5	25.7	22.5	58.5	19.0
Lower segment above	60.0	21.5	49.7	28.8	24.5	56.2	19.3
Upper segment above	59.2	16.6	51.8	31.6	20.3	56.4	23.3
Landholding Groups							
Landless wage earner	59.1	24.5	49.6	26.0	21.1	57.3	21.6
Marginal	58.3	21.0	50.7	28.3	23.6	58.0	18.5
Small	62.2	22.3	46.6	31.1	22.9	55.0	22.1
Medium	63.1	22.2	50.9	27.0	27.2	54.6	18.2
Large	60.5	23.3	47.0	29.7	27.2	50.8	22.0
Landless others	56.5	18.4	53.3	28.3	21.6	58.6	19.8
Landowners	60.4	21.8	49.1	29.1	24.3	55.8	19.8
Landless	57.9	21.7	51.3	27.0	21.3	57.9	20.8
Occupational Groups							
Cultivators	60.8	22.2	50.1	27.6	24.9	57.3	17.8
Salaried+Prof.+S.Empl.	55.2	16.0	51.3	32.7	20.7	54.1	25.2
Wage earners	59.9	23.9	49.5	26.6	22.3	57.0	20.7
All others	59.1	21.4	48.4	30.2	22.6	55.4	22.0
Social Groups							
Caste							
STs	64.8	23.5	43.4	33.2	21.6	49.8	28.6
SCs	58.4	26.3	48.9	24.9	26.6	55.4	17.9
Religion							
Hindus	60.5	22.4	49.8	27.8	23.3	56.6	20.1
Muslims	57.1	17.0	53.8	29.2	23.1	59.4	17.5
Christians	34.2	19.9	42.5	37.6	24.2	53.5	22.3
Other Minorities	57.2	23.2	36.9	39.9	27.2	41.5	31.4
Household Size Groups							
Up to 4	58.5	21.6	52.3	26.1	19.4	62.2	18.5
5–7	61.7	22.2	47.7	30.1	24.0	54.3	21.7
8 and above	57.4	21.4	51.5	27.2	24.3	56.8	18.8

(Contd.)

Adult Literacy Groups							
None literate	60.8	27.1	50.0	22.8	25.4	56.5	18.1
Female literate	56.0	17.2	51.6	31.1	17.7	62.7	19.6
Male literate	60.1	23.1	50.2	26.6	26.9	55.2	17.9
Both literate	58.2	16.3	49.2	34.5	18.8	57.3	23.9
Village Development Groups							
Low	62.3	22.9	52.1	25.0	26.4	53.8	19.8
Medium	58.9	24.7	46.7	28.6	26.2	53.7	20.0
High	57.1	15.8	51.6	32.6	14.8	64.4	20.8
All India	**59.5**	**21.8**	**49.8**	**28.4**	**23.4**	**56.5**	**20.1**

Facilities for Treatment of Diarrhoea Occurring During the Last Year (%) by States

Regions/ States	Cases Referred After			Source of Facility for Treatment		
	Many Watery Stools	Repeated Vomiting	Getting More Sick/ Not Getting Better	Govern- ment	Private	No Outside Care
North						
Haryana	18.7	80.4	0.9	31.7	51.8	15.6
Himachal Pradesh	25.9	63.4	10.7	54.6	17.3	26.2
Punjab	3.7	84.3	11.9	28.1	33.4	37.3
Upper Central						
Bihar	12.0	86.7	1.3	23.2	32.1	40.6
Uttar Pradesh	9.9	76.3	13.8	24.3	23.5	50.5
Lower Central						
Madhya Pradesh	18.8	78.2	3.0	39.4	26.8	33.4
Orissa	32.1	66.5	1.3	41.6	10.4	46.4
Rajasthan	3.6	88.5	7.9	27.6	21.7	49.4
East						
North-eastern Rg.	7.2	92.8	–	73.2	14.4	12.4
West Bengal	34.7	64.5	0.8	23.4	50.4	24.7
West						
Gujarat	4.2	90.9	4.9	56.8	17.1	26.1
Maharashtra	32.4	64.2	3.5	31.0	49.8	18.0
South						
Andhra Pradesh	11.2	84.1	4.6	50.3	34.4	15.3
Karnataka	24.0	71.7	4.3	62.9	21.5	15.6
Kerala	5.2	93.8	1.1	46.7	46.6	6.1
Tamil Nadu	31.1	63.1	5.8	39.0	45.7	15.2
All India	**16.0**	**78.8**	**5.3**	**35.5**	**30.2**	**33.0**
C.V.	64.7	13.9	87.4	36.3	43.9	51.0

Facilities for Treatment of Diarrhoea Occurring during the Last Year (%) by Population Groups

Population Groups	Sources of Facility for Treatment		
	Government	Private	No Outside Care
Household Income Groups			
Up to 20,000	34.3	31.3	32.8
20,001–40,000	36.1	29.0	33.8
40,001–62,000	39.6	26.0	33.3
62,001–86,000	39.5	27.5	32.3
Above 86,000	35.0	33.9	29.4
Poverty Line Groups			
Lower segment below	32.1	31.2	34.7
Upper segment below	33.6	29.9	34.2
Lower segment above	36.8	29.7	32.8
Upper segment above	41.1	30.3	28.0
Landholding Groups			
Landless wage earner	33.8	34.9	29.9
Marginal	35.5	28.8	34.5
Small	39.5	25.3	34.0
Medium	38.8	25.9	34.0
Large	34.6	31.3	32.7
Landless others	30.1	36.6	31.5
Landowners	37.1	27.6	34.1
Landless	32.1	35.6	30.6
Occupational Groups			
Cultivators	36.4	28.1	34.0
Salaried+Prof.+S.Empl.	35.3	30.7	33.7
Wage earners	34.7	32.5	31.3
All others	34.2	32.0	32.2
Social Groups			
Caste			
STs	47.6	19.4	31.6
SCs	31.6	30.1	37.4
Religion			
Hindus	36.1	29.4	33.3
Muslims	31.0	35.9	30.7
Christians	33.4	31.4	35.1
Other Minorities	33.5	29.7	32.2
Household Size Groups			
Up to 4	37.8	32.2	29.0
5–7	36.8	30.3	31.5
8 and above	32.7	29.1	36.7
Adult Literacy Groups			
None literate	30.7	28.9	37.8

(Contd.)

Female literate	40.7	41.7	17.6
Male literate	34.0	27.4	37.6
Both literate	40.5	33.1	25.6
Village Development Groups			
Low	30.8	26.1	41.5
Medium	38.0	27.9	32.7
High	38.0	39.2	21.7
All India	**35.5**	**30.2**	**33.0**

APPENDIX A.8.26

Children (Under 3 Years) who had Diarrhoea and Knowledge and Use of ORS (%) by States

Regions/States	Child Having Diarr.	Distribution of Occurrence			Mothers Having	
		Last one Month	1–12 Months	One Year Ago	ORS Knowledge	Given ORS
North						
Haryana	94.5	31.3	49.1	19.6	47.2	44.0
Himachal Pradesh	71.4	51.3	39.7	9.0	66.0	60.1
Punjab	53.2	40.5	46.5	13.0	26.4	22.4
Upper Central						
Bihar	68.4	28.9	59.6	11.5	51.0	27.8
Uttar Pradesh	54.9	48.1	45.8	6.1	38.0	29.9
Lower Central						
Madhya Pradesh	91.4	48.0	44.6	7.4	27.3	20.4
Orissa	70.9	39.7	44.0	16.3	51.7	39.1
Rajasthan	61.2	58.4	35.7	5.9	28.0	22.7
East						
North-eastern Rg.	57.4	13.3	79.5	7.3	48.3	47.2
West Bengal	31.7	22.8	58.1	19.2	72.0	58.2
West						
Gujarat	43.6	27.2	56.0	16.8	59.5	49.0
Maharashtra	48.7	25.5	60.8	13.7	75.1	63.2
South						
Andhra Pradesh	64.3	39.7	49.0	11.3	58.5	39.2
Karnataka	38.9	20.7	68.1	11.2	49.8	39.9
Kerala	45.6	17.7	62.6	19.7	78.7	58.1
Tamil Nadu	62.0	17.9	62.0	20.1	65.4	49.3
All India	**59.5**	**36.4**	**52.5**	**11.1**	**47.9**	**36.0**
C.V.	27.8	39.9	20.7	37.9	30.8	32.8

Children (Under 3 Years) who had Diarrhoea and Knowledge and Use of ORS (%) by Population Groups

Population Groups	Child Having Diarr.	Distribution of Occurrence			Mothers Having	
		Last one Month	1–12 Months	One year Ago	ORS Knowledg	Given ORS
Household Income Groups						
Up to 20,000	59.6	36.6	52.2	11.2	44.9	32.6
20,001–40,000	61.4	36.8	52.5	10.7	51.1	39.7
40,001–62,000	58.2	32.8	57.5	9.7	51.9	40.2
62,001–86,000	53.8	37.0	46.2	16.9	50.4	43.0
Above 86,000	54.7	40.0	48.8	11.2	59.6	47.8
Poverty Line Groups						
Lower segment below	58.0	37.3	51.4	11.3	42.2	29.4
Upper segment below	60.6	36.2	53.3	10.5	44.9	33.9
Lower segment above	60.0	36.6	52.8	10.6	49.9	38.6
Upper segment above	59.2	34.6	51.9	13.5	57.8	44.5
Landholding Groups						
Landless wage earner	59.1	33.3	53.4	13.3	44.5	31.1
Marginal	58.3	36.5	53.6	9.9	47.3	34.1
Small	62.2	35.8	53.8	10.4	48.7	38.7
Medium	63.1	41.3	47.4	11.3	44.5	35.3
Large	60.5	44.2	45.4	10.4	50.5	39.4
Landless others	56.5	33.7	54.1	12.3	53.1	41.2
Landowners	60.4	37.8	51.9	10.3	47.6	36.2
Landless	57.9	33.5	53.7	12.8	48.4	35.7
Occupational Groups						
Cultivators	60.8	38.0	51.8	10.1	46.1	34.9
Salaried+Prof.+S.Empl.	55.2	33.6	56.2	10.2	55.7	45.1
Wage earners	59.9	35.6	51.6	12.7	43.6	30.7
All others	59.1	35.4	52.7	11.9	53.7	40.8
Social Groups						
Caste						
STs	64.8	31.7	57.1	11.2	40.1	32.1
SCs	58.4	37.4	51.3	11.2	44.5	34.6
Religion						
Hindus	60.5	37.6	51.6	10.8	47.8	36.2
Muslims	57.1	29.1	59.3	11.6	48.4	34.9
Christians	34.2	29.0	58.3	12.7	63.7	43.6
Other Minorities	57.2	31.3	48.1	20.6	41.1	30.8
Household Size Groups						
Up to 4	58.5	35.5	51.7	12.8	48.6	36.4
5–7	61.7	35.2	53.8	11.0	48.0	36.7
8 and above	57.4	38.4	51.0	10.6	47.3	34.9

(Contd.)

Adult Literacy Groups						
None literate	60.8	39.2	50.4	10.4	36.7	25.4
Female literate	56.0	32.7	55.3	11.9	59.4	42.7
Male literate	60.1	38.4	50.9	10.7	42.3	32.4
Both literate	58.2	32.5	55.4	12.1	61.5	47.8
Village Development Groups						
Low	62.3	44.5	46.0	9.5	37.1	27.9
Medium	58.9	34.8	54.4	10.9	47.9	35.8
High	57.1	28.0	58.2	13.7	62.5	47.3
All India	**59.5**	**36.4**	**52.5**	**11.1**	**47.8**	**36.0**

APPENDIX A.8.28
Sources of ORS Packets for Diarrhoea (%) by States

Regions/States	Sources of Availability of ORS			
	Govern-ment	Private	Gen. Shop	Friend/ Relative
North				
Haryana	59.3	34.2	2.2	0.0
Himachal Pradesh	78.5	5.4	5.2	2.4
Punjab	60.6	25.9	12.6	0.0
Upper Central				
Bihar	22.0	37.0	23.5	5.4
Uttar Pradesh	63.5	6.9	12.5	0.7
Lower Central				
Madhya Pradesh	86.8	5.2	3.0	0.0
Orissa	63.6	13.5	14.5	0.9
Rajasthan	55.6	21.4	13.2	1.2
East				
North-eastern Rg.	87.1	10.4	–	0.0
West Bengal	29.8	47.3	9.2	0.0
West				
Gujarat	77.6	10.5	–	0.7
Maharashtra	63.8	30.0	0.4	0.1
South				
Andhra Pradesh	70.5	24.0	–	0.0
Karnataka	69.8	22.8	1.6	1.7
Kerala	69.0	29.0	1.0	0.6
Tamil Nadu	63.5	32.4	0.9	0.1
All India	**58.7**	**23.4**	**8.2**	**1.2**
C.V.	26.5	54.8	110.4	157.1

Sources of ORS Packets for Diarrhoea (%) by Population Groups

Population Groups	Sources of Availability of ORS			
	Govern-ment	Private	Gen. Shop	Friend/ Relative
Household Income Groups				
Up to 20,000	59.1	22.2	9.0	1.1
20,001–40,000	57.0	24.8	7.9	1.0
40,001–62,000	60.4	24.6	5.5	2.9
62,001–86,000	61.0	21.7	7.3	0.0
Above 86,000	58.2	28.1	7.6	2.1
Poverty Line Groups				
Lower segment below	59.4	19.9	10.9	0.8
Upper segment below	58.2	24.2	7.5	1.5
Lower segment above	58.3	24.1	7.9	0.9
Upper segment above	59.3	25.0	6.7	2.2
Landholding Groups				
Landless wage earner	60.8	23.6	6.9	0.0
Marginal	57.7	22.2	9.3	1.5
Small	61.0	21.3	9.1	1.2
Medium	63.8	22.6	4.3	1.5
Large	64.9	20.5	7.3	0.7
Landless others	49.6	29.5	9.3	2.0
Landowners	60.3	21.8	8.3	1.3
Landless	55.2	26.6	8.1	1.0
Occupational Groups				
Cultivators	60.9	22.1	7.4	1.1
Salaried+Prof.+S.Empl.	57.1	23.4	7.3	2.6
Wage earners	62.2	22.8	6.9	0.3
All others	50.1	27.2	12.7	1.6
Social Groups				
Caste				
STs	81.0	7.8	2.2	0.4
SCs	59.3	23.7	8.6	0.9
Religion				
Hindus	59.8	22.9	7.9	1.1
Muslims	50.4	24.9	11.2	2.4
Christians	60.1	28.7	3.6	0.0
Other Minorities	56.0	31.1	7.1	1.5
Household Size Groups				
Up to 4	59.9	25.3	6.9	0.5
5–7	60.4	22.8	7.1	1.4
8 and above	55.9	23.2	10.4	1.3
Adult Literacy Groups				
None literate	57.7	19.0	11.0	1.2

(Contd.)

Female literate	57.1	19.8	7.8	0.5
Male literate	60.6	21.5	9.5	0.6
Both literate	58.0	26.9	6.1	1.7
Village Development Groups				
Low	59.0	19.5	10.0	1.2
Medium	56.5	22.5	9.8	1.7
High	60.9	27.4	4.9	0.7
All India	**58.7**	**23.4**	**8.2**	**1.2**

Advisory Committee

Mr Han-C-Von Sponeck
UNDP

Dr Erlin Dessau
Resident Representative
UNDP

Dr R. Sudarshan
UNDP

Dr J.E. Rode
Resident Representative
UNICEF

Dr E. Watanabe
Resident
UNICEF

Mr Gordon Alexander
UNICEF

Dr A.K. Shiva Kumar
UNICEF

Mr T. Abrams
Resident Representative
UNFPA

Mr V.G. Pandey
International Development
Research Centre

Dr S.N. Ray
Director General
Central Statistical Organization

Dr R.N. Panday
Central Statistical Organization

Mr Satya Bhusan
Director, NIEPA

Dr N. K. Gupta
Secretary
Planning Commission

S.V. Giri
Secretary
Department of Education
Ministry of Human Resource Development

The Registrar General
Census Commission of India

Mr S. Vardachary
Representative Joint Secretary
Department of Economic Affairs

Mr R.L. Mishra
Secretary
Ministry of Health

Mr A.B. Bose
Planning Commission

Dr B.N. Sahay
Planning Commission

Mr Madan Mohan Jha
Joint Registrar General
Office of the Census Commissioner of India

Dr Shri Prakash
National Institute of Educational
Planning & Administration